THE HISTORY

OF

ENGLISH LAW

THE HISTORY

OF

ENGLISH LAW

BEFORE THE TIME OF EDWARD I

BY

SIR FREDERICK POLLOCK

AND

FREDERIC WILLIAM MAITLAND

SECOND EDITION

Reissued
with a new introduction and select bibliography by
S. F. C. MILSOM

VOLUME II

CAMBRIDGE

AT THE UNIVERSITY PRESS

1968

Published by the Syndics of the Cambridge University Press
Bentley House, 200 Euston Road, London, N.W. 1
American Branch: 32 East 57th Street, New York, N.Y. 10022

Library of Congress Catalogue Card Number: 68-21197

Standard Book Numbers:
521 07062 7 clothbound
521 09516 6 paperback

First edition 1895
Second edition 1898
Reprinted 1911 1923 1952

Reissued with a new introduction
and select bibliography by
S. F. C. Milsom 1968

Printed in Great Britain
at the University Printing House, Cambridge
(Brooke Crutchley, University Printer)

CONTENTS.

BOOK II.

CHAPTER IV.

§ 3. *Conveyance,* pp. 80—106.

CHAPTER V.

CONTRACT, pp. 184—239.

CHAPTER VI.

§ 3. *The Last Will*, pp. 314—356.

§ 4. *Intestacy*, pp. 356—363.

CHAPTER VII.

CHAPTER VIII.

CRIME AND TORT, pp. 448—557.

§ 1. *The Ancient Law*, pp. 449—462.

§ 2. *Felony and Treason*, pp. 462—511.

§ 3. *The Trespasses*, pp. 511—543.

§ 4. *Ecclesiastical Offences*, pp. 543—557.

CHAPTER IX.

PROCEDURE, pp. 558—673.

§ 1. *The Forms of Action*, pp. 558—573.

§ 2. *Self-help*, pp. 574—578.

§ 3. *Process*, pp. 578—597.

§ 4. *Pleading and Proof*, pp. 598—673.

ADDITIONS AND CORRECTIONS.

p. 149. As to the ownership and possession of movables, the articles by Mr J. B. Ames in Harv. L. R. vol. xi. pp. 277 ff. should be consulted.

p. 360, note 1. As to the forfeiture of the goods of a man who dies desperate, see Art. 30 of the Preston Custumal (Harland, Mamecestre, vol. iii. p. xxxviii.).

p. 363, note 2. Add a reference to Records of Leicester, p. 219. In 1293 the burgesses decide that the heir is to have the best cauldron, the best pot and so forth. In Scotland the 'heirship movables' were of considerable importance. In the seventeenth century the heir would take, among other things, 'the great House Bible, a Psalm-book, the Acts of Parliament.' See Hope's Minor Practicks, ed. 1734, p. 538.

p. 372, note 1. An interesting historical account of the Scottish law of marriage by Mr F. P. Walker will be found in Green's Encyclopædia of the Law of Scotland. Pre-Tridentine catholicism seems to find its best modern representative in this protestant kingdom.

p. 485, note 5, and p. 636, note 2. The Annals of Winchester, p. 25, and Thomas Wykes, p. 235, differ about the number of the compurgators, which may have been 25 or 50.

p. 500, side-note, should read 'Treason contrasted with felony.'

p. 537, note 5. So the burgess of Preston who has charged a married woman with unchastity must proclaim himself a liar holding his nose with his fingers : Harland, Mamecestre, vol. iii. p. xl.

CHAPTER IV.

OWNERSHIP AND POSSESSION.

[p. 1] WE have already spoken at great length of proprietary The law of property. rights in land. But as yet we have been examining them only from one point of view. It may be called—though this distinction is one that we make, rather than one that we find made for us—the stand-point of public law. We have been looking at the system of land tenure as the framework of the state. We have yet to consider it as a mesh of private rights and duties. Another change we must make in the direction of our gaze. When, placing ourselves in the last quarter of the thirteenth century, we investigate the public elements or the public side of our land law, we find our interest chiefly in a yet remoter past. We are dealing with institutions that are already decadent. The feudal scheme of public law has seen its best or worst days; homage and fealty and seignorial justice no longer mean what they once meant. But just at this time a law of property in land is being evolved, which has before it an illustrious future, which will keep the shape that it is now taking long after feudalism has become a theme for the antiquary, and will spread itself over continents in which homage was never done. Our interest in the land law of Henry III.'s day, when we regard it as private law, will lie in this, that it is capable of becoming the land law of the England, the America, the Australia of the twentieth century.

§ 1.   *Rights in Land.* [p. 2]

Distinction between movables and immovables.   One of the main outlines of our medieval law is that which divides material things into two classes. Legal theory speaks of the distinction as being that between 'movables' and 'immovables'; the ordinary language of the courts seldom uses such abstract terms, but is content with contrasting ' lands and tenements' with 'goods and chattels[1].' We have every reason to believe that in very remote times our law saw differences between these two classes of things; but the gulf between them has been widened and deepened both by feudalism and by the evolution of the ecclesiastical jurisdiction. We shall be better able to explore this gulf when, having spoken of lands, we turn to speak of chattels; but even at the outset we shall do well to observe, that if in the thirteenth century the chasm is already as wide as it will ever be, its depth has yet to be increased by the operation of legal theory. The facts to which the lawyers of a later day will point when they use the word 'hereditaments' and when they contrast 'real' with 'personal property' are already in existence, though some of them are new; but these terms are not yet in use. Still more important is it to observe that Glanvill and Bracton—at the suggestion, it may be, of foreign jurisprudence—can pass from movables to immovables and then back to movables with an ease which their successors may envy[2]. Bracton discourses at length about the ownership of things (*rerum*), and though now and again he has to distinguish between *res mobiles* and *res immobiles,* and though when he speaks of a *res* without any qualifying adjective, he is thinking chiefly of land, still he finds a great deal to say about things and the ownership of things which is to hold good whatever be the nature of the things in question. The tenant in fee who holds land in demesne, is, like the owner of a chattel, *dominus rei*; he is *proprietarius*; he has *dominium et proprietatem rei.* That the law of England knows no ownership of land, or will concede such ownership only to the king, is a dogma that has never entered the head of Glanvill or of Bracton.

Is land owned?   We may well doubt whether had this dogma been set [p. 3]

[1] But in certain contexts it is common to speak of movable and immovable goods; in particular the usual form of a bond has 'obligo omnia bona mea mobilia et immobilia.'

[2] See for example Glanvill, x. 6; Bracton, f. 61 b.

before them, they would have accepted it without demur.
It must be admitted that medieval law was not prepared to
draw the hard line that we draw between ownership and ruler-
ship, between private right and public power; and it were
needless to say that the facts and rules which the theorists of
a later day have endeavoured to explain by a denial of the
existence of land-ownership, were more patent and more important in the days of Glanvill and Bracton than they were
at any subsequent time.   But those facts and rules did not cry
aloud for a doctrine which would divorce the tenancy of land
from the ownership of chattels, or raise an insuperable barrier
between the English and the Roman *ius quod ad res pertinet.*
This cry will only be audible by those who sharply distinguish
between the governmental powers of a sovereign state on the
one hand, and the proprietary rights of a supreme landlord
on the other: by those who, to take a particular example,
perceive a vast difference between a tax and a rent, and while
in the heaviest land-tax they see no negation or diminution
of the tax-payer's ownership, will deny that a man is an owner
if he holds his land at a rent, albeit that rent goes into the
royal treasury.   In the really feudal centuries it was hard to
draw this line; had it always been drawn, feudalism would
have been impossible.   The lawyers of those centuries when
they are placing themselves at the stand-point of private law,
when they are debating whether Ralph or Roger is the better
entitled to hold Blackacre in demesne, can regard seignorial
rights (for example the rights of that Earl Gilbert of whom
the successful litigant will hold the debatable tenement) as
bearing a political rather than a proprietary character.   Such
rights have nothing to do with the dispute between the two
would-be land-owners; like the 'eminent domain' of the
modern state, they detract nothing from ownership.   All land
in England must be held of the king of England, otherwise he
would not be king of all England.   To wish for an ownership
of land that shall not be subject to royal rights is to wish for
the state of nature.

And again, any difficulty that there is can be shrouded
from view by a favourite device of medieval law.   As we shall
see hereafter, it is fertile of 'incorporeal things.'   Any right or
group of rights that is of a permanent kind can be thought of
as a thing.   The lord's rights can be treated thus; they can be

Ownership
and
lordship.

converted into 'a seignory' which is a thing, and a thing quite
distinct from the land over which it hovers. The tenant in
demesne owns the land; his immediate lord owns a seignory;
there may be other lords with other seignories; ultimately [p. 4]
there is the king with his seignory; but we have not here
many ownerships of one thing, we have many things each with
its owner. Thus the seignory, if need be, can be placed in the
category that comprises tithes and similar rights. The tithe-
owner's ownership of his incorporeal thing detracts nothing
from the land-owner's ownership of his corporeal thing[1].

Ownership and feudal theory.   By some such arguments as these Bracton might endeavour
to defend himself against those severe feudalists of the seven-
teenth and later centuries, who would blame him for never
having stated the most elementary rule of English land law,
and for having ascribed *proprietas* and *dominium rei* to the
tenant in demesne. Perhaps as a matter of terminology and
of legal metaphysics the defence would not be very neat or
consistent. The one word *dominium* has to assume so many
shades of meaning. The tenant *qui tenet terram in dominico,* is
dominus rei and has *dominium rei*; but then he has above him
one who is his *dominus,* and for the rights of this lord over
him and over his land there is no other name than *dominium.*
When we consider the past history of the *feodum,* and the
manner in which all rights in land have been forced within the
limits of a single formula, we shall not be surprised at finding
some inelegances and technical faults in the legal theory which
sums up the results of this protracted and complex process.
But we ought to hesitate long before we condemn Bracton,
and those founders of the common law whose spokesman he
was, for calling the tenant in demesne an owner and proprietor
of an immovable thing[2]. Only three courses were open to

---

[1] See, for example, Bracton's emphatic statement on f. 46 b. The tenant
makes a feoffment without his lord's consent. The lord complains that the
feoffee has 'entered his fee.' No, says Bracton, he has not. The lord's fee is
the 'service' (the seignory) not the land.

[2] The double meaning of *dominus* is well illustrated by a passage in Bracton,
f. 58, where in the course of one sentence we have *capitalis dominus* meaning
chief lord, and *verus dominus* meaning true owner. A gift made by a *verus
dominus* [= true owner] is confirmed by the *capitalis dominus* [= the owner's
immediate lord] *vel ab alio non domino* [= or by some one else who is not the
owner]. We shall have to remark below that the English language of Bracton's
day had not the word *ownership*, nor, it may be, the word *owner.* In a sense
therefore the law knew no ownership either of lands or of goods. We are only

[p. 5] them : (1) to deny that any land in England is owned : (2) to ascribe the ownership of the whole country to the king : (3) to hold that an owner is none the less an owner because he and his land owe services to the king or to some other lord. We can hardly doubt that they were right in choosing the third path ; the second plunges into obvious falsehood ; the first leads to a barren paradox. We must remember that they were smoothing their chosen path for themselves, and that social and economic movements were smoothing it for them. As a matter of fact, the services that the tenant in fee owed for his land were seldom very onerous ; often they were nominal ; often, as in the case of military service, scutage and suit of court, they fell within what we should regard as the limits of public law. Again, it could hardly be said that the tenant's rights were conditioned by the performance of these services, for the lord, unless he kept up an efficient court of his own, could not recover possession of the land though the services were in arrear[1]. The tenant, again, might use or abuse or waste the land as pleased him best. If the lord entered on the land, unless it were to distrain—and distress was a risky process— he was trespassing on another man's soil ; if he ejected the tenant 'without a judgment,' he was guilty of a disseisin[2]. As against all third persons it was the tenant in demesne who represented the land ; if a stranger trespassed on it or filched part of it away, he wronged the tenant, not the lord. And then the king's court had been securing to the tenant a wide liberty of alienation—for an owner must be able to alienate what he owns[3]. The feudal casualties might indeed press heavily upon the tenant, but they need not be regarded as restrictions on ownership. An infant land-owner must be in ward to some one, and to some one who as a matter of course will be entitled to make a profit of the wardship[4]; but if a boy's ownership of his land would not be impaired by his being in ward to an uncle, why should it be impaired by his being in ward to his lord ? If the tenant commits felony, his lands will escheat to his lord ; but his chattels also will be forfeited, and

contending that the lawyers of the time see no great gulf between rights in movables and rights in land. In Anglo-French the owner of a chattel is *le seignur de la chose*; see *e.g.* Britton, i. 60.

[1] See above, vol. i. p. 352.   [2] Bracton, f. 217.
[3] See above, vol. i. p. 329.   [4] See above, vol. i. p. 322.

it may well be that this same lord (since he enjoys the franchise known as *catalla felonum*) will take them. It is very possible that Bracton saw the Roman land-owner of the classical age holding his land 'of' the emperor by homage and service; it [p. 6] was common knowledge that the modern Roman emperor was surrounded by feudatories; but at any rate there was no unfathomable chasm between the English tenancy in fee and that *dominium* of which the Institutes speak. On the whole, so it seems to us, had Bracton refused to speak of the tenant in demesne as the owner of a thing, or refused to treat his rights as essentially similar to the ownership of a movable, he would have been guilty of a pedantry far worse than any that can fairly be laid to his charge, a retrograde pedantry. But, be this as it may, the important fact that we have here to observe is that he and his contemporaries ascribed to the tenant in demesne ownership and nothing less than ownership. Whether he would have ascribed 'absolute ownership,' we do not know. Might he not have asked whether in such a context 'absolute' is anything better than an unmeaning expletive[1]?

Tenancy in fee and life tenancy.

And now, taking no further notice of the rights of the lord, we may look for a while at those persons who are entitled to enjoy the land. For a while also we will leave out of account those who hold for terms of years and those who hold at the will of another, remembering that into this last class there fall, in the estimation of the king's court and of the common law, the numerous holders in villeinage. This subtraction made, those who remain are divisible into two classes: some of them are entitled to hold in fee, others are entitled to hold for life. As already said, 'to hold in fee' now means to hold heritably. The tenant in fee 'has and holds the land to himself and his heirs' or to himself and some limited class of heirs. This last qualification we are obliged to add, because, owing to 'the form of the gift' under which he takes his land,

---

[1] Foreign feudists attempted to meet the difficulty by the terms *directum* and *utile*, which they borrowed from Roman law. The lord has the *dominium directum*, the vassal a *dominium utile*. This device is quite alien to the spirit of English law. The man who is a tenant in relation to some lord, is *verus dominus* (true owner) in relation to the world at large. We shall hereafter raise the question whether English law knew any property either in land or goods that was *absolute*, if we mean to contrast *absolute* with *relative*. We shall also have to point out that the ownership of lands was a much more intense right than the ownership of movables.

the rights of the tenant in fee may be such that they can be inherited only by heirs of a certain class, in particular, [p. 7] only by his descendants, 'the heirs of his body,' so that no collateral kinsman will be able to inherit that land from him. A donor of land enjoys a wide power of impressing upon the land an abiding destiny which will cause it to descend in this way or in that and to stop descending at a particular point. But this does not at present concern us. We may even for a while speak as though the only 'kind of fee' that was known in Bracton's day—and it was certainly by far the commonest—was the 'fee simple absolute' of later law, which, if it were not alienated, would go on descending among the heirs of the original donee, from heir to heir, so long as any heir, whether lineal or collateral, existed; if at any time an heir failed, there would be an escheat.

A person who is entitled to hold land in fee and demesne *The tenant* may be spoken of as owner of the land. When in possession of *in fee.* it he has a full right to use and abuse it and to keep others from meddling with it; his possession of it is a 'seisin' protected by law. If, though he is entitled to possession, this is being withheld from him, the law will aid him to obtain it; his remedy by self-help may somewhat easily be lost, but he will often have a possessory action, he will always have a proprietary action.

The rights of a person who is entitled to hold land for *The life* his life are of course different from those just described. But *tenant.* they are not so different as one, who knew nothing of our land law and something of foreign systems, might expect them to be. The difference is rather of degree than of kind; nay, it is rather in quantity than in quality. Before saying more, we must observe that when there is a tenant for life there is always a tenant in fee of the same land. In the thirteenth century life-tenancies are common. Very often they have come into being thus—one man *A*, who is tenant in fee, has given land to another man *B* for his, *B*'s, life; or he has simply given land 'to *B*' and said nothing about *B*'s heirs, and it is a well-settled rule that in such a case *B* will hold only for his life, or in other words, that in order to create or transfer a fee, some 'words of inheritance' must be employed[1]. Then on *B*'s death, the land will 'go back' or 'revert' to *A*. Very

---

[1] See above, vol. i. p. 308.

possibly an express clause in the charter of gift will provide for this 'reversion'; but this is unnecessary. Despite the gift, *A* will still be tenant in fee of the land; he will also be *B*'s lord; *B* will hold the land of *A*; an oath of fealty can [p.8] be exacted from *B*, and he and the land in his hand may be bound to render rent or other services to *A*. These services may be light or heavy; sometimes we may find what we should call a lease for life at a substantial rent; often a provision is being made for a retainer or a kinsman, and then the service will be nominal; but in any case, as between him and his lord, the tenant for life will probably be bound to do the 'forinsec service[1].' But more complicated cases than this may arise :— for example, *A* who is tenant in fee may give the land to *B* for his life, declaring at the same time that after *B*'s death the land is to 'remain' to *C* and his heirs. Here *B* will be tenant for life, and *C* will be tenant in fee; but *B* will not hold of *C*; there will be no tenure between the tenant for life and the 'remainderman'; both of them will hold of *A*. Or again, we may find that two or three successive life-tenancies are created at the same moment : thus—to *B* for life, and after his death to *C* for life, and after his death to *D* and his heirs. But in every case there will be some tenant in fee. Lastly, we may notice that family law gives rise to life-tenancies; we shall find a widower holding for his life the lands of his dead wife, while her heir will be entitled to them in fee; and so the widow will be holding for her life a third part of her husband's land as her dower, while the fee of it belongs to his heir.

Position of the tenant for life.

Now any one who had been looking at Roman law-books must have been under some temptation to regard the tenant for life as an 'usufructuary,' and to say that, while the tenant in fee is owner of the land, the tenant for life has a *ius in re aliena* which is no part of the *dominium* but a servitude imposed upon it. Bracton once or twice trifled with this temptation[2]; but it was resisted, and there can be little doubt that it was counteracted by some ancient and deeply seated ideas against which it could not prevail. Let us notice some of these ideas and the practical fruit that they bear.

[1] See above, vol. i. p. 238.

[2] Bracton, f. 30 b: 'propter *servitutem* quam firmarius sibi acquisivit...de usu fructuum habendo ad terminum vitae vel annorum.' And so on f. 32 b. Usually however Bracton reserves the term *usufructuary* for the tenant for years.

In the first place, it seems probable that in the past a Tenant for life and the law of waste. tenant for life has been free to use and abuse the tenement as [p. 9] pleased him best : in other words, that he has not been liable for waste.   The orthodox doctrine of later days went so far as to hold that, before the Statute of Marlborough (1267), the ordinary tenant for life—as distinguished from tenant in dower and tenant by the curtesy—might lawfully waste the land unless he was expressly debarred from so doing by his bargain[1]. This opinion seems too definite.   For some little time before the statute actions for waste had occasionally been brought against tenants for life[2].   Still the action shows strong signs of being new.   The alleged wrong is not that of committing waste, but that of committing waste after receipt of a royal prohibition.   Breach of such a prohibition seems to have been deemed necessary, if the king's court was to take cognizance of the matter[3].   At any rate, repeated legislation was required to make it clear that the tenant for life must behave *quasi bonus pater familias.*

Secondly, for all the purposes of public law, the tenant for Tenant for life and public law. life in possession of the land seems to have been treated much as though he were tenant in fee.   He was a freeholder, and indeed the freeholder of that land, and as such he was subject to all those public duties that were incumbent upon free-holders.

Thirdly, his possession of the land was a legally protected Seisin of tenant for life. seisin.   Not merely was it protected, but it was protected by precisely the same action—the assize of novel disseisin —that sanctioned the seisin of the tenant in fee.   His was no *iuris quasi possessio*; it was a seisin of the land.   He was a freeholder of the land :—so plain was this, that in some contexts to say of a man that he has a freehold is as much as to say that he is tenant for life and not tenant in fee[4].

---

[1] Stat. Marlb. c. 23 ; Stat. Glouc. c. 5.   See Coke's comments on these chapters in the Second Institute, and Co. Lit. 53 b, 54 a ; also Blackstone, Comm. ii. 282.   The matter had been already touched by Prov. Westm. c. 23.

[2] Note Book, pl. 443, 540, 607, 1304, 1371.   It is possible also that the reversioner had a remedy by self-help, might enter and hold the tenement until satisfaction had been made for past and security given against future waste : Bracton, f. 169 ; Britton, i. 290.

[3] Bracton, f. 315 ; Note Book, pl. 574.

[4] See *e.g.* Bracton, f. 17 b : 'desinit esse feodum et iterum incipit esse liberum tenementum.'   The estate ceases to be a fee and becomes a [mere] freehold.

Tenants
for life in
litigation. Fourthly, in litigation the tenant for life represents the land. Suppose, for example, that A is holding the land as tenant for life by some title under which on his death the land will revert or remain to B in fee. Now if X sets up an adverse [p. 10] title, it is A, not B, whom he must attack. When A is sued, it will be his duty to 'pray aid' of B, to get B made a party to the action, and B in his own interest will take upon himself the defence of his rights. Indeed if B hears of the action he can intervene of his own motion[1]. But A had it in his power to neglect this duty, to defend the action without aid, to make default or to put himself upon battle or the grand assize, and thus to lose the land by judgment. We can not here discuss at any length the effect which in the various possible cases such a recovery of the land by X would have upon the rights of B; it must be enough to say that in some of them he had thenceforth no action that would give him the land, while in others he had no action save the petitory and hazardous writ of right: —so completely did the tenant for life represent the land in relation to adverse claimants[2].

We see then very clearly that a tenant for life is not thought of as one who has a servitude over another man's soil; he appears from the first to be in effect what our modern statutes call him, 'a limited owner,' or a temporary owner.

The
doctrine of
estates. We thus come upon a characteristic which, at all events for six centuries and perhaps for many centuries more, will be the most salient trait of our English land law. Proprietary rights in land are, we may say, projected upon the plane of time. The category of quantity, of duration, is applied to them. The life-tenant's rights are a finite quantity; the fee-tenant's rights are an infinite, or potentially infinite, quantity; we see a difference in respect of duration, and this is the one fundamental difference. In short, to use a term that we have as yet

---

[1] Bracton, f. 393 b.

[2] Littleton, sec. 481. Before Stat. Westm. II. c. 3: 'If a lease were made to a man for term of life, the remainder over in fee, and a stranger by a feigned action recovered against the tenant for life by default, and after the tenant died, he in remainder had no remedy before the statute, because he had not any possession of the land.' The remainderman can not use the writ of right because neither he, nor any one through whom he claims *by descent*, has been seised of the land. See Second Institute, 345. Even the reversioner could be driven to the cumbrous and risky writ of right in order to undo the harm done by a collusive recovery against tenant for life.

carefully eschewed, we are coming by a law of 'estates in land.'
We have as yet, though not without a conscious effort, refrained
from using that term, and this because, so far as we can see, it
[p. 11] does not belong to the age of Bracton.   On the other hand, so
soon as we begin to get Year Books, we find it in use among
lawyers[1].   As already said[2], it is the Latin word *status*; an
estate for life is, in the language of our records, *status ad
terminum vitae*, an estate in fee simple is *status in feodo
simplici*; but a very curious twist has been given to that word.
The process of contortion can not at this moment be fully
explained, since, unless we are mistaken, it is the outcome of a
doctrine of possession; but when once it has been accomplished,
our lawyers have found a term for which they have long been to
seek, a term which will serve to bring the various proprietary
rights in land under one category, that of duration.   The
estate for life is finite, *quia nihil certius morte*; the estate in fee
is infinite, for a man may have an heir until the end of time.
The estate for life is smaller than the estate in fee; it is
infinitely smaller; so that if the tenant in fee breaks off and
gives away a life estate, or twenty life estates, he still has a fee.
Thus are established the first elements of that wonderful
calculus of estates which, even in our own day, is perhaps the
most distinctive feature of English private law.

In the second half of the thirteenth century this calculus is   The estate
just beginning to take a definite shape; but in all probability   and the
forma
some of the ideas which have suggested it and which it employs   *doni.*
are very ancient.   One of them is that which attributes to the
alienator of land a large power of controlling the destiny of the
land that he is alienating.   By a declaration of his will expressed at the moment of alienation—in other words, by the
forma doni—he can make that land descend in this way or
in that, make it 'remain,' that is, stay out, for this person or for
that, make it 'revert' or come back to himself or his heirs upon
the happening of this or that event.   His alienation, if such
we may call it, need not be a simple transfer of the rights
that he has enjoyed; it is the creation of new rights, and
the office of the law is to say what he may not do, rather than
what he may do in this matter; it has to limit his powers,
rather than to endow him with them, for almost boundless

[1] See, for example, Y. B. 20-1 Edw. I. p. 39.
[2] See above, vol. i. p. 408.

powers of this kind seem to be implied in its notion of ownership. Not that land has been easily alienable; seignorial
and family claims must be satisfied before there can be any
alienation at all; but when a man is free to give away his land, [p. 12]
he is free to do much more than this; he can impose his will on
that land as a law that it must obey[1].

The power
of the
gift.

In this context we ought to remember that the power to
alienate land is one that has descended from above. From all
time the king has been the great land-giver. The model gift of
land has been a governmental act; and who is to define what
may or may not be done by a royal land-book, which, if it is a
deed of gift, is also a *privilegium* sanctioned by all the powers
of state and church? The king's example is a mighty force;
his charters are models for all charters. The earl, the baron,
the abbot, when he makes a gift of land will consult, or profess
that he has consulted, his barons or his men[2]. This influence
of royal *privilegia* goes far, so we think, to explain the power of
the *forma doni*. Still it would not be adequate, were we not
to think of the hazy atmosphere in which it has operated. The
gift of land has shaded off into the loan of land, the loan into
the gift; the old land-loan was a temporary gift, the gift was a
permanent loan; and if the donee's heirs were to inherit the
land, this was because it had been given not only to him, but
also to them[3]. This haze we believe to be very old; it is not
exhaled by feudalism but is the environment into which feudalism is born. And so in the thirteenth century every sort and
kind of alienation (that word being here used in its very
largest sense) is a 'gift,' and yet it is a gift which always, or
nearly always, leaves some rights in the giver[4]. In our eyes the
transaction may be really a gift, for a religious house is to hold
the land for ever and ever, and the only service to be done to
the giver is one which he and his will receive in another world;
or it may in substance be a sale or an exchange, since the

[1] Bracton, f. 17 b: 'Modus enim legem dat donationi, et modus tenendus est
contra ius commune et contra legem, quia modus et conventio vincunt legem.'

[2] See above, vol. i. p. 346.

[3] See Brunner's two essays, Die Landschenkungen der Merowinger, and
Ursprung des droit de retour, which are reprinted in his Forschungen zur
Geschichte des deutschen und französischen Rechts. Also, Maitland, Domesday
Book, 299.

[4] The exception is when there is 'substitution' not 'subinfeudation.'

so-called donee has given money or land in return for the so-called gift; or it may be what we should call an onerous lease for life, the donee taking the land at a heavy rent :—but in all these cases there will be a 'gift,' and precisely the same two [p.13] verbs will be used to describe the transaction; the donor will say 'I have given and granted (*sciatis me dedisse et concessisse*)[1].'

If then 'the form of the gift' can decide whether the donee is to hold in fee or for life, whether he is to be a heavily burdened lessee, or whether we must have recourse to something very like a fiction in order to discover his services, we can easily imagine that the form of the gift can do many other things as well. Why should it not provide that one man after another man shall enjoy the land, and can it not mark out a course of descent that the land must follow? The law, if we may so put it, is challenged to say what the gift can not do; for the gift can do whatever is not forbidden.

The form of the gift a law for the land.

One of the first points about which the law has to make up its mind is as to the meaning of a gift to a man 'and his heirs.' The growing power of alienation has here raised a question. Down to the end of the twelfth century the tenant in fee who wished to alienate had very commonly to seek the consent of his apparent or presumptive heirs[2]. While this was so, it mattered not very greatly whether this restraint was found in some common-law rule forbidding disherison, or in the form of a gift which seemed to declare that after the donee's death the land was to be enjoyed by his heir and by none other. But early in the next century this restraint silently disappeared. The tenant in fee could alienate the land away from his heir. This having been decided, it became plain that the words 'and his heirs' did not give the heir any rights, did not decree that the heir must have the land. They merely showed that the donee had 'an estate' that would endure at least so long as any heir of his was living. If on his death his heir got the land, he got

The gift to a man and his heirs.

---

[1] The medieval 'gift' is almost as wide as our modern 'assurance.' Bracton, f. 27 : 'Item *dare* poterit quis alicui terram ad voluntatem suam et quamdiu ei placuerit, de termino in terminum, et de anno in annum.' However Bracton, f. 17, says that a lease for years is rather a grant (*concessio*) than a *donatio*, and gradually the scope of *dare* is confined to the alienation or creation of freehold estates ; one demises or bails (Fr. *bailler*) for a term of years.

[2] Of this more fully below in the chapter on Inheritance.

it by inheritance and not as a person appointed to take it by the form of the gift[1].

This left open the question whether the donee's estate was [p. 14] one which might possibly endure even if he had no heir. Of course if the estate was not alienated, then if at any time an heir failed, the land escheated to the lord. But suppose that it is alienated: then will it come to an end on the failure of the heirs of the original donee? We seem to find in Bracton's text many traces of the opinion that it will. Early in the century it became a common practice to make the gift in fee, not merely to the donee 'and his heirs,' but to the donee, 'his heirs and assigns[2].' What is more, we learn that if the donee is a bastard, and consequently a person who can never have any heirs save heirs of his body, and the gift is to him 'and his heirs' without mention of 'assigns,' it is considered that he has an estate which, whether alienated or no, must come to an end so soon as he is dead and has no heir[3]. However, this special rule for gifts to bastards looks like a survival; and the general law of Bracton's time seems to be that the estate in fee created by a gift made to a man 'and his heirs' will endure until the person entitled to it for the time being—be he the original donee, be he an alienee—dies and leaves no heir. This was certainly the law at a somewhat later time[4].

[1] Bracton, f. 17 : 'et sic acquirit donatorius rem donatam ex causa donationis, et heredes eius post eum ex causa successionis; et nihil acquirit [heres] ex donatione facta antecessori, quia cum donatorio non est feoffatus.'

[2] Generally in a collection of charters we shall find two changes occurring almost simultaneously soon after the year 1200:—(1) the donor's expectant heirs no longer join in the gift ; (2) the donee's 'assigns' begin to be mentioned.

[3] Bracton, f. 12 b, 13, 20 b, 412 b ; Note Book, pl. 402, 1289, 1706; Britton, i. 223 ; ii. 302.

[4] Alienation would chiefly be by way of subinfeudation, and Bracton on more than one occasion discusses the case in which a mesne lordship escheats but leaves the demesne tenancy existing; f. 23 b, 48. But unless the donor expressly contracted to warrant the donee's 'assigns' he was not bound to warrant them; f. 17 b, 20, 37 b, 381. See also Note Book, pl. 106, 332, 617, 804, 867, 1289, 1906 ; also Chron. de Melsa, ii. 104. The position of a tenant who had no warrantor was very insecure, for he could be driven to stake his title on battle or the grand assize ; hence the great importance of 'assigns' in the clause of warranty. It was important also in the grant of an advowson : Bracton, f. 54. Apparently too it might be valuable if the donor's apparent heir was convicted of felony : Ibid. f. 134. But by this time the word in its commonest context was becoming needless : Y. B. 33-5 Edw. I. p. 363. The writer of the Mirror (Selden Soc.), pp. 175, 181, holds that no one should be able to alienate unless his assigns have been mentioned. On the whole we

Another matter that required definition was the effect of attempts to limit the descent of the land to a special class [p. 15] of heirs, to the descendants of the original donee, 'the heirs of his body.' It is possible that the process which made *beneficia* or *feoda* hereditary had for a while been arrested at a point at which the issue of the beneficed vassal, but no remoter heirs of his, could claim to succeed him; but this belongs rather to French or Frankish than to English history. So far as we can see, from the Conquest onwards, collateral heirs, remote kinsmen, can claim the ordinary *feodum*, if no descendants be forthcoming. But a peculiar rule arose concerning the marriage portions of women.

It is necessary here to make a slight digression. Our English law in its canons of inheritance postponed the daughter to the son; it allowed her no part of her dead father's land if at his death he left a son or the issue of a dead son. In such a case the less rigorous Norman law gave her a claim against her brothers; she could demand a reasonable marriage portion, if her father had not given her one in his lifetime[1]. Even in England her father was entitled to give her one, and this at a time when as a general rule he could not alienate his fee without the consent of his expectant heirs, who in the common case would be his sons. Whether the Norman rule that he could give but one-third of his land away in *maritagia* ever prevailed in this country, we do not know. But we must further observe that in this case he might make a free, an unrequited gift. Of course a free gift was far more objectionable than a gift which obliged the donee to an adequate return in the shape of services; for in the latter case the donor's heir, though he would not inherit the land in demesne, might inherit an equivalent for it. To this state of things it apparently is that the term 'frank-marriage' (*liberum maritagium*) takes us back. A father may provide his daughter, not merely with a *maritagium*, but with a *liberum maritagium* :— his sons can not object to this. If land is given in frank-marriage it will be free from all service; as between donor and donee it will even be free from the forinsec service until it has

can not doubt that the use of this term played a large part in the obscure process which destroyed the old rules by which alienation was fettered. See Williams, Real Property, 18th ed., pp. 66–70.

[1] Très ancien coutumier, pp. 10, 83; Ancienne coutume, p. 84; Somma, p. 83.

been thrice inherited by the heirs of the body of the donee [1]. When that degree has been passed, the tenant will be bound to do homage to the donor's heir and perform the forinsec service. [p. 16] Probably under twelfth century law the estate of the donee was deemed inalienable, at all events until this degree had been passed. The *maritagium* was a provision for a daughter— or perhaps some other near kinswoman—and her issue. On failure of her issue, the land was to go back to the donor or his heirs [2].

Gifts to a man and the heirs of his body.

Meanwhile about the year 1200 gifts expressly limited to the donee 'and the heirs of his body' and gifts made to a husband and wife 'and the heirs of their bodies' begin to grow frequent [3]. Before the end of Henry III.'s reign they are

---

[1] Bracton, f. 21 b.

[2] The *maritagium* appears already in D. B., *e.g.* i. 139 b: 'dedit cum nepte sua in maritagio.' It appears in Henry I.'s coronation charter as *maritatio*; see also Round, Ancient Charters, p. 8, for an example from 1121. Glanvill discusses it in lib. i. 18; Bracton, f. 21–23. During the period between Glanvill and Bracton it causes a good deal of litigation; see cases in Note Book, indexed under 'Marriage Portion' and Select Civil Pleas (Selden Soc.), pl. 184. It has been said that 'Frank marriage is the name not of a species of tenure but of a species of estate' (Challis, Real Property, 2nd ed. p. 12). This is hardly true of the early period with which we are dealing. The most striking feature of the *liberum maritagium* is a tenurial quality, namely, tenure which for three generations is tenure without service. The term *maritagium* points, we may say, to a peculiar kind of estate; but *liberum maritagium* points also to a highly peculiar kind of tenure. See Y. B. 30–31 Edw. I. 388. In later days the gift in frank marriage is deemed to create an estate in special tail for the husband and wife, and the main interest of it lies in the creation of such an estate without any words of inheritance; see Challis, Real Property, 2nd ed. pp. 12, 265. But from an early time it was usual, as a matter of fact, to employ words marking out a line of descent, and in Bracton's day this was not always that of an estate in tail special for husband and wife. The *maritagium* may be given to husband and wife and the heirs of their two bodies, or to the wife and the heirs of her body, or to the husband and the heirs of his body; and there are other variations. See Bracton, f. 22, 22 b. So long as feudal services are grave realities it is important to maintain that the marriage portion, whichever of these forms it may take, may be a *liberum maritagium*. In 1307 counsel urges that a gift to a woman and the heirs of her body can not be frank marriage. A judge replies 'Why so? If I give you a tenement in frank marriage can I not frame the entail as I please?' See Y. B. 33–5 Edw. I. p. 398.

[3] Fines (ed. Hunter), i. 34, 85, 95, 102, 110, 160, 251; ii. 78, 91, 100. These are instances from the reigns of Richard and John. An instance of a royal marriage settlement is this:—in 1252 Henry III. gave land to his brother Richard, to hold to him and his heirs begotten of his wife Sanchia, with an express clause stating that the land was to revert on the failure of such heirs to the king and his heirs; Placit. Abbrev. 145.

common. An examination of numerous fines levied during the first years of Edward I. and the last of his father brings us to the conclusion that every tenth fine or thereabouts contained a limitation of this character. The commonest form of such [p.17] gifts seems to have been that which designated as its objects a husband and wife and the heirs springing from their marriage; but a gift to a man and the heirs of his body, or to a woman and the heirs of her body, was by no means unusual. On the other hand, a form which excludes female descendants, any such form as created the 'estate in tail male' of later days, was, if we are not mistaken, rare[1]. These expressly limited gifts begin to be fashionable just at the time when the man who holds 'to himself and his heirs' is gaining a full liberty of alienation both as against his lord and as against his apparent or presumptive heirs. No doubt the two phenomena are connected. It has become evident that if a provision is to be made for the children of a marriage, or if the donor is to get back his land in case there be no near kinsman of the donee to claim the bounty, these matters must be expressly provided for.

Now before the end of Henry III.'s reign the judges seem to have adopted a very curious method of interpreting these gifts. They held that they were 'conditional gifts.' We may take as an example the simplest, the gift 'to X and the heirs of his body.' They held that so soon as X had a child, he had fulfilled a condition imposed upon him by the donor, could alienate the land, could give to the alienee an estate which would hold good against any claim on the part of his (X's) issue, and an estate which would endure even though such issue became extinct. Even before the birth of a child, X could give to an alienee an estate which would endure so long as X or any descendant of X was living. On the other hand, they stopped short of holding that, so soon as a child was born, X was just in the position of one holding 'to himself and his heirs'; for if he afterwards died without leaving issue and without having alienated the land, his heir (who of course would not be an 'heir of his body') had no right in the land, and it reverted to the donor[2].

The conditional fee.

---

[1] Calendarium Genealogicum, i. 111; Robert de Quency before 48 Hen. III. enfeoffed the Earl of Winchester and the heirs male of his body.

[2] The preamble of Stat. West. II. c. 1 has been supposed to show—and this

[p. 18]

History of the conditional fee.

How the lawyers arrived at this odd result we do not know; but a guess may be allowable. When men were making their first attempts to devise these restricted gifts, they seem to have not unfrequently adopted a form of words which might reasonably be construed as the creation of a 'conditional fee.' In the first years of the century a gift 'to X and his heirs if he shall have an heir of his body' seems to have been almost as common as the gift 'to X and the heirs of his body[1].' At first little difference would be seen between these two forms. In either case the donor, with no precedents before him, might well suppose that he had shown an intention that the land should descend to the issue, if any, of X, but to no other heirs. But without doing much violence to the former of these clauses ('to X and his heirs if he shall have an heir of his body') we can make it mean 'to X and his heirs' upon condition that he shall have a child born to him. If then X has a child, the condition is fulfilled for good and all; X is holding the land simply to himself and his heirs[2]. A mode of interpretation established for the one form of gift may then have extended itself to the other, namely, 'to X and the heirs of his body': intermediate and ambiguous forms were possible[3].

The leaning in favour of alienability.

But explain the matter how we will, we can not explain it sufficiently unless we attribute to the king's court a strong bias

(see Challis, Real Property, 2nd ed. p. 239) is now the received opinion—that in certain cases the birth of issue of the prescribed class made it possible for the estate to descend to issue outside the prescribed class. This goes further than Bracton would have gone; see Bracton, f. 22. As to the second husband's curtesy, see Bracton, f. 437 b, 438 b; Note Book, pl. 487, 1921.

[1] See for example Rot. Cart. Joh. p. 209 : charter of king John (1215) : gift to H to hold to him and his heirs, and we will that if he has an heir begotten on a wife he shall hold as aforesaid, but if not the land is to revert to us. Fines (ed. Hunter), i. 85, 95, 110, 160, 251; Note Book, pl. 429, 948.

[2] Bracton, f. 18, 47. Bracton was evidently familiar with gifts of this kind. It is to be remembered that in the past the maxim *Nemo est heres viventis* had not been observed. In the most formal documents an heir apparent or presumptive had been simply *heres*.

[3] This is no new explanation; it is given in Plowden, Comment. p. 235. The transition may have been made the easier by the clauses which attempted to define the event upon which a reverter is to take place :—'but if he shall not have—but if he shall not leave—but if he shall die without leaving—without having had—an heir of his body, then the land shall revert.' Such a clause might be regarded as defining a condition. When the deed says that the land is to revert if the donee never has an heir of his body, we may argue that only in this case is there to be a reversion; also that a man has an heir of his body directly he has a child.

in favour of free alienation. Bracton apparently would have
held that if the gift is 'to X and the heirs of his body,' the
rights, if rights they can be called, of his issue are utterly at
his mercy. An heir is one who claims by descent what has
[p. 19] been left undisposed of by his ancestor; what his ancestor has
alienated he cannot claim. Others may think differently, may
hold that the issue are enfeoffed along with their ancestor; but
this, says Bracton, is false doctrine[1]. Whether he would have
taken the further step of holding that X, so soon as he has a
child, can make an alienation which, even when his issue have
failed, will defeat the claim of the donor—that is, to say the
least, very doubtful[2]. But that step also was taken at the
latest in the early years of Edward I.[3] Gifts in 'marriage' and
gifts to the donee and the heirs of his body were to be treated
as creating 'conditional fees.'

But this doctrine was not popular; it ran counter to the
intentions of settlors; 'it seemed very hard to the givers that
their expressed will should not be observed.' Already in 1258
there was an outcry[4]. In 1285 the first chapter of the Second
Statute of Westminster, the famous *De donis conditionalibus*,
laid down a new rule[5]. The 'conditional fee' of former times
became known as a fee tail (Lat. *feodum talliatum*, Fr. *fee
taillé*), a fee that has been carved or cut down, and about the
same time the term *fee simple* was adopted to describe the
estate which a man has who holds 'to him and his heirs.' But
the effect of this celebrated law can not be discussed here[6].

Statutory protection of conditional gifts.

---

[1] Bracton, f. 17 b; Note Book, pl. 566.   [2] Bracton, f. 17 b.

[3] The clearest contemporary authorities are Stat. West. II. c. 1 and Y. B. 32–3
Edw. I. 279 = Fitzherbert, *Formedon*, 62.

[4] Oxford Petition, c. 27 (Select Charters). This is one of the first proofs
that these *dona* are being regarded as *conditionalia*. The petitioners seem to
complain not of this, but of some doctrine which they regard as permitting an
infringement of the 'condition.'

[5] Stat. 13 Edw. I. c. 1.

[6] It seems that the term *fee tail* was already in use before the statute was
passed; it occurs in the statute (c. 4) though not in the famous first chapter.
We have found it on a roll slightly older than the statute; De Banco Roll, Mich.
11–12 Edw. I. m. 70 d: 'Emma non habuit...nisi feodum talliatum secundum
formam donationis praedictae.' At any rate it was in common use within a very
few years afterwards. See *e.g.* Y. B. 21–2 Edw. I. 365, 574, 641. It is about
the same time that *fee simple*, alternating with (Fr.) *fee pur*, (Lat.) *feodum
purum*, becomes very common. In Bracton we read rather of *donatio pura* or
donatio simplex as opposed to *donatio conditionalis*. The modern learning of
'conditional fees at the common law' can be found in Co. Lit. 18 b; Second

Settle-
ments in
cent. XIII.

These are the three principal elements which the settlors [p. 20] of the thirteenth century have in their hands. To give them their modern names they are (1) the fee simple absolute, given to a person and his heirs, (2) the fee simple conditional, given to a person and the heirs, or some class of the heirs, of his body, and (3) the estate for life. Already there are settlors. As the old restraints which tended to keep land in a family dropped off, men became more and more desirous of imposing their will upon land and making family settlements. Such settlements seem to have been made for the more part by fines levied in the king's court or by a process of feoffment and refeoffment. How much could be done by these means may for a long time have been doubtful, but we can see that a good deal could be done.

Joint-
tenancies.

Something could be done by the creation of co-ownership or co-tenancy. About this there is not much to be said, except that the form known in later days as 'joint tenancy' seems decidedly older than that known as 'tenancy in common.' If land is given to two men and their heirs, there is a *ius accrescendi* between them: when one dies, the survivor takes the whole. The conditional fee given to the husband and wife and the heirs of their marriage is not uncommon. Also we may sometimes find land settled upon a father, a mother, a son, and the heirs of the son. The object thereby gained seems to have been that of defeating the lord's claim to the wardship of an infant heir or to a relief from an heir of full age[1]. Already conveyancers had hopes of circumventing the lord; already the legislator had set himself to defeat their schemes[2]. But

Inst. 331; *Paine's Case*, 8 Rep. 34; *Barkley's Case*, Plowden, 223; and is excellently summed up in Challis, Real Property, c. 18. On the whole it is well borne out by such authorities as we have from the thirteenth century. These are chiefly Bracton, f. 17 b, 47; Britton, i. 236; ii. 152; Fleta, f. 185; the cases in the Note Book indexed under 'Fee Conditional,' of some of which a partial knowledge descended through Fitzherbert to Coke; a few cases of Edward's reign collected by Fitzherbert under 'Formedon,' several of which with others appear now in Horwood's Year Books; and lastly the long and important recital in the statute. About one small point we speak in a note at the end of this section.

[1] Coke, 2nd Inst. 110.

[2] Stat. Marlb. c. 6. Even by taking a joint tenancy with one's wife something could be done to hurt the lord. Gilbert of Umfravill holds of the king in chief in fee simple. He and his wife have a son who is one year old. He wants to enfeoff a friend and take back an estate limited to himself and his

we must pass to more ambitious enterprises, devices for making
one estate follow upon another.

[p. 21]   Two technical terms are becoming prominent, namely, Reversion
and re-
mainder.
'revert' and 'remain.'   For a long time past the word *reverti*,
alternating with *redire,* has been in use both in England and
on the mainland to describe what will happen when a lease of
land expires:—the land will 'come back' to the lessor. We
find this phrase in those 'three life leases' which Bishop
Oswald of Worcester granted in King Edgar's day[1]. We find
it also in a constitution issued by Justinian, which is the
probable origin of those 'three life leases' that were granted by
the Anglo-Saxon churches[2]. But occasionally in yet remote
times men would endeavour to provide that when one person's
enjoyment of the land had come to an end, the land should not
'come back' to the donor or lessor, but should 'remain,' that is,
stay out for, some third person[3]. The verb *remanere* was a
natural contrast to the verb *reverti* or *redire*[4]; the land is to
stay out instead of coming back.   Both terms were in common
use in the England of the thirteenth century, and though we
may occasionally see the one where we should expect the other[5],
they are in general used with precision.   Land can only 'revert'
to the donor or to those who represent him as his heirs or
assigns : if after the expiration of one estate the land is not to

wife and their heirs. An inquest finds that this will be to the king's damage.
If Gilbert dies in his wife's lifetime the king may lose a wardship. Cal. Geneal.
ii. 650.

   [1] See, *e.g.* Kemble, Cod. Dipl. vol. iii. p. 4 : ' ad usum primatis redeat ';
Ibid. p. 22 : ' ad usum revertatur praesulis.' In these leases *redeat* and *resti-
tuatur* are the common terms.

   [2] Nov. 7, cap. 3, § 2 : in the Greek ἐπανιέναι : in the Latin *redeat* : in the
'Authentic' *reverti*. For the connexion between this Novel and the practice of
the English prelates, see Maitland, Domesday Book, 303.

   [3] See the will (A.D. 960) of Count Raymond of Toulouse, in Mabillon,
De Re Diplomatica, p. 572, where numerous remainders are created by use of the
verb *remanere*. Thus : ' et post decessum suum *R.* filio suo remaneat, et si *R.*
mortuus fuerit, *B* et uxori suae *A* remaneat, et si infans masculus de illis
pariter apparuerit ad illum remaneat, et si illi mortui fuerint qui infantem non
habuerint, *H* remaneat, et si *H* mortuus fuerit...' See also Hübner, Donationes
post obitum (Gierke's Untersuchungen, No. xxvi.), p. 70.

   [4] This contrast appears in the classical Roman jurisprudence. Ulpiani
Fragmenta, vi. §§ 4–5 : ' Mortua in matrimonio muliere, dos a patre profecta ad
patrem *revertitur*......Adventicia autem dos semper penes maritum *remanet*.'

   [5] Thus Bracton, f. 18 b, uses *reverti* where we should expect *remanere*. So
in Hunter, Fines, i. 99 (temp. Ric. I.), we may find what we should describe as
the converse mistake.

come back to the donor, but is to stay out for the benefit of another, then it 'remains' to that other. Gradually the terms 'reversion' and 'remainder,' which appear already in Edward I.'s day[1], are coined and become technical; at a yet later date we have 'reversioner' and 'remainderman[2].'

Remainders after life estates.

When creating a life estate, it was usual for the donor to [p. 22] say expressly that on the tenant's death the land was to revert. But there was no need to say this: if nothing was said the land went back to the donor who had all along been its lord. But the donor when making the gift was free to say that on the death of the life tenant the land should remain to some third person for life or in fee. As a matter of fact this does not seem to have been very common; but in all probability the law would have permitted the creation of any number of successive life estates, each of course being given to some person living at the time of the gift[3].

Reversion and escheat.

If an estate in 'fee conditional' came to an end, then the land would go back to the donor. We have seen that the king's court did something towards making this an uncommon event, for the tenant so soon as issue of the prescribed class had been born to him, might if he pleased defeat the donor's claim by an alienation. Still even when this rule had been established, such an estate would sometimes expire and then the land would return to the donor; it would 'revert' or 'escheat' to the donor and lord. Now in later days when the great statutes of Edward I. had stopped subinfeudation and defined the nature of an estate tail, no blunder could have been worse than that of confusing a reversion with an escheat. These two terms had undergone specification:—land 'escheated' to the lord *propter defectum tenentis* when a tenant in fee simple died without heirs, and the lord in this case could hardly ever be the donor from whom that tenant acquired his

---

[1] Y. B. 33–5 Edw. I. p. 429.

[2] As a matter of history it is a mistake to think that a remainder is so called because it is what remains after a 'particular estate' has been given away. The verb is far older than the noun and is applied to the land. Indeed in our law Latin the infinitive of the verb has to do duty as a noun; a remainder is a 'remanere.' The words 'reversioner' and 'remainderman' are yet newer. In the thirteenth century one says 'he to whom the reversion or remainder belongs' or 'he who has the reversion or remainder.'

[3] An early case of successive life estates will be found in Cart. Rams. **i.** p. 150.

estate[1]; while, on the other hand, on the death of a tenant for life, or the death without issue of a tenant in tail, land 'reverted' to the donor who had created that tenant's estate. But at an earlier time there was not this striking contrast. In the common case, so long as subinfeudation was permissible, the tenant in 'fee simple absolute' just like the tenant in 'fee conditional' held of his donor. If the heirs of the one or the [p. 23] heirs of the body of the other fail, the land goes back to one who is both lord and giver. The two cases have very much in common, and the words 'revert' and 'escheat' are sometimes indiscriminately used to cover both[2].

According to the orthodoxy of a later age what the donor has when he has created a conditional fee is not a reversion but a 'possibility of reverter.' Whether the lawyers of 1285 had come in sight of this subtle distinction we may doubt, without hinting for a moment that it is not now-a-days well established. As a matter of fact the land reverts to the donor. So early as 1220 it is possible for the donor to get a writ which will bring the land back to him[3], and before the end of Henry's reign a writ for this purpose seems to have taken its place among the writs of course[4]. But it is further said that after the

Remainders after conditional fees.

---

[1] If the king made a feoffment he was both lord and donor.

[2] Bracton, f. 23, speaks plainly of an absolute fee simple reverting to its donor on failure of the heirs of a tenant. And on the other hand gives, f. 160 b, a writ of escheat suitable for a case in which tenant in fee conditional dies without an heir of his body. In a MS. Registrum Brevium of Henry III.'s reign a writ which answers the purpose of 'formedon in the reverter'—and we have seen no earlier specimen of any such writ—is called a writ of escheat: H. L. R. iii. 170. Fitzherbert, *Formedon*, 63, gives a record of 13 Edw. I. (the year of *De donis*): 'T. petit versus A. unam carucatam terrae in quam non habet ingressum nisi per R. cui praedictus T. illam dimisit in liberum maritagium suum cum A. filia sua et heredibus qui de praedicta A. exierint, et quae ad ipsum reverti debet *tanquam eschaeta sua* eo quod praedicta A. obiit sine herede de se.' It is to be remembered that even in later days the writ of escheat contained the words *reverti debet*: Reg. Brev. Orig. 164 b. Also we may observe that the word *escheat* (*excadere*) had no special aptitude for expressing a seignorial right. In medieval French law land *descends* to a lineal, but *escheats* to a collateral heir; Beaumanoir, vol. i. pp. 225, 296.

[3] Note Book, pl. 61 = Fitz. *Formedon*, 64.

[4] Stat. Westm. II. c. 13 and see above note 2. Coke in Co. Lit. 22 a, b, seems to say that even after the Statute *De donis*, there had been a doubt as to whether there could be a reversion on a fee tail. The references to ancient authorities that he gives in his margin seem for the more part to be misprinted; as they stand they are beside the mark. The Second Statute of Westminster itself (c. 4) speaks of a *reversio* where there is a *feodum talliatum*. So far as we

conditional fee there could be no remainder. To this, without the slightest wish to disturb the well settled law of later days[1], we can not unreservedly assent. In the first place, such a remainder had come before the court as early as 1220 and to all appearance had not shocked it[2]. In the second place, Bracton [p. 24] distinctly says that land can be given to *A* and the heirs of his body, and on failure of such heirs to *B* and the heirs of his body, and on failure of such heirs to *C* and the heirs of his body[3]. In the third place, during the first years of Edward and the last of Henry such gifts were common. So far as we can see, about one out of every two fines that create a conditional fee will in plain language create a remainder after that estate. To judge by these fines, of which many hundreds are preserved, a remainder on a conditional fee was commoner than a remainder on a life estate. In the fourth place, directly the Year Books begin—and they begin about seven years after the statute *De donis*—the lawyers are treating a remainder after a conditional fee or estate tail as a very natural thing[4]. Fifthly, though that statute did not by any express words take notice of the remainderman or do anything for him, we find that while Edward was still alive the remainderman was enjoying that full protection which the statute had conferred on the reversioner[5]. Lastly, Bracton distinctly says that the remainderman has an action to obtain the land when the previous estate has expired. This action, he says, can not be an assize of *mort d'ancestor*, nor can it be a writ of right, for the remainderman claims nothing by way of inheritance; but *ut res magis valeat quam pereat* the remainderman will have an 'exception' if he is in possession, while if he is out of possession he will have a writ founded on the 'form of the gift[6].'

have observed in the Year Books of Edward I. and II. (which were not printed in Coke's day) the lawyers invariably speak in this context of a reversion, never of a 'possibility of reverter.' See *e.g.* 21–2 Edw. I. pp. 58, 187 ; 30–1 Edw. I. p. 124 ; 32–3 Edw. I. p. 100.

[1] Challis, Real Property (ed. 2), Appendix II.

[2] Note Book, pl. 86.

[3] Bracton, f. 18 b. On f. 18 he has spoken of a gift to husband and wife and their common heirs, and if such heirs fail then to the heirs of the survivor.

[4] Y. B. 21–2 Edw. I. pp. 58, 196, 266. Three cases from two terms.

[5] Y. B. 33–5 Edw. I. pp. 20, 130, 157. The last two of these cases are formedon in the remainder on the expiration of an estate tail. The first is formedon in the remainder on the death of tenant for life. Of this hereafter.

[6] Bracton, f. 69, and again on f. 262 b. 263.

However, it must be confessed that though Bracton says Their va-
lidity ques-
tionable. that he is going to give us the words of this writ[1], he does not fulfil this promise, also that we have looked through a good many plea rolls without finding any instance of such a writ being brought into court before the statute of 1285. On the whole we must leave it a doubtful question whether before [p. 25] that statute the remainderman had any writ adapted to his case. But the want of an appropriate writ is one thing, the want of right another. Such certainly was the case in the thirteenth century. New writs could be made when they were wanted; lawyers were not yet compelled to argue always from writ to right, never from right to writ. For some forty years past such remainders as we have in view had been frequently created by instruments drawn up by officers of the court. Bracton had expressed his approval of them, had said that defences ('exceptions') could be founded upon them, had said that an action could be given for their protection. Whether that action was first given a few years after or a few years before the statute is a small question; the action was not given by the statute, but was the outcome of pure common law doctrine and the practice of conveyancers. It is quite as difficult to prove that the remainderman whose estate was preceded by an estate for life had any action, as to prove that there was a writ for the remainderman whose estate was preceded by a conditional fee; yet no one doubts that the common law of the thirteenth century allowed the creation of a remainder after a life estate[2].

But—to leave this disputable point—the creation of re- Gifts upon
condition. mainders is only one illustration of the power of the *forma doni.* The gage of land, the transaction which makes land a security for money lent, was being brought under the rubric 'Conditional Gifts' or 'Gifts upon Condition.' A creditor might be given a term of years in the land, which upon the happening of a specified event, to wit, the non-payment of the debt at a certain date, would swell into a fee[3]. Again, it was becoming a common practice for a feoffor or a lessor to stipulate that if the services due

---

[1] Bracton, f. 96 : 'breve autem tale est ut liquere poterit'; no writ follows. In the Digby ms. a large blank space is left at this point as if for the reception of the writ. See Bracton and Azo, 243.

[2] See the note at the end of this section.

[3] See below, the section on The Gage of Land.

to him were in arrear for a certain time, he might reenter on the land and hold it as of old :—he made his gift subject to the express condition that rent should be duly paid. Again, the liberty of disposition which the king's courts had conceded to landholders was so large that it sometimes gave rise to new forms of restraint. As the common law about alienation became definite, feoffors sought to place themselves outside of it by express bargains. Sometimes the stipulation is that the lord shall have a right of preemption[1], sometimes that the land shall not be conveyed to men of religion[2], sometimes that it shall not be [p. 26] conveyed at all. A man who took land from the Abbot of Gloucester had, as a matter of common form, to swear that he would neither sell, nor exchange, nor mortgage the land, nor transfer it to any religious house without the consent of the monks[3]. Bracton regarded such conventions as binding on the land : a purchaser can be evicted on the ground that he has purchased land which the vendor had covenanted not to sell[4]. The danger of the time was not that too little, but that too much, respect would be paid to the expressed wills of feoffors and feoffees, so that the newly acquired power of free alienation would involve a power of making land absolutely inalienable.

The form of the gift and testamentary power.

On the other hand, the form of the gift, if it could restrain alienation, might give to the donee powers of alienation that he would not otherwise have enjoyed. We have already noticed that the introduction of the word 'assigns' had at one time been of importance. But just about the middle of the century we find for a short while a more ambitious clause in charters of feoffment. It strives to give the feoffee that testamentary power which the common law denies him. The gift is made not merely to him, his heirs and assigns, but to him, his

---

[1] Cart. Glouc. i. 222. See also Cart. Rams. ii. 279.

[2] Cart. Glouc. i. 302 ; Chron. de Melsa, i. 361.

[3] Cart. Glouc. i. 179, 181, 188, 194, 195, 337, 370. See also Chron. de Melsa, i. 376 : *N* gives to the abbot the homage and service of *T*, who pledges faith that he will not mortgage or sell, or permit any of his freeholders to mortgage or sell, save to the abbot (A.D. 1210–1220).

[4] Bracton, f. 46, 46 b. At one point a doubt is expressed as to the necessity for some words expressly giving the donor power to reenter on an unauthorized 'alienation. This hardly assorts with the rest of the text and may be an addition.' But at any rate if apt words be used, the land can be made inalienable. See Note Book, pl. 18, 36, 543, 680.

heirs, assigns and legatees[1]. Whether any writ was ever penned which would enable the legatee—or as we should now call him 'devisee'—to recover the land from the heir, we may doubt. Bracton's opinion as to the validity of such clauses seems to have fluctuated. At one time he thought them good and was prepared to draw up the writ which would have sanctioned [p. 27] them. At another he thought them ineffectual, and we may guess that this was his final doctrine[2]. However, just in his time a famous case occurred in which an enormous tract of land was effectually devised. In 1241 Henry III. gave the honour of Richmond to Peter of Savoy 'to hold to him and his heirs or to whomsoever among his brothers or cousins he should give, assign, or bequeath it.' In 1262 the king amplified this power of bequest; he declared by charter that Peter might bequeath the honour to whomsoever he would. A few years afterwards Peter died and the honour passed under his will to Queen Eleanor[3]. It is possible that the discussion of this famous case convinced the king and the great feudatories that they would lose many wardships and marriages if land became devisable *per formam doni.* At any rate, so far as we have observed, it is just about the moment when the honour of Richmond actually passed under a will, that the attempt to create a testamentary power was abandoned[4]. But that men were within an acc of obtaining such a power in the middle of the thirteenth century is memorable; it will help to explain those devisable 'uses' which appear in the next century.

We have dwelt for some while on the potency of the *forma doni.* To our minds it is a mistake to suppose that our common law starts with rigid, narrow rules about this matter, knows only a few precisely defined forms of gift and rejects everything that deviates by a hair's-breadth from the established models. On the contrary, in the thirteenth century it is elastic and liberal, loose and vague. It has a deep reverence for the expressed wish of the giver, and is fully prepared to accept any

Influence of the forma doni.

---

[1] An early example from John's reign is found in Rot. Cart. 160. Almost any monastic cartulary which contains deeds of the middle of the century will give instances, *e.g.* Gloucester, i. 204; Malmesbury, ii. 101; Whalley, i. 319; Sarum, p. 217; Note Book, pl. 1906; Northumberland Assize Rolls, p. 198.

[2] Bracton, f. 18 b, 49, 412 b.

[3] Foedera, i. 417, 475, 482.

[4] The clause appears in a precedent book compiled after 1280; but at that date it may have been a belated form: L. Q. R. vii. 63–4.

new writs which will carry that wish into effect. From Henry III.'s day onwards, for a long time to come, its main duty in this province will be that of establishing some certain barriers against which the *forma doni* will beat in vain[1].

We have now taken a brief survey of those 'estates,' those [p. 28] modes of ownership, which were known to the law. Much yet remains to be said, but we can make no further progress without introducing a new idea, that of 'seisin.' In order to understand our English ownership, we must understand our English possession.

Additional Note.

The conditional fee.

We will here state shortly the results obtained by a search among the unprinted plea rolls for writs of formedon. (1) Writs of *formedon in the reverter* after a conditional fee are quite common a few years before the statute. We have seen five in one eyre of 9 Edw. I. Late in Henry's reign such writs appear rarely and still speak of the land as 'escheating' for want of heirs of the prescribed class. (2) We have seen no writ of *formedon in the descender* before the statute. It has been a matter of controversy whether such a writ existed. See Challis, Real Property, ed. 2, p. 74. It is, we think, fairly certain that the issue in tail (it is convenient to give him this name, even if we are guilty of an anachronism) could use the *mort d'ancestor* if he was also heir general and if his ancestor died seised. It is also clear from Bracton, f. 277 b, 278, that as early as 1227 Pateshull had given the issue in tail an 'exception' against a *mort d'ancestor* brought by the heir general. In the case stated at the end of the present note we see the issue in tail, who is not heir general, recovering in a *mort d'ancestor* against the heir general; but whether he could have done this if the heir general wisely abstained from special pleading seems to us very doubtful. We have seen no direct proof that the issue in tail had any other writ than the *mort d'ancestor*. (3) As said above, we have seen no instance of *formedon in the remainder* where the remainder follows a conditional fee. (4) We have seen no instance of *formedon in the remainder* where the remainder follows a life estate, earlier than the clear case in Y. B. 33–5 Edw. I. p. 21. The position of any and every remainderman if he has not yet been seised, is for a long time precarious, because the oldest actions, in particular, the writ of right and the *mort d'ancestor*, are competent only to one who can allege a seisin in himself or in some ancestor from whom he claims by hereditary right.

---

[1] To take one more example, Bracton (f. 13) distinctly contemplates the possibility of a gift to unborn children; Britton follows him; a glossator of the fourteenth century has to point out that this is against the law. See the interesting note to Britton, i. 231.

Lastly, we must confess that we have but glided over the surface of a few
of the many plea rolls. All our conclusions therefore are at the mercy of
any one who will read the records thoroughly.

About one small point we are able to quote a case which runs counter
to the received doctrine as to what was law before the statute *De donis*.
If land was given to husband and wife 'and the heirs of their bodies,' and
after her husband's death the wife married again, the issue of the second
marriage could not inherit, nor could the second husband have an estate
by the curtesy, although the 'condition' had been fulfilled by the birth of
[p. 29] issue of the first marriage. Such is the law that is laid down very
positively in 7 Edw. I. (Assize Rolls, No. 1066, m. 20). We have this
pedigree :—

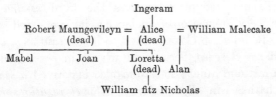

Ingeram enfeoffed Robert and Alice and the heirs of their bodies. In
an assize of *mort d'ancestor* brought by Mabel, Joan and William fitz
Nicholas against William Malecake, to which Alan was also made a party,
it is adjudged that Alan can not inherit, nor can William Malecake have
curtesy. When the statute speaks of the curtesy of the second husband,
it probably has in view a gift to the wife and the heirs of her body begotten by her first husband, but it speaks largely, and was soon supposed
to have had that wider meaning which is attributed to it now-a-days.

§ 2.   *Seisin*.

In the history of our law there is no idea more cardinal than Seisin.
that of seisin. Even in the law of the present day it plays a
part which must be studied by every lawyer; but in the past it
was so important that we may almost say that the whole
system of our land law was law about seisin and its consequences[1].

Seisin is possession. A few, but only a few words about Seisin and
etymology may be ventured. The inference has been too hastily possession.

---

[1] Langlois, Le règne de Philippe le Hardi, 267: 'La saisine avait, au moyen
âge, une valeur extraordinaire, supérieure même, en quelque sorte, à celle
du droit de propriété.' Among students of medieval law on the Continent few
questions have been more debated than those which we touch in this section.
It will be sufficient to refer here to Heusler's Gewere, and the same writer's
Institutionen.

drawn that this word speaks to us of a time of violence, when
he who seized land was seised of it, when seizing land was the
normal mode of acquiring possession. Now doubtless there is
an etymological connexion between 'seizing' and being 'seised,'
but the nature of that connexion is not very certain. If on the
one hand 'seisin' is connected with 'to seize,' on the other hand
it is connected with 'to sit' and 'to set':—the man who is
seised is the man who is sitting on land; when he was put in
seisin he was set there and made to sit there. Thus seisin [p. 30]
seems to have the same root as the German *Besitz* and the Latin
possessio. To our medieval lawyers the word *seisina* suggested the very opposite of violence; it suggested peace
and quiet. It did so to Coke. 'And so it was said as *possessio*
is derived *a pos et sedeo*, because he who is in possession may
sit down in rest and quiet; so *seisina* also is derived *a sedendo*,
for till he hath seisin all is *labor et dolor et vexatio spiritus*;
but when he has obtained seisin, he may *sedere et acquiescere*[1].'

Sitting on
land.

The would-be Latin words *seisina, seisire,* came in with the
Conqueror; but in all probability they did but translate cognate
English terms. When in a famous passage the Saxon Chronicle
tells us that 'ealle tha landsittende men' swore fealty to
William[2], it tells what was done by all who were seised of
land. 'To sit upon land' had been a common phrase, meaning
to possess land; in the cartularies we read of *landseti, cotseti,
ferlingseti, undersetles,* as of various classes of tenants. To this
day we call the person who takes possession of land without
having title to it a 'mere squatter'; we speak of 'the sitting
tenant,' and such a phrase as 'a country seat' puts us at the

---

[1] 6 Co. Rep. 57 b. Skeat, s. v. *seize*, thinks that 'to seize or seise' in the
sense of 'to grasp' is posterior to 'to seize or seise' in the sense of 'to put into
possession.' Diez, s. v. *sagire*, holds that the idea of taking to oneself probably
preceded that of putting into possession. See also Brunner, Geschichte d.
Röm. u. Germ. Urkunde, p. 242, where the earliest instances of the word are
given. The problem can not be worked out on English soil; but in the time
immediately following the Norman Conquest, the verb meaning 'to put into
possession' was commoner than the verb meaning 'to take possession'; *e.g.* in
D. B. i. 208 : 'comitatus negat se vidisse sigillum vel saisitorem qui eum inde
saisisset'; in D. B. the 'saisitor' is one who delivers seisin to another. The
use of the one verb may be illustrated from Mag. Carta, 1215, c. 9 : 'Nec nos
nec ballivi nostri seisiemus terram aliquam'; that of the other from Glanv. ii. 4,
'Praecipio tibi quod seisias M. de una hida terrae'; the latter disappeared
in course of time in favour of 'facias M. habere seisinam.'

[2] A.-S. Chron. ann. 1085.

right point of view. The seated man is in quiet enjoyment. We reverence the throne, the bishop's see, 'the Right Reverend Bench,' the bench of judges, we obey the orders of the chair; the powers that be are seated.

Now in course of time *seisin* becomes a highly technical word; but we must not think of it having been so always. Few, if any, of the terms in our legal vocabulary have always been technical terms. The licence that the man of science can [p. 31] allow himself of coining new words is one which by the nature of the case is denied to lawyers. They have to take their terms out of the popular speech; gradually the words so taken are defined; sometimes a word continues to have both a technical meaning for lawyers and a different and vaguer meaning for laymen; sometimes the word that lawyers have adopted is abandoned by the laity. Such for a long time past has been the fate of *seisin*. Technica-lities of seisin.

The process by which words are specified, by which their technical meaning is determined, is to a first glance a curious, illogical process. Legal reasoning seems circular:—for example, it is argued in one case that a man has an action of trespass because he has possession, in the next case that he has possession because he has an action of trespass; and so we seem to be running round from right to remedy and then from remedy to right. All the while, however, our law of possession and trespass is being more perfectly defined. Its course is not circular but spiral; it never comes back to quite the same point as that from which it started. This play of reasoning between right and remedy fixes the use of words. A remedy, called an assize, is given to any one who is disseised of his free tenement: —in a few years lawyers will be arguing that X has been 'disseised of his free tenement,' because it is an established point that a person in his position can bring an assize. The word *seisin* becomes specified by its relation to certain particular remedies. Seisin and remedies.

What those remedies were it will be our duty to consider. But first we may satisfy ourselves that, to begin with, seisin simply meant possession. Of this we may be convinced by two observations. In the first place, it would seem that for at least three centuries after the Norman Conquest our lawyers had no other word whereby to describe possession. In their theoretical discussions, they, or such of them as looked to the Roman Possession.

books as models of jurisprudence, could use the words *possessio* and *possidere*; but these words are rarely employed in the formal records of litigation, save in one particular context. The parson of a church is 'in possession' of the church :—but then this is no matter for our English law or our temporal courts; it is matter for the canon law and the courts Christian; and it is all the more expedient to find some other term than 'seised' for the parson, since it may be necessary to contrast the rights of the parson who is possessed of the church with those of the [p. 32] patron who is seised of the advowson[1].

Seisin of chattels.

In the second place, this word 'seisin' was used of all manner of things and all manner of permanent rights that could be regarded as things. At a later date to speak of a person as being seised, or in seisin of, a chattel would have been a gross solecism. But throughout the thirteenth century and in the most technical documents men are seised of chattels and in seisin of them, of a fleece of wool, of a gammon of bacon, of a penny. People were possessed of these things; law had to recognize and protect their possession; it had no other word than 'seisin' and therefore used it freely[2]. It may well be, as some think, that the ideas of seisin and possession are first developed in relation to land; one sits, settles, squats on land, and in early ages, preeminently during the feudal time, the seisin of chattels was commonly interwoven with the seisin of land. Flocks and herds were the valuable chattels; 'chattel' and 'cattle' are the same word; and normally cattle are possessed by him who possesses the land on which they are levant and couchant. Still when the possession of chattels was severed from the possession of land, when the oxen were stolen or were sold to a chapman, there was no word to describe the possession of this new possessor, this thief or purchaser, save seisin[3]. Sometimes we meet with the phrase 'vested and

---

[1] For a somewhat similar reason it is not uncommon to speak of a guardian as having possession of the wardship, while the ward is seised of the land. Plac. Abbrev. p. 165 : 'in pacifica possessione custodiae praedictae.'

[2] Maitland, The Seisin of Chattels, L. Q. R. i. 324. Numerous other instances will be found in the indexes to Bracton's Note Book, and to vols. i., ii. of the Selden Society's Publications.

[3] Heusler, Institutionen, i. 333, discoursing of the German equivalent for our seisin (*Gewere*), says that one never spoke of a man having the *Gewere* of a movable, though one said that it was in his *Gewere*. So in England as regards chattels it seems to have been much commoner to say 'equus fuit in seisina sua,' or 'seisitus fuit de equo' than 'habuit seisinam de equo.'

seised,' which was common in France; this however seems to mean no more than 'seised,' and though we may now and then read of 'investiture,' chiefly in relation to ecclesiastical offices, this does not become one of the technical terms of the common law[1].

[p. 33]

When we say that seisin is possession, we use the latter term in the sense in which lawyers use it, a sense in which possession is quite distinct from, and may be sharply opposed to, proprietary right. In common talk we constantly speak as though possession were much the same as ownership. When a man says 'I possess a watch,' he generally means 'I own a watch.' Suppose that he has left his watch with a watchmaker for repair, and is asked whether he still possesses a watch, whether the watch is not in the watchmaker's possession, and if so whether both he and the watchmaker have possession of the same watch at the same time, he is perhaps a little puzzled and resents our questions as lawyers' impertinences. Even if the watch has been stolen, he is not very willing to admit that he no longer possesses a watch. This is instructive:—in our non-professional moments *possession* seems much nearer to our lips than *ownership*. Often however we slur over the gulf by means of the conveniently ambiguous verbs 'have' and 'have got'—I have a watch, the watchmaker has it—I have a watch, but some one else has got it. But so soon as there is any law worthy of the name, right and possession must emerge and be contrasted:—so soon as any one has said 'You have got what belongs to me,' the germs of these two notions have appeared and can be opposed to each other. Bracton is never tired of emphasizing the contrast. In so doing he constantly makes use of the Roman terms, *possessio* on the one hand, *proprietas* or *dominium* on the other. These are not the technical terms of English law; but it has terms which answer a like purpose, *seisina* on the one hand, *ius* on the other. The person who has right may not

Contrast between seisin and proprietary rights.

---

[1] Note Book, pl. 1539: a thief is 'vested and seised' of some stolen tin. This phrase appears more frequently in French than in Latin. The Latin rolls give *seisitus*, where the precedents for oral pleadings give *vetu et seisi*. *Investura* or *investitura* is occasionally found, but rather in chronicles than in legal documents. Hist. Abingd. ii. 59: 'investituram, id est saisitionem accepit.' Madox, Formulare, p. ix., supplies some instances. As yet we are far from any talk of 'vested estates.'

be seised, the person who is seised may not be seised of right[1].

Seisin and enjoyment. The idea of seisin seems to be closely connected in our ancestors' minds with the idea of enjoyment. A man is in seisin of land when he is enjoying it or in a position to enjoy it; he is seised of an advowson (for of 'incorporeal things' there may be seisin) when he presents a parson who is admitted to [p. 34] the church; he is seised of freedom from toll when he successfully resists a demand for payment. This connexion is brought out by the interesting word *esplees* (*expleta*). In a proprietary action for land the demandant will assert that he, or some ancestor of his, was 'seised of the land in his demesne as of fee 'and of right, by taking thence esplees to the value of five 'shillings, as in corn and other issues of the land.' The man who takes and enjoys the fruits of the earth thereby 'exploits' his seisin, that is to say, he makes his seisin 'explicit,' visible to the eyes of his neighbours[2]. In order that a seisin may have all its legal effects it must be thus exploited. Still a man must have seisin before he can exploit it, and therefore in a possessory action it is unnecessary for the plaintiff to allege this taking of esplees. The moment at which he acquires his seisin may not be the right moment for mowing hay or reaping corn. Seisin of land therefore is not the enjoyment of the fruits of the earth; it is rather that state of things which in due time will render such an enjoyment possible[3]

Who is seised? Law must define this vague idea, and it can not find the whole essence of possession in visible facts. It is so now-a-days[4]. We see a man in the street carrying an umbrella; we can not at once tell whether or no he possesses it. Is he its owner, is he a thief, is he a borrower, a hirer, is he the owner's servant? If he is the owner, he possesses it; if he is a thief, he possesses it. If he is the owner's servant, we shall probably

---

[1] The terms *possessio* and *proprietas* are used even in judicial records, *e.g.* Note Book, pl. 240: 'differtur actio super proprietate quousque discussum fuerit super possessione.' Indeed the word *possession* is frequently used in describing a possessory writ; it is 'bref de possession'; rarely, if ever, is it 'bref de seisine.' See *e.g.* Y. B. 33–5 Edw. I. p. 469: 'We are in a writ of possession, not a writ of right, and it is sufficient for us to maintain possession.'

[2] Skeat, Dict., s.v. *explicit, exploit.* The history of these words begins with the Latin *explicare.*

[3] Bracton, f. 40, 284, 373; Note Book, pl. 1865.

[4] Pollock and Wright, Possession in the Common Law, p. 11.

deny his possession. If he is a borrower, we may have our doubts; the language of every-day life may hesitate about the matter; law must make up its mind. Before we attribute possession to a man, we must apparently know something about the intentions that he has in regard to the thing, or rather about the intentions that he must be supposed to have when the manner in which he came by the thing has been taken into consideration. Probably the better way of stating the matter is not to speak of his real intentions, which are often beside the mark, nor of the intentions that he must be supposed to have, which are fictions, but to say at once that we require [p. 35] to know how he came by the thing[1]. This being known, problems await us. If the carrier of the umbrella is its owner, he possesses it; if he is a thief making off with a stolen chattel, he possesses it; if he has by mistake taken what he believes to be his own, he probably possesses it; if he has borrowed it or hired it, the case is not so plain; law must decide—and various systems of law will decide differently—whether possession shall be attributed to the borrower or to the lender, to the letter or the hirer

When deciding to whom it would attribute a seisin, our medieval law had to contemplate a complex mass of facts and rights. In the first place, the actual occupant of the soil, who was cultivating it and taking its fruits, might be so doing in exercise, or professed exercise, of any one of many different rights. He might be there as tenant at will, tenant for term of years, tenant in villeinage, tenant for life, tenant in dower, tenant by the curtesy, tenant in fee simple, guardian of an infant, and so forth. But further, at the same moment many persons might have and be actually enjoying rights of a proprietary kind in the same plot of ground. Giles would be holding in villeinage of Ralph, who held in free socage of the abbot, who held in frankalmoin of the earl, who held by knight's service of the king. There would be the case of the reversioner to be considered and the case of the remainderman. *Seisin and medieval land law.*

In the thirteenth century certain lines have been firmly drawn. The royal remedies for the protection of seisin given *Case of tenant in villeinage.*

---

[1] A servant who is carrying his master's goods can not become a possessor of them by merely forming the intent to appropriate them. If we say that he must be supposed to have an honest intent until by some act he shows the contrary, we are introducing a fiction.

by Henry II. were given only to those who were seised 'of a
free tenement:' the novel disseisin lies when a man has been
disseised *de libero tenemento suo.* Doubtless these words were
intended to exclude those who held in villeinage. This is
well brought out by a change in the language of Magna Carta.
The original charter of 1215 by its most famous clause declares
that no free man is to be disseised, unless it be by the lawful
judgment of his peers or the law of the land. The charter of
1217 inserts the words 'de libero tenemento suo vel libertatibus
vel liberis consuetudinibus suis[1].' It is not intended, it would
not be suffered, that a man holding in villeinage, even though [p. 36]
personally *liber homo*, should have a possession protected by the
king's court. Such a tenant is not seised of free tenement,
and, as royal justice is now beginning to supplant all other
justice, it is said that he has no seisin recognized by the
common law. The lord of whom he holds is the person protected by the common law, and is seised *de libero tenemento*; if
you eject the villein tenant, you disseise the lord. But within
the sphere of manorial justice this tenant is seised—seisin has
been delivered to him by the rod according to the custom of
the manor—and when he pleads in the manorial court he will
say that he is seised according to the custom of the manor.
Here then already we have a dual seisin:—the lord seised
quoad the king's courts and the common law, the tenant seised
quoad the lord's court and the manorial custom.

Case of the
termor.   In the past the tenant for term of years, though he was in
occupation of the soil, had not been considered to be seised of
it. In the days of Henry II. when the great possessory
remedy, the assize of novel disseisin, was being invented,
tenancies for terms of years seem to have been novelties, and
the lawyers were endeavouring to treat the 'termor'—this is
a conveniently brief name for the tenant for term of years—
as one who had no right in the land, but merely the benefit
of a contract. His lessor was seised; eject the lessee, and
you disseise the lessor. Already in Bracton's day, however,
this doctrine was losing its foundation; the termor was acquiring a remedy against ejectors. But this remedy was a
new action and one which in no wise affected the old assize of
novel disseisin. For a while men had to content themselves
with ascribing a seisin of a certain sort to both the termor

[1] Charter, 1215, c. 39; Charter, 1217, c. 35.

and his lessor[1].   Eject the termor, you lay yourself open to two actions, a *Quare eiecit infra terminum* brought by him, an assize of novel disseisin brought by his lessor.   The lessor still has the assize; despite the termor's occupation, he is seised, and seised in demesne, of the land; and he is seised, while the termor is not seised, 'of a free tenement'—this is proved by his having the assize.   Thus the term 'free tenement' is getting a new edge; the termor has no free tenement, no freehold, no seisin of the freehold.   At a later date lawyers will meet this difficulty by the introduction of 'possession' as a new technical term; they will deny 'seisin' of any sort or kind to the termor, and, on the other hand, will allow him possession. But of tenancies for years we shall have more to say hereafter.

[p. 37]

An infant's guardian, though the wardship was a profitable, vendible right, was not seised of the infant's land; his occupation of the land was the infant's seisin[2].   It is true that about this matter language might hesitate and fluctuate[3].   It is, for example, common enough to speak of the lord and guardian putting the ward into seisin of the land when he has attained his majority; but for the main purposes of the law the guardian's own right, the *custodia*, is converted into an incorporeal thing, an incorporeal chattel, of which there may be a seisin or possession, and for the protection of such a seisin there is a special possessory action.   If a person who is in occupation of the land as guardian is ejected from the land, and wishes to make good his own rights, he will complain, not of having been disseised of the land, but of having been ejected from the wardship[4].

Case of the guardian.

---

[1] Note Book, i. p. 91; L. Q. R. i. 341.

[2] Bracton, f. 165, 167 b; Britton, i. 287.   Y. B. 30–31 Edw. I. p. 245: 'car nous tenoms la seisine le gardeyn lor seisine'; so also Y. B. 21–2 Edw. I. p. 369.

[3] This is due to the fact that the current language has no term whereby to express that 'occupation' or 'detention' which is not a legally protected seisin. Hence we are driven to such phrases as 'The seisin of the termor, or the guardian, is the seisin of the lessor, or ward.'   Bracton endeavours to meet the case by distinguishing between *esse in seisina* and *seisitus esse*: the guardian *est in seisina*, the ward *seisitus est*.   But this slip of Romanism does not take root in England.

[4] See *e.g.* Note Book, pl. 1709.   The law of Glanvill's time speaks of the guardian as 'seisitus de terra illa ut de warda': Glanv. xiii. 13, 14.   This phrase gives way to 'seisitus fuit de custodia' or 'habuit custodiam terrae illius,' or 'fuit in possessione custodiae illius.'   But the guardian is seised of the ward as well as of the wardship, 'seisitus de corpore heredis.'

Case of
tenant for
life.

As to the tenant for life—including under that term tenant in dower and tenant by the curtesy—our law seems never to have had any doubt. The tenant for life, if he is in occupation of the land by himself, his servants, his villein tenants or his termors, is seised, seised of the land, seised in demesne, seised of a free tenement. If ejected, he will bring exactly the same possessory action that he would have brought had he been a tenant in fee.

Case of
the lord.

Then we must consider the ascending series of lords and tenants. Let us suppose that Ralph holds in fee and in free socage of the earl, who holds in fee by knight's service of the king. If all is as it should be, then both Ralph and the earl [p. 38] may be said to be seised of the land. Ralph, who is occupying the land by himself, his servants, his villein tenants or his termors, is seised in demesne. The earl, to whom Ralph is paying rent, also is seised; he is seised of the land, not in demesne but in service[1]. We have here to remember that if the feudal idea of seignorial justice had been permitted to develop itself freely, this ascending series of seisins would have had as its counterpart an ascending series of courts. The king's court would have known of no seisin save that of the earl, the tenant in chief. The seisin of Ralph, the earl's immediate tenant, would have found protection—at least in the first instance—only in the earl's court; and so downwards, each seisin being protected by a different court. The seisin of the tenant in villeinage protected only in the manorial court is an illustration of this principle[2]. But then Henry II. had restrained and crippled this principle; he had given a remedy in his own court to every one who could say that he had been disseised of a free tenement. The result of this is for a while a perplexing use of terms. Ralph, the tenant in demesne, he who has no freeholder below him, is indubitably seised of the land, however distant he may be in the feudal scale from the king. Eject him, and he will bring against you the assize of novel disseisin; indeed if his lord, the earl, ejects him or even distrains him outrageously, he will bring the assize against his lord, thus showing that as between him and his lord the seisin of the land is with him[3]. It is possible that at one time by ejecting Ralph, a stranger would have disseised both Ralph and

---

[1] For this use of words see Bracton, f. 81, 392.

[2] Heusler, Institutionen, ii. 32.   [3] Bracton, f. 217–8.

his lord and exposed himself to two actions; but this does not
seem to have been the law of Bracton's day. The lord was
ceasing to have any interest in what we may call the person-
ality of his tenant. If Ralph is ejected by Roger, the earl can
not complain of this; he is in no way bound to accept Roger as
a tenant; he can distrain the tenement for the services due to
him from Ralph; he is entitled to those services but to nothing
else[1]. More and more an incorporeal thing or group of in-
[p. 39] corporeal things supplants the land as the subject matter of the
lord's right and the lord's seisin. He is entitled to and seised
of, not the land itself, but a seignory, the services, fealty,
homage of a tenant. As the earl can be guilty of disseising
Ralph of the land, so Ralph can be guilty of disseising the earl
of the rent or other service that the earl has heretofore received,
and an assize of novel disseisin lies for such incorporeals; he
disseises the earl if he resists a lawful distress for services in
arrear[2]. So a stranger by compelling Ralph to pay rent to him
instead of to the earl, can be guilty of disseising the earl[3]. The
existence as legal entities of those complex units known as
'manors,' a seisin of which when analyzed consists in part of
the actual occupation by oneself or one's villein tenants of
certain parcels of land, and in part of the receipt of rents or
other services from freehold tenants, sadly complicates the
matter; but on the whole the 'seisin of land in service' is
ceasing to be spoken of as a seisin of the land, and is being
regarded more and more as the seisin of the service, an incorporeal thing.

This sort of seisin could be attributed to a 'reversioner,' for
in truth a reversioner was a lord with a tenant below him.
The tenant for life was seised, but he was capable of disseising
the reversioner; he would, for example, be guilty of this, if he
made a feoffment in fee, an act incompatible with his lawful
position and injurious to the reversioner[4]. On the other hand,
we can not find that any sort or kind of seisin was as yet
attributed to the remainderman. He was not seised of the

Case of the rever-sioner.

---

[1] If the lord's tenant is disseised and dies out of seisin and without heirs, it
seems doubtful whether at this time the lord has any action by which as against
the disseisor, his heirs or feoffees, he can insist on his right to an escheat. Note
Book, pl. 422; The Mystery of Seisin, L. Q. R. ii. 487.

[2] Bracton, f. 203; Britton, i. 275, 281.

[3] Bracton, f. 169, 203 b.   [4] Bracton, f. 161 b.

land in demesne, and he was not, like the reversioner, seised of it 'in service,' for no service was due to him.

Infants etc. We can not find that our law ever saw the slightest difficulty in an attribution of seisin to infants or to *communitates*. It is common also to speak of a church as being seised.

General doctrine. On the whole we may say that the possession of land which the law protects under the name of a 'seisin of freehold,' is the occupation of land by one who has come to it otherwise than as tenant in villeinage, tenant at will, tenant for term of years or guardian, that occupation being exercised by himself, his servants, guardians, tenants in villeinage, tenants at will or tenants for term of years. This seems the best statement of the matter:—occupation of land is seisin of free tenement unless it has been obtained in one of certain particular ways. If, how- [p. 40] ever, we prefer to look at the other side of the principle, we may say that the *animus* required of the person who is 'seised of free tenement' is the intent to hold that land as though he were tenant for life or tenant in fee holding by some free tenure.

Protection of possession. More remains to be said of the nature of seisin, especially of that element in it which we have spoken of as occupation; but this can best be said if we turn to speak of the effects of seisin, its protection by law, its relation to proprietary rights.

Modern theories. We may make our task the lighter if for one moment we glance at controversies which have divided the legal theorists of our own day. Why does our law protect possession? Several different answers have been, or may be, given to this question. There is something in it that attracts the speculative lawyer, for there is something that can be made to look like a paradox. Why should law, when it has on its hands the difficult work of protecting ownership and other rights in things, prepare puzzles for itself by undertaking to protect something that is not ownership, something that will from to time come into sharp collision with ownership? Is it not a main object of law that every one should enjoy what is his own *de iure*, and if so why are we to consecrate that *de facto* enjoyment which is signified by the term *possession*, and why, above all, are we to protect the possessor even against the owner?

It is chiefly, though not solely, in relation to the classical Roman law that these questions have been discussed, and, if any profitable discussion of them is to be had, it seems essential that some definite body of law should be examined with an accurate heed of dates and successive stages of development. If, scorning all relations of space and time, we ask why law protects possession, the only true answer that we are likely to get is that the law of different peoples at different times has protected possession for many different reasons. Nor can we utterly leave out of account motives and aims of which an abstract jurisprudence knows nothing. That simple justice may be done between man and man has seldom been the sole object of legislators; political have interfered with juristic interests. An illustration may make this plainer. We may well believe that Henry II. when he instituted the possessory assizes was not without thought of the additional strength that [p. 41] would accrue to him and his successors, could he make his subjects feel that they owed the beatitude of possession to his ordinance and the action of his court. Still, whatever may be the legislator's motive, judges must find some rational principle which shall guide them in the administration of possessory remedies; and they have a choice between different principles. These may perhaps be reduced in number to four, or may be said to cluster round four types.

In the first place, the protection given to possession may be merely a provision for the better maintenance of peace and quiet. It is a prohibition of self-help in the interest of public order. The possessor is protected, not on account of any merits of his, but because the peace must be kept; to allow men to make forcible entries on land or to seize goods without form of law, is to invite violence. Just so the murderer, whose life is forfeited to law, may not be slain, save in due form of law; in a civilized state he is protected against irregular vengeance, not because he deserves to live, for he deserves to die, but because the permission of revenge would certainly do more harm than good to the community. Were this then the only principle at work, we should naturally expect to find the protection of possession in some chapter of the criminal law dealing with offences against public order, riots, affrays, and the like. *Possession and criminal law.*

Others would look for it, not in the law of crimes, but in the law of torts or civil injuries. The possessor's possession is protected, not indeed because he has any sort of right in the thing, but because in general one can not disturb his possession without being guilty, or almost guilty, of some injury to his *Possession and the law of tort.*

person, some act which, if it does not amount to an assault, still comes so dangerously near to an assault that it can be regarded as an invasion of that sphere of peace and quiet which the law should guarantee to every one of its subjects. This doctrine which found expression in Savigny's famous essay has before now raised an echo in an English court :—'These rights of action are given in respect of the immediate and present violation of possession, independently of rights of property. They are an extension of that protection which the law throws around the person[1].'

Possession as a bulwark of property. A very different theory, that of the great Ihering, has gained ground in our own time. In order to give an adequate protection to ownership, it has been found necessary to protect [p. 42] possession. To prove ownership is difficult, to prove possession comparatively easy. Suppose a land-owner ejected from possession; to require of him to prove his ownership before he can be reinstated, is to require too much; thieves and land-grabbers will presume upon the difficulty that a rightful owner will have in making out a flawless title. It must be enough then that the ejected owner should prove that he was in possession and was ejected; the ejector must be precluded from pleading that the possession which he disturbed was not possession under good title. Possession then is an outwork of property. But though the object of the law in protecting possession is to protect the possession of those who have a right to possess, that object can only be obtained by protecting every possessor. Once allow any question about property to be raised, and the whole plan of affording easy remedies to ousted owners will break down. In order that right may be triumphant, the possessory action must be open to the evil and to the good, it must draw no distinction between the just and the unjust possessor. The protection of wrongful possessors is an unfortunate but unavoidable consequence of the attempt to protect rightful possessors. This theory would make us look for the law of possession, not in the law of crimes, nor in the law of torts, but in very close connexion with the law of property.

Possession as a kind of right. There is yet another opinion, which differs from the last, though both make a close connexion between possession and proprietary rights. Possession as such deserves protection, and really there is little more to be said, at least by the lawyer.

[1] *Rogers* v. *Spence*, 13 Meeson and Welsby, 581.

He who possesses has by the mere fact of his possession more right in the thing than the non-possessor has; he of all men has most right in the thing until someone has asserted and proved a greater right. When a thing belongs to no one and is capable of appropriation, the mere act of taking possession of it gives right against all the world; when a thing belongs to A, the mere fact that B takes possession of it still gives B a right which is good against all who have no better.

An attempt might be made, and it would be in harmony with our English modes of thought, to evade any choice between these various 'abstract principles' by a frank profession of the utilitarian character of law. But the success which awaits such an attempt seems very doubtful; for, granted that in some way or another the protection of possession promotes the welfare of the community, the question still arises, why and in what measure this is so. Under what sub-head of 'utility' shall we bring this protection? Shall we lay stress on the public disorder which would be occasioned by unrestricted 'self-help,' on the probability that personal injuries will be done to individuals, on the necessity of providing ready remedies for ousted owners, on the natural expectation that what a man possesses he will be allowed to possess until some one has proved a better title? This is no idle question, for on the answer to it must depend the extent to which and the mode in which possession ought to be consecrated. Measures, which would be quite adequate to prevent any serious danger of general disorder, would be quite inadequate to give the ejected owner an easy action for recovering what is his. If all that we want is peace and quiet, it may be enough to punish ejectors by fine or imprisonment; but this does nothing for ejected possessors, gives them no recovery of the possession that they have lost. Again, let us grant that the ejected possessor should be able to recover the land from the ejector if the latter is still in possession; but suppose that the land has already passed into a third hand; shall the ejected possessor be able to recover it from him to whom the ejector has given or sold it? If to this question we say Yes, we shall hardly be able to justify our answer by any theory which regards injury to the person, or something very like injury to the person, as the gist of the possessory action, for here we shall be taking possession away from one who has come to it without violence.

Contrast between various principles

[p. 43]

The
various
principles
in English
law.
Now we ought—so it seems to us—to see that there well
may be a certain truth in all these theories. That the German
jurists in their attempts to pin the Roman lawyers down to
some one neat doctrine of possession and of the reasons for
protecting it, may have been engaged on an impossible task, it is
not for us to suggest in this place; but so far as concerns our
own English law we make no doubt that at different times and
in different measures every conceivable reason for protecting
possession has been felt as a weighty argument and has had
its influence on rights and remedies. At first we find the
several principles working together in harmonious concert;
they will work together because as yet they are not sharply
defined. Gradually their outlines become clearer; discrepancies
between them begin to appear; and, as the result of long [p. 44]
continued conflict, some of them are victorious at the expense
of others.

Disseisin
as an
offence.
A glance at the law books of the thirteenth century is
sufficient to tell us that this is so. The necessity of keeping
the peace is often insisted on by those who are describing the
great possessory action, the assize of novel disseisin. Every
disseisin is a breach of the peace; a disseisin perpetrated with
violence is a serious breach. In any case the disseisor is to be
amerced, and the amount of the amercement is never to be less
than the amount of the damages. But the justices will inquire
whether he came with force and arms, and, if he did so, he will
be sent to prison and fined. Besides this he has to give the
sheriff an ox, 'the disseisin ox' or five shillings[1]. If he repeats
his offence, if he disseises one who has already recovered seisin
from him by the assize, this of course is a still graver affair; he
must go to prison because he has broken the king's peace, and
because he has contemned the king's court[2]. The necessity for
a statute against these 'redisseisors' shows us how serious a
danger to the state was the practice of 'land-grabbing'; men
did not scruple to eject those who had been put in seisin by
the king's court.

Disseisin
as a tort.
In the second place, the disseisor can be condemned to pay
damages to the disseisee. This is a notable point, for in the
first quarter of the thirteenth century the assize of novel
disseisin was the only action in which both land and damages
could be recovered. The man who merely possessed land

---

[1] Bracton, f. 161 b, 186 b, 187.   [2] Bracton, f. 236; Stat. Mert. c. 3.

without having any right to possess it did not incur any liability for damages, and it would seem that he was entitled to the fruits of the land taken by him before judgment; but the disseisor was guilty of an *iniuria*, of a tort, for which he had to pay damages. Bracton is very clear that a disseisin is an *iniuria*; the assize of novel disseisin, when it is brought against the disseisor himself, is a personal action founded on tort; and this is the reason why if the disseisor dies there can be no assize against his heir; that heir in taking possession of what his ancestor possessed is guilty of no tort; the tort dies with the person who committed it[1].

[p. 45]   But in the third place, the possessory assizes extend far beyond what is necessary for the conservation of the peace and the reparation of the wrong done by violent ejectment. Suppose that *A* is seised; *B* disseises *A* and enfeoffs *C*; *A* can bring the assize of novel disseisin against *B* and *C* jointly; against *B* it is an action for damages founded on tort; against *C* it is an action for the recovery of the land; *C* will not have to pay damages, for he has not been guilty of any *iniuria*, unless indeed the feoffment followed so close on the disseisin that *C* must be treated as a participator in *B*'s guilt; but in any case *C* will have to give up the land[2]. It is obvious that a doctrine which treats the possessory action as an action founded on delict, will hardly account for this; still less, as we shall see hereafter, will it account for the assize of mort d'ancestor.

Possessory action against the third hand.

There is a great deal in our ancient law that countenances a different theory, namely, that which looks upon possession as 'an outwork of property.' In the thirteenth century the proprietary action for land is regarded as cumbrous and risky. It has been urged[3] against this theory that 'in ninety-nine cases out of a hundred, it is about as easy and cheap to prove at least a *prima facie* title as it is to prove possession.' That may be so in modern times; but our ancestors would not have accepted the

Proof of seisin and proof of ownership.

---

[1] Bracton, f. 164 b, 175 b–179, 187. This doctrine comes out strongly in a small tract found in MSS. (*e.g.* Camb. Univ. Lib. Ll. 4. 17, f. 181) *Articuli qui in narrando indigent observari*: 'Item breve novae disseisinae currit in dominico tantum, quum breve illud supponit arduam transgressionem; et ne quis ex tam recenti iniuria videatur commodum portare, conceditur in odium spoliatoris seu disseisitoris quod disseisitus statum suum, etiam non coloratum de feodo aut iure, propter personale factum illatum sibi disseisito, possit recuperare, dummodo per assisam seu per recognitionem constet de abiectione.'

[2] Bracton. f. 175 b.   [3] Holmes, The Common Law, 211.

saying. The procedure in an assize of novel disseisin was incomparably more speedy than the procedure in a writ of right, and in the latter the tenant could always refuse the foreknowable verdict of men and put himself upon the unforeknowable judgment of God. But further, it seems constantly assumed in our books that the possessory remedy exists chiefly for the benefit of those who have good title: that normally the possessor is one who has a right to possess. If he is disseised, he can bring a writ of right; but he will not do so, because he has a far more expeditious and certain remedy[1].

Seisin as a root of title.

But in the fourth place, the protection of seisin and of rights begotten by seisin seems to be carried far beyond what is necessary for the adequate protection of ownership. Seisin, we may say, generates a title to the land, a title good against all who have no better because older title. Suppose that A, who of all men has best right, is seised; B disseises him; B has a title good against all but A; C disseises B; C has a title good against all but A and B; and so on; Z the last of a series of disseisors will have a title good against all, save those signified by the other letters of the alphabet. And these titles are descendible; B's heir will have a worse title than A's heir but a better title than C's heir. English law both medieval and modern seems to accept to the full this theory:—Every title to land has its root in seisin; the title which has its root in the oldest seisin is the best title. We have not to deal with two persons and no more, one of whom has *dominium* while the other has *possessio*; we may have to deal with an indefinitely large number of titles relatively good and relatively bad.

Introduction of possessory actions.

This by way of preface. We must now trace the growth of a set of definitely possessory actions, actions for the protection of seisin or of that sort of title which is begotten by seisin. We can hardly pursue this matter beyond the assizes of Henry II. We are told, however, by German historians that a distinctly possessory action is not native in the law of our race[2]. Wherever it appears, whether in France or Germany or England, it

[p. 46]

---

[1] Thus in the popular tract *Cum sit necessarium:* 'In omni casu de placito terrae ubi aliquis petit tenementum aliquod de seisina propria vel per descensum hereditarium potest fieri breve de recto patens quod est omnium aliorum in sua natura supremum. Set propter istius brevis de recto *nimiam dilacionem et manifesta pericula evitanda* possunt fieri per alia brevia remedia celeriora.'

[2] Heusler, Gewere, 255.

bears witness to the influence of Roman law, acting either immediately, or through the medium of canon law.   Of course under the old formal procedure the position of a defendant in an action must as a general rule have been preferable to that of a plaintiff.   It is so now-a-days; but while we describe the defendant's beatitude by saying that the burden of the proof lies on the plaintiff, our remote ancestors would have said that the benefit of the proof is enjoyed by the defendant.   And the benefit of the proof was often enormous; the party to whom it is adjudged may have merely to swear to his right and find others who will swear formally and in set phrase that his oath is true.   Therefore when there is to be litigation every one would wish to be defendant.   Normally the possessor of the thing must be the defendant; but it must soon have been apparent that the unqualified action of this rule would lead to [p. 47] gross injustice.   Both *A* and *B* assert a title to land; *A* is in possession; *B* turns *A* out in order that he (*B*) may play the easy part of defendant in the forthcoming action.   To prevent this flagrant wrong it might become necessary to inquire whether the defendant in the action was really entitled to the advantages normally given to defendants, to inquire whether *B* had ejected *A*, as a preliminary to deciding whether *A* or *B* had the better right.   The possessory question would here appear as a mere preliminary to the proprietary question. It is said that German law without foreign help got as far as this, and there are passages in the *Leges Henrici* which suggest that this is true of English law also[1].   Even the definitely possessory actions which Henry II. made general both in Normandy and in England, may have had forerunners[2].

Be this as it may, in Henry II.'s day, and seemingly in the year 1166[3], we came by a distinctly possessory action, the assize

The novel disseisin.

---

[1] Leg. Hen. 29, § 2: 'et seisiatus placitet.' Ibid. 61, § 21: 'et nemo placitet dissaisiatus.'   Ibid. 53, § 3: 'Nullus a domino suo inplegiatus, vel inlegiatus, vel iniuste dissaisiatus ab eodem implacitetur ante legitimam restitutionem.' Ibid. 53, § 5: 'Et nemo dissaisiatus placitet, nisi circa ipsam dissaisiationem agatur.'   But even these passages seem to show the influence of the canonists' *exceptio spolii*. William of Malmesbury, Gesta Regum, ii. 553, makes the legate say to King Stephen, 'Rex itaque faciat quod etiam in forensibus iudiciis legitimum est facere, ut revestiat episcopos de rebus suis; alioquin iure gentium dissaisiti non placitabunt.'   This is the *exceptio spolii*, and apparently by *ius gentium* is meant the temporal law.

[2] Bigelow, Placita, 128.   [3] See above, vol. i. p. 145.

of novel disseisin. There can we think be no doubt that this action was suggested by the canonist's *actio spolii*, which itself had its origin in the Roman interdict *unde vi*[1]. But when once adopted, English law very speedily made it her own. It soon became an exceedingly popular action. The plea rolls of Richard's reign and John's are covered with assizes of novel disseisin, many of which are brought by very humble persons and deal with minute parcels of land.

A summary action. It was, according to the notions of the time, and it would [p. 48] be even according to our own notions, a summary action. At every point it was sharply contrasted with the proprietary action for land, the writ of right. The writ by which the plaintiff begins his action bids the sheriff summon twelve men to declare (*recognoscere*) whether since some recent date, for instance, the king's last voyage to Normandy, the defendant has unjustly and without judgment disseised the plaintiff of 'his free tenement' in a certain vill[2]. We need not here speak of the expeditious procedure, the exclusion of essoins, of vouchers to warranty and so forth; but must notice that if the defendant does not appear, the assize will be taken by default, and that if he does appear there need be no pleading between the parties. There is properly speaking no pleading to issue[3]. The question to be addressed to the jurors has been formulated before the defendant appeared. On the earliest rolls we seldom see any pleadings in this action. The question is put to the jurors. They answer with a monosyllable, Yes or No, and judgment is given; in the one case the plaintiff recovers his seisin with damages, in the other his action is dismissed. Sometimes, however, the defendant will plead some *exceptio*, some special plea: that is, he will allege some reason why the assize should

---

[1] The terms 'iniuste et sine iudicio' point to the *actio spolii*. They are to be found in the Leges Henrici, 74, § 1, though oddly enough in connexion with homicide: 'qui iniuste vel sine iudicio fuerint occisi.' They occur also in a writ of Henry I.; Bigelow, Placita, 128, 130: 'unde ipsi sunt iniuste et sine iudicio dissaysiti.' A similar phrase often occurs in John of Salisbury's legal correspondence with the Pope touching English ecclesiastical causes; thus *e.g.* Opera, ed. Giles, i. p. 5, 'violenter et absque ordine iudiciario expulisset'; p. 10, 'spoliatum......absque iudicio'; p. 13, 'violenter et sine iudicio destitutus'; p. 18, 'absque ordine iudiciario spoliatum.'

[2] Glanvill, xiii. 33; Bracton, f. 179; Summa, p. 220; Ancienne coutume, c. 94 (ed. de Gruchy, p. 214).

[3] Brevia Placitata, ed. Turner, p. 27.

not be taken, why the formulated question should not be
answered; and this grows more frequent in course of time.
Also—and this is the practice of Bracton's day—the justices
begin to require that the plaintiff shall explain his case,
explain how he came to be seised[1]. Sometimes again a special
plea (*exceptio*) will lead the litigants down a bye path, and
they will come to issue about some question which is not that
which was formulated in the writ. Thus the assize may be
converted into a jury (*assisa vertitur in iuratam*); the verdict
of the twelve men who have been summoned, or it may be of
another twelve, will be taken about the new question which
has arisen out of the pleadings[2]. In all these ways what were
[p. 49] by this time regarded as questions of law, were being withdrawn from the jurors; they were often questions about the
nature of 'seisin,' 'disseisin,' 'free tenement.' A great deal of
law was growing up around these matters. Still even in
Edward I.'s day the question stated in the writ was often left
to the jurors, and they answered it as of old by a monosyllable.

But the most important point for us to observe is that in
Bracton's day this assize protects a thoroughly wrongful, un-
titled and vicious possession. Any special pleas that are
regarded as pleas of proprietary right are strictly excluded[3].
It is perfectly possible that a true owner should be guilty of
having disseised 'unjustly and without a judgment' one who not
merely was a wrongful possessor, but obtained his possession
by unlawful force, and unlawful force directed against the true
owner. We will suppose that *A*, the lawful tenant in fee, or
for life, is ejected by *X*, who has no right whatever; the assize
sets a strict limit to *A*'s right of self-help. He must re-eject
X at once or not at all; if he does this after a brief delay,
then he is guilty of disseising *X* unjustly and without a
judgment from his (*X*'s) free tenement; *X* will bring an assize
against him; *A* will not be permitted to plead his better
right; *A* will lose the land and will be amerced; if he has

Protection of wrongful seisin.

---

[1] Bracton, f. 183 b.

[2] The distinction between a verdict given *in modo assisae* and one given *in modo iuratae* was of great importance in Bracton's day (f. 288 b, 289 b), for in the former case the jurors might be attainted, while in the latter there could be no attaint, since both parties had put themselves upon the verdict.

[3] This has been argued at length in The Beatitude of Seisin; L. Q. R. iv. 24.

come with force and arms, he will be imprisoned. Now
Bracton seems to have inherited an ancient set of rules as to
the time within which a re-ejectment is a lawful act and no
disseisin. If *A* in person was expelled from the land, he has
but four days for the re-ejectment. We are elsewhere told that
he may ride one day east, another west, another north, another
south, to collect friends and arms, and must perpetrate the
re-ejectment on the fifth day at the latest[1]. If he was away
from the land when the disseisin was done, then he has a
somewhat longer time, which is reckoned from the moment
when he hears of the disseisin. A reasonable time must be
allowed him for hastening to the tenement, and then he will
have his four days. Bracton, however, seems inclined to make
light of these rules, which look old, and to explain them away
in terms that he has learned from the glossators. The ejected
A so soon as he is ejected has ceased to possess *corpore,* but [p. 50]
he has not ceased to possess *animo*; he has lost the *possessio
naturalis,* but not the *possessio civilis.* This 'possession in
law' he does not lose until in some mode or another he has
acquiesced in the fact of the disseisin. This thought, that the
disseisor gets his seisin by the acquiescence or negligence of
the ousted possessor, becomes prominent in after times. Under
its influence the justices begin to require that a plaintiff shall
show something more than mere possession, that he shall show
either that he came to the land by title, for example, by a
feoffment, or else that he has been in possession for some little
time. But there seems no doubt that in Edward I.'s day,
though the old rule about the four days may have been disregarded in practice, the disseisor, and the disseisor who had
no title whatever, could still somewhat easily acquire a 'seisin
of free tenement,' a seisin protected by the assize, even as
against the ejected owner[2].

Relativity
of seisin.
　　　　Protected even as against the ejected owner—this we say,
for in the very moment of the disseisin, the disseisor, so soon as
de facto he has the land to himself, is protected against all
others. As against them he is seised of free tenement, and it
is nothing to them, says Bracton, that his seisin is slight
(*tenera*) and wrongfully acquired[3]. Here we come upon a very
curious idea, but one which is to become of great importance

[1] L. Q. R. iv. 30.　　　　　　　　[2] L. Q. R. iv. 287.
[3] Bracton, f. 209 b.

hereafter, the relativity of seisin. One may be seised as regards the world at large, and yet not seised as regards him whom one has ejected.

The disseisin must be 'novel.' In Normandy the action Novelty must be brought within a year after the wrongful act. The of the question for the jurors is whether the defendant has disseised disseisin. the plaintiff since the last harvest[1]. Harvest is the time when a man exploits his seisin in a very obvious fashion under the eyes of all his neighbours. Every one knows who it was that garnered the last crop. In England—unfortunately, as we well may think,—the matter was otherwise settled. From time to time a royal ordinance set a limit to the action. When Glanvill was writing, the king's last passage to Normandy fixed the boundary; and this can hardly have given the disseised even a [p. 51] year for his action[2]. But kings forget to make such ordinances and the action is showing itself to be useful. When our plea rolls begin in 1194, the limiting date is that of Richard's first coronation in 1189. In 1236 a period of near twenty years, that which has elapsed since Henry III.'s first coronation, has been open to plaintiffs. In 1236 or 1237 a statute or ordinance gave them a term of some six or seven years by confining them to the time that had passed since the king's voyage to Britanny in 1230[3]. No change was made until 1275, when a day in 1242 was chosen, and that day limited the assize of novel disseisin until the reign of Henry VIII.[4]. Somewhat the same fate had befallen the mort d'ancestor. In Normandy it was an annual action[5]. In England it was never so straitly limited. When Glanvill wrote, a plaintiff could still go back to 1154[6]. In 1236 or 1237 he was allowed to go back to 1210[7]. In 1275 he was allowed to go back to 1216, and this he might do

---

[1] Somma, p. 220; Ancienne coutume, c. 94 (ed. de Gruchy, pp. 214, 218).

[2] Glanvill, xiii. 32, 33. Henry crossed to Normandy in February 1187, returned to England in January 1188, and crossed once more in July 1188.

[3] Stat. Merton c. 8 (Statutes, i. 4); Note Book, i. p. 106; iii. p. 230. The best evidence points to *Britanniam* not *Vasconiam*.

[4] In 1236 or 1237 Henry's first voyage to Britanny was mentioned; in 1275 by Stat. West. I. c. 39, his first voyage into Gascony. Now in 1230 Henry went to Britanny and passed thence through Anjou and Poitou into Gascony; but this can not we think be the first voyage to Gascony of the Statute of 1275. We take that voyage to be the expedition of 1242. Coke, Sec. Inst. 238, speaks of a voyage to Gascony in 5 Hen. III. There was no such voyage.

[5] Somma, p. 239; Ancienne coutume, c. 99.

[6] Glanvill, xiii. 3.   [7] Note Book, pl. 1217.

until 1540[1]. These are not uninteresting details. A possessory action is likely to lose some of its possessory characteristics if the plaintiff is suffered to rely on ancient facts.

'Unjustly and without judgment.'

The words of the writ charge the defendant not merely with a disseisin, but with a disseisin perpetrated 'unjustly and without a judgment.' We might think perhaps that the word *iniuste* left open a door for pleas of proprietary right, and that though a man has done a disseisin, he has not done it unjustly if he has but ejected from possession a man who acquired it by unlawful force. But it is very doubtful whether the word was intended to have this effect. The model for possessory actions was the interdict *unde vi* of Justinian's day, which would protect one who had acquired his possession by force and by force used against the true owner[2]. At any rate, in Bracton's day the [p. 52] construction put upon this term left no room for proprietary pleas. He who disseises another without judgment—unless he is but re-ejecting an ejector who has not as yet acquired seisin as against him—does this unjustly; in one sense he may have *ius*, proprietary right, on his side, but he infringes a right given by possession[3]. As to the words *sine iudicio*, which are equivalent to the *absque ordine iudiciario* of the canonists, we may translate them by 'without process of law,' noticing, however, that a disseisin done 'by judgment' may still be an unjust and an actionable disseisin[4].

Rigorous prohibition of self-help.

The maintenance of a possessory action as rigorous as that which we are considering requires of those who control it a high degree of that quality which we may call lawyerly courage. They will often be called upon to do evil that good may come, to protect the land-grabber against his victim in order that land may not be grabbed. They must harden their hearts and enforce the rule. We can not say that the judges of Bracton's age, or Bracton himself, always hardened their hearts sufficiently, always closed their ears to the claims of 'better right'; they would sometimes lean towards 'substantial justice.' Still it seems to us that they had no other theory of the novel

---

[1] Stat. West. I. c. 39; 32 Hen. VIII. c. 2.

[2] Inst. iv. 15. 6; Bracton, f. 210 b. However, the Norman assize seems to have been denied to one who obtained possession by force; Somma, p. 234; Ancienne coutume, c. 95. It is possible that the words of the Institutes may have influenced the English practice.

[3] Note Book, i. p. 85–6.   [4] Bracton, f. 205 b.

disseisin than that which we are endeavouring to explain, and the thought that violent self-help is a contempt of the king's court helped to prevent any wide aberrations from this theory[1].

A few other traits of this action deserve notice. Besides serving as 'an interdict for the recovery of possession,' it will often serve as 'an interdict for the retention of possession.' To constitute an actionable disseisin, a successful ejectment of the possessor is not indispensable; an unsuccessful attempt, a repelled invasion, will be enough. But further, if without [p.53] attempting to eject, one troubles the possessor in his possession, this will often be disseisin enough, if he chooses to treat it as such[2]. An action in the king's courts founded on mere trespass and aiming merely at the exaction of damages is a comparatively new phenomenon; such actions only become common late in the reign of Henry III. Many mere trespasses, as we should think them, have been treated as disseisins; at all events repeated trespassing can be so treated, if the possessor elects to consider himself disseised[3]. To meet that troubling of possession which is caused by nuisances as distinguished from trespasses, that is, by things that are erected, made, or done, not on the soil possessed by the complainant but on neighbouring soil, there has all along been an 'assize of nuisance' which is a supplement for the novel disseisin[4]. Law endeavours to protect the person who is seised of land, not merely in the possession of the land, but in the enjoyment of those rights against his neighbours which he would be entitled to were he seised under a good title.

In the first age of its operation the novel disseisin seems to have been directed against acts which could be called ejectments in the strictest sense of the word, though, as just said, any persistent interference with possession might fall within it.

Trespass and disseisin.

Disseisin of an absent possessor.

---

[1] Occasionally Bracton suggests an examination of the plaintiff's *causa possidendi*, which can not be justified by his general principle. See in particular f. 169 b. A woman is in seisin as doweress; then it is proved in an ecclesiastical court that she was never married; she may be ejected, for her *causa possidendi* is proved to be false. This is a very dangerous decision if the assize is to keep its possessory rigour.

[2] Bracton, f. 161 b. The 'disseisin at election' of later law was an elaborate outgrowth of this idea.

[3] Bracton, f. 216 b: 'Frequentia enim mutat transgressionem in disseisinam.' Y. B. 20–1 Edw. I. p. 393.

[4] Glanvill, xiii. 34–5–6; Bracton, f. 233; Reg. Brev. Orig. f. 198 b.

English law was perfectly ready to say with the Roman text that, if a man goes to market and returns to find on his land an interloper who resists his entry, he has been ejected[1]. Probably it was prepared to hold that a person who has once acquired seisin always retains seisin until he dies, or is disseised, or in some formal manner gives up his seisin, and that for another to take to himself the land of which seisin is being thus retained is a disseisin[2]. But it had to consider other cases, cases in which some person who is in occupation of the land, but who is not seised of it, takes upon himself to deliver seisin to another. [p. 54] For example, the land is occupied by a bailiff, by a villein tenant, by a termor or by a guardian, who takes upon himself to sell the land and enfeoff a stranger. This feoffee is now seised; but is there here a disseisin; is the feoffee a disseisor? The answer that our law gives to this question in later days is, 'Yes; there is a disseisin; both feoffor and feoffee are disseisors.' A statute of 1285 was needed to make the matter plain, but the law of Bracton's day seems to have been inclining towards this answer. This however was, to all seeming, an extension of the original notion of disseisin, and it was one that was likely to occasion many a difficulty in the future[3].

The scope of the assize.

A still more momentous matter is the treatment of those who have come to the possession of the land after the perpetration of the disseisin. Suppose that M disseises A and enfeoffs X; or that M disseises A and that X disseises M. Can A in either of these cases recover the land by this assize from X?

[1] Bracton, f. 161 b; Dig. 43, 16, 1, § 24.

[2] Bracton (see f. 38 b, 39), adopting what is now regarded as a misinterpretation of a famous passage of Paulus, Dig. 50, 17, 153, would hold that the man who has once been seised can retain seisin *animo solo*, and so remain seised though he never cultivates nor goes near the land. It seems very doubtful whether a man could (or can) get rid of a seisin once acquired, except by delivering seisin to some one else.

[3] Stat. West. II. c. 25; 2nd Inst. 412; Ibid. 154; L. Q. R. iv. p. 297. The law of Bracton's day provides for these cases writs of entry—even for the case where the feoffor is a mere bailiff; Bracton, f. 323 b. These writs afterwards dropped out from the Register; see Reg. Brev. Orig. p. 231, where it is noted that the writ of entry on alienation by a villein has given way to the assize; for the actual use of such a writ see Note Book, pl. 713. We may say pretty confidently that in Bracton's day no one would ever have used a writ of entry if he could have brought the assize. But Bracton, f. 161 b (this passage is marginal in some MSS.), is coming to the opinion that a feoffment by guardian or termor is a disseisin, and even that a feoffment in fee by tenant for life is a disseisin of the reversioner.

The answer to this question is very instructive. The writ must say of the plaintiff that he has been disseised by the defendant or defendants. These words are to be construed with some strictness. The action lies for the disseisee against the disseisor. It does not lie for the heir of the disseisee; it does not lie against the heir of the disseisor; nor, if the disseisor is dead, does it lie against the feoffee of the disseisor, or against the disseisor of the disseisor. But suppose the disseisor still alive, then this action can be brought by the disseisee against the disseisor and any person who has come to the land through or under the disseisor or by disseising the disseisor. In the cases that we have just now put, if M is still alive, A can, and indeed, if he would succeed, must bring the assize against M and X jointly. He will say in his writ that M and X have disseised him. Upon

[p. 55] M will fall the punishment due to disseisors. Whether X also has laid himself open to that punishment, is a question as to the time that had elapsed after the disseisin and before X came to the land. If, for example, M enfeoffed X during the time allowed to A for self-help—normally, as we have seen, four days—then X is treated as a participator in the disseisin; A might have ejected him by force, and if A sues both M and X both can be punished. If, on the other hand, the feoffment to X was made after the interval which debarred A from self-help, then X can not be punished. But—and this is what chiefly concerns us—in any case if X is sued along with M, he can be compelled to restore the tenement to A[1].

Now here our law is answering a vital question. It is decreeing that a person who has come to the possession of land fairly and honestly and by feoffment, one who, as it admits, is no disseisor[2], can be compelled to give up the land merely because he acquired the land—it may be at a distant remove—from one who was guilty of a disseisin; and no opportunity will be allowed him of pleading any proprietary right that he may have. It is very possible that when the assize was first instituted this result was not intended or not foreseen. The writ which brings this feoffee before the court will accuse him of having perpetrated or joined in the perpetration of a disseisin. Practice has been extending the scope of the assize. The

A possessory action against the third hand.

---

[1] Bracton, f. 175 b–177.

[2] Bracton, f. 175 b: 'quia illi non sunt disseisitores.' Yet the writ will distinctly charge them with having joined in a disseisin.

outcome is capricious. Whether the assize will lie against the feoffee (*X*) is a question that is made to depend on the, to our minds, irrelevant question, whether the original disseisor (*M*) is yet alive and is comprehended in the writ; for it is absolutely essential to the success of the assize that the original disseisor should be a defendant[1]. This caprice, however, is becoming more apparent than real, for if the original disseisor is dead, and the feoffee can no longer be hit by the assize, he can be hit by a newer action, called a 'writ of entry sur disseisin.' Of that writ we shall have to speak hereafter, and shall then be in a position to consider the whole policy of our law in giving possessory actions against those who have been guilty of no disseisin. Meanwhile we will follow the chronological order of [p. 56] development and speak of the second possessory assize.

The assize of mort d'ancestor. The mort d'ancestor is a few years younger than the novel disseisin[2] and is a much more distinctive product of Norman and English law[3]. Its formula runs as follows:

Whether *M* the father [mother, uncle, aunt, brother, sister] of *A* (the plaintiff) was seised in his demesne as of fee of so much land [rent, or the like] in such a vill on the day on which he died; and whether he died since the period of limitation; and whether *A* is his next heir; which land *X* (the defendant) holds[4].

If all these questions are answered in the plaintiff's favour he recovers the land.

A summary action. The action is summary; not indeed so summary as the novel disseisin; there may be more essoining and the defendant may vouch a warrantor who is not named in the writ; but still it is summary when compared with the proprietary action begun by writ of right. Before there has been any pleading, before the defendant has appeared, twelve recognitors are summoned to answer the formulated question; the assize

---

[1] Note Book, pl. 336.   [2] See above, vol. i. p. 147.

[3] We are not aware of any foreign model after which this assize was fashioned. The plaint of *nouvelle dissaisine*, or more briefly of *nouvelleté*, became a well-known action in French customary law. On the other hand, we do not know that the *mort d'ancestor* is found outside Normandy. Bracton, f. 103 b, 104, while he compares the one to the *unde vi*, sees in the other a *possessoria hereditatis petitio*. However ingenious this may be (see Ihering, Besitzesschutz, pp. 85–87), it is probably an afterthought.

[4] Glanvill, xiii. 3; Bracton, f. 253 b. There are variations adapted to the case of civil death by monastic profession and death on pilgrimage.

can be taken and the plaintiff can get judgment even though
the defendant does not appear.

It is regarded as a strictly possessory action. The plaintiff
asserts that, within some recent time fixed by ordinance, one,
whose next heir he is, died seised of the tenement in question.
He has to make out not merely that he is this ancestor's next
heir, but that there was a very near relationship between them.
The plaintiff must be son, daughter, brother, sister, nephew or
niece of this ancestor. This restriction of the assize is curious.
There can be no principle of jurisprudence involved in the
denial of this action to one who is grandson or cousin of the
ancestor; a next heir is a next heir however remote he may be.

[p. 57] But in the history of our forms of action we have frequently to
notice that law begins by providing for common cases, and will
often leave uncommon cases unprovided for, even though they
fall within an established principle. In this particular instance,
however, there is more to be said. The mort d'ancestor is a
blow aimed at feudalism by a high-handed king. Not only
does it draw away business from the seignorial courts, but it
strikes directly at those lords who, for one reason or another, are
apt to seize the land that is left vacant by the death of a
tenant[1]. But even a high-handed king must, as the phrase
goes, draw the line somewhere, and may have to draw it without
much regard for legal logic. Besides if the plaintiff must rely
on remote kinship, we can not urge that, since the relevant
facts must be known to the neighbours, there is no place for
trial by battle. About half-a-century later, after a dispute
between the justices and the magnates, the former succeeded
in instituting the actions of aiel, besaiel, tresaiel and cosinage
(*de avo, de proavo, de tritavo, de consanguinitate*) as supplements
for the assize of mort d'ancestor[2].

The mort d'ancestor possessory.

---

[1] Assize of Northampton, c. 4. The words of this ordinance do not expressly
give the assize against any one but the lord, and as a matter of fact the lord
was a common defendant.

[2] Bracton, f. 281-2; Note Book, pl. 1215. These new actions do not take
the shape of formulated assizes; they begin with a *Praecipe quod reddat.* Even
they did not cover the whole ground. Bracton, f. 281, seems to have thought
that an action might be brought on the seisin of any lineal ancestor however
remote, 'ad triavum et ulterius si tempus permittat.' But at a little later date
we find it said that one can not go back further than one's besaiel, one's grandfather's father; Nichols, Britton, ii. 164, 300: Northumberland Assize Rolls, p.
260. Ultimately, so it would seem, one might go back to one's tresaiel, but no
further; Fitzherbert, Natura Brevium, f. 221. This question can hardly have

Seisin as of fee.

The action, we say, was possessory; but of course in this case the heir had to allege something more than a seisin, a seisin in demesne, or a seisin of free tenement, on the part of his ancestor. He had to allege a seisin 'as of fee' (*ut de feodo*). On the other hand, he had not to assert, as the demandant in a writ of right always had to assert, a seisin 'as of right' (*ut de iure*). A man may well be seised 'as of fee' though he be not seised 'as of right.' Seemingly we may put the matter thus:—every person who is seised is seised as of fee, unless he has come to his seisin by some title which gives him no more than an estate for life. A disseisor who has, and knows that he has, no right whatever, becomes seised in fee[1].

Exclusion of proprietary pleas.

Consequently the defendant is not suffered to urge pleas [p. 58] (*exceptiones*) of a proprietary character. To insist on this is the more necessary, for at a yet early time this assize gives occasion for a good deal of special pleading[2]. In the first place, the defendant may wish to plead and establish some fact inconsistent with the plaintiff's possessory case. Thus, for example, instead of saying, 'I deny that you are next heir of the ancestor named in your writ,' he may well wish to say, 'You have an elder brother living,' and thus concentrate the attention of the jurors on this fact. But this of course is not a proprietary plea. Then, again, he may admit that the plaintiff's case is true and yet may have a possessory defence to urge. Thus he may say, 'True your ancestor died seised as of fee; true also that you are now his next heir; but he left at his death a nearer heir, who by means of a release conveyed his rights to me, and in whose shoes I now stand[3].' In this last case if the assize were taken by default or without special pleading, the defendant would succumb; but he has a perfectly good defence if he pleads it properly. It has already become apparent, as this

---

had any interest so long as the action was confined by a decent statute of limitations. It had the same limit of time as the mort d'ancestor.

[1] Bracton, f. 264: 'Item dicitur *ut de feodo* ita quod *ut* ponatur pro *quasi* et denotet similitudinem, vel quod *ut* denotet ipsam veritatem. Ipsam veritatem, sicut de ipsis dici poterit qui iustum habent titulum, et iustam causam possidendi ab eis qui ius habent conferendi; et tunc pro *sicut ut* supra. Item similitudinem, pro *quasi*, sicut de illis dici poterit qui ingrediuntur sine causa et sine iusto titulo.' And see the strong words on f. 262: it matters not what sort of seisin the ancestor had, whether by disseisin or by intrusion, whether acquired from an owner or from a non-owner, if only he was seised *quasi* of fee.

[2] Glanvill, xiii. 11.   [3] Bracton, f. 270 b.

case shows, that the formula of the assize does not fully state all those positive and negative conditions, a fulfilment of which will of necessity entitle the plaintiff to recover the land[1]. But here there is no proprietary pleading; the defendant does not seek to go behind the 'seisin as of fee' of the ancestor. He would not be allowed to do that. He would not be allowed to say, 'Yes, your ancestor was seised as of fee when he died; but I, or some third person, had a better right to the land than he had[2].'

[p. 59] The principle then which is the foundation for this assize Principle of this assize. seems to be this, that whenever a man dies seised and did not come to his seisin by some title which would make him only a life-tenant, his heir is of all the world the person best entitled to be put into seisin. If any other person, no matter that he had better right than the dead man, forestalls the heir and acquires seisin, he shall be turned out in favour of the heir, be told to bring some action against the heir, be told that he ought not to have helped himself. On the whole this principle seems to be well maintained throughout the enormous number of actions which are brought in the thirteenth century. The 'dying seised' is strictly insisted upon, and the physical element of seisin is brought prominently forward. For a short period after the *de facto* ejectment an ejected possessor is, we have seen, allowed recourse to self-help, and if he dies within this period then his heir can say that he died seised. But this period is very short in our eyes; according to Bracton it should be in the commonest case but four days[3].

---

[1] By means of a special plea, to take another example, the defendant may allege that the ancestor's fee was a fee conditional (estate tail), and thus the heir *per formam doni* may protect himself against the heir general; Bracton, f. 268 b, 277 b, 283.

[2] Bigelow, Hist. Procedure, 178: 'Even in the time of Glanvill......the course of a cause begun by a writ for the trial of a question of seisin could be entirely deflected by the defendant's plea on the appearance of the recognitors. From a simple question of seisin, the cause might turn into a question of the right of property.' With this we can not wholly agree. No one of the pleas to the *mort d'ancestor* suggested by Glanvill or Bracton is proprietary; no one of them goes behind the seisin of the ancestor at the time of his death. Such pleas as, 'You have released to me,' 'You have already brought an assize against me and failed,' 'You were seised since your ancestor's death,' and the like, are possessory. Of course, however, the plaintiff may consent to the introduction of a proprietary question.

[3] Bracton, f. 262.

Is seisin heritable?

Now how are we to explain this matter? Are we to say that seisin can be transmitted from ancestor to heir; that the heir is seised so soon as the ancestor dies; that the defendant who succumbs in an assize of mort d'ancestor has been found guilty of disseising the heir? Such is not the theory, and of this we may be easily convinced. For one thing, were seisin itself a heritable right there could be no place for the mort d'ancestor, since its whole province would be covered by the novel disseisin. The stranger who entered on the ancestor's death would always be a disseisor. But this he was not if he entered before the heir entered; and throughout the first half of the thirteenth century it was a matter of much importance to him that this distinction should be observed. In the novel disseisin he could be compelled to pay damages; it was not until 1259 that damages could be given in the mort d'ancestor, and to all appearance until that date the man who forestalled [p. 60] the heir and entered on a vacant tenement, the 'abator' of later law, could not by any procedure be forced to make compensation in money for what he had done[1]. Secondly, in an assize of mort d'ancestor the objection that the plaintiff heir has himself been seised since his ancestor's death is an objection that is often urged and that can sometimes be urged successfully. If he himself has been seised of free tenement since his ancestor's death, he should be bringing the novel disseisin and not the mort d'ancestor[2].

Seisin in law.

The law of a later age ascribes to the heir at the moment of his ancestor's death a certain 'seisin in law' which it contrasts with that 'seisin in deed' which he will not acquire until he has entered on the land; and this seisin in law is good enough seisin for a few, but only a few purposes[3]. We can not find that the law of Bracton's day held this language[4]. It knew such a thing as vacant seisin. So soon as the ancestor died, or, at all events, so soon as his corpse was carried from the house,

---

[1] Bracton, f. 253 b, 285, would have liked to give damages. They were given as against the lord by Prov. Westminster, c. 9, and Stat. Marlb. c. 16.

[2] Glanvill, xiii. 11; Bracton, f. 273. An heir ejected almost immediately after his ancestor's death might have his choice between the two assizes.

[3] Littleton, sec. 448.

[4] Bracton, f. 434 b: 'Et quandoque dividitur ius proprietatis a possessione, quia proprietas statim post mortem antecessoris descendit heredi propinquiori ...sed tamen non statim acquiritur talibus possessio quia alius......se ponere possit in seisinam.'

seisin was vacant until some one assumed it—unless indeed the heir had been dwelling along with his ancestor, in which case seisin would not be vacant for a moment. We have said that the vacancy began at latest as soon as the dead man's body was carried out for burial. Bracton has some curious words about this matter[1]. He thinks himself bound by the authority of Paulus[2] to hold that a man can not lose possession until he has given it up both *animo* and *corpore*; but it is not impossible that his ascription of possession to a corpse, grotesque though it may seem to us, had a real foundation, and that until the funeral no stranger could acquire a seisin:—this might prevent unseemly struggles in the house of mourning and give the heir an opportunity of entering[3]. The heir again acquires seisin with [p. 61] great ease; so soon as he sets foot on the land he is seised; still he must enter[4]. Seisin is not heritable; but the man who dies seised as of fee transmits a heritable right to his heir; his seisin generates this heritable right. The substance of a famous French maxim, ' le mort saisit le vif,' we accept, though the phrase is not quite that which is sanctioned by our books[5].

The ' abator '—that is, the person who excludes the heir— *Acquisition of seisin by an abator.* does not very easily acquire a seisin that is protected against the heir's self-help. An occupation for four days which will protect the disseisor seems not long enough to protect this interloper. The reason for this distinction may be that, though disseisin is a more serious offence and a graver wrong than an abatement, the heir must be allowed some reasonable time for hearing of his ancestor's death and of the interloper's entry. An opinion current in Bracton's day would have given him a year for self-help, but some would have given less[6].

This assize can be brought against any person who is *Against whom does the assize lie?* holding the land, however remote he may be from the original ' abator.' He is not accused of having been guilty of an

---

[1] Bracton, f. 51 b, 262.   [2] Dig. 50, 17, 153.

[3] Y. B. 33–5 Edw. I. 53–5.

[4] Y. B. 33–5 Edw. I. 53–5: 'sola pedis posicio vero heredi seisinam contulit.'

[5] The general opinion seems to be that the French *saisine* and the German *Gewere*, unlike the Roman *possessio*, were heritable. See Heusler, Gewere, 172. Ihering, Besitzwille, p. 33, has good remarks on the controversy as to whether what passes to the possessor's heir should be called possession or a right to possession.

[6] Bracton, f. 160 b, 161; Britton, i. 288; ii. 2; Somersetshire Pleas, pl. 1433 a case decided by Bracton.

unlawful act; he may have come to his seisin by inheritance, or
by feoffment and purchase in good faith, and none the less he
may be turned out by this action. In this direction the scope
of the assize is unlimited. On the other hand, it will not serve
to decide disputes between two would-be heirs. If both parties
claim the land as heir to the ancestor named in the writ, the
procedure by way of assize is out of place[1]. One reason for
this limitation may be found in the existence of another remedy
adapted for the settlement of such controversies. In a writ of
right between kinsmen, if both litigants claim as heirs of the
same man and their pedigrees are not disputed, then there will
be neither duel nor grand assize; the question will be decided
on the pleadings, or, as the phrase goes, 'by count counted and
plea pleaded': the question must be one of pure law. But
also, as will appear more fully when we speak of the law of
inheritance, our courts, influenced, so it seems, by King John's [p. 62]
usurpation of the throne, were in some cases very unwilling to
turn out of possession a would-be heir at the suit of a kinsman
who had a better, but only a slightly better, right[2].

The writs of entry.   We see then our common law starting on its career with
two possessory actions for land. In sharp contrast to these it
keeps a definitely proprietary action, that begun by writ of
right. Had the development of forms stopped here, we should
have had a story to tell far simpler than that which lies before
us. It is to be regretted that we can not state the law about
seisin and proprietary right without speaking at length of what
we would fain call mere matters of procedure; but we have no
choice; unless we can understand the writs of entry we cannot
understand seisin.

The writ of right.   Let us cast one glance at the proprietary action. It is
begun either in a seignorial court by a *breve de recto tenendo* or
in the king's court by a *Praecipe*. Both of these writs are
often spoken of as 'writs of right.' They deal not merely with
seisina but with *ius*. The demandant will appear and claim
the land as his right and inheritance. He will go on to assert
that either he or some ancestor of his has been seised not
merely 'as of fee' but also 'as of right.' He will offer battle by
the body of a champion who theoretically is also a witness, a

---

[1] Glanvill, xiii. 11; Bracton, f. 266; Britton, ii. 115.
[2] Bracton, f. 267 b, 268, 282, 327 b.

witness who testifies this seisin either of his own knowledge or in obedience to the injunction of his dead father. The person attacked in the action (he is called the tenant) may be able to plead some special plea (*exceptio*), but he always has it in his power to deny the demandant's case and to put himself on battle or the grand assize[1]. If he chooses the grand assize, the recognitors will swear in answer to a question which leaves the whole matter of fact and of law to them—namely, whether the demandant has greater right to demand the land than the tenant has to hold it. As a result of the trial a very solemn judgment is pronounced. The land is adjudged to the one party and his heirs, and abjudged (*abiudicata*) from the other [p. 63] party and his heirs for ever. Nothing could be more conclusive. We may notice in passing that such an action is a tedious affair, that it may drag on its slow length for many years; men are not lightly to be abjudged for ever, they and their heirs, from their seisin. But it is more important to observe that, even if all goes swiftly, the tenant has great advantages. He can choose between two modes of trial. He can insist that the whole question of better right, involving, as it may, the nicest questions of law, shall be left all in one piece to the knights of the neighbourhood; and then, if he fears their verdict, he can trust to the God of battles; he can force the demandant to a *probatio divina*, which is as much to be dreaded as any *probatio diabolica* of the canonists.

The law is too hard upon a demandant, who, it may well be, has recent and well-known facts in his favour. This is keenly felt and a remedy is provided. The change, however, is effected not by any express legislation, but by the gradual invention of a whole group of writs which shall, as it were, stand mid-way between the indubitably possessory assizes and the indubitably proprietary writ of right. The basis for this superstructure is found in the simple writ of *Praecipe quod reddat*, which is the commencement of a proprietary action. That writ bids the tenant give up the land which the demandant claims, or appear in the king's court to answer why he has not done so. All the new writs have this in common

Invention of writs of entry.

---

[1] It seems that occasionally a demandant could drive the tenant to an issue of fact; Note Book, pl. 17; but as a general rule he could not. The whole development of special pleas in writs of right seems to be post-Glanvillian and for a long time they are by no means common.

that they add some definite suggestion of a recent flaw in the tenant's title. This they do by the phrase :—

'in quam [terram] non habuit ingressum nisi....'

The tenant, it is alleged, had no entry into the land except in a certain mode, which mode will be described in the writ and is one incapable of giving him a good title. The object of this formula is to preclude the tenant from that mere general denial of the demandant's title which would be appropriate in a writ of right, and to force him to answer a certain question about his own case :—'Did you or did you not come to the land in the manner that I have suggested?' If the tenant denies the suggestion, then here is a question of fact that ought to be sent to a jury.

Entry sur disseisin. For a moment we may isolate from the rest of these writs one small class which is very closely connected with the assize of novel disseisin. We have seen that the assize can only be [p. 64] employed if both the disseisor and the disseisee are still alive. But in principle our law has admitted that an ejected possessor ought to be able to pursue his land into the hands of those who have come to it through or under the disseisor. This can be done by the assize if the disseisor is still living, and clearly his death ought not to shield his feoffees. Furthermore, if we hold that a possessory action should lie even against one who comes to the land by feoffment and in good faith, then we can no longer say that the action is admissible only against one who has been guilty of a delict, an act of unlawful violence, and there can be no reason why the heir of the disseisee should not have a possessory action against any one in whose hands he finds the land.

Scope of the action. Slowly this principle bears practical fruit in the evolution of the 'writs of entry sur disseisin.' In this instance we may enjoy the rare pleasure of fixing a precise date. A writ of entry for the disseisee against the heir of the disseisor was made a 'writ of course' in the autumn of the year 1205[1]. Very soon after this, we may find a writ for the heir of the disseisee[2]. For a while such actions seem only to have been allowed where an assize of novel disseisin had been begun, but

[1] Rot. Cl. Joh. p. 32: 'Hoc breve de cetero erit de cursu.' But already in Richard's day we find 'in quam ecclesiam nullum habet ingressum nisi per ablatorem suum.'

[2] Note Book, pl. 383 (A.D. 1230); pl. 993 (A.D. 1224).

had been brought to naught by the death of one of the parties[1].
This limit was transcended without legislation, but another
and a very curious limit was discovered. A writ of entry
can be made for the disseisee or his heir against the third
hand or against the fourth hand, but not against the fifth
or any remoter hand. We count the disseisee's hand as the
first, the disseisor's as the second. The action will lie against
the disseisor's heir or the disseisor's feoffee; his is the third
hand. It will also lie against the heir's feoffee, the feoffee's
heir, the feoffee's feoffee; but it will go no further; it is only
[p. 65] effectual within these 'degrees[2].' Why so? We must probably
find our answer to this question in politics rather than in jurisprudence. These writs of entry draw away litigation from the
feudal courts and impair the lord's control over his tenantry;
they are but too like evasions, or even infringements, of the
Great Charter[3]. Some barriers must be maintained against
them and the legal logic which impels them forward. A temporary defence may be found in the argument that the only
excuse for these writs is that the questions raised by them are
questions about recent facts, and therefore to be solved by
verdict rather than by battle. When, however, there have
been three or four feoffments since the disseisin, the facts are
elaborate and remote. Jurors should testify to what they have
seen; on the other hand, the champion in the writ of right can
testify to what his father has told him. The new procedure
must not encroach on the proper sphere of the old and sacral
procedure. Another defence for the frontier that lies between
the fourth hand and the fifth may perhaps have an ancient
rule about warranty of which we shall speak hereafter[4]. But
in truth this frontier was not defensible. Bracton was for

---

[1] This seems the state of things represented by Bracton, f. 218 b, and the
Note Book.

[2] Bracton, f. 219 b: 'usque ad tertiam personam inclusivam.' The first
stage is 'into which he had not entry save by (*per*) X, who demised it
to him and who had disseised the demandant [or his ancestor].' The second
stage is 'into which etc. save by (*per*) X, to whom (*cui*) Y demised it, who
had disseised etc.' The first form is a writ in the *per*, the second in the
per and *cui*.

[3] Charter, 1215, c. 34: 'Breve quod vocatur *Praecipe* de cetero non fiat
alicui de aliquo tenemento unde liber homo amittere possit curiam suam.' But
the writ of entry does begin with *Praecipe*.

[4] See below, p. 70.

crossing it[1], and the statute of Marlborough crossed it[2]. That statute gave the disseisee or his heir 'a writ of entry sur disseisin in the *post*,' an action, that is, in which he might allege that his adversary 'had no entry into the land save after (*post*) the disseisin' that some one or another (*X*) perpetrated against the demandant or his ancestor. In such an action it was unnecessary for the demandant to trace the process by which the land passed from the disseisor (*X*) to the tenant whom the action attacked.

The English possessorium and the canon law.

Thus by a series of gradual concessions we arrive at the result that if a disseisin has been committed and the time—an ever lengthening time—allowed for an action based upon that disseisin has not yet elapsed, an action can be brought for the recovery of the land by the disseisee or his heir against [p. 66] any person who has come to that land through or under the disseisor or by disseising the disseisor: and this action will be possessory. This is a matter of great interest in the general history of law, for hardly a question of jurisprudence has caused fiercer combats than the question whether a possessory action for the recovery of land should lie against 'the third hand,' or, to use our English terms, against the disseisor's feoffee; and these combats have not yet ceased. Just in the reign of our King John, when the writs of entry were becoming writs of course, his antagonist Pope Innocent III. was issuing a memorable decree[3]. It often happens, he said, that because the despoiler transfers the thing to a third person, against whom a possessory action will not lie, the despoiled loses, not only the benefit of possession, but even his property, owing to the difficulty of proof; and so, notwithstanding the rigour of the civil law (whose *unde vi* will not lie against the third hand), we decree that the despoiled shall have the remedy of restitution against one who receives the thing with knowledge of the spoliation. Thus a possessory action was given against the *mala fide* possessor. But the canonists were not content with

---

[1] Bracton, f. 219 b, as is often the case, suggests his own opinion under a 'nisi sit qui dicat.'

[2] Stat. Marlb. c. 29: Second Institute, 153.

[3] c. 18. X. de restitut. spol. (2. 13); Lateran Council of 1215. To some modern Romanists this famous canon is the abomination of desolation. To Ihering it is an exploit worthy of the greatest of the popes, a genuine development of Roman law: Besitzwille, p. 459.

this; they found or thought that they found in ancient texts authority enough for a possessory action even against the *bona fide* possessor[1]. English law seems never to have taken any notice of this distinction. Psychical researches, inquiries as to good faith, as to knowledge or ignorance, were beyond its powers. If its possessory action is to be given against any, it must be given against every third hand; but it felt with Pope Innocent that to refuse a possessory action was often enough to obliterate proprietary right '*propter difficultatem probationum*[2].'

[p. 67]   The possessory character of the English action by 'writ of entry sur disseisin' can be best shown by means of a very curious case reported by Bracton. Great people were concerned in it. William Marshall, Earl of Pembroke, the famous regent, had a wife; that wife was entitled to land which was being withheld from her by one Richard Curpet. The earl took the law into his own hands and disseised Curpet. The earl died; his wife held the land; she died; his heir and her heir, William Marshall the younger, entered. A writ of entry was brought against him, and he had to give up the land. He had to give up what was his own because he and his mother before him had come to it by virtue of a disseisin. To-morrow he may bring his writ of right and get back this land; but at present he must give it up, for into it he had no entry save as the successor of a disseisor, and he is precluded from going behind the disseisin and pleading proprietary right[3].

That seems to be the principle of this action. You are not to go behind the entry with which you are charged. If you admit that entry you may still have many defences open to you, as for example a deed of release executed by the disseisee; but behind that entry you are not to go.

The actions of which we have been speaking are possessory

Illustration of the English doctrine.

The other writs of entry.

---

[1] By the side of the action given by the canon of Innocent III. (condictio ex c. 18) they develop a condictio ex c. *Redintegranda*, which they trace back to a passage in the Decretum, c. 3. C. 3. qu. 1. The process is described at length by Bruns, Recht des Besitzes, 163–262.

[2] Bracton, f. 282 b. It would, says Bracton, be hard to send a man to his writ of right when he has on his side so recent a seisin; 'quod grave esset petenti de tam recenti seisina.'

[3] Bracton, f. 219; Fleta, p. 364; Britton, ii. 299. Later law met some of the cases in which a man having good title came to the land under a bad title, by holding that when once he was seised he was 'remitted' to his good title. See Littleton, lib. 3, cap. 12. But this seems to belong to the future.

in this amongst other senses, namely, that they presuppose what may fairly be called an infringement of possession and have that infringement for their foundation. This is obviously the case with the assize of novel disseisin and the writs of entry sur disseisin. There has been a disseisin, the dispossession of a possessor. We may say the same of the mort d'ancestor, if we give the name 'seisin in law' to that right which a man who dies seised 'as of fee' transmits to his heir. But the same can not be said of the large group of writs of entry which is now to come before us. We shall have before us actions which are, and well may be, called possessory, and yet they do not presuppose any violation of seisin, not even of a 'seisin in law.'

The various forms of writs.

Most of these writs suggest that the person who is attacked in the action has come to the land by virtue of an alienation made by someone who, though he was occupying and rightfully occupying, had no power to alienate it. He was a bailiff or a [p. 68] tenant in villeinage, a termor or a guardian, and took upon himself to make a feoffment; he was a tenant for life, tenant in dower or by the curtesy, and made a feoffment in fee; he was a husband who alienated his wife's land; he was a bishop or an abbot who without the consent of chapter or convent alienated the land of his church; he was of unsound mind; he was an infant. For one reason or another the alienation was voidable from the moment when it was made, or has become voidable. The person who is entitled to avoid it seeks to do so, and seeks to do so by a possessory action.

Historical evolution of the writs.

Some of these cases attracted attention at an early time. A tenant in fee lets or pledges (*vadiare*) the land for a term of years. That term expires; but the termor holds on, and insists perhaps that he is tenant in fee. It seems hard that the lessor should not be able to get back his land without battle or grand assize. And so too if this termor makes a feoffment, it seems hard that when the term has expired his feoffee should hold on and force the lessor to a difficult proof. In Glanvill's day English law was apparently showing an inclination to meet some of these cases by actions similar to that which was competent to the disseisee, that is to say, by formulated assizes, and in Norman law we find several actions of this kind[1]. But

---

[1] Norman law has a recognition *Utrum de feodo vel de vadio*, another *Utrum de feodo vel de firma*, another *Utrum de feodo vel de warda*, also an *Utrum de maritagio* which answers to our *Cui in vita*. See Brunner, Schwurgerichte,

soon in this country a flexible and comprehensive formula was adopted, namely, that of a *Praecipe* qualified by a suggestion as to the tenant's mode of entry. Thus: 'into which land he (*A*) had not entry save by *B*, the father of the demandant (whose heir the demandant is) who demised it to him (*A*) for a term that has expired[1].' This form was flexible. Any kind of invalid 'entry' might be suggested. For example, one of the earliest and commonest of these writs was that which enabled a widow to recover land which had belonged to her but had been alienated by her husband. During his life this alienation was valid; during his life she could not oppose him in any thing —*cui in vita sua contradicere non potuit*; but when he died leaving her alive, she could avoid the alienation, and a possessory action was given to her for this purpose. These two are old forms, the *ad terminum qui praeteriit* and the *cui in vita*; but many others were soon invented as, for instance, the *dum fuit infra aetatem,* by which after attaining his majority a man could recover the land that he had alienated while an infant; the *sine assensu capituli* which aided the successor of a bishop who without the consent of his chapter had made away with the lands of his church, and those writs called the writs *ad communem legem* (to distinguish them from others given by Edwardian statutes) which lay when a tenant for life had alienated in fee and had died[2]. Between the days of Glanvill and the days of Bracton the chancery was constantly adding to the number of these writs. In Bracton's day the process was almost

[p. 69]

c. 15. Glanvill, xiii. 26–31, knows some of these recognitions; but in general the writs which direct them to be taken are 'judicial' rather than 'original' writs: that is to say, litigants came to these recognitions only in the course of actions begun by other writs. In very early plea rolls a jury summoned in course of the pleadings is occasionally called an assize.

[1] The evolution of the writ *ad terminum qui praeteriit* which supplies the place of several Norman recognitions can be traced in the earliest plea rolls, *e.g.* Curia Regis Rolls (Pipe Roll Society), 50, 66, 67, 74, 123; Rot. Cur. Regis (Palgrave), i. 341; ii. 37, 38, 85, 211, 227; Select Civil Pleas (Selden Society), pl. 143, 192; and so on into Bracton's Note Book where the fully developed form appears. The evolution of the *cui in vita* may be similarly traced; already in John's reign its characteristic formula is seen; Rot. Cur. Regis (Palgrave) ii. 168. These are for a while the commonest writs of entry.

[2] They are *ad communem legem* to distinguish them from the writ (*in casu proviso*) given by Stat. Gloucester, 6 Edward I. c. 7, and other writs (*in consimili casu*) framed after its likeness, which enabled one to insist that an alienation in fee by tenant in dower, tenant by the curtesy, or tenant for life, was a forfeiture of the alienor's estate.

complete; he knew nearly all those writs of entry which in
after ages were reckoned as common law writs, and he knew
some which soon went out of use owing to statutory extensions
of the assize of novel disseisin[1]. The scheme of writs of entry
had crystallized; what more could be done for it was done
explicitly by statutes of Edward I.

Principle of these writs.

Now we must not discuss these actions at any length; we
could not do so without losing our chief theme, the nature of
seisin, in a maze of obscure details. But a few main principles
should be understood. These we may bring to light by means
of the question: How far will these possessory actions extend;
to whom and against whom are they competent?

Active transmission.

To the first part of this question we answer that as a general [p. 70]
rule they are hereditarily transmissible on the demandant's side.
If the ancestor had an action, the heir has an action. I can
base my action on the fact that I, or that my father (whose heir
I am) demised this land for a term that has expired. If the
widow has an action (*cui in vita*) to avoid an alienation made
by her husband and dies without using it, her heir has an
action (*sur cui in vita*) for the same purpose[2].

Passive transmission.

Turning to the other side of the question, we see that no
good faith, no purchase for value, will protect the man who is
attacked by the action; but we also see that curious boundary
which has been mentioned above. Until the Statute of Marlborough otherwise ordained, a writ of entry could only be

The doctrine of degrees.

brought 'within the degrees[3].' To take one example, the
widow can bring her action against her husband's feoffee, or
against that feoffee's feoffee; but if there has been a third
feoffment, then her only remedy is by writ of right. This
limitation seems illogical, though it may have for its excuse
some rule limiting the number of warrantors who may be
called. At any rate, the Statute of Marlborough removed

---

[1] Bracton, f. 317 b. As already said, writs of entry on alienations by bailiffs,
guardians, termors, and tenants in villeinage went out of use, since in such
cases alienor and alienee could be treated as disseisors.

[2] There seems to have been some doubt as to the possibility of a writ of
entry in case the demandant would have had to go back for a seisin to his
grandfather's grandfather. See Nichols, Britton, ii. p. 300. Such a case would
be exceedingly rare; but in 1306 a man has attempted to get from the chancery
a writ on the seisin of his great-grandfather's grandfather, and failed in his
endeavour: Y. B. 33–35 Edw. I. 125.

[3] Bracton, f. 318: 'Non enim excedit tertium gradum.'

it[1]. Thenceforward the widow, or her heir, could bring the writ of entry against any one (however remote from the wrong-doing husband) who was holding the land in consequence of the wrongful alienation. And what we say of the widow's writ might be said of the other writs of entry. The writ of right fell into the background; and, though still popular in Edward I.'s day, it was hardly needed by any but those whose claims were of a rare character, or who had allowed so long a time to elapse that they were debarred from writs of entry by the extremely patient statutes of limitation that were in force[2].

---

[1] Stat. Marlb. c. 29. This speaks only of writs sur disseisin; but seems to have been construed to give a general authority for writs 'in the *post*.' See Fleta, p. 360; Britton, ii. 297.

[2] The boundary set by the common law to the writs of entry we can not thoroughly explain, but a suggestion about it may be ventured. Bracton, f. 320 b, 321, seems to connect it with two rules, (1) that vouching to warranty never goes beyond the fourth degree, (2) that in a writ of entry the tenant may only vouch the persons named in the writ. This latter rule is of some interest. A widow (*A*) charges *O* with having come to the land as feoffee of *N*, who was the feoffee of her husband *M*. Now the only person whom *O* may vouch is *N* (or *N*'s heir), and the only person whom *N* may vouch is *M*'s heir. The reason is that *O* could only be entitled to vouch another person, *e.g. X*, if *O* acquired the land from *X*, and the mere assertion that he acquired it from *X* would be an answer to *A*'s action, for it would deny the entry by *N*, on which *A* relies. This rule was still observed after the Statute of Marlborough and served to differentiate the old action 'within the degrees' from the statutory action 'beyond the degrees.' In the latter you might 'vouch at large,' vouch whom you would; in the former you could only vouch along the line of alienors mentioned in the writ. See Stat. West. I. c. 40. So much as to Bracton's second rule. As to the rule which would bring the process of voucher to an end when the third warrantor had been called, we are not certain that Bracton means to lay this down as a general rule which will extend even to writs of right, for he elsewhere (f. 260, 388) suggests that the chain of warrantors may be traced to infinity. But the rule seems to have existed in all its generality both in Normandy and in Scotland; it had been applied in England to the case of chattels; similar rules are found in Lombardy, France, Germany, Anglo-Saxon England, Scandinavia, Wales (Ancienne coutume de Normandie, c. 101; Somma, p. 132; Regiam Maiestatem, i. 22; Quoniam Attachiamenta, c. 6; Glanvill, x. 15, where *quotum warrantum* should be *quartum warrantum*; Laws of Cnut, ii. 24; Leg. Henrici, 64, § 6; Brunner, D. R. G. ii. 502; Ancient Laws of Wales, i. 439). Now assuming these two rules, namely, (1) there may be three vouchers but no more, and (2) the defendant may only vouch along the line suggested in the writ of entry, we come to the result that this line must be limited in length. There are difficulties in the way of this explanation, for apparently our writs within the degrees allow only two vouchers; thus, in the case put above, when *O* has vouched *N*, and *N* has vouched the husband's heir, there can seemingly be no further vouching, unless the chance of rebutting a demandant by his own or his ancestor's warranty is reckoned as a third voucher. There is something to be

[p. 71]

Are the writs of entry possessory?

Now were these actions possessory or were they not? The lawyers of the thirteenth century hardly knew their own minds about this question. Bracton seems to have thought that the writs *sur disseisin* and a few others were possessory, but that in general the writs of entry were proprietary[1]. A little later some justices of Henry III.'s reign record their opinion that a writ of entry, since it touches property, is of a higher nature than an assize of novel disseisin which only touches possession[2]. Fleta and Britton tell us that the causes, [p. 72] pleaded by writs of entry have something of possession in them, but in part 'savour' of property[3]. About the same date a lawyer says that a writ of entry is a writ mixed of right and possession[4]. At a later time it seems generally agreed that these writs are possessory. We must attempt to make up our minds as to what this term implies.

No violation of possession necessary.

If it be of the essence of a possessory action that the plaintiff complains of a violated possession, then none of the actions with which we have been dealing are possessory, except the assize of novel disseisin and the writs of entry *sur disseisin*, to which, as we have explained above, we may perhaps add the mort d'ancestor and its attendant writs of cosinage and the like; but even these can be brought against persons who have not been concerned in the violation of possession; they can be brought against those who have come to possession by honest and legitimate means, even against those who have purchased in good faith.

The right of defence is limited.

When, however, we are speaking of actions in which the possession of land may be adjudged to the plaintiff—and with actions which aim at mere damages we have at present no concern—the term 'possessory' may very rightly be used in another sense. For the moment it will be enough to say that such an action is possessory if the defendant in it may find

discovered in this obscure region; we can not profess to have thoroughly explored it. It is darkened by inconsistent methods of counting the degrees.

[1] Bracton, f. 218 b, treats the writs *sur disseisin* as mere supplements for the assize: so also, f. 160, the writs of intrusion; but, f. 317 b, the other writs of entry lie 'in causa proprietatis.'

[2] Placit. Abbrev. 183 (Kanc.).

[3] Fleta, p. 360; Britton, ii. 296.

[4] Y. B. 20–21 Edw. I. p. 27. So in Y. B. 33–5 Edw. I. p. 125: 'our action is mixed in the possession.' Ibid. 421: 'the writ is mixed, to wit, in the possession and in the right.'

himself precluded by a rule of law from relying upon his proprietary right in the land. To put the matter another way: the action is possessory if it will leave open the question whether the successful plaintiff has better right to the land than the vanquished defendant.

Now in this sense all our writs of entry seem to be posses- The writs of entry possessory. sory. We will put a case: Alice who was seised in fee simple married Adam; during the marriage Adam enfeoffed Roger in fee simple, who enfeoffed William in fee simple; Adam died leaving Alice his widow; Alice now seeks to recover the land from William. She brings a writ of entry. 'She claims the land as her right and inheritance and as that into which William had no entry save through Roger to whom Adam her [p. 73] husband (whom in his lifetime she could not contradict) demised it[1].' Now William is at liberty to deny that this was his entry; he is at liberty to assert that he entered in quite different fashion, for example that he was enfeoffed by Peter. If a jury is against Alice on this point, if it finds that she has not correctly stated the means by which William came to the land, then she fails; but—and here we see an illustration of the possessory character of the action—she can at once begin another action by writ of right and in that she may prove by the arm of her champion or the verdict of a grand assize that after all she has better right than William[2]. But—to go back to Alice's writ of entry—William has other defences open to him. He may admit the suggestion that Alice has made; he may say 'True it is that I entered in the manner that you have described; but you in your widowhood have released your rights to me; see here your charter.' And other defences may be open to him. If, for example, we suppose the action to be brought not by Alice, but by one Benedict who calls himself her heir, then William may say 'You are not Alice's heir, for she is yet alive,' or 'You are not Alice's heir, for you have an elder brother Bertram[3].' All this William may do; but there

---

[1] In the writs of entry the term 'demise' is used in its very largest sense: it will *e.g.* cover a feoffment in fee.

[2] Bracton, f. 319 b: 'remanebit tenens in seisina quousque petens sibi perquisierit per breve de recto.' And yet Bracton treats these writs of entry as being rather proprietary than possessory.

[3] This is all that Bracton means when he says, f. 320 b, 'Item excipi poterit contra petentem quod alius ius maius habet quam ille qui petit.' He does not

is one thing that he must not do:—if he does not dispute the entry suggested in the writ, he must not go behind it; he must not 'plead higher up' than the facts upon which Alice has based her claim. Thus, for example, he must not say, 'All that you urge is very true, but I tell you that you obtained your seisin in this or that illegitimate manner and that when you married your husband I, or some ancestor of mine, or some stranger to this action, was the true owner of this land.' The whole object of that clause in the writ which suggests a particular mode of entry, is to impose an artificial limitation upon the defendant in his defence. By an artificial limitation we mean one which prevents him from asserting in this action rights which he really has, rights which to-morrow he can assert [p. 74] in another action. The writ of entry does not finally decide the dispute between the parties; the vanquished tenant may hereafter be a victorious demandant[1].

The hierarchy of actions. A graduated hierarchy of actions has been established. 'Possessoriness' has become a matter of degree. At the bottom stands the novel disseisin, possessory in every sense, summary and punitive. Above it rises the mort d'ancestor, summary but not so summary, going back to the seisin of one who is already dead. Above this again are writs of entry, writs which have strong affinities with the writ of right, so strong that in Bracton's day an action begun by writ of entry may by the pleadings be turned into a final, proprietary action. The writs of entry are not so summary as are the assizes, but they are rapid when compared with the writ of right; the most dilatory of the essoins is precluded; there can be no battle or grand assize[2]. Ultimately we ascend to the writ of right. Actions are higher or lower, some lie 'more in the right' than

mean that every *ius tertii* can be pleaded. The only *ius tertii* that can be pleaded is one that is inconsistent with the demandant's possessory claim.

[1] A good illustration occurs in Y. B. 33–5 Edw. I. p. 359: 'Maud first disseised Robert while she was sole and then took a husband, who alienated to Nicholas; Nicholas was seised; Robert released and quit-claimed to Nicholas; Maud's husband died, and she deraigned these tenements from Nicholas by the *cui in vita.*' Nicholas had a better right than Maud, for by the release he had Robert's right; but he could not set this up in Maud's action; he had come to the land by an alienation made by her husband which she could avoid.

[2] As to the conversion of the writ of entry into a writ of right, see Bracton, f. 318, 319. This doctrine seems to have become obsolete and so the possessoriness of the writs of entry became more apparent.

others. You may try one after another; begin with the novel disseisin, go on to the mort d'ancestor, then see whether a writ of entry will serve your turn and, having failed, fall back upon the writ of right[1].

Now we can not consent to dismiss these rules about writs of entry as though they were matters of mere procedure. They seem to be the outward manifestation of a great rule of substantive law, for this graduated hierarchy of actions corresponds to a graduated hierarchy of seisins and of proprietary rights. The rule of substantive law we take to be this:— Seisin generates a proprietary right—an ownership, we may even say—which is good against all who have no better, because [p. 75] they have no older, right[2]. We have gone far beyond the protection of seisin against violence. The man who obtains seisin obtains thereby a proprietary right that is good against all who have no older seisin to rely upon, a right that he can pass to others by those means by which proprietary rights are conveyed, a right that is protected at every point by the possessory assizes and the writs of entry. At one and the same moment there may be many persons each of whom is in some sort entitled in fee simple to this piece of land :—*C*'s title is good against all but *B* and *A* ; *B*'s title is good against all but *A* ; *A*'s title is absolute.

The hierarchy of seisins.

But is even *A*'s title absolute? Our law has an action which it says is proprietary—the writ of right. As between the parties to it, this action is conclusive. The vanquished party and his heirs are 'abjudged' from the land for ever. In the strongest language that our law knows the demandant has to assert ownership of the land. He says that he, or his ancestor, has been seised of the land as of fee 'and of right' and, if he relies on the seisin of an ancestor, he must trace the descent of 'the right' from heir to heir into his own person. For all this, we may doubt whether he is supposed to prove a right that is good against all the world. The tenant puts himself upon the grand assize. What, we must ask, will be the question submitted to the recognitors? It will not be this, whether the demandant is owner of the land. It will be this,

Is the writ of right possessory?

---

[1] The final form of this doctrine will be found in *Ferrer's Case*, 6 Rep. 7 a.

[2] Of course to generate a hereditary right the seisin must be 'as of fee.' But there are writs of entry that can be used even by one who has been seised as life tenant ; Bracton, f. 326.

whether the demandant or the tenant has the greater right to the land[1]. Of absolute right nothing is said; greater right is right enough. Next we must observe that the judgment in this action will not preclude a third person from claiming the land. The judgment if it is followed by inaction on his part for some brief period—ultimately year and day was the time allowed to him—may preclude him, should he be in this country and under no disability; but the judgment itself is no bar[2]. But lastly, as we understand the matter, even in the writ of right the tenant has no means of protecting himself by an assertion that the ownership of the land belongs neither to him nor to [p. 76] the demandant but to some third person. This needs some explanation, for appearances may be against what we have here said.

Clement brings a writ of right against William. He pleads that his grandfather Adam was seised in fee and of right, that from Adam the right descended to Bernard as son and heir, and from Bernard to Clement as son and heir. William may put himself upon battle or upon the grand assize; in the latter case a verdict will decide whether Clement or William has the greater right. But a third course is open. William may endeavour to plead specially and to bring some one question of fact before a jury. In this way he may attack the pedigree that Clement has pleaded at any point; he may, for example, assert that Bernard was not Adam's son or was a bastard. In so doing he may seem at times to be setting up *ius tertii*, to be urging by way of defence for himself the rights of a stranger. But really he is not doing this. He is proving that Clement's right is not better than his own. For example, he says: 'Bernard was not Adam's heir, for Adam left an elder son, Baldwin by name, who is alive.' Now if this be so, Clement has no right in the land whatever; Clement does not allege that he himself has been seised and he is not the heir of any one who has been seised. But what, as we think, William can not do is this, he can not shield himself by the right of a stranger to the action whose title is inconsistent with the statement that Adam was seised in fee and of right. He can not, for example, say, 'Adam your ancestor got his

[1] This form goes back to the first days of the grand assize; Glanvill, ii. 18.

[2] The exception against him will be not *exceptio rei iudicatae*, but *exceptio ex taciturnitate*; Bracton, f. 435 b; Co. Lit. 254 b.

seisin by disseising Odo, or by taking a feoffment from Odo's guardian, and Odo, or Odo's heir, has a better right than either of us[1].'

Thus our law of the thirteenth century seems to recognize in its practical working the relativity of ownership. One story is good until another is told. One ownership is valid until an older is proved. No one is ever called upon to demonstrate an ownership good against all men; he does enough even in a proprietary action if he proves an older right than that of the person whom he attacks. In other words, even under a writ of right the common law does not provide for any kind of judgment *in rem*.

Relativity of ownership.

The question whether this idea—'the relativity of proprietary right'—should be called archaic, is difficult[2]. A discussion of it might lead us into controversies which are better left to those who have more copious materials for the history of very remote ages than England can produce. For our own part we shall be willing to allow that the evolution of the writs of entry, a process to be explained rather by politics than by jurisprudence, has given to this idea in England a preternatural sharpness. The proprietary action by writ of right is cumbrous and is irrational, for it permits trial by battle. Open attacks upon it can not be made, for it brings some profit to the lords and is supported by a popular sentiment which would gladly refer a solemn question of right to the judgment of the Omniscient. But covert attacks can be made, and they take the form of actions which protect the title begotten by seisin, actions in which artificial limits are set to the right of defence. On the other hand, we can not but think that this idea of relatively good proprietary right came very naturally to Englishmen. It developed itself in spite of cosmopolitan jurisprudence and a

Remote history of ownership and possession.

[p. 77] *(marginal, left)*

---

[1] It is very difficult to offer any direct proof of this doctrine, more especially as Bracton never finished his account of the writ of right. But see the remarkable passage on f. 434 b, 435, which culminates in 'plura possunt esse iura proprietatis et plures possunt habere maius ius aliis, secundum quod fuerint priores vel posteriores.' After reading the numerous cases of writs of right in the Note Book and many others as well, we can only say that we know no case in which the tenant by special plea gets behind the seisin of the demandant's ancestor. As to later times there can be no doubt. See *e.g.* Littleton, sec. 478, quoted below, p. 78. See also Lightwood, Possession of Land, 74.

[2] Dr Brunner in a review of the first edition of our book (Political Science Quarterly, xi. 540) gave an affirmative answer, and vouched early Frankish law.

romanized terminology. The lawyers themselves believe that there is a wide gulf between possessory and proprietary actions; but they are not certain of its whereabouts. They believe that somewhere or another there must be an absolute ownership. This they call *dreyt dreyt*[1], mere right, *ius merum.* Apparently they have mistaken the meaning of their own phrases; their *ius merum* is but that *mere dreit* or *ius maius* which the demandant asserts in a writ of right[2]. Bracton more than once protests with Ulpian that possession has nothing in common with property[3], and yet has to explain how successive possessions beget successive ownerships which all live on [p. 78] together, the younger being invalid against the older[4]. The land law of the later middle ages is permeated by this idea of relativity, and he would be very bold who said that it does not govern us in England at the present day, though the 'forms of action' are things of the past and we have now no action for the recovery of land in which a defendant is precluded from relying on whatever right he may have[5].

Seisin and 'estates.' We can now say our last word about that curious term 'estate[6].' We have seen that the word *status*, which when it falls from Bracton's pen generally means personal condition, is soon afterwards set apart to signify a proprietary right in land or in some other tenement :—John atte Style has an estate of fee simple in Blackacre. We seem to catch the word in the very act of appropriating a new meaning when Bracton says that the estate of an infant whether in corporeal or in

---

[1] Bracton, f. 434 b.

[2] It is probable that the Latin *ius merum* is a mistaken translation of the Anglo-French *mere dreit*, or as it would stand in modern French *majeur* (**maire*) *droit.* We have Dr Murray's authority for this note.

[3] Bracton, f. 113, 284 : 'nihil commune habet possessio cum proprietate.' Dig. 41, 2, 12, § 1.

[4] Bracton, f. 434 b, 435.

[5] Holmes, Common Law, p. 215; Pollock and Wright, Possession, 93–100; Lightwood, Possession of Land, 104–127. One of the most striking statements of this doctrine is in Littleton, sec. 478. 'Also if a man be disseised by an infant, who alien in fee, and the alienee dieth seised and his heir entreth, the disseisor being within age, now it is in the election of the disseisor to have a writ of entry *dum fuit infra aetatem* or a writ of right against the heir of the alienee, and, which writ of them he shall choose, he ought to recover by law.' In other words, a proprietary action is open to the most violent and most fraudulent of land-grabbers as against one whose title is younger than his own; 'and he ought to recover by law.'

[6] See above, vol. ii. p. 10.

incorporeal things must not be changed during his minority[1]. A person already has a status in things; that status may be the status of tenant for life or the status of tenant in fee. It is of course characteristic of this age that a man's status—his general position in the legal scheme—is closely connected with his proprietary rights. The various 'estates of men,' the various 'estates of the realm,' are supposed to be variously endowed with land; the baron, for example, ought in theory to be the holder of a barony; he has the status of a baron because he has the estate of a baron. But a peculiar definiteness is given to the term by that theory of possession which we have been examining. Seisin generates title. At one and the same time there may be many titles to one and the same piece of land, titles which have various degrees of validity. It is quite possible that two of these titles should meet in one man and [p. 79] yet maintain an independent existence. If a man demands to be put into the possession of land, he must not vaguely claim a certain piece of land, he must point out some particular title on which he relies, and if he has more than one, he must make his choice between them. For example, he must claim that 'status' in the land which his grandfather had and which has descended to him. It becomes possible to raise the question whether a certain possessor of the land was on the land 'as of' one status, or 'as of' another status; he may have had an ancient title to that land and also a new title acquired by disseisin. What was his status; 'as of' which estate was he seised[2]? One status may be heritable, another not heritable; the heritability of a third may have been restricted by the *forma doni*. And so we pass to a classification of estates; some are estates in fee, some are estates for life; some estates in fee are estates in fee simple, others are estates in fee conditional; and so forth. We have come by a word, an idea, in which the elements of our proprietary calculus can find utterance.

---

[1] Bracton, f. 423 b, 424.

[2] A good example is given by Y. B. 33–5 Edw. I. p. 197: 'By his entering into warrantry he is, as it were, in the estate which he received by the feoffment of Eustace and of that estate he pleads.' 'By your entering into warranty alone you are in your first estate.' Ibid. p. 467: 'Although you had alienated the estate that you had by Simon and had afterwards retaken that estate...you are in your first estate.'

Seisin and title.

One other principle should be noticed. Every proprietary right must have a seisin at its root. In a proprietary action the demandant must allege that either he or some ancestor of his has been seised, and not merely seised but seised with an exploited seisin, seised with a taking of esplees. Nor is this all; every step in his title, if it be not inheritance, must comprise a transfer of seisin. Every owner of land must have been seised of it or must have inherited it from one who was seised. Such, at all events, was the old and general rule, as we shall now see when we turn to speak of the means whereby proprietary rights could be conveyed[1].

§ 3. *Conveyance.*

Modes of acquiring rights in land.

De acquirendo rerum dominio—this is the title of what is [p. 80] printed as Bracton's second book. In the main that book deals with but two modes of acquisition, namely, gift and inheritance, and if for a while we concern ourselves only with the ownership of land, and if we relegate the whole subject of inheritance to a later chapter, we shall find that practically a projected essay *de acquirendo rerum dominio* will become an essay *de donationibus.*

No title by occupation.

Of the occupation of unowned land we have not to speak, for no land is or can be unowned. This rule seems to be implied in the principle that the king is lord of all England. What is not held of him by some tenant of his is held by him in demesne. In all probability no tenant can abandon the land

---

[1] In closing this section we have to say that the account here given of the relation of the writs of entry to the possessory assizes is utterly at variance with the traditional doctrine sanctioned by Blackstone (Comment. iii. 184), which makes 'our Saxon ancestors' acquainted with writs of entry. Now, however, that large selections from the early plea rolls have been printed, there can be no doubt at all that the assizes are older than the writs of entry, though even a comparison of Bracton with Glanvill should have made this clear. To this must be added that throughout the thirteenth century there is no writ of entry for the disseisee against the disseisor. No one would think of using such a writ, because the assize of novel disseisin is far more summary. At a much later period when the assize procedure was becoming obsolete—obsolete because too rude—such a writ of entry, 'the writ in the nature of an assize,' or 'writ in the *quibus*' was invented. But in Bracton's time the writs of entry presuppose the assizes. The credit of having been the first to explain the relation between the assizes and the writs of entry is due to Dr Brunner's Entstehung der Schwurgerichte.

that he has been holding in such wise as to leave it open to the
occupation of any one who sees fit to take it to himself. The
tenant can indeed 'waive' his tenancy; he can, says Bracton,
do this even though his lord objects; but, this done, there will
be no vacant ownership; the lord will be entitled to hold the
land in demesne[1]. Later law discovered one narrow sphere
within which rights in land could be acquired by occupation.
Suppose that *A* a tenant in fee simple gives land to *B* for his
(*B*'s) life, and that *B* gives this land to *C* (saying nothing of *C*'s
heirs), for his (*B*'s) life, thus making *C* 'tenant pur autre vie';
and suppose that *C* dies during *B*'s lifetime; who is entitled to
enjoy the land while *B* still lives? Not *C*'s heirs, for they have
not been mentioned; not *B*, for he has given away all that he
had to give, an estate for his life; not *A*, for he has given away
the land for the whole of *B*'s lifetime. Whoever chooses may
occupy the land and enjoy it during this unforeseen interval.
But, old though this rule may look, it does not seem to belong
[p. 81] to the thirteenth century. Bracton has a different solution for
this difficult case. He does not regard the 'estate pur autre
vie' as a freehold; it is only a chattel like a term of years; *C*
can dispose of it by will, and, if he fails to do this, the land will
revert to *B*[2]. Thus even here there was no room for a lawful
occupation.

Again, our law knew no acquisitive prescription for land, it ~No acquisi-~
merely knew a limitation of actions. Even to the writ of right ~tive pre-~
a limit was set. Before 1237 claimants had been allowed to go ~scription.~
back to a seisin on the day in 1135 when Henry I. died; then
they were restricted to the day in 1154 when Henry II. was
crowned; in 1275 the boundary was moved forward to the
coronation of Richard I. in 1189, and there it remained during
the rest of the middle ages[3]. Thus actions are barred by lapse
of time; but acquisitive prescription there is none. On the
other hand, we have to remember that every acquisition of
seisin, however unjustifiable, at once begets title of a sort, title
good against those who have no older seisin to rely upon.

[1] Bracton, f. 382, § 5.

[2] Bracton, f. 13 b, 27, 263; Fleta, p. 193, 289. In Hengham Parva, c. 5,
there is a transitional doctrine:—If a tenant for his own life alienates, the
alienee, the tenant *pur autre vie*, has a freehold. If a tenant in fee demises for
his own life, the lessee has a freehold 'according to some'; but the question
seems to be open.

[3] Note Book, pl. 280, 1217; Stat. Merton, c. 8; Stat. West. I. c. 39.

Alluvion etc.

Bracton copies from the Institutes and Azo's Summa passages about alluvion and accession, the emergence of islands and the like[1]. It is not very probable that English courts were often compelled to consider these matters, and a vacant field was thus left open for romanesque learning[2].

Escheat, forfeiture, reversion.

Escheat, again, and forfeiture and reversion, can hardly be described as modes by which proprietary rights are acquired. The lord's rights have been there all along; the tenant's rights disappear; the lord has all along been entitled to the land; he is entitled to it now, and, since he has no tenant, he can enjoy it in demesne. As yet, again, there can be no seizure and sale of land for the satisfaction of debts, and so we have not to speak of what is sometimes called 'involuntary alienation.' Thus in truth we are left with but few modes of acquisition, and, if we set on one side inheritance and marriage, we are left with but one mode. That mode can be described by the wide word 'gift,' which, as already said[3], will cover sale, exchange, gage [p. 82] and lease.

The gift of land.

How can land be given? We will begin with the simple and common case. A tenant in fee simple wishes to give to another for life or in fee. In the latter case he may wish either to create a new tenancy by way of subinfeudation or to substitute the donee for himself in the scale of tenure. He must make a feoffment with livery of seisin. What, we must ask, does this mean?

Feoffment.

Feoffment is a species of the genus gift[4]. A gift by which the donee acquires a freehold is a feoffment. It is common to speak of such a gift as a feoffment, but in making it the donor will seldom use the verb 'enfeoff' (*feoffare*); the usual phrase is 'give and grant' (*dare et concedere*). Also we may note— for this is somewhat curious—that the feoffee (*feoffatus*) need not acquire a fee (*feodum*); the gift that creates a life estate is a feoffment.

The expression of the donor's will.

Now, of course, if there is to be a gift there must be some expression of the donor's will. It is unnecessary that this

---

[1] Bracton, f. 9; Bracton and Azo, 99.

[2] Smyth, Lives of the Berkeleys, i. 112, gives a curious and early case touching land torn by the Severn from one of its banks, added to the opposite shore and afterwards restored.

[3] See above, vol. ii. p. 12.

[4] Britton, i. 221: 'Doun est un noun general plus qe n'est feffement.'

expression should take the form of a written document[1]. It is,
to say the least, very doubtful whether the Norman barons of
the first generation, the companions of the Conqueror, had
charters to show for their wide lands, and even in Edward I.'s day
men will make feoffments, nay settlements, without charter[2].
Later in the fifteenth century Littleton still treats them as
capable of occurring in practice. Furthermore, the charter of
feoffment, if there be one, will, at all events in the thirteenth
century and thenceforward, be upon its face an evidentiary,
not a dispositive, document. Its language will be not 'I hereby
give,' but 'Know ye that I have given.' The feoffor's intent
then may be expressed by word of mouth; but more than this
is necessary. It is absolutely essential—if we leave out of
account certain exceptions that are rather apparent than real—
—that there should be a livery of seisin. The donor and the The livery of seisin.
donee in person or by attorney must come upon the land.
There the words of gift will be said or the charter, if there
be one, will be read. It is usual, though perhaps not necessary,
that there should be some further ceremony. If the subject of
[p. 83] gift is a house, the donor will put the hasp or ring of the door
into the donee's hand (*tradere per haspam vel anulum*); if there
is no house, a rod will be transferred (*tradere per fustem et
baculum*) or perhaps a glove[3]. Such is the common and the
safe practice; but it is not indispensable that the parties
should actually stand on the land that is to be given. If that
land was within their view when the ceremony was performed,
and if the feoffee made an actual entry on it while the feoffor
was yet alive, this was a sufficient feoffment[4]. But a livery of
seisin either on the land or 'within the view' was necessary.

---

[1] Bracton, f. 33 b.

[2] See *e.g.* Y. B. 20–1 Edw. I. p. 32, and Stat. Marlb. c. 9.

[3] Bracton, f. 40; Britton, i. 261–2.

[4] Bracton, f. 41: 'Ex hoc enim quod patior rem meam esse tuam ex aliqua
causa, vel apud te esse, videor tradere. Idem est de mercibus in orreis. Idem
etiam dici poterit et assignari, quando res vendita vel donata est in conspectu,
quam venditor vel donator dicit se tradere, ut si ducatur in orreum vel campum.'
This is romanesque and goes back to Dig. 41. 1. 9, § 6, and Dig. 41. 2. 1, § 21;
but it probably fell in with English ideas; and the requirement that in such a
case the feoffee must enter while the feoffor is still alive—a requirement to be
discovered rather in later law than in Bracton's text—is not Roman. In 1292
(Y. B. 20–1 Edw. I. p. 256) Cave J. asks the jurors whether the feoffor was so
near the land that he could see it or point it out with his finger.

Until such livery had taken place there was no gift; there was nothing but an imperfect attempt to give. We may for purposes of analysis distinguish, as Bracton does, the *donatio* from the *traditio*, the feoffment from the livery, the declaration of the donor's will from the induction of the donee into seisin; but in law the former is simply nothing until it has been followed by the latter. The *donatio* by itself will not entitle the donee to take seisin; if he does so, he will be guilty of disseising the donor[1]. Nor does the *donatio* by itself create even a contractual right and bind the donor to deliver seisin. The charter of feoffment, which professedly witnesses a completed gift, will not be read as an agreement to give[2]. Until there has been livery, the feoffee, if such we may call him, has not even *ius ad rem*. Furthermore, the courts of Bracton's day are insisting with rigorous severity that the livery of seisin shall be no sham. Really and truly the feoffor must quit possession; really and truly the feoffee must acquire posses- [p. 84] sion. No charter, no receipt of homage, no transference of symbolic rods or knives, no renunciation in the local courts, no ceremony before the high altar, can possibly dispense with this, for it is the essence of the whole matter—there must be in very truth a change of possession, and rash is the feoffee who allows his feoffor's chattels to remain upon the land or who allows the feoffor to come back into the house, even as a guest, while the feoffment is yet new[3].

The ancient German conveyance.

It seems probable that in this respect our law represents or reproduces very ancient German law, that in the remotest age to which we can profitably recur a transfer of rights involved of necessity a transfer of things, and that a conveyance without livery of seisin was impossible and inconceivable. Of

[1] Bracton, f. 40, 44, holds that, in such a case, if the donor dies without having objected to the donee's assumption of seisin, he may be deemed to have ratified it.

[2] In Edward I.'s day a covenant to enfeoff was not uncommon; it formed part of the machinery of a settlement by way of feoffment and refeoffment; but the courts seem never to think of reading a charter of feoffment as a covenant to enfeoff.

[3] In the Note Book and the earliest Year Books hardly a question is commoner than whether there was a real and honest change of possession. The justices examine the jurors about the relevant facts and will not be put off with ceremonies. See *e.g.* Note Book, pl. 780, 871, 1209, 1240, 1247, 1294, 1850; Somersetshire Pleas, pl. 1440, 1491, 1497.

the ancient German conveyance we may draw some such picture as this:—The essence of the transaction may be that one man shall quit and another take possession of the land with a declared intention that the ownership shall be transferred; but this change of possession and the accompanying declaration must be made in formal fashion, otherwise it will be unwitnessed and unprovable, which at this early time is as much as to say that it will be null and void. An elaborate drama must be enacted, one which the witnesses will remember. The number and complexity of its scenes may vary from time to time and from tribe to tribe. If we here speak of many symbols and ceremonies, we do not imply that all of them were essential in any one age or district. The two men each with his witnesses appear upon the land. A knife is produced, a sod of turf is cut, the twig of a tree is broken off; the turf and twig are handed by the donor to the donee; they are the land in miniature, and thus the land passes from hand to hand. Along with them the knife also may be delivered, and it may be kept by the donee as material evidence of the transaction; perhaps its point will be broken off or its blade twisted in order that it may differ from other knives. But before this

[p. 85] the donor has taken off from his hand the war glove, gauntlet or thong, which would protect that hand in battle. The donee has assumed it; his hand is vested or invested; it is the *vestita manus* that will fight in defence of this land against all comers; with that hand he grasps the turf and twig. All the talk about investiture, about men being vested with land, goes back, so it is said, to this impressive ceremony. Even this is not enough; the donor must solemnly forsake the land. May be, he is expected to leap over the encircling hedge; may be, some queer renunciatory gesture with his fingers (*curvatis digitis*) is demanded of him; may be, he will have to pass or throw to the donee the mysterious rod or *festuca* which, be its origin what it may, has great contractual efficacy[1].

We are told that at a yet remote time this elaborate 'mode   Symbolic
livery.

---

[1] Heusler, Gewere, p. 7 ff.; Heusler, Institutionen, ii. 65; Brunner, Geschichte der Röm. u. Germ. Urkunde, i. 263 ff.; Schröder, D. R. G., 59, 270. The talk about 'vesting' can be traced back to the sixth century. As to broken and twisted knives, see Baildon, Select Civil Pleas, p. xv. The gesture with curved fingers was a Saxon practice; it is described by Schröder *op. cit.* p. 59, and was employed in Holstein within recent years.

of assurance' began to dissolve into its component parts, some
of which could be transacted away from the land. It is not
always very convenient for the parties to visit the land. In
particular is this the case when one of them is a dead saint.
One may indeed, if need be, carry the reliquary that contains
him to the field that he is to acquire; but some risk will thus
be run; and if the saint can not come to the field, the field
must come to the saint. In miniature it can do so; turf and
twig can be brought from it and placed with the knife upon
the shrine; the twig can be planted in the convent garden.
And then it strikes us that one turf is very much like another,
and since the bishop, who has just preached a soul-stirring
sermon, would like to secure the bounties of the faithful while
compunction is still at work, a sod from the churchyard will
do, or a knife without any sod, or a glove, or indeed any small
thing that lies handy, for the symbolical significance of sods
and knives and gloves is becoming obscure, and the thing thus
deposited is now being thought of as a gage or *wed* (*vadium*),
by which the donor can be constrained to deliver possession of
the land[1]. When, under Roman influence, the written document comes into use this also can be treated as a symbol; it is
delivered in the name of the land; the effectual act is not the [p. 86]
signing and sealing, but the delivery of the deed, and the
parchment can be regarded as being as good a representative
of land as knife or glove would be. Just as of old the sod
was taken up from the ground in order that it might be
delivered, so now the charter is laid on the earth and thence
it is solemnly lifted up or 'levied' (*levatio cartae*); Englishmen
in later days know how to 'levy a fine[2].' And lastly there
are, as we shall see hereafter, advantages to be gained by a
conveyance made before a court of law after some simulated
litigation; and one part of the original ceremony can be performed there; the donor or vendor can in court go through the
solemnity of surrendering or renouncing the land; the rod or
festuca can be passed from hand to hand in witness of this
surrender.

Symbolic
livery on
the Con-
tinent.

It seems to be now generally believed that long before the
Norman conquest of England this stage of development had

---

[1] Heusler, Gewere, 18.
[2] Brunner, Geschichte d. Urkunde, 104, 303.

been traversed by the continental nations. Land, it is said, could be conveyed without any transfer of possession, by a symbolical investiture, by the delivery of a written charter, by a surrender in court; and we suppose that this must be considered as proved, though, had our fully developed common law stood alone, we might have come to another conclusion.

As regards the Anglo-Saxon law, our evidence is but very slight. We know nothing about the conveyance of any land that was not book-land, and book-land we take to be an alien, ecclesiastical institution, from which few inferences can be drawn. Even as to this book-land some questions might be raised which could not easily be answered. On the whole, though the books may speak of the gift in the perfect or in the future as well as in the present tense, it seems probable that the signing or the delivery of the parchment was the effectual act. It would even seem that, when once land had been booked, a delivery of the original deed was sufficient to transfer proprietary rights from one man to another[1]. Occasionally, though but rarely, we hear of a turf being placed upon the altar[2]. *Anglo-Saxon-law.*

For some time after the Norman Conquest the shape that our law will take seems somewhat uncertain. In the first place, throughout the Norman period we often come upon royal and other charters which assume the air of dispositive documents and speak of the gift in the present tense. It is only by degrees that the invariable formula of later days, 'Know ye that I have given and granted,' finally ousts 'I give and grant[3].' In the second place, we read a good deal about the use of symbolical knives, rods and other such articles. Thus, for example, we are told that when the Conqueror gave English land to a Norman abbot by a knife, he playfully made as though he were going to dash the point through the abbot's hand and exclaimed, 'That's the way to give land[4].' Often it is clear *Law of the Norman age.*

[p. 87]

---

[1] Brunner, *op. cit.*, 149–209.

[2] Pollock, Land Laws, 3rd ed., p. 199. This, or something equivalent, may well have been done in other cases where it is not mentioned.

[3] For one instance see Round, Ancient Charters, p. 6; but there are many examples among the earliest charters in the Monasticon.

[4] Cartulaire de l'abbaye de la Sainte Trinité du Mont de Rouen (Documents inédits), p. 455: 'Haec donatio facta est per unum cultellum, quem praefatus Rex iosulariter dans Abbati quasi ejus palmae minatus infigere, Ita, inquit, terra dari debet.'

that the transfer of the symbol did not take place upon the
land that was in question; it took place in a church or a court
of law. The donor is said to put the land upon the altar by
a knife (*mittere terram super altare per cultellum*)[1]. Charters
are preserved which still have knives attached to them, and
in some cases a memorandum of the gift is scratched on the
haft of the knife[2]. Now and again this symbol is spoken of as
a *vadium,* or gage, and this may for a moment suggest that,
even if a real transfer of possession is necessary to complete
the conveyance, the transaction with the knife constitutes a
contractual obligation and gives the donee *ius ad rem*[3]. On
the other hand, such a transaction, which takes place far away
from the land, is sometimes, though rarely, spoken of as though
it were itself a delivery of seisin[4]. It is thus that a chronicler
describes how a dispute between the Abbot of St Albans and
the Bishop of Lincoln was compromised in the king's court:
'Then the bishop arose and resigned into the king's hand by [p. 88]
means of his head-gear (which we call a *hura*) whatever right
he had in the abbey or over the abbot Robert. And the king
took it and delivered it into the abbot's hand and invested the
church of St Alban with complete liberty by the agency of
the abbot. And then by his golden ring he put the bishop
in ownership and civil possession of the land at Tynhurst with
the consent of the abbot and chapter[5].' Thirdly, we have to
remember that at a later time, within the sphere of manorial
custom, seisin was delivered in court 'by the rod' which the
steward handed to the new tenant.

A real
livery
required.

When all this has been considered—and it is not of rareties
that we have been speaking—we shall probably come to the
conclusion that some external force has been playing upon our
law when it recurs to the rigorous requirement of a real transfer

[1] Madox, Formulare, p. x.; Cart. Glouc. i. 164, 205; ii. 74, 86; Cart. Rams.
i. 256; ii. 262. But examples are numerous.

[2] Selby Coucher Book, ii. 325.

[3] Hist. Abingd. ii. 100, 168; Winchcombe Landboc, i. 212: 'et per cultellum
super altare posuerunt signum pactionis huius.'

[4] This is so even in records of the king's court. Thus so late as 28 Hen. III.
it is recorded that John de Bosell came before the barons of the Exchequer and
in their presence put Robert Gardman in full seisin of lands and houses in
Lincoln; Madox, Formulare, p. xii.

[5] Gesta Abbatum, i. 156. For the *hura* see E. C. Clark, English Academical
Costume, p. 39.

of possession and a ceremony performed upon the land[1]. We have not far to seek for such a force. In bygone times Roman influence had made in favour of conveyance by charter, for, though the classical jurisprudence demanded a *traditio rei*, the men of the lower empire had discovered devices by which this requirement could be evaded and the ownership of land might practically, though not theoretically, be conveyed by the execution of a written instrument—devices curiously similar to those which Englishmen would be employing for a similar purpose in the nineteenth century[2]. It was a world in which ownership was apparently being transferred by documents that the barbarians invaded. If the Anglo-Saxon land-book passes ownership, it derives its efficacy, not indeed from classical Roman law, but from Italian practice. But when our common law was taking shape the Roman influence was of another and a more erudite kind and made for an opposite result. 'Traditionibus et usucapionibus dominia rerum, non nudis pactis, transferuntur[3]'—no text could be more emphatic. At the same time there is a great deal in our law, especially in the law relating to incorporeal things, which shows that Englishmen even of the thirteenth century found much difficulty in conceiving a transfer of rights unembodied in a transfer of things, and what we must ascribe to the new Roman influence is, not the requirement of a *traditio rei*, but the conviction that when land is to be given the delivery of no rod, no knife, no charter will do instead of a real delivery of the land. To this we may add that the king's justices seem to have felt very strongly that *donner et retenir ne vaut*. They are the same judges who, as we shall see, stamped out testamentary dispositions of land. Besides, their new instrument for the discovery of truth, a jury of the country, would tell them of real transfers of possession, but could not reveal transactions which took place in private[4].

[p. 89]

---

[1] In Edward I.'s day there were some jurors, 'simplices personae, qui cum non essent cognoscentes leges et consuetudines Anglicanas,' supposed that a charter might suffice without livery of seisin : Calendar. Genealog. ii. 659.

[2] Brunner, *op. cit.* p. 113 ff. The conveyance with reservation of a nominal usufruct evaded the *traditio* as the conveyance by 'lease and release' evaded the livery of seisin.

[3] Cod. 2. 3. 20 ; Bracton, f. 38 b, 41.

[4] Ecclesiastical law knew the symbolic investiture. Jocelin of Brakeland (Camden Soc.), p. 69, tells how the pope appointed judges delegate to hear the

Practice in
cent. xiii.
As a matter of fact, in the first half of the thirteenth century it was still common for the feoffor and the feoffee to
attend the county or hundred court, to have their charter read
there and to procure its attestation by the sheriff and the
leading men of the district[1]. In addition to this, if the gift was
to be made to a monastery, the charter would be read in the
chapter house and then it would be carried into the church and
offered upon the altar along with knife or rod. Beside this
there would be a ceremony on the land, including sometimes a
perambulation of boundaries in the presence of witnesses; and
this was the more necessary because the charter rarely described the many small strips of land which made up that hide
or virgate which had been bestowed. One could not be too
careful; one could not have too many ceremonies. But what
the king's court demanded was a real delivery of a real possession[2].

Royal con-
veyances.
No exception was made in the king's case. Even a royal [p. 90]
charter did not by itself confer seisin. With it there went out
a writ to the sheriff directing a livery. If the king made two
inconsistent gifts, a later charter with an earlier seisin would
override an earlier charter with a later seisin[3].

The
release.
To the rule that requires a *traditio* it is hardly an exception
that a *traditio brevi manu* is possible. The English *traditio
brevi manu* is the 'release.' Suppose that X is occupying the

---

cause of the Coventry monks. The monks were successful and 'a simple
seisin' was given to them in court by means of a book, the corporal institution
being delayed for a while. So, Chron. de Melsa, i. 294, in John's day judges
delegate restore land *per palmam viridem,* and some time after *corporalis
possessio* is delivered in their presence. In our own day the ceremonies
observed at the induction of a parson are good illustrations of medieval law.

[1] See the Brinkburn Cartulary (Surtees Soc.) *passim,* where many of the
charters are witnessed by the sheriff of Northumberland.

[2] The Winchcombe Landboc in particular is full of evidence of these
accumulated ceremonies. Very often there is a transaction before the county or
the hundred court of a renunciatory character. In 1182 (p. 197), on the day
after the ceremony on the land involving a perambulation of boundaries with
one set of witnesses, the donor attends the chapter house and executes his
charter before another set of witnesses, then he goes into the church and
'renews his gift' on the altar of St Kenelm. Note Book, pl. 375, seisin is given
in the county court; pl. 754, in the hundred court and afterwards on the land.
In Abbrev. Placit. 266, there is an odd and untranslatable story; a man delivers
seisin of a house *per haspam,* 'et reversus versus parietem cepit mingere.' Was
this a renunciatory act?

[3] Bracton, f. 56 b.

land as tenant for years or for life, that A has the fee simple; or suppose that X is holding the land adversely to A; and then suppose that in either of these cases A wishes to pass his rights to X. It would be an idle multiplication of ceremonies to oblige X to quit possession merely in order that he might be put into possession once more by a feoffment[1]. In the thirteenth century English law is meeting these cases by holding that A can pass his rights to X by a written document without any change in possession. As yet there is no well-defined specific term for such a transaction. It belongs to the great genus 'gift'; it is effected by such verbs as 'grant, render, remit, demit, quit-claim' (*concedere, reddere, remittere, dimittere, quietum clamare*)[2]. Hereafter 'release' (*relaxare, relaxatio*) will become the technical word, and there will be subtle learning about the various kinds of releases. The curious term *quietum clamare*, the origin of our 'to cry quits,' is extremely common, especially when the right that is to be transferred is an adverse right; for example, a disseisee will quit-claim his disseisor. Very possibly in the past such transactions have been effected without written instruments. We often read of the transfer of a rod in connexion with a quit-claim, and the term itself may point to some formal renunciatory cry; but in the thirteenth century a sealed deed or the record of a court was becoming necessary, and so in these cases we see proprietary rights transferred, or (it may be) extinguished, by the execution and delivery of a written document[3].

The quit-claim.

[p. 91]

[1] Bracton, f. 41: 'Quandoque sine traditione transit dominium et sufficit patientia; ut si tibi vendam quod tibi accommodavi, aut apud te deposui vel ad firmam vel ad vitam, et si quod ad vitam, vendo tibi in feodo, et sic mutaverim casum [*corr.* causam] possessionis, hoc fieri poterit sine mutatione possessionis.' This passage is based on Dig. 41. 1. 9, § 5, but is in harmony with English practice. See Littleton, sec. 460: 'for it shall be in vain to make an estate by a livery of seisin to another, where he hath possession of the same land by the lease of the same man before.'

[2] See *e.g.* the releases in Madox, Formulare; also Bracton, f. 45. Littleton, sec. 445: 'And it is to be understood that these words *remisisse et quietum clamasse* are of the same effect as these words *relaxasse* etc.'

[3] As to the grammatical use of the term, what I quit-claim is usually my right, thus I quit-claim my right (*ius meum*) in Blackacre to William; but I may also be said to quit-claim the land to William, or, but more rarely, to quit-claim William. It would seem from Ducange that the term was hardly in use out of England and Normandy, but elsewhere *quietare* was used in much the same sense. A solemn 'abjuration' of claims in court or in church had been common in England, as any cartulary will show; *e.g.* Melsa, i. 309: 'et illam postmodum

The surrender.

Another case in which a feoffment would have been unnecessary, and indeed misplaced, was that in which the tenant made a surrender to his lord. Here if the tenant was but tenant for term of years, his lord was already seised in demesne of the land, and if the tenant held for life or in fee, the lord was already seised of the land 'in service.' It is probable that in such a case the transaction could be accomplished in an informal fashion without deed or other ceremony[1]. But deeds of surrender are by no means uncommon. The verbs that were commonly used for this purpose seem to have been *reddere et quietum clamare*[2].

Change of estate.

For what may be called the converse case to that in which the release was used our law made no special provision. Suppose, for example, that *A* is seised in fee simple and desires to become a mere tenant for life or to acquire a conditional fee; no course seems open save that which necessitates two feoffments; he must enfeoff *X* in order that *X* may re-enfeoff him. In Edward I.'s day this machinery is being frequently employed for the manufacture of family settlements[3]. To take one famous [p. 92] example, the earl marshal surrenders office and lands to the king in fee simple, and after a few months is re-enfeoffed in tail, and, as it is clear that he is going to die without issue, King Edward has thus secured for himself the fief of the Bigods[4]. Probably in this case our law has had to set its face against looser practices. There is a great deal to show that men have thought themselves able by a single act or instrument to transfer the fee while retaining a life estate, and to make those *donationes post obitum* which have given rise to prolonged discussion in other countries. It is by no means impossible that many of the so-called Anglo-Saxon 'wills' were really instruments of this kind, irrevocable conveyances which were to operate at a future time. Our law will now have none of these[5].

sicut ius proprium nostrum in pleno wapentagio de Hedona, tactis sacrosanctis evangeliis, coram omnibus penitus abiuravit. Insuper se et heredes suos carta sua obligavit etc.' For the use of a stick, see Guisborough Cartulary, p. 71: 'Noveritis me...lingno et baculo reddidisse.' But this is common enough.

  [1] It was so in later law; Co. Lit. 338 a.
  [2] See *e.g.* Guisborough Cartulary, pp. 50–3–4–5, 70, 156.
  [3] See *e.g.* Calendar. Genealog. ii. 650, 702. The feoffee does not make the refeoffment until he has had a 'full and peaceful seisin.'
  [4] Foedera, i. 940–1.
  [5] Of this more hereafter in our section on The Last Will.

Another case which requires some special treatment is that **Gifts when the donor is not in occupation.** in which neither the donor nor the donee is in occupation of the land, but the occupier is a tenant of the donor.   Here we must distinguish.   If the tenant is holding in villeinage, the common law pays no heed to any customary rights that he may have; he is simply occupying in the name of his lord, and in this case a regular feoffment with livery of seisin is possible.   That livery, however, will very likely include a recognition by the tenant of the transfer of lordship.   Thus we may see one Richard de Turville giving seisin to the Abbot of Missenden; he sends his steward with letters patent to the villeins; they are congregated; seisin of them and of their tenements is delivered to the abbot; the abbot takes their fealty and demands rent, but, as no rent is due, some pence are lent to them and they each pay a penny for leave to remain in occupation[1].   If, however, the

[p. 93] tenant on the land was a freeholder whether for life or in fee, the case was not so simple.   The lord would have no business to enter on the land and make a feoffment there.   Slowly the doctrine is evolved that the seignory or reversion which is to be transferred can be treated as one of those incorporeal things which ' lie in grant,' as distinguished from that corporeal thing the land itself which 'lies in livery.'   Still even here men will not allow that there can be a transfer of proprietary right until there has been what can be pictured as a transfer of a thing. A deed of grant is executed—the word ' grant ' (Fr. *graunter*, Lat. *concedere*) becomes the term appropriate to such a transaction[2]—but this leaves the transaction incomplete; the tenant who is on the land must attorn himself to the grantee; pro- **Attornment.** bably an oral acceptance of his new lord is enough; often a nominal payment is made[3].   In most cases he can be compelled to attorn himself; if he will not do it, the court will attorn him[4]; but, until there has been attornment, the transaction is incomplete and ineffectual.   The case in which the tenant is a termor stands midway between the two that we have already mentioned.   He has a possession, or even a certain sort of

[1] Note Book, pl. 524.

[2] Among ancient documents it is difficult to distinguish those which, according to later theory, are deeds of grant from those which are charters of feoffment. All are charters of gift and commonly employ the same verbs: 'Sciatis me dedisse, et concessisse, et hac mea carta confirmasse.'

[3] An oral statement was enough in later days: Littleton, sec. 551.

[4] See above, vol. i. p. 347.

seisin, which the law has begun to protect; but still his lord is seised of the land and seised in demesne. It seems to be thought that two courses are open to the lord. There may be a deed of grant followed by an attornment; but a feoffment with livery of seisin may perhaps be possible. Bracton argues that the lord has a right to enter on the tenement for the purpose of making a feoffment: thereby he does no wrong to the termor, for the two concurrent seisins, that of the lord and that of the tenant, are compatible with each other[1]. However, in later days, the lord could not proceed by way of feoffment, unless he obtained the termor's consent or waited for some moment when the termor and all his family were absent from the land[2].

Feoffments with remainders.
When making a feoffment it was possible for the giver to impose conditions or to establish remainders, and all this by [p. 94] word of mouth. It is probable, however, that a charter was executed if anything elaborate was to be done, and, if we mistake not, remainders were seldom created in the thirteenth century except by those 'fines' of which we are about to speak. The remainder-man is for a while in a somewhat precarious position. This is due to two facts:—(1) he is usually no party to that transaction which gives him his rights; (2) neither he nor any ancestor of his has ever been seised. Thus if his rights are to be protected he must have special remedies.

Charters of feoffment.
The charter of feoffment or of grant is generally a very brief and simple affair. We seldom find after the end of the twelfth century any examples which depart far from the common form, though a few new devices, such as the mention of 'assigns' and the insertion of a well-drawn clause of warranty, were rapidly adopted in all parts of the country. It is almost always an unilateral document, a *carta simplex*, or as we should say 'deed poll,' not a bilateral document, a *carta duplicata, carta cyrographata.*

The fine.
There is something of mystic awe in the tone which already in Edward I.'s time lawyers and legislators assume when they speak of the 'fine,' or, to give it its full name, the final concord levied in the king's court. It is a sacred thing, and its sanctity is to be upheld at all cost[3]. We may describe it briefly and

[1] Bracton, f. 27, 44 b, 220 b; Note Book, pl. 1290.

[2] Litt. sec. 567; Co. Lit. 48 b; *Bettisworth's Case*, 2 Co. Rep. 31, 32.

[3] See the so-called Statute de Modo levandi Fines (Statutes of the Realm, i. 214); the Statute de Finibus levatis, 27 Edw. I. (Ibid. 126); Placit. Abbrev. 182; Rot. Parl. i. 67.

roughly as being in substance a conveyance of land and in form
a compromise of an action. Sometimes the concord puts an
end to real litigation; but in the vast majority of cases the
litigation has been begun merely in order that the pretended
compromise may be made.

'For the antiquity of fines,' says Coke, 'it is certain that they were frequent before the Conquest[1].' We do not think that this can be proved for England, but in Frankland the use of litigious forms for the purpose of conveyancing can be traced back to a very distant date; and in the Germany of the later middle ages a transaction in court which closely resembled our English fine became the commonest, some say the only[2], 'mode of assurance.' The advantages to be gained by employing it instead of an extrajudicial conveyance are in the main two. In the first place, we secure indisputable evidence of the transaction. In the second place, if a man is put into seisin by the judgment of a court he is protected by the court's ban. A short term, in general a year and day, is given to adverse claimants for asserting their rights; if they allow that to elapse and can offer no reasonable excuse for their inertness, such as infancy or absence, they are precluded from action; they must for ever after hold their peace, or, at all events, they will find that in their action some enormous advantage will be allowed to the defendant, as, for example, that of proving his case by his own unsupported oath. When Bracton charges with negligence and 'taciturnity' all those persons living in England who are silent while the land upon which they have claims is being dealt with by the king's court, this may look absurd enough, for how is a man in Northumberland to know of all the collusive suits that are proceeding at Westminster[3]? But the courts of old times had been local courts; the freeholders of the district had been bound to attend them; and to the man who alleged that he was not at the moot when his land was adjudged to another, there was this reply—'But it was your duty to be there[4].'

Marginal note: Origin of fines.

Marginal note: [p. 95]

---

[1] Second Institute, 511. Plowden, Comment, 369. The lawyers of the Elizabethan age seem to have been imposed upon by some of the forgeries that proceeded from Croyland. See Madox, Formulare, p. xiii; Hunter, Fines, i. p. 11.

[2] See Heusler, Institutionen, ii. 88.　　　　[3] Bracton, f. 435 b.

[4] It has been customary among English writers to find 'the origin of fines' in the *transactio* of the civilians and canonists. But this leaves unexplained the one thing that really requires explanation, the peculiar preclusive effect of a fine, or rather of seisin under a fine.

In England after the Conquest we soon begin to see men attempting to obtain incontestable and authoritative evidence of their dealings with land. While as yet the great roll of the exchequer is the only roll that is regularly kept, men will pay money to the king for the privilege of having their compromises and conveyances entered among the financial accounts rendered by the sheriffs—a not too appropriate context; and at a much later time we may still see them getting their charters of feoffment copied onto the plea rolls of the king's court. In Henry II.'s day one William Tallard solemnly abandoned a claim that he had been urging in the county court of Oxfordshire against the Abbot of Winchcombe. The abbot obtained a royal charter confirming this 'reasonable fine' of the suit, and [p. 96] he further obtained testificatory charters from the Abbots of Oseney and Ensham, and yet another charter to which the sheriff set his seal 'by the counsel and consent of the county[1].'

Evidence of a transaction is one thing; a special protection of the seisin that is held under that transaction is another. To obtain this men at one time allowed a simulated action to go as far as a simulated battle. The duel was 'waged, armed and struck'; that is to say, some blows were interchanged, but then the justices or the friends of the parties intervened and made peace, 'a final peace,' between them[2]. This had the same preclusive effect as a duel fought out to the bitter end. All whom it might concern had notice that they must put in their claims at once or be silent for ever. This might happen in the county court or in a seignorial court, and when the king's court has developed a model form of *concordia* we may see this closely imitated by less puissant tribunals[3].

But our interest has its centre in the king's court. After some tentative experiments[4] a fixed form of putting compromises on parchment seems to have been evolved late in

---

[1] Winchcombe Landboc, i. 186–192.

[2] Note Book, pl. 147, 168, 316 ('concordati fuerunt in campo'), 363, 815 ('concordati fuerunt in campo'), 851, 1035, 1619. Chron. de Melsa, ii. 99 (compromise while the battle is being fought); Ibid. 101 (the battle has been going on all day; our champion is getting worsted; Thurkelby J., who is a friend of ours, intervenes).

[3] For example, in Camb. Univ. Lib. Ee. iii. 60, f. 206 b, a regular fine levied in the court of the Abbot of St Edmunds in the seventh year of John. Guisborough Cartulary, ii. 333. Madox, Formulare, p. xv. Dugdale, Origines, 93. See also Note Book, pl. 992, 1223, 1616, 1619.

[4] See *e.g.* Note Book, pl. 1095; Dugdale, Origines, 50.

Henry II.'s reign, just about the same time when the first plea
roll was written. From the year 1175 onwards we begin to
get, in a few cases at first hand, in many cases at second hand,
chirographs, that is, indented documents, which have as their
first words what is to be the familiar formula: 'This is a final
'concord made in the court of our lord the king[1].' Glanvill
writing a few years afterwards has already much to say of these
[p. 97] final concords[2]. Then there is happily preserved for us a
document of this kind dated on the 15th of July, 1195,
which bears an endorsement saying that this was the first
chirograph that was made in the form of three chirographs, of
which one was to remain in the treasury to serve as a record;
it adds that this innovation was due to the justiciar Hubert
Walter and the other barons of the king[3]. What is new seems
to be this:—heretofore when a compromise was made, its terms
were stated in a bipartite indenture, one 'part' of which was
delivered to each litigant; henceforth there is to be a tripartite indenture and one 'part' of it is to be preserved in
the treasury. This 'part' or copy (perhaps owing to some
confusion between the French *pes* which means peace, concord,
and the Latin *pes* which means foot) soon becomes known as
the 'foot' of the fine, and with the summer of 1195 begins that
magnificent series of *pedes finium* which stretches away into
modern times and affords the best illustrations that we have of
medieval conveyancing[4]. Soon the fines became very numerous;

---

[1] See Round, Feudal England, 509, and E. H. R. xii. 293. Some other early
fines were mentioned in Select Pleas of the Crown, Selden Society, p. xxvii.
Since then others have come before us. The Winchcombe Landboc, i. 201–
211 has six. There are five more in a Register of St Edmunds, Camb. Univ.
Lib. Ee. iii. 60, f. 183 d, 187, 189, 205. All these fines ought to be collected in
one place.

[2] Glanvill, lib. viii.

[3] Feet of Fines, Hen. II. and Rich. I. (Pipe Roll Soc.) p. 21: 'Hoc est
primum cyrographum quod factum fuit in curia domini Regis in forma trium
cyrographorum secundum quod...dominum Cantuariensem et alios barones
domini Regis ad hoc ut per illam formam possit fieri recordum. Traditur
Thesaurario ad ponendum in thesauro, anno regni Regis Ricardi vi° die
dominica proxima ante festum beate Margarete coram baronibus inscriptis.'
The fine itself is dated on the previous day. The Pipe Roll Society is publishing
such of the fines of Richard's reign as are not in Hunter's collection. That
collection (2 vols. Record Commission) contains fines of Richard's and of John's
day; it will be of great service to us.

[4] This suggestion as to the origin of the 'foot' is due to Horwood, Y. B.
21-2 Edw. I. p. x; but, so far as we are aware, the *pes* was always the lowest

every term, every eyre (for a fine can be levied before justices
in eyre as well as in the central court) supplies a large number
of *pedes*; often they are beautiful examples of both exquisite
caligraphy and accurate choice of words. The curious term
'levy' soon comes into use. It may take us back to the
Frankish *levatio cartae*, the ceremonial lifting of a parchment
from the ground[1]; but the usual phrase is, not that the litigants
levy a fine, but that a fine levies between them[2].

Procedure
when a fine
is to be
levied.

An action was begun between the parties by writ. Many [p. 98]
different forms of writ were used for this purpose, but ultimately
one of the less cumbrous actions, the writ of covenant, or the
writ of *warantia cartae*, was usually chosen[3]. In the earliest
period the parties seem often to plead and to go so far as the
summoning of a grand assize[4]; and of course the fine is at
times the end of serious litigation; but in general so soon as
they are both before the court, they ask for leave to compromise their supposed dispute (*petunt licentiam concordandi*):—
compromising a suit without the leave of the court is an offence
to be punished by amercement, and the king makes money out
of the licences that his justices sell[5]. Having obtained the
requisite permission, the litigants state to the court (four
justices at least should be present) the terms of their compact[6].

'part' of the indenture, and our phrase 'the foot of the page' deserves
consideration. Already in Henry III.'s reign we have 'quesiti sunt pedes
cyrographorum...et nullus pes inveniri potuit': Placit. Abbrev. 182.

[1] See above, p. 86.

[2] The common phrase on the rolls of Edward I. seems to be 'et finis levavit
[*not* levavit se] inter eos.' Coke, Second Institute, 511, remarks that 'finis se
levavit' is better than 'J. S. levavit finem.'

[3] In Richard's and John's reigns the action is often a mort d'ancestor, often
a writ of right. Coke, *Tey's Case*, 5 Rep. 39, says that any writ by which land
is demanded, or which in any sort concerns land, will do. *Warantia cartae*
and *Covenant* are according to thirteenth century ideas personal actions, and
the process in them is simple. There is in manuscript (*e.g.* Camb. Univ. Add.
3097 *ad fin.*) a tract on the practice of levying fines, which seems as old as the
fourteenth century. It should be printed.

[4] Fines, ed. Hunter, i. 89, 91, 109 etc.

[5] The payments due to the king as ultimately fixed are described by Coke,
Second Institute, 510. He gets in all a quarter of one year's value of the land.

[6] Modus levandi Fines, Statutes of the Realm, i. 214. This document was
long called a statute of 18 Edw. I. In the Commissioners' edition it has been
relegated to the *Tempus Incertum*. Its style and the fact that we have no
better warrant for it than private MSS. make its statutory origin exceedingly
doubtful. It may however have been sanctioned by the judges and have
been what we should call a rule of court. It is to be distinguished from the

Throughout the middle ages the justices exercise a certain supervision over the fines that are levied before them. When a married woman is concerned, they examine her apart from her husband and see that she understands what she is doing. In other cases they do not inquire into the subject matter of the compromise; they have not to protect the material interests of the parties or of strangers, but they do pretty frequently interfere to maintain formal correctness and the proprieties of conveyancing: they refuse irregular fines. Even the formal correctness of the arrangement they do not guarantee, but they are not going to have their rolls defaced by obviously faulty instruments[1]. Then the indenture is drawn up by an officer of the court; one 'part' of it is delivered to each party, and the *pes* is sent to the royal treasury, there to remain until its conclusive testimony is required[2].

A fine is generally a bilateral instrument: that is to say, each of the parties professedly does something for the other. The one whom we may for the moment call the conveyor grants or releases his rights in the land or the incorporeal thing, for example, the advowson, which is the subject matter of the suit, or else he solemnly confesses (*cognoscit*) that the said thing 'is the right' of the other party. In this last case we may speak of the party who makes the confession or 'conusance' as the 'conusor' while his adversary in the suit becomes a 'conusee.' Then a separate clause will state that, in return for what he has thus done, the conveyor receives some benefit. This may be 'the fraternity and prayers' of a convent[3]; very often it is a sum of money paid down: in some cases a trivial sum, in others so large that the transaction seems to be a sale of the land for its full value. But again,

Form of the fine.

[p. 99]

---

unquestionable Statute de Finibus Levatis of 27 Edw. I. In the last years of Henry III. many fines were levied before but two justices.

[1] Many instances of fines rejected for irregularity can be found in the Year Books. Some are collected in Fitz. Abr. tit. *Fines.* See *Tey's Case*, 5 Rep. 38 *b*; also *Barkley's Case*, Plowden, 252, where great weight is given to the argument that the fine in question would never have been received by such learned judges as Brian and his fellows if it had been invalid on its face.

[2] This is but a rough statement. The somewhat complicated relationship between the 'concord,' the 'note,' and the 'foot' as described in *Tey's Case* would be of no interest here; it must be enough to say that for some purposes the fine is valid before the chirograph has been drawn up. This was so already under Edward I.: Y. B. 33–5 Edw. I. p. 487.

[3] Fines, ed. Hunter, i. 60, 128.

it is possible that this recompense will take the form of some right in the land; *A* having confessed that the land belongs to one *X*, this *X* will grant the whole or part of it to *A* to hold of him (*X*) by some service more or less onerous. Thus a way is opened for family settlements, for we can sometimes see that *X* is a mere friend of the family, who is brought into the transaction for the purpose of enabling *A* to exchange an estate in fee simple for a life estate with a remainder to his son. It will be for future ages to distinguish accurately between the various classes of fines[1].

Advantages of a fine.

Evidence secured.

Of the advantages that could be obtained by the use of a [p. 100] fine a little can now be said.

(1) Incontestable evidence of the transaction was thus secured, and this was no small boon at a time when forgeries, or at all events charges of forgery, were common. Men would not scruple to forge even the chirograph of a fine, but then, owing to the retention of the *pes* in the treasury, the forgery could be detected[2]. In the old days, before the reform that we have attributed to Hubert Walter, the justices might indeed have borne record of a fine that was levied before them, and, if they did so, their record was conclusive; but their record was based upon their memory, not upon parchment, and, if they were uncertain about the matter, then the question whether or no there had been a fine was open to contest, and we may see it contested[3]. When, however, the practice of retaining *pedes* had been introduced, a search in the treasury would settle this question for good and all[4].

Action on the fine.

(2) A man who was party to a fine was bound by a stringent obligation to perform and respect its terms. If he infringed them, an action lay against him and he could be sent to prison; seemingly in Glanvill's day he could be compelled

---

[1] In the early fines either the demandant (*D*) or the tenant (*T*) may be the conveyor; thus in Hunter's collection, *D* quit-claims to *T* (p. 1), grants to *T* (p. 6), confesses to *T* (p. 14), while *T* quit-claims to *D* (p. 6–7), grants to *D* (p. 109), confesses to *D* (p. 8). An early specimen of a settlement effected by fine is this from 1202 (Hunter, p. 34):—Bartholomew demandant, Maria tenant; Maria confesses the land to be the right of Bartholomew; in return he grants half of it to Maria for life, with remainder to her son Hugh and the heirs of his body, with remainder to her son Stephen and his heirs.

[2] Placit. Abbrev. 182.

[3] Glanvill, viii. 5–8; Note Book, pl. 715, 1095.

[4] Placit. Abbrev. 182.

to find security for the future; but at any rate he could be imprisoned[1]. At a time when contractual actions, actions on mere covenants, were but slowly making their way to the royal court, the action *Quod teneat ei finem factum* was already popular[2].

(3)   We come to the most specific quality of the fine. Like a final judgment in a writ of right, it sets a short preclusive term running against the whole world 'parties, privies and strangers.' If there be any person who thinks that he has a right to the land comprised in the fine, he must assert that right at once; otherwise—unless he has been under one of the recognized 'disabilities,' such as infancy or absence beyond sea—he will be barred for ever. This statement needs some qualification. In order that the fine shall have this preclusive effect, it is necessary that one of the parties to it be seised: a seisin acquired by wrong will be good enough, but a seisin there must be. It is not to be suffered that a man who is in peaceful seisin of land in Yorkshire, and who may be the true owner, should be done out of his rights by a collusive ceremony perpetrated at Westminster by two tricksters who 'have nothing in the land.' Our law may have doubted for a while whether such a fine, one levied between persons neither of whom was seised, would have any effect at all, would bind even those persons or their heirs. A statute of 1299 decided that the parties and those claiming under them were bound; but strangers were not affected by the fine[3]. We have further to notice that in many cases the preclusive term did not begin to run until the fine took effect in a change of seisin. It is difficult to speak in general terms of this matter because there were various kinds of fine; but just as, when there had been judgment on a writ of right, the fateful year and day did not start until seisin had been delivered by the sheriff to the victorious demandant, so, when a fine was levied, it was often necessary that a writ of seisin should be sued out and that seisin should be delivered[4]. Seisin under the order of the king's court; seisin under the king's ban,—it is this rather

The preclusive bar.

[p 101]

---

[1] Glanvill, viii. 5; Note Book, pl. 454, 496.

[2] Note Book, vol. i. p. 186.

[3] Stat. de Finibus Levatis, 27 Edw. I.   See Coke's commentary in Second Institute, 521; also Bracton, f. 436 b.

[4] See Coke, 1 Rep. 96 b, 97 a, and the books there cited.

than the mere compromise of an action that, if we look far enough back, seems the cause of preclusion[1].

The year and day.
As to the length of the preclusive term, Bracton seems to hold that the bar is established so soon as the chirograph is delivered to the parties. This is never done until fifteen days after the concord has been made in court, and fifteen days is the time usually allowed to a litigant who has been summoned[2]. A little later we find that year and day are allowed[3], and as this was the period allowed from of old in Germany[4], we may perhaps infer that the judges of Bracton's day had been attempting to abbreviate an ancient term[5]. In order to prevent his right being barred, a man must either bring an action or else enter his claim upon the *pes* of the fine. On ancient *pedes* it is [p. 102] common to see a claim entered, or even two or three claims; this seems to show that what went on at Westminster was soon noised abroad[6].

Value of the bar.
Now here of course we see an advantage of enormous importance that the fine has over any extrajudicial transaction, and, when we remember how easily seisin begets proprietary rights, how at one and the same moment half-a-dozen possessory titles to the same piece of land—titles which are more or less valid—may be in existence, we shall not be surprised at the reverential tones in which the fine is spoken of. It is a piece of firm ground in the midst of shifting quicksands.

The married woman's fine.
(4) In Bracton's day the fine had already become the married woman's conveyance. If her land was to be lawfully and effectually conveyed, she and her husband were made parties to an action, and before the 'concord' was accepted by the court, the justices examined her and satisfied themselves that she was acting freely[7].

---

[1] And therefore it is that we find it doubtful whether judgment in a writ of right in favour of the tenant can have a preclusive effect; Y. B. 7 Edw. III. f. 37 (Trin. pl. 41).   [2] Bracton, f. 436.

[3] Fleta, p. 443 ; Modus levandi, Statutes of the Realm, i. p. 214.

[4] Laband, Die vermögensrechtlichen Klagen, 295 ; Heusler, Gewere, 237.

[5] Throughout the Note Book those who plead 'non-claim' make no mention of year and day. It seems possible that an old rule was for a while thrown into confusion by the new practice of making chirographs and retaining *pedes*.

[6] On the back of the *pes* we read '*A* de *B* apponit clamium suum.' In later days one might assert one's right by action, by claim on the *pes*, or by entry. In Bracton's day entry would have been dangerous owing to the severe prohibition of self-help.

[7] Bracton, f. 321 b.   Of the married woman we speak in a later chapter.

(5) If what was to be conveyed was a seignory or a Convey-
ance of
reversions
reversion, a fine was useful[1]. It was possible that the tenant
who was in possession of the land would make some difficulty
about attorning himself to the purchaser. But if a fine was
levied, there was a regular procedure in common use for compelling such tenants to appear before the court and confess the
terms of their tenure, and then they would be forced to attorn
themselves or would be attorned by the court, unless they could
show some good reason for their refusal[2].

(6) Lastly, it might seem that family settlements could be Family set-
tlements.
effected more simply and more securely by fine than by other
means. If *A* is tenant in fee simple and wishes to obtain a life
estate followed by remainders, or a conditional fee limited to
the heirs of his body, or the like, he may be able to effect this
[p. 103] by enfeoffing *X* in order that he may be re-enfeoffed. But there
are obvious objections to this practice. For one thing, *X* may
be dishonest and do much harm by enfeoffing a stranger; and
then again, someone may hereafter urge that *X* never acquired
a real and true seisin of the land and that the transaction was
therefore but a sham. On the other hand, it may be that by
fine the whole settlement can be effected at one moment.

This leads us to speak of the relation between the law about The fine
and seisin.
fines and the law about seisin. Can a fine transfer seisin? Is the
operation of a fine an exception to the general rule that land
can not be conveyed without a *traditio rei*, a transfer of seisin?

To the first of these questions we must answer, No. Seisin A judg-
ment can
give no
seisin.
is for the men of the thirteenth century a fact; the physical
element in it is essential. It can not be transferred by a written
instrument, nor by a compromise however solemn, nor even by
the judgment of a court. The judgment awarded to a successful
demandant does not even confer upon him a right to enter and
to acquire seisin; if he enters without waiting for the sheriff,
who is to execute the judgment, he will be guilty of disseising
the defeated tenant[3]. And so the preclusive term, the year and

---

[1] Britton, f. 229.

[2] There seem to be in Bracton's day two writs for this purpose:—*Per quae
servitia* and *Quid iuris clamat;* proceedings upon them are common in the Note
Book; see vol. i. p. 184–5. There is some learning about the latter of them in
Tey's Case, 5 Rep. 39 b.

[3] See *e.g.* the strong statement of Berwick, J. in Y. B. 20–1 Edw. I. p. 52;
also Y. B. 33–5 Edw. I. p. 200. Whether a judgment can confer the *Gewere*
(seisin) has been a question much debated among the Germanists. See Heusler,
Gewere, p. 186.

day, does not begin to run in favour of a victorious demandant until he has been put in seisin.

A fine gives no seisin.

It is so also with the fine. It does not transfer seisin of the land. We have already seen that some one who is no party to the fine may be seised at the time when the fine is levied, and in that case his seisin and his rights will remain unaffected by the collusive action and the feigned compromise. But we must pass to the case in which one of the two parties to the fine is seised of the land, and even here we shall see that the fine standing by itself—the mere recorded compromise—is incapable of transferring seisin of the land. Of course in many cases there can be no talk of any transfer of seisin. The parties are merely doing by fine what they could have done, though not so effectually, by a deed : that is to say, the one of them who is not seised is releasing or quit-claiming some right to the one who is seised. Also of 'things incorporeal' we are not speaking; but the mere fine is incapable of transferring seisin of land. This [p. 104] we shall see if we turn from our first to our second question.

The fine does not convey land.

Just because the mere fine is incapable of transferring seisin, it is incapable of conveying land. This may seem a startling statement to those who have been bred up to consider the fine as one of the most potent of the 'common assurances' of the common law. But what we have said seems to be true in the thirteenth century. We put a simple case :—*A* is seised in fee simple; in an action brought against him by *X* he solemnly confesses that the land is the right of *X*[1], or goes further and confesses (what is not true) that he, *A*, has given it to *X* by feoffment[2]; nevertheless *A* remains in occupation of the land. Now, at any moment during *A*'s lifetime *X* can obtain execution of the fine; thereby he will obtain seisin and so the conveyance will be perfected. But suppose that *A* dies seised, it seems exceedingly doubtful whether his confession, his false confession of a feoffment, can according to the doctrines of the thirteenth century bar the claim of his heir[3]. Of another case we may speak with greater certainty. It was very common. The tenant in fee simple, *A*, wishes to make a settlement; by the fine he

---

[1] This is the fine *sur conusance de droit tantum*.

[2] This is the fine *sur conusance de droit come ceo que il ad de son don*.

[3] Bracton, f. 242 b. At all events if the conusee after the conusor's death entered and forestalled the heir, the heir would have the assize of mort d'ancestor against him ; Bracton, f. 262.

confesses that he has enfeoffed X, and then the chirograph will
go on to say that X grants and renders the land to A for some
estate (for example a life estate) which will entitle him (A) to
remain seised as heretofore, and then some remainders are
created[1]. Really there has been no feoffment; X has never for
a moment been on the land; A has occupied it all along and
continues to occupy it until his death. Now his heir is not
bound by that fine. If an attempt is made to enforce it against
the heir, he will plead that A was seised at the date of the fine
and continued seised until his death; and this plea will be
good. We learn this from a statute of 1299 which alters the
law; it takes away this plea from the heir of any one who was
party to the fine. Thereafter such a fine as we have supposed
will be effectual as against those who stand in A's shoes.
[p. 105] Taken by itself and without a transmutation of seisin it will be
effectual. But this operation it owes to a statute. According
to the law as it stood at the end of Henry III.'s reign, a fine
unaccompanied by a *de facto* change of seisin could never be a
substitute for a feoffment; and so we have to qualify a statement with which we started, namely, that a fine is a conveyance[2].

Thus have we once more been brought back to seisin. Our
conception of the seisin of land which our law knew in the
thirteenth century is being made clearer by negative propositions. Seisin of land can not pass from man to man by

Return to seisin.

---

[1] This would be a fine *sur grant, don et render*.

[2] This is the best opinion that we can offer about a difficult matter. The
Statute de Finibus Levatis, 27 Edw. I., states that for some time past, during
the present king's reign and that of his father, the parties to fines and their
heirs have been suffered to annul them by the plea of continuous seisin.
This practice, it says, was contrary to the old law. A tradition current in
Edward III.'s reign ascribed the innovation to 'the maintenance of the great':
Coke improved upon this by an allusion to the Barons' War. See Y. B.
6 Edw. III. f. 28, Pasch. pl. 75; Second Institute 522. But the heir's plea is
sanctioned by Bracton, f. 242 b, 262, 270, and can be traced back to very near
the beginning of Henry III.'s reign; Note Book, pl. 125, 778, 853. See also
Y. B. 33–5 Edw. I. pp. 201, 435. The Statute speaks of the plea as having been
used not merely by the heir, but even by the person who was party to the fine.
This may have been a recent innovation, and one hardly to be reconciled with
sound principle; for certainly it seems strange that a man should be allowed to
dispute a solemn confession that he has made in court. We seem to see here
as elsewhere that the justices of the first half of the century have been insisting
rigorously on a *traditio rei* as an essential part of every conveyance. In this instance they may have overshot the mark. But further investigation of this obscure
tract of history is needed. In later days a large mass of intricate learning
clustered round the fine. Here we have merely tried to find its original germ.

inheritance, by written instrument, by confession in court, by judgment; it involves a *de facto* occupation of the land. On the other hand, without a transmutation of seisin—which may however in appropriate cases take the form of a *traditio brevi manu*—there is no conveyance of land.

§ 4. *The Term of Years.*

The term
of years.

From time to time we have been compelled to speak of the curious treatment that the tenancy for a term of years has received at the hands of our law[1]; we must now discuss it at some length. And in the first place we observe that the law has drawn a hard line which does not of necessity coincide with any economic distinction. A feoffment for life may in substance be an onerous lease, a lease for years may be granted for so long a term and at so trivial a rent that the lessee's rights [p. 106] will be very valuable. For all this, the tenant for life will be a freeholder, while the tenant for years, or 'termor,' will be no freeholder.

Attempt to
treat the
term as a
personal
right.

At the end of the twelfth century the law was apparently endeavouring to regard the termor as one who has no 'real' right, no right in the land; he enjoys the benefit of a covenant (*conventio*); he has a right *in personam* against the lessor and his heirs. His action is an action of covenant (*quod teneat ei conventionem factam*), an action which seems to have been invented chiefly for the enforcement of what we should call leases[2]. In this action he can recover possession, or rather seisin (for such is the phrase commonly used), of the land. The judgment is, we may say, a judgment for the 'specific performance' of the covenant[3]. Frequently, if not always, the termor enjoys the benefit of a warranty. If he is evicted by some third person, he can claim from the lessor an equivalent for the benefit of which he

[1] See above, vol. i. p. 357, vol. ii. p. 36.

[2] A plea of covenant appears on the earliest plea roll: Curia Regis Rolls (Pipe Roll Soc.), p. 53. The writ occurs in very early registers: Harv. L. R. iii. 113, 169. Actions of covenant are fairly common in the Note Book; see vol. i. p. 186.

[3] Note Book, pl. 1739 (A.D. 1226): 'et ideo consideratum est quod convencio teneatur et quod Hugo habeat seisinam suam usque ad terminum suum decem annorum.'

has been deprived[1]. Add to this that if his lessor attempts to turn
him out, he is allowed *vim vi repellere;* a speedy re-ejectment
would be no disseisin, no wrong to the lessor[2]. But as against
the world at large he is unprotected. At all events he is
unprotected against ejectment. Eject him, and you disseise the
freeholder under whom he is holding; that freeholder will bring
the assize of novel disseisin against you. How far the termor is
protected by an action for damages against mere trespassers who
stop short of ejectment, we can not say. The action of trespass
only becomes common in the king's courts near the middle
of the thirteenth century, and of what went on in the local
courts about the year 1200 we know very little.

[p. 107]   Even if no ejector appeared from without, the termor was
not very secure in his holding. His rights had to yield to those
of the guardian in chivalry, as well as to those of the lessor's
widow. If the doweress, as she might, turned him out of one-
third of the land, he was allowed to hold the other two-thirds
for an additional period by way of compensation[3]. If his lessor's
lord, who had got his lessor's heir in ward, turned him out, his
term was, not indeed destroyed, but it was 'deferred[4].' The
lessor's assigns were not bound by the lessor's covenant; the
lessor's feoffee could oust the termor and leave him to his
remedy against the lessor or the lessor's heir.

Insecurity of the termor.

But, at all events in this last particular, the law was not
expressing the common sense of mankind. About the year
1235 a new action was given to the termor, the *Quare eiecit
infra terminum.* This reform is attributed to Bracton's master,
William Raleigh, who was then presiding in the king's court.
Bracton was loud in its praise[5]. Writing a few years afterwards,
he distinctly says that this new action, which will restore the
ejected termor to the land, will lie against all manner of
ejectors, and he appeals to the broad principle that to eject

Failure of the old doctrine.

---

[1] Note Book, pl. 106, 638. The doctrine that a demise for years implies a
warranty seems to flow as a natural consequence from the original character of
such a demise. The lessor gives the lessee no right in the land, but covenants
that the lessee shall enjoy the land; this covenant he must fulfil *in specie*, if
that be possible: otherwise he must render an equivalent.

[2] Hengham Parva, c. 7.

[3] Bracton, f. 312; Note Book, pl. 658, 767, 970; Y. B. 33–5 Edw. I. p. 267.

[4] Bracton, f. 30: 'custodia non adimit terminum sed differt.' Britton, ii. 8.

[5] Bracton, f. 220; Maitland, History of the Register, Harv. L. R. iii. 173,
176; Note Book, pl. 1140.

a termor is as unjustifiable as to disseise a freeholder[1]. However, as has not unfrequently happened, some words got into the new writ which restricted its efficacy. The most scandalous case of ejectment is that in which the termor is turned out by one who has purchased the land from the lessor. Not only may it be urged that the purchaser should be in no better position than that which the vendor has occupied, but an obvious door is opened to fraud:—the lessor, who dares not himself eject the lessee, effects his object by the mediation of a collusive purchaser, and contrives that an action on the covenant shall be of no value[2]. The new writ in the form which it takes when it crystallizes in the register, contains [p. 108] words which strike directly at this particular case. It supposes that the defendant has purchased the land from the lessor. In spite of what Bracton says, the golden opportunity has been missed. This action can not be used against ejectors in general; it will only lie against one who has purchased from the lessor[3].

The termor and the writ of trespass. For protection against ejectors who were in no way connected with his lessor, the termor had to look to another quarter: to the development of the new, and for a long time semi-criminal action which accuses the defendant of having entered and broken another man's close 'with force and arms and against the king's peace,' the action of 'trespass *quare clausum fregit.*' Such actions were becoming popular during the last years of Henry III.'s reign. Apparently they were for a while held in check by the doctrine that they ought not to be used as substitutes for the assize of novel disseisin[4]. Nor was this doctrine unnatural. By choosing an action of trespass instead of an assize one was threatening the defendant with all the terrors of outlawry and using a weapon which had in the past been reserved for felons. Now at what moment of time

---

[1] Bracton, f. 220.

[2] See the reasoning in the printed Register : Reg. Brev. Orig. 227 : 'Et quia multotiens contingit quod dimisor non habet unde conventionem teneat, et fraus et dolus nemini debent patrocinari.' The printed book ascribes the writ to William of Merton, apparently a person compounded out of William of Raleigh and Walter of Merton. The older MSS. speak of Raleigh.

[3] It is remarkable that while Fleta, f. 275, follows Bracton pretty closely, Britton, i. 417, apparently denies the existence of any writ that will avail the ejected termor against his lessor's feoffee. Perhaps there were some who had doubts as to the validity of the writ. In Y. B. 18 Edw. II. p. 599 there is question as to whether the allegation of sale to the defendant is traversable or no.

[4] Bracton, f. 413.

the termor became entitled to this new action, it is very difficult to say, for in the action of trespass the plaintiff but rarely asserts by express words any title, or seisin or possession. He simply says that 'his' close has been entered and broken by the defendant. We should not be surprised at discovering that from the very first, that is, so soon as actions of trespass became common, the termor was allowed to say in this context that the land in question was 'his' close[1]. The principle that he ought to be protected against the world at large had been fully conceded by Bracton. An investigation of this matter would take us far beyond the moment of time that we have [p. 109] chosen for our survey. It must suffice if we here say that the termor did acquire the action of trespass, an action for damages against all who unlawfully disturbed him in his possession; that a specialized writ of trespass *de eiectione firmae* (which is to be carefully distinguished from the old *quare eiecit infra terminum*) was penned to meet his particular case; and that just at the close of the middle ages it was decided that in this action he could recover, not merely damages, but his possession of the land—he could 'recover his term[2].'

In another quarter a statute of **1278** gave the termor some much needed protection. In the old actions for land he had no *locus standi* either as the active or as the passive party. He did not represent the land. If you brought a writ of right or writ of entry against him, he would plead that he was but a termor and your action would be dismissed. Consequently his interest could be destroyed by a collusive action. Some one sued his lessor; that lessor allowed judgment to go by default, and the recoveror, who had by supposition shown a title

Further protection of the termor.

---

[1] If the lessor attempts to eject the termor, the latter may use force in the defence of his possession : Hengham Parva, c. 7. We may argue *a fortiori* that he may use force against the mere trespasser who endeavours to eject him; and from the concession of a right to maintain possession by force to the concession of an action for damages, the step seems short.

[2] It seems to us that the relation between the two writs is often misrepresented in modern books owing to a mistake which can be traced to Fitzherbert. He knew from the note about 'William of Merton' in the Register that the *Quare eiecit* was a modern action, but seems to have supposed that *De eiectione firmae* was primeval. This has led Blackstone (Comment. iii. 207) to represent the *Quare eiecit* as a mere supplement for the *De eiectione*. But the writ whose invention is recorded by Bracton and Fleta is the *Quare eiecit*, while the growth of the action of trespass is post-Bractonian. In the MS. Registers the *Quare eiecit* appears long before the *De eiectione firmae*.

superior to the lessor's, ousted the termor. Already, however, in Edward I.'s day the Statute of Gloucester empowered the termor in divers cases to intervene in the action for the protection of his interest. This statute required a supplement in Henry VIII.'s reign; but during the interval a vigilant termor who had a written lease was fairly well defended against the easiest devices of chicane[1].

Seisin and possession.

From the thirteenth century onwards English law has on its hands the difficult task of maintaining side by side two different possessions or seisins, or (to adopt the convenient distinction which is slowly established during the fourteenth and later centuries) a seisin and a possession[2]. There is the old seisin protected by the assize, there is the new possession protected [p. 110] by the writ of trespass. Of course one and the same man may have both. The tenant in fee or for life, who occupies his own land, is both seised and possessed of it. But the two may be divided; they are divided when there is a termor occupying the land; he is possessed, but the freeholder is seised. Even at the present day, though the old possessory remedies which protected seisin are things of the past, we have still to be always distinguishing between seisin and possession[3].

Explanation of termor's history.

It is natural therefore that we should ask how it came about that in the twelfth century the courts arrived at the conclusion that the ejected termor was not to have the assize of novel disseisin. Why is he not seised of a free tenement? The question is not easy. If in such a context we are entitled to speak of the natural inclination of English law, we ought apparently to say that this was in favour of attributing a legally protected possession to any person who is in enjoyment of the land and can take the fruits as his own, albeit he is there only for a time and is paying rent to a lord. The tenant for life, however heavily he may be burdened with rent or other service, is indubitably seised of free tenement. We are told also that Germanic law, when left to itself, always displays this inclination. It does not require of the man to whom it attributes

---

[1] Stat. Glouc. c. 11; Stat. 21 Hen. VIII. c. 15; Co. Lit. 46 a.

[2] In Bracton's day and much later seisin is habitually ascribed to the termor; *e.g.* Note Book, pl. 1739 : 'et ideo consideratum est quod convencio teneatur et quod Hugo habeat seisinam suam usque ad terminum suum decem annorum.' See L. Q. R. i. 332. As already said, in pleadings and judgments the word *possessio* is rare. See above, p. 31.

[3] See Pollock and Wright, Possession, p. 49.

possession that he shall behave as owner of the thing possessed ; if he takes the fruits as his own, that is quite enough. We are told also that when this inclination is not manifested, then the operation of a Roman influence may be suspected[1].

The requisite explanation we shall hardly find in the mere rarity of tenancies for terms of years. No doubt in the year 1150 they were still uncommon, and it is not until 1200 that we begin to read much about them. How rare they had been in yet older times we can not tell. For example, the fact that they are hardly ever mentioned in the Anglo-Saxon land-books will not prove that they were practically unknown in England before the Conquest. The solemn ' book ' would hardly have been used for so humble a purpose as that of creating short tenancies. Still we can see enough both in England and on the continent to say that during the dark age leases for determinate periods were not very common. They seem to imply a pecuniary speculation, a computation of gain and loss, which is impossible where there is little commerce. The man who was in quest of land was looking out, not for a profitable investment, but for a home and the means of livelihood. He had to think of the days when he would no longer be able to work, and, if he could not obtain a secure provision for his whole life, he would take land on precarious terms and trust to a lord's generosity or inertness : very likely his precarious estate would become hereditary. The Roman *locatio conductio* of land disappeared ; it was overwhelmed by the *precarium* which tended to become a *beneficium* or a lease for life[2]. We can not say for certain that none of the *locationes* and *commendationes terrae* mentioned in Domesday Book were leases for years[3]; such leases begin to appear very soon after the Conquest[4]; but it is noticeable that the first of such tenancies of which we obtain definite tidings are rarely, if ever, what we should call ' husbandry leases.' In the Conqueror's reign the Abbot of St Albans leased the manor of Aldenham to the Abbot of Westminster for twenty years at the rent of a hundred shillings :

Early leases for years.

[p. 111]

[1] Heusler, Gewere; Heusler, Institutionen, ii. 22 ff.

[2] Brunner, D. R. G. i. 210. The *precarinm* (so-called) for a fixed term of years was not utterly unknown.

[3] D. B. i. 260 : ' ibi ij. homines reddunt iiij. solidos de locatione terrae. '

[4] Cart. Burton, 21, 23 : temp. Hen. I., two manors are already leased for sixteen years.

such at least was the story current at St Albans[1]. In the reign of Rufus land is being let for years to secure a debt of £20[2]. In the twelfth century the beneficial lease was by no means unknown; it was one of the expedients employed for raising money. Thus under Henry II. William Fossard obtains a large sum from the Abbot of Meaux, and, by way of return, grants him among other things, two whole vills for a term of fifteen years[3]. A little later the abbot obtains a lease of thirteen bovates for forty years at the cost of a heavy sum[4]. In 1181 a gross sum is paid down for a lease for twenty-nine years and no rent is reserved[5]. What is more, as we shall see [p. 112] hereafter, the lease for years had become a common part of the machinery whereby land was gaged for money lent. In the first half of the thirteenth century the termor is often visible[6]. He holds for fairly long terms and his rights are valuable; he has often paid a 'premium,' as we should call it, for his lease[7]. Nor is the sub-lessee unknown, and the sub-lessee may be an abbey[8]. It is possible that for a while the notion prevailed that a lease should not be for a longer term than forty years. The writer of the Mirror protests that this was the old law[9], and it would certainly have been very dangerous to make a longer lease by word of mouth, for, when the witnesses to the transaction were dead, the termor would have been much tempted to claim the fee and drive his lessor to battle or the grand assize[10].

---

[1] Gesta Abbatum, i. 43.   [2] Hist. Abingd. ii. 40.

[3] Chron. de Melsa, i. 174–5.

[4] Ibid. i. 231: 'acceptis inde multis denariis.' Cart. Rams. ii. 268 (A.D. 1149) lease for seven years to the abbot; he is to educate the lessor's son; in return he pays thirty marks.

[5] Newminster Cartulary, p. 73.

[6] The writ of entry *ad terminum qui praeteriit* is common on early plea rolls. See above, p. 69.

[7] Select Civil Pleas, pl. 177: lease of sixty acres for seven years in consideration of 5 marks paid down. Note Book, pl. 106: lease of a manor for seventeen years at a rent of £16. Ibid. 638: lease for twenty-two years. Ibid. 970: lease of a house for forty years. Ibid. 1140: lease of a messuage and thirty acres for twenty years in consideration of 50 marks paid down. Madox, Formulare, No. 220: lease for thirty years. Ibid. 122: lease for two years; no rent; consideration, 20 shillings paid down. Ibid. 223: lease for thirty-two years at a rent of a mark per year, but the whole 32 marks are paid in advance. Ibid. 228: lease for two years in consideration of 24 shillings paid down

[8] Whalley Coucher, i. 24 (A.D. 1271); Chron. de Melsa, ii. 183 (A.D. 1286).

[9] Mirror (Selden Soc.), p. 75; Blackstone, Comment. ii. 142.

[10] Bracton, f. 318 b, 319.

But Bracton contemplates the possibility of a lease for a term which exceeds that of human life; Britton speaks of a lease for a hundred years[1]; and in 1270 such a lease was granted[2]. It must be allowed, however, that in the days when the assize of novel disseisin was yet new—and this for our present purpose is the critical moment—tenancies for terms of years were very rare when compared with tenancies for life or in fee. Still we can not find our explanation in this rarity, for we have not to say why no special remedy was granted to the termor; we have to say why he was excluded from a very general remedy. Why has he no free tenement?

Assuredly in asking this question we must not lay an accent on the word 'free.' The termor's tenement, if he can be said to have one, is in no sense unfree. Abbots of West-minster, Newminster, Meaux, men who have paid large sums for their leases, have not done anything 'unworthy of a free man.' Nor can we dispose of them as 'mere farmers or husbandmen...who were considered as the bailiffs or servants of the lord[3].' All the evidence that we can collect tends to show that the husbandry lease is a late institution when compared with the beneficial lease purchased by a premium. Again, we shall hardly help ourselves by saying that the tenancy is not 'feudal.' The termor had no *feodum*; but the tenant for life had none. The termor did no homage; the tenant for life even of a military fee did none; the tenant of a socage fee was not in general bound to do it[4]. On the other hand, it seems fairly plain that the tenant for years swore fealty[5].

Why has the termor no free-hold?

[p. 113]

We must further notice that the language of everyday life and the language of pleading refused to fit in with the only theories which the lawyers put forward to justify their denial of the assize to the termor. Indubitably the termor, like the tenant in fee, holds a tenement: there is no other phrase by which his position can be described. Men do not say, lawyers do not say when they are dealing with concrete cases, that he has the benefit of an obligation, nor that he has an usufruct, nor that he has a servitude comparable to a right of way; they say

Arbitrary distinc-tions.

1 Bracton, f. 27; Britton, ii. 302.
2 Gloucester Corporation Records, ed. Stevenson, p. 253.
3 Blackstone, Comm. ii. 141.
4 Bracton, f. 77 b.
5 Bracton, f. 80; Co. Lit. 67 b.

boldly that he holds a tenement[1]. They add that he is seised
of a tenement; he is not merely in seisin, he is seised. They
have no verb specially appropriated to the act which creates a
tenancy for years, they use 'grant,' and even 'give,' as well as
'deliver' (*tradere, bailler*) and 'demise'; and a 'lease' may be
for life[2]. What is more, they have a word in common use
which throws rent-paying termors into one class with rent-
paying freeholders. People who pay full rents are farmers,
firmarii. This word describes an economic fact. But many
firmarii are not termors; they are freeholders holding for life
or in fee. Through this natural class of *firmarii* a hard [p. 114]
line is drawn, an arbitrary line, for many termors hold on far
easier terms than those to which the fee farmer is subjected[3].
As a matter of economic fact it is untrue that while the freeholder always holds *nomine proprio,* the termor always holds
nomine alieno.

Influence
of Roman
theory.
Lastly, the only explanation that the lawyers have to give is
a romanesque explanation. They go back to Paulus:—the term
is an usufruct, and the usufruct is no part of the *dominium*;
it is a servitude like a right of way. All Europe over, lawyers
were being at once attracted and puzzled by the Roman
doctrine of possession. They could not conceive it in all its
simplicity. They could not deny every sort of *dominium* and
every sort of *possessio* to the vassal who held of a lord. In
England an attempt to do this would have led to the useless
dogma that the king owns and possesses every inch of land.
They do what they can with the adjectives *civilis* and *naturalis,*
directus and *utilis*; there must be several *dominia,* several
possessiones. But a line must be drawn somewhere, for clearly
Roman law compels us to hold that there are some occupiers
who are not possessors[4]. In an evil hour the English judges,

---

[1] It is possible to find talk of usufruct in a few very early deeds: but there
it will stand for a life tenancy. Thus in Cart. Rams. i. 121 (A.D. 1088).

[2] Bracton, f. 27: 'si autem fiat donatio ad terminum annorum......concedere
ad terminum annorum.' Note Book, pl. 1140 (A.D. 1235–6): A termor pleads—
'Robertus tradidit et *concessit* ei...mesuagium et fecit ei *donum*...ita quod
positus fuit inde in seisinam...et fuit in seisina.' Ibid. pl. 1739: a leaseholder
recovers his seisin. On the other hand, a feoffment could be made by the word
'demise'; see Second Institute, 295.

[3] For the fee farmer, see above, vol. i. p. 293.

[4] See Bruns, Recht des Besitzes, 106–8; Heusler, Gewere, 300. Some of
the Italian jurists come very near to our English result. The vassal possesses,

who were controlling a new possessory action, which had been suggested by foreign models, adopted this theory at the expense of the termor.   He must be the *conductor* who does not possess, or he must be the usufructuary who does not possess the land but has '*quasi* possession' of a servitude.   But they can not go through with their theory.   In less than a century it has broken down.   The termor gets his possessory action; but it is a new action.   He is 'seised,' but he is not 'seised of free tenement,' for he can not bring an assize.   At a somewhat later time he is not 'seised' but is 'possessed.'   English law for six centuries and more will rue this youthful flirtation with Romanism[1].

p. 115]   Some compensation was made to the termor, and at the same time the gulf that divided him from the freeholder was widened, by the evolution of another doctrine.   In the first half of the thirteenth century lawyers were already beginning to say that his interest in the land is a *quasi* chattel[2]; soon they were saying boldly that it is a chattel[3].   The main import of this doctrine is that he has something to bequeath by his will. There was a writ in common use which prohibited the ecclesiastical courts from meddling with lay fee (*laicum feodum*), but the termor's interest was no 'lay fee,' and, if he bequeathed it by his will, the spiritual tribunal would not be prevented from enforcing the bequest.   On the other hand, the time had not yet come when the term would be treated as a chattel by the law of intestate succession.   It was common to make the lease for years to the lessee 'and his heirs,' and, at all events if this were done, the term would pass to the heir if it were not bequeathed by the lessee's will.   However, he was able to bequeath it.   We can see the analogy between the term and the chattel at work in another quarter: if the termor commits a felony, his interest does not escheat to his lord, it is forfeited to

The term as a chattel.

at least *naturaliter*; the *colonus* does not possess, at least unless he has a long lease; whether the usufructuary possesses or no is for them very uncertain.

[1] The most instructive passage on this matter is Bracton, f. 220 b, where a romanizing gloss has invaded the text.   See L. Q. R. i. 341.   The gloss is from Paulus, Dig. 50. 16. 25 pr.   So in Bracton, f. 167 b, the termor does not possess, because he is an usufructuary.   Bracton there says that the *firmarius* does not possess, but has immediately to qualify this by allowing possession to the fee farmer.

[2] Bracton, f. 407 b.

[3] Y. B. 33–5 Edw. I. p. 165: 'la terme nest qe chattel.'

the king *quasi catallum*[1]. Indeed the analogy was beginning to work in many quarters. This is not a purely English peculiarity. In Normandy also the term of years is accounted a movable; it is *firma mobilis,* as contrasted with fee farm (*feodi firma,*[2].

Chattels real.

At first sight it is strange that the termor should be able to do what the tenant in fee can not do, namely, to give his right by testament. We can not explain this by painting him as a despised creature for whom the feudal land law can find no proper place, for he is thus being put into one category with those who are exercising the most distinctively feudal of all rights in land. To a modern Englishman the phrase 'chattel real' suggests at once the 'leasehold interest,' and probably it suggests nothing else. But in the middle ages the phrase covers a whole group of rights, and the most prominent member of that group is, not the leasehold interest, but the seignorial right of marriage and wardship[3]. When a wardship falls to [p. 116] the lord, this seems to be treated as a windfall; it is an eminently vendible right, and he who has it can bequeath it by his will. At all events in the hands of a purchaser, the wardship soon becomes a bequeathable chattel: already in John's reign this is so[4]. The analogy between his right and that of the termor is very close. The purchaser of the wardship, though he is in occupation of the land, has no seisin of free tenement; he can bring no assize. On the other hand, he obtains possessory protection by the writ *Quare eiecit de custodia*[5], which is a parallel writ to the termor's *Quare eiecit infra terminum.* What then, we must ask, have these two cases in common? Is there any economic reason for this assimilation of a term of years to a wardship, and for the treatment of both of them as bequeathable chattels? We believe that there is, namely, the investment of capital, and by the way we will remark that the word *catallum,* if often it must be translated by our *chattel,* must at others be rendered by our *capital*[6]. Already

---

[1] Bracton, f. 131.

[2] Somma, p. 284; Ancienne coutume (ed. de Gruchy), c. 114.

[3] Y. B. 32–3 Edw. I. p. 245. In a writ of wardship the demand is for 'no more than a chattel.'

[4] Rot. Cart. Joh. p. 108.

[5] For an early example see Note Book, pl. 1709.

[6] In the Jewish mortgage deeds the principal sum is the *catallum* the interest is *lucrum;* so in Magna Carta, 1215, c. 10.

in the year 1200 sums of money that we must call enormous
were being invested in the purchase of wardships and marriages[1].
There was a speculative traffic in these things at a time when
few other articles were being bought and sold on a large scale.
Now it is very natural that a man who invests a round sum
should wish for a power of bequest. The invested sum is an
utterly different thing from the landed estate which he would
desire to keep in his family. And then, as to the term of years,
we believe that in the twelfth century and yet later, this
stands often, if not generally, in the same economic category.
It is a beneficial lease bought for a sum of ready money; it is
an investment of capital, and therefore for testamentary purposes
it is *quasi catallum*[2]. If this explanation be thought untrue—
and perhaps it runs counter to some traditional theories—we
must once more ask attention to the close similarity that there
[p. 117] is between our law's treatment of the termor and its treatment
of one who has purchased a wardship. Such a purchaser was
no despised 'husbandman,' no 'mere bailiff'; in John's day an
archbishop who had been chief justiciar invested four thousand
marks in a wardship[3].

§ 5.   *The Gage of Land.*

Closely connected with the lease for years is the gage of   The gage.
land. A single root has sent out many branches which over-
shadow large fields of law. Gage, engagement, wage, wages,
wager, wed, wedding, the Scottish wadset, all spring from one
root. In particular we must notice that the word 'gage,' in
Latin *vadium*, is applied indiscriminately to movables and
immovables, to transactions in which a gage is given and to
those in which a gage is taken. When a lord has seized his
tenant's goods in distress they are in his hands a gage for
the payment of the rent that is in arrear, and the sheriff is
always taking gages from those who have no mind to give

---

[1] See above, vol. i. p. 324.   [2] See above, vol. ii. pp. 111–2.

[3] Rot. Cart. Joh. p. 108. For some long leases granted in the thirteenth
century, see Gloucester Corporation Records, ed. Stevenson. The doubts,
expressed by some modern lawyers as to whether a term of years is a 'tenement,'
imply a conception of a metaphysical 'tenement' which Bracton had not
apprehended. See Challis, Real Property, 2nd ed. p. 55 and App. I.

them. The notion expressed by the word seems to be that expressed by our 'security'; some thing has either been given or been seized, and the possession of it by him in whose hands it now is, secures the payment of money or the performance of some act by the person by whom it was given or from whom it was taken. But it is the given gage of land that concerns us now[1].

Antiquity of gages.

Such transactions had long been known. We read of them in some of the Anglo-Saxon land-books, and it is highly probable that in England as elsewhere we might from a very early age distinguish several different methods by which land was made to serve as a security for money lent. We seem to see the conveyance which is subject to a condition, also the beneficial lease for years which enables a lender to satisfy himself by taking the fruits of the land, also a form of gage which does not set off the fruits against the debt[2]. Already in Domesday Book we may see land in the possession of one to whom it has been gaged[3]. Soon afterwards the duke of [p. 118] the Normans had gaged his duchy to the king of the English[4]. Before the end of the twelfth century very large sums of money had been lent upon gage. The crusaders wanted ready money and there were Jews who would supply it. In Henry II.'s day

[1] The term *pignus* is occasionally used both of movables and immovables, *e.g.* by Bracton, f. 268: and *impignorare* sometimes takes the place of the common *invadiare*, *e.g.* Cart. Guisborough, 144. The term *hypotheca* will hardly be found except in instruments executed in favour of foreigners; the Abbot of Winchcombe hypothecates lands and goods to the pope; Winchcombe Landboc, i. 255. The chapter of York binds a manor *ypotecae seu pignori* to secure money lent by the succentor; Historians of Church of York, iii. 174. What is seized by the distraining landlord is more frequently a *namium* than a *vadium*, but *divadiare* or *devadiare* often describes the act of distraining, *e.g.* in *Leg. Henrici*. In Germany *Pfand* seems to have covered the wide field of our *vadium*, and the *genommenes Pfand* has to be distinguished from the *gesetztes Pfand*: Franken, Französiches Pfandrecht, 11. See also Wigmore, The Pledge Idea, Harv. L. R. vol. x. xi., for the early history of gage and pledge in various systems of law.

[2] Brunner, Zur Rechtsgeschichte der röm. u. germ. Urkunde, 193; Brunner, Political Science Quarterly, xi. 541; Crawford Charters, ed. Napier and Stevenson, pp. 9, 77.

[3] D. B. ii. 137, 141, 217; in the last of these cases one Eadric has gaged land to the Abbot of St Benet; in the first a woman is ready to prove by ordeal that a debt, for which land was gaged, has been paid.

[4] See Freeman, William Rufus, i. 155. The chroniclers differ widely in their accounts of this transaction. According to some there was rather a rentless lease for three years than a gage.

William Fossard had gaged his land to the Jews for some twelve hundred pounds[1].

The forms which these early gages took are not in all respects so clear as might be wished. Glanvill, who perhaps leaves out of sight the conditional feoffment which required no special treatment, draws several distinctions. One of these is famous: that between the *mort gage* and the *vif gage*[2]. The specific mark of the mortgage is that the profits of the land received by the creditor are not to reduce the debt. Such a bargain is a kind of usury; but apparently it is a valid bargain, even though the creditor be a Christian. He sins by making it, and, if he dies in his sin, his chattels will be forfeited to the king; but to all seeming the debtor is bound by his contract[3]. As to the Jew, he was not prohibited from taking usury from Christians; he took it openly. Even the Christian, if we are not much mistaken, was very willing to run such risk [p. 119] of sin and punishment as was involved in the covert usury of the mortgage. The plea rolls of the thirteenth century often show us a Christian gagee in possession of the gaged land, but we have come upon no instance in which he was called upon to account for the profits that he had received. We infer that the gagee was usually a mortgagee in Glanvill's sense of that term[4].

Glanvill's mortgage and vifgage.

[1] Chron. de Melsa, i. 173.

[2] *Mortgage* seems to imply *vifgage*, and the latter term occurs in the Norman Grand Coutumier, ed. de Gruchy, p. 274: but we know of no direct proof that it was used in England.

[3] The words 'dead' and 'living' seem to have been applied to the gage in several different senses. To Glanvill (x. 8) the deadness of the mortgage consists in the fact that the gaged thing is not by its profits reducing the debt. Beaumanoir, c. 68, § 11, agrees with this. See also Somma, pp. 54, 279. Littleton (sec. 332) has a different explanation. If the debt is not paid off, the land is dead to the debtor; if the debt is paid off, the land is dead to the creditor. Then, by way of contrast, we find that the German *Todsatzung* is the gage which is gradually 'amortizing' or killing the debt. As to all this see Franken, Französisches Pfandrecht, 8, 123. Glanvill's words about the validity of the *mortuum vadium* are not quite plain. A bargain which provides for the reduction of the debt by the profits which the creditor receives 'iusta est et tenet.' The other sort of bargain 'inhonesta est...sed per curiam domini Regis non prohibetur fieri.' Having said this, he speaks of the forfeiture of the chattels of the usurer who dies in his sin. The next following words 'cetera serventur ut prius de vadiis in rebus mobilibus consistentibus dictum est' (in which case 'stabitur conventioni,' c. 6. *ad fin.*) appear to mean that the court will enforce the terms of the *mortuum vadium*. Compare Dial. de Scac. lib. ii. c. 10; Somma, p. 54.

[4] An early instance of a Jewish gagee accounting for profits in reduction of

Glanvill's
gage.
Then again (to return to Glanvill) the gage is given either
'for a term' or 'without a term.' In the former case we have
another distinction. There may be an express bargain that, if
at the fixed term the debtor does not pay, the creditor shall
hold the gaged thing, be it land or chattel, for ever. In this
instance the creditor has no need of a judgment to make the
thing his own. Or there may be no such express bargain, and
in that case the nature of the transaction is apparently this,
that when the term has elapsed the creditor can sue the debtor
and obtain a judgment which will order the debtor to pay
the debt within some 'reasonable' time, and will declare that,
should he make default, the gaged thing will belong to the
creditor. If the gage be given 'without a term,' then, to all
seeming, the creditor can at any time obtain a judgment which
will order the debtor to pay within some fixed and 'reasonable'
period, and will declare that if this be not done, the creditor
may do what he pleases with the gaged thing[1]. It will be
noticed that we have here something very like those 'decrees
of foreclosure' which courts of equity will make in much
later days.

Disappear-
ance of the
Glanvillian
gage.
But of the practice described by Glanvill we know exceedingly little; it is not the root of our classical law of mortgage,
which starts from the conditional feoffment[2]. It seems to have
soon become antiquated and the cause of its obsolescence is
not far to seek. The gagee of Glanvill's day is put into possession of the land. Unless the gagor has put the gagee into
possession, the king's court will pay no heed to the would-be
gage. It will be one of those mere 'private conventions' which
that court does not enforce[3]. So the gagee must be put into [p. 120]
possession. His possession is called a seisin, a *seisina ut de
vadio*[4]. For all, this, however, it is unprotected. If a stranger

---

the debt is found on the Pipe Roll of 10 Ric. I.: see Madox, Formulare, No. 142.
See also the very interesting transaction in Round, Ancient Charters, p. 93.

[1] Glanvill, x. 8: compare Ancienne coutume, c. 111 (ed. de Gruchy, p. 269);
Somma, p. 277.

[2] Glanvill, it will be seen, gives the creditor something that is not very
unlike an 'equity of redemption': that is to say, there are forms of gage which
compel the creditor to go to court before he can become owner of the gaged
thing, and the court will give the debtor a day for payment. For this purpose
the gagee has a writ calling upon the debtor to 'acquit' the gage (Glanvill, x. 7).
We can not find this writ even in the earliest Registers.

[3] Glanvill, x. 8.   [4] Glanvill, xiii. 28.

casts the gagee out, it is the gagor who has the assize. But
more; if the gagor casts the gagee out, the gagee can not
recover the land. The reason given for this is very strange:—
What the creditor is really entitled to is the debt, not the
land. If he comes into court he must come to ask for that
to which he is entitled. If he obtains a judgment for his
debt, he has obtained the only judgment to which he has
any right[1].

Now, if a court of law could always compel a debtor to pay *Position of the Glanvillian gagee.*
his debt, there would be sound sense in this argument. Why
should the court give a man a security for money when it can
give him the money? But a court can not always compel a
debtor to pay his debt, and the only means of compulsion that
a court of the twelfth century could use for such a purpose
were feeble and defective. Thus the debtor of Glanvill's day
could to all appearance reduce his gagee from the position of
a secured to that of an unsecured creditor by the simple
process of ejecting him from the gaged land. Such a state
of things can have been but temporary. The justices were
learning to use those new instruments, the possessory actions,
and they may have been distracted by foreign theories of
possession. They did not well know whether the gagee's seisin
was really a seisin or no[2].

Soon after this English law seems to abandon the attempt *Later law.*
to treat the rights of the gagee in the land as rights of a
peculiar character. If he is to have any right of any sort or
kind in the land, he must take his place in some category of
tenants. He must be tenant for years, or for life, or in fee.
In the first case he will obtain his rights under a demise for
years and will have the termor's remedies. In the other
cases he must be enfeoffed and he will have the freeholder's
remedies.

[p. 121] Now in our records it is not always easy to mark off the *The gage for years and the beneficial lease.*
gage for years from those beneficial leases of which we have

---

[1] Glanvill, x. 11.

[2] If it be urged that Roman law would have taught them that the creditor
with a *pignus* has possession, the reply is that the Roman law of the Italian
glossators would have taught them the reverse. At all events Placentinus
denied the creditor possession: Savigny, Besitz, § 24; Bruns, Recht des
Besitzes, p. 106. Bracton, f. 263, follows this lead; the usufructuary (termor)
and the creditor do not possess.

spoken above[1]. Both of them will serve much the same purpose, that of restoring to a man a sum of money which he has
placed at the disposal of another, though in the case of the
beneficial lease there is nothing that can be called a debt. As
already said the beneficial lease was common[2]. It was particu-
larly useful because it avoided the scandal of usury. There
was no usury, because there was no debt; and yet the terms of
the lease might be such as to provide that the money paid for
it by the lessee should be returned to him out of the profits
of the land with handsome interest.

The Bractonian gage for years.

But the true gage for years is a different thing:—In consideration of money lent, A demises land to X for a term of
years, and there is a provision that, if at the end of that term A
does not pay the debt, then X is to hold the land in fee. This
seems to have been the usual gage of Bracton's day. It gives
the gagee a term of years which, on the fulfilment of a certain
condition, becomes a fee; the condition is that at the end of
the term default is made in payment of the debt. During the
term the gagee is entitled to have, and usually has, that sort of
possession or seisin of the land that a termor can have, while
the gagor remains seised in fee; but, on the fulfilment of the
condition, the fee shifts to the gagee, and his possession or
seisin becomes a seisin in fee[3]. The lawyers as yet see nothing
shocking in this, because 'demise' and 'feoffment' both belong
to the great genus 'gift' and they have a deep reverence for
the *forma donationis*: it can enlarge a term of years into a fee
on the happening of a certain event, or reduce a fee to a term
of years on the fulfilment of a condition[4].

The classical mortgage.

At a later time straiter notions prevail. In substance the
termor has become as well protected as the freeholder is;
freeholders indeed begin to wish that they had the termor's
remedies. But the age which sees this, sees the lawyers
deepening the theoretic gulf which lies between the 'mere [p. 122]

---

[1] See, *e.g.* Note Book, pl. 50, 370, 1140, 1770. The transaction that is
called an *invadiatio* seems in some cases to be a beneficial lease. See Kemble,
Cod. Dip. 924 (iv. 263) for an early instance of this kind.

[2] See above, vol. ii. p. 111.

[3] Bracton, f. 20, 268–9; Britton, ii. 125–9; Madox, Formulare, No. 509;
Cart. Guisborough, p. 144; Note Book, pl. 889. Variants on this form may be
found in Madox, Formulare, No. 230; Chron. de Melsa, i. 303; Round, Ancient
Charters, No. 56. It appears in Y. B. 21–2 Edw. I. p. 125.

[4] Bracton, f. 268 b.

chattel' and the freehold. They begin to see great difficulties
in the way of a transaction whereby a man obtains a term of
years which will swell into a fee so soon as something is or is
not done[1]. The mortgage of our classical common law employs
a different machinery. The debtor enfeoffs the creditor and his
heirs upon condition that, if upon a certain day the debt be
paid, then the feoffor or his heirs may re-enter and hold the
land[2].

The gage, whatever form it took, could be effected without
deed. In the thirteenth century it is not uncommon to find a
dispute as to whether or no there has been a gage, and yet
neither disputant produces a charter[3]. We believe that as a
general rule the gagee, or at least the Christian gagee, not only
took but kept possession. It was only by taking the profits of
the land that he could get anything in the nature of interest
for his money. Perhaps he sometimes redemised the land to
the gagor. Thus the Abbot of Meaux in consideration of 800
marks demised a manor to William and Andrew Hamelton for
twenty years without rent; they redemised to the Abbot for
nineteen years at a rent of £100 and covenanted that their
gage should come to an end when they had received by way of
rent the capital sum that they had advanced[4]. We may see
Isaac the Jew of Northampton demising the gaged land to the
gagor's wife at a rent which is to go in reduction of the debt
due from her husband[5]. But the Jew in these matters was a
highly privileged person, privileged because what belonged to
him belonged potentially to the king. Certainly the Jewish
gagee was not always in possession, and it seems possible that,
under the system of registration which had been introduced in
Richard's reign, a valid gage could be given to him, though

The mortgagee in possession.

---

[1] See the long discussion in Co. Lit. 216–8. The thirteenth century lawyers
have hardly come in sight of the difficulty. See Fitz. Abr. *Feffements*, pl. 119.

[2] It is very possible that this form of gage, the conditional feoffment, had
been in use from an early time, but that the text-writers found little to say of it,
because it fell under the general doctrine of conditional gifts.

[3] See *e.g.* Y. B. 30–1 Edw. I. p. 210, where the gagee has a charter
testifying an absolute feoffment, but the gagor establishes a condition by the
country.

[4] Chron. de Melsa, ii. 183 (A.D. 1286).

[5] Madox, Formulare, p. xxii., from a chirograph of 1207 or thereabouts.
Madox mentions this among demises 'which appear pretty singular.' See also
Round, Ancient Charters, No. 56.

the gagor never went out of possession for a moment. Very early in the thirteenth century we may see an abbot searching [p. 123] the register, or rather the chest, of Jewish mortgages at York in quite modern fashion[1]. A little later an abbot of the same house, when buying land, has to buy up many incumbrances that have been given to Jews, but has difficulty in doing so because some of them have been transferred[2]. The debts due to Israelites were by the king's licence freely bought and sold when as yet there was no other traffic in obligations[3]. We may guess that, if the Jews had not been expelled from England, the clumsy mortgage by way of conditional conveyance would have given way before a simpler method of securing debts, and would not still be incumbering our modern law.

§ 6. *Incorporeal Things.*

Incorporeal things.
The realm of medieval law is rich with incorporeal things. Any permanent right which is of a transferable nature, at all events if it has what we may call a territorial ambit, is thought of as a thing that is very like a piece of land. Just because it is a thing, it is transferable. This is no fiction invented by speculative jurists. For the popular mind these things are things. The lawyer's business is not to make them things but to point out that they are incorporeal. The layman who wishes to convey the advowson of a church will say that he conveys the church; it is for Bracton to explain to him that what he means to transfer is not that structure of wood and stone which belongs to God and the saints, but a thing incorporeal, as incorporeal as his own soul or the *anima mundi*[4].

Their thinglikeness.
A complete list of incorporeal things would be long and miscellaneous. Blackstone's list may serve us as a starting point. 'Incorporeal hereditaments are principally of ten sorts; 'advowsons, tithes, commons, ways, offices, dignities, franchises, 'corodies or pensions, annuities and rents[5].' Now with such a

---

[1] Chron. de Melsa, i. 377.   [2] Ibid. ii. 115.

[3] Curia Regis Rolls (Rec. Office), No. 115, m. 10 (18–9 Hen. III.). Complaints are made against Robert Passelew, justice of the Jews. The 'ark' has been tampered with; 'pedes quorundam cyrographorum exposita fuerunt venalia apud Weschep per garciones ipsius Roberti.'

[4] Bracton, f. 53; f. 10 b.   [5] Comment. ii. 21.

[p. 124] catalogue before us, one which puts the 'way' next to the 'office,' it would be only too easy for us to digress into remote fields of legal history, to raise once more that eternal question about the origin of tithes and then to wander off to pasture rights and the village community. If we are to keep our discussion of these things within reasonable bounds it must be devoted to that quality which they have in common. To describe that quality such terms as 'real' and 'reality' are too feeble; we must be suffered to use 'thinglike' and 'thinglikeness.' They are thinglike rights and their thinglikeness is of their very essence[1].

We may begin by observing that the line between the corporeal and the incorporeal thing is by no means so clear in medieval law as we might have expected it to be, could we not remember that even our modern institutional writers have shown some uncertainty as to its whereabouts[2]. We must return to the case in which a lord has a freehold tenant and that tenant has been duly performing his services. How shall we describe this lord's position? Shall we say that he is seised of the tenant's homage and fealty and services, or shall we say that he is seised of the land? We may take whichever course we please; but if we say that he is seised of the land, we ought to add that he is seised of it, not in demesne, but in service[3]. On the other hand, if we say that he is seised of services, we must understand that these services are a thing, and a thing that is exceedingly like an acre of land. This we shall understand the better if we give a few words to (1) the means by which the lord's rights are enforced against his tenant, (2) the means by which they are protected against the world at large, (3) the means by which they can be transferred.

The seignory as a thing.

(1) The tenant will not perform his services; they are in arrear. The lord can distrain him; but distress is not always a safe or easy remedy, more especially if there is reason to fear that the tenant will deny his liability. The lord must have an action. He has an action: the writ of customs and services

Rights of lord against tenant.

---

[1] See Heusler's treatment of the incorporeal things of German law (Institutionen, i. 329). Almost every item in our English list has its parallel in Germany. We have to envy our neighbours such a word as *Dinglichkeit*.

[2] Joshua Williams, for example, treated 'reversions and remainders' in land as incorporeal things; and this treatment is inevitable if we say that whatever 'lay in grant' was an incorporeal thing.

[3] See above, vol. i. p. 233; vol. ii. p. 38.

(*de consuetudinibus et servitiis*)[1]. It is an action of the 'realest' [p.125] kind, closely similar to the proprietary action for land that is begun by the writ of right.   The lord—we will suppose that he can not rely upon a recent seisin—will have to say that some ancestor of his was seised of these services as of fee and of right by taking esplees to such or such a value in rents or in pleas or the like.   Then he will trace the descent to himself and then he will offer battle[2].   The tenant can accept this offer or he can put himself upon the grand assize.   Should the lord be victorious, he will 'recover his seisin' of the services[3].   In the thirteenth century the lord has often to use this cumbrous and dilatory, because proprietary, action.   But he enjoys possessory protection even as against his tenant.   If once this lord has been seised of this tenant's services, this tenant can be guilty of disscising this lord.   Mere default in render of services will not be a disseisin, but the tenant will probably become a disseisor if he resists the lord's distraint, and he will certainly be such if he without coercion renders the services to an adverse claimant[4].   Whether in the latter case he will not also be forfeiting his tenancy, that is another question which he should seriously consider[5]; in the past he would have left himself open to a charge of 'felony[6].'   But at any rate he is a disseisor. The lord will bring against him an assize of novel disseisin. The writ will be word for word the same as that which a man brings when he is ejected from the occupation of land.   It will report how the plaintiff alleges that he has been disseised of 'his free tenement' in such a vill, and only at a later stage will come the explanation that the thing to be recovered is, not so many acres of land, but so many shillingsworth of rent.

Contract between lord and tenant.

We have here no enforcement of an obligation; we have the recovery of a thing.   Of course between lord and tenant there often is an obligation of the most sacred kind, that begotten by homage and fealty; a breach of it has borne the name of felony. The tenant will often have sworn to do these services.   Nevertheless, the idea of a personal obligation or contract plays but

---

[1] Glanvill, ix. 9 ; Bracton, f. 329 ; for numerous instances see Note Book, vol. i. p. 177.

[2] See *e.g.* Note Book, pl. 895, 1738.   [3] Note Book, pl. 960.

[4] Bracton, f. 169, 203 ; Note Book, pl. 1239 ; Britton, i. 281, 290.

[5] Bracton, f. 203 b ; Note Book, pl. 109.

[6] Note Book, pl. 1687.

[p. 126] a subordinate part in the relation between lord and tenant. We see this when we say that as a general rule that relation never gives rise to an action of debt. We shall hereafter raise the question whether the action of debt was contractual; but it seems to have had about it too strong a trait of personalness to be an appropriate action for the landlord. The landlord who demands the rent that is in arrear is not seeking to enforce a contract, he is seeking to recover a thing[1].

(2) After all that has been said, it will be needless to repeat that the lord has rights which are good against the world at large. He is entitled to a thing with which other people ought not to meddle. True that an ejectment of his freehold tenant is no disseisin to him; it is no invasion of his right, it is an invasion of the tenant's right, and the disseisor will find that the seignory is subsisting when his cattle are taken because the land owes rent or other services. But suppose that we have *A* as the well entitled lord and *M* as his tenant, and that *X* has succeeded in obtaining from *M* those services that are due to *A*; then *X* is detaining a thing that belongs to *A*. It may be that *A* will have to bring a proprietary action by writ of right. Litigation between great lords is often carried on, if we may so speak, over the heads of their freehold tenants. This fact is sometimes obscured from view by the convenient term 'manor.' We may find *A* demanding from *X* a manor, just as though it were a physical object like a field, and yet there may well be freehold tenants of this manor, and neither *A* nor *X* is asserting any right to disturb them; the suit passes over their heads[2]. What is more, *A* will say that some ancestor of his was seised in demesne of this manor. He will not thereby mean that at the time of which he

Rights of lord against the world.

---

[1] Very grudgingly our law in later days allowed an action of debt for rent due from a freeholder in some cases in which there was no other remedy; see *Ognel's Case*, 4 Coke's Reports, 48 b; Co. Lit. 47 a; Blackstone, Comment. iii. 231, and (for the doctrine has been important even in recent years) *Thomas* v. *Sylvester*, L. R. 8 Q. B. 368; *In re Blackburn etc. Society*, 42 Ch. Div. 343. See also Cyprian Williams, Incidence of Rent, Harv. L. R. xi. 1. and L. Q. R. xiii. 288. Even the action of debt against the termor, which became common, seems rare in Bracton's day. As early as 1225, Note Book, pl. 946, it is brought after the term has expired.

[2] When a writ of right for land is brought against *X* and he wishes to plead non-tenure, *i.e.* to escape from the action by alleging that he does not hold the land, he has to say that he holds it neither in demesne nor in service. Bracton, f. 433; Note Book, pl. 102, 1067, 1164.

speaks there were no freeholders, and that his ancestor held every parcel of the land in demesne; he will mean that of this [p. 127] composite thing, the manor taken as a whole, his ancestor had an immediate seisin; he held the whole manor in demesne, though of some parcels of the land which are within the precincts of the manor he was seised in service[1]. The county palatine of Chester[2], nay, for the matter of that, the kingdom of Scotland, can be demanded in a proprietary action, just as Blackacre can be demanded.

Seisin of services.

Very often, however, there is no need for a proprietary action, because the seisin of services is fully protected by possessory actions. It is protected by the same actions that protect a seisin of land. If M has hitherto been paying his rent to A, and is coerced by distress into paying it to X, then A has been disseised by X and can bring the assize of novel disseisin against X and recover his seisin[3]. If M has paid unwillingly, then he ought not to be made a party to the action; the litigation should go on over his head[4]. The wrong complained of is not in our modern phrase 'a malicious interference with contractual rights'; it is a disseisin, the ousting of another from that of which he is possessed. A possessory protection of a receipt of money-dues or other services naturally gives rise to far more difficulties than such as are incident to a possessory protection of those who sit upon land. Cases arise in which we have to say that A has a choice between behaving as one who has been disseised and behaving as one who is still seised; 'disseisin at election' becomes the title for an intricate chapter of law[5]. Nevertheless, a gallant attempt is made to press this thought through all obstacles:—a seisin of services, however it may have been obtained, ought to be protected.

Conveyance of seignory.

(3) Then as to the conveyance of the lord's rights, we have but to repeat once more[6] that the attornment of the tenant is an essential element in the transaction. Somehow or another a seisin of the thing that is to be conveyed must be transferred, and when that thing is the feudal superiority with

---

[1] See Littleton, sec. 587–9, which are full of instruction as to the sort of seisin and disseisin that there can be of that composite entity a 'manor.'

[2] Note Book, pl. 1227, 1273.

[3] Bracton, f. 203 b; Co. Lit. 323 b.　　　[4] Note Book, pl. 1239.

[5] Littleton, sec. 589.　　　[6] See above, vol. ii. p. 93.

its accompanying right to services, we can naturally say that [p. 128] there has been such a transfer when the occupier of the land has confessed that, instead of holding it under the grantor, he now holds it under the grantee[1].

In the case that we have been discussing we see an incor-   Rents as things.
poreal thing that is very closely implicated with a corporeal thing; to sunder the two is not easy. Now, starting from this point, we may notice various degrees of incorporeality This may seem a strange phrase, and yet it will serve to describe a phenomenon which deserves attention. Starting with the rent which is a service rendered by tenant to landlord, a rent which has been 'reserved' when the tenancy was created and is thought of as something which remains to the giver or lessor after he has made the gift or lease, we may pass by three steps to a rent or annuity which is quite unconnected with land.

In this country the one word *rent* (Lat. *redditus*) was used   Various kinds of rents.
to cover several things which were of different kinds. In other countries such a rent as that of which we have been speaking, a rent payable by tenant to landlord, was generally known as *census, cens, zins*, while *redditus* or *rent* was reserved for those rents of which we are now to speak. In England the term *census*, though by no means unknown in old times, failed to gain a permanent place in the legal vocabulary. The tenurial rent was a *redditus*: to use a term which comes into use somewhat late in the day, it was 'rent service.' But there were other rents; we may call them 'non-tenurial,' there being no technical term which covers them all. These non-tenurial rents fall into two classes, for each of which in course of time lawyers invent a name. If the non-tenurial rent can be exacted by distress, it is a *rent charge*; if not, it is a *rent seck, redditus siccus*, a dry rent. Bracton knew these distinctions, though he had not the names that mark them in after ages[2].

---

[1] The word *feoffment* is sometimes applied to such a transaction even in formal pleadings. Northumberland Assize Rolls, p. 271: 'ipse feoffavit praedictum Johannem de servitio praedictorum tenementorum recipiendo per manus ipsius Angnetis.'

[2] Bracton, f. 203 b, after dealing with rent due from tenant to lord (*rent service*) says: 'Si autem sit redditus qui detur alicui ex tenemento...aut datur cum districtione (*rent charge*) vel sine (*rent seck*)...Si autem redditus sit proveniens ex camera (*personal annuity*)'......The terms *rent service* and *rent charge* were already current in Edward I.'s day: Y. B. 33–5 Edw. I. p. 211, 352.

[p. 129]

Non-tenu-
rial rents.

A non-tenurial rent often comes into being by virtue of a grant. The holder of land imposes such a rent upon his land in favour of some other person. It may be a rent for life or a rent in fee. If he expressly concedes to the grantee a power of distress, there is a rent charge; otherwise there is a rent seck. The creation of a rent charge was by no means uncommon. The purchase of a rent was a favourite mode of investing money at a time when any receipt of interest for a loan was sinful, and a religious house would have many rents constituted in its favour by those whose piety or whose wealth fell short of a gift of land. Sometimes again a rent which had started by being a rent service would become a rent seck. Thus *A*, who has a rent-paying tenant *M*, may grant the rent to *X*, but continue to be *M*'s lord and retain for himself any other services that are due, together with the feudal casualties. In that case, when *M* has attorned himself to *X*, the rent will no longer be a rent service, it will no longer be due from tenant to lord, it will be a rent seck[1].

Rents
charge as
things.

Now these non-tenurial rents, whether they be rents charge or rents seck, are treated as things. They are exceedingly like rents service. Often in a record of litigation about a rent we can see nothing that tells us to what class that rent belongs. Two people are disputing about the title to an existing rent; nothing is said about its origin; the person who will have to pay it, the 'terre tenant,' the occupant of the land, is no party to the action. The 'thinglikeness' of the rent charge may not surprise us, for in one most important respect it resembles the rent service:—it carries with it the power to distrain, and this power manifests itself in a procedure that attacks the land. Into the land the rent-owner enters; he takes the chattels that are found there; they may or may not be the chattels of the tenant; they are on the burdened land and that is enough. In such a case it is easy for us to picture the rent 'issuing out of' the land and incumbering the land. The thinglikeness of a rent seck is therefore a more striking phenomenon. This right does not empower him who has it to make any attack upon the land by way of distress. The most that he is entitled to do to the land is to enter on it for the purpose of demanding payment of his rent. And yet the rent seck is very truly a thing.

[1] Littleton, sec. 225.

(1)   In the first place the governing idea is that the land is Rents owed by the land.
bound to pay the rent, and it is by no means necessary to the
[p. 130] existence of the rent that any person should be bound to pay it.
In later days the creator of a rent seck or rent charge was in
general personally bound to pay it, and, if he had expressly
bound his heirs to pay it, then his heirs were bound; but it was
always open to the creator of a rent to exclude this personal
liability[1].   The personal liability was enforced by an action of
annuity, an action in which the plaintiff demanded the arrears
of an annual rent that was due to him.   But this action is by
no means one of our oldest.   If we mistake not, it was very new
when Bracton was writing[2].   To the last, protection by this
writ is not of the essence of a valid rent; there often may be a
rent which no person is bound to pay.   Of course, if we must
be analytic, a payment is always made by a person and is never
made by land, and if a payment is due some person must be
bound to make it.   But the terre tenant has only to pay the
rent that becomes due while he is terre tenant.   We may
almost go the length of saying that the land pays it through
his hand.   The rent-owner's weapon against him is not a contractual action, it is an assize of novel disseisin.   When the
rent-owner has received an instalment of rent and the terre
tenant refuses another, the rent-owner has been disseised of his
free tenement in a certain vill.   Another refusal to pay will
make the tenant a redisseisor; he will be sent to gaol and will
have to pay double damages[3].

(2)   The assize of novel disseisin enables the rent-owner to The rent-owner's rights against the world.
coerce the tenant of the land into paying the rent as it becomes
due.   It also protects him as against the world at large in the
enjoyment of his incorporeal thing.   The rent is a thing about
which there can be litigation between adverse claimants.   One
of them is possessed of it, the other claims possession and

---

[1] Littleton, sec. 220–1.   See Cyprian Williams, The Incidence of Rent, Harv.
L. R. xi. 1, and L. Q. R. iii. 288.

[2] The *breve de annuo redditu* is mentioned in Bracton, f. 203 b.   We do not
think that the Note Book supplies a single instance of it, unless pl. 52, which
hovers between 'debt' and 'annuity,' be one.   It seems to get into the Register
late in Henry III.'s reign.   Harv. L. R. iii. 173.

[3] Littleton, sec. 233 and Coke's comment.   Heusler, Institutionen, i. 347,
asserts the same principle for Germany.   The rent-owner's action against the
terre tenant is a real, not a contractual action.   Its foundation is not ' dare
mihi debes,' but ' malo ordine retines.'

perhaps alleges that he has been unlawfully disseised. Every sort of action that can be brought for the recovery of land can be brought for the recovery of rent ; one has but to put in the writ ten shillingsworth of annual rent instead of ten acres of [p. 131] land[1]. Even a writ of entry can be used ; there is not the least impropriety in saying that a man entered into a rent charge[2], or was ejected from it[3].

Creation and transfer of rents.(3) Next we see that in order to create one of these non-tenurial rents a transaction that is closely akin to a livery of seisin is necessary. In the thirteenth century the execution and delivery of a deed is becoming an essential element in the transaction, and, since the creation of such rents can hardly be traced beyond the time when the use of sealed writings had become common, we may perhaps treat the requirement of a deed as aboriginal. Such a deed will be closely similar to a charter of feoffment ; the creator or transferor of the rent will say, 'Know ye that I have given and granted a rent,' and very possibly the transaction is actually spoken of as a feoffment[4]. But the execution and delivery of the deed were not sufficient. If we suppose A, the tenant of the land, to be creating a rent in favour of X, the delivery of the deed may be enough to give X a power to distrain for the rent if the rent be a rent charge ; but, in order to give him an action for a rent charge and in order to give him any remedy whatever for a rent seck, he must obtain a 'seisin in deed' of the rent. This will be given to him if A hands to him a penny or, it is said, any other valuable thing in name of seisin of the rent[5]. Next we suppose that the rent has been created, that A is still the terre tenant and that X wishes to convey the rent to Y. The mere execution and delivery of a deed will do nothing effectual. In order to give Y the power to distrain for the rent, which for the moment we suppose to be a rent charge, A must attorn to Y. But more than attornment—which may be made by mere words without act—is required if Y is to have an action for a rent charge or any means whatever of exacting a rent seck. The

---

[1] Littleton, sec. 236 and Coke's comment.

[2] See *e.g.* Y. B. 18 Edw. II. p. 588.

[3] Northumberland Assize Rolls, p. 151.

[4] See the model charter in Britton, i. 270. As to the use of the word *feoffment* see Pike, L. Q. R. v. 29–32.

[5] Littleton, sec. 235, 565.

terre tenant *A* must pay something to *Y* in name of seisin of
the rent. The right is not completely transferred until there
[p. 132] has been some act that can be regarded as a manual transfer
of the thing[1].

We have been gradually leaving the land behind us. The ^{Annuities} rent service is part of a lordship over land; the rent charge
authorizes a distress upon land similar to that which a landlord
makes; the rent seck does not authorize a distress but still it
'issues out of,' it is owed by, land. One more step we must
make, for we have yet to speak of rents that do not issue out of
land. Of 'rents' we say. At a later time they will generally
be called 'annuities,' 'personal annuities.' But let an action be
brought for such an annuity, then in the precise language of
pleading it will be called an annual rent, *annuus redditus*[2].
Such annuities were known in the thirteenth century, and it
was allowed that they did not 'issue out of' land. Did they
then issue out of nothing? No, that would have been inconceivable. A permanent right of this kind, a right to receive
money year by year, could not exist unless it had some point of
contact with the physical world; it must issue out of some
thing. These annuities issue out of the grantor's 'chamber,' the
place where he keeps what treasure he has[3]. To our eyes they
are merely personal annuities, unsecured annuities; the grantee
has nothing to trust to but the grantor's honesty and solvency.
Still they are things, incorporeal things, and in the thirteenth
century they must be thought of as having in some sort a
visible fountain-head in the world of sense.

Our materials give us but little information as to the ^{Annuities} treatment of these personal annuities by the law of Bracton's ^{lose their thinglike-} age. Probably the only things of this sort that were at all ^{ness.} common were the corodies granted by religious houses, of which
we must speak hereafter. But it was decided that the actions
for land could not be made to serve for the recovery of these
'chamber rents.' The writ of novel disseisin was inapplicable,

---

[1] The great repertory of learning about the seisin of rents is *Bevill's Case*,
4 Coke's Reports, 8. The general rule is, 'As to an avowry [*i.e.* right to
distrain], seisin in law is sufficient; but as to have an assize, actual seisin is
requisite.'

[2] Reg. Brev. Orig. f. 158 b.

[3] Bracton, f. 180, 203 b; Note Book, pl. 52, 439. We find the writ of annuity
called *Bref de rente de chambre*: Camb. Univ. MS. Ee. i. 1. f. 247 b. See also
Brevia Placitata, ed. Turner, 31.

because there was no land of which a view could be given to the jurors. The grantor's chamber was no fixed place[1]. Therefore the person who is deforced of such a rent has not been disseised of his free tenement; therefore such a rent is not a [p. 133] tenement[2]. Late in Henry's reign an appropriate action, the writ of annuity, or rather of 'annual rent,' was given for their recovery. They fell apart from land, and in course of time they slowly assumed the guise of merely contractual rights; but in the earlier Year Books their thinglikeness is visible. For many reasons it was important for the annuitant that he should be able to allege a seisin of his annuity[3].

Corodies as things.

One class of annuities has an instructive history of its own. It consists of the corodies (*conredia*) granted by religious houses. In consideration, as we should say, of some benefit conferred, or some services done or to be done, a religious house undertakes to supply some man at stated intervals with victuals and clothes or other commodities. Sometimes he may be a distinguished canonist and the corody is his retaining fee. Sometimes one of the abbey's land agents, steward or woodward, is to be thus rewarded for his labours. Sometimes the king will exact a corody for one of his chancery clerks from a house of royal foundation. Sometimes a man will invest ready money in the purchase of a corody and thus provide for his old age. In many cases an elaborate document will be executed. The quantity and quality of the meat, drink, clothes, candles, firewood, that the grantee is to receive will be carefully defined; even the mustard and garlic will not be forgotten. Perhaps he will be entitled to the use of one of the convent's horses or to stabling for his own horse. Perhaps a room in the house must be found for the use of him or of his servants if he requires it[4].

Treatment of corodies.

In Bracton's day the temporal courts were leaving the corody alone. It was very like a rent seck. It 'issued out of' a fixed place, and in this respect it differed from the mere personal annuity which was supposed to issue from the grantor's 'chamber.' Such a chamber may be here to-day and

[1] Rot. Cart. p. 14: King John grants an annuity of forty marks 'to be received from our chamber until we assign them in some certain and competent place.'

[2] Bracton, f. 180, 203 b. Cf. Heusler, Institutionen, i. 343, as to the 'chamber rent' in Germany.

[3] See *e.g.* Y. B. 21–2 Edw. I. pp. 129, 541.

[4] The Winchcombe Landboc has many good specimens of corody deeds.

gone to-morrow, but the religious house is permanent. The corody, however, issued from a house which was on consecrated soil, a house which, to use Bracton's phrase, was *in bonis Dei.* Therefore it is a spiritual thing and its exaction must be left to the ecclesiastical court[1].

[p. 134]   A new rule was introduced by statute in 1285[2]. A temporal action was given for the corody, and this action was the assize of novel disseisin. If an annual supply of victuals or other necessaries is to be received in some certain place, the right to receive it is to be treated like land. To us this treatment of what in our eyes is but the benefit of a contract may seem very awkward. It was deliberately chosen as the proper treatment by the great lawyers who surrounded King Edward. They might have given an action of annuity, of debt, of covenant; they gave an assize of novel disseisin; they told the man whose corody was in arrear to complain of an ejectment from his free tenement; they sent the jurors to view the monastery whence the corody issued. A better example of medieval realism could hardly be given.

Disseisin of corodies.

If rights that appear to us to be merely contractual are thus dealt with, we shall not be surprised to find that where the contractual element is wanting, incorporeal things are very easily created. If 'offices' are to fall within the pale of private law at all, if they are to be heritable and vendible, perhaps we can not do better than treat them as being very like pieces of land.

Offices as things.

The statute that we have just mentioned gave the assize of novel disseisin for 'the wardenship of woods, parks, chases, warrens and gates, and other bailiwicks and offices in fee.' Some have said that this was no innovation[3]. Be that as it may, at the end of the century the assize which protects the possessor of land seems the natural defence for the possession of an office, at all events if that office has a local sphere, if the jurors can be shown some place in which it has its home or its being. Our law is following in the wake of the canon law. The canonists have been carrying their doctrine of 'the possession of rights' into almost every province of jurisprudence.

---

[1] Bracton, f. 180.   [2] Stat. West. II. c. 25.

[3] Coke, Second Institute, 412 ; Coke, 8 Reports, 47. We have not found an assize for an office before the statute; but in 47 Hen. III. a *Praecipe quod reddat* was brought for the stewardship of a manor: Placit. Abbrev. 154.

By a famous decretal the Archbishop of York gained a possessory and provisional protection for the right, if right it were, of carrying his cross erect in the province of Canterbury; and in days when the two primates were hardly to be kept from [p. 135] fisticuffs, this *iuris quasi possessio* made for decency[1].

The advowson as a thing.

But we shall learn most about the thinglikeness of our incorporeal things if we turn to the advowson. The advowson is a thing of great value and importance, the subject-matter of frequent litigation and copious law. Generally[2] an advowson is the right to present a clerk to the bishop for institution as parson of some vacant church; the bishop is bound to institute this presented clerk or else must show one of some few good causes for a refusal. There can be little doubt that historically the patron's right has it origin in an ownership of the land upon which the church stands[3]. The law of the thirteenth century regards the advowson as being normally an appurtenance of some manor. Make a feoffment of the manor, and the advowson is conveyed. Disseise a man of the manor, and you become seised of the advowson. But advowsons are often severed from the manors to which, in legal theory, they have at some time or another belonged. The lord gives the manor but retains the advowson, or else he gives the advowson but retains the manor. The latter transaction is common; numerous advowsons are detached from their manors by being given to religious houses. An advowson thus detached becomes, to use a phrase which is current in the last years of the century, 'a gross,' that is, a thing by itself, a thing which has an independent existence[4].

Where is the advowson?

We may see Bracton struggling with the notion that such a right can not exist unless it exists somewhere. There must be some corporeal thing in which it inheres. It no longer inheres in a manor. It must inhere in the church itself, the structure of wood and stone. Every day advowsons are being taken into

---

[1] c. 1. X. 2. 16; Bruns, Recht des Besitzes, 208; Historians of the Church of York, iii. 73. The Abp. of York asserted that he had been despoiled 'de possessione huius rei.'

[2] Of collatives and donatives we need not here speak.

[3] See above our section on Corporations and Churches.

[4] The phrase 'this advowson is a gross' seems older than the to us more familiar 'it is in gross.' See *e.g.* Y. B. 21–2 Edw. I. p. 609. So too it was but slowly settled that an advowson is *appendant* rather than *appurtenant* to a manor. See Co. Lit. 121 b.

the king's hands; this is a common episode in litigation. The
sheriff goes to the church and declares before witnesses that he
seizes the advowson. The advowson must be there, in the
church, or how could he seize it[1]? Still Bracton knows that
the advowson is incorporeal, invisible, impalpable, and speaks
with some pity of the layman who says that he gives a church
when he means that he gives a right of patronage[2].

[p. 136]   If, however, the advowson is incorporeal it is none the less Actions for advowsons.
a thing—a thing for the purposes of litigation, a thing for the
purposes of conveyance. In the first place, there is a proprietary
action for the recovery of the advowson, a writ of right of
advowson, which is closely parallel to the writ of right for land;
it leads to battle or the grand assize[3]. In the second place,
there is definite possessory protection for the possessor of the
advowson. This takes the form of an assize of darrein presentment (*de ultima presentatione*) which is almost, if not quite, as
old as the analogous novel disseisin[4]. To apply the idea of
seisin or possession to an advowson is not altogether easy. The
only actual exercise that there can be of this right is a successful presentation. If you have presented the man who is now
parson of the church, then it may well be said that, rightfully
or wrongfully, you are seised of the advowson. But you can
not exercise such a right just when you please, nor can you
exercise it periodically. Now and again at longish intervals
a man has a chance of showing that he is seised. Nevertheless,
seisin there is, and it ought to be protected. The question
addressed to the recognitors of the assize is this:—

> Who was the patron who in time of peace presented
> the last parson, who is now dead, to the church of
> Middleton, which is vacant, and the advowson whereof
> Alan claims against William?

The principle of law which lies at the root of this formula

---

[1] Bracton, f. 378 b.

[2] Bracton, f. 53; Note Book, pl. 1418.   See c. 7. X. 3. 24 (Innocent III. to
the Bp. of Ely).

[3] Glanvill, ii. 13; iv. 2; Note Book, vol. i. p. 178; Reg. Brev. Orig. f. 29 b.
The classical writ of right of advowson is a *Praecipe quod reddat*, which at once
brings the case before the king's court; but in an early Registrum a *breve de
recto tenendo* addressed to the feudal lord may be found, though it is there
called a rare writ. See Harv. L. R. iii. 170.

[4] Glanvill, xiii. 18; Bracton, f. 237 b; Summa, p. 265; see above, vol. i.
p. 148.

seems simple. The person who, by himself or his ancestors, presented on the last occasion, ought to present upon this occasion also. But this principle is too simple, or rather, the formula that enshrines it is too rude. The jurors may be compelled to answer the question in favour of Alan, and yet William ought to prevail, even in a possessory action. For one thing, since the last presentation Alan may have granted the advowson of the church to William, and already in Glanvill's day such a grant will entitle the grantee to the next presenta- [p. 137] tion[1]. But William, if he wishes to rely upon such a grant, must plead it by way of *exceptio* (special plea); if the original question be answered by the recognitors, Alan will succeed in his action and present a clerk. At a comparatively early time special pleas became common in this assize[2]. Probably it was for this reason that, while the novel disseisins and mort d'ancestors were disposed of in their proper counties by justices of assize, darrein presentments were reserved (except when there was a general eyre) for the justices of the bench[3]. For all this, however, the action was a purely possessory action. The defendant could not go behind the last presentation. The victor in to-day's assize may succumb to-morrow before a writ of right brought by the very adversary whom he has vanquished.

Convey-
ance of
advowsons. An advowson can be conveyed by one person to another. Often it passes from one person to another as appendant to a manor which is being conveyed. In such a case no deed is requisite; there will be a feoffment; seisin of the manor will be delivered, and, when the church next becomes vacant, the feoffee will be entitled to present; in the meantime he will have a seisin in law, a 'fictitious seisin.' But we have more concern with the case in which the advowson is to be conveyed by itself as 'a gross.' Probably in this case also, whatever could be done by deed could be done without deed. Late in the next century all the justices agree that in order to grant an advowson it is sufficient that the two parties shall go to the door of the church and that the grantor shall there speak the words of grant and deliver 'seisin of the door[4].' However, the common practice certainly was that a deed should be executed. But the

---

[1] Glanvill, xiii. 20.   [2] Note Book, vol. i. p. 184.

[3] Charter of 1217, c. 15, amending Charter of 1215, c. 18.

[4] Y. B. 43 Edw. III. f. 1. (Hil. pl. 4); Pike, Livery of Incorporeal Things, L. Q. R. v. 35; Pollock and Wright, Possession, p. 54.

mere delivery of the deed can not be for all purposes a sufficient conveyance. In Bracton's eyes such a deed transfers a 'fictitious' or 'imaginary' seisin[1]. This is effectual for some purposes. We will suppose that Alan, who made the last presentment, has by deed granted the advowson to William. Now if the church falls vacant and William has not parted with the advowson, he will be entitled to present. Against an assize of [p. 138] darrein presentment brought by Alan he can protect himself by an exception. Further, he has himself an action which will enable him while the church is vacant to enforce his right against Alan or a third person. This is the *Quare impedit*, a possessory action invented for the sake of those who can not (and William can not) use the assize[2]. But we will suppose that, before the church falls vacant, William by a deed grants the advowson to Roger. Then the parson dies. Who is entitled to present? Four times over Bracton, with many references to decided cases, has given us the answer, and curious it is[3]. Alan is entitled to present. The 'quasi-possession,' the imaginary or fictitious seisin, that his deed gave to William was not transferable, and therefore Roger has got nothing. On the other hand, William has succeeded in depriving himself of whatever he had or seemed to have. The only real seisin is with Alan, and he is entitled to present. Until the grantee of an advowson has obtained an actual seisin by a successful presentment, he has nothing that he can give to another.

But further, the grantee until he has successfully presented is in an extremely insecure position. The church falls vacant; he is entitled to present, and he can make good this right by means of the *Quare impedit*. But suppose that he does not seize this opportunity. Suppose that some mere wrong-doer presents and gets his clerk instituted. Then our grantee's rights are gone for ever. Of course he can have no possessory action, for seisin is now with the usurper. But he can have no proprietary action, for he can not allege—and this in a writ of right he would have to do—that either he or some ancestor of

Seisin of advowsons.

---

[1] Bracton, f. 54, 55, 242-3, 246.

[2] Coke, Second Institute, 356, finds the *Quare impedit* in Glanvill; we can not see it there; but it appears very early in the thirteenth century and is common in the Note Book. See Bracton, f. 245.

[3] Bracton, f. 54, 54 b, 242 b, 243. Most of his cases are in the Note Book. The law is the same if the advowson has been given as appendant to a manor.

his has been seised with an exploited seisin. Such was the law until a statute of 1285 allowed him six months after the usurpation for his *Quare impedit;* but down to Queen Anne's day an usurpation followed by inaction for more than six months would utterly destroy his right[1].

Rights of common as things.

The same ideas are applied to other incorporeal things, more especially to those rights that are known as rights of common. If a feoffment is made of a piece of land to which a right of [p. 139] common belongs, the feoffee, says Bracton, at once acquires a fictitious seisin by viewing the ground over which the right of pasturage or the like extends[2]. It may be that he has at the moment no beasts to turn out; it may be that the season of the year during which the right is exercisable has not yet come. But he ought to take the first opportunity that occurs of converting this imaginary into a real seisin; if he lets that slip, he may well find that he can no longer turn out his beasts without being guilty of a disseisin[3]. To this we must add that, so long as his seisin is fictitious, he has nothing that he can convey to another. Such at all events is the case if the right of pasturage was granted to him 'as a gross[4].'

Possessory protection of rights of common.

Then again, there is a possessory protection for these incorporeal things. The novel disseisin for common of pasture is coeval with the novel disseisin for land[5]. The practice of Bracton's day was extending the same remedy to rights of turbary and fishery[6]. The Second Statute of Westminster sanctioned this extension and carried it further. The right to take wood, nuts, acorns is to be included, also the right to take toll and similar dues. The assize of novel disseisin is regarded as a most successful institution; the best method of enforcing these rights is to protect those who are seised of them[7].

Law of prescription.

Seisin itself is protected, seisin of the incorporeal thing. We see this best if we consider the modes in which the ownership of such a thing can be acquired. It can be acquired by inheritance; it can be acquired by conveyance,

---

[1] Bracton, *l.c.*; Stat. West. II. c. 5; 7 Anne, c. 18; Blackstone, Comment. iii. 243–4.

[2] Bracton, f. 225.   [3] Bracton, f. 223 b.   [4] Bracton, f. 225.

[5] Glanvill, xiii. 37; Harv. L. R. iii. p. 114. There are good illustrations in Mr Chadwyck-Healey's Somersetshire Pleas.

[6] Bracton, f. 231; Note Book, pl. 1194, 1915.

[7] Stat. West. II. c. 25; Second Institute, 411.

though, as we have just seen, the grantee has never got full and secure ownership until he has got possession, actual exploited possession; it can also be acquired by long-continued user. Of the effects of long-continued user Bracton speaks somewhat obscurely; his romanesque terms, *usucapio* and the like, perplex his doctrine[1]. We must, however, draw a marked line between [p. 140] land and incorporeal things. Our medieval law knows no acquisitive prescription for land; all it knows is a limitation of actions. This principle seems to be implicit in the form which every demand for land by proprietary action must take. The claimant must allege that he or some ancestor of his was seised as of right; he must deduce his title from a seisin that was rightful. He must not indeed 'plead higher up' than a certain limiting period. In Bracton's day he must allege a seisin as of right on this side of Henry II.'s coronation. That date will leave him a hundred years or thereabouts. He will have to tender a champion prepared to swear to this rightful seisin, as one who either saw it, or was enjoined to bear witness of it by a dying father[2]. Thus a limit is set to the action. Mere lapse of time may serve as a shield for the tenant, but it can not serve as a sword for the demandant. He can not say, 'I claim this land because my ancestors were seised of it for twenty, thirty, a hundred years.' He must begin with some ancestor who was seised as of right. But further, we may doubt whether for land there is any extinctive prescription. The man who can not allege a seisin on this side of Henry II.'s day has lost every action for the land; but it does not follow that his right is extinct. Hereafter it may prove its vitality, if this man, having obtained seisin under some new and defeasible title, is 'remitted' to the oldest title that he has. We can not say with certainty that this was so in Bracton's day; but at a later time 'it is commonly said that a right can not die[3]' and this we may well believe to be an old, as well as a common, saying.

By way of contrast we may see that many incorporeal things can be acquired by prescription, by long-continued user[4]. In

Incorporeals acquired by prescription.

---

[1] Bracton, f. 51 b, 52. When Bracton is speaking of this matter, it is not always easy to say whether he is dealing with the acquisition of good right or with the acquisition of protected seisin. He has a, to us misleading, habit of calling the short period which protects the disseisor against the self-help of the disseisee (it may be but four days) 'longum tempus,' 'longum intervallum,' etc.

[2] Bracton, f. 373; Note Book, pl. 1217.   [3] Littleton, sec. 473.

[4] See Salmond, Essays in Jurisprudence, p. 99.

particular we may see this in the case of rights of common. There is an action by which the landowner calls upon the person who asserts such rights to prove his title, the action *Quo iure clamat communam*[1]. It is regarded as a thoroughly proprietary action; it may lead to a grand assize. Now one of the usual answers to this action is a prescriptive claim— 'I and those whom I represent have commoned here—always —from before the Norman Conquest—from time immemorial.' In most cases the Norman Conquest is mentioned. Behind the great resettlement of the land one must not go; on the [p. 141] other hand one can, to all seeming, be required to allege a continuous seisin ever since that remote event[2].

Possessory protection of an inchoate right. This is a proprietary action; but it is fairly evident that a man can acquire a legally protected possession of an incorporeal thing on much easier terms. We put this case:— For some time past a man openly and peaceably, and as though asserting a right, has been turning his beasts out on my land; he may have been doing it for so long a time that I can no longer bring an assize against him as against one who has been disseising me of my land; still he can not assert a user that goes back nearly as far as the Conqueror's days. The question is whether this man is protected against my self-help. May I bar out his beasts from the pasture or seize them if they are there? To this question the answer that Bracton gives is that against self-help this man is protected. My proper course is to bring against him some more or less proprietary action. Possibly I may have to bring the *Quo iure,* and then there may be a grand assize. It is very possible that this man should one day 'recover the common' in an assize and the next day be made a defendant in a proprietary action which will deprive him of the common for good and all[3]. This idea of a purely possessory protection for those who are enjoying 'incorporeal things,' but who can not yet

---

[1] Bracton, f. 229 b; Note Book, i. 185.

[2] Note Book, pl. 223, 274, 392, 628, 971, 1624. In pl. 818 (A.D. 1293) the assertion 'Seised since the Conquest' is met by 'No, seised only since the war of 1216.' In pl. 135 the defendant only goes back to Henry II.'s day. In pl. 843 a way is claimed by user since the Conquest.

[3] Bracton, f. 230: 'Cum igitur quis per iudicium seisinam suam recuperaverit per assisam propter usum, amittere debet illam, nisi doceat *quo iure* illam exigat.' So on f. 52 b, a man by continuous user obtains possession of a servitude 'ita quod taliter utens sine brevi et iudicio eici non debet.'

say that those things are their own, is one that can not be easily managed. We seem to have before us a pasture right that is only half a right, an incorporeal thing that exists and yet does not exist[1]. But the lawyers of the thirteenth century made a strenuous endeavour to pursue this idea through all speculative difficulties[2].

[p. 142]

It is by no means certain that both prescription and the possessory protection of inchoate 'things' were not extended to 'things' which in our eyes consist wholly or in part of the benefit of a contractual obligation. In the Year Book period it is possible to prescribe for rents, and the courts seem to be engaged rather in setting new limits to this doctrine than to widening its scope. One ecclesiastical corporation is allowed to prescribe against another for a mere personal annuity. In 1375 the judges draw a line at this point; they will not hold that a natural person can be bound to pay an annuity merely because from time immemorial his ancestors have paid it[3]. We have but little evidence as to the opinions which the lawyers of Henry III.'s reign held about this matter; but the canonical influence was making for the widest extension both of the sphere of prescription and of the possessory protection of inchoate things[4]; and English law would take little account of the canonist's requirement of *bona fides*. Certainly it was very dangerous for any man to make any payment which could possibly be construed as being made in discharge of a permanent duty, unless he wished to go on making similar payments at periodical intervals to the end of time. You should never attend the county court unless you want to attend it every month, for you will be giving the king and his sheriff the seisin of 'a suit.' But in this region it is not very easy to distinguish between what we may call the generative and the merely evidentiary effects of seisin.

Can annuities be prescribed for?

---

[1] See Pollock, First Book of Jurisprudence, 184.

[2] We have been dealing with a case which in Holmes, Common Law, 241, 384, is rightly treated as a good test of the so-called 'possession of rights,' and we believe that, if this test is applied to the law of Bracton's age, the result is that an user which falls far short of establishing an indefeasible right obtains a possessory protection.

[3] Y. B. 49 Edw. III. f. 5 (Hil. pl. 9).

[4] Bruns, Recht des Besitzes, p. 123: Azo, as advocate in a cause, argued that there could be no possession of a rent until that rent (which had not been created in any other way) had been created by prescription; but the great canonist Huguccio, who was acting as judge, overruled this argument.

Even when seisin does not beget a right, it will often be good evidence that the right exists.

How far prescription can be carried in another direction, that in which the 'franchises' lie, was a burning question. The royal lawyers were asserting that the franchises, or at all events such of them as had to do with the administration of justice, could not be gained by continuous user[1]. As regards these, *Nullum tempus occurrit Regi.* They can only be acquired by express grant; a grant will be construed in a manner favourable to the king; if once acquired they are inalienable[2]; they are very easily lost. The man who has the franchise of *utfangthief*, for example, must be vigilant in acquiring and retaining a seisin thereof[3]; if he lets the sheriff hang even one thief who is within the terms of the privilege, he will have forfeited that privilege by non-user and will have to repurchase it by a fine. Edward I was forced to make concessions in this quarter[4]; many of the franchises, even many of the justiciary franchises, became prescriptible; but so long as they were of any real importance there were frequent debates about this matter.

Many of the incorporeal things inhere in corporeal things; indeed the notion that they can exist by themselves, that they can exist 'in gross' or 'as a gross' has had difficulties to encounter. Where can the advowson be, if it is not inherent in a manor[5]? A tract of land has rights pertaining to it; they are as much a part of it as the trees that grow out of it and the houses that are built upon it. In a charter of feoffment it is not usual to describe these rights; to say that the land has been conveyed *cum pertinentiis* is quite enough, and very probably even this phrase is needless. Occasionally however we may come upon a copious stream of 'general words.' One example may suffice. Just about the time of Edward I.'s accession the Abbot of Ramsey purchased a manor from Berengar le Moigne for the very large sum of £1666. 13*s.* 4*d.* (this instance of a great sale for ready money

[1] Bracton, f. 56; Select Pleas in Manorial Courts (Selden Soc.), p. xxiv.

[2] Note Book, pl. 1271–2.

[3] Ann. Tewkesbur. p. 511: An amusing and spirited story tells of the difficulties that the abbot had to meet before he could hang John Milksop, it being doubtful whether the right had not been lost by non-user.

[4] Select Pleas in Manorial Courts, p. lxxvii.

[5] See above, vol. ii. p. 136.

is remarkable), and it was conveyed to him 'with the homages, rents, services, wardships, reliefs, escheats, buildings, walls, banks, in whatsoever manner constructed or made, cultivated and uncultivated lands, meadows, leys, pastures, gardens, vineyards, vivaries, ponds, mills, hedges, ways, paths, copses, and with the villeins, their chattels, progeny and customs, and all that may fall in from the said villeins, merchets, gersums, leyrwites, heriots, fines for land and works, and with all easements and commodities within the vill and without[1].' A manor is a highly complex and organized aggregate of corporeal and incorporeal things. This aggregate may be broken up, but, while it remains intact, the thought that it is a single [p. 144] thing is maintained with consistency, even in favour of a violent wrong-doer. You are seised of a manor to which an advowson belongs; I disseise you of that manor; if the church falls vacant before you have recovered the manor, it will be for me, not for you, to present a clerk[2].

One large class of incorporeal things consists of rights to be exercised *in alieno solo*. Normally these inhere in a dominant tenement; but our law does not deny the possibility of their existing as 'grosses[3].' It is as yet vaguely liberal about these matters. It does not make any exhaustive list of the only 'praedial servitudes' that there can be. Men are very free to strike what bargains they please, and the result of such a bargain will be, not an enforceable contract, but the creation and grant of an incorporeal thing. The most elaborate and carefully worded of the private documents that have come down to us are those which create or regulate pasture rights and rights of way. Our law seems to look at these rights from the stand-point of the person who enjoys them, not from that of the person who suffers by their exercise. They are not 'servitudes,' they are 'easements,' 'profits,' 'commodities[4].' A distinction is being established between the 'easement' which does not authorize one to take anything, and the 'profit' that

Easements and profits.

---

[1] Cart. Rams. ii. 339.

[2] Bracton, f. 243 b ; Note Book, pl. 49 ; Holmes, Common Law, pp. 382–6.

[3] In Bracton's exposition the rights in gross fall into the background, though they are visible. He likes to speak of 'servitudes,' 'dominant and servient tenements,' and so forth. The common in gross he will hardly call common, it is rather a right of 'herbage.'

[4] Note Book, pl. 720 (A.D. 1225): 'asiamentum de aqua de Pittes.'

authorizes a taking; the typical instance of the one is the right
of way, of the other the right to take grass 'by the mouths of
one's cattle.' The term common (*communa*) is not confined to
cases in which many neighbours have a right to some profit, by
fishing, taking turf, depasturing cattle, on the soil of their lord,
though it may be that the term has its origin in cases of this
sort. You may grant to me 'common of pasture' in your soil,
and I may be your one commoner, and it is by no means
essential that you should be my lord. Such grants were not
unusual and very often they defined with minute particularity
the number of beasts that might be turned out and the other
terms of the bargain[1]. Nor is it very rare to find the grant
of a right to take wood; this is often limited to such wood [p. 145]
as may be requisite for the repair or the warming of a certain
house or the maintenance of fences on a certain tract of land[2].
The yet feeble law of contract is supplemented by a generous
liberality in the creation of incorporeal things. The man of the
thirteenth century does not say, 'I agree that you may have
so many trees out of my copse in every year,' he says, 'I give
and grant you so much wood[3].' The main needs of the agricultural economy of the age can be met in this manner without
the creation of any personal obligations.

Liberty and serfage as things. 'Liberty,' again, and 'serfship' can be treated as things of
which there is possession or seisin[4]. The lord of a villein owns
a corporeal thing and ought to be seised of it, and in the thirteenth century, though a feoffment of a 'manor' will transfer
the ownership of men as well as of other things, still in an
action for reducing a man to villeinage, the would-be lord
claims that man as a thing by itself and seldom, if ever, makes
any mention of manor or land. 'My grandfather,' he will say,
'was seised of your grandfather as of his villein, and took
esplees of him as by taking merchet from him, tallaging him
high and low and making him reeve,' and then the descent
of the right and the transmission of the villein blood will be

---

[1] The Meaux chronicle (Chron. de Melsa) has much about rights of way and
of pasture.

[2] Winchcombe Landboc, p. 81: 'husbote et heibote et huswerminge.'

[3] Sometimes the language of the charter is curiously materialistic; *e.g.*
Winchcombe Landboc, p. 205: 'I have granted you twelve beasts in my pasture';
this means—'I have granted you a right to turn out twelve beasts in my
pasture.'

[4] See above, vol. i. p. 417.

traced step by step. But the lord is only driven to this proprietary pleading if the man whom he claims is 'in seisin of liberty.' This seisin of liberty the villein may somewhat readily gain, if he has the courage to flee. Apparently the lapse of four days will preclude his lord from self-help. After that, he may not seize the body of the fugitive, unless he has returned to 'his villein nest,' nor may the chattels of the fugitive be taken, since they can for this purpose be regarded as appurtenances of his body, and when one loses seisin of the principal thing, one loses seisin of its appurtenances. On the other hand, a man who is free *de iure* may be a villein *de facto*. Until by flight or litigation he destroys this *de facto* relationship, he can, it would [p. 146] seem, be lawfully treated as a villein, be tallaged, for example, or set in the stocks[1].

But even to the conjugal relationship the idea of seisin is extended. Possibly we might expect that a husband would be seised of his wife; but, as a matter of fact, we more commonly read in our English records of a wife being seised of her husband. The canon law in its desire to suppress sin has made marriage exceedingly easy; no nuptial ceremony is necessary. The result is that many *de facto* marriages are of doubtful validity, since it is only too possible that one of the parties has some more legitimate spouse. The canon law has been constrained to divide the *possessorium* from the *petitorium.* I can be compelled to live with my *de facto* wife until by reason of an earlier marriage, or of consanguinity, or the like, I have obtained a divorce from her[2]. With this our temporal law is not concerned; but it is by no means improbable that, when a man dies, two women will claim dower, and that one of the would-be widows will put forward a definitely possessory claim : 'I was seised of this man when he died as of a lawful husband ; possession of one-third of his lands should be awarded to me, and when I have got that, then let this lady assert her proprietary rights[3].' The position of defendant is coveted and medieval judges will not decide a question of best right if they can help it.

The marital relationship and possessory protection.

---

[1] The attempt to treat the villein himself as an 'incorporeal hereditament' belongs to a later age.

[2] Bruns, Recht des Besitzes, 191.

[3] Note Book, pl. 642, 1142 ('seisinam habuit de corpore ipsius Thoraldi antequam traditum esset sepulturae'), 1564, 1597, 1703 ; Bracton, f. 306.

Wardships
as things.

The guardian can and ought to be seised of the body of the ward, and the seisin of a *de facto* guardian is protected against the self-help of a more rightful claimant. As to the wardship of land, this is treated as an incorporeal thing which is distinct from the land. One may, rightfully or wrongfully, have possession of this *custodia*, but this will not give one a seisin of the land. For testamentary purposes the *custodia* is an incorporeal chattel.

Landlike-
ness of the
incor-
poreals.

For the more part, however, our incorporeal things are conceived as being very like pieces of land. Gradually a word is being told off to express this similarity. That word is 'tenements.' Unless we are mistaken, that word first came into use for the purpose of comprising meadows, pastures, woods and wastes, for at an early time the word *terra* will [p. 147] hardly cover more than the arable land[1]. But *tenementum* will also comprise any incorporeal thing which can be holden by one man of another. Thus in particular it will comprise an advowson, even when that advowson exists 'in gross,' for it will be held of the king or of some mesne lord. Probably the advowson 'in gross' was generally held by frankalmoin, since it was chiefly for the benefit of religious houses that advowsons were severed from their manors; but it might be held by knight's service[2]. Then, as the assize of novel disseisin was extended to one class of incorporeal things after another, the term 'tenements' was extended to things that were not holden of another person, for the writ of assize always supposed that the plaintiff had been disseised 'of his free tenement' in a certain vill. Thus, for example, rents charge, rents seck, rights of common, become tenements. Statutes of Edward I.'s day gave the word a sharper edge[3]. On the whole the analogy is persistently pursued; the incorporeal thing as regards proprietary and

---

[1] In writs and other legal documents of the thirteenth century *terra* is constantly used in the narrow sense; *e.g.* a demandant claims 'xx. acras terrae et v. acras prati.' Y. B. 33-5 Edw. I. p. 149: meadow can not be demanded as 'land.'

[2] See Co. Lit. 85 a.

[3] In particular Stat. Westm. II. c. 1 *de donis conditionalibus*, and c. 24 extending the scope of the novel disseisin. Under the influence of the first of these chapters the word 'tenement' becomes more metaphysical. It becomes possible to say that a termor has no tenement because he has nothing that he can entail. See above p. 117, note 3. This is a spiritualizing doctrine; the first tenement was of the earth earthy.

possessory remedies, as regards conveyance, as regards succession, as regards the 'estates' that may exist in it, shall be made
as like an acre of land as the law can make it.   The mere
personal or unsecured annuity, when it is no longer conceived
as a 'cameral rent,' falls apart from the other incorporeal things;
its contractual nature becomes more and more apparent.   It is
like land for the purposes of succession on death, but not for
other purposes; in the language of a later time it is a 'hereditament' but no 'tenement.'   That land should have been the
model after which these things were fashioned, will not surprise
us, when we have turned, as now we must, from the rich land-
law to the poor and backward law of movable goods; but we
[p. 148] can not leave behind us the law of incorporeal things, the most
medieval part of medieval law, without a word of admiration
for the daring fancy that created it, a fancy that was not afraid
of the grotesque.

§ 7. *Movable Goods.*

Of the manner in which our English law of the thirteenth
century treated the ownership and the possession of movable
goods, we know but little.   Against the supposition that in the
feudal age chattels were of small importance so that there was
hardly any law about them, a protest should be needless.   Not
even in the feudal age did men eat or drink land, nor, except in
a metaphorical sense, were they vested with land.   They owned
flocks and herds, ploughs and plough-teams and stores of hay
and corn.   A Cistercian abbot of the thirteenth century, who
counted his sheep by the thousand, would have been surprised
to hear that he had few chattels of any value.   Theft has never
been a rare offence; and even on the land-owner the law brought
its pressure to bear chiefly by seizures of his movable goods.
Indeed the further we go back, the larger seems the space which
the possession of chattels fills in the eye of the law.   An action
for the recovery of cattle seems as typical of the Anglo-Saxon
age as an action for the recovery of land is of the thirteenth
century, or an action on a contract is of our own day.   It is, no
doubt, worthy of remark that in the feudal time the title to
chattels was often implicated with the title to land.   The

*Ownership
and posses-
sion of
chattels.*

ownership of a manor usually involved the lordship over villeins and the right to seize their chattels; and so when two men were litigating about a 'manor,' the subject of the dispute was not a bare tract of land, but a complex made up of land and of a great part of the agricultural capital that worked the land, men and beasts, ploughs and carts, forks and flails[1]. For all this, however, by the operation of sales and gifts, by the operation of our dual law of inheritance or succession—to say nothing of the nefarious operations of the cattle lifter,—the ownership and the possession of movables were often quite distinct from the ownership and the possession of any land.

Obscurity of the subject. In part our ignorance may be explained by the fact that [p. 149] litigation about chattels was prosecuted chiefly in those local courts which kept no written records of their doings, or whose records have not been preserved or have not been published. Even when in Edward I.'s day the competence of those courts had been restricted within a pecuniary limit, they could still entertain by far the greater number of the actions for the recovery of chattels that were brought; for a chattel worth forty shillings was in those days a costly thing[2]. But to this cause of ignorance we must add another, namely, a want of curiosity. It has been common knowledge that medieval land-law was unlike modern land-law and that it would repay the investigator. On the other hand, we have but too easily believed that the medieval law of chattels was simple and straightforward and in all probability very like modern law. A little acquaintance with foreign books would teach us that this can hardly be true. In France and Germany, in countries which are not overwhelmed by such voluminous records of the land-law as those that we have inherited, few questions about legal history have given rise to keener debates than those which touch the ownership and possession of movables. Did medieval law know an ownership of movables? Even this fundamental question has been raised.

The medieval chattel. A few characteristics of the typical medieval chattel demand our attention. In the first place, we can speak of a typical

---

[1] The chattels of the villeins are sometimes expressly mentioned in the charter which testifies to the feoffment of a manor; *e.g.* Cart. Rams. ii. 340: 'et cum villanis, catallis, sequelis et cum consuetudinibus eorum.'

[2] In Henry II.'s day for forty shillings one might have bought some thirteen oxen or eighty sheep: Hall, Court Life, p. 221.

chattel; the very word *chattel* tells us this. The typical chattel
is a beast. The usage which has differentiated *chattel* from
cattle is not very ancient; when Englishmen began to make
their wills in English a gift of one's 'worldly catell' was a gift
of all one's movables. Then, in the second place, this typical
chattel was perishable; the medieval beast, horse, ox, sheep,
had but a short life, and in this respect but few chattels
departed far from the type. With the exception of armour,
those things that were both costly and permanent were for
the more part outside the ordinary province of litigation;
books, embroidered vestments, jewelled crowns and crucifixes,
these were safe in sanctuary or in the king's treasure house;
there was little traffic in them. Thirdly, the typical chattels
had a certain 'fungibility.' Time was when oxen served as
[p. 150] money, and rules native in that time will easily live on into
later ages. The *pecunia* of Domesday Book is not money but
cattle. When cattle serve as money, one ox must be regarded
as being for the purposes of the law exactly as good as another
ox. Of course a court may have to decide whether an ox is a
good and lawful ox, just as it may have to decide whether a
penny is a good and lawful penny; but, granted that two
animals are legally entitled to the name of ox, the one in the
eye of the law can be neither better nor worse than the other.
It was by slow degrees that beasts lost their 'pecuniary'
character. A process of differentiation went on within each
genus of animals; the genus *equus* contains the *dextrarius*, the
iumentum, the *palefridus*, the *runcinus*. All horses are not of
equal value, but all palfreys are or may for many legal purposes
be supposed to be, and the value of the destrier can be
expressed in terms of rounceys. Rents are payable in oxen,
sheep, corn, malt, poultry, eggs. The royal exchequer has a
tariff for the commutation of promised hawks and hounds into
marks and shillings[1]. We may expect therefore that the law of
the twelfth and thirteenth centuries will draw no very sharp
line between coins and other chattels; but this means that one
important outline of our modern law will be invisible or obscure.

We are not arguing that the typical chattels of the middle *Pecuniary*
ages were indistinguishable from each other, or were supposed *character of chattels.*
to be so by law. When now-a-days we say that 'money has no
ear-mark,' we are alluding to a practice which in all probability

[1] As to what the law understands by a hawk, see Dialogus, ii. c. 25.

played a large part in ancient law. Cattle were ear-marked or branded, and this enabled their owner to swear that they were his in whosesoever hands he might find them[1]. The legal supposition is, not that one ox is indistinguishable from another ox, but that all oxen, or all oxen of a certain large class, are equivalent. The possibility of using them as money has rested on this supposition.

Possession of chattels.

In one other particular a chattel differs from a piece of land. As we have seen, when several different persons, lords and tenants of divers orders, have rights in a piece of land, medieval [p. 151] law can attribute to each of them a certain possession or seisin. One is seised 'in service,' the other 'in demesne'; one is seised of the land, the other of a seignory over the land; one is seised while the other possesses—and so forth. The consequence is that in the case of land a great legal problem can be evaded or concealed from view. If we ascribe possession or seisin to a hirer of land, this will not debar us from ascribing a certain sort of possession or seisin to the letter: *istae duae possessiones sese compatiuntur in una re*[2]. But it is otherwise with chattels. As between letter and hirer, lender and borrower, pledgor and pledgee—in short, to use our convenient general terms, as between bailor and bailee—we must make up our minds, and if we concede possession to the one, we must almost of necessity deny it to the other. The lord's seisin of his seignory becomes evident when he enters to distrain for services that the land owes him, when he enters as the heir's guardian and the like. In the case of goods we can hardly have any similar phenomenon, and if, as we may be apt to do, we attribute possession to the bailee, we shall have to refuse it to the bailor. We may then be compelled to face a case which will tax to the uttermost the forces of our immature jurisprudence. The ownership of a chattel may be divorced, not only from possession, but from the right to possess. Can it in such a case really continue to be ownership? May it not undergo such a transmutation that it will be reduced to the rank of a mere right *in personam*?

Englishmen are accustomed to hear it said that our medieval

---

[1] See Homeyer, Haus- und Hofmarken; Ihering, Vorgeschichte, 30; Brunner, D. R. G., ii. 500. Modern Australia seems to have reproduced some very ancient phenomena. At all events in romances, the bush-ranger who has confined his operations to the taking of 'clear-skins' (unmarked beasts), and therefore has not been put to the risky process of 'faking a brand,' is pretty safe.

[2] Note Book, i. p. 92.

law knew, and even that our modern law knows, no absolute ownership of land. To many of them the statement that our medieval law knew no absolute ownership of chattels may be new, and yet we shall see that the ownership of land was a much more intense and completely protected right than was the ownership of a chattel. Indeed we may be left doubting whether there was any right in movable goods that deserved the name of ownership[1].

[p. 152] In the course of our investigation, we must distinguish two questions, the one about a remedy, the other about a

---

[1] As to the words *owner* and *ownership*:—Dr Murray has kindly informed us that the earliest known example of the former occurs in 1340: Ayenbite of Inwyt, p. 27. The verb to own, *áȝnian, áhnian*, can be traced much further back and, says Dr Murray, 'there is no etymological reason why *áȝnere*, owner, should not have been formed from it and used in Old English, but no examples appear to be known.' After 1340 it is increasingly common. 'Of *ownership*, which might, etymologically, have been formed so soon as *owner* existed, had there been a want felt for it (since *-ship* has been a living movable suffix for a thousand years or more), we have no instance before 1583.' Coke therefore is making an early use of it when he says (Co. Lit. 17 b), 'Of an advowson wherein a man hath an absolute ownership and propertie as he hath in lands or rents.' So far as we are aware, the term *absolute ownership* was very new when Coke thus applied it to the tenant in fee of English land. In the past the place of *owner* and *ownership* seems to have been filled in common discourse by such terms and phrases as 'possessor,' 'possessioner,' 'he to whom the thing belongs or pertains,' 'he who has the thing.' In the translation of Isaiah i. 3, where the A. V. gives 'The ox knoweth his *owner*' one of the Wiclifite versions gave *welder* [wielder, governor, from A.-S. *gewealdan*] and the other gave *lord*. So these versions speak of the lord of the ox (Exod. xxi. 28), the lordis of the colt (Luke xix. 33), the lord of the ship (Acts xxvii. 11). In the A. V. neither *ownership* nor *property* appears (teste Cruden); on the other hand *possess* and its derivatives are exceedingly common. The things that a man owned were often described as his *possessions*. This usage of *possessiones* is very ancient; witness Paulus, Dig. 50, 16, 78; it runs through the middle ages. The Bankruptcy Act of 1623 (21 Jac. I. c. 19) did much towards giving legal currency to the term *owner* by its famous 'order and disposition clause'; but it occurs in an English statute as early as 1487 (4 Hen. VII. c. 10, sec. 3); in 1494 a statute speaks of the owner of land (11 Hen. VII. c. 17); in 1530 we find owners and occupiers of ground (21 Hen. VIII. c. 11). As to *property*, though throughout the middle ages the French and Latin forms of this word occasionally occur, and the use of it is insured by the writ *de proprietate probanda*, we believe that until the last century it was far less frequent than would be supposed by those who have not looked for it in the statute book. Instead of *property* in the vaguer of the two senses which it now bears, men used *possessions* and *estate*. In a narrower sense *property* was used as an equivalent for best right (*e.g.* Co. Lit. 145 b: 'But there be two kinde of properties; a generall propertie, which every absolute owner hath; and a speciall propertie'), but in the Year Books it is by no means common. We find *owner or proprietary* in 1509 (1 Hen. VIII. c. 5, sec. 4).

substantive right. Our common law in modern times has refused, except in rare cases, to compel the restitution of a chattel[1]. Having decided that the chattel belongs to the plaintiff and that the defendant's possession is wrongful, it nevertheless stopped short of taking the thing by force from the defendant and handing it over to the plaintiff. Its judgment was that the plaintiff should recover from the defendant [p. 153] the chattel or a sum of money that a jury had assessed as its value. This left to the defendant the choice between delivering up the thing and paying a sum of money, and if he would do neither the one nor the other, then goods of his were seized and sold, and the plaintiff in the end had to take money instead of the very thing that he demanded. This odd imperfection in the remedy may suggest to us that there are some historical problems to be solved, still it affected not the plaintiff's right but only his remedy:—he obtained the value of the thing because he had shown that the thing belonged to him. On the other hand, for some time past the ownership of chattels that our common law has sanctioned has reached a high grade in the scale of intensity. That law has been very favourable to the owner, unduly favourable, so our legislators have thought[2]. It has maintained that, except in the case of a sale in market overt—an exception which was more important in the later middle ages than it is in the present century—the owner can not be deprived of his ownership by any transaction between other persons, even though he has parted with possession, and for a time with the right to possess. The owner, A, lends, lets, deposits, pledges, his chattel,—in short he 'bails' it—to B; if B, in breach of the contract between him and A, sells this chattel to C, the sale, unless it took place in market overt, will not deprive A of his ownership, even though C has acted with the utmost good faith, paid a full price and made every inquiry that he could be expected to make.

[1] The first statutory inroad on this rule was made in 1854 by Stat. 17–8 Vic. c. 125, sec. 78. In stating the rule quite accurately it would be necessary to take notice of the writ for the restitution of stolen goods; but this writ was given by common law only where there was an appeal of larceny; it was given in the case of an indictment by Stat. 21 Hen. VIII. c. 11. Also the Court of Chancery in exercise of its equitable jurisdiction would sometimes compel restitution of a chattel of exceptional value.

[2] Legislation adverse to owners and favourable to those who in good faith deal with possessors, begins with the Factors' Act of 1823, Stat. 4 Geo. IV. c. 83. Even at the present day (52–3 Vic. c. 45) such legislation has not gone very far.

If, however, we may draw inferences from foreign systems, we may say with some certainty that the favour thus shown to *Mobilia* ownership can not be very ancient.   When French and German *non habent sequelam.* law take shape in the thirteenth century, they contain a rule which is sometimes stated by the words *Mobilia non habent sequelam* (*Les meubles n'ont pas de suite*), or, to use a somewhat enigmatical phrase that became current in Germany, *Hand muss Hand wahren*.   Their scheme seems to be this:—If my goods go out of my possession without or against my will—if they are unlawfully taken from me, or if I lose them,—I may recover them from any one into whose possession they have come; but if, on the other hand, I have of my own free will [p. 154] parted with the possession of them—if I have deposited them, or let or lent or pledged, or 'bailed' them in any manner— then I can have no action for their recovery from a third possessor.   I have bailed my horse to *A*; if *A* sells or pledges it to *X*, or if *X* unlawfully takes it from *A*, or if *A* loses and *X* finds it—in none of these cases have I an action against *X*; my only action is an action against my bailee, against *A* or the heirs of *A*[1].   'Where I have put my trust, there must I seek it.'   We have not here to deal with rules which in the interest of free trade protect that favourite of modern law, the *bona fide* purchaser.   Neither the positive nor the negative rule pays any heed to good or bad faith.   If my goods go from me without my will, I can recover them from the hundredth hand, however clean it may be; if they go from me with my will, I have no action against any one except my bailee[2].

To account for this state of things many ingenious theories have been devised.   It has been contended that we have to deal with an imperfect conception of ownership.   The owner who of his own free will parts with the possession of his chattel, parts also with the ownership of it.   In exchange he takes a

---

[1] Any one who by testamentary or intestate succession represents the bailee, is not a 'third possessor' for the purposes of this rule.

[2] Heusler, Gewere, 487; Heusler, Institutionen, ii. 209; Laband, Die Vermögensrechtlichen Klagen; Sohm, Process der Lex Salica, p. 55; Hermann, Die Grundelemente der Altgermanischen Mobiliarvindication; Schröder, D. R. G., 266, 682; Brunner, D. R. G. ii. 495; Jobbé-Duval, Revendication des meubles. The meaning of *Hand muss Hand wahren* seems to be that the bailee's hand wards the bailor's hand; it is only from the bailee's hand that the bailor can demand restitution.   The same doctrine, to all appearance, may be found in the Ancient Laws of Wales, i. 249.

mere right *in personam,* a mere contractual right, a promise
that in certain events, or after the lapse of a certain time, the
chattel shall be returned to him. On the other hand, it has
been argued that we have before us not imperfect ownership
but defective remedies. The bailor is still owner of the thing
that he has bailed; but the law has hitherto been so much
occupied with the difficult task of suppressing theft, that it
has omitted to supply him with a 'real' action, a vindication:
many plausible reasons may be suggested for this neglect. To
an Englishman bred up to believe that 'there is no right
without a remedy,' some of the controversies that have raged
over this matter may seem idle. There may come a time when [p. 155]
those legal rules of which we have been speaking no longer
express men's natural thoughts about right and wrong. In
such a time it may be allowable to say that the defect is in
the remedy rather than in the right, more especially if the
law courts are beginning to treat the old rules as antiquated
and to circumvent them whenever this can be done. But by
this means we only throw back the question into a remoter
age. If there was any age in which these rules seemed an
adequate protection for ownership, then we are bound to say
that the ownership known to that age was in one most important particular different from the ownership that is known
to us.

English
law.

Of late years learned writers have asserted that the negative
or restrictive half of this scheme was at one time a part of
English law. There is much, it is said, in the Year Books,
something even in our modern law, which can not be explained
unless we suppose that the rule *Mobilia non habent sequelam*
held good in this country, and that the man who had bailed his
goods had no action against any save his bailee[1]. But more
than this has been said. It has been pointed out that in the
Year Books 'possession has largely usurped not only the substance but the name of property[2],' and that the justices have a
perplexing habit of ascribing the *propretie* to the trespasser
and even to the thief[3]. A thorough treatment of this difficult
topic is impossible to those who are debarred from discussing

[1] Holmes, Common Law, Lect. v.; Laughlin in the Essays in A.-S. Law,
197 f.

[2] Pollock and Wright, Possession, p. 5.

[3] Ames, Disseisin of Chattels, Harv. L. R., vol. iii.

in detail the texts of the later middle ages. Still something about it must be said[1].

I. Leaving out of sight for a while the cases in which there has been a bailment, we may consider the position of the owner whose goods have been taken from him, in order that we may if possible come to some understanding of that puzzling phenomenon, the ascription of property to the trespasser and even to the thief, which we find in the later Year Books.

The 'property' of the thief.

Cattle lifting is our starting point. It is a theme to which the Anglo-Saxon dooms and the parallel 'folk laws' of the continental nations are ever recurring. If only cattle lifting could be suppressed, the legislators will have done all or almost all that they can hope to do for the protection of the owner of movables. The typical action for the recovery of a movable is highly penal. It is an action against a thief, or at any rate it is an action which aims at the discovery and punishment of a thief as well as at the restitution of stolen goods. An action we call it, but it is a prosecution, a prosecution in the primary sense of that word, a pursuit, a chase; a great part of the legal procedure takes place before any one has made his way to a court of law. My cattle have been driven off; I must follow the trail; it is the duty of my neighbours to assist me, to ride with me. If we catch the marauder still driving the beasts before him, we take him as a 'hand-having' thief and he is dealt with in a summary fashion; 'he can not deny' the theft. The practice of ear-marking or branding cattle, and the legal duty that I am under of publicly exposing to the view of my neighbours whatever cattle I have, make it a matter of notoriety that these beasts, which this man is driving before him, have been taken from me. Even if we can not catch a thief in the act, the trail is treated as of great importance. If it leads into a man's land, he must show that it leads out again; otherwise it will 'stand instead of a foreoath'; it is an accusing fact[2]. If the possessor has no unbroken trail in his favour, then, when he discovers the thing, he lays his hand upon it and claims it. He declares the ox to be his and

Ancient action for the recovery of stolen goods.

[p. 156]

---

[1] Had Bracton finished his work with chapters on the personal actions, our position would have been very different. As it is, he has given us a valuable account of the *actio furti*, but as regards the bailments we have only some romanesque generalia in which we dare not place a perfect trust.

[2] Æthelst. v. 2.

calls upon the possessor to say how he came by it. The possessor has to give up the thing or to answer this question. He may perhaps assert that the beast is his by birth and rearing; a commoner answer will be that he acquired it from a third person whom he names. Then the pursuer with his left hand grasping one of the beast's ears, and his right upon a relic or a sword, swears that the beast is his and has been stolen from him, and the possessor with his left hand grasping the other ear swears that he is naming the person from whom he purchased[1].

The procedure in court.

Now at length there may be proceedings before a court of law. The possessor must produce this third person in court; [p. 157] he has vouched a warrantor and must find him. If this vouchee appears and confesses the warranty, then the beast is delivered over to him and the accusation is made against him. He can vouch another warrantor, and so, by following backwards the course along which the beast has passed, we may come at length to the thief. The rules about proof we need not here consider, only we must notice that the possessor, though he is not convicted of theft, may often have to give up the thing to the pursuer. The elaborate law of warranty, the attempts made in England and other countries to prevent undue delay by a restriction of the process to some three or four vouchers, these show plainly enough that the man whose beasts have been stolen can claim them from any one in whose possession they are. If the possessor can name no warrantor, it is still possible that he should protect himself against the charge of theft by showing that he purchased the thing in open market before the proper witnesses; but he will have to surrender that thing; it is not his though he bought it honestly[2]. Sales and purchases ought to take place before official witnesses, and the possessor who has neither warrantor nor witness has himself to blame if he is treated as a thief[3].

---

[1] For this seizure of the ear see Brunner, D. R. G., ii. 500, and (for the ceremony appears in Celtic as well as in Teutonic law) Ancient Laws of Wales, ii. 725.

[2] However in the very early laws of Hlothœre and Eadric, c. 16, the man who has publicly bought in London need not give up the goods unless the price that he paid is offered to him. This seems a curious testimony to the commercial importance of London. Liebermann, Gesetze, p. 11.

[3] It will be sufficient to refer to Brunner, *op. cit.* p. 495, where this old procedure is fully described and due attention is paid to the Anglo-Saxon texts.

When there has been a bailment and the chattel has been The bailee
pursues
the thief.
taken from the bailee's possession, it is natural that, so long
as prosecution means speedy pursuit, the right and duty of
prosecution should be his.   The bailor, it may be, will never
hear of the theft until it is some days old and the tell-tale
hoof-marks have been effaced.   When the pursuer makes his
claim he will say that the thing is 'his'; but this is an
assertion of possession rather than of ownership; he means
that the thing was taken from him[1].

[p. 158]   Of any other procedure for the recovery of goods we read The
bailor's
action
against the
bailee.
little or nothing in our old dooms.   No doubt the bailor had
some action against the bailee for the return of the goods; but
whether this action was conceived as based upon ownership or
as based upon contract, whether that distinction could have
been clearly drawn, whether the bailee could be compelled to
deliver back the very thing that had been bailed, or whether
the bailor had to be content if he got its value—these are
questions about which we have no certain information[2].

In the thirteenth century this ancient procedure was not Bracton's
actio furti
yet obsolete; but it was assuming a new form, that of the
appeal of larceny.   Bracton called it the *actio furti*[3].   We
should do wrong were we to reject this name as a scrap of
romanizing pedantry.   English law knew an action based upon
theft, and, if we would speak of such an action in Latin, we
can but call it *actio furti*.   It still had about it many antique
traits, though, as already said, it was assuming a new form,
that of the appeal of larceny[4].   We are wont to think of the
appeal as of a criminal prosecution, though one that was

The A.-S. verb which describes the voucher is *týman*.   The *team* of the Anglo-
Norman charters seems to be the right to hold a court into which foreigners,
i.e. persons not resident within the jurisdiction, may be vouched.   See Acts of
Parliament of Scotland, i. 742.

    [1] Brunner, *op. cit.* ii. 510.

    [2] Essays in A.-S. Law, pp. 199, 200.   The two passages there cited as
bearing on this action are (1) Alfred, Introd. c. 28, which comes from the book
of Exodus, (2) William, I. 37, which is a reminiscence of the *Lex Rhodia de
iactu*.   But we might argue from analogy that there must have been an action
for the restoration of the *res praestita*; Lex Salica, c. 51 (ed. Hessels, col. 334);
Sohm, Process der Lex Salica, 34.

    [3] Bracton, f. 151 b.

    [4] Dial. de Scac. lib. ii., cap. 10.   In the twelfth century the owner who
prosecuted the thief to conviction might still obtain 'double value.'   Of this we
shall speak in our chapter on Criminal Law.

instituted by a private prosecutor. A criminal prosecution it was, and if the appellee was convicted, he would as a general rule be sentenced to death; but still throughout the middle ages it had in it a marked recuperatory element; it was constantly spoken of as a remedy competent to the man whose goods had been stolen: it would restore those goods to him[1]. But in Bracton's day the recuperatory element was even more visible than it was in later centuries, and we can see a close connexion between the appeal and that old procedure which we have endeavoured to describe. A little time spent over this matter will not be lost, for it is only through procedural forms that we can penetrate to substantive rights.

Procedure in the action of theft.

The trail has not yet lost its importance. The sheriff and men of Shropshire were wont to trace it into the borough of Bridgenorth and to charge the burgesses with the difficult task [p. 159] of showing its exit[2]. The summary mode of dealing with 'hand-having' thieves, thieves who are 'seised of their thefts' was still maintained; the prosecutor in such a case bore the ancient name of *sakeber*; the fresh suit and capture being proved, a local court sentenced the prisoner to decapitation, giving him no opportunity of denying the theft; in some cases the duty of beheading him was committed to the *sakeber*[3]. But even if such summary justice was out of the question, even if there was to be a regular appeal, a great part of the procedure took place, or was supposed to take place, out of court. The appellor had to allege 'fresh suit' after the criminal. He ought at once to raise the hue and cry, he ought to go to the four nearest townships, 'the four quarters

---

[1] See *e.g.* Y. B. 4 Hen. VII. f. 5 : 'l'appel est a reaver ses biens et affirme proprieté continualment en le party.'

[2] Select Pleas of the Crown, pl. 173.

[3] Bracton, f. 150 b; Fleta, f. 54; Britton, i. 56. In the note by Mr Nichols to the last of these passages the meaning of the mysterious word *sakeber* is discussed. See also Spelman's Glossary. The true form of the word seems to be very uncertain. A Scottish book, Quoniam Attachiamenta (Acts of Parl. i. 647), speaks of the pleas of wrong and unlaw which are prosecuted *per sacreborgh*. In this form the last syllable seems to be the word *borh*, which means a pledge. In the English books the term *sakeber* is applied to the prosecutor. In very early Frankish law the *sacebaro* appears as an officer of some sort; little is known of him, and the name disappears on the Continent at a very remote date. Oddly enough however it does appear in our English Quadripartitus, while *sagemannus* occurs both there and in Leg. Henr. 63. See Brunner, D. R. G., ii. 151–4; Liebermann, Quadripartitus, p. 32. Of summary justice we shall speak in another chapter.

of the neighbourhood' and proclaim his loss[1]. At the next county court the appellor must make, and at court after court he must repeat his appeal, until the accused either appears or is outlawed. The king's justices may not hold themselves very straitly bound by the letter of old rules, but they are fond of quashing appeals that have not been prosecuted with the utmost diligence[2].

[p. 160]   A far more important point is this, that an *actio furti*, we may almost say an appeal of larceny, may very properly be brought against one who is not a thief. We are assured by Bracton and his epitomators that the plaintiff may if he chooses omit the 'words of felony' from his count[3]. He may, even though he thinks that his adversary is a thief, demand his chattels, not as stolen chattels, but as goods that somehow or another have gone from him against his will; they have been *adirata* from him[4]. In the course of his action, and perhaps in consequence of the defendant's answer, he may add the charge of felony. This is permissible; one may thus raise a civil into a criminal, though one may not lower a criminal into a civil charge. Of such a procedure we can, it is true, find but few instances upon our records; but that this should be so is natural, for it is the procedure of local courts, and is not commenced by royal writ. We must not confuse it with that action of 'trespass *de bonis asportatis*' which is being slowly developed by the king's courts. We can see enough, however, to say that Bracton is not misleading us. For one moment in 1233 we catch a glimpse of the court of the royal manor of Windsor. Edith of Wackford charged

Scope of the action of theft

---

[1] Bracton, f. 139 b. Even in very late precedents for appeals the allegation of pursuit is retained: 'dictusque J. ipsum W. recenter insecutus fuit de villa in villam usque ad quatuor villas propinquiores.' As to the 'four neighbouring vills,' see Gross, Coroners' Rolls, pp. xxxvii.–xl.

[2] Any collection of criminal cases from this age will show many appeals quashed for want of a timely and incessant prosecution. The Statute of Gloucester, c. 9, mitigated the requirements of the common law.

[3] Bracton, f. 150 b, 140 b; Fleta, f. 55; Britton, i. 57.

[4] In the Norman books as well as our own, *adiratum* (*adiré*) is contrasted with *furatum* (*emblé*); Somma, p. 28. It occurs elsewhere in French law-books. It is said to have its origin in a low Latin *adextratum*, meaning 'that which is gone from my hand'; but whether in legal texts it means specifically 'lost by accident' or more generally 'lost, whether by accident, wrongful taking, or otherwise' seems to be a moot point. See Jobbé-Duval, Revendication, pp. 91–4; also Y. B. 21–2 Edw. I. p. 467.

William Nuthach with detaining from her three pigs, which were *adirati* from her. William denied that the pigs were hers. She left the court to seek counsel, and on her return counted against William as against a thief, and, as she did so she, in true archaic fashion, held one of the pigs in her hand[1]. A few years earlier, in one of the hundred courts of Gloucestershire, Adam of Throgmorton demanded some hay from Clement Bonpas. It was adjudged that Clement should purge himself with oath-helpers in the county court. When Clement was upon the point of swearing, Adam 'levied him from the oath' and made a charge of felony[2]. But a regular [p. 161] appeal might be properly commenced against one who was not the thief. The appellor was not bound to say to the appellee, 'You stole these goods'; it was enough if he said, as in old days his English or Frankish ancestor might have said, 'These goods were stolen from me, and I can name no other thief than you[3].' We may expand this charge. 'These goods were stolen from me; I have pursued them into your possession; upon you now lies the burden of proving, (1) that you are not a thief, (2) that I ought not to have these goods back again.' At any rate, however, and by whatever words it may be commenced, the English *actio furti* can be effectually used against one who is no thief, but an honest man.

Defences to the action of theft.

We have to consider the appellee's means of defence. The appellor offers battle, and to all appearance the appellee can always, if he pleases, accept the offer[4]. In later days he can

---

[1] Note Book, pl. 824.

[2] Gloucestershire Pleas of the Crown (ed. Maitland), p. 6. The practice known as levying a man from an oath (*a sacramento levare*) is referred to in Glanvill, x. 5. When he is just going to swear, you charge him with being on the point of committing perjury or theft by perjury, and thus what has as yet been a civil is turned into a criminal suit. The procedure is described by Brunner, D. R. G., ii. 434. Another early instance of it occurs in Rot. Cur. Reg. (Palgrave) i. 451; the hand which the would-be swearer has stretched out is seized by his adversary and the charge of attempted perjury is made. Late in Henry III.'s day the Brevia Placitata (Camb. Univ. Lib. Ee. i. 1. f. 243 b) still teaches us how to catch our adversary's hand when he is on the brink of the oath, and to make the charge of perjury against him with an offer of battle.

[3] Select Pleas of the Crown, pl. 192 : 'nescivit alium latronem quam ipsum Edwardum.' Note Book, pl. 1539: 'quod ipse fuit latro vel latronem nominare scivit.' Fleta, p. 55: 'latro est aut latronem inde sic [*corr.* scit] nominare.' See the A.-S. oaths, Schmid, App. x.

[4] Bracton, f. 140. It would be otherwise if the appellor were maimed or too old to fight.

always, if he pleases, put himself upon his country for good and ill.   The permission thus accorded to him of submitting to the verdict of a jury tends to change the character of the appeal, to strengthen the criminal or accusatory at the cost of the civil or recuperatory element.   This we shall see if we observe that in the days of Bracton the appellee who does not wish to fight has to defend himself in one of three ways; (i) he proves the goods to have been his from the first moment of their existence; (ii) he vouches a warrantor; (iii) he admits the appellor's title, surrenders the goods and confines his defence to a proof of [p. 162] honest and open purchase.   Of each of these modes of meeting the action a few words must be said.

(i)   The appellee says that the goods have been his from the first: for instance, that the horse in question was the foal of his mare[1].   He enforces this by the production of a 'suit' of witnesses.   The appellee may meet this by a counter suit, and in Bracton's day these rival suits can be examined by the court. Each witness can be severed from his fellows and questioned about ear-marks and so forth.   The larger and more consistent suit carries the day[2].

Defence of 'birth and rearing.'

(ii)   But what is regarded as the common defence is the voucher of a warrantor[3].   The appellee asserts that he acquired the goods from a third person, whom he calls upon to defend the appeal.   There is a writ enabling him to compel the appearance of the vouchee[4].   The vouchee appears.   If he denies that the goods passed from him to the appellee, there may be battle between him and the appellee, and should he succumb in this, he will be hanged as a thief[5].   If he admits that the goods passed from him to the appellee, then the appellee retires from the action[6].   We see the goods placed in the warrantor's hand, and, when he is seised of them, then the appellor counts against him as against the thief or one who can name the thief[7].   The warrantor can vouch another warrantor.   The process of voucher can be repeated until a third, or perhaps a

Defence by voucher.

---

[1] Bracton, f. 151.   In Welsh law, which in its treatment of this subject is very like English law, the proof of 'birth and rearing' is one of the three normal defences.

[2] Note Book, pl. 1115.

[3] Glanvill, x. 15; Bracton, f. 151; Fleta, p. 55; Britton, i. 57.

[4] Glanvill, x. 16; Bracton, f. 151.   [5] Note Book, pl. 1435.

[6] Glanvill, x. 15; Bracton, f. 151; Britton, i. 59.

[7] Select Pleas of the Crown, pl. 192.

fourth, warrantor is before the court[1]. There a doom of Cnut
drew a line; similar lines are drawn in other ancient bodies of
law, both Teutonic and Celtic:—some limit must be set to this
dilatory process[2]. But the point that we have to observe is that
the *actio furti* is put to a legitimate use when it is brought
against one who is no thief. The convicted warrantor is hanged;
the appellor recovers his chattel; but meanwhile the first ap-   [p.163]
pellee has gone quit; he is no thief, but he has lost the
chattel[3].

Defence of honest purchase.

(iii)   If the appellee can produce no warrantor, and can not
assert that the thing was his from the first moment of its
existence, then he must, if he would avoid battle, confine his
defence to an assertion of honest acquisition. He may prove
by witnesses a purchase in open market. If he does this, he
goes quit of the charge of theft, but must surrender the
chattel. The law has still a great suspicion of secret sales. It
is no longer so rigid as it used to be; perhaps by this time
an appellee will be allowed to prove his honesty though he
can not prove a purchase in open market; but the man who can
not allege such a purchase is, says Bracton, in peril.' He
will probably have to fight if he would escape the gallows[4].

Stolen goods recovered from honest purchasers.

We have spoken at some length of these ancient modes
of meeting the *actio furti*, because they are soon overwhelmed
by the verdicts of jurors, and because they enable us to lay
down a proposition about the substantive law of the thirteenth
century, which, regard being had to what will be said in later
days, is of no small value:—Stolen goods can be recovered by

---

[1] Glanvill, x. 15: read 'ad quartum (*not* quotum) warrantum erit standum.'
In such reckonings it is never very clear whether the original defendant is
reckoned as one of the warrantors.

[2] See above, p. 71.

[3] Actual instances of warranty are Select Pleas of the Crown, pl. 124, 192;
Note Book, pl. 67, 1138, 1435, 1461. By the kindness of Dr Jessopp we are
enabled to give the following entry from a manorial roll of 1259: 'Postea venit
praedictus Willelmus et calumpniavit, dicens quod praedictus bidens ei furatus
fuit;...Johannes de venditione dictae pellis vocavit ad warantum praedictum
David; qui venit et warentizavit. Et pro distancia inter praedictos Willelmum
et David tradita fuit Thomae le Cu in equali manu ad custodiendum.' We see
here the deposit of the debatable chattel 'en uele main,' according to the practice
described in Leg. Will. I. 21, § 2.

[4] This recovery of stolen goods from an appellee who has proved honest
purchase is attested by Glanvill, x. 17; Bracton, f. 151; Fleta, p. 55; Britton,
i. 59, 60.

legal action, not only from the hands of the thief, but from the hands of the third, the fourth, the twentieth possessor, even though those hands are clean and there has been a purchase in open market.

Now this old procedure, which is Glanvill's *petitio rei ex causa furtiva*[1] and Bracton's *actio furti*, underwent a further change. The appellee against whom a charge of larceny was brought was expected, if he would not fight, to put himself upon his country. This we may regard as a concession to appellees. The accused had no longer to choose between some two or three [p. 164] definite lines of defence; he could submit his case as a whole to the verdict of his neighbours, and hope that for one reason or another—which reason need not be given—they would acquit him. The voucher of a warrantor disappeared, and with it the appellor's chance of recovering his goods from a hand which was not that of the thief. Men were taking more notice than they once took of the psychical element of theft, the dishonest intention, and it was no longer to be tolerated that a burden of disproving theft should be cast upon one against whom no more could be asserted than that he was in possession of goods that had been taken from another. The appeal had become simply a criminal prosecution; it failed utterly if the appellee was not convicted of theft. If he was convicted, and the stolen goods had been seized by the king's officers, the appellor might, as of old, recover them; a writ of restitution would be issued in his favour, if he proved that he made 'fresh suit.' But more and more this restitution is regarded as a mere subordinate incident in the appeal, and when it is granted, it is granted rather as a favour than as a matter of strict right. The man who has been forward in the prosecution of a malefactor deserves well at the hands of the state; we reward him by giving him his own. In order to explain this view of the matter we must add that our law of forfeiture has been greedy. The felon forfeits his chattels to the king; he forfeits what he has; he forfeits 'that which he seemeth to have.' If the thief is indicted and convicted, the king will get even the stolen goods[2]; if he is appealed, then the appellor will perhaps, if he has shown himself a diligent subject, receive a prize for good

---

[1] Glanvill, x. 15.
[2] This was altered by Stat. 21 Hen. VIII. c. 11.

conduct[1]. Men will begin to say that the thief has 'property' in the stolen goods and that this is the reason why the king takes them. As a matter of history we believe this to be an inversion of logic:—one of the reasons why the thief is said to have 'property' in those goods is that the king has acquired a habit of taking them and refusing to give them up[2].

Action of trespass de bonis asportatis.

But more than this must be said before we can understand [p. 165] the ascription of property to a thief or other wrongful taker[3]. So long as the old practice of bringing an *actio furti* against the third hand obtained, such an ascription would have been impossible. As already said, that practice went out of use. The king's court was putting something in its place, and yet not exactly in its place, namely, a writ of trespass. This became common near the end of Henry III.'s reign. It was a flexible action; the defendant was called upon to say why with force and arms and against the king's peace he did some wrongful act. In course of time the precedents fell into three great classes; the violence is done to the body, the lands, the goods of the plaintiff. The commonest interference with his goods is that of taking and carrying them away; a well-marked sub-form of trespass, is trespass *de bonis asportatis*. If, however, we look back at the oldest precedents, we shall see that the destruction or asportation of goods was generally complained of as an incident which aggravated the invasion of land, the entry and breach of a close, and this may give us a clue when we explore the remedy which this action gives[4].

Scope of the action of trespass.

It is a semi-criminal action. The procedure against a contumacious defendant aims at his outlawry. The convicted defendant is imprisoned until he makes fine with the king. He also is condemned to pay damages. The action is not recuperatory; it is not *rei persecutoria*[5]. In the case of

---

[1] The law is well stated in Staunford, Pleas of the Crown, lib. iii. c. 10. See also Ames, Disseisin of Chattels, Harv. L. R. iii. 24.

[2] That the thief does not really get property in the goods is proved by this, that if a second thief steals from the first thief, the owner can still obtain restitution by appealing the second thief. Y. B. 13 Edw. IV. f. 3 (Mich. pl. 7); 4 Hen. VII. f. 5 (Pasch. pl. 1). The result is curious, for the owner has had no action against the second non-felonious trespasser.

[3] Two striking illustrations are given by Ames, Harv. L. R. iii. 24.

[4] See Placit. Abbrev. for the last years of Henry III.

[5] There may have been a brief hesitation about this; Maitland, Harv. L. R. iii. 173.

assault and battery a compensation in money is the appropriate
remedy. But it is so also if the plaintiff complains of an
invasion of his land. Whatever may happen at a later day, the
writ of trespass is as yet no proper writ for a man who has been
disseised of land. A whole scheme of actions, towering upwards
from the novel disseisin to the writ of right, is provided for
one who is being kept out of land that he ought to possess.
To have made the action recuperatory (*rei persecutoria*) in the
case of chattels would have been an anomaly; in Henry III.'s
day it might even have been an improper interference with
[p. 166] the old *actio furti;* but at any rate it would have been
an anomaly. Therefore the man whose goods have been
taken away from him can by writ of trespass recover, not
his goods, but a pecuniary equivalent for them; and the writ
of trespass is beginning to be his only remedy, unless he is
hardy enough to charge the defendant with larceny[1].

This is not all. Whatever subsequent ages may think, an
action of trespass *de bonis asportatis* is not an action that should
be brought against the third hand, against one who has come to
the goods through or under the wrongful taker, or against one
who has wrongfully taken them from one who is not the
plaintiff[2]. The man who has bought goods from the trespasser,
how has he broken the king's peace and why should he be sent
to gaol? As to the second trespasser, the action *de bonis
asportatis* would have fallen out of touch with its important
and influential neighbour the action *de clauso fracto*, if it could
have been brought against any one but the original wrong-doer.
If I am disseised of land and one disseises my disseisor, a writ
of trespass is not my remedy against him; I want land, not
money, and a proper action is provided for me. It would be
an anomaly to suffer the writ of trespass to do for the disseisee
of a chattel what it will not do for the disseisee of land. The
mischief is that the two cases are not parallel. The disseisee
of land has plenteous actions though the writ of trespass be
denied him, while the disseisee of a chattel, when the barbaric
actio furti was falling into oblivion, had none. And so we
arrive at this lamentable result which prevails for a while:—
If my chattel be taken from me by another wrongfully but not

No action
of trespass
against the
third hand.

---

[1] Britton, i. 123, cautions his readers against the appeal; it is perilous; the writ of trespass is safer.

[2] See Ames, Harv. L. R. iii. 29.

feloniously, then I can have no action against any third person
who at a subsequent time possesses it or meddles with it; my
one and only action is an action of trespass against the original
taker[1].   A lamentable result we call this, not so much because
it may have done some injustice to men who are long since [p. 167]
dead and buried, as because for centuries it bewildered our
lawyers, made them ascribe 'property' to trespassers and even
to thieves, and entailed upon us a confused vocabulary, from
the evil effects of which we are but slowly freeing ourselves[2].

Self help.   As to self-help, we must not suppose that the owner's
rights of action were supplemented by a right of recapture.
The old procedure was a procedure by way of self-help and
recapture; but it was no formless procedure; it was a solemn
legal act.   In the presence of the possessor the pursuer laid
hand on the beast and in set phrase he claimed it.   We may be
pretty certain that if, neglecting ceremonies, he just took his
own behind the possessor's back, he was laying himself open to
a charge of theft.   Even at the end of the thirteenth century
he was hazarding the loss of his rights.   Britton supposes that
John appeals Peter of stealing a horse, and that Peter says,
'The horse was mine and as mine I took it.'   If Peter succeeds
in proving this assertion, he escapes the gallows, but he loses
the horse for good and all, 'for' (King Edward is supposed to

---

[1] In the case of two felonious takings I can still obtain restitution by
appealing the second thief. See above, p. 166. We shall see hereafter that for a
long time 'detinue' can not be brought against any but the plaintiff's bailee, and
to say that the owner has neither trespass nor detinue, is to say that he has no
action against the third hand, unless there be felony. Gradually 'detinue' is
extended and 'trover' is invented; but a great deal of harm has been done in
the meanwhile.

[2] In the foregoing paragraphs we have had in view Mr J. B. Ames's papers
on the Disseisin of Chattels, Harv. L. R. vol. iii. The two criticisms that we
have to make on those masterly articles are these. (1) Their learned author
has hardly offered a sufficient explanation of the fact that at one point the
analogy between land and chattels breaks down. The disseisee of land has, the
disseisee of chattels has not, an action against the third hand. (2) It seems to
us that this difference can not be regarded as being of vast antiquity or as having
its origin among the ideas of substantive law. The old *actio furti* with its chain
of warrantors shows that the disseisee once had an action against the twentieth
hand. Whatever may be thought of our argument about the scope of trespass,
it seems to us clear that at this point we have to deal, not with a defective
conception of ownership, but with an unfortunate accident, which has momentous
effects because it happens just at the time when the writs are crystallizing for
good and all. The old action disappears; a new one is put in its place, but
can not fill that place.

say) 'we will that every one shall have recourse to judgment
rather than to force[1].' Our common law, which in later days
has allowed a wide sphere to recapture[2]—a sphere the width of
which would astonish foreign lawyers—seems to have started in
the twelfth and thirteenth centuries with a stringent prohibition of informal self-help, and a rigorous exclusion of proprietary pleas from the possessory action of trespass. Thus far it
applied a common rule to land and to chattels; but while in the
[p. 168] one case the disseisor, after being ousted from the land, might
fall back upon those legal methods that he had despised, in the
other case no place of penitence was allowed him; he lost for
good and all the thing that was his, because he had taken it to
himself.

Thus far we have been dealing with what in our eyes
is an unlucky chapter of mishaps, which in the fourteenth
century has deprived the owner of a remedy which he would
have had in the twelfth century, namely, of an action against
the third hand for the recovery of goods that had been wrongfully taken. We have now to speak of a more vital rule and
one that appears in many lands besides our own.

II. Hitherto we have supposed that the thing in question   The
was taken from the owner's possession. We have next to   bailment
suppose that the owner has bailed the thing to another. And
here we may remark that our medieval law has but a meagre
stock of words that can be used to describe dealings with
movable goods. The owner, whenever and for whatever purpose he delivers possession of his chattel to another, is said to
bail it to that other (Fr. *bailler*, Lat. *tradere, liberare*). This
word is used even when he is indubitably parting with ownership, when he delivers a sold thing to the buyer, or when he
makes a 'loan for consumption' (*mutui datio*)[3]. In more modern
times we have restricted the term *bailment* to cases in which
there is no transfer of ownership, to cases in which the goods,
after the lapse of a certain time or upon the happening of a
certain event, are to be delivered by the bailee to the bailor or
his nominee. Even these cases are miscellaneous; but our

---

[1] Britton, i. 115-6.

[2] *Blades* v. *Higgs*, 10 C. B. N. s. 713; Pollock, Law of Torts (5th ed.), p. 362.
It is far from clear that the decision would now be approved by a higher Court.

[3] A plaintiff who sues for a money debt usually counts that he 'bailed' a
certain sum to the defendant; *e.g.* Y. B. 21-2 Edw. I. p. 255.

lawyers found no great need of words which would distinguish
between the various forms of bailment, the pledge, the deposit
for safe custody, the delivery to a carrier or to an artizan who
is to do work upon the thing, the gratuitous loan for use and
return, the letting for hire. All these transactions are regarded as having much in common; one term will stand for
them all[1]. And all these transactions were known in the
thirteenth century: for example, the deposit for safe custody [p. 169]
of those valuable chattels, the title-deeds of land was not
uncommon.

The bailee
has the
action
against
the wrong-
doer.

Now if goods were unlawfully taken from the possession of
the bailee, it was he that had the action against the wrong-
doer; it was for him to bring the appeal of larceny or the
action of trespass[2]. And, having thus given the action to the
bailee, we must in all probability deny it to the bailor. As
already said, in the days when the *actio furti* still preserved
many of its ancient characteristics, when it began with hue and
cry and hot pursuit, it was natural that the bailee, rather than
the bailor, should sue the wrongful possessor. But already in
the thirteenth century a force was at work which tended to
disturb this arrangement.

Liability
of bailees.

The nature of this force we shall understand if we turn to
the question that arises between the bailor and the bailee when
the goods have been taken from the bailee by a third person.
We are likely to find the rule that the bailee has the action
against the stranger in close connexion with a rule that makes
the bailee absolutely responsible to the bailor for the safe
return of the goods:—if they are taken from him, he, however
careful he may have been, must pay their value to the bailor.
We have good reason to believe that this rule had been law in

---

[1] Even the *mutuum* is not kept apart from the *commodatum*, though Bracton,
f. 99, knows the difference. Very often the lender is said *commodare* or
accommodare pecuniam, which the borrower is said *mutuare*; see *e.g.* Note Book,
pl. 568, 830. To this day we Englishmen are without words which neatly mark
the distinction. We *lend* books and half-crowns to *borrowers*; we hope to see
the same books again, but not the same half-crowns; still in either case there
is a *loan*. Gibbon, Decline and Fall, c. 44: ' The Latin language very happily
expresses the fundamental difference between the *commodatum* and the *mutuum*,
which our poverty is reduced to confound under the vague and common appel-
lation of a loan.'

[2] Bracton, f. 151: ' et non refert utrum res quae ita subtracta fuerit, extiterit illius appellantis propria vel alterius, dum tamen de custodia sua.'

England[1]. In 1200 a plaintiff asserts that two charters were delivered to the defendant for custody; the defendant pleads that they were robbed from him when his house was burnt and that he is appealing the robbers; the plaintiff craves judgment on this admission by the defendant that the charters were lost out of his custody; the defendant makes default and judgment is given against him[2]. Glanvill holds that the commodatary is absolutely bound to restore the thing or its value[3]. Bracton, however, with the Institutes before him, seems inclined to mitigate the old rule. Apparently he would hold the depositary liable only in the case of *dolus;* the *conductor* can escape if he has shown a due diligence, and so can the pledgee, and it seems that even the commodatary may escape, though we can not be very certain as to the limits of the liability that Bracton would [p.170] cast upon him[4]. There is much in later history to make us believe that Bracton's attempt to state this part of our law in romanesque terms was premature[5]; but none the less it is plain that already in his day English lawyers were becoming familiar with the notion that bailees need not be absolutely responsible for the return of the chattels bailed to them, and that some bailees should perhaps be absolved if they have attained a certain standard of diligence[6]. Now this notion may easily begin to react upon the rule which equips every bailee with the action against the wrongful taker and denies that action to the bailor. Perhaps we come nearest to historical truth if we say that between the two old rules there was no logical priority. The bailee had the action because he was liable

[1] Holmes, Common Law, p. 175. To the contrary, Beale, Harv. L. R. xi. 158.

[2] Select Civil Pleas (Selden Society), pl. 8.   [3] Glanvill, x. 13.

[4] Bracton, f. 62 b, 99; Fleta, p. 120–1; Güterbock, Bracton and his Relation to Roman Law (tr. Coxe), pp. 141, 175; Scrutton, Law Quarterly Review, i. 136. We have examined many MSS of Bracton's work for the purpose of discovering the true reading of the well-known passage on f. 99; but, so far as we can see, the vulgate text is right in representing him as applying to a case of *commodatum* the words which the Institutes apply to a case of *mutuum.* See Bracton and Azo, p. 146.

[5] Holmes, Common Law, p. 176.

[6] In 1299 the Prior of Brinkburn brings detinue for charters bailed to the defendant for safe custody. The defendant alleges that the charters had been seized by robbers along with his own goods, and that they cut off the seals; he tenders the charters which have now no seals. The Prior confesses the truth of the defence and the action is dismissed. See the record in Brinkburn Cartulary, p. 105.

and was liable because he had the action[1]. But, when once a
limit is set to his liability, then men will begin to regard his
right of action as the outcome of his liability, and if in any case
he is not liable, then they will have to reconsider the position
of the bailor and perhaps will allow him to sue the wrongful
taker.   In Bracton's text and in the case-law of Bracton's day
we may see this tendency at work, a tendency to require of the
bailee who brings an appeal of larceny or an action of trespass
something more than mere possession, some interest in the
thing, some responsibility for its safety.   But as yet it has not
gone very far[2].

The bailor
and the
third hand.
That the bailor has no action against any person other than [p. 171]
his bailee, no action against one who takes the thing from his
bailee, no action against one to whom the bailee has sold or
bailed the thing—this is a proposition that we nowhere find
stated in all its breadth. No English judge or text-writer hands
down to us any such maxim as *Mobilia non habent sequelam.*
Nevertheless, we can hardly doubt that this is the starting-
point of our common law. We come to this result if one by
one we test the several actions which the bailor might attempt
to use.   These are but three[3]: (1) the appeal of larceny, (2) the
action of trespass, and (3) the action of detinue. The first two
would be out of the question unless there had been an unlawful
taking, and in that case, as already said, there seem to be

---

[1] Mr Justice Holmes, Common Law, p. 167, maintains the priority of the rule
that gives the action to the bailee. But we may at all events believe that at an
early date the refusal to the bailor of an action against the taker was justified
by the argument that he must look to his bailee.   It seems to be this argument
that is embodied in the German proverb *Hand muss Hand wahren.* See Heusler,
Gewere, p. 495.

[2] Bracton, f. 103 b, 146, more than once seems to require that the appellor
shall complain of a theft of his own goods or of goods for which he has made
himself responsible, for which *intravit in solutionem erga dominum suum.* This
phrase is actually used by appellors in 1203, Select Pleas of the Crown, pl. 88, 126.
It is to be remembered that at this time the limit between the servant's *custody*
and the bailee's *possession* is not well marked; both are often called *custodia.*
The law has to be on its guard to prevent masters from setting their servants to
bring appeals which they dare not bring themselves.   A servant is not to bring
an appeal for the theft of his master's goods unless he has in some definite way
become answerable for their safe keeping.   But it is also to be remembered that
Bracton is thinking of Inst. 4. 2. 2, where it is required of the plaintiff in an
action *bonorum raptorum* that he shall have some interest in the thing, 'ut
intersit eius non rapi.' See Bracton and Azo, p. 183.

[3] At present the action of replevin needs no mention, for its scope is very
limited. See Ames, Harv. L. R. iii. 31.

ample reasons for believing that the taker could be successfully attacked by the bailee and by him only[1].

But at first sight there seems to be one action open to the bailor, the action of detinue. This action slowly branches off from the action of debt. The writ of debt as given by Glanvill is closely similar to that form of the writ of right for land which is known as a *Praecipe in capite.* The sheriff is to bid the defendant render to the plaintiff so many marks or shillings, 'which, so the plaintiff says, the defendant owes him, and whereof he unjustly deforces him'; and if the defendant will not do this, then he is to give his reason in the king's court. The writ is couched in terms which would not be inappropriate were the plaintiff seeking the restoration of certain specific coins, of which he was the owner, but which were in the defendant's keeping. Very shortly after Glanvill's day this form gave way to another somewhat better fitted to express the relation between a debtor and a creditor:—the word 'deforces' was dropped; the debtor is to render to the creditor so many pounds or shillings 'which he owes and unjustly detains[2].' This was the formula of 'debt in the *debet et detinet,*' a formula to be used when the original creditor sued the original debtor. If, however, there had been a death on the one side or on the other, then the word *debet* was not in place; the representative of the creditor could only charge the debtor with 'unjustly detaining' money, and only with an unjust detention could the representative of the debtor be charged. In such cases there is an action of debt 'merely in the *detinet*[3].' At the same time the claim for a particular chattel is being distinguished from the claim for a certain quantity of money, or of corn or the like. If a man claims a particular object, he ought not to use the word *debet*; he should merely say *iniuste detinet.*

The action of detinue.

[p. 172]

---

[1] A century later, in 1374, Y. B. 48 Edw. III. f. 20 (Mich. pl. 8), it is allowed that either the bailor or the bailee can sue in trespass. See Holmes, Common Law, p. 171. But this applies only to a bailment at will. If the bailment was for a fixed term, the bailor could not bring trespass.

[2] A few cases of debt are to be found in the Plea Rolls of Richard I.; Rot. Cur. Reg. (Palgrave), i. 39, 380; ii. 9, 106; and of John; Select Civil Pleas (Baildon), pl. 38, 83, 102, 146, 173, 174. They become commoner in the Note Book, yet commoner on the latest rolls of Henry III. The writ appears in the earliest Registers; see Harv. L. R. iii. 112, 114, 172, 215. We shall speak of it again in the next chapter.

[3] Reg. Brev. Orig. 139 b.

Roughly this distinction may seem to us to correspond with
that between contractual and proprietary claims; the action of
debt may look like the outcome of contract, while the action of
detinue is a vindication based upon proprietary right. The
correspondence, however, is but rough. A nascent perception
of 'obligation' seems to be involved in the rules that prevail as
to the use of the word *debet*, but this is struggling with a cruder
idea which would be satisfied with a distinction between current
coins on the one hand and all other movable things upon the
other. It is with detinue, not with debt, that we are here
concerned; but it was very needful that the close connexion
between these two actions should not escape us.

Scope of
detinue.

Now at first sight the writ of detinue seems open to every
one who for any cause whatever can claim from another the
possession of a chattel:—*X*, the defendant, is to give up a thing
which he wrongfully detains (*iniuste detinet*) from *A*, the
plaintiff, or to explain why he has not done so. But so soon as [p. 173]
we begin to examine the scope and effect of the action, two
remarkable phenomena meet our eye. In the first place, if *X*
chooses to be obstinate, he can not be compelled to deliver the
chattel—let us say the ox—to *A*. In his count *A* will be
bound to put some value upon the ox:—*X*, he will say, is
detaining from me an ox worth five shillings. If he makes
good his claim, the judgment will be that he recover his ox
or its value assessed by a jury, and if *X* chooses to pay the
money rather than deliver up the ox, he will by so doing satisfy
the judgment. If he is still obstinate, then the sheriff will be
bidden to sell enough of his chattels to make the sum awarded
by the jurors and will hand it over to the plaintiff. In a
memorable passage Bracton has spoken of this matter: memorable for to it we may trace all our talk about 'real and personal
property.' 'It would seem at first sight,' he says, 'that the
action in which a movable is demanded should be as well *in
rem* as *in personam* since a specific thing is demanded and the
possessor is bound to restore that thing; but in truth it is
merely *in personam*, for he from whom the thing is demanded
is not absolutely bound to restore it, but is bound alternatively
to restore it or its price; and this, whether the thing be forthcoming or no. And therefore, if a man vindicates his movable
chattel as having been carried off for any cause, or as having
been lent (*commodatam*), he must in his action define its price,

and propound his claim thus :—I, such an one, demand that such an one do restore to me such a thing of such a price :—or —I complain that such an one detains from me, or has robbed me of, such a thing of such a price :—otherwise, no price being named, the vindication of a movable thing will fail[1].'

For a moment we may think that Bracton has gone astray among the technical terms of a foreign system. We may argue against him that the 'vindication' of a chattel, if it really be a vindication, if it be an assertion of ownership, is not the less an action *in rem* because the court will not go all lengths to restore that chattel to its owner, but will do its best to give him what is of equal value. But there is a second phenomenon to be [p.174] considered. Bracton says nothing about it, though possibly it was in his mind when he wrote this passage. No one, so far as we know, says anything about it for a long time to come, and yet in our eyes it will be strange. It is this :—despite the generality of the writ, the bailor of a chattel can never bring this action against any one save his bailee or those who represent his bailee by testate or intestate succession. In later days there are but two modes of 'counting' in detinue[2]. The plaintiff must say either, 'I lost the goods and you found them,' or, 'I bailed the chattel to you[3].' The first of these counts (*detinue sur trover*) was called a 'new found haliday' in the fifteenth century[4]. We have, however, some reason for believing that it had been occasionally used in earlier times[5]. In the present context it is of no great interest to us, for if the owner has accidentally lost his chattel, that chattel has gone from him against his will, and we are here dealing with cases in which the owner has given up possession to another. In such cases there is clearly no place—if words mean anything—for *detinue sur trover*, for there has been no loss and finding. We must see what can be done with *detinue sur bailment*; and we come to the result that this action will not lie against the third

^{No real action for movables.}

---

¹ Bracton, f. 102 b ; Bracton and Azo, p. 172.

² We may here neglect the action by the widow or child for a 'reasonable part' of a dead man's goods.

³ A variation on the latter count will be required in an action against the bailee's executor or administrator.

⁴ Y. B. 33 Hen. VI. f. 26–7 (Trin. pl. 12) ; Holmes, Common Law, p. 169.

⁵ Y. B. 21–2 Edw. I. 466 ; 2 Edw. III. f. 2 (Hil. pl. 5) ; Ames, Harv. L. R. iii. 33. In yet earlier times the finder who did not take the witness of his neighbours to the finding would have stood in danger of an *actio furti*.

hand. In other words, *A* bails a chattel to *M*, and *M* wrongfully gives or sells or bails it to *X*, or *X* wrongfully takes it from *M*:—in none of these cases has *A* an action against *X*; his only action is against *M*. In times much later than those with which we are dealing, lawyers will have begun to say that these phrases about trover and bailment, though one of them must be used, are not 'traversable': that the defendant must not catch hold of them and say, 'You did not lose, I did not find,' or, 'You did not bail to me,' but must deny that wrongful detention which has become the gist of the action. It was not always so; it was not so in the thirteenth century[1]. Early in the fifteenth a man bailed chattels for safe custody to a woman; she took a husband and died; her husband would not restore the goods; the bailor went to the chancery saying that he had no remedy at the common law[2]. Apparently in this instance, as in some other instances, the common law held to its old rule until an interference of the chancellor's equity was imminent.

Has the bailor property? How shall we explain this? Shall we say that the man who [p. 175] bails his chattel to another parts with the ownership of it, that in exchange for ownership he takes a promise, and that the refusal to call his action an action *in rem* is fully justified, for he has no right *in rem* but only a right *in personam*? There is much to attract us in this answer. It has the plausible merit of being definite; it deals with modes of thought to which we are accustomed. What is more to the purpose, it seems to explain the close relation—in form it is almost identity—between detinue and debt. But unfortunately it is much too definite. Were it true, then the bailee ought consistently to be thought of and spoken of as the owner of the thing. But this is not the case. For example, Bracton in the very sentence in which he concedes to the bailee the appeal of larceny, denies that he is the owner of the things that have been bailed to him. Such things are in his keeping, but they are the things of another[3]. Indeed the current language of

---

[1] Already in 1292 we see a slight tendency to regard the detainer rather than the bailment as the gist of the action. Y. B. 20–1 Edw. I. p. 192: it is not enough to say, 'You did not bail to me': one must add, 'and I do not detain from you.' But there are much later cases which show that it is impossible, or at least extremely hard, for the bailor to fashion any count that will avail him against the third hand: Y. B. 16 Edw. II. f. 490; Ames, Harv. L. R., iii. 33.

[2] Select Cases in Chancery (Seld. Soc.) p. 113.

[3] Bracton, f. 151: 'et non refert utrum res quae ita subtracta fuerit, extiterit

the time is apt to speak of the bailee as having but a *custodia* (Fr. *garde*) of the goods and to avoid such terms as *possessio* and *seisina*, though the bailee has remedies against all who disturb him. The thought has even crossed men's minds that a bailee can commit theft. Glanvill explains that this is impossible since the bailee comes to the thing by delivery[1]; but he would not have been at pains to tell us that a man can not steal what he both possesses and owns. The author of the Mirror recounts among the exploits of King Alfred that 'he hanged Bulmer because he adjudged Gerent to death, by colour of larceny of a thing which he had received by title of bailment[2].' This romancer's stories of King Alfred have for the more part some point in the doings of the court of Edward I., and it is not inconceivable that some of its justices had shown an inclination to anticipate the legislators of the nineteenth century by [p.176] punishing fraudulent bailees as thieves. But to us the convincing argument is that, if once the bailee had been conceived as owner, and the bailor's action as purely contractual, the bailor could never have become the owner by insensible degrees and without definite legislation. We know, however, that this happened; before the end of the middle ages the bailor is the owner, has 'the general property' in the thing, and no statute has given him this. Lastly, we must add that, as will appear in the next chapter, to make the bailor's right a mere right *ex contractu* is to throw upon the nascent law of contract a weight that it will not bear. The writ of detinue is closely connected with the writ of debt; but then the writ of debt is closely connected with the writ of right, the most proprietary and most 'real' of all actions.

The explanation we believe to be that the evolution of legal Evolution remedies has in this instance lagged behind the evolution of of ownership. morality. The law of property in land may be younger than the law of property in chattels, but has long ago outstripped its feebler rival. There may have been a time when such idea of ownership as was then entertained was adequately expressed in a mere protection against theft. From century to century the

---

illius appellantis propria vel alterius, dum tamen de custodia sua.' So Glanvill, x. 13: 'Ex causa quoque commodati solet res aliqua quandoque deberi, ut si rem meam tibi gratis commodem ad usum inde percipiendum in servitio tuo; expleto quidem servitio, *rem meam* mihi teneris reddere.'

[1] Glanvill, x. 13.   [2] Mirror (Seld. Soc.), p. 169.

pursuit and punishment of thieves and the restoration of
chattels to those from whom they have been stolen were the
main objects which the law had set itself to attain. Meanwhile
'bailments,' as we call them, of goods were becoming common.
As against the thief and those who receive the goods from the
thief, it was the bailee who required legal weapons. They were
given him, and, when he has assumed them, he looks, at least
to our eyes, very like an owner. But men do not think of him
as the owner; they do not think of his bailor as one who has a
mere contractual right. At all events so long as the goods are
in the possession of the bailee, they are the goods of the bailor.
If the men of the thirteenth century, or of yet earlier times,
had been asked why the bailor had no action against the third
hand, they would not have said, 'Because he has only a contract
to rely upon and a contract binds but those who make it'; they
would, we believe, have said, 'We and our fathers have got on
well enough without such an action.' Their thoughts are not
our thoughts; we can not at will displace from our minds the
dilemma '*in rem* or *in personam*' which seems to have been put
there by natural law. We can not rethink the process which
lies hidden away in the history of those two words *owe* and
own. What is owing to me, do I not own it, and is it not my
own? Nevertheless what has already been said about the
'pecuniary' character of chattels may give us some help in [p. 177]
our effort to represent the past.

Pecuniary
character
of chattels.
We have seen that when a man claims a chattel our law
will make no strenuous effort to give him the very thing that
he asks for. If he gets the value of the thing, he must be satisfied, and the thing itself may be left to the wrong-doer. Absurd
as this rule might seem to us now-a-days, it served Englishmen well enough until the middle of the nineteenth century;
it showed itself to be compatible with peace and order and an
abundant commerce[1]. In older times it was a natural rule because of the pecuniary character of chattels. If one man has
deposited a sovereign with another, or has lent that other a
sovereign, the law will hardly be at pains to compel the
restitution of that particular coin; an equivalent coin will do
just as well. Our language shows that this is so. When we

---

[1] See above, p. 154. Though the Court of Chancery was prepared to compel
the delivery of chattels of exceptional value, applications for this equitable
remedy were not very common.

speak of money being 'deposited,' we almost always mean that
money is 'lent,' and when we speak of money being 'lent,' we
almost always mean that the ownership of the coins has passed
from the lender to the borrower; we think of *mutuum* not of
commodatum. But more than this can be said. True 'bailments' of coins do sometimes occur; coins may be deposited in
the hands of one who is bound not to spend them but to keep
them safely and restore them; they may even be 'commodated,'
that is, lent for use and return, as if one lends a sovereign in
order that the borrower may perform some conjuring trick with
it and give it back again. In these cases our modern criminal
law marks the fact that the ownership in the coins has not been
transferred to the bailee, for it will punish the bailee as a thief
if he appropriates them[1]. But then, this is the result, sometimes of a modern statute[2], sometimes of the modern conception
of delivery for a strictly limited purpose not being a bailment
at all; and if we carry back our thoughts to a time when
the bailee will not be committing theft or any other crime in
appropriating the bailed chattel, then we shall see that a
bailment of coins can hardly be distinguished for any practical
purpose from what we ordinarily call a loan (*mutui datio*) of
money. In the one case the ownership in the coins has been, in
the other it has not been, transferred; but how can law mark
this difference? The bailee does all that can be required of
him if he tenders equivalent coins, and those who, dealing with
him in good faith, receive from him the bailed coins, will
become owners of them. Some rare case will be required to
show that the bailee is not the owner of them. And now if we
repeat that the difference seen by modern law between coins
and oxen is not aboriginal, we come almost of necessity to the
result that there was a time when the lender of an ox or other
thing might be called and thought of as its owner and yet have
no action to recover it or its value, except one which could be
made to look very like an action for a debt created by contract.

[p. 178]

---

[1] Pollock and Wright, Possession, 161-3.

[2] Stat. 20-1 Vic. c. 54, sec. 4; 24-5 Vic. c. 96, sec. 3. The doctrine that a
bailee might be guilty of theft if he 'determined the bailment' before he
misappropriated the goods, has not been traced back beyond the celebrated
carrier's case in 1474 (Y. B. 13 Ed. IV. f. 9, Pasch. p. 5), where it seems to
have been forced upon the judges by the chancellor for the satisfaction of
foreign merchants.

An elementary question.

We must not be wise above what is written or more precise than the lawyers of the age. Here is an elementary question that was debated in the year 1292:—I bail a charter for safe custody to a married woman; her husband dies; can I bring an action of detinue against her, it being clear law that a married woman can not bind herself by contract? This is the way in which that question is discussed:—

Huntingdon. Sir, our plaint is of a tortious detinue of a charter which this lady is now detaining from us. We crave judgment that she ought to answer for her tort.

Lowther. The cause of your action is the bailment; and at that time she could not bind herself. We crave judgment if she must now answer for a thing about which she could not bind herself.

Spigurnel. If you had bailed to the lady thirty marks for safe custody while she was coverte for return to you when you should demand them, would she be now bound to answer? I trow not. And so in this case.

Howard. The cases are not similar; for in a writ of debt you shall say *debet,* while here you shall say *iniuste detinet.* And again, in this case an action arises from a tortious detainer and not from the bailment. We crave judgment.

Lowther. We repeat what we have said[1].

Any one who attempts to carry into the reign of Edward I. [p. 179 a neat theory about the ownership and possession of movables must be prepared to read elementary lectures on 'general jurisprudence' to the acutest lawyers of that age.

Conveyance of movables.

There are other questions about movables that we should like to ask; but we shall hardly answer them out of the materials that are at hand. We think it fairly certain that the ownership of a chattel could not be transferred from one person to another, either by way of gift, or by way of sale, without a *traditio rei,* also that the only known gage of movables was what we should call a pawn or pledge, which has its inception in a transfer of possession. In Bracton's eyes the necessity for a livery of seisin is no peculiarity of the land law[2]. In order to transfer the ownership of any corporeal thing we must transfer

---

[1] Y. B. 20–1 Edw. I. p. 191. The question what was the nature of the action of detinue remained open till our own time. See *Bryant* v. *Herbert,* 3 C. P. D. 389.

[2] Bracton, f. 38 b; f. 41: 'idem est de mercibus in orreis.

the possession of it.   Naturally, however, we hear much less of
the livery of goods than of the livery of land.   When land is
delivered it is highly expedient that there should be some
ceremonies performed which will take root in the memory of the
witnesses.   In the case of chattels formal acts would be useless,
since there is no probability that the fact of transfer will be
called in question at a distant day.   Besides, in this case the
court has not to struggle against the tendency to substitute a
sham for the reality, a 'symbolical investiture' for a real change
of possession; there is not much danger that the giver of
chattels will endeavour both to give and to keep.   At a later
time our common law allowed that the ownership of a chattel
could be transferred by the execution, or rather the delivery, of
a sealed writing; but as this appears to have been a novelty
in the fifteenth century[1], we can hardly suppose that it was
already known in the thirteenth.   Nor is it clear that even
at the later time a gift by deed was thought to confer more
than an irrevocable right to possess the goods.   We doubt
whether, according to medieval law, one could ever be full
owner of goods, unless as executor, without having acquired
actual possession.   We do not doubt that the modern refinements of 'constructive delivery' were unthought of, at all
events in the thirteenth century.   Of sales we shall speak in
the next chapter.

In dealing with chattels we have wandered far from the Land and
beaten track of traditional exposition.   Had we followed it we chattels.
should have begun by explaining that chattels are not 'real
property,' not 'hereditaments,' not 'tenements.'   But none of
the distinctions to which these terms point seem to go to the
root of the matter.   If by a denial of the 'realty' of movable
goods we merely mean (as is generally meant) that their owner,
when he sues for them, can be compelled to take their value
instead of them, this seems a somewhat superficial phenomenon,
[p. 180] and it is not very ancient.   So long as the old procedure for the
recovery of stolen goods was in use, so long even as the appellor
could obtain his writ of restitution, there was an action, and at
one time a highly important action, which would give the owner
his goods.   Also, as modern experience shows, a very true and
intense ownership of goods can be pretty well protected by

---

[1] Y. B. 7 Ed. IV. f. 20, pl. 21.

P M II

actions in which nothing but money can with any certainty be obtained. Indeed when our orthodox doctrine has come to be that land is not owned but that 'real actions' can be brought for it, while no 'real action' can be brought for just those things which are the subjects of 'absolute ownership,' it is clear enough that this 'personalness' of 'personal property' is a superficial phenomenon. Again, in the thirteenth century —this we shall see hereafter—the distinction which in later days was indicated by the term 'hereditaments' was not as yet very old, nor had it as yet eaten very deeply into the body of the law. Lastly, the fact that movables are not made the subjects of 'feudal tenure,' though it is of paramount importance, is not a fact which explains itself. It is not unlikely that some of the first stages in the process which built up the lofty edifice of feudalism were accomplished by loans of cattle, rather than by loans of land. Of course we must not seem to deny that rights in land played a part in the constitution of society and in the development of public law which rights in chattels did not and could not play; but we have not told the whole of the story until we have said that the dogma of retrospective feudalism which denies that there is any absolute ownership of land (save in the person of the king) derives all such truth as it contains from a conception of ownership as a right that must be more complete and better protected than was that ownership of chattels which the thirteenth century and earlier ages knew. On the land *dominium* rises above *dominium*; a long series of lords who are tenants and of tenants who are lords have rights over the land and remedies against all the world. This is possible because the rights of every one of them can be and is realized in a seisin; *duae possessiones sese compatiuntur in una re.* It is otherwise with the owner of a chattel. If he bails it to another, at all events if he bails it on terms that deprive him of the power to reclaim it at will, he abandons every sort and kind of seisin; this makes it difficult for us to treat him as an owner should be treated, for it is hard for us to think of an ownership that is not and ought not to be realized in a seisin. [p. 181] We may call him owner or say that the thing belongs to him, but our old-fashioned law treats him very much as if he had no 'real' right and no more than the benefit of a contract. Hence the dependent tenure of a chattel is impossible. This, if we approach the distinction from the side of jurisprudence, rather than from the side of constitutional or economic history, seems to be its core. The compatibility of divers seisins permits the rapid development of a land law which will give to both letter and hirer, feoffor and feoffee, rights of a very real and intense kind in the land, each protected by its own appropriate action, at a time when the backward and meagre law of personal property can hardly sanction two rights in one thing, and will not be dissatisfied with itself if it achieves the punishment of thieves and the restitution of stolen goods to those from whose seisin they have been taken.

CHAPTER V.

CONTRACT.

Late development of a law of contract.

THE law of contract holds anything but a conspicuous place among the institutions of English law before the Norman Conquest. In fact it is rudimentary. Many centuries must pass away before it wins that dominance which we at the present day concede to it. Even in the schemes of Hale and Blackstone it appears as a mere supplement to the law of property. The Anglo-Saxon dooms tell us but little about it; they tell us less the more carefully we examine them. For example, certain provisions which may seem at first sight to show a considerable development in this department turn out, on closer scrutiny, to have a wholly different bearing. There are many ordinances requiring men who traffic in cattle to make their purchases openly and before good witnesses[1]. But they really have nothing to do with enforcing a contract of sale between the parties. Their purpose is to protect an honest buyer against possible claims by some third person alleging that the beasts were stolen from him. If the Anglo-Saxon *teám* was an ancestor of the later law of warranty in one line, and of rules of proof, ultimately to be hardened into rules of the law of contract, in another, the results were undesigned and indirect. Anglo-Saxon society barely knew what credit was, and had no occasion for much regulation of contracts. We find the same state of things throughout northern and western Europe. Ideas assumed as fundamental by this branch of law in modern times and so familiar to modern lawyers as apparently to need no explanation had perished in the general breaking up of the

---

[1] Schmid, Gesetze, Glossar, s. v. *Marktrecht.*

[p. 183] Roman system, and had to be painfully reconstructed in the middle ages. Further, it is not free from doubt (though we have no need to dwell upon it here) how far the Romans themselves had attained to truly general conceptions. In any case the Germanic races, not only of the Karolingian period, but down to a much later time, had no general notion whatever of promise or agreement as a source of civil obligation. Early Germanic law recognized, if we speak in Roman terms, only Formal and Real Contracts. It had not gone so far as to admit a Consensual Contract in any case. Sale, for example, was a Real, not a Consensual transaction. All recent inquirers seem to concur in accepting this much as having been conclusively established[1].

Beyond this there is much ground that is debatable, and we have no reason for believing that the order of events was exactly the same in all the countries of western Europe; indeed it is plain that at latest in the thirteenth century our English law was taking a course of its own. One main question is as to the derivation of the 'formal contract' of old Germanic law from the 'real contract.' Some 'real contracts,' or transactions that we should regard as such, must appear at a very early time. Sale and exchange, it may be, are as yet only known to the law as completed transactions, which leave no outstanding duty to be enforced; no credit has been given on either side; the money was paid when the ox was delivered and the parties have never been bound to deliver or to pay. But loans there must soon be, and the borrower ought to return what is lent him. Also a gage (*wed, vadium, gagium*), or as we should now call it a pledge, will sometimes be given[2]. Even in these cases, however, it is long before any idea of contractual obligation

The Real and the Formal Contract.

---

[1] Sohm, Recht der Eheschliessung; Heusler, Institutionen, ii. 225; Schröder, D. R. G., p. 283; Franken, Französisches Pfandrecht, 43; Esmein, Études sur les contrats dans le très-ancien droit français; Viollet, Histoire du droit civil français, 599; Pertile, Storia del diritto italiano, iv. 465: Amira in Paul's Grundriss der Germanischen Philologie, vol. ii. pt. 2, p. 161.

[2] In modern times we use the word *pledge* when a thing is given by way of security. But throughout the middle ages such a thing is a gage, a *vadium*. On the other hand the word *pledge*, which answered to the A.-S. *borh*, was reserved for cases in which there was what we now call *suretyship*; the *plegius* was a surety. Thus the common formula *Pone per vadium et salvos plegios* would, according to our modern use of words, become 'Exact a pledge and safe sureties.' In this chapter we shall give to *gage* and *pledge* their old meanings: a gage is a thing, a pledge is a person.

emerges. The lender claims not what has been promised him [p. 184] but what belongs to him. He does so in the case of the loan for use (*commodatum*); but he does so also in the case of the loan for consumption (*mutuum*); we have already seen how slowly these two cases are distinguished[1]. Then in the case of the gage there probably was at first no outstanding duty on the side of the debtor when once the gage had been given. He had become indebted for a *wergild* or a *bót*; he handed over some thing of sufficient value to cover and more than cover the debt; the debt was satisfied; the only outstanding duty was that of the recipient of the gage, who was bound to hand it back if within due time its giver came to redeem it. But here again, if the gage was not restored, the claim for it would take the form, ' You unjustly detain what is mine[2].' Again, a pledge or surety was in the beginning but an animated gage, a hostage delivered over to slavery but subject to redemption. The *wed* or gage, however, was capable of becoming a symbol; an object which intrinsically was of trifling value might be given and might serve to bind the contract. Among the Franks, whom we must regard as being for many purposes our ancestors in law, it took the shape of the *festuca*.

Fides facta. The formal contract.
Whether this transition from the 'real' to the 'formal' can be accomplished without the intervention of sacral ceremonies seems doubtful. There are some who regard the *festuca* as a stout staff which has taken the place of a spear and is a symbol of physical power[3]. Others see in it a little bit of stick on which imprecatory runes have been cut[4]. It is hard to decide such questions, for, especially under the influence of a new religion, symbols lose their old meanings and are mixed up. Popular etymology confounds confusion. When a straw takes the place of a stick, this we are told is the outcome of speculations which derive the Roman *stipulatio* from *stipula*[5]. Our

---

[1] See above, vol. ii. p. 169.

[2] Wigmore, The Pledge Idea, Harv. L. R. x. 326 ff.

[3] Schröder, D. R. G., p. 60.

[4] Heusler, Institutionen, i. 76.

[5] Heusler, Institutionen, i. 77. It is not unknown in England that in the surrender of copyholds a straw will sometimes take the place of the rod. A straw is inserted in the top of the document which witnesses the surrender of a copyhold and is fixed in that place by seals. The person who is making the surrender holds one end of the straw when he hands the document to the steward. We owe this note to Dr Kenny.

English documents come from too late a time to throw much [p. 185] light upon these archaic problems. The Anglo-Saxon is constantly finding both *wed* and *borh*; but what his *wed* is we do not know. In later times 'the rod' plays a part in the conveyance of land, and is perhaps still more often used when there is a 'quit-claim,' a renunciation of rights[1]; but we sometimes hear of it also when 'faith' is 'made.' Hengham tells us that when an essoiner promises that his principal will appear and warrant the essoin, he makes his faith upon the crier's wand[2], and we find the free miner of the Forest of Dean making his faith upon a holly stick[3]. But at any rate the Franks and Lombards in yet early times came by a binding contractual ceremony, the *fides facta*. At first it seems to be usually performed in court. The duty of paying *wergild* or other *bót* seems to have been that which first led to a legal process of giving credit. Where the sum due was greater (as must have often happened) than the party buying off the feud could raise forthwith, or at any rate produce in a convenient form, he was allowed to pay by instalments on giving security. Originally he must give either gages or hostages which fully secure the sum; at a later time he makes faith 'with gage and pledge'; and among the Franks his gage is a *festuca*. He passes the *festuca* to the creditor who hands it to the pledge. The pledge is bound to the creditor; for a while he is still regarded as a hostage, a hostage who is at large but is bound to surrender himself if called upon to do so. He holds the debtor's *wed* and this gives him power to constrain the debtor to pay the debt. Here is a general form of contract which can be used for a great variety of purposes, and the forms can be abandoned one by one or take weaker shapes. A man may make himself his own pledge by passing the *festuca* from the one hand to

---

[1] See above, vol. ii. p. 91.

[2] Hengham Magna, cap. 6: 'affidatis in manibus vel super virgam clamatoris.' The *clamator* is the crier of the court.

[3] See the Book of Dennis, a custumal of the Forest, of which we have only an English version made in 1673 from an ancient original. It is printed by H. G. Nicholls, Iron Making in the Olden Times (1866), p. 71. 'And there the debtor before the Constable and his Clarke, the Gaveller and the Miners, and none other Folke to plead right but onely the Miners, shall be there and hold a stick of holly and then the said Myner demanding the debt shall putt his hand upon the sticke and none others with him and shall sweare upon his Faith that the said debt is due to him.'

the other[1]. The *festuca* with its runes may be rationalized into a tally stick[2]. If sticks and straws will do, why not any [p. 186] other trifle? A glove becomes the gage of battle. Even this trifle may disappear and leave nothing save an empty hand to be grasped; but this in turn becomes indistinguishable from the distinct and very ancient form of faith-plight by the right hand which we now must mention.

The hand-grasp.

In many countries of western Europe, and in other parts of the world also, we find the mutual grasp of hands (*palmata, paumée, Handschlag*) as a form which binds a bargain. It is possible to regard this as a relic of a more elaborate ceremony by which some material *wed* passed from hand to hand; but the mutuality of the hand-grip seems to make against this explanation. We think it more likely that the promisor proffered his hand in the name of himself and for the purpose of devoting himself to the god or the goddess if he broke faith. Expanded in words, the underlying idea would be of this kind: ' As I here deliver myself to you by my right hand, 'so I deliver myself to the wrath of Fides—or of Jupiter 'acting by the ministry of Fides, *Dius fidius*—if I break faith 'in this thing '[3]. Whether the Germans have borrowed this symbolic act from the Roman provincials and have thus taken over a Roman practice along with the Roman term *fides*, or whether it has an independent root in their own heathen religion, we will not dare to decide[4]. However, the grasp of

---

[1] This is the *Selbstbürgschaft* of German writers; Heusler, Institutionen, ii. 242; Schröder, D. R. G., p. 286.

[2] Heusler, Instit., i. 76, 92.

[3] For the special connexion of Fides with Jupiter, see Ennius, ap. Cic. Off. 3, 29, 104: 'O Fides alma apta pinnis et iusiurandum Iovis.' Cp. Leist, Altarisches Ius Civile, pp. 420 ff. Leist has no doubt (p. 449) that the hand itself was the gage. Promises by oath were said to have been put by Numa under the protection of all the gods, *ib.* 429. Cicero's comment, 'qui ius igitur iurandum violat, is fidem violat' *etc.*, deriving the force of a formal oath from the natural obligation of *fides* implied in it, is a reversal, perhaps a conscious reversal, of the process of archaic morality. Other passages in Cicero show that the cult of Fides was treated as deliberate ethical allegory by educated Romans of his time.

[4] There is abundant authority to show that the Roman custom was both ancient and popular. *Fides* is the special name of *iustitia* as applied *creditis in rebus*: Cic. Orat. Part. c. 22, § 78, cf. Dig. 12, 1, 1. '[Populus Romanus] omnium [virtutum] maxime et praecipue fidem coluit': Gell. 20, 1. See Muirhead, Private Law of Rome, 149, 163; Dion. H. 2, 75; Livy, 1, 21, § 4; and (as to the right hand) Plin. H. N. xi. 45, 103; Servius on Aen. 3. 607; Pacchioni,

[p.187] hands appears among them at an early time as a mode of contracting solemn, if not as yet legally binding, obligations[1]. Probably we ought to keep the mutual grasp apart from another act of great legal efficacy, that of placing one's folded hands within the hands of another in token of subjection. This act, which as the act of homage is to transform the world, appears among our English forefathers in the days of Edward the Elder[2]. But at any rate the feudal, or rather the vassalic, contract is a formal contract and its very essence is *fides*, faith, fealty.

We must, however, remember that agreements sanctioned by sacral forms are not of necessity enforced by law; indeed so long as men firmly believe that the gods interfere with human affairs there may be something akin to profanity in the attempt to take the vow out of their hands and to do for them what they are quite capable of doing for themselves. But the Christian church could not leave sinners to the wrath of God; it was her duty to bring them to repentance. Her action becomes of great importance, because she is beginning to hold courts, to distribute penances according to fixed rules, to evolve law. She transmutes the *fides facta* and makes it her own. She was glad to find a form which was not an oath, but which, even if it did not already involve an ancient sacral element, could be regarded as a transaction directly concerning the Christian faith. She was bound to express some disapprobation of oaths, that is, of unnecessary oaths; she could not blot out the 'Swear not at all' from her sacred books. True that she invented new oaths, the oath upon the relics, the oath upon the gospels. These new oaths took their place beside and then began to drive out the ancient German imprecations. This process was very slow; the heathen oaths

The Church and the fides facta.

Actio ex sponsu (repr. from Archivio Giuridico) Bologna, 1888, on the distinct history of the Stipulation. Brunner, Röm. u. Germ. Urkunde, 222, holds that very possibly the Franks found the provincials using the phrase *fidem facere* to describe the ceremony of stipulation, and borrowed it (they borrowed the word *stipulatio* also) for the purpose of describing their own formal contract. Caesar, B. G., iv. 11, makes certain Germans employ the phrase *iureiurando fidem facere*; Esmein, Études sur les contrats, 73.

[1] See Ducange, s. v. *Dextrae*. Esmein, Études sur les contrats, 98.

[2] Laws of Edward, ii. 6. If a thief forfeits his freedom 'and his hand on hand sylle (*et manum suam in manum mittat*),' he is to be treated as a slave. See Brunner, D. R. G. ii. 270.

on weapons and on rings lived on, though they now occupied a secondary place in the hierarchy of assertions; men would still swear upon a sword in Christian England[1]. True also [p. 188] that the church would enforce oaths by penance and did not nicely distinguish between the assertory and the promissory oath. Already in the seventh century Archbishop Theodore has a graduated scheme of penances for a graduated scheme of oaths. He was not prepared to define a censure for a breach of an oath that was sworn upon the hand of a mere layman; but an oath sworn upon a priest's hand was a different matter[2].

Oath and faith.

Still, as already said, the church was bound to express some disapprobation of unnecessary swearing. The clergy at all events ought to refrain from it. At times it is asserted that even in court a priest should not be compelled to swear; no more should be exacted of him than 'Veritatem in Christo dico, non mentior[3].' A new and a Christian tinge is therefore given to the old contract with *wed* and *borh*. It may look like an oath; we may think that it implicitly contains all the essentials of an oath; but no relic or book or other thing is sworn upon and no express words of imprecation are used[4]. A gage is given; that gage is *fides*; that *fides* is the giver's Christianity; he pawns his hope of salvation. If, on the one hand, the *wed* is spiritualized and becomes incorporeal, on the other hand a man's Christianity is 'realized'; it becomes a thing, an object to be given and returned[5]. An 'age of faith'

---

[1] Brunner, D. R. G. ii. 428; Schmid, Gesetze, App. vii. 1 § 4: when a blood feud is being compromised the peace is sworn 'on ánum wæpne.' The oath on the sword was itself invested with a Christian character by association with the cross of the guard. In the 16th century the oath of admission to the gild of Spanish fencing-masters was taken 'super signum sanctae crucis factum de pluribus ensibus'; Rev. archéol. vi. 589.

[2] Theodore's Penitential, i. 6 (Haddan and Stubbs, iii. 182): 'Quis periurium facit in aecclesia, xi. annos peniteat. Qui vero necessitate coactus sit, iii. quadragesimas. Qui autem in manu hominis iurat, apud Graecos nihil est. Si vero iuraverit in manu episcopi vel presbiteri aut diaconi seu in alteri [*corr.* altari] sive in cruce consecrata, et mentitus est, iii. annos peniteat.'

[3] Laws of Wihtræd, 18. So after several centuries, 'Clericus non debet iurare in iudicio coram iudicibus saecularibus'; Protest of Grosseteste, Ann. Burton, 426.

[4] The process whereby in England the word *affidavit* has come to imply an actual oath upon the gospels would be worthy of investigation. But it does not fall within our period.

[5] Rievaulx Cartulary, p. 164: Henry archbishop of York declares to his successors and to the cathedral chapter how in his presence Robert de Ros

[p. 189] uses daring phrases about these matters. When a man makes a vow to God he will place his faith upon an altar and will find sureties who are to have coercive power over him[1]. But more, when he makes a promise to another man, he will sometimes offer God as his surety[2]. We must remember that in very old times the surety or pledge had in truth been the principal debtor, the creditor's only debtor, while his possession of the *wed* gave him power over the person whose *plegius* he was. Hence it is that when we obtain details of the ceremony by which faith is 'made' or 'given' or 'pledged,' we often find that the manual act takes place, not between the promisor and the promisee, but between the promisor and a third person who is sometimes expressly called a *fideiussor*. He is generally one whose station gives him coercive power over the promisor; he is the bishop of the diocese or the sheriff of the county. He does not accept any legal liability for the promise; but he holds the promisor's faith in his hands and can constrain him to redeem it by ecclesiastical censure or temporal distress[3]. We are far from saying that whenever faith was pledged, even in the most ancient times, three persons took part in the transaction. It may well be that sometimes the promisor put his faith directly into the hands of the promisee, and in this form the ceremony would become

confirmed to Rievaulx Abbey the lands given by Walter Espec; 'et primum haec omnia sacramento firmavit, deinde Christianitatem in manu mea qua se obsidem dedit et me plegium constituit de his omnibus'; therefore if he infringes the pact, he is to be coerced by ecclesiastical censures. Another good instance will be found in Madox, Formulare, p. 3. See also Ducange, s. v. *Christianitas.* For some political pacts sanctioned by affidation, see Round, Geoffrey de Mandeville, p. 384.

[1] Eadmer. Hist. Nov. p. 31: Rufus in a moment of terrified repentance promises to restore the good laws; 'spondet in hoc fidem suam, et vades inter se et Deum facit episcopos suos, mittens qui hoc votum super altare sua vice promittant.'

[2] Letters of John of Salisbury, ed. Giles, ii. 224: Henry II. promises to forgive Becket; 'primo Deum et (ut dici solet) Christianitatem suam obsidem dabat; deinde patruum suum......et omnes qui convenerant constituebat fideiussores.'

[3] Rievaulx Cartulary, 33 : Roger de Mowbray says, 'Hanc donationem [a gift to Rievaulx] ego et Nigellus filius meus manu nostra affidavimus tenendam in manu Roberti Decani [Eboracensis]...et ipsam ecclesiam Eboracensem testem et fideiussorem inter nos et monachos constituimus, ita ut si aliquando ego vel heredes mei ab hac conventione deviaverimus ipsa ecclesia ad haec exequenda nos ecclesiastica revocet disciplina.' For other instances see ibid. pp. 37, 39, 159, 169.

fused with that mutual grasp of hands which, as already said, may have had a somewhat different origin. And like a man's religious faith, so his wordly honour can be regarded as an [p. 190] object that is pawned to a creditor. Of pledges of honour which have definite legal results much may be read in the German documents of the later middle ages[1]. To this day we speak as though we could pledge our faith, our honour, our word, while the term *borrow* tells us of a time when men rarely, if ever, lent without receiving sufficient *borh*. Here, however, we are concerned to notice that a form of contract has been devised which the ecclesiastical tribunals may fairly claim to enforce:—a man has pawned his religion ; very often, he has placed it in the hand of the bishop[2].

The written document as a form.

Meanwhile the written document is beginning to present itself as a validating form for transactions. To the eye of the barbarians the Roman provincials seemed to be conveying land by means of documents and to be stipulating by means of documents[3]. It is broadly stated that according to the 'Lex Romana' any one who contravenes or will not perform a written agreement is infamous and to be punished[4]. The written document, which few have the art to manufacture, is regarded with mystical awe ; it takes its place beside the *festuca*[5]. The act of setting one's hand to it is a *stipulatio*[6] ; it is delivered over as a symbol along with twig and turf and glove[7]. For a long time, however, it is chiefly used as a means of creating or

---

[1] Kohler, Shakespeare vor dem Forum der Jurisprudenz, p. 62.

[2] See an article by Sir Edward Fry, Specific Performance and Laesio Fidei, L. Q. R. v. 235. The *godborh* should be compared with the practice of 'taking God to witness' and inscribing His name at the head of a list of witnesses who attest a charter. See the ancient Welsh documents written in the Book of St Chad and reproduced by Gwenogvryn Evans in his edition of the Liber Landavensis, p. xlv, where the first witness is 'Deus Omnipotens.'

[3] See Brunner, Röm. u. Germ. Urkunde.

[4] Rozière, Recueil des formules, i. 152: 'Romanamque legem ordinantem ut quicumque in aetate perfecta pactionem vel diffinitionem per scripturam fecerit, et hoc quod fecit implere neglexerit, aut contra eam ire praesumpserit, infames vocetur et ipsam causam agere non permittatur, atque poenam statutam cogetur exsolvere.' See Esmein, Études, 17.

[5] Heusler, Institutionen, i. 87–92.

[6] Brunner, Urkunde, 224. Kemble, Cod. Dip. vol. v. p. 54 (A.D. 791): 'cunctis astipulantibus et confirmantibus nominatis atque infra descriptis.' Charter of Henry I., Monasticon, iv. 18: 'Hanc donationem confirmo ego Henricus rex et astipulatione sanctae crucis et appositione sigilli mei.'

[7] See above, vol. ii. p. 86.

transferring rights in land by way of gift, sale, lease or gage ; it
is rarely used for the purpose of creating or attesting the
[p. 191] creation of purely personal rights[1]. But it has a future before
it. The belief that the Romans stipulated by writing, the
argument *a fortiori* that if men can be bound by question and
answer they must be bound by their charters, will not easily be
dispelled[2]. The most carefully worded documents that will be
sealed in the England of the thirteenth century, the bonds
given to Lombard merchants, will speak of stipulation[3].

It would be idle to inquire what stage of development these
various institutions had attained in the England or the
Normandy of the year 1066. The *God-borh* flits before us in
Alfred's laws[4], and we have other evidence that a 'wedded'
promise was under the sanction of the church[5]. We may see
the solemn contract of betrothal[6] and may read of promises
secured by oath and *wed* and *borh*[7]. But, for example, we can
not tell in what, if any, cases a merely symbolic gage will have
the effect of binding a bargain. To all appearance writing has
hardly been used for any legal purpose except when land is to
be conveyed or a last will is to be made. There is no sure
ground earlier than Glanvill's book. But that book reminds us
that in the twelfth century two new forces are beginning to
play upon the law of contract: the classical Roman law is being
slowly disinterred and the canon law is taking shape. Glanvill
knows a little, Bracton knows much more about both. For a
moment we may glance at them, though the influence that they
exercise over English law is but superficial and transient.

English law in cent. xii.

---

[1] See Rozière's collection of formulas *passim*.

[2] Bracton, f. 100 b ; Bracton and Azo (Selden Soc.), 155. It should be
remembered that Justinian (Inst. 3, 21) had done his very best to lead the
medieval lawyers astray.

[3] Cart. Rievaulx, p. 410; a bond given in 1275 by the abbot to a Florentine
firm: 'promittimus et tenemur per legitimam stipulationem.........tenemur per
praedictam stipulationem.' Camb. Univ. Libr. MS. Ee. 5. 31, f. 12 b; the
convent of Christ Church, Canterbury, gives a bond to the Frescobaldi: 'Nos
vero dictas xxx. marcas vel consimiles praedictis Johanni, Coppo, Rutto et
Tedaldo stipulantibus tam pro se ipsis quam pro praedictis Gyno et aliis sociis
suis .....promittimus reddere.' In 1214 the Earl of Ferrers becomes a surety
for a debt due by King John to the Pope; in his charter he says 'constitui me
fideiussorem......per solempnem stipulationem promittens quod......satisfaciam';
Rot. Pat. Joh. p. 139.

[4] Alfred, 33.   [5] Alfred, 1. § 8.

[6] Schmid, Gesetze, App. VI.

[7] Schmid, Gesetze, Glossar, s. v. *Eid, wed, borh*.

Medieval
Roman
law.
In the twelfth century the revived study of Justinian's
books, though it urged men to rediscover or to construct some
general law about the validity of agreements, tended also to [p. 192]
confirm the notion that something more than a formless expression of agreement must be required if an action is to be given[1].
Nudum pactum non parit actionem—so much at least was clear
beyond a doubt, and the glossators set themselves to describe,
sometimes in picturesque phrases, those various 'vestments'
which will keep the pact from perishing of cold[2]. The Roman
formal contract, the *stipulatio*, might be dead past resuscitation,
yet they were neither prepared to put a new ceremony in its
place nor to declare that ceremonies are needless. The mere
pactum in their eyes derives its name from that mutual grasp of
hands (*palmarum ictus*) whereby men were wont to bind a
bargain[3]. Even in countries where 'the imperial laws' had a
claim to rule because they were imperial, the civilian's doctrine
of contract was too remote from traditional practice to sway the
decisions of the courts, and the civilian was beginning to find in
the canonist a rival who had a simpler doctrine and one less
hampered by ancient history. Bracton makes a half-hearted
attempt to engraft the theory of the legists upon the stock of
English law. No part of his book has of late attracted more
attention than the meagre chapters that he gives to contract;
none is a worse specimen of his work[4]. It is a scholastic exercise poorly performed. Here and there half unwillingly he lets
us see some valuable truth, as when, despite Justinian and Azo,
he mixes up the *mutuum* and the *commodatum* and refuses to
treat sale as 'consensual.' But there is no life in this part of
his treatise because there is no practical experience behind it.
The main lesson that we learn from it is that at the end of
Henry III.'s reign our king's court has no general doctrine of
contract[5].

[1] Seuffert, Geschichte der obligatorischen Verträge.

[2] Azo, Summa Cod. de pactis (2, 3), paints for us a shivering pact which
nestles among the furs, the 'vair and grise,' of some well-dressed contract and
becomes *pactum adiectum*. Bracton and Azo, 143.

[3] Azo, *l. c.*: 'vel dicitur [pactum] a percussione palmarum; veteres enim
consentientes palmas ad invicem percutiebant in signum non violandae fidei.'

[4] Salmond, Essays in Jurisprudence, p. 174.

[5] As to the character of this part of Bracton's work, see Bracton and Azo
(Selden Soc.), 142 ff. Britton, i. 156, and Fleta, p. 120, repeat the learning of
vestments. Fleta, however, has some valuable passages about the action of
debt. It is not unlikely that Bracton intended to give a chapter to that action.

[p. 193] We have seen that ecclesiastical law gained a foot-hold The canon law. within the province of contract by giving a Christian colouring to the old formal agreement, the pledge of faith. This having been accomplished, the canonists began to speak slightingly of ceremonies. The sacred texts, which teach that the Christian's Yea or Nay should be enough, may have hastened the change, but we believe that the motive force had its origin elsewhere. The law of marriage had fallen into the canonist's hand, and in the middle of the twelfth century, after long hesitation, he was beginning to teach that a bare interchange of words was sufficient to constitute a marriage. This doctrine was not due to any contempt for ceremonies, but to quite other causes of which we must speak elsewhere[1]. Nevertheless, it could not but exercise a powerful influence outside the sphere of marriage law, and some small counterpoise to the enormous harm that it did within that sphere may be found in the effects that it produced in other quarters. If, not merely a binding contract to marry, but an indissoluble marriage can be constituted without any formalities, it would be ridiculous to demand more than consenting words in the case of other agreements. In the course of the thirteenth century the canonists were coming to this opinion, and could cite in its favour two sentences which had found a place in the Gregorian statute-book. Even the 'nude pact' should be enforced, at any rate by penitential discipline[2].

From this point onward the process of arriving at a general Evolution of a law of contract on the continent. law of contract was different in England and on the continent, although some curious particular coincidences may be found. Both here and elsewhere the secular courts were put on their mettle, so to speak, by the competition of the spiritual forum. In Italy, where the power of the revived Roman law was at its strongest, the development of the new doctrine, which would cast aside the elaborate learning of 'vestments' and enforce the naked agreement, was to some extent checked by the difficulty

---

[1] See below, the section on Marriage.

[2] cc. 1. 3. X., de pactis, 1. 35; Seuffert, *op. cit.* 47. One of the first writers who proclaim this doctrine is that Hostiensis, who (see above, vol. i. pp. 122, 214) had made himself but too well known in England. Hostiensis, ad tit. *de pactis.* § *quid sit effectus*: 'Ut modis omnibus servetur, etiamsi sit nudum secundum canones......quia inter simplicem loquelam et iuramentum non facit Deus differentiam.' See Seuffert, *op. cit.* p. 50.

of stating it in a Roman form of plausible appearance, even for [p. 194]
the use of ecclesiastical judges, while, on the other side, the
problem for the civilian was to find means of expanding or
evading the classical Roman rules and of opening the door
of the secular tribunal to formless agreements by practically
abolishing the Roman conception of *nudum pactum*[1]. In
Germany and in northern France the old Teutonic formalism
was but slowly undermined by the new principle, and in one
and the same book we may find the speculative *Pacta sunt
servanda* lying side by side with the practical demand for
formalities[2]. In England the Courts Christian were early in
occupation of the ground and bold in magnifying their jurisdiction, and the king's judges were rather slow to discover how
profitable a field their rivals were occupying. It is not a little
remarkable that Bracton, in search for principles, preferred
importing the system of the glossators, which at all events
preached the sterility of the naked pact, to adopting the novel
and ecclesiastical doctrine. His efforts ended in a sad failure.
English law went on its way uninfluenced by Italian learning,
but confirmed in its belief that pacts require vestments. The
problem of constructing a general law of contract was not
faced until a much later day, when the common-law system
of pleading was mature, and what was then sought was a new
cause and form of action which could find a place within limits
that were already drawn.

Influence of Roman and canon law in England. In Italy we find some jurists holding that an action *de dolo*
will lie for damage caused by breach of an informal pact[3].
This offers a striking parallel to the influence of the action of
deceit in forming that English action of *assumpsit* which was
to become by slow degrees the ordinary means of enforcing an
informal contract. But the method which found most favour
among the Italians was to hold that an additional express
promise (*pactum geminatum* or *duplex*) was a sufficient 'clothing' of the natural obligation of a *nudum pactum* to make it
actionable. The opinion formerly current in our courts that an
express promise, founded on an existing moral duty, is a sufficient
cause of action in *assumpsit*, is not unlike this. But all this lies
in the future. Gradually upon the continent the new principle [p. 195]

---

[1] Seuffert, *op. cit. passim.*

[2] Franken, Das französische Pfandrecht, pp. 43 ff.

[3] Seuffert, *op. cit.* 77, 80.

that had been proclaimed by the canonists gained ground; the French lawyers of the sixteenth century, going back as humanists to the original Roman authorities, held out latest of all. From the seventeenth century onwards German writers boldly appealed to the law of nature. The modern philosophic lawyers of Germany do not seem wholly satisfied with the results[1]. But, before the thirteenth century was out, both Roman and canon law had lost their power to control the development of English temporal law. The last effective words that they had spoken here were contradictory. About one point Bracton and his epitomators are clear—*Nudum pactum non parit actionem;* but the words sculptured on the tomb of 'the English Justinian' are the canonical *Pactum serva.*

Our task now becomes that of tracing the fortunes of three different institutions, the germs of which we have already seen, namely (1) the pledge of faith, (2) the action of debt, and (3) the action of covenant. We shall be compelled to speak chiefly of the doctrines of the king's court. These were to be in the future the English law of contract; but we must remember that in the twelfth and even in the thirteenth century that court was not professing to administer the whole law. There were other courts for the recovery of debts, and both Glanvill and Bracton seem willing to admit that there may be many binding agreements which royal justice will not enforce or will only enforce as a matter of grace and favour[2].

(1) We have seen how 'an interposition of faith' accomplished by some manual act could be converted into a vestment for pacts, and how this vestment was sanctified by a doctrine which saw in the faith that was pledged the pledgor's Christianity. This interpretation brought the ceremony within the cognizance of the ecclesiastical tribunals, which in the twelfth [p. 196] century were seeking to enlarge their borders. The ceremony is often mentioned in deeds of that age, and it must frequently have taken that elaborate form which involved the action of

English law in cent. xiii.

(1) The pledge of faith.

----

[1] Seuffert, *op. cit. ad fin.*

[2] Glanvill, **x.** 8: 'Curia domini Regis huiusmodi privatas conventiones de rebus dandis vel accipiendis in vadium vel alias huiusmodi, extra curiam, sive etiam in aliis curiis quam in curia domini Regis, factis, tueri non solet nec warantizare.' Ibid. **x.** 18: 'Praedictos vero contractus qui ex privatorum consensu fiunt breviter transigimus, quia, ut praedictum est, privatas conventiones non solet curia domini Regis tueri.' See also the passage from Bracton, cited below, p. 218, note 3.

three persons, the faith being deposited in the hands of some *mediator* or *fideiussor* who was often the bishop and judge ordinary, but often the sheriff of the county or the steward of a lord who kept a court[1]. The letters of John of Salisbury allow us to see that in the earliest years of Henry II.'s reign the ecclesiastical tribunals, even the Roman curia, were busy over agreements made by Englishmen with pledge of faith[2]. Then came the quarrel between Henry and Becket.

The church's jurisdiction in case of broken faith.

We hardly need explain, after all that we have elsewhere said, that there was no question of a war all along the line between the spiritual and the temporal power. The king never disputed that many questions belonged of right to the justice of the church, nor the bishop that many belonged to the justice of the king. But there was always a greater or less extent of border-land that might be more or less plausibly fought for. In this region the mastery was with the party which could establish the right to draw the boundary. This was as clearly perceived by Henry and Becket as by any modern theorist; and the controversy centred round the question: who in doubtful cases should decide where a cause should be tried. The Constitutions of Clarendon (1164) mark the king's determination that his justices, not the bishops, shall be the persons to say what matters are for the royal court and what are not. The fifteenth article, which alone concerns us here, is in these terms : 'Placita de debitis, quae fide interposita debentur, vel absque interpositione fidei, sint in iustitia regis.'

Struggle between ecclesiastical and temporal justice.

We can not be certain about the precise meaning that the king's advisers attributed to these words. Becket and his friends interpreted them to mean that the ecclesiastical tribunals were deprived of all jurisdiction of every kind over breaches of oath or breaches of faith[3]. This article was among those that [p. 197]

---

[1] Northumberland Assize Rolls (Surtees Soc.) 56: in 1253 a marriage settlement is secured by faith deposited in the hands of the abbot of Newminster and the prior of Hexham. Winchcombe Landboc, i. 204: A. W., on quit-claiming land to the abbot, pledges his faith in the hands of E. R. Rievaulx Cartulary, 39: S. and his wife, releasing land to their lord, pledge faith in the hands of the lord's steward in full court : they then go before the sheriff and pledge faith in his hands. See ibid., 69, 76, 77, 89, 100–1–2, 139.

[2] Letters of John of Salisbury, ed. Giles, vol. i. pp. 1, 3, 8, 21 etc.

[3] Hoveden, i. 238, and Materials for the Life of Becket, v. 294 : 'Quod non liceat episcopo coercere aliquem de periurio vel fide laesa.' See also Materials, ii. 380, vi. 265. William Fitz Stephen (Mater. iii. 47) gives this version :—' Ne

the pope condemned[1]. After the murder Henry was compelled to renounce his 'innovations'; but here as in other cases we are left to guess how much he conceived to be covered by that term. A few years afterwards we have Glanvill's statement of the law[2]. He admits that *fidei laesio vel transgressio* is a proper subject of criminal cognizance in the ecclesiastical court; but is careful to add that by statute (*per assisam regni*, that is, by the Constitutions of Clarendon) the 'interposition of faith' must not be so used as to oust the king's jurisdiction over the debts of the laity or their tenements. Thenceforward there were two subjects of debate. We have seen that the spiritual courts claimed a civil, that is, a non-criminal jurisdiction over all personal actions in which a clerk was defendant. We have seen how this claim was resisted and slowly abandoned[3]; still there can be little doubt that during the thirteenth century clerks were often sued upon their contracts in the courts Christian[4].

But what concerns us here is the assertion of a criminal jurisdiction to be exercised *in foro externo* over all causes of broken oath or broken faith. Now the lay courts did not deny that this jurisdiction had a legitimate sphere. They defined that sphere by two writs of prohibition; the one forbad the ecclesiastical judges to meddle with 'lay fee,' the other forbad them to meddle with chattels or debts except in matrimonial and testamentary causes[5]. How wide a province was [p. 198] left to them is by no means clear. It is plain that a creditor who had a claim which the king's court would enforce was not to hale his opponent before the ordinary on a charge of

The writs of prohibition.

omnis controversia de fidei vel sacramenti trangressione sit in foro ecclesiastico; sed tantum de fide adacta pro nuptiis vel dote vel huiusmodi, quae non debent fieri nisi in facie ecclesiae. De aliter dato fidei sacramento, ut de debitis vel sic, statuit rex causam esse in foro laico.' Anonymus II. (Mater. iv. 102) says: 'Quod apud iudicem ecclesiae non conveniatur aliquis laicus super laesa fide vel periurio de pecunia.'

[1] Materials, v. 79.   [2] Glanvill, x. 12.   [3] See above, vol. i. p. 446.

[4] In John of Oxford's collection of precedents (circ. 1280) the example of an ecclesiastical libel (*littera editionis*) is one in which a plaintiff, who has transcribed a book for the defendant, claims an unliquidated sum, the amount of which is to be determined by the estimate of good men; Maitland, A Conveyancer in the Thirteenth Century, L. Q. R. vii. 67.

[5] Glanvill, xii. 21, 22; Select Civil Pleas (Selden Soc.), pl. 83. History of the Register, Harv. L. R. iii. 112, 114; Reg. Brev. Orig. f. 34. The ordinaries must not hold plea concerning chattels or debts 'quae non sunt de testamento vel matrimonio.'

violated faith. That a man might sometimes wish to do this is also evident; he might thus attain his end more speedily than by an action of debt[1]. In such cases a promise not to seek a prohibition, a renunciation of the *privilegium fori*, would not stay the issue of the writ, for no one could renounce the king's right to protect his own jurisdiction, though the man who thus went against his own act might be sent to gaol, and a certain validity was thus conceded to those renunciatory clauses which are not uncommon in the charters of this age[2]. But there were as yet numerous agreements which the king's court did not profess to enforce. Might the court Christian punish a breach of these when they involved a gage of faith? We doubt it. They must in almost every case have fallen within the words of the writ of prohibition. At any rate the clergy were profoundly dissatisfied with the law administered by the royal justices, and spoke as though the spiritual forum was prohibited from punishing a breach of faith in any pecuniary matter if it were not of a testamentary or matrimonial character[3]. Certainly these writs were always buzzing about the ears of the ecclesiastical judges[4]; they retaliated with excommunications, and we may see Northampton laid under an interdict because its mayor enforced a prohibition[5].

Circumspecte agatis.

A document attributed to the year 1285, which in after days was ranked among the statutes, the *Circumspecte agatis*, suggests that at some time or another some concession was made in this matter by the lay power[6]. This document may

[1] Note Book, pl. 351: 'quia ibi maturius iusticiam habere potuit.'

[2] Bracton, f. 401 b. In 1303 Bereford J. remarks that not long ago such clauses had been frequent in mercantile documents, but that they were against law; Y. B. 30–1 Edw. I. 493. Sometimes the promisor had expressly obliged himself 'sub poena anathematis'; Selby Coucher, ii. 140.

[3] Grosseteste's articles (1258), Ann. Burton, 423: 'Item sub colore prohibitionis placiti in curia Christianitatis de pecunia, nisi sit de testamento vel matrimonio, impedit et perturbat [Rex] processum in foro ecclesiastico super fidei laesione, periurio......in magnum animarum detrimentum.'

[4] Note Book, pl. 50, 351, 670, 683, 1361, 1464, 1671, 1893.

[5] Note Book, pl. 351.

[6] Statutes of the Realm, i. 101. The editors of this volume seem to have failed to find any authentic text of this writ. It certainly ought to be enrolled somewhere. The author of the Mirror treats it as a statute. Possibly Britton, i. 28, alludes to it. A reason for giving it to the year 1285 is that it appears to be issued in consequence of a petition presented in that year by the bishops; Wilkins, Concilia, ii. 117. In this they complain in general terms that they are prohibited from entertaining causes *de fidei vel sacramenti laesione*.

[p. 199] be described as a royal circular sent to the judges; perhaps it was issued along with a set of commissions, or sent to the judges after they had already started on their circuits. The bishop's court is not to be interfered with in matters of spiritual discipline (*pro hiis quae sunt mere spiritualia*); and it is laid down as already settled that violent laying of hands upon a clerk, defamation, and (according to some, but by no means all copies) breach of faith, are good subjects of ecclesiastical jurisdiction, so long as, not the payment of money, but spiritual correction is the object of the suit. The words about breach of faith may possibly be authentic[1]; but there were lawyers in the fourteenth century who protested that this document was concocted by the prelates and of no authority[2]. In any case the quarrelling went on as before; no change was made in the writs of prohibition. Both parties were in their turn aggressors. In 1373 the commons in parliament complain that the courts Christian are encroaching to themselves pleas of debt even where there has been no lesion of faith[3], and it seems plain that the ecclesiastical judges did not care to inquire whether a complainant could have found a remedy in a lay court[4]. On the other hand, the king's justices would [p. 200] concede but a small territory to the canonists; their doctrine is that the only promises that are subjects for spiritual jurisdiction are promises which concern spiritual matters[5]. That

---

[1] Such MSS. as we have consulted leave this very doubtful. Curiously enough Coke gives while Lyndwood, p. 97, omits the important words. The Articuli Cleri of 1315 (Statutes, i. 171) mention assaults on clerks and defamation as offences proper for ecclesiastical punishment, but say no word of breach of faith. See also Makower, Const. Hist., 434.

[2] Fitzherbert, Abr. *Jurisdiction*, pl. 28. See also Prynne, Records, iii. 336.

[3] Rot. Parl. ii. 319 : 'eaux ont encroché plee de dette ov une addition q'est appellé fide-lesion la ou unqes nul ne fust.' This injures the lords who have courts.

[4] Thus in 1378 Richard vicar of Westley is cited in the bishop of Ely's court at the instance of a Cambridge tailor to answer for perjury and breach of faith which apparently consist in his not having paid a loan of eight shillings : Register of Bp. Arundel (in the Palace at Ely), f. 88 b. See the cases from Hale's Precedents and Proceedings collected in Harv. L. R., vi. 403. Also Depositions and other Ecclesiastical Proceedings in the Courts of Durham (Surtees Soc.), p. 50 (A.D. 1535); the agreement enforced is for the purchase of a horse.

[5] Lib. Ass. f. 101. ann. 22. pl. 70; Y. B. 2 Hen. IV. f. 10 (Mich. pl. 45); 11 Hen. IV. f. 38 (Trin. pl. 40) ; 36 Hen. VI. f. 29 (Pasch. pl. 11) ; 20 Edw. IV. f. 10 (Mich. pl. 9) ; 22 Edw. IV. f. 20 (Trin. pl. 47) ; Second Inst. 493.

one court, if it has received no prohibition, should have a right to do what another court can prohibit it from it doing, need not surprise us: this in the middle ages is no antinomy.

The formal pledge of faith in the ecclesiastical court.

Within the limits assigned to their civil or non-penal jurisdiction the English courts Christian were in all probability able and willing to enforce the doctrines of the Italian decretists, who, as already said, were slowly coming to the opinion that the 'nude pact' will support an action. These limits however were not very wide, though they included testamentary and matrimonial causes and other matters 'merely spiritual.' No English canonist, so far as we are aware, achieved anything for the law of contract. Outside the limits just mentioned the very most that the ecclesiastical judge could do was to punish by corporal penance a breach of promise which was also a breach of faith, and the king's courts would not have allowed him to whittle away the requirement of 'form.' To the end there must be at least a hand-shake in order to bring the case within his cognizance[1].

The king's court and the pledge of faith.

One curious result of this bickering over 'faith' seems to have been that already in Glanvill's day the king's justices had set their faces against what might otherwise have become the English formal contract. Glanvill gives us to understand that a plaintiff who claims a debt in the royal court must produce some proof other than an interposition of faith[2]. In other words, the grasp of hands will not serve as a sufficient vestment for a contract. The same may be said of the gage. If a thing be given by way of gage, the creditor can keep it and can call upon the debtor to 'acquit' it by paying the debt; but, if the debtor will not do this, then no worse will happen to him than [p. 201] the loss of the gage[3]. This prevents our treating the delivery of a rod or a glove as a validating ceremony. Within a sphere marked out for it by ancient law, the symbolic *wed* was still

[1] Depositions and other Ecclesiastical Proceedings in the Courts of Durham (Surtees Soc.), 50; in 1535 a deponent in a case of breach of faith says that he heard the oral agreement made; 'et desuper idem [reus] fidem fecit dicto actori —vidit dictum reum ponentem manum suam dextram in manu dextra ipsius actoris in supplementum promissi sui.'

[2] Glanvill, x. 12: 'creditor ipse si non habeat inde vadium neque plegium, neque aliam disrationationem nisi sola fide, nulla est haec probatio in curia domini Regis.'

[3] Glanvill, x. 6. 7.

used. This sphere we may call that of the 'procedural contract' made in the course of litigation, the contract to appear
before the court, the contract to abide by and fulfil its award.
By this time justice had grown so strong that these engage-
ments were hardly regarded as contracts; but, at least in
theory, men found gage as well as pledge for their appearance
in court, and when they were there they 'waged' battle, or
'waged' their law, or 'waged' an amercement, by the delivery
of a glove or some other symbol[1]. In the exchequer[2] and
in other courts men were constantly pledging their faith
(*affidare*) that essoins would be warranted, that pleas would
be prosecuted and the like[3]; but they were ceasing to think
that in such cases the court's power to punish a defaulter
was given to it by agreement. We should be rash were we
to assume that the local courts of the twelfth century paid
no heed to these ceremonies. Blackstone has recorded how
in his day men shook hands over a bargain[4]; they do it still;
but already in Henry II.'s reign the decisive step has been
taken; common as these manual acts may be, they are not
to become the formal contract of English temporal law.

(2) We must now turn to the action of debt. But first
we ought to notice that in the thirteenth century a prudent
creditor was seldom compelled to bring an action for the
recovery of money that he had lent. He had not trusted
[p. 202] his debtor's bare word nor even his written bond, but had
obtained either a judgment or a recognizance before the loan
was made. We see numerous actions of debt brought merely
in order that they may not be defended, and we may be pretty
sure that in many cases no money has been advanced until a
judgment has been given for its repayment. Still more often

(2) The action of debt.

The recognizance.

---

[1] *Pone per vadium et salvos plegios*—when the sheriff is bidden to do this,
he, so far as we can see, merely exacts pledges (sureties). Of the wager of law
we have this account in ms. Brit. Mus. Egerton, 656, f. 188 b : 'Il gagera la ley
de sun gaunt plyee e le baylera en la meyn cely e puys reprendra arere sun
gaunt, e dunke trovera il plegges de la ley.' When in later times we find that
the glove is 'thrown down' as a gage of battle, we may perhaps suspect that
some act of defiance has been confused with the act of wager.

[2] Dialogus, ii. 12, 19, 21, 28.

[3] See *e.g.* Hengham Magna, c. 6 : Select Pleas in Manorial Courts (Selden
Soc.), p. 6.

[4] Blackstone, Comm. ii. 448 : 'Antiently, among all the northern nations,
shaking of hands was held necessary to bind the bargain ; a custom which we
still retain in many verbal contracts.'

there is upon the plea rolls what purports to be the compromise of an action of debt. The defendant confesses (*cognoscit, recognoscit*) that he owes a sum of money, promises to pay it upon a certain day and 'grants' that, if he does not pay it, the sheriff may levy it from his lands and goods; in return the plaintiff is sometimes said to remit the damages which are supposed to be already due to him from his debtor[1]. Still more often the parties go into the chancery or the exchequer and procure the making of an entry upon the close roll or some other roll. The borrower confesses (*recognoscit*) that he owes a certain sum which is to be paid upon a certain day, and grants that, if default be made, the money may be levied by the sheriff. This practice, which is of some importance in the history of the chancery, may have its origin in the fact (for fact it is) that some of its officers were money lenders on a great scale; but no doubt it has ancient roots; it is analogous to the practice of 'levying fines'; indeed we ought to notice that at this period the 'fine of lands' sometimes involves an agreement to pay money and one which can be enforced by summary processes. Now the recognizance is aptly called a 'contract of record'; we might also call it an 'executory' contract, if we used this adjective in an unfamiliar sense, but one that it will bear. The recognizance is equivalent to a judgment; nothing remains to be done but execution. Within a year from the date fixed for payment, a writ of execution will issue as a matter of course on the creditor's applying for it, unless the debtor, having discharged his duty, has procured the cancellation or 'vacation' of the entry which describes the confession. The legislation of Edward I. in favour of merchants instituted a new and popular 'contract of record,' the so-called 'statute merchant.' This we must not examine; but already before his accession the recognizance was in common use and large sums of money were being lent upon its security.

The action of debt in Glanvill. Glanvill knows an action of debt in the king's court[2]. The [p. 203] original writ is a close copy of that form of the writ of right for land which is known as a *Praecipe in capite*. The sheriff is to bid the debtor render a hundred marks which he owes to the plaintiff 'and whereof the plaintiff complains that the

---

[1] Select Civil Pleas (Selden Soc.), pl. 102. This has begun as early as 1201.

[2] Glanvill, x. 2.

defendant unjustly deforces him'; if the debtor will not
obey this order, then he is to be summoned before the king's
court.   The creditor is being 'deforced' of money just as the
demandant who brings a writ of right is being 'deforced' of
land.   There may be trial by battle in the one case as in the
other.   The bold crudity of archaic thought equates the repayment of an equivalent sum of money to the restitution of
specific land or goods.   To all appearance our ancestors could
not conceive credit under any other form.   The claimant of a
debt asks for what is his own.   After all, we may doubt
whether the majority of fairly well-to-do people, even at this
day, realize that what a man calls 'my money in the bank' is a
mere personal obligation of the banker to him[1].   The gulf that
we see between *mutuum* and *commodatum* is slurred over.   If
we would rethink the thoughts of our forefathers we must hold
that the action of debt is proprietary, while at the same time
we must hold, as we saw in the last chapter, that there is no
action for the recovery of a chattel that would be called
proprietary by a modern lawyer[2].

Though Glanvill gives a writ of debt and though the action
of debt occasionally appears on the very earliest plea rolls[3], it
long remains a rare action in the king's court.   In the case of
debts any royal writ, whether it takes the form of a *Praecipe* or
of a *Iusticies*[4], seems to be regarded as a luxury which the king
is entitled to sell at a high price.   Even in the earlier years of
[p. 204] Henry III.'s reign the plaintiff must often promise the king a
quarter or a third of all that he recovers before he will get his
writ[5].   That men are willing to purchase the king's interference
at this extravagant price seems to tell us that the justice of the

An action of debt in the king's court is rare.

---

[1] See Langdell, Contracts, §§ 99, 100.

[2] The doctrine that we are here maintaining about old English law had, we
believe, become the orthodox doctrine about old German law.   Of late
Dr Heusler (Institutionen, i. 377–396) has vigorously attacked it, declaring that
the German at a very remote time saw a difference between real and personal
rights and between real and personal actions.   We wish that he had considered
the English actions of debt and detinue.   What we have here said is in accord
with Holmes, Common Law, p. 252; Salmond, Essays on Jurisprudence, 175.

[3] Rolls of the King's Court, (Pipe Roll Soc.) pp. 24, 25 ; Rot. Cur. Reg. (ed.
Palgrave), i. 5.   See above, p. 173.

[4] A *Praecipe* brings the case to the royal court, a *Iusticies* commits it to the
sheriff.

[5] Maitland, Register of Original Writs, Harv. L. R., iii. 112, 114 ; Excerpta
e Rot. Fin. i. 29, 49, 62, 68 ; Glanvill Revised, Harv. L. R., vi. 15.

local courts is feeble and that credit is seldom given. All the entries relating to Staffordshire cases that appear upon the rolls of the king's court during this long reign of fifty-six years are in print; some eight actions of debt are all that we find among innumerable novel disseisins[1]. Staffordshire was a poor and backward county and our series of rolls is by no means perfect; but still this is a significant fact. In the last years of the reign, however, the action was becoming much commoner; fifty-three entries on the plea roll of one term speak of it, and some of the loans to which they testify are large[2]. First from the Jew, then from the Lombard, Englishmen were learning to lend money and to give credit for the price of goods.

Proprietary character of the action. We may see the action gradually losing some of its proprietary traits; we may see the notion of personal obligation slowly emerging. The offer of battle in proof of debt vanishes so early that we are unable to give any instance in which it was made; thus one link between the writ of right for land and what we might well call the writ of right for money is broken. Then the eloquent 'deforces' of Glanvill's precedent disappears. In the king's courts one says 'detains' not 'deforces'; but late in the thirteenth century the old phrase was still being used in local courts and the deforcement was even said to be a breach of the peace[3]. But 'debt' was falling apart from 'detinue': in other words, lawyers were beginning to feel that there are certain cases in which the word *debet* ought, certain in which it ought not to be used[4]. They were beginning to feel that the two forms of 'loan,' the *commodatum* and the *mutuum*, are not all one, and this although the judgment in detinue gave the defendant a choice between returning the thing that he had borrowed and paying an equivalent in money[5]. One ought not to say *debet* when there is a *commodatum*. But further—and [p. 205] this is very curious—even when there is a money loan the word *debet* should only be used so long as both parties to the transaction are alive; if either dies, the money may be

---

[1] Staffordshire Historical Collections, vol. iv.

[2] Curia Regis Roll for Pasch. 55 Hen. III. (No. 202).

[3] Select Pleas in Manorial Courts, 140, 144, 150, 152.

[4] See above, vol. ii. p. 173.

[5] In the language which the royal chancery employs in describing the loans of money made to the king by Italian bankers a change occurs about the middle of Henry III.'s reign ; *commodare* gives place to *mutuo tradere, mutuo liberare* and the like. See Archæologia, xxviii. 261.

'unlawfully detained' by the representative of the one or from
the representative of the other, but there is no longer any
'owing' of the money. This looks like a clumsy struggle on the
part of the idea of obligation to find its proper place in the legal
system[1]. Centuries will pass away before it comes by its just
rights. Well worthy of remark is the fate of the Roman term.
It is useless for Bracton to talk of *obligationes ex contractu vel
quasi, ex maleficio vel quasi*; an obligation, or in English a
'bond,' is a document written and sealed containing a confession
of a debt; in later times 'contract' is the genus, 'obligation'
the species[2].

By far the commonest origin of an action of debt is a loan of
money. But soon we begin to see the same action used for the
price of goods. The contract of sale as presented by Glanvill
is thoroughly Germanic[3]. Scraps of Roman phraseology are
brought in, only to be followed by qualification amounting to
contradiction. To make a binding sale there must be either
delivery of the thing, payment of the whole or part of the price,
or giving of earnest[4]. The specially appointed witnesses, the
'transaction witnesses' of the Anglo-Saxon laws, have by this
time disappeared or are fast disappearing, and we must think of
them as having provided, not an alternative form or evidence of
the contract, but a collateral precaution :—the man who bought
[p. 206] cattle without their testimony was exposed to criminal charges.
In substance the conditions mentioned by Glanvill are the very
conditions which in the seventeenth century our Statute of
Frauds will allow as alternatives in a case of sale to a note
or memorandum in writing[5].

Debts arising from sale.

---

[1] Y. B. 21–2 Edw. I. p. 615 ; 30–1 Edw. I. p. 391 ; 33–5 Edw. I. p. 455. In
the last of these cases it is said that the heir of the original creditor is not a
creditor, and therefore he can not say *debes mihi*. In the early records of debt
and detinue the active party does not complain (*queritur*) he demands (*petit*) ;
in other words he is a 'demandant' rather than a 'plaintiff' and the action is
'petitory.' See Note Book, pl. 645, 732, 830.

[2] So in French customary law *obligation* has a similar narrow meaning :
Esmein, Études sur les contrats, pp. 151, 177.

[3] Glanvill, x. 14 ; Bracton, f. 61 b. In this instance Bracton has worked
into his book almost the whole of Glanvill's text.

[4] Glanvill, x. 14 : 'Perficitur autem emptio et venditio cum effectu ex quo
de pretio inter contrahentes convenit, *ita tamen* quod secuta fuerit rei emptae et
venditae traditio, *vel quod* pretium fuerit solutum totum sive pars, *vel saltem
quod* arrhae inde fuerint datae et receptae.'

[5] Stat. 29 Car. II. c. 3. sec. 17: 'except the buyer shall accept part of the

We must observe that the giving of earnest is treated as a quite different thing from part payment. Earnest, as modern German writers have shown[1], is not a partial or symbolic payment of the price, but a distinct payment for the seller's forbearance to sell or deliver a thing to any one else. In the Statute of Frauds, 'something in earnest to bind the bargain' and 'part payment' are distinguished indeed, but thrown into the same clause as if the distinction had ceased to be strongly felt. In Glanvill's time earnest was still, as it was by early Germanic law, less binding than delivery of the goods or part-payment of the price, for if the buyer did not choose to complete his bargain, he only lost the earnest he had given. The seller who had received earnest had no right to withdraw from the bargain, but Glanvill leaves it uncertain what penalty or compensation he was liable to pay. In the thirteenth century Bracton and Fleta state the rule that the defaulting seller must repay double the earnest[2]. In Fleta the law merchant is said to be much more stringent, in fact prohibitory, the forfeit being five shillings for every farthing of the earnest, in other words 'pound for penny[3].' It is among the merchants that the giving of earnest first loses its old character and becomes a form which binds both buyer and seller in a [p. 207] contract of sale. To all appearance this change was not accomplished without the intermediation of a religious idea. All over western Europe the earnest becomes known as the God's penny or Holy Ghost's penny (*denarius Dei*)[4]. Sometimes we

---

goods so sold and actually receive the same, or give something in earnest to bind the bargain, or in part payment, or that some note or memorandum in writing of the said bargain be made' etc. These words appear almost unchanged in sec. 4 of our new Sale of Goods Act, 56–7 Vic. c. 71.

[1] Heusler, Institutionen, i. 76–86 ; ii. 253–7.

[2] Bracton, f. 61 b, 62 ; Fleta, pp. 126–7. Bracton here uses the words of Inst. 3. 23, and it is possible that this definition of the vendor's liability is due to Roman influence. Glanvill was uncertain as to the penalty that should be inflicted upon him. But the rule that the defaulting vendor shall lose the same sum that the buyer has risked is not unnatural. At any rate we can not think that the law of earnest as known to Glanvill and Bracton is derived from the Roman law books, though this is the opinion expressed by Sir Edward Fry in *Howe* v. *Smith*, 27 Chan. Div. 89, 102. The origin of the word *earnest* or *ernes* seems very obscure. The editors of the Oxford English Dictionary think that it may be traced to *arrula*, a diminutive of *arra*, through the forms *arles*, *erles*, *ernes*.

[3] A penalty of five *solidi* is denounced by French law books of this age in a somewhat similar case ; Franken, Das französische Pfandrecht, 57.

[4] For England see Select Pleas in Manorial Courts, p. 151; for Germany,

find that it is to be expended in the purchase of tapers for the patron saint of the town or in works of mercy[1]. Thus the contract is put under divine protection. In the law merchant as stated by Fleta we seem to see the God's penny yet afraid, if we may so speak, to proclaim itself as what it really is, namely a sufficient vestment for a contract of sale. A few years later Edward I. took the step that remained to be taken, and by his *Carta Mercatoria,* in words which seem to have come from the south of Europe[2], proclaimed that among merchants the God's penny binds the contract of sale so that neither party may resile from it[3]. At a later day this new rule passed from the law merchant into the common law[4].

Returning however to Glanvill's account of sale, we must notice that in case a third person claims the object as stolen from him, the seller must be prepared to warrant the buyer's [p. 208] right, or, if he refuses to do this, to be himself impleaded by the buyer, and in either case there may be a trial by battle[5]. We have seen above how the old rules which set a limit to the voucher of warrantors were still being maintained; the fourth, or perhaps the third, warrantor is not allowed to vouch[6]. That

Law of sale continued.

Heusler, Institutionen, ii. 255; for France, Esmein, Études sur les contrats, 24; Franken, *op. cit.* 61; for Italy, Pertile, Storia del diritto, iv. 473.

[1] St Trophimus had the benefit of it at Arles; St Lawrence at Salon.

[2] Thus in the statutes of Avignon (quoted by Esmein, *op. cit.* 24): 'Item statuimus quod quaelibet mercadaria, cuiuscumque rei emptio, et in re locata, et in quolibet alio contractu, postquam pro eis contrahendis contrahentes inter se dederint vel alius pro eis denarium dei, firma et irrevocabilis habentur, et contrahentes teneantur precise solvere precium et rem tradere super quam celebratus est contractus ultro citroque adimplere.'

[3] Munimenta Gildhallae, ii. 206: 'Item quod quilibet contractus per ipsos mercatores cum quibuscunque personis undecunque fuerint, super quocunque genere mercandisae initis, firmus sit et stabilis, ita quod neuter praedictorum mercatorum ab illo contractu possit discedere vel resilire postquam denarius dei inter principales personas contrahentes datus fuerit et receptus.' See also the charter for the Gascon wine-merchants, Lib. Rub. Scac. iii. 1061.

[4] Noy, Maxims, c. 42: 'If the bargain be that you shall give me ten pounds for my horse, and you do give me one penny in earnest, which I do accept, this is a perfect bargain; you shall have the horse by an action on the case and I shall have the money by an action of debt.' In Madox, Form. Angl. No. 167, we find a payment of a penny *racione ernesii* mentioned in a deed relating to the sale of growing crops which are not to be carried away until the residue of the price is paid. This from 1322; the earnest is here spoken of as though it were part of the price. This happens in some earlier cases also; Select Pleas in Manorial Courts, p. 140.

[5] Glanvill, x. 15.   [6] See above, vol. ii. p. 164.

the ownership of the purchased goods did not pass to the buyer until they were delivered to him seems plain. We may gather from Bracton and Fleta that this was so even when the whole price had been paid[1]. Unless there was some special agreement to the contrary, the risk remained with the party who was in possession of the goods[2]. At the same time the question about the transfer of ownership has not as yet taken that sharp form with which we are familiar, because, as we endeavoured to show in an earlier chapter[3], it is but slowly that an owner of goods who is not also the possessor of them acquires legal remedies against thieves or trespassers who meddle with them. For this reason our law was able to reconsider this question about the effect of the contract of sale at a time when its notion of ownership had become more precise than it was in Bracton's day.

Scope of the action of debt.

Even in Edward I.'s time, whatever may have been the potential scope of the action of debt, it seems (if we may judge from the plea rolls, the Year Books and some manuscript precedents that have come to us) to have been used but rarely save for five purposes: it was used, namely, to obtain (1) money lent, (2) the price of goods sold, (3) arrears of rent due upon a lease for years, (4) money due from a surety (*plegius*), and (5) a debt confessed by a sealed document[4]. We can not say that any theory hemmed the action within these narrow limits. As anything that we should call a contract was not its essence, we soon find that it can be used whenever a fixed sum, 'a sum certain,' is due from one man to another. Statutory penalties, forfeitures under by-laws, amercements inflicted by inferior courts, money adjudged by any court, can be recovered by it. This was never forgotten in England so long as the old system of common law pleading was [p. 209] retained[5]. Already in 1293 the bailiff of one of the bishop of

---

[1] Bracton, f. 62; Fleta, p. 127: 'quia revera qui rem emptori nondum tradidit adhuc ipse dominus erit, quia traditionibus et usucapionibus etc.'

[2] Glanvill, x. 14. Bracton, f. 62, with Glanvill and the Institutes both open before him, deliberately contradicts the latter and copies the former.

[3] See above, vol. ii. pp. 170 ff.

[4] In a few cases it would perhaps be used to recover arrears of a freehold rent; but this was exceptional. See above, vol. ii. p. 127.

[5] In the sixteenth century, however, the word *contract* had acquired a special association with the action of debt. See Fitz. Abr. *Dett, passim.*

Ely's manors has paid a sum of money to the bishop's steward
for him to pay over to the bishop; the steward has neglected
or refused to do his duty; the bailiff seeks restitution by
action of debt[1]. In the next year we are told that if the
purchaser of land pays his money and the vendor will not
enfeoff him, an action of debt will lie[2]. An action of debt
against his father's executors is considered the appropriate
remedy for the child who claims a *legitima portio* of his
father's goods[3]. If however we look only at the cases in which
the action is used for what modern lawyers would regard as
the enforcement of a contract, and if we put aside for a while
the promise under seal, we have the money loan, the sale of
goods, the lease of land and the surety's undertaking, as the
four main causes for an action of debt. The action against
the surety has had its own separate history; the surety has
been a hostage and in later days a formal ceremony with a
wed or *festuca* has been the foundation of the claim against
him[4]. In the three other cases the defendant has received
something—nay, he has received *some thing*—from the plaintiff.
To use the phrase which appears at a later day, he obviously
has *quid pro quo,* and the *quid* is a material thing. We do
not say that the doctrine rested here even for a moment.
Probably the king's court would have put services rendered
on an equality with goods sold and delivered. The fact that
we can not give an instance of an action brought by a servant
to recover his wages may well be due to the existence of local
courts which were fully competent to deal with such matters.
But we much doubt whether at the end of the thirteenth
[p. 210] century the action extended beyond those cases in which the
defendant had received some material thing or some service
from the plaintiff[5].

---

[1] Y. B. 21–2 Edw. I. p. 39. This was a notable action. The count in it is
preserved in a collection of precedents, MS. Lansdowne, 652, f. 223 b.

[2] Y. B. 21–2 Edw. I. p. 599.

[3] This is given as a precedent in MS. Lansdowne, 652, f. 223 b. We shall
speak of this action in another chapter.

[4] So late as 1314 (Y. B. 7 Edw. II. f. 242) an action of debt is brought against
a surety who has not bound himself by sealed instrument. See Holmes, Common
Law, pp. 260, 264, 280; Salmond, Essays in Jurisprudence, 182.

[5] In 1292 (Y. B. 21–2 Edw. I. p. 111) we find an action which departs from
the common precedents. The plaintiff let land to the defendant for fourteen
years; the defendant was to build a house worth £14 and in default was to pay

Any formulated doctrine of *quid pro quo* was still in the future. Therefore we are not concerned to explore the history of the generalization which in after days is expressed by that curious term. The courts are proceeding outwards from a typical debt. In its earliest stage the action is thought of as an action whereby a man 'recovers' what belongs to him. It has its root in the money loan; for a very long time it is chiefly used for the recovery of money that has been lent. The case of the unpaid vendor is not—this is soon seen—essentially different from that of the lender: he has parted with property and demands a return. It enters no one's head that a promise is the ground of this action. No pleader propounding such an action will think of beginning his count with ' Whereas the defendant promised to pay '; he will begin with ' Whereas the plaintiff lent or (as the case may be) sold or leased to the defendant.' In short he will mention some *causa debendi* and that cause will not be a promise[1]. The Norman custumal which lies parallel to, but is much less romanized than, Bracton's book, puts this very neatly:—' Ex promisso autem nemo debitor constituitur, nisi causa precesserit legitima promittendi[2].' Our English writers give us nothing so succinct as this, because unfortunately the Italian glossators have led them astray with a theory of 'vestments' which will not fit the English facts; but we can not doubt that the Norman maxim would have commanded the assent of every English pleader. No one thinks of transgressing it. If you sue in debt you must rely on loan, or sale, or some other similar transaction. At a later time, various transactions have been [p. 211] pronounced to be similar to loan and sale, and an attempt is made to define them by one general phrase, or, in other words, to discover the common element in the *legitimae causae debendi.*

that sum, or (so it seems) such part of it as was not covered by the value of any house that he had built. He built a house worth £6. 10*s.* The plaintiff brings an action of debt for £7. 10*s.* The objection that this is a case of covenant, not debt, is overruled.

[1] Glanvill, x. 3: ' Is qui petit pluribus ex causis debitum petere potest, aut enim debetur ei quid ex causa mutui, aut ex causa venditionis, aut ex commodato, aut ex locato, aut ex deposito, aut ex alia iusta debendi causa.'

[2] Summa, p. 215; Ancienne coutume (ed. de Gruchy), c. 91 (90). The French text says—' Aulcun n'est estably debteur pour promesse qu'il face, se il ny eust droicte cause de promettre.' The whole of the chapters relating to debts and contracts is very instructive.

That this should be found in *quid pro quo* is not unnatural. We may take it as a general principle of ancient German law that the courts will not undertake to uphold gratuitous gifts or to enforce gratuitous promises[1]. The existence of this principle is shown by the efforts that are made to evade it. We can trace back the manufacture of what an English lawyer would call 'nominal considerations' to the remotest period. In the very old Lombard laws we see that the giver of a gift always receives some valueless trifle in return, which just serves to make his gift not a gift but an exchange[2]. At a much later time both in France and in England we see the baby, who as expectant heir is brought in to take part in a sale of land, getting a penny or a toy. The buyer gives the seller a coin by way of earnest, otherwise the seller's promise would not bind him. The churches would not acquire their vast territories if they had nothing to offer in return; but they have the most 'valuable' of 'considerations' at their disposal. As regards the conveyance of land, the principle is concealed by feudalism, but only because it is so triumphant that a breach of it is hardly conceivable. Every alienation of land, a sale, an onerous lease in fee farm, is a 'gift' but no 'gift' of land is gratuitous; the donee will always become liable to render service, though it be but the service of prayers. Every fine levied in the king's court will expressly show a *quid pro quo*; often a sparrow-hawk is given in return for a wide tract of land; and this is so, though here the bargain takes the solemnest of solemn forms[3].
[p. 212] Perhaps we may doubt whether in the thirteenth century a purely gratuitous promise, though made in a sealed instrument,

---

[1] Heusler, Institutionen, i. 81; Schröder, D. R. G. 61. The statement current in English books of recent times that the solemnity of a deed 'imports consideration' is historically incorrect, but shows the persistence of this idea.

[2] This is the Lombard *launichild* (*Lohngeld*); see Heusler, Institutionen, i. 81; Val de Lièvre, Launegild und Wadia. Is the modern custom of nominally selling, not giving, a knife or other weapon or weapon-like thing to be regarded as a mere survival of this? Or has the *launichild* coalesced with some other and perhaps even older superstitious form? Dr Brunner, Pol. Sci. Quarterly, ix. 542, suggests that if the donee were cut by the knife, he might under ancient law hold the donor answerable for the wound.

[3] See Fines, ed. Hunter, *passim*. When a fine is levied in favour of a religious house, the 'consideration' stated in the chirograph is very often the admission of the benefactor into the benefit of the monks' prayers; see *e.g.* Selby Coucher, ii. 329, 333. The sparrow-hawk is a 'common form' in fines of Edward I.'s day.

would have been enforced if its gratuitous character had stood openly revealed[1]. We are not contending that the principle had as yet been formulated. It is long before men formulate general negations of this kind. They proceed outwards from a type such as the loan of money: they admit one *causa debendi* after another, until at last they have to face the task of generalization. Still we think that all along there is a strong feeling that, whatever promises the law may enforce, purely gratuitous promises are not and ought not to be enforceable[2].

Proof of debt.

In the action of debt, unless the plaintiff relied on a sealed document, the defendant might as a general rule wage his law: that is to say, he might undertake to deny the debt by an oath with oath-helpers[3]. A wager of battle there had seldom been in such cases, and in the thirteenth century it was no longer allowed. In the earlier years of that age a defendant would sometimes meet the charge by demanding that the 'suitors' [p. 213] who were produced by the plaintiff should be examined, and, if

---

[1] The ordinary bond of this period generally states that there has been a loan of money, and, even when both parties are Englishmen, it often contains a renunciation of the *exceptio non numeratae pecuniae*. See, *e.g.* Selby Coucher, ii. p. 243, where this occurs in a quit-claim. This probably was an unnecessary precaution learnt from the Italian bankers; for see Bracton, f. 100 b. But in any case the bond is no mere promise; it is the confession of a legal debt. It says, *Sciatis me teneri*. As Bracton puts it, the obligor *scripsit se debere* and is bound by his confession.

[2] We can not accept the ingenious theory advocated by Mr Justice Holmes, Common Law, pp. 255–9, which would connect the requirement of *quid pro quo* with the requirement of a *secta*, and this with the requirement of transaction witnesses. The demand for a *secta* is no peculiarity of the action of debt. The plaintiff who complains (*e.g.*) of an assault, must produce a *secta*, but his suitors will not be 'official witnesses.' Again, the action to recover money lent is for a long while the typical action of debt; but we have no reason to believe that money loans were contracted before official witnesses. Lastly, we have no proof that the official witnesses were ever called in by the plaintiff to establish a contract; they were called in by a defendant to protect him against a charge of theft. The history of 'consideration' lies outside the period with which we are dealing. Few points in English legal history have been more thoroughly discussed within recent times. See Holmes, Common Law, Lecture vi.; Salmond, Essays in Jurisprudence, iv.; Hare on Contracts, ch. vii.; Ames, History of Assumpsit, Harv. L. R. ii. 1, 53; Jenks, Doctrine of Consideration; Pollock, Principles of Contract, App. Note E; Esmein, Un chapitre de l'histoire des contrats en droit anglais, Nouvelle revue historique de droit français et étranger, 1893, p. 555. Mr Ames has put the subject, from the fifteenth century downwards, on a new footing.

[3] Even in debt for rent when there is no deed a wager of law is permitted; Y. B. 20–1 Edw. I. p. 304.

they failed to tell a consistent story, the action was dismissed; but the tender of 'suit' was, at least in the king's court, rapidly becoming a mere form[1]. Efforts were made from time to time to place the tally, at all events if it bore writing and a seal, on an equality with the sealed charter. In cases between merchants a royal ordinance decreed that, if the defendant denied the tally, the plaintiff might prove his case by witnesses and the country in the same way as that in which the execution of a charter could be proved[2]. The common law, however, allowed the defendant to meet a tally by wager of law. In mercantile cases, when a tally of acquittance was produced against a tally of debt, the defendant was allowed to make good his assertion by an oath sworn upon nine altars in nine churches[3]. In the city of London the 'foreigner' who could not find oath-helpers was allowed to swear away a debt by visiting the six churches that were nearest the gildhall[4]. The ease with which the defendant could escape was in the end the ruin of this old action.

In the action of debt the plaintiff demands a sum of money together with 'damages' for the unjust detention. The damages claimed by the plaintiff are often very high[5], and he has a chance of getting all that he claims, for if the defendant wages, [p. 214] but fails to make his law, there will be no mitigation or

Damages in debt.

---

[1] Note Book, pl. 1693; Fleta, p. 138, allows an examination. So late as 1324 a plaintiff fails because he has no 'suitors' ready; Y. B. 18 Edw. II. f. 582.

[2] Fleta, p. 138; this boon was conceded to merchants 'ex gratia principis.' Select Civil Pleas, pl. 146; Note Book, pl. 645; Y. B. 20–1 Edw. I. p. 305; 21–2 Edw. I. p. 457; 30–1 Edw. I. p. 235; 32–3 Edw. I. p. 185. A collection of cases, MS. Harley, 25. f. 179, 188, contains an interesting discussion about sealed tallies. Plaintiff produces a tally. Defendant wishes to wage his law. Plaintiff asks 'Is this your deed?' Defendant answers 'We need not say.' Then a judge says 'Coment qil seient taillés, vus les avez aforcé par le planter de vostre seel, et icy vostre fet.' To this it is replied that in the time of Sir John Metingham (temp. Edw. I.) a sealed tally was admitted but the judgment was reversed.

[3] Fleta, pl. 138.

[4] Munimenta Gildhallae, i. 203. In the Laws of Alfred, 33, we read of an oath in four churches outsworn by an oath in twelve.

[5] See *e.g.* Northumberland Assize Rolls, p. 169: the plaintiff claims seven marks, the price of a horse sold about four years ago, and ten marks damages. At a little later time the civic court in London by general rule allowed damages at the rate of 20 per cent. per annum unless the debt was confessed at the first summons. See Munim. Gildh. i. 471.

'taxation' of the amount that the plaintiff has mentioned[1]. In other cases the jurors under the control of the justices seem to be free to award what damages they please, provided that they do not give more than has been demanded. There is no usury here, for there has been no bargain that the creditor shall receive any certain sum for the use of his money, still, so far as we can see, the plaintiff gets damages though he has only proved that the debt was not paid when it was due.

Limit to the action.

One boundary of the action of debt is fixed from the first and can not be removed. The plaintiff must claim some fixed sum that is due to him. We must have a quite different action if 'unliquidated' sums are to be claimed by way of damages for breach of contract.

(3) Action of covenant.

(3) The writ of covenant (*breve de conventione*) is not mentioned by Glanvill; but it appears within a short time after the publication of his book[2] and already in the early years of Henry III. it can be had 'as of course,' at all events when the tenement that is in question is of small value[3]. Before Henry's death it has become a popular writ. On the roll for the Easter term for 1271 we found thirty-five actions of covenant pending[4]. But the popularity of the writ is due to the fact that men are by this time commonly employing it when they want to convey land by way of fine[5]. The great majority of actions of covenant are brought merely in order that they may be compromised. We doubt whether any principle was involved in the choice; but may infer that the procedure instituted by this writ was cheap and expeditious for those who wished to get to their

---

[1] Y. B. 33–5 Edw. I. p. 397. Hence a would-be verse found in MS. precedent books: 'Qui legem vadiat, nisi lex in tempore fiat, Mox condemnetur, taxatio non sibi detur.'

[2] Rolls of the King's Court (Pipe Roll Soc.), p. 53 (A.D. 1194, the earliest extant plea roll); an essoin is cast in a 'placitum convencionis per cirographum'; but this may be an action on a fine. Select Civil Pleas (Selden Soc.), pl. 89 (A.D. 1201) seems an indubitable specimen. Brevia Placitata, ed. Turner, 21.

[3] Maitland, Register of Writs, Harv. L. R. iii. 113–5. The writ first appears in the Registers as a *Iusticies*, which can be had as of course when the annual value of the land is worth less than 40 shillings. See also Excerpta e Rot. Fin. i. 31.

[4] Curia Regis Rolls (Rec. Off.), No. 202, Pasch. 55 Hen. III.

[5] See above, vol. ii. p. 98. The writ of *warantia cartae* is for this purpose its principal rival. Blackstone, Comm. ii. 350, mentions as alternatives the *warantia cartae* and the *de consuetudinibus et servitiis*.

[p. 215] final concord.   In all the oldest specimens that we have seen, whether on the plea rolls or in the registers, the subject matter of the *conventio* is land or one of those incorporeal things that are likened to land.

The specific want that this action has come to meet is that which is occasioned by the growing practice of letting lands for terms of years.   The *placitum conventionis* is almost always what we should call an action on a lease.   We have seen above how an unsuccessful attempt was made to treat the termor as having no rights in, no possession or seisin of, the land, but merely the benefit of an agreement.   This attempt, as already said, we are inclined to regard as an outcome of misdirected Romanism; at any rate it failed.   The termor, however, is protected by the writ of covenant and for a while this is his only protection; the action therefore becomes popular as leases for terms of years become common[1].   At a little later time it finds another employment.   Family settlements are being made by way of feoffment and refeoffment; the settlor takes a covenant for refeoffment from his feoffee.   Again, there is some evidence that in the course of the thirteenth century attempts were made to establish a kind of qualified tenure in villeinage by express agreements[2].   In all these cases, however, the writ mentions a certain piece of land, an advowson or the like, as the subject matter of the *conventio* and the judgment will often award this subject matter to the successful plaintiff[3].   As may well be supposed, in days when the typical *conventio* was a lease of land for a term of years and the lessee was gaining a 'real' right in the land, men were not very certain that other *conventiones* concerning land would not give real rights, that a covenant to enfeoff, or a covenant not to alienate might not bind the land and hold good against a subsequent [p. 216] feoffee[4].   However, in 1284 the *Statutum Walliae* made it

Covenants and leases.

---

[1] See above, vol. ii. p. 106.   [2] See above, vol. i. p. 405.

[3] Note book, pl. 1739; action by ejected termor: 'Et ideo consideratum est quod conventio teneatur et quod Hugo habeat seisinam suam usque ad terminum suum x. annorum.'

[4] See Note Book, pl. 36.   Bracton, f. 46; if a feoffment be made upon condition that the feoffee is not to alienate, the lord can eject one who purchases from the feoffee 'propter modum et conventionem in donatione appositam.'   Bracton does not here distinguish between condition and covenant. See also Y. B. 21-2 Edw. I. p. 183, where the objection is taken that one can not recover a freehold in a writ of covenant; and Note Book, pl. 1656, where the action is refused to one who could bring the novel disseisin.   In Y. B. 30-1

clear that a feoffment can not thus be set aside in favour of an earlier *conventio*, and specified this case as one of those in which the freehold can not be recovered and judgment must be for damages[1].

Scope of
the action. The same great statute assures us that in an action of covenant sometimes movables, sometimes immovables are demanded, also that the enforceable covenants are infinite in number so that no list of them can be made[2]; and, though we believe that the covenants which had as yet been enforced by the king's court had for the more part belonged to a very few classes, still it is plain that the writ was flexible and that no one was prepared to set strict limits to its scope. Bracton speaks as though the royal justices had a free hand in the enforcement of 'private conventions' and might in this particular do more than they were actually doing[3]. We can produce a few examples in which the plaintiff is not claiming land or an incorporeal thing such as a rent or an advowson[4].

Edw. I. p. 145, we read how 'this action is personal and is given against the person who did the trespass and the tort.' Thus the conception of the writ has been fluctuating between opposite poles. The statement that a breach of covenant is 'tort' and 'trespass' is of some importance when connected with the later history of *assumpsit*.

[1] Statutes of the Realm, vol. i. p. 66.

[2] Ibid. : 'et quia infiniti sunt contractus conventionum difficile esset facere mentionem de quolibet in speciali.'

[3] Bracton, f. 34, 100; Bracton and Azo, p. 152 : 'Iudicialis autem poterit esse stipulatio, vel conventionalis.........Conventionalis, quae ex conventione utriusque partis concipitur......et quarum totidem sunt genera, quot paene rerum contrahendarum, de quibus omnino curia regis se non intromittit nisi aliquando de gratia.' It is not very plain whether by this last phrase, which is a reminiscence of Glanvill, x. 8, Bracton means to say that the court sometimes as a matter of grace enforces unwritten agreements, or that it only enforces written agreements occasionally and as a matter of grace. On the same page, following the general tendency of medieval Roman law, he explains that a *stipulatio* may well be made *per scripturam*. In the passage here quoted the printed book gives *poenae* instead of *paene*, which (though every MS. of this age would give *pene* even if the word was *poenae*) is indubitably the true reading; see Inst. 3. 18. § 3.

[4] Y. B. 21–2 Edw. I. p. 111 : it is said that an action of covenant will lie for not building a house. Y. B. 21–2 Edw. I. p. 183 : a Prioress has convenanted to provide a chaplain to sing service in the plaintiff's chapel. But even here there is 'a chantry' of which 'seisin' is alleged. Y. B. 20–1 Edw. I. p. 223 : covenant to return a horse that has been lent or to pay £20. But for reasons given below (p. 220) some doubt hangs over this case. Note Book, pl. 1053 (A.D. 1225) : covenant that the plaintiff and his wife may live with the defendant, and that, if they wish to depart, he will cause them to have certain lands.

[p. 217] However, in the Statute of Wales we have a sufficient declaration that, as regards the subject matter of the agreements
that can be enforced by this action, no boundaries have been
or can be drawn.   One limitation however soon becomes apparent, and is curious.   The action of covenant can not be
employed for the recovery of a debt, even though the existence
of the debt is attested by a sealed instrument.   A debt can
not have its origin in a promise or a *conventio*; it must arise
from some transaction such as loan, or sale or the like; and
the law is economical; the fact that a man has one action is
a reason for not giving him another[1].

But what of form?   Before the end of Edward I.'s reign
the king's court had established the rule that the only *conventio*
that can be enforced by action is one that is expressed in a
written document sealed 'by the party to be charged therewith.'
Thenceforward the word *conventio* and the French and English
covenant, at least in the mouths of Westminster lawyers, imply
or even denote a sealed document.   There had been some
hesitation; nor is this to be wondered at.   *Pacta sunt servanda*
was in the air; *Pactum serva* was Edward's chosen motto.
The most that the Romanist could do for the written agreement
was to place it alongside the *stipulatio* or to say that it was a
stipulatio, and he knew that according to the latest doctrine of
mature Roman law a *stipulatio* could be made by a simple
question and answer without the use of any magical or
sacramental phrases.   Again, the king's court had refused to
attribute any special efficacy to what we may call the old
Germanic forms, the symbolic *wed* and the grasp of hands;
these had fallen under the patronage of the rival tribunals
of the church.   There was a special reason for hesitation and
confusion, for it was chiefly for the protection of lessees of land
that the writ of covenant had come into being; for some time

The covenant must be written.

Note Book, pl. 1129: covenant that plaintiff may have a hundred pigs in a
certain wood.   But here the plaintiff seems to be claiming a 'profit.'   Warranties
or agreements of a similar kind seem to be occasionally enforced by writ of
covenant; but usually they are enforced either by voucher or by the writ of
warantia cartae.   In Edward I.'s time it is thought that there are some cases in
which a plaintiff can choose between debt and covenant; Y. B. 20–1 Edw. I.
p. 141; 21–2 Edw. I. pp. 111, 601.

[1] Ames, Harv. L. R. ii. 56: 'The writer has discovered no case in which a
plaintiff succeeded in an action of covenant, where the claim was for a sum
certain, antecedent to the seventeenth century.'

it was the termor's only writ, and no one had yet said or would ever say that the 'term of years' could not (apart from statute) be created by word of mouth and delivery of possession. To [p. 218] require a charter for a lease would have been to require more than was demanded where there was to be a feoffment in fee simple. And so for a while we seem to see some unwritten agreements enforced as *conventiones,* and, even when it is plain that the unwritten agreement will bear no action, men think that it will bear an 'exception:' in other words, that it can be set up by way of defence. What is more, the lawyers do not think that they are laying down a rule of substantive law about the form that a covenant must take; they are talking about evidence. The man who relies upon a covenant must produce in proof some 'specialty' (*especialté, aliquid speciale*); the production of 'suit' is not enough. Thenceforward, however, it is only a short step to holding as a matter of law that a 'deed'—and by a deed (*fet, factum*) men are beginning to mean a sealed piece of parchment—has an operative force of its own which intentions expressed, never so plainly, in other ways have not. The sealing and delivering of the parchment is the contractual act. Further, what is done by 'deed' can only be undone by 'deed[1].'

---

[1] The period of hesitation is illustrated by Note Book, pl. 890, 1129, 1549. But as early as 1234–5 we have found (Record Office, Curia Regis Roll, No. 115, m. 7) a fairly clear case of an action of covenant dismissed because the plaintiff has no deed: 'et quia dictus H. non protulit cartam nec cyrographum de praedicta terra, consideratum est quod loquela illa vacua est.' On the roll for Pasch. 34 Hen. III. (Record Office, Curia Regis Roll, No. 140), m. 15 d, W. E. sues the Abbot of Evesham 'quod teneat ei conventionem'; the plaintiff counts that the abbot came before the justices in eyre, granted the plaintiff an elaborate corody, and further granted that he would execute a deed (*conficeret cartam*) embodying this concession; suit is tendered and no appeal is made to any record. The abbot confesses the *conventio,* denies the breach and wages his law. In Y. B. 20–1 Edw. I. p. 223—as late therefore as 1292—we seem to see that whether 'suit' will support an action of covenant is still doubtful, while it will support an action of debt. (See however, p. 487; we can not be quite certain that one of the reporters has not blundered.) In Y. B. 21–2 Edw. I. p. 621, a defendant sets up an agreement by way of defence; on being asked what he has to prove the covenant, he appeals to 'the country.' 'Nota' says the reporter 'ke la ou un covenant est aleggé cum chose incident en play yl put estre detrié par pays.' In Y. B. 32–3 Edw. I. p. 297, an action of covenant is brought against tenant *pur autre vie* for wasting the tenement; he demands judgment as the plaintiff has nothing to prove the covenant or the lease; but is told to find a better answer. This case shows the point of contact between the covenant and the lease. Ibid. p. 201, a writ of covenant is brought against

One other action remains to be mentioned, namely, the action of account. Here, again, the writ was modelled upon the proprietary writs. The defendant must 'justly and without delay render to the plaintiff' something, namely, an account for the time during which he was the plaintiff's bailiff and receiver of the plaintiff's money. Even in the modern theory of our law 'the obligation to render an account is not founded upon contract, but is created by law independently of contract[1].' The earliest instance of this action known to us dates from 1232[2]: the writ seems to come upon the register late in Henry III.'s reign[3], and much of its efficacy in later times was due to the statutes of 1267 and 1285[4]. These statutes sanctioned a procedure against accountants which was in that age a procedure of exceptional rigour. We gather that the accountants in question were for the more part 'bailiffs' in the somewhat narrow sense that this word commonly bore, manorial bailiffs. In Edward I.'s day the action was being used in a few other cases; it had been given by statute against the guardian in socage[5], and we find that it can be used among traders who have joined in a commercial adventure: the trade of the Italian bankers was being carried on by large 'societies' and

---

a termor who is holding beyond his term; he promised to execute a written agreement, but has not; the defendant at first relies on the want of a 'specialty,' but is driven to claim a freehold. The rule that what is done by 'deed' can in general only be undone by 'deed' appears in Y. B. 33–5 Edw. I. pp. 127, 331, 547. See Bracton, f. 101: 'eisdem modis dissolvitur obligatio......quibus contrahitur, ut si conscripserim me debere, scribat creditor se accepisse.' This is romanesque (see the passages collected by Moyle in his comment on Inst. 3. 29) but is quite in harmony with English thought, and was rigorously enforced. See Ames, Specialty Contracts and Equitable Defences, Harv. L. R. ix. 49. The technical use of the word *deed* seems the outcome of the very common plea *Non est factum meum, Nient mon fet*, i.e. I did not execute that document. As a word which will stand for the document itself, it slowly supplants *carta*; it is thus used in Y. B. 33–5 Edw. I. p. 331: 'nous avoms vostre fet.' As to specialty (*aliquid speciale*), this comes to the front in *quo waranto* proceedings; the claimant of a franchise must have something special to show for it. In relation to contract, the demand for specialty seems a demand for some proof other than a verdict of 'the country.'

1 Langdell, Survey of Equity Jurisdiction, Harv. L. R. ii. 243.

2 Note Book, pl. 859.

3 Maitland, Register of Original Writs, Harv. L. R. iii. 173. Brevia Placitata, ed. Turner, 23.

4 Stat. Marlb. c. 23; Stat. West. II. c. 11.

5 See above, vol. i. p. 322.

Eng'ishmen were beginning to learn a little about partnership[1]. Throughout the fourteenth and fifteenth centuries the action was frequent enough, as the Year Books and Abridgements show. In after times the more powerful and convenient [p. 220] jurisdiction of equity superseded the process of account at common law, though the action lingered on in one application, as a remedy between tenants in common, late enough to furnish one or two modern examples. But on the whole it did very little for our law of contract.

Covenant in the local courts.
We have been speaking of actions in the king's court; but we imagine that in the thirteenth century the local courts were still very free to go their own way about such matters as contract. There is evidence that some of them enforced by action of 'covenant' agreements that were not in writing[2]. It is possible that these agreements had been fastened by a grasp of hands; as yet we know but too little of what was done by the municipal and manorial tribunals. *Pacta sunt servanda* was, as we have said, already in the air. The scheme of actions offered by the king's court had become rigid just too soon, and in later centuries the Westminster lawyers were put to strange and tortuous devices in their attempt to develop a comprehensive law of contract. They had to invent a new action for the enforcement of unwritten agreements, and its starting point was the semi-criminal action of trespass. Of their bold and ingenious inventions we must not here speak. At present we see them equipped with the actions of debt, covenant and account; each has its own narrow sphere and many an

---

[1] Y. B. 32–3 Edw. I. p. 377, where 'la manere de la companye des Lombars' is mentioned; 33–5 Edw. I. p. 295.

[2] Select Pleas in Manorial Courts, p. 157: action in the Fair of St Ives (A.D. 1275) by a master against a servant who has left his service; the breach of contract is admitted; the judgment is that John do serve Richard to the end of the term; no written document is mentioned. See also The Court Baron (Selden Soc.), p. 115; unwritten agreement enforced in a manorial court of the bishop of Ely. We have seen several such cases on the rolls of the court of Wisbech now preserved in the palace at Ely. In one case of Edward I.'s time the plaintiff alleges an agreement (*conventio*) for the sale of two acres of land for one mark. The plaintiff has paid the price but the defendant has refused to enfeoff him. No word is said of any writing. The defendant denies the agreement and asks for an inquest. The jurors find that the agreement was made, and the plaintiff has judgment for damages. For the civic courts in London, see Munimenta Gildhallae, i. 214; Fitz. Nat. Brev. 146 a. For Nottingham, see Records of Nottingham, i. 161, 167, 207. We may well believe that in the larger towns unwritten covenants were commonly enforced.

agreement though, as we should say, made for valuable consideration, finds no remedy in the king's court.

The English formal contract, therefore, is no product of ancient folk-law. The 'act and deed' that is chosen is one that [p. 221] in the past has been possible only to men of the highest rank. The use of the seal comes to us from the court of Frankish kings. At the date of the Conquest the Norman duke has a seal and his cousin the late king of England had a seal; but in all probability very few of William's followers, only the counts and bishops, have seals[1]. Even in the chancery of our Norman kings the apposition of a seal had to struggle with older methods of perfecting a charter. A seal sufficed for writs, but a solemn 'land-book' would as of old bear the crosses of the king and the attesting magnates, ink crosses which they had drawn, or at least touched, with their own hands[2]. This old ceremony did not utterly disappear before Stephen's day; but men were beginning to look for a seal as an essential part of a charter. The unsealed 'books' of the Anglo-Saxon kings are called in question if they have not been confirmed by a sealed document[3]. Gilbert de Balliol called in question the charters granted by his ancestors to Battle Abbey; Richard de Lucy the justiciar replied that it was not the fashion of old time that every petty knightling should have a seal[4]. For some time to come we meet with cases in which a man who had land to give had no seal of his own and delivered a charter which had passed under the seal of the sheriff or of some nobleman. In the France of Bracton's day the privilege of using a seal was confined to 'gentixhomes'; a man of lower degree would execute his bond by carrying it before his lord and

The sealed document.

---

[1] Bresslau, Urkundenlehre, i. 521 ff; Giry, Manuel de diplomatique, 636 ff.

[2] The Monasticon testifies to the existence of many charters granted by the Norman kings, including Stephen, which either bore no seals, or else were also signed with crosses in the old fashion. Maitland, Domesday Book, p. 265. The Exeter Charter of William I. (Facsimiles of Anglo-Saxon Charters, vol. i. no. 16) will serve as a specimen. Sometimes the cross is spoken of as more sacred than the seal; see Monast. ii. 385–6 : 'non solum sigillo meo sed etiam sigillo Dei omnipotentis, id est, sanctae crucis.'

[3] Gesta Abbatum, i. 151. In Henry II.'s time the unsealed charters of St Albans are considered to be validated by the sealed confirmation obtained from Henry I.

[4] Bigelow, Placita, 177 : 'Moris antiquitus non erat quemlibet militulum sigillum habere, quod regibus et praecipuis tantum competit personis.'

procuring the apposition of his lord's seal[1]. But in England, as we have often seen, the law for the great became the law for all, and before the end of the thirteenth century the free and [p. 222] lawful man usually had a seal. It is commonly assumed that jurors will as a matter of course have seals. We must not think of the act of sealing as a mere formality; the impressed wax was treated as a valuable piece of evidence. If a man denied a charter that was produced against him and the witnesses named in it were dead, the seal on it would be compared with the seals on instruments the genuineness of which he admitted, and thus he might be convicted of a false plea[2]. 'Nient mon fet' was a very common defence, and forgery, even the forgery of royal writs and papal bulls, was by no means rare.

Growth of written documents. In the twelfth century charters of feoffment had become common; they sometimes contained clauses of warranty. In the next century leases for years and documents which dealt with easements, with rights of pasturage, with tithes and the like, were not unfrequent; they sometimes contained penal clauses which were destined to create money debts[3]. Occasionally there was an agreement for a penal sum which was to go to the king or to the sheriff, to the fabric fund of Westminster abbey or to the relief of the Holy Land[4]. In John's reign the Earl of Salisbury, becoming surety for the good behaviour of Peter de Maulay, declares that, if Peter offends, all the earl's hawks shall belong to the king; and so Gilbert Fitz Remfrey invokes perpetual disherison on himself should he adhere to

---

[1] Beaumanoir, c. 35. § 18: 'Trois manieres de lettres sunt: le premiere entre gentix homes de lor seaus, car il poent fere obligation contr'eus par le tesmognage de lor seaus; et le second, si est que tous gentil home et home de poeste poent fere reconnisances de lor convenances par devant lor seigneurs dessoz qui il sont couquant et levant, ou par devant le sovrain.'

[2] The trial by collation of seals is illustrated in Note Book, pl. 1, 51, 102, 234, 237 etc.

[3] Winchcombe Landboc, i. 239: if J. S. breaks the water pipe of the abbot of Winchcombe, which runs through his land, he will repair it, and in default of repair will pay half a mark for each day's neglect. Reg. Malmesb. ii. 83: if rent falls into arrear the lessee will pay an additional 10 shillings *pro misericordia.*

[4] Winchcombe Landboc, i. 239: the sheriff may distrain and take a half-mark for the king's use. Newminster Cartulary, 98: a penal sum to be paid *in subsidium terrae sanctae.* See also the precedents of John of Oxford, L. Q. R. vii. 65; Madox, Formulare, p. 359, and Archæologia, xxviii. p. 228.

Magna Carta which the pope has quashed[1]. But documents of a purely obligatory character were still rare. They seem to come hither with the Italian bankers. They generally took the form of the 'single bond[2]'; the bond with a clause of defeasance seems to be of later date. The creditor confesses himself to be bound (*se teneri*) in respect of money lent, and obliges himself and all his goods, movable and immovable, for its repayment on a fixed day or after the lapse of so many days from the presentation of the bond. Sometimes we may see (at all events when the lender is an Italian) a distinct promise to pay interest (*interesse*)[3]; more often there is a promise to pay all damages and costs which the creditor shall incur, and this is sometimes coupled with a promise that the creditor's sworn or unsworn assertion shall fix their amount[4]. When a rate of interest was fixed, it was high. With the pope's approval, Henry III. borrowed 540 marks from Florentine merchants, and, if repayment were not made after six months or thereabouts, the debt was to bear interest at sixty per cent.[5] Often the debtor had to renounce in advance every possible 'exception' that civil or canon or customary law might give him. The cautious Lombard meant to have an instrument that would be available in every court, English or foreign. But even an English lawyer might think it well to protect himself by such phrases. Thus when Mr Justice Roubury lent the Bishop of Durham £200, the bishop submitted himself to every sort of jurisdiction and renounced every sort of exception[6]. Often the

The single bond.

[p. 223]

---

[1] Rot. Cart. Joh. pp. 191, 221.

[2] See Blackstone, Comm. ii. 340. Not one of the commentators, so far as we know, has rightly understood this term in the place where Shakespeare has made it classical (Merch. of Venice, Act i. Sc. 3). Shylock first offers to take a bond without a penalty, and then adds the fantastic penalty of the pound of flesh, ostensibly as a jesting afterthought.

[3] Cart. Riev. p. 410: the abbot is to pay one mark on every ten marks for every delay of two months, *i.e.* sixty per cent. per annum 'pro recompensatione, interesse, et expensis.' This pact is secured by recognizance in the king's court. See also Mat. Par. Chron. Maj. iii. 330.

[4] See *e.g.* Registr. Palatin. Dunelmense, i. 91: 'super quibus iuramento eorundem vel eorum unius socii, fidem volumus adhiberi.' Madox, Formulare, p. 359: 'damnis et expensis quae vel quas se simplici verbo suo dixerint sustinuisse.'

[5] Prynne, Records, ii. 1034; see also ibid. 845.

[6] Registr. Palatin. Dunelmense, i. 276 (A.D. 1311): 'Et ad haec omnia fideliter facienda obligamus nos et omnia bona nostra mobilia et immobilia, ecclesiastica et mundana, ubicunque locorum inventa, iurisdictioni et coercioni

debtor is bound to pay the money either to the creditor or to any attorney or mandatory of his who shall produce the bond.

Mercantile
documents.　　The clause which promises payment to the creditor ' or his attorney' is of great interest.　Ancient German law, like ancient Roman law, sees great difficulties in the way of an assignment of a debt or other benefit of a contract[1].　The assignee who sued the debtor would be met by the plea 'I never bound myself to pay money to *you.*'　But further, men do not see how there can be a transfer of a right unless that right is embodied in some corporeal thing.　The history of [p. 224] the 'incorporeal things' has shown us this; they are not completely transferred until the transferee has obtained seisin, has turned his beasts onto the pasture, presented a clerk to the church or hanged a thief upon the gallows[2].　A covenant or a warranty of title may be so bound up with land that the assignee of the land will be able to sue the covenantor or warrantor.　At an early time we may see the assignee of a lease bringing an action of covenant against the lessor[3].　But, even in the region of warranty, we find that much depends on the use of the word *assigns*; the feoffor will only be bound to warrant the feoffee's assigns if he has expressly promised to warrant them[4].

Assign-
ment of
debts.　　In the case, however, of the mere debt there is nothing that can be pictured as a transfer of a thing; there can be no seisin or change of seisin.　In course of time a way of escape was found in the appointment of an attorney.　In the thirteenth century men often appear in the king's court by attorney; but they do not even yet enjoy, unless by virtue of some special favour purchased from the king, any right of appointing attorneys to conduct prospective litigation; when an action

cuiuscunque iudicis ecclesiastici vel civilis quem idem dominus Gilbertus adire vel eligere voluerit in hac parte: exceptioni non numeratae, non traditae, non solutae, nobis pecuniae, et in nostram et ecclesiae nostrae utilitatem non conversae, et omni iuri scripto canonico et civili, ac omni rationi et privilegio per quam vel quod contra praemissa, vel aliquod praemissorum, venire possemus, renunciantes penitus et expresse.'　The finest specimen of a renunciatory clause that we have seen is in a bond given in 1293 by the abbot of Glastonbury to some merchants of Lucca for the enormous sum of £1750; Archaeologia, xxviii. 227; it must have been settled by a learned civilian.　A good instance of a bond for the delivery of wool sold by the obligor is in Prynne, Records, iii. 185.

[1] Pollock, Principles of Contract, App. Note F; Brunner in Holtzendorff's Encyklopädie (5th ed.) p. 279.

[2] See above, vol. ii. p. 139.　　[3] Note Book, pl. 804.　　[4] See Bracton, f. 37 b.

has been begun, then and not until then, an attorney can be appointed[1]. The idea of representation is new[2]; it has spread outwards from a king who has so many affairs that he can not conduct them in person. However, it has by this time spread so far that the debtor who in express written words promises to pay money either to the creditor or to the mandatory (*nuntius*) or attorney of the creditor is bound by his promise; he has himself given the creditor power to appoint a representative for the exaction of the debt. Often in the bonds that are before us the debtor promises to pay the creditor or 'his certain attorney producing these letters.' The attorney will have to produce the bond and also evidence, probably in the form of a 'power of attorney,' that he is the attorney of the original creditor[3]. It seems probable that the process which in [p. 225] the end enables men to transfer mere personal rights has taken advantage, if we may so speak, of the appearance of the contract in a material form, the form of a document. That document, is it not itself the bond, the obligation? If so, a bond can be transferred. For a very long time past the Italians have been slowly elaborating a law of negotiable paper or negotiable parchment; they have learnt that they can make a binding promise in favour of any one who produces the letter in which the obligation is embodied. Englishmen are not yet doing this, but under Italian teaching they are already promising to pay the Florentine or Sienese capitalist or any attorney of his who produces the bond[4].

---

[1] See above, vol. i. p. 213. [2] Heusler, Institutionen, i. 203.

[3] On a roll of 1285 we read how the executors of the countess of Leicester have attorned Baruncino Gualteri of Lucca to receive certain moneys due to her; this in consideration of a loan from Baruncino. When he demands payment he will have to produce 'litteras praedictorum executorum dictam assignationem testificantes.' See Archaeologia, xxviii. 282. By this time the king is frequently 'assigning' the produce of taxes not yet collected.

[4] The clause 'vel suo certo attornato [*vel* nuntio] has litteras deferenti' is quite common. The only English instance that we have seen of a clause which differs from this is in Select Pleas in Manorial Courts, p. 152, where in 1275 a merchant of Bordeaux sues on a bond which contains a promise to pay to him 'vel cuicunque de suis scriptum obligatorium portanti.' But here the person who demands the debt can apparently be required to show that he is a partner or the like (*de suis*) of the creditor named in the bond. For the history of such clauses, see Brunner, Forschungen, p. 524 fol.; Heusler, Institutionen, i. 211; Jenks, Early History of Negotiable Instruments, L. Q. R. ix. 70. Apparently Bracton, f. 41 b, knew these mercantile documents under the name *missibilia*.

The whole law of agency is yet in its infancy. The king indeed ever since John's day has been issuing letters of credit empowering his agents to borrow money and to promise repayment in his name[1]. A great prelate will sometimes do the like[2]. It is by this time admitted that a man by his deed can appoint another to do many acts in his name, though he can not appoint an attorney to appear for him in court until litigation has been begun[3]. Attorneys were appointed to deliver and to receive seisin[4]. Among the clergy the idea of procuration was striking root; it was beginning to bear fruit in the domain of public law; the elected knights and burgesses must bring with them to parliament 'full powers' for the representation of the shires and boroughs. But of any informal agency, of any implied agency, we read very little[5]. We seem to see the beginning of it when an abbot is sued [p. 226] for the price of goods which were purchased by a monk and came to the use of the convent[6].

The germ of agency is hardly to be distinguished from the germ of another institution which in our English law has an eventful future before it, the 'use, trust or confidence.' In tracing its embryonic history we must first notice the now established truth that the English word *use* when it is employed with a technical meaning in legal documents is derived, not from the Latin word *usus*, but from the Latin word *opus*, which in old French becomes *os* or *oes*[7]. True that the two words are in course of time confused, so that if by a Latin document land is to be conveyed to the use of John, the scribe of the charter will write *ad opus Johannis* or *ad usum*

---

[1] Archaeologia, xxviii. 217.

[2] Registr. Palatin. Dunelmense, i. 69 (A.D. 1311): appointment of an agent to contract a large loan.

[3] One can not do homage by attorney; Note Book, pl. 41.

[4] Bracton, f. 40. The passage in which Bracton, f. 100 b, tells us 'per quas personas acquiritur obligatio' is a piece of inept Romanism. See Bracton and Azo, p. 160.

[5] Note Book, pl. 873: a plaintiff claims a wardship sold to her by the defendant's steward: 'et quia ipsa nihil ostendit quod ipse Ricardus [*the defendant*] ei aliquid inde concesserit, consideratum est quod Ricardus inde sine die.'

[6] Y. B. 33–5 Edw. I. p. 567. Already in Leg. Henr. 23 § 4, we read that the abbot must answer for the acts of the obedientiaries (*i.e.* the cellarer, chamberlain, sacrist, etc.) of the house. The legal deadness of the monks favours the growth of a law of agency.

[7] L. Q. R. iii. 116.

Johannis indifferently, or will perhaps adopt the fuller formula *ad opus et ad usum*; nevertheless the earliest history of 'the use' is the early history of the phrase *ad opus*[1]. Now this both in France and in England we may find in very ancient days. A man will sometimes receive money to the use (*ad opus*) of another person; in particular, money is frequently being received for the king's use. A king must have many officers who are always receiving money, and we have to distinguish what they receive for their own proper use (*ad opus suum proprium*) from what they receive on behalf of the king. Further, long before the Norman Conquest we may find a man saying that he conveys land to a bishop to the use of a church, or conveys land to a church to the use of a dead saint. The difficulty of framing a satisfactory theory touching the whereabouts of the ownership of what we may loosely call 'the lands of the churches' gives rise to such phrases. In the thirteenth century we commonly find that where there [p. 227] is what to our eyes is an informal agency, this term *ad opus* is used to describe it. Outside the ecclesiastical sphere there is but little talk of 'procuration'; there is no current word that is equivalent to our *agent*; John does not receive money or chattels 'as agent for' Roger; he receives it to the use of Roger (*ad opus Rogeri*).

Now in the case of money and chattels that haziness in the conception of ownership to which we have often called attention[2] prevents us from making a satisfactory analysis of the notion that this *ad opus* implies. William delivers two marks or three oxen to John, who receives them to the use of Roger. In whom, we may ask, is the ownership of the coins or of the beasts? Is it already in Roger; or, on the other hand, is it in John, and is Roger's right a merely personal right against John? This question does not arise in a clear form, because possession is far more important than ownership. We will suppose that John, who is the bailiff of one of Roger's manors, has in the ordinary course of business gone to a market, sold Roger's corn, purchased cattle with the price of the corn and is now driving them home. We take it that if a thief or trespasser swoops down and drives off the

Chattels held to the use of another.

---

[1] See the note appended to the end of this chapter. Mr Justice Holmes, L. Q. R. i. 162, was the first to point to the right quarter for the origin of 'uses.'
[2] See above, vol. ii. pp. 153, 177.

oxen, John can bring an appeal or an action and call the
beasts his own proper chattels. We take it that he himself
can not steal the beasts; even in the modern common law he
can not steal them until he has in some way put them in his
employer's possession[1]. We are not very certain that, if he
appropriates them to his own use, Roger has any remedy
except an action of debt or of account, in which his claim
can be satisfied by a money payment. And yet the notion
that the beasts are Roger's, not John's, is growing and destined to grow. In course of time the relationship expressed
by the vague *ad opus* will in this region develop into a law
of agency. In this region the phrase will appear in our own
day as expressing rights and duties which the common law
can sanction without the help of any 'equity.' The common
law will know the wrong that is committed when a man 'converts to his use' (*ad opus suum proprium*) the goods of another; and in course of time it will know the obligation which
arises when money is 'had and received to the use' of some
person other than the recipient.

Lands held
to the use
of another.
It is not so in the case of land, for there our old law had [p. 228]
to deal with a clearer and intenser ownership. But first we
must remark that at a very remote period one family at all
events of our legal ancestors have known what we may call
a trust, a temporary trust, of lands. The Frank of the *Lex
Salica* is already employing it; by the intermediation of a third
person, whom he puts in seisin of his lands and goods, he
succeeds in appointing or adopting an heir[2]. Along one line
of development we may see this third person, this 'saleman,'
becoming the testamentary executor of whom we must speak
hereafter; but our English law by forbidding testamentary
dispositions of land has prevented us from obtaining many
materials in this quarter. However, in the England of the
twelfth century we sometimes see the lord intervening between
the vendor and the purchaser of land. The vendor surrenders
the land to the lord 'to the use' of the purchaser by a rod, and
the lord by the same rod delivers the land to the purchaser[3].
Freeholders, it is true, have soon acquired so large a liberty of

---

[1] See Mr Justice Wright's statement and authorities, in Pollock and Wright,
Possession, p. 191.

[2] Lex Salica, tit. 46, *De adfathamire.* Heusler, Institutionen, i. 215.

[3] See above, vol. i. p. 345.

alienation that we seldom read of their taking part in such surrenders; but their humbler neighbours (for instance, the king's sokemen) are often surrendering land 'to the use' of one who has bought it. What if the lord when the symbolic stick was in his hand refused to part with it? Perhaps the law had never been compelled to consider so rare an event; and in these cases the land ought to be in the lord's seisin for but a moment. However, we soon begin to see what we can not but call permanent 'uses.' A slight but unbroken thread of cases, beginning while the Conquest is yet recent, shows us that a man will from time to time convey his land to another 'to the use' of a third. For example, he is going on a crusade and wishes that his land shall be held to the use of his children, or he wishes that his wife or his sister shall enjoy the land, but doubts, it may be, whether a woman can hold a military fee or whether a husband can enfeoff his wife. Here there must be at the least an honourable understanding that the trust is to be observed, and there may be a formal 'interposition of faith.' Then, again, we see that some of the lands and revenues of a religious house have often been devoted to some special object; they have been given to the convent 'to [p. 229] the use' of the library or 'to the use' of the infirmary, and we can hardly doubt that a bishop will hold himself bound to provide that these dedications, which are sometimes guarded by the anathema, shall be maintained. Lastly, in the early years of the thirteenth century the Franciscan friars came hither. The law of their being forbad them to own anything; but they needed at least some poor dormitory, and the faithful were soon offering them houses in abundance. A remarkable plan was adopted. They had come as missionaries to the towns; the benefactor who was minded to give them a house, would convey that house to the borough community 'to the use of' or 'as an inhabitation for' the friars. Already, when Bracton was writing, plots of land in London had been thus conveyed to the city for the benefit of the Franciscans. The nascent corporation was becoming a trustee. It is an old doctrine that the inventors of 'the use' were 'the clergy' or 'the monks.' We should be nearer the truth if we said that, to all seeming, the first persons who in England employed 'the use' on a large scale were, not the clergy, nor the monks, but the friars of St Francis.

Now in few, if any, of these cases can the *ad opus* be regarded as expressing the relation which we conceive to exist between a principal and an agent. It is intended that the 'feoffee to uses' (we can employ no other term to describe him) shall be the owner or legal tenant of the land, that he shall be seised, that he shall bear the burdens incumbent on owners or tenants, but he is to hold his rights for the benefit of another. Such transactions seem to have been too uncommon to generate any definite legal theory. Some of them may have been enforced by the ecclesiastical courts. Assuredly the citizens of London would have known what an interdict meant, had they misappropriated the lands conveyed to them for the use of the friars, those darlings of popes and kings. Again, in some cases the feoffment might perhaps be regarded as a 'gift upon condition,' and in others a written agreement about the occupation of the land might be enforced as a covenant. But at the time when the system of original writs was taking its final form 'the use' had not become common enough to find a comfortable niche in the fabric. And so for a while it lives a precarious life until it obtains protection in the 'equitable' jurisdiction of the chancellors. If in the [p. 230] thirteenth century our courts of common law had already come to a comprehensive doctrine of contract, if they had been ready to draw an exact line of demarcation between 'real' and 'personal' rights, they might have reduced 'the use' to submission and assigned to it a place in their scheme of actions: in particular, they might have given the feoffor a personal, a contractual, action against the feoffee. But this was not quite what was wanted by those who took part in these transactions; it was not the feoffor, it was the person whom he desired to benefit (the *cestui que use* of later days) who required a remedy, and moreover a remedy that would secure him, not money compensation, but enjoyment of the land. 'The use' seems to be accomplishing its manifest destiny when at length after many adventures it appears as 'equitable ownership.'

We have been laying stress on the late growth of a law of contract, so for one moment we must glance at another side of the picture. The master who taught us that 'the movement of the progressive societies has hitherto been a movement from Status to Contract,' was quick to add that feudal society

was governed by the law of contract[1]. There is no paradox
here. In the really feudal centuries men could do by a contract, by the formal contract of vassalage or commendation,
many things that can not be done now-a-days. They could
contract to stand by each other in warfare 'against all men
who can live and die'; they could (as Domesday Book says)
'go with their land' to any lord whom they pleased; they
could make the relation between king and subject look like
the outcome of agreement; the law of contract threatened
to swallow up all public law. Those were the golden days
of 'free,' if 'formal,' contract. The idea that men can fix their
rights and duties by agreement is in its early days an unruly,
anarchical idea. If there is to be any law at all, contract must
be taught to know its place.

Note on the phrase 'ad opus,' and the Early History of the Use.

p. 231] I. The employment of the phrase *ad opus meum* (*tuum, suum*) as
meaning on my (your, his) behalf, or for my (your, his) profit or advantage,
can be traced back into very early Frankish formulas. See Zeumer's
quarto edition of the Formulae Merovingici et Karolini Aevi (Monumenta
Germaniae), index s. v. *opus*. Thus, *e.g.*:—

p. 115 'ut nobis aliquid de silva ad opus ecclesiae nostrae . . . dare
iubeatis.' (But here *opus ecclesiae* may mean the fabric of the church.)

p. 234 'per quem accepit venerabilis vir ille abba ad opus monasterio
suo [=monasterii sui] . . . . masas ad commanendum.'

p. 208 'ad ipsam iam dictam ecclesiam ad opus sancti illius . . . dono.'

p. 315 (An emperor is speaking) 'telonium vero, excepto ad opus
nostrum inter Q et D vel ad C [*place names*] ubi ad opus nostrum decima
exigitur, aliubi eis ne requiratur.'

II. So in Karolingian laws for the Lombards. Mon. Germ. Leges, IV.
Liber Papiensis Pippini, 28 (p. 520): 'De compositionibus quae ad palatium
pertinent: si comites ipsas causas convenerint ad requirendum, illi
tertiam partem ad eorum percipiant opus, duos vero ad palatium.' (The
comes gets 'the third penny of the county' for his own use.)

Lib. Pap. Ludovici Pii 40 (p. 538): 'Ut de debito quod ad opus
nostrum fuerit wadiatum talis consideratio fiat.'

---

[1] Maine, Ancient Law, 6th ed. pp. 170, 305.

III. From Frankish models the phrase has passed into Anglo-Saxon land-books. Thus, *e.g.*:—

Cenwulf of Mercia, A.D. 809, Kemble, Cod. Dipl. v. 66 : 'Item in alio loco dedi eidem venerabili viro ad opus praefatae Christi ecclesiae et monachorum ibidem deo servientium terram ...'

Beornwulf of Mercia, A.D. 822, Kemble, Cod. Dipl. v. 69 : 'Rex dedit ecclesiae Christi et Wulfredo episcopo ad opus monachorum .... villam Godmeresham.'

Werhard's testament, A.D. 832, Kemble, Cod. Dipl. i. 297: the arch-bishop acquired lands for the use of the cathedral convent : 'ad opus ... familiae [Christi].'

IV. It is not uncommon in Domesday Book. Thus, *e.g.*:—

D. B. i. 209 : 'Inter totum reddit per annum xxii. libras .... ad firmam regis .... Ad opus reginae duas uncias auri ... et i. unciam auri ad opus vicecomitis per annum.'

D. B. i. 60 b : 'Duae hidae non geldabant quia de firma regis erant et ad opus regis calumniatae sunt.'

D. B. ii. 311 : 'Soca et saca in Blideburh ad opus regis et comitis.'

V. A very early instance of the French *al os* occurs in Leges Willelmi, I. 2. § 3 : 'E cil francs hom .... seit mis en forfeit el cunté, afert al os le vescunte en Denelahe xl. ores .... De ces xxxii. ores averad le vescunte al os le rei x. ores.' The sheriff takes certain sums for his own use, others for the king's use. This document can hardly be of later date than the early years of cent. xii.

VI. In order to show the identity of *opus* and *os* or *oes* we may pass to Britton, ii. 13 : 'Villenage est tenement de demeynes de chescun seignur baillé a tenir a sa volunté par vileins services de emprouwer al oes le seignur.' [p. 232]

VII. A few examples of the employment of this phrase in connexion with the receipt of money or chattels may now be given.

Liberate Roll 45 Hen. III. (Archaeologia, xxviii. 269): Order by the king for payment of 600 marks which two Florentine merchants lent him, to wit, 100 marks for the use (*ad opus*) of the king of Scotland and 500 for the use of John of Britanny.

Liberate Roll 53 Hen. III. (Archaeologia, xxviii. 271): Order by the king for payment to two Florentines of money lent to him for the purpose of paying off debts due in respect of cloth and other articles taken 'to our use (*ad opus nostrum*)' by the purveyors of our wardrobe.

Note Book, pl. 177 (A.D. 1222): A defendant in an action of debt con-fesses that he has received money from the plaintiff, but alleges that he was steward of Roger de C. and received it *ad opus eiusdem Rogeri*. He vouches Roger to warranty.

Selby Coucher Book, ii. 204 (A.D. 1285): 'Omnibus ... R. de Y. ballivus domini Normanni de Arcy salutem. Noveritis me recepisse duodecim libras ... de Abbate de Seleby ad opus dicti Normanni, in quibus idem Abbas ei tenebatur ... Et ego ... dictum abbatem ... versus dominum meum de supradicta pecunia indempnem conservabo et adquietabo.'

Y. B. 21–2 Edw. I. p. 23: 'Richard ly bayla les chateus a la oeus le Eveske de Ba.'

Y. B. 33–5 Edw. I. p. 239: 'Il ad conté qe eux nous livererent meyme largent al oes Alice la fille B.'

VIII. We now turn to cases in which land is concerned:—

Whitby Cartulary, i. 203–4 (middle of cent. xii.): Roger Mowbray has given land to the monks of Whitby; in his charter he says 'Reginaldus autem Puer vendidit ecclesiae praefatae de Wyteby totum ius quod habuit in praefata terra et reliquit michi ad opus illorum, et ego reddidi eis, et saisivi per idem lignum per quod et recepi illud.'

Burton Cartulary, p. 21, from an 'extent' which seems to come to us from the first years of cent. xii.: 'tenet Godfridus viii. bovatae [corr. bovatas] pro viii. sol. praeter illam terram quae ad ecclesiam iacet quam tenet cum ecclesia ad opus fratris sui parvuli, cum ad id etatis venerit ut possit et debeat servire ipsi ecclesiae.'

Ramsey Cartulary, ii. 257–8, from a charter dated by the editors in 1080–7: 'Hanc conventionem fecit Eudo scilicet Dapifer Regis cum Ailsio Abbate Rameseiae . . . . de Berkeforde ut Eudo habere deberet ad opus sororis suae Muriellae partem Sancti Benedicti quae adiacebat ecclesiae Rameseiae quamdiu Eudo et soror eius viverent, ad dimidium servitium unius militis, tali quidem pacto ut post Eudonis sororisque decessum tam partem propriam Eudonis quam in eadem villa habuit, quam partem ecclesiae Rameseiae, Deo et Sancto Benedicto ad usum fratrum eternaliter . . . possidendam . . . relinqueret.' In D. B. i. 210 b, we find 'In Bereforde tenet Eudo dapifer v. hidas de feodo Abbatis [de Ramesy].' So here we have a 'Domesday tenant' as 'feoffee to uses.'

[p. 233]   Ancient Charters (Pipe Roll Soc.) p. 21 (*circ.* A.D. 1127): Richard fitz Pons announces that having with his wife's concurrence disposed of her marriage portion, he has given other lands to her; 'et inde saisivi Milonem fratrem eius loco ipsius ut ipse eam manuteneat et ab omni defendat iniuria.'

Curia Regis Roll No. 81, Trin. 6 Hen. III. m. 1 d. Assize of mort d'ancestor by Richard de Barre on the death of his father William against William's brother Richard de Roughal for a rent. Defendant alleges that William held it in *custodia*, having purchased it to the use of (*ad opus*) the defendant with the defendant's money. The jurors say that William bought it to the use of the defendant, so that William was seised not in fee but in wardship (*custodia*). An attempt is here made to bring the relationship that we are examining under the category of *custodia*.

Note Book, pl. 999 (A.D. 1224): *R*, who is going to the Holy Land, commits his land to his brother *W*. to keep to the use of his (*R*'s) sons (*commisit terram illam W. ad opus puerorum suorum*); on *R*'s death his eldest son demands the land from *W*, who refuses to surrender it; a suit between them in a seignorial court is compromised; each of them is to have half the land.

Note Book, pl. 1683 (A.D. 1225): *R* is said to have bought land from *G* to the use of the said *G*. Apparently *R* received the land from *G* on the understanding that he (*R*) was to convey it to *G* and the daughter of *R* (whom *G* was going to marry) by way of a marriage portion.

Note Book, pl. 1851 (A.D. 1226–7): A man who has married a second wife is said to have bought land to the use of this wife and the heirs of her body begotten by him.

Note Book, pl. 641 (A.D. 1231): It is asserted that *E* impleaded *R* for certain land, that *R* confessed that the land was *E*'s in consideration of 12 marks, which *M* paid on behalf of *E*, and that *M* then took the land to the use (*ad opus*) of *E*. Apparently *M* was to hold the land in gage as security for the 12 marks.

Note Book, pl. 754 (A.D. 1233): Jurors say that *R* desired to enfeoff his son *P*, an infant seven years old; he gave the land in the hundred court and took the child's homage; he went to the land and delivered seisin; he then committed the land to one *X* to keep to the use of *P* (*ad custodiendum ad opus ipsius Petri*) and afterwards he committed it to *Y* for the same purpose; *X* and *Y* held the land for five years to the use of *P*.

Note Book, pl. 1244 (A.D. 1238–9): A woman, mother of *H*, desires a house belonging to *R*; *H* procures from *R* a grant of the house to *H* to the use (*ad opus*) of his mother for her life.

Assize Roll No. 1182, m. 8 (one of Bracton's Devonshire rolls): 'Iuratores dicunt quod idem Robertus aliquando tenuit hundredum illud et quod inde cepit expleta. Et quaesiti ad opus cuius, utrum ad opus proprium vel ad opus ipsius Ricardi, dicunt quod expleta inde cepit, sed nesciunt utrum ad opus suum proprium vel ad opus ipsius Ricardi quia nesciunt quid inde fecit.'

Chronicon de Melsa, ii. 116 (an account of what happened in the middle of cent. xiii. compiled from charters): Robert confirmed to us monks the tenements that we held of his fee; 'et insuper duas bovatas [p. 234] cum uno tofto ... ad opus Ceciliae sororis suae et heredum suorum de corpore suo procreatorum nobis concessit; ita quod ipsa Cecilia ipsa toftum et ii. bovatas terrae per forinsecum servitium et xiv. sol. et iv. den. annuos de nobis teneret. Unde eadem toftum et ii. bovatas concessimus dictae Ceciliae in forma praescripta.'

Historians of the Church of York, iii. 160: In 1240 Hubert de Burgh in effect creates a trust for sale. He gives certain houses to God for the defence of the Holy Land and delivers them to three persons 'ad disponendum et venditioni exponendum.' They sell to the archbishop of York.

IX. The lands and revenues of a religious house were often appropriated to various specific purposes, e.g. *ad victum monachorum*, *ad vestitum monachorum*, to the use of the sacrist, cellarer, almoner or the like, and sometimes this appropriation was designated by the donor. Thus, *e.g.* Winchcombe Landboc, i. 55, 'ad opus librorum'; i. 148, 'ad usus infirmorum monachorum'; i. 73, certain tithes are devoted 'in usum operationis ecclesiae,' and in 1206 this devotion of them is protected by a ban pronounced by the abbot ; only in case of famine or other urgent necessity may they be diverted from this use. So land may be given 'to God and the church of St German of Selby to buy eucharistic wine (*ad vinum missarum emendum*)' ; Selby Coucher, ii. 34.

In the ecclesiastical context just mentioned *usus* is a commoner term than *opus*. But the two words are almost convertible. On Curia Regis Roll No. 115 (18–9 Hen. III.) m. 3 is an action against a royal purveyor. He took some fish *ad opus Regis* and converted it *in usus Regis*.

X. In the great dispute which raged between the archbishops of Canterbury and the monks of the cathedral monastery one of the questions at issue was whether certain revenues, which undoubtedly belonged to 'the church' of Canterbury, had been irrevocably devoted to certain specific uses, so that the archbishop, who was abbot of the house, could not divert them to other purposes. In 1185 Pope Urban III. pronounces against the archbishop. He must restore certain parochial churches to the use of the almonry. 'Ecclesiae de Estreia et de Munechetun . . . . ad usus pauperum provide deputatae fuissent, et a . . . praedecessoribus nostris eisdem usibus confirmatae . . . Monemus quatenus . . . praescriptas ecclesias usibus illis restituas.' Again, the prior and convent are to administer certain revenues which are set apart 'in perpetuos usus luminarium, sacrorum vestimentorum et restaurationis ipsius ecclesiae, et in usus hospitum et infirmorum.' At one stage in the quarrel certain representatives of the monks in the presence of Henry II. received from the archbishop's hand three manors 'ad opus trium obedientiariorum, cellerarii, camerarii et sacristae.' See Epistolae Cantuarienses, pp. 5, 38, 95.

XI. Historians of the Church of York, iii. 155: In 1241 we see an archbishop of York using somewhat complicated machinery for the creation of a trust. He conveys land to the chapter on condition that (*ita quod*) they will convey it to each successive archbishop to be held by him at a rent, which rent is to be paid to the treasurer of the cathedral and expended by him in the maintenance of a chantry. The event that an archbishop may not be willing to accept the land subject to this rent is provided for. This 'ordination' is protected by a sentence of excommunication.

XII. We now come to the very important case of the Franciscans.

Thomas of Eccleston, De adventu Fratrum Minorum (Monumenta Franciscana, i.), p. 16 : 'Igitur Cantuariae contulit eis aream quandam et aedificavit capellam . . . Alexander magister Hospitalis Sacerdotum ; et quia fratres nihil omnino appropriare sibi voluerunt, facta est communitati civitatis propria, fratribus vero pro civium libitu commodata . . . Londoniae autem hospitatus est fratres dominus Johannes Ywin, qui emptam pro fratribus aream communitati civium appropriavit, fratrum autem usumfructum eiusdem pro libitu dominorum devotissime designavit . . . Ricardus [p. 235] le Muliner contulit aream et domum communitati villae [Oxoniae] ad opus fratrum.' This account of what happened in or about 1225 is given by a contemporary.

Prima Fundatio Fratrum Minorum Londoniae (Monumenta Franciscana, i.), p. 494. This document gives an account of many donations of
land made to the city of London in favour of the Franciscans. The first
charter that it states is one of 1225, in which John Iwyn says that for the
salvation of his soul he has given a piece of land to the *communitas* of
the city of London in frankalmoin 'ad inhospitandum [*a word missing*]
pauperes fratres minorum [minores ?] quamdiu voluerint ibi esse.'

XIII. The attempt of the early Franciscans to live without property
of any sort or kind led to subtle disputations and in the end to a world-
shaking conflict. At one time the popes sought to distinguish between
ownership and usufruct or use; the Franciscans might enjoy the use but
could not have ownership; the *dominium* of all that was given to their
use was deemed to be vested in the Roman church and any litigation
about it was to be carried on by papal procurators. This doctrine was
defined by Nicholas III. in 1279. In 1322 John XXII. did his best to
overrule it, declaring that the distinction between use and property was
fallacious and that the friars were not debarred from ownership (Extrav.
Jo. XXII. 14. 3). Charges of heresy about this matter were freely flung
about by and against him, and the question whether Christ and His
Apostles had owned goods became a question between Pope and Emperor,
between Guelph and Ghibelline. In the earlier stages of the debate there
was an instructive discussion as to the position of the third person, who
was sometimes introduced as an intermediary between the charitable
donor and the friars who were to take the benefit of the gift. He could
not be treated as agent or procurator for the friars unless the ownership
were ascribed to them. Gregory IX. was for treating him as an agent for
the donor. See Lea, History of the Inquisition, iii. 5–7, 29–31, 129–154.

XIV. It is very possible that the case of the Franciscans did much
towards introducing among us both the word *usus* and the desire to
discover some expedient which would give the practical benefits of ownership to those who could yet say that they owned nothing. In every large
town in England there were Minorites who knew all about the stormy controversy, who had heard how some of their foreign brethren had gone to the
stake rather than suffer that the testament of St Francis should be overlaid
by the evasive glosses of lawyerly popes, and who were always being
twitted with their impossible theories by their Dominican rivals. On the
continent the battle was fought with weapons drawn from the armoury of
the legist. Among these were *usus* and *usufructus*. It seems to have been
thought at one time that the case could be met by allowing the friars a
usus or *usufructus*, these terms being employed in a sense that would not
be too remote from that which they had borne in the old Roman texts.
Thus it is possible that there was a momentary contact between Roman
law—medieval, not classical, Roman law—and the development of the
English *use*. Englishmen became familiar with an employment of the
word *usus* which would make it stand for something that just is not,
though it looks exceedingly like, *dominium*. But we hardly need say that [p. 236]
the *use* of our English law is not derived from the Roman 'personal

servitude'; the two have no feature in common. Nor can we believe that the Roman *fideicommissum* has anything to do with the evolution of the English *use*. In the first place, the English *use* in its earliest stage is seldom, if ever, the outcome of a last will, while the *fideicommissum* belongs essentially to the law of testaments. In the second place, if the English *use* were a *fideicommissum* it would be called so, and we should not see it gradually emerging out of such phrases as *ad opus* and *ad usum*. What we see is a vague idea, which developing in one direction becomes what we now know as agency, and developing in another direction becomes that *use* which the common law will not, but equity will, protect. It is only in the much later developments and refinements of modern family settlements that the English system of *uses* becomes capable of suggesting *Fideicommiss* to modern German inquirers as an approximate equivalent. Where Roman law has been 'received' the *fideicommissum* plays a part which is insignificant when compared with that played by the trust in our English system. Of course, again, our 'equitable ownership,' when it has reached its full stature, has enough in common with the praetorian *bonorum possessio* to make a comparison between the two instructive; but an attempt to derive the one from the other would be too wild for discussion.

CHAPTER VI.

INHERITANCE.

§ 1. *Antiquities.*

The history of the family: a controversial theme.

IF before we speak of our law of inheritance as it was in [p. 237] the twelfth and thirteenth centuries, we devote some small space to the antiquities of family law, it will be filled rather by warnings than by theories. Our English documents contain little that can be brought to bear immediately or decisively on those interesting controversies about primitive tribes and savage families in which our archæologists and anthropologists are engaged, while the present state of those controversies is showing us more clearly every day that we are yet a long way off the establishment of any dogmas which can claim an universal validity, or be safely extended from one age or one country to another. And yet so long as it is doubtful whether the prehistoric time should be filled, for example, with agnatic *gentes* or with hordes which reckon by 'mother-right,' the interpretation of many a historic text must be uncertain.

The family as an unit.

It has become a common-place among English writers that the family rather than the individual was the 'unit' of ancient law. That there is truth in this saying we are very far from denying—the bond of blood was once a strong and sacred bond—but we ought not to be content with terms so vague as 'family' and 'unit.' It may be that in the history of every nation there was a time when the men and women of that nation were grouped together into mutually exclusive clans, when all the members of each clan were in fact or in fiction bound to each other by the tie of blood, and were accounted strangers in blood to the members of every other clan. But [p. 238] let us see what this grouping implies. It seems to imply almost of necessity that kinship is transmitted either only by males or only by females. So soon as it is admitted that the bond of blood, the bond which groups men together for the purpose of blood-feud and of *wergild,* ties the child both to his father's brother and to his mother's brother, a system of mutually exclusive clans is impossible, unless indeed each clan is strictly endogamous. There is a foray; grandfather, father and son are slain; the *wer* must be paid. The *wer* of the grandfather must be paid to one set of persons; the *wer* of the father to a different set; the *wer* of the son to yet a third set. If kinship is traced only through males or only through females, then we may have permanent and mutually exclusive units; we may picture the nation as a tree, the clans as branches; if a twig grows out of one branch, it cannot grow out of another. In the other case each individual is himself the trunk of an *arbor consanguinitatis.*

Now it is not contended that the Germans, even when they first come within the ken of history, recognize no bond of blood between father and son. They are for the more part monogamous, and their marriages are of a permanent kind. The most that can be said by ardent champions of 'mother-right' is that of 'mother-right' there are distinct though evanescent traces in the German laws of a later day. On the other hand, we seem absolutely debarred from the supposition that they disregarded the relationship between the child and its mother's brother[1]. So soon as we begin to get rules about inheritance and blood-feud, the dead man's kinsfolk, those who [p. 239] must bear the feud and who may share the *wergild,* consist in part of persons related to him through his father, and in part of persons related to him through his mother.

No clans in England.

---

[1] Tacitus, Germania, c. 20 : 'Sororum filiis idem apud avunculum qui apud patrem honor.' The other stronghold of the upholders of 'mother-right' is the famous tit. 59 of the Lex Salica (ed. Hessels, col. 379). This in its oldest form gives the following order of inheritance : (1) sons, (2) mother, (3) brothers and sisters, (4) mother's sister, thus passing by the father. The force of the passage is diminished by the omission of the mother's brother. One can not tell how much is taken for granted by so rude a text. Among modern Germanists 'mother-right' seems to be fast gaining ground; but the evidence that is adduced in favour of a period of exclusive 'mother-right' is sparse and slight. The word *matriarchy* should be avoided. A practice of tracing kinship only through women is perfectly compatible with a man's despotic power over his household. See Dargun, Mutterrecht und Vaterrecht, p. 3.

Spear-kin
and spin-
dle-kin.

It was so in the England of Alfred's day; the maternal kinsfolk paid a third of the *wer*. The *Leges Henrici*, which about such a matter will not be inventing new rules, tell us that the paternal kinsfolk pay and receive two-thirds, the maternal kinsfolk one-third of the *wer*; and this is borne out by other evidence[1]. Also it is clear that marriage did not sever the bond between a woman and her blood-kinsmen; they were responsible for her misdeeds; they received her *wer*, and we are expressly told that, if she committed homicide, vengeance was not to be taken on 'the innocent family' of her husband[2]. It would even seem that her husband could not remove her from the part of the country in which her kinsmen lived without giving them security that he would treat her well and that they should have an opportunity of condoning her misdeeds by money payments[3]. Now when we see that the wives of the members of one clan are themselves members of other clans, we ought not to talk of clans at all[4]. If the law were to treat the clan as an unit for any purpose whatever, this would surely be the purpose of *wer* and blood-feud; but just for that purpose our English law does not contemplate the existence of a number of mutually exclusive units which can be enumerated and named; there were as many 'blood-feud groups' as there were living persons; at all events each set of brothers and sisters was the centre of a different group.

No per-
manent
organiza-
tion of the
blood-feud
group.

From this it follows that the 'blood-feud group' cannot be a permanently organized unit. If there is a feud to be borne or *wer* to be paid or received, it may organize itself *ad hoc*; but the organization will be of a fleeting kind. The very next deed of violence that is done will call some other blood-feud group into existence. Along with his brothers and paternal uncles a man goes out to avenge his father's death and [p. 240] is slain. His maternal uncles and cousins, who stood outside the old feud, will claim a share in his *wer*.

---

[1] Alf. 27; Æthelst. II. 11; Leg. Henr. 75 § 8–10; Schmid, App. VII. 1, § 3. The passage in the Laws of Alfred is an exceedingly difficult one, because it introduces us to those *gegyldan* of whom no very satisfactory explanation has ever been given. But, especially if read along with the *Leges Henrici*, it seems to tell us that, if the slayer has both paternal and maternal kinsfolk, the paternal pay two-thirds, the maternal one-third. See Brunner, D. R. G. i. 218.

[2] Schmid, App. VI. § 7; Leg. Henr. 70 § 12, 13, 23.

[3] Schmid, App. VI. § 7.

[4] See Gierke, Genossenschaftsrecht, i. 27.

This is what we see so soon as we see our ancestors. About what lies in the prehistoric time we can only make guesses. Some will surmise that the recognition of the kinship that is traced through women is a new thing, and that in the past there have been permanently coherent agnatic *gentes* which are already being dissolved by the action of a novel principle. Others will argue that the movement has been not from but towards agnation, and has now gone so far that the spear-cousins are deemed nearer and dearer than the spindle-cousins. Others, again, may think that the great 'folk-wandering' has made the family organization of the German race unusually indefinite and plastic, so that here it will take one, and there another form. What seems plain is that the exclusive domination of either 'father-right' or 'mother-right'—if such an exclusive domination we must needs postulate—should be placed for our race beyond the extreme limit of history. To this, however, we may add that the English evidence as to the wife's position is a grave difficulty to any theory that would start with the patriarchal family as a primitive datum. That position we certainly cannot ascribe to the influence of Christianity. The church's dogma is that the husband is the head of the wife, that the wife must forsake her own people and her father's house; and yet, despite all preaching and teaching, the English wife remains, for what has once been the most important of all purposes, a stranger to her husband's kin, and even to her husband.

It is quite possible that in England men as a matter of fact dwelt together in large groups tilling the land by co-operation, that the members of each group were, or deemed themselves to be, kinsmen in blood, and that as a force for keeping them in these local groups spear-sibship was stronger than spindle-sibship:—their relative strength could be expressed by the formula 2 : 1. We get a hint of such permanent cohesive groups when we find King Æthelstan legislating against the *mægð* that is so strong and so mickle that it denies the king's rights and harbours thieves. The whole power of the country is to be called out to ride against these offenders[1]. The law will, if possible, treat such a *mægð* as an 'unit' by crushing it [p. 241] into atoms. But in no other way, so far as we can see, will its unity be legally recognized. The rules of blood-feud that the

[1] Æthelst. VI. 8 § 2, 3.

law sanctions are a practical denial of its existence. Unless it be endogamous, it can have no claim to the whole *wer* of any one of its members; every one of its members may have to pay *wer* along with persons who stand outside it.

The kindred as land-owning unit.
Again, if we accept the common saying that the land-owning unit was not an individual but a *mægð*, a clan, or *gens*, we must meet the difficulty that at an early period land was being inherited through women. The rules of inheritance are very dark to us, but, so far as we can see, the tendency in the historic period is not towards an admission of the 'spindle-kin,' but towards a postponement of their claims to those of the 'spear-kin'[1]. Already in the eighth century the Anglo-Saxon thegn wishes to create something like the estate in tail male of later times[2]. And the law takes his side; it decrees that the form of the gift shall be respected[3]. Now if for a moment we suppose that a clan owns land, we shall see a share in this land passing through daughters to their children, and these children will be on their father's side members of another clan. Our land-owning clan, if it still continues to hold its old lands, will soon cease to be a clan in any tolerable sense of the term; it will be a mere group of co-proprietors, some of whom are bound by the sacred tie of blood-feud more closely to those who stand outside than to those who stand inside the proprietary group.

The kindred no corporation.
We must resist the temptation to speak of 'the *mægð*' as if it were a kind of corporation[4], otherwise we have as many corporations as there are men and women. The collective word *mægð* is interchangeable with the plural of the word *mǽg*, which signifies a kinsman. When a man has been slain, those who are bound and entitled to avenge his death will, it is probable enough, meet together and take counsel over a plan of campaign; but so far as we can see, the law, when first it knows a *wergild*, knows the main outlines of a system which divides the *wergild* among individual men. There is in the first place a sum called the *healsfang*, which is due only to those who are [p. 242] very closely related to the dead man[5]; then there is the rule that gives two thirds to the spear and one to the spindle. Again, when the 'kindred' of a lordless man is ordered to find

---

[1] See the instances collected by Kemble, Cod. Dipl. i. p. xxxiii.
[2] Kemble, Cod. Dipl. 147 (i. 177); 299 (ii. 94).
[3] Alf. c. 41.   [4] See Heusler, Institutionen, i. 259.
[5] Brunner, D. R. G. i. 219.

him a lord, we need not think of this as of a command addressed to corporations, or even to permanently organized groups of men; it may well be addressed to each and all of those persons who would be entitled to share the *wergild* of this lordless man: every one of them will be liable to perform this duty if called upon to do so[1]. A fatherless child 'follows its mother'; apparently this means that, as a general rule, this child will be brought up among its maternal, not its paternal, kinsmen; the guardianship however of its paternal goods is given by ancient dooms to its paternal kinsmen[2]. But such texts do not authorize us to call up the vision of a *mægð* acting as guardian by means of some council of elders; the persons who would inherit if the child died may well be the custodians of the ancestral property. But even if in any given case a person's kinsmen act together and, for example, find a lord or appoint a guardian for him, it is only by reason of their relationship to him that they constitute an unit. There may be a great deal to show that in England and elsewhere strong family groups formed themselves and that the law had to reckon with them; but they were contending against a principle which, explain it how we will, seems to be incompatible with the existence of mutually exclusive *gentes* as legal entities[3].

We turn to the popular theory that land was owned by families or households before it was owned by individuals. This seems to mean that at a time when a piece of land was never owned by one man, co-ownership was common. Now [p. 243] co-ownership may take various forms. In the later middle ages it took here in England at least four. There was the tenancy in common. In this case when one co-tenant died, his own undivided share descended to his heir[4]. There was the joint tenancy. In this case when one co-tenant died, his share did not descend to his heir, but 'accrued' to the surviving co-tenant or co-tenants. There was the co-parcenary occasioned by

The household as land-owner.

---

[1] Æthelstan, II. 2.   [2] Hloth. and Ead. 6; Ine, 38.

[3] Heusler, Institutionen, i. 259, argues that the German sib does not show us even the germ of a juristic person. The contrary, and at one time more popular, opinion is stated with special reference to the Anglo-Saxon evidence by Gierke, Genossenschaftsrecht, i. 17 ff. When Bracton, f. 87 b, says that an infant sokeman is *sub custodia consanguineorum suorum propinquorum*, we do not see a family council; why should we see one when a similar phrase occurs in an Anglo-Saxon doom?

[4] We are speaking briefly, and are therefore supposing that the co-tenants hold in fee simple.

the descent of lands to co-heiresses. In this case there had been doubt whether on the death of one co-tenant without issue there would be inheritance or 'accruer by survivorship.' The intimate union between husband and wife gave rise to a fourth form, known as tenancy by entireties. We can not *a priori* exhaust the number of forms which co-ownership may take. Nor is it only on the death of one of the co-owners that the differences between these forms will manifest themselves. In a modern system of law, and in many a system that is by no means modern[1], every one of the co-owners may in general insist on a partition either of the land itself or, it may be, of the money that can be obtained by a sale of it; or again, without any partition being made, he can without the consent of his fellows transfer his aliquot share to one who has hitherto stood outside the co-owning group. Demonstrably in some cases, perhaps in many, these powers are of recent origin[2]. Let us [p. 244] for a moment put them out of account. Let us suppose that on a father's death his land descends to his three sons, that no son can force his brothers to a physical partition of the inheritance, and that no son can sell or give away his share. Let us make yet another supposition, for which there may be warrant in some ancient laws. Let us suppose that if one of the three sons dies leaving two sons, these two will not of necessity inherit just their father's share, no more, no less. Let us suppose that there will be a redistribution of the shares into which the land has hitherto been ideally divided, so (for example) that these four persons, namely the two uncles and their two nephews, will have equal shares. The land is still owned by four men[3]. Let the number of co-tenants increase

---

[1] Heusler, Institutionen, i. 240. In India there are traces of a period when partition could not be enforced, and 'in Malabar and Canara, at the present day, no right of partition exists' : Mayne, Hindu Law, § 218.

[2] It is not until the reign of Henry VIII. (Stat. 31 Hen. VIII. c. 1) that one of several joint tenants can compel his fellows to make partition. But the co-parcener has had this power from a remote age. This is remarkable : the co-ownership created by inheritance can, the co-ownership created by the act of a feoffor can not, be destroyed against the wish of one of the co-owners.

[3] Some such plan of a repeated redistribution *per capita* among brothers, first-cousins and second-cousins seems to have prevailed in Wales; but the redistributions of which we read in Welsh law seem to be redistributions of physically divided shares. Apparently in ancient Germany the rule was that within the joint family the sons, however numerous, of a dead co-proprietor would upon partition get no larger share than their father would have taken had he lived. In

until there are forty of them; the state of the case is not
altered. Individuals do not cease to be individuals when there
are many of them. But if there are many of them, we shall
often spare ourselves the trouble of enumerating them by the
use of some collective name. If John Smith's land has
descended to his seven daughters who are holding it as co-
parceners, we shall in common discourse speak of it as the land
of the Smiths or of the Smith family, or, if we prefer medieval
Latin to modern English, we shall say that the land belongs to
the *genealogia Johannis Fabri*. If these ladies quarrel with
their neighbours about a boundary, there may be litigation
between two families (*inter duas genealogias*), the Smiths, to
wit, and the Browns; but it will be a quarrel between
'individuals'; this will be plain enough so soon as there is
any pleading in the action.

[p. 245]   Now no one is likely to maintain, even as a paradox, that Is co-
the ownership of aliquot shares of things is older than the ownership older than
ownership of integral things. If nothing else will restrain him, several owner-
he may at least be checked by the reflection that the more ship?
ancient institution will inevitably become the more modern
within a few years. He distributes the land to families. So
soon as by the changes and chances of this mortal life any one
of those families has but a single member, 'individual ownership' will exist, unless to save his dogma he has recourse to
an arbitrary act of confiscation.

To deny that 'family ownership' is an ownership by indi- Co-owner-
viduals of aliquot shares is another expedient. But this in ship and aliquot
truth is a denial of the existence of any law about partition. shares.
If there is any law which decides how, if a partition be made,
the physically distinct shares ought to be distributed, then
there is already law which assigns to the members of the group
ideal shares in the unpartitioned land[1]. But to seek to go

other words, while the family is still 'joint' there is inheritance of ideal quotas.
Heusler, Institutionen, i. 240. Maine, Early History of Institutions, p. 195, speaks
of a distribution *per capita* occurring in the most archaic forms of the joint family.

[1] Heusler, Institutionen, i. 238. We read of two rival schools of Hindu
lawyers, the one maintaining the theory of 'aggregate ownership,' the other
that of 'fractional ownership.' The same two theories have divided the
German antiquaries. But it seems reasonable to say with Heusler that if there
is law which upon a partition will assign to each co-proprietor some definite
aliquot share of the land, then there is law which gives him an ideal fraction of
the land while it still remains undivided, though it assigns him no certain
share in the profits.

behind a law for the partition of family estates without passing
into a region in which there is no ownership and no law does
not in Western Europe look like an endeavour that is destined
to succeed. Such evidence as we have does not tend to prove
that in ancient times the 'joint family' was large. Seldom
did it comprise kinsmen who were not the descendants of a
common grandfather: in other words, the undivided family
rarely lived through three generations[1]. But supposing that
there is no law about partition, we still have before us something
which, if we agree to call it ownership, is ownership by individuals. We have land owned by four, or by forty individuals,
and at any moment a war, a plague or a famine may reduce
their number to one.

Birth-
rights.

To our thinking then, the matter that has to be investigated
is not well described as the non-existence of 'individual ownership.' It would be more correctly described as the existence [p. 246]
and the origin of 'birth-rights.' Seemingly what we mean
when we speak of 'family ownership,' is that a child acquires
rights in the ancestral land, at birth or, it may be, at adolescence;
at any rate he acquires rights in the ancestral land, and this
not by gift, bequest, inheritance or any title known to our
modern law.

History
of birth-
rights.

Now that such rights once existed in England and many
other parts of Western Europe is not to be denied. When the
dark age is over, they rarely went beyond this, that the land-
holder could not utterly disinherit his expectant heirs either
by will or by conveyance; the father, for example, could not
sell or give away the ancestral land without the consent of
his sons, or could only dispose of some 'reasonable' part of
it. If he attempted to do more, then when he was dead his
sons could revoke the land. However, it was not unknown in
some parts of Germany that, even while the father lived, the
sons could enforce their rights and compel him to a partition[2].

Birth-
rights and
inherit-
ance.

It is natural for us to assume without hesitation that those
forms of birth-right which are least in accord with our own
ideas are also the most archaic, that the weaker forms are
degenerate relics of the stronger, that originally the child was

---

[1] Heusler, Instit. 229, says that in the oldest German documents even first-
cousins are seldom 'joint.'

[2] In Germany within historic times the stronger forms of birth-right seem
to have been peculiar to the South German (Alaman and Bavarian) nations.

born a landowner, that a law which only allows him to recall
the alienated land after his father's death is transitional, and
that his right has undergone a further and final degradation
when it appears as a mere *droit de retrait,* a right to redeem
the alienated land at the price that has been given for it.
According to this theory, the law of intestate succession has
its origin in 'family ownership.' It is an old and a popular
doctrine[1]. Before however we allow to it the dignity of a
proved and universal truth, we shall do well to reflect that
it attributes to barbarous peoples a highly commendable care
for the proprietary rights of the *filius familias,* and if for his
proprietary rights then also for his life and liberty, for the
state of things in which a father may lawfully reduce the
number of his co-proprietors by killing them or selling them
into slavery is not one that we can easily imagine as a normal
or stable stage in the history of mankind.

[p. 247]   The suggestion therefore may be admissible that at least
in some cases 'family ownership,' or the semblance of it, may
really be, not the origin, but the outcome of intestate succession[2].
We have but to ask for a time when testamentary dispositions
are unknown and land is rarely sold or given away. In such a
time a law of intestate succession will take deep root in men's
thoughts and habits. The son will know that if he lives long
enough he will succeed his father; the father will know that
in the ordinary course of events his land will pass from him to
his sons. What else should happen to it? He does not want
to sell, for there is none to buy; and whither could he go and
what could he do if he sold his land? Perhaps the very idea
of a sale of land has not yet been conceived. In course of
time, as wealth is amassed, there are purchasers for land; also
there are bishops and priests desirous of acquiring land by
gift and willing to offer spiritual benefits in return. Then
the struggle begins, and law must decide whether the claims
of expectant heirs can be defeated. In the past those claims
have been protected not so much by law as by economic conditions. There is no need of a law to prohibit men from doing
what they do not want to do; and they have not wanted to

Birth-rights begotten by a law of inhe-ritance.

[1] Gaius, ii. 157; Paulus, Dig. 28. 2. 11.
[2] See Ficker, Untersuchungen zur Erbenfolge, i. 229. No student of 'family
ownership' should neglect this book. See also Baden-Powell, Indian Village
Community, 416.

sell or to give away their land. But now there must be law. The form that the law takes will be determined by the relative strength of conflicting forces. It will be a compromise, a series of compromises, and we have no warrant for the belief that there will be steady movement in one direction, or that the claims of the heirs must be always growing feebler. That this is so we shall see hereafter. The judges of Henry II.'s court condemned in the interest of the heir those testamentary or *quasi*-testamentary dispositions of land which Englishmen and Normans had been making for some time past, though the same judges or their immediate successors decided that the consent of expectant heirs should no longer be necessary when there was to be an alienation *inter vivos*. Thus they drew up the great compromise which ruled England for the rest of the middle ages. Other and different arrangements were made elsewhere, some more, some less favourable to the heirs, and we must not assume without proof that those which are most favourable to the heirs are in the normal order of events the most primitive. They imply, as already said, that a son can [p. 248] hale his father before a court of law and demand a partition; when this can be done there is no 'patriarchalism,' there is little paternal power[1].

Antiquity of inheritance. In calling to our aid a law of intestate succession we are not invoking a modern force. As regards the German race we can not go behind that law; the time when no such law existed is in the strictest sense prehistoric. Tacitus told his Roman readers that the Germans knew nothing of the testament, but added that they had rules of intestate succession. These rules were individualistic: that is to say, they did not treat a man's death as simply reducing the number of those persons who formed a co-owning group. Again, they did not give the wealth that had been set free to a body consisting of persons who stood in different degrees of relationship to the dead man. The kinsmen were called to the inheritance class by class, first the children, then the brothers, then the uncles[2]. The *Lex Salica*

---

[1] A brief account of the various theories which have prevailed in modern Germany about the relation of 'family ownership' or 'birth-rights' to inheritance is given by Adler, Ueber das Erbenwartrecht nach den ältesten Bairischen Rechtsquellen (Gierke, Untersuchungen, No. xxxvii.).

[2] Germania, c. 20: 'heredes tamen successoresque sui cuique liberi et nullum testamentum. si liberi non sunt, proximus gradus in possessione, fratres, patrui, avunculi.'

has a law of intestate succession; it calls the children, then the
mother, then the brothers and sisters, then the mother's sister[1].
These rules, it may be said, apply only to movable goods
and do not apply to land; but an admission that there is an
individualistic law of succession for movable goods when as yet
anything that can be called an ownership of land, if it exists
at all, is new, will be quite sufficient to give us pause before
we speak of 'family ownership' as a phenomenon that must
necessarily appear in the history of every race. Our family
when it obtains a permanent possession of land will be familiar
with rules of intestate succession which imply that within the
group that dwells together there is mine and thine. But the
Lex Salica already knows the inheritance of land; the dead
man's land descends to his sons, and an express statement
that women can not inherit it is not deemed superfluous.

Now as regards the Anglo-Saxons we can find no proof of
the theory that among them there prevailed anything that ought
to be called 'family ownership.' No law, no charter, no record
[p. 249] of litigation has been discovered which speaks of land as being
owned by a *mægð*, a family, a household, or any similar group of
kinsmen. This is the more noticeable because we often read of
familiae which have rights in land; these *familiae*, however,
are not groups of kinsmen but convents of monks or clerks[2].

Family ownership in England.

But, further, the dooms and the land-books are markedly
free from those traits which are commonly regarded as the
relics of family ownership[3]. If we take up a charter of
feoffment sealed in the Norman period we shall probably find
it saying that the donor's expectant heirs consent to the gift.
If we take up an Anglo-Saxon land-book we shall not find
this; nothing will be said of the heir's consent[4]. The denun-
ciatory clause will perhaps mention the heirs, and will curse
them if they dispute the gift; but it will usually curse all

Birthrights in England.

---

[1] Lex Sal. 59.

[2] See *e.g.* Cod. Dipl. 156 (i. 187) where the 'senatores familiae' are
mentioned.

[3] What can be said on the other side has been said by Mr Lodge, Essays on
Anglo-Saxon Law, pp. 74–7.

[4] Cod. Dipl. 1017 (v. 55), Birch, i. 394, on which Mr Lodge relies, is a forgery.
It is to be remembered that we have but very few land-books which do not come
from kings or bishops, but we seem to have just enough to enable us to say
with some certainty that a clause expressive of the heir's consent was not part
of the 'common form,' and that the best forgers of a later time knew this.

and singular who attack the donee's title, and in any system
of law a donee will have more to fear from the donor's heirs
than from other persons, since they will be able to reclaim the
land if for any cause the conveyance is defective[1]. Occasionally
several co-proprietors join to make a gift; but when we consider that in all probability all the sons of a dead man were
equally entitled to the land that their father left behind him,
we shall say that such cases are marvellously rare. Co-ownership, co-parcenary, there will always be. We see it in the
thirteenth century, we see it in the nineteenth; the wonder
is that we do not see more of it in the ninth and tenth than
our Anglo-Saxon land-books display.

In the days before the Conquest a dead man's heirs some- [p. 250]
times attempted to recover land which he had given away, or
which some not impartial person said that he had given away.
They often did so in the thirteenth century; they sometimes
do so at the present day. At the present day a man's expectant heirs do not attempt to interfere with his gifts so long
as he is alive; this was not done in the thirteenth century;
we have no proof that it was done before the Conquest[2].

Expectant heirs do not like to see property given away by
will; they sometimes contest the validity of the will which
contains such gifts; not unfrequently, as every practitioner
in a court of probate will know, the legatees are compelled
to compromise their claims. All this happened in the days

---

[1] In the middle of the eighth century Abbot Ceolfrith with the king's
consent gives to the church at Worcester land which has descended to him as
heir of his father. The charter ends with this clause: 'Si quis autem, quod
absit, ex parentela mea vel externorum, malivola mente et maligno spiritu
instigatus, huius donationis nostrae munificentiam infringere nititur et contraire,
sciat se in die tremendo......rationem redditurum.' Here is a man who has
inherited land from his father, who gives it away though he has a *parentela*,
and who is no more careful to protect the church against claims urged by his
kinsmen than he is to protect it against the claims of *externi*. See Cod. Dipl.
127 (i. 154).

[2] Mr Lodge relies on Cod. Dipl. 195 (i. 238). King Egbert gave land to
Aldhun, who gave it to the church of Canterbury. King Offa took it away,
'quasi non liceret Ecgberhto agros hereditario iure scribere.' Another and an
earlier charter, Cod. Dipl. 1020 (v. 61), distinctly alleges that Offa's resumption
was based, not on an infraction of family law, but on a royal or seignorial claim.
Egbert had given the land to his *minister* Aldhun; Offa revoked it, 'dicens
iniustum esse quod minister eius praesumpserit terram sibi a domino distribu-
tam absque eius testimonio in alterius potestatem dare.'

before the Conquest; but when we consider that the testamentary or *quasi*-testamentary gift was in that age a new thing, we can not say that such disputes about wills were common[1].

A doom of King Alfred speaks thus:—'If a man has book-land which his kinsmen left him, we decree that he is not to alienate it outside his kindred, if there is writing or witness that this was forbidden by those who first acquired it and by those who gave it to him; and let this be declared with the witness of the king and the bishop in the presence of his kinsfolk[2].' We may argue, if we will, that this is an attempt to impose upon the alienable book-land some of those fetters which have all along compressed the less alienable folk-land or 'family-land'; the *forma donationis* is to be observed and restrictive forms are not unknown[3]. Nevertheless, here, about the year 900, we see the current of legislation moving, at least for the moment, in favour of the expectant heirs. Either a new law is made for their benefit or a new precision is given to an old law.

We may well suppose that often enough a man's co-heirs left his land unpartitioned for some time, and that for more than one generation his male descendants and such of his female descendants as were not married continued to live together under one roof or within one enclosure as a joint, undivided household. We may guess that when, to take one

[marginal notes: The restraint on alienation. / [p. 251] / Partition of inheritances.]

---

[1] The best cases are collected at the end of the Essays on Anglo-Saxon Law, Nos. 4, 8, 14, 16, 30. Mr Lodge's argument (p. 76) about Æthelric's will (Cod. Dipl. 186; Birch, i. 438, 440) we cannot adopt. 'The necessity of family consent is shown by the provision in Æthelric's will, that the land could be alienated *cum recto consilio propinquorum*.' There is no such provision. Æthelric gives land to his mother for life, and on her death it is to go to the church of Worcester. But he has reason to fear that a claim will be put in by the church of Berkeley. So he desires that the church of Worcester shall protect the mother, and adds 'et si aliquis homo in aliqua contentione iuramentum ei decreverit contra Berclingas, liberima erit ad reddendum cum recto consilio propinquorum meorum, qui mihi donabant hereditatem et meo quo ei dabo.' Whatever this may mean, it is not the land but an oath in defence of title that is to be given (*reddendum*). Apparently the *propinqui* who have given Æthelric his *hereditas* are already dead: the testator himself, by whose 'counsel' the oath is to be given, will be dead before it is given. The devisee is to be free to swear that she acquired the land by the gift of Æthelric, and that he came to it by the gift of ancestors who had it to give.

[2] Alf. 41; cf. Leg. Hen. 70, § 21; 88, § 14.

[3] Cod. Dipl. 147 (i. 177).

out of many examples, ten thegns hold three hides in parage, they are cousins[1]; but the partition of an inheritance among co-heirs, or rather as it happens co-heiresses, appears at an early time[2], and we have nothing to show that when an inherited estate remained undivided and one of the parceners died, his share did not pass to his own descendants according to the same rules of inheritance that would have governed it had it been physically partitioned and set out by metes and bounds. No one word is there to show that a son at birth was deemed to acquire a share of the land that his father held. Need we say that there is no one word to show that the law treated the father as a trustee for his children, or as the attorney or procurator of his family?

The appointment of heirs.

'Only God can make a *heres,* not man'—said Glanvill[3]. But far back in remote centuries Englishmen had seen no difficulty in giving the name *heres* to a person chosen by a land-holder to succeed him in his holding at his death. And so with the English word for which *heres* has been an equivalent. It was not inconceivable that a man should name an *yrfeweard* [p. 252] to succeed him. We are far from believing that this could be done of common right, or that this nominated *yrfeweard* was a *heres* in the Roman sense of that term; but, while in Glanvill's day it would have been a contradiction in terms to speak of an heir who was not of the blood of the dead man, this had not been so in the past[4].

The restraint on alienation before and after the Conquest.

We must admit that most of our evidence relates to book-land, and we have often argued that in all likelihood book-land is an exotic and a superficial institution, floating, as it were, on the surface of English law. Of what went on below the surface among those men who had no books we can learn little; it is very likely that a restraint in favour of the expectant heirs was established. But what we see happening

---

[1] D. B. i. 79.   [2] Cod. Dipl. 232 (i. 300); Birch, i. 572; A.D. 833.
[3] Glanvill, vii. 1.

[4] Cod. Dipl. 675 (iii. 255). It is possible to contend that the clause in the land-books which enables the donee to bestow the land upon such *heres* as he pleases, gives him what modern lawyers would describe as a limited power of testamentary appointment among his kinsmen. But the history of the clause does not favour this interpretation. We start with forms that say nothing of heirs. See *e.g.* Cod. Dipl. 79, 80, 83, 90 : 'et cuicumque voluerit tradere vel in vita illius vel post obitum eius [potestatem] habeat tradendi.' We do not think that the 'cuicumque ei karorum' (Cod. Dipl. 216) or 'cuicumque heredum' of later documents are restrictive phrases.

among the great folk is not unimportant, and it is this :—the Anglo-Saxon thegn who holds book-land does not profess to have his heir's consent when he gives part of that land to a church ; his successor, the Norman baron, will rarely execute a charter of feoffment which does not express the consent of one heir or many heirs. Our record is miserably imperfect, but as it stands it tends to prove that among the rich and noble there was a period when the rights of the expectant heir were not waning but waxing. In the end, as we shall see hereafter, the heir succeeds in expelling from the common law the testamentary or *quasi*-testamentary gift of land.

We have not been arguing for any conclusion save this, that in the present state of our knowledge we should be rash were we to accept 'family ownership,' or in other words a strong form of 'birth-right,' as an institution which once prevailed among the English in England. That we shall ever be compelled to do this by the stress of English documents is improbable ; nor at this moment does it seem likely that comparative jurisprudence will prove that dogma the universal validity of which we have ventured to doubt. To suppose that the family law of every nation must needs traverse the same route, this is an unwarrantable hypothesis. To construct some fated scheme of successive stages which shall comprise every arrangement that may yet be discovered among backward peoples, this is a hopeless task. A not unnatural inference from their backwardness would be that somehow or another they have wandered away from the road along which the more successful races have made their journey. *Last words on family ownership.*

About the rules of intestate succession which prevailed here in the days before the Conquest we know little ; they may have been different in the different folks, and at a later time they may have varied from shire to shire. We know much more of the rules that obtained among our near cousins upon the mainland, and by their aid we may arrive at a few cautious conclusions. But we are here met by a preliminary question as to the nature of inheritance. For a time we must disregard that canon of later English law which bids us use the words 'inheritance' and 'heir' only when we are describing the fate which awaits the lands, or to speak more nicely, the 'real estate,' of the dead. This canon we can not take back with us into the distant age that is now before us ; but, *Nature of inheritance.*

[p. 253]

applying these terms to movables as well as to immovables, and assuming for a while that we know who the dead man's heirs must be, we have still to ask, What is the nature of inheritance?

Inherit-
ance and
represen-
tation of
the dead.

It is the more necessary to ask this question because we might otherwise be misled by modern law and Roman law into giving it a tacit answer that would not be true. To us it must seem natural that when a man dies he should leave behind him some representative who will bear, or some few representatives who will jointly bear, his *persona*. Or again, we may be inclined to personify the group of rights and duties which are, as it were, left alive, though the man in whom they once inhered is dead: to personify the *hereditas*. We Englishmen do something of this kind when we speak of an executor owing money to or having claims against 'the estate' of his testator. To do something of this kind is so natural, that we can hardly imagine a time when it was not done.

Represen-
tation of
the dead
in modern
law.

But our own modern law will remind us that even in the nineteenth century there is no absolute necessity compelling the whole *persona*, or whole estate, of the dead man to devolve upon one representative, or one set of representatives who will act in unison. In the case of intestacy the 'realty' will go one way and the 'personalty' another. This is not all: [p. 254] it is conceivable that the realty itself should fall into fragments, each of which will descend in a different course. Not only does our law respect local customs, but it also retains in an obscured form the old rule which gives *paterna paternis, materna maternis*. As an exercise for the imagination we might construct a case in which the intestate's realty would be broken into twelve portions, each of which would follow a different path[1]. Thus even in our own day we have not yet found it needful to decree that some one man or some set of conjoint persons shall succeed *in universum ius defuncti*[2].

Why must
the dead
be repre-
sented?

But why do we demand that the dead shall be represented? The law of inheritance seems to answer two purposes, which can be distinguished, though in practice they are blended.

[1] The *propositus* inherited land from his (1) paternal grandfather, (2) paternal grandmother, (3) maternal grandfather, (4) maternal grandmother, and in every case the land inherited contained acres subject to (*a*) the common law, (*b*) the gavelkind rule, (*c*) the Borough English custom.

[2] A long step in this direction has been taken by the Land Transfer Act, 1897.

The dead man has left behind him a mass of things, and we must decide what is to be done with them. But further, he has gone out of the world a creditor and a debtor, and we find it desirable that his departure should make as little difference as may be to his debtors and creditors. Upon this foundation we build up our elaborate system of credit. Death is to make as little difference as may be to those who have had dealings with him who has died, to those who have wronged him, to those whom he has wronged.

Now the first of these needs must be met at an early stage in legal history. If there is to be peace, a scramble for the dead man's goods can not be suffered; law must have some rule for them. On the other hand, we can not say with any certainty that the second purpose will become perceptible until there is a good deal of borrowing and lending. But it is only this second purpose that requires any representation of the dead. It may be allowed indeed that so soon as land is inherited the heir will in some sort fill the place of his ancestor. The land, when it becomes his, must still bear the same burdens that it has hitherto borne. But here there seems to be no representation of the ancestor; rather we have a personification of the plot of land; it has sustained burdens and enjoyed easements in the past, and must sustain and enjoy them still. *(margin: Representation not necessary in early times.)*

[p. 255] We have therefore grave doubts as to whether any widely general dogma about these matters will deserve a ready assent. So much will depend upon religion. In this province of law the sacral element has in various ages and various lands been strong. We have to think not only of what is natural but also of what is supernatural. Among one rude people the representation of the ancestor by the heir may appear at an early time, because the son must perform sacrificial duties which have been incumbent on his father. Among another and a less rude people there may be no representation until commerce and credit demand it. Of Germanic heathenry we know little, but the Christianity which the Germans have adopted when first they are writing down their laws is not a religion which finds its centre at the family hearth. Much might be done by a pious heir for the good of his ancestor's soul, and the duty of doing this was sedulously preached; but the heir could not offer the expiatory sacrifice, nor would *(margin: Representation and religion.)*

it be offered in his house; no priesthood had descended upon him. There is therefore no religious nucleus that will keep together the *universum ius defuncti*; the churches would prefer that the dead man's lands and goods should never reach the hands of the heir but be dissipated by pious gifts.

Inherit-
ance of
debts and
credits.

In the old time the person or persons who succeeded to the lands and goods of the dead man had few, if any, debts to pay or to receive. Most of the pecuniary claims that could be made good in a court of law would perish at the death of the creditor and at the death of the debtor. We may perhaps gather from the so-called 'wills' of this age that there were some claims of which this was not true, for a testator some-times says that his debtors are to be forgiven or that his creditors are to be paid[1]. In the former case, however, we can not be certain that there has not been an express promise that the creditor 'or his heir' shall have the money. In later days this phrase becomes part of the common form of a written bond for the payment of money; and there is much both in English and in continental documents to suggest that the mention of the heirs has not been idle verbiage[2]. A promise to pay money to Alfred is no promise to pay money to Alfred's heir, just as a gift of land to Alfred will hardly give him heritable rights unless something be said of his heirs. As [p. 256] to the hereditary transmission of a liability, this we take it was not easily conceived, and when an Anglo-Saxon testator directs that his debts be paid, this, so far from proving that debts can normally be demanded from those who succeed to the debtor's goods, may hint that law is lagging behind morality. If the heir paid the ancestor's debts, he did a pious and laudable act, perhaps an act as beneficial for the departed soul as would be the endowment of a chantry:—this is a feeling that grows stronger as time goes on. At any rate our law, when at the end of the thirteenth century it takes a definite form, seems to tell us that in the past many debts have died with the debtors. We have every reason to believe that claims *ex delicto* would seldom, if ever, survive the death of the wrong-doer or of the wronged. For one moment the blood-feud and the wergild may induce us to think otherwise; but in truth there is here no representation. The wergild was

[1] Thorpe, Diplomatarium, pp. 550–1, 558, 561, 567–8.
[2] Heusler, Instit. i. 60; ii. 541.

not due to the slain man and is not paid to one who represents him.   At least in the common case it is not even paid
only to those persons who are his heirs, for many persons are
entitled to a share in the wergild who take no part of the
inheritance.   The slain man's brothers, uncles and cousins, as
well as his children, have been wronged and atonement must
be made with them.   And when an attack is made upon
the slayer's kinsmen or the wergild is demanded of them,
they are not pursued as his representatives—he himself may
be alive—they are treated rather as his belongings, and all
that belongs to him is hateful to those who hate him.   Gradually as the feud loses its original character, that of a war,
the heirs of the slayer may perhaps free themselves from all
liability by rejecting the inheritance; but this is an infringement of the old principle, and in the region of blood-feud
there is not much room for the development of representation[1].
Lastly, as regards the wrongs which do not excite a lawful
feud, such as insults, blows, wounds, damage to land or goods,
we must think of them as dying with the active and dying
with the passive party.   Only by slow degrees has our law
come to any other rule, and even now-a-days those causes of
action which were the commonest in ancient times still die
with the person.

[p. 257]   If there is to be no representation of the dead man for the
purpose of keeping obligations alive, then there is no great
reason why the things that he leaves behind him should all
go one way, and early Germanic law shows a tendency to allow
them to go different ways.   It sees no cause why some one
person or some set of conjoint persons should succeed *in universum ius defuncti.*   Thus the chattels may be separated from
the land and one class of chattels from another.   Among some
tribes the dead man's armour, his 'heriot,' follows a course
of its own and descends to his nearest kinsman on the sword
side.   Then it is said that in the *Lex Salica* we may see the
last relics of a time when movable goods were inherited
mainly or only by women; and all along through the middle
ages there are German laws which know of certain classes
of chattels, the clothes and ornaments of a woman's person,
which descend from woman to woman to the neglect of males.
At all events, already in the *Lex Salica* there is one set

*The in-
heritance
need not
descend in
one mass.*

---

[1] As to the whole of this subject see Heusler, Instit. ii. 540.

of canons for chattels, another for land; a woman can not inherit land.

Transition.

But the little more that can be said of these obscure matters will be better said hereafter. It is time that we should turn to an age which is less dark and speak of the shape that our law of inheritance takes when first it becomes plain in the pages of Glanvill and Bracton and the rolls of the king's court. And the first thing that we have to do is to leave off using the words 'inheritance' and 'heir' in that wide sense in which we have hitherto used them:—they point only to the fate of land and of those incorporeal things that are assimilated to land; they point to a succession which is never governed by testament.

§ 2.　*The Law of Descent.*

Primary
rules.

At the end of Henry III.'s reign our common law of inheritance was rapidly assuming its final form. Its main outlines were those which are still familiar to us, and the more elementary of them may be thus stated:—The first class of persons called to the inheritance comprises the dead person's descendants; in other words, if he leaves an 'heir of his body,' no other person will inherit. Among his descendants, precedence [p. 258] is settled by six rules. (1) A living descendant excludes his or her own descendants. (2) A dead descendant is represented by his or her own descendants. (3) Males exclude females of equal degree. (4) Among males of equal degree only the eldest inherits. (5) Females of equal degree inherit together as co-heiresses. (6) The rule that a dead descendant is represented by his or her descendants overrides the preference for the male sex, so that a grand-daughter by a dead eldest son will exclude a younger son. Here for a while we must pause, in order to comment briefly upon these rules[1].

Preference
of descend-
ants.

The preference of descendants before all other kinsfolk we may call natural: that is to say, we shall find it in every system

---

[1] This topic has been discussed at great length by Hale, History of the Common Law, ch. xi., and Blackstone, Comm. Bk. ii. ch. 14; also by Brunner, Das Anglo-Normannische Erbfolgesystem. The main fault to be found in Blackstone's classical exposition is the tendency to treat the Lombard *Libri Feudorum* as a model to which all feudal law ought to correspond.

that is comparable with our own.   A phrase that is common in the thirteenth century makes it prominent.   A man who dies without leaving a descendant, though he may have other kinsfolk who will be his heirs, is often said to die 'without an heir of (or from) himself' (*obiit sine herede de se*).   It is only when a man has no heir *de se*, that his brother or any other kinsman can inherit from him.

A preference for males over females in the inheritance of land is strongly marked in several of the German folk-laws. The oldest form of the *Lex Salica* excludes women altogether. Some of the later codes postpone daughters to sons and admit them after sons, but a postponement of daughters even to remoter male kinsmen is not unknown.   As to England, we may say with some certainty that, in the age which immediately preceded Harold's defeat, women, though they could inherit land, were postponed at least to their brothers. Domesday Book seems to prove this sufficiently.   In every zone of the system of landholdership as it stood in the Confessor's day we may find a few, but only a few, women as tenants[1].   On the other hand, already at the beginning of the ninth century we see a clear case of a king's daughter [p. 259] inheriting his land[2], and other cases of female heirs are found at an early date[3].

Preference of males.

In later days the customs which diverge from the common law, for instance the gavelkind custom of Kent, agree with it about this matter:—males exclude females of equal degree[4].

Influence of feudalism.

[1] There are some three or four cases in which a sister seems to be holding in common with brothers, but these may be due to gifts or bequests.

[2] King Cenwulf of Mercia died leaving as his heiress his daughter Cwenthryth and was succeeded in the kingship by Ceolwulf, who seems to have been his brother.   A legend gives Cenwulf a son (St Kenelm) whom Cwenthryth, aiming at the kingdom, treacherously slays.   This is a late fable, but the fact that she inherited some of her father's land seems beyond doubt.   See Kemble, Cod. Dipl. 220 (i. 280); Haddan and Stubbs, Councils, iii. 596.

[3] Kemble, Cod. Dipl. 232 (i. 300).   The position of women in the systems of inheritance laid down by the 'folk laws' is the subject of a monograph by Opet, Erbrechtliche Stellung der Weiber (Gierke, Untersuchungen, xxv.).   Sketches of these systems are given by Stobbe, Privatrecht, v. 84.   Opet argues that the Anglo-Saxon law did not postpone women to men of equal degree.   For reasons given in the first edition of this book we do not think that he has proved his case.

[4] Customs which put the daughters on a level with the sons seem to be uncommon.   The instances alleged in modern books (*e.g.* Robinson, Gavelkind, 45) namely the customs of Wareham, Taunton and Exeter, are borough customs.

This precedence is far older than feudalism, but the feudal influence made for its retention or resuscitation[1]. At the same time, the feudalism with which we are concerned, that of [p. 260] northern France, seems to have somewhat easily admitted the daughter to inherit if there was no son. In England, so soon after the Norman invasion as any law becomes apparent, daughters, in default of sons, are capable of inheriting even military fees. In 1135 it is questionable—and this is the extreme case—whether a king's daughter can not inherit the kingdom of England[2].

Primo-
geniture.

A rule which gives the whole of a dead man's land to the eldest of several sons is not a natural part of the law of inheritance. In saying this we are not referring to any fanciful 'law of nature,' but mean that, at all events among the men of our own race, the law of inheritance does not come by this rule if and so long as it has merely to consider what, as between the various kinsmen of the dead man, justice bids us do. When it decides that the whole land shall go to one son—he may be the eldest, he may be the youngest—and that his brothers shall have nothing, it is not thinking merely of the dead man and his sons, and doing what would be fair among them, were there no other person with claims upon the land; it has in view one who is a stranger to the inheritance, some king or some lord, whose interests demand that the land shall not be partitioned. It is in the highest and the lowest of the social strata that 'impartible succession' first appears. The great fief which is both property and office must, if it be inherited at all, descend as an integral whole;

---

[1] The law of the Lombard *Libri Feudorum* excludes women as a general rule; but the original feoffment may make the *feudum* a *feudum femineum.* In Germany also women were excluded from the inheritance of fiefs for some time after fiefs had become heritable among males. Stobbe, Privatrecht, iv. 325-7.

[2] That in 1100 women could inherit knights' fees is sufficiently proved by a clause in the coronation charter:—'Et si mortuo barone vel alio homine meo filia heres remanserit, illam dabo consilio baronum meorum cum terra sua.' The Pipe Roll of 31 Hen. I. shows the sale of female wards. We must leave to genealogists the discussion of the few cases in which Domesday Book shows that already since the Conquest a great lady has acquired lands. A daughter of Ralph Tailbois and a daughter of Roger de Rames (Ellis, Introduction, i. 419) appear among the tenants in chief; but the father of the latter seems to be living. The English fief of William of Arques, a Domesday tenant, seems to have passed to his daughter and then to her daughters: Round, Geoffrey de Mandeville, 397.

the more or less precarious rights which the unfree peasant has in a tenement must, if they be transmissible at all, pass to one person[1]. But these tendencies have to struggle against [p. 261] the dictate of what seems to be natural justice, the obvious rule that would divide the inheritance among all the sons. Perhaps we see this best in the case of the kingship. So soon as the kingship became strictly hereditary it became partible. Over and over again the Frankish realm was partitioned; kings and the younger sons of kings were slow to learn that, at least in their case, natural justice must yield to political expediency[2]. Brothers are equals, they are in parage; one of them can not be called upon to do homage to his peer[3].

Happily for the England of the days before the Conquest, the kingship had never become so strictly hereditary as to become partible. On the other hand, we have every reason to believe that the landowner's land was divided among all his sons. We are here speaking of those persons who in the Norman classification became *libere tenentes*. It is not improbable that among those who were to be the *villani* and the *servi* of Domesday Book a system of impartible succession, which gave the land to the eldest or to the youngest son, was prevalent; but for a while we speak of their superiors. In the highest strata, among the thegns, though we do not see primogeniture, we do see causes at work which were favouring its growth. Causes were at work which were tying military service to the tenure of land, and it would be natural that the king, who had theretofore looked to one man for an unit of fighting power, should refuse to recognize an arrangement which would split that duty into fractional parts: he must have some one man whom he can hold responsible for the production of a duly armed warrior. It is to this that point the numerous entries in

Primogeniture in England.

---

[1] Stobbe, Privatrecht, iv. p. 104.

[2] It is possible, as argued by Maine (Ancient Law, c. 7) that 'the examples of succession by primogeniture which were found among the benefices may have been imitated from a system of family-government known to the invading races, though not in general use.' But the link has yet to be found, and had such a system of family-government been known to the Frankish nation, those ruinous partitions of the kingdom would hardly have taken place.

[3] Richard Cœur de Lion refused to do homage to his brother Henry, 'the young king,' saying, 'It is not meet that the son of the same father and the same mother should admit that he is in any way subject to his elder brother':— Viollet, Établissements, i. 125.

Domesday Book which tell us of two, three, four, nine, ten thegns holding land 'in parage.' They are, we take it, co-heirs holding an undivided inheritance, but one of them is answerable to the king for the military service due from the land. This is the meaning of 'tenure in parage' in later Norman law. The younger heirs hold of the eldest 'in parage'; they do him no homage; they swear to him no fealty; they are his peers, equally entitled with him to enjoy the inheritance; but he and he alone does homage to the lord and is responsible for the whole service of the fee[1]. As will be said below, this arrangement appears in the England of the twelfth and thirteenth centuries when an inheritance falls to co-heiresses. There are several texts in Domesday Book which seem to show that the Norman scribes, with this meaning of the term in their minds, were right in saying that some of the Anglo-Saxon thegns had been holding in parage. It is not unnatural that, if one of several brothers must be singled out to represent the land, this one should usually be the eldest. In Buckinghamshire eight thegns were holding a manor, but one of them was the *senior* of the others and was the man of King Edward[2]. Probably he was their *senior* in every sense of the word, both their elder and their superior; he and only he was the king's man for that manor. The king then is beginning to look upon one of several brothers and co-heirs, usually the eldest, as being for one very important purpose the only representative of the land, the sole bearer of those duties to the state which were incumbent on his father as a landholder. The younger sons are beginning to stand behind and below their elder brother. By a powerful king this somewhat intricate arrangement may be simplified. He and his court may hold that the land is adequately represented by the firstborn son, not merely for one, but for all purposes. This will make the collection of reliefs and aids and taxes the easier, and gradually the claims of the younger sons upon their eldest brother may become merely moral claims which the king's court does not enforce.

[p. 262]

Primo-
geniture in
Normandy.
It is by no means certain that in 1066 primogeniture had gone much further in Normandy than in England[3]. True that

---

[1] Somma, p. 97; Ancienne coutume, c. 30 (ed. de Gruchy, p. 95).

[2] D. B. i. 145 b: 'Hoc manerium tenuerunt octo teigni et unus eorum Alli homo Regis Edwardi senior aliorum fuit.'

[3] See Stapleton, Norman Exchequer Rolls, i. pp. lvi. lxxii.

in all probability a certain traditional precariousness hung about
the inheritance of the military fiefs, a precariousness which
might become a lively force if ever a conquering duke had a
vast land to divide among his barons.   But we can not argue
[p. 263] directly from such precariousness to primogeniture.   We may
say, if we will, that primogeniture is a not unnatural outcome
of feudalism, of the slow process which turns an uninheritable
beneficium into a heritable *feodum*.   It is as a general rule
convenient for the lord that he should have but one heir to
deal with ; but as already said, the lord's convenience has here
to encounter a powerful force, a very ancient and deep-seated
sense of what is right and just, and even in the most feudal age
of the most feudal country, the most feudal inheritances, the
great fiefs that were almost sovereignties, were partitioned
among sons, while as yet the king of the French would hardly
have been brought to acknowledge that these *beneficia* were
being inherited at all.   It is the splendid peculiarity of the
Norman duchy that it was never divided[1].   And, as this
example will show, it was not always for the lord's advantage
that he should have but one heir to deal with: the king at
Paris would not have been sorry to see that great inheritance
split among co-heirs.   And so we can not believe that our
Henry III. was sorry when his court, after prolonged debate,
decided that the palatinate of Chester was divisible among
co-heiresses[2].   A less honest man than Edward I. would have
lent a ready ear to Bruce and Hastings when they pleaded for
a partition of Scotland[3].   That absolute and uncompromising
form of primogeniture which prevails in England belongs, not
to feudalism in general, but to a highly centralized feudalism,
in which the king has not much to fear from the power of his
mightiest vassals, and is strong enough to impose a law that
in his eyes has many merits, above all the great merit of
simplicity.

In Normandy the primogenitary rule never went beyond *Primo-
*securing the impartibility of every military tenement, and even *geniture
*this impartibility was regarded as the outcome of some positive *under later
Norman
*ordinance[4].   If the inheritance consisted of one hauberk-fief, or *law.*
of a barony, or of a serjeanty, the eldest son took the whole ; he
was bound to provide for his brothers to the best of his ability ;

---

[1] Luchaire, Institutions monarchiques, i. 64–65.   [2] Note Book, pl. 1273.
[3] Foedera, i. p. 779.   [4] Très ancien coutumier, p. 9.

but this was only a moral duty, for an ordinance had forbidden the partition of a fief[1]. If there were two fiefs in the inheritance and more than one son, the two eldest sons would get a [p. 264] fief apiece. Other lands were equally divided; but the eldest son would have no share in them unless, as we should say, he would 'bring into account' the military fief that he was taking. It is put as a possible case that the value of a share in the other lands will exceed that of the fief; if so, the eldest son need not take the fief; he has first choice, and it is possible that the knightly land will be left to the youngest and least favoured son. In short, Norman law at the end of the twelfth century prescribes as equal a partition of the inheritance among sons as is compatible with the integrity of each barony, serjeanty or military fief, and leaves the sons to choose their portions in order of birth[2]. Indeed, subject to the rule about the impartibility of military fiefs, a rule imposed by the will of the duke, Norman law shows a strong desire for equality among sons. Any gift of land made by a father to one of his sons is revoked by the father's death; no one is to make one of his expectant heirs better off than the rest[3]. Not upon the Normans as Normans can we throw the burden of our amazing law of inheritance, nor can we accuse the Angevin as an Angevin[4].

Primo-geniture in England under the Norman kings. We may believe that the conquest of England gave William an opportunity of insisting that the honour, the knight's fee, the serjeanty, of the dead man, was not to be divided; but what William and his sons insisted on was rather 'impartible succession' than a strict application of the primogenitary rule. The Conquest had thrown into their hands a power of reviving that element of precariousness which was involved in the inheritance of a *beneficium* or *feodum*. There is hardly a strict right to inherit when there is no settled rule about reliefs, and the heir must make the best bargain that he can with the king[5]. What

---

[1] Both of the tracts of which the Très ancien coutumier consists (pp. 9, 92) lay stress on the duty of the eldest son to provide for his brothers.

[2] Très ancien coutumier, pp. 8, 91.

[3] Somma, p. 114; Ancienne coutume, c. 36 (ed. de Gruchy, p. 111).

[4] Viollet, Établissements, i. 122–5.

[5] See above, vol. i. pp. 308, 314. In Germany the old rule seems to have been that all the sons had equal claims upon the dead man's fief; the lord, however, was only bound to admit one of them, and, if they could not agree who that one should be, then the choice was in the lord's hand. At a later time the primogenitary rule was gradually adopted; but the eldest son, if he took the

we see as a matter of fact in the case of the very great men is
[p. 265] that one son gets the Norman, another the English, fief. On
the death of William Fitz Osbern, for example, 'the king distributed his honour among his sons and gave Breteuil and the
whole of the father's possessions in Normandy to William and
the county of Hereford in England to Roger[1].' 'Roger of
Montgomery died; his son Hugh of Montgomery was made earl
in England, and Robert of Bellême acquired his whole honour
in Normandy, while Roger of Poitou, Arnulf, Philip and Everard
had no part of the paternal inheritance[2].' We may believe also
that in the outer zones of the feudal system the mesne lords
insisted on the impartibility of the knight's fee and of the
serjeanty, and that these as a general rule passed to the eldest
son; but we can not say with any certainty that, if the dead
man held two different fees of different lords, his eldest son was
entitled to both of them. Norman law, as already said, is in
favour of as much equality as is compatible with the integrity
of each military fee.

Two of the authors who have left us *Leges* for the Anglo-
Norman period approached the topic of inheritance; neither of
them knew what to make of it. The *Leis Williame* say, 'If a
man dies without a devise, let his children divide the inheritance equally;' but this occurs among sentences of Roman origin,
and, if its maker had any warrant for it, he may perhaps have
been speaking only of movables[3]. The author of the *Leges
Henrici* goes all the way to the ancient *Lex Ribuaria* for a canon
of inheritance, and fetches thence a rule which we should be rash
in applying to the England of the twelfth century, for it would
exclude a daughter in favour of the remotest male kinsman, to
say nothing of admitting father and mother[4]. He says this

Inherit-
ance in the
Anglo-
Norman
Leges.

---

fief, had to 'collate' its value if he wished to share in the general inheritance.
Stobbe, Privatrecht, iv. 322.

[1] Ordericus Vitalis (ed. le Prevost), ii. 405.

[2] Ibid. iii. 425.

[3] Leg. Will. i. c. 34: 'Si home mort senz devise, si depertent les enfans
lerité entre sei per uwel.' See above, vol. i. p. 103, as to the Romanesque
character of the context. The Latin translation gives *pueri* for *enfans*; but
pueri may stand for children of either sex (Calend. Genealog. i. 204: 'omnes alii
pueri eius erant filiae'), and perhaps *enfans* may stand for *sons*. But we can
allow hardly any weight to this part of the *Leis*.

[4] Leg. Henr. 70 § 20. The writer tampered with the end of the passage
that he borrowed, and it is possible that what looks at first sight like an

however, and it is to the point:—In the first place the eldest [p. 266] son takes the father's *feodum*. What exactly he would have given to the eldest son, or what he would have done if the inheritance comprised two *feoda*, we do not know[1]. The conquest and the clash of national laws have thrown all into confusion, and the king will profit thereby.

Primo-
geniture
under the
Angevins.

It may well be that Henry II. spoke his mind in favour of primogeniture both in England and in Normandy; his son Geoffrey in 1187, just when Glanvill was writing, decreed that in Britanny the knight's fee should pass intact to the eldest son[2]. But already in Glanvill's day English law had left Norman law behind it. 'According to the law of the realm of England,' he says—and probably he is here contrasting the kingdom with the duchy—the eldest son of the knight or of one who holds by knight's service succeeds to all that was his father's[3]. With such a military tenant he contrasts the 'free sokeman.' The free sokeman's land is divided among all his sons, but only if it be 'socage and partible from of old.' If it has not been partible from of old, then by some customs the eldest, by others the youngest son will inherit it.

Primo-
geniture
in Glanvill
and
Bracton.

In the many commentaries on this text it has hardly been sufficiently noticed that the sphere of primogeniture is already defined by very wide, and the sphere of equal division by very narrow words. Glanvill does not say that a knight's fee is impartible among sons; he says that land held by military service is impartible. Of the serjeanties he here says nothing; of them it were needless to speak, for a serjeanty is the most

exclusion of women is merely the rule 'paterna paternis.' 'Et dum virilis sexus extiterit, et hereditas ab inde sit, femina non hereditetur':—an inheritance which comes down the paternal line will not fall to the maternal line if there be any paternal kinsman living.

[1] Leg. Henr. 70 § 21: 'Primo patris feodum primogenitus filius habeat.' See Kenny, Primogeniture, p. 16. At present there seems to be no warrant for the reading *Primum* which some of our older writers have adopted. The rubric to c. 70, *Consuetudo Westsexae*, probably refers only to the first sentence of the chapter, and neither the rubrics nor the division into chapters can be treated as of high authority. Here the writer is thinking primarily, not of the order of inheritance, but of the law concerning alienation; the *feodum* is contrasted with the acquests and may mean the family land, the *hereditas aviatica*. On the other hand, it may mean a military fee.

[2] Brunner, Erbfolgesystem, p. 31.

[3] Glanv. vii. 3: 'Quia si miles fuerit vel per militiam tenens, tunc secundum ius regni Angliae primogenitus filius patri succedit in totum.'

impartible of all tenements, impartible (so men are saying) even among daughters[1].   But if we leave serjeanty and frankalmoin [p. 267] out of account, by far the greater number of the free tenures that exist in England at the end of the twelfth century fall within the sphere of primogeniture; they are in name and in law military tenures[2].   True that the tenant may be a mere peasant who will never go to the wars; but if he pays one penny by way of scutage his tenure is military[3], and usually when lords make feoffments they take care that the burden of scutage shall fall upon their tenants.   By far the greater number of the countless new feoffments that are being made day by day are creating military tenures, for it is not usual for the feoffor to assume as between himself and his tenant the ultimate incidence of the uncertain war-tax.   The greater number of those very numerous tenures in 'free and common socage' which exist in the last of the middle ages, have, we believe, their origin in the disappearance of scutage and the oblivion into which the old liability for scutage fell[4].   But then again, Glanvill does not say that socage land is partible among sons. For one thing, it is partible only if it has been treated as partible in time past.   Every new tenure therefore that is created after Henry II.'s day, albeit a tenure in socage, adds to the number of estates which obey the primogenitary rule. But more; the estates which according to Glanvill are partible, are only the estates of the 'free sokemen.'   Now while in his day the term 'socage' was just beginning to have that wide meaning which would ultimately make it cover whatever tenure was non-military, non-elemosinary, non-serviential, there was no similar extension of the term 'sokeman[5].'   The free sokemen whom he has in view are a small class that is not increasing.   They are to be found chiefly on the ancient demesne of the crown.   A few may be found on other manors, for the more part in the eastern counties; but these are disappearing.   On the one hand, many are lapsing into villeinage; on the other hand, some are obtaining charters, which perhaps make them in name and in law military tenants, but at any rate give them a new estate and one that has never been partitioned.   Therefore after Glanvill's day there was no further

---

[1] See above, vol. i. p. 290.   Select Civil Pleas, pl. 112.

[2] See above, vol. i. pp. 277, 356.   [3] Note Book, pl. 703, 795, 1663.

[4] See above, vol. i. p. 355.   [5] See above, vol. i. pp. 294, 394.

change in the law; Bracton uses almost the selfsame words [p. 268] that his predecessor used[1].

Consequently there is very little litigation about this matter, and what there is comes from very few counties. We can refer to seventeen cases from the reign of John and the early years of Henry III. which make mention of partible land; of these seven come from Kent, five from Norfolk, three from Suffolk, one from Northamptonshire, one from Rutland[2]. Leaving Kent out of account, it is the land which the Domesday surveyors found well stocked with 'free men' and sokemen that supplies us with our instances. In later days it may be possible to find a few isolated examples of partible land in many shires of England; but, outside Kent, the true home of partibility is the home of that tenure which the lawyers of Edward I.'s day distinguished from 'socage' by the term 'sokemanry[3].'

[1] A comparison of the following passages will prove what we have said.

Glanvill, vii. 3.

Si vero fuerit liber sokemanus, tunc quidem dividetur hereditas inter omnes filios, quotquot sunt, per partes equales, *si fuerit socagium et id antiquitus divisum*, salvo tamen capitali mesuagio primogenito filio pro dignitate aesnesciae suae, ita tamen quod in aliis rebus satisfaciet aliis ad valentiam. Si vero non fuerit antiquitus divisum, tunc primogenitus secundum quorundam consuetudinem totam hereditatem obtinebit; secundum autem quorundam consuetudinem postnatus filius heres est.

Bracton, f. 76.

Si liber sokemanus moriatur, pluribus relictis heredibus et participibus, *si hereditas partibilis sit et ab antiquo divisa*, heredes, quotquot erunt, habeant partes suas equales, et si unicum fuerit mesuagium, illud integre remaneat primogenito, ita tamen quod alii habeant ad valentiam de communi. Si autem non fuerit hereditas divisa ab antiquo, tunc tota remaneat primogenito. Si autem fuerit socagium villanum, tunc consuetudo loci erit observanda. Est enim consuetudo in quibusdam partibus quod postnatus prefertur primogenito et e contrario.

It seems clear that Bracton had Glanvill's text before him, and we can not think that by shifting the words here printed in italics from one place to another he changed, or meant to change, the meaning of the passage. With Glanvill, as with Bracton, the only partible land is the socage land of a sokeman which has been divided from of old. Thus the common opinion that there was a change in the law after Glanvill's day, does not seem to us to be warranted. The judges in the early Year Books do not lean strongly against partibility. If the plaintiff asserts partibility he must prove partition; but if he proves partition he may perhaps succeed in making even a knight's fee partible :—Y. B. 30–1 Edw. I. 57; 33–5 Edw. I. 515. Glanvill's rule needs no extension; it is so very wide.

[2] Placit. Abbrev. 28 (Rutland); Select Civil Pleas (Seld. Soc.) pl. 6, 107, 123. 157; Note Book, 154, 499, 703, 704, 795, 1009, 1023, 1048, 1074, 1565, 1663, 1770.

[3] A great deal of Norfolk seems to have been partible, and partibility reigned

p. 269] The problem which is set before us by the gavelkind of Gavelkind.
Kent is not a problem in the history of the law of inheritance,
but a difficult problem in the general history of English law,
and one which is of an economic rather than of a purely legal
character. It belongs to the twelfth century. It is this :—
How does it come about that at the end of that period there
is in Kent, and not elsewhere, a strong class of rent-paying
tenants who stand well apart from the knights on the one side
and the villeins on the other, a class strong enough to maintain
a *lex Kantiae* which differs at many points from the general law
of the land? We have already given such answer as we can
give to this hard question[1]. On the one hand, it seems to us
that the matter of the Kentish custom is in part very old.
The law of inheritance shows a curious preference for the
youngest son. When his father's house has to be divided, the
hearth (*astre*) is reserved for him[2]. We may say with some
certainty that a rule which had its origin in the twelfth century,
if it gave a preferential share to any son, would give it to the
eldest[3]. Again, some parts of the custom enshrined ancient
English proverbs, which the scribes of the fourteenth century
could not understand and which make reference to institutions
that must have been obsolescent in the twelfth, obsolete in the
thirteenth century[4]. On the other hand, we can not think that

in several of the great 'sokes' of the Danelaw, *e.g.* the soke of Rothley in
Leicestershire and the soke of Oswaldsbeck in Nottinghamshire. See Robinson,
Gavelkind (ed. 1822), pp. 42–6. For 'sokemanry,' see above, vol. i. p. 394.

[1] See above, vol. i. p. 186.

[2] Statutes of the Realm, i. p. 224.

[3] Glanvill, vii. 3; Bracton, f. 76: the free sokeman's house goes to the eldest
son.

[4] We find a proverb about the wife who loses her free-bench by unchastity,
another about the descent of the felon's land, a third about the process called
gavellet. The last of these is obscure. The lord after a long forbearance has
had the tenement adjudged to him, because of the tenant's failure to pay his
rent. The tenant has however a *locus poenitentiae* allowed him. The proverb
seems to say that, if he will get back his land, he must pay the arrears of rent
nine times (or perhaps eighteen times) over, and, in addition to this, must pay a
wergild of five pounds. In the Anglo-Norman reckoning five pounds will do well
enough as a ceorl's *wer* (Leg. Will. I. c. 8), and the nine-fold payment is like the
eleven-fold payment which we find in the account of the Bishop of Worcester's
customs in Domesday Book, i. 174. According to old Kentish law a nine-fold
geld was payable to the king in some cases (Schmid, App. IV. c. 6, 7). Seemingly
the proverb means in truth that the tenant will lose the land for good and all.
It is one of those humorous rules of folk-law which, instead of telling a man
that he can not have what he wants, tell him that he may have it if he will

the Kent of 1065 was a county in which the tillers of the soil [p. 270] were peculiarly well off. Unless the terminology of the Domesday surveyors was far more perverse and deceptive than we can believe it to have been, Kent differed little from Sussex, widely from Norfolk, and in 1086, not Kent, but the shires of the Danelaw must have seemed the predestined home of a strong free yeomanry tenacious of ancient customs. Nor, again, can we think that Kent suffered less than other districts at the hands of the Norman invaders. The best theory that we can suggest is that in the twelfth century the unrivalled position of Kent as the highway of commerce induced a widespread prosperity which favoured the tillers of the soil. An old system of 'provender rents' may have passed into the modern system of money rents without passing through the stage in which the lord places his main reliance on the 'week work' of his tenants. A nucleus of old customs expanded and developed; even the lowest classes of tenants were gradually brought within their range, until at length it was said that every child born in Kent was born free[1].

Dis-gavelling.

It is only to modern eyes that the inheritance partible among sons is the main feature of gavelkind. In the thirteenth century a custom which allowed the sons of the hanged felon to inherit from their father may have seemed a more striking anomaly. Still the partible inheritance was beginning to attract attention. Archbishop Hubert Walter,

perform an impossible condition. As to the more famous proverb 'the father to the bough, the son to the plough,' the oldest form of this sends the father to the bowe, the son to the lowe, that is apparently, to the fireside, the *astre*, which is, if we may so say, the centre of the inheritance. See above, vol. i. p. 187.

[1] The printed custumal professes to be a record of the customs approved in the eyre of 1293; but no official or authoritative text of it has been found. See Robinson, Gavelkind (ed. 1822), p. 355. Almost all the customs mentioned in it are however evidenced by earlier records. Somner, Gavelkind, Appendix, gives several ancient charters conveying land to be held in gavelkind. In the earliest of our plea rolls we find brothers sharing land in Kent and the name 'gavelingude' appears: Rolls of King's Court (Pipe Roll Society), pp. 39, 43. Thenceforward we often find the name. Thus in John's reign, Select Civil Pleas (Selden Society), pl. 157; Placit. Abbrev. p. 56. The peculiarities of the widow's free-bench soon appear: Select Civil Pleas, pl. 128; Note Book, pl. 9, 1338. So the peculiarities of the widower's free-bench: Robinson, Gavelkind, p. 179. Bracton speaks of gavelkind on f. 276 b, 311, 313, 374. On the whole, most of the known peculiarities can be traced as far back as Bracton's time. The statement that there is no villeinage in Kent is made in 1302: Y. B. 30–1, Edw. I. p. 169, as well as in the custumal of 1293: Statutes, vol. i. p. 224.

p. 271] who presided in the king's court during years critical in our legal history, obtained from King John a charter empowering him and his successors to convert into military fees the tenements that were holden of their church in gavelkind[1]. The archbishop's main object may have been to get money in the form of rents and scutages, instead of provender and boon-works, 'gavel-corn' and 'gavel-swine,' 'gavel-erth' and 'gavel-rip'; and we have here an illustration of those early commutations of which we have been speaking, and an important illustration, for a great part of Kent was under the archbishop and his example would find followers[2]. It is possible, however, that Glanvill's nephew and successor also intended to destroy, so far as he could, the partible inheritance. Such at any rate was the avowed object of Edward I. when in 1276 he 'disgavelled' the lands of John of Cobham. In the charter by which he did this we have perhaps the oldest argument in favour of primogeniture that has come down to us, for when Bracton tells us that the first-born son is 'first in the nature of things' this is hardly argument. 'It often happens,' says Edward, 'that tenements held in gavelkind, which so long as they remained whole were sufficient for the maintenance of the realm and provided a livelihood for many, are divided among co-heirs into so many parts and fragments that each one's part will hardly support him'; therefore as a special favour Cobham's gavelkind lands are to descend for ever as though they were held by knight's service[3].

We are far from saying that there were no sound reasons of state to be urged for the introduction and extension of the primogenitary rule. Englishmen in course of time began to

Introduction of primogeniture.

[1] This most interesting charter is given in Lambard, Perambulation of Kent (ed. 1596), p. 531. The charter roll for this year is not forthcoming.

[2] Robinson, Gavelkind (ed. 1822), p. 66: Hubert Walter grants that a certain tenant, who hitherto has held a yoke and ten acres in gavelkind, shall henceforth hold in frank fee by the service of a twentieth part of a knight's fee and an annual rent of 28 shillings. In after days the power of the king and of the archbishop to change the mode of descent was denied. See Elton, Tenures of Kent, chap. xvi.

[3] Robinson, p. 76. Already in 1231 we hear that one messuage is often divided into three or four messuages 'sicut gavelikinde': Note Book, pl. 666. Edward allowed the Welsh to retain the partible inheritance, insisting only that bastards must not be admitted, and that women must be admitted in default of males; but then, as has been well said (Kenny, Primogeniture, p. 32), 'Edward's power lay in the strength of Kentishmen and the weakness of Welshmen.'

glory in it, and under its sway the England of Edward I.'s [p. 272
day had become a strong, a free, and a wealthy state. But
we miss one point in the history of our law unless we
take account of its beautiful simplicity. Granted that each
military fee should descend as an impartible whole, a hundred
difficulties will be evaded if we give all the dead man's lands to
his eldest son—difficulties about 'hotchpot,' difficulties about
the contribution of co-heirs to common burdens, difficulties
about wardships and marriages to which a 'parage' tenure
must, as we shall see hereafter, give rise. We cut these
knots. That when one man leaves the world one other should
fill the vacant place, this is an ideally simple arrangement.
The last years of Henry II. were the years that decided the
matter for good and all, and they were years in which a newly
fashioned court, unhampered by precedents, was with rude,
youthful vigour laying down its first principles. Here as
elsewhere its work is characterized by a bold, an almost
reckless, simplicity. Nor must we fail to notice that here as
elsewhere it generalized the law of the great folk and made
it common law for all free and lawful men, except some ancient
and dwindling classes which had hardly come within its ken.
When we balance the account of our primogenitary law we
must remember that it obliterated class distinctions[1].

Inherit-
ance by co-
heiresses.

The manner in which our law deals with an inheritance
which falls to the dead man's daughters may give us some
valuable hints about the history of primogeniture. If we look
merely at the daughters and isolate them from the rest of the
world, their claims are equal and the law will show no
preference for the first-born. This principle was well maintained, even though some of the things comprised in the

[1] It is fairly clear that in Henry II.'s day the primogenitary rule was not
popular among those classes with which the royal court had to deal. Glanvill
(vii. 1) has to regret that men are too fond of their younger sons. A French
chronicler tells a curious story of a parliament held by Henry III. and Simon de
Montfort in which there was debate as to the abolition of primogeniture and the
adoption of the French rule. England, so it was said, was being depleted and
agriculture was suffering since the younger sons of the English gentry were
driven to seek their fortunes in France. This chronicler shows himself very
ignorant of English history, and the story, as he tells it, must be false. What
we learn from him is that a Frenchman of the fourteenth century thought the
English rule unjust and impolitic. As to this passage, see Bémont, Simon de
Montfort, p. 201.

[p. 273] inheritance were not such as could be easily divided, or were likely to become of less value in the process of division. For example, if there was but one house, the eldest daughter had no right to insist that this should fall to her share, even though she were willing to bring its value into account. No, unless the parceners could agree upon some other plan, the house itself was physically divided[1]. And so again, if there was but one advowson, the eldest sister could not claim the first presentation as her own; all the parceners must join in a presentation, otherwise it will lapse to the ordinary[2]. There were, however, certain indivisible things; a castle could not be partitioned, nor the messuage which was the head of a barony. This passed as a whole to the eldest of the sisters, but she accounted for its value in the division of the rest of the inheritance. To explain this a maxim of public law is introduced:—were partitions made of these things, earldoms and baronies would be brought to naught, and the realm itself is constituted of earldoms and baronies[3]. So again, Bracton's opinion is that a tenement held by serjeanty ought not to be divided, and this opinion seems to have been warranted at all events by the practice of an earlier age[4]. But the king's claim to prevent the partition of a great fee has in the past gone far. In 1218 a litigant pleads that ever since the conquest of England it has been the king's prerogative right that, if one of his barons dies leaving daughters as his heirs, and the elder-born daughters have been married in their father's lifetime, the king may give the youngest daughter to one of his knights with the whole of her father's land to the utter exclusion therefrom of the elder daughters[5]. There is a good deal in the history of the twelfth century to show that the king had held himself free to act upon some such rule. The law of later times about the abeyance of titles of honour is but a poor remnant of the right which he has thus assumed. When of old he 'determined an abeyance in favour of one of the

---

[1] Bracton, f. 76.

[2] Bracton, f. 76 b.   But for later law see Co. Lit. 166 b.

[3] Bracton, f. 76 b.

[4] Bracton, f. 77.   Placit. Abbrev. pp. 34, 39 (temp. Joh.).   But in 1221 Henry III. permits co-heiresses to hold a serjeanty: Excerpt. e Rot. Fin. i. 67. See above, vol. i. p. 290.

[5] Note Book, pl. 12; but this contention seems to be overruled, and as a matter of fact a partition seems to have been made: Excerpt. e Rot. Fin. i. 141.

parceners,' he disposed not merely of a 'title of honour' and [p. 274]
a 'seat in the House of Lords,' but of a great tract of land[1].

Co-heirs
and
parage.

But, though the division among the co-heiresses was in
general a strictly equal division, we see the eldest daughter
or her husband standing out as the representative of the
whole inheritance for certain feudal purposes. The law about
this matter underwent an instructive change. We will suppose
that Henry, who holds of Roger, dies leaving three daughters,
whom in order of birth we call Alice, Barbara and Clara, and
that a partition of the land is made among them. Now two
different feudal schemes may be applied to this case. On the
one hand, we may decide that each of the three women holds
her land of Roger; on the other, that Alice holds the whole
inheritance of Roger, while her sisters hold their shares of her.
Roger has apparently something to gain and something to lose
by the adoption of either scheme. On the one hand, he may
wish to treat Alice as his only tenant, for he will thus have one
person to whom he can look for the whole service due from the
whole land[2]; but then, if this theory is adopted, can he fairly
claim any wardships or marriages in the lines of which Barbara
and Clara are the starting points? This, however, seems to
have been the old theory; Alice will hold of Roger; her
husband, and no one else, will do homage to Roger for the
whole land; her sisters will hold of her; they will 'achieve'
(*accapitare*) to her, that is, will recognize her as their head.
For three generations (of which they are the first) they and
their descendants will do no homage, swear no fealty, and pay
no reliefs; but the third heir of Barbara or Clara must pay
relief to, and become the man of, Alice or her heir[3]. We have
here the Norman tenure in parage[4].

---

[1] Round, Ancient Charters, 97–9: Geoffrey Fitz Peter, the chief justiciar,
having married one of the co-heiresses of the last of the Mandeville earls cf
Essex, obtained the whole Mandeville fief.

[2] Bracton, f. 78: 'particularis enim solutio non minimum habet incom-
modi.'

[3] Glanvill, vii. 3.

[4] Somma, p. 97; Ancienne coutume, cap. 30. In Normandy the parage
endures until the 'sixth degree of lineage' has been past. It seems possible
that this means much the same as what Glanvill means, and that the discrepancy is caused by divers modes of reckoning. According to Glanvill the
great-great-grandson of the dead man is the first person who does homage to a
cousin. Six degrees of Roman computation divide the great-grandson in the
one line from the great-grandson in the other line; thus in the normal case

The reason why no homage is done until a third heir has Fluctua-
tions in
inherited we can not here discuss; but it soon becomes apparent the law as
to parage.
that the king is dissatisfied with this arrangement and that the
law is beginning to fluctuate. In 1236 the English in Ireland
sent to Westminster for an exposition of the law. Of whom do
the younger sisters hold? The answering writ, which has
sometimes been dignified by the title *Statutum Hiberniae de
Coheredibus*, said that if the dead man held in chief of the king,
then all the co-heirs hold in chief of the king and must do him
homage[1]. If the lands were held of a mesne lord, then that
lord has the marriages and wardships of all the parceners, but
only the eldest is to do homage, and her younger sisters are to
do their services through her hands. The eldest daughter, the
writ says, is not to have the marriage and wardship of her
sisters, for this would be to commit the lambs to the wolf[2].
This last provision looks like new law, if it means that the
wardships and marriages of Barbara's descendants are to belong
to Roger, and not to Alice or her descendants. In 1223 we may
find the daughter of an elder sister claiming the marriage of
the son and heir of a younger sister[3]. A judge of Edward I.'s
day tells us of a *cause célèbre* in which the wardships and
marriages of the heirs in the younger line had in generation
after generation gone to the representatives of the older line;
but all this was held null and void at the suit of the lord[4].
Bracton gives the law as it was laid down by the writ of 1236,
and in his day we still see the younger daughters holding of

there would be seven (Roman) degrees at least between the person who first does
and the person who first receives homage. According to Bracton, f. 78, the
younger sisters swear fealty to the elder; according to Glanvill they do not.
For the parage of Anjou, see Viollet, Établissements, i. 125.

   [1] For some time past the king had habitually taken the homage of all the
parceners: Excerpta e Rot. Fin. i. 32, 48, 67, 72, 164 etc.

   [2] Statutes of the Realm, i. p. 5; Praerogativa Regis, c. 5, 6; Britton, ii. 23.

   [3] Note Book, pl. 1596. The law is also illustrated by pl. 667, 869, 1053,
1765.

   [4] Y. B. 32–3 Edw. I. p. 301: Bereford, J. says, 'I have seen a case where the
father, grandfather and great-grandfather have been seised of the homage,
wardship and marriage of their parceners, and yet all this was set aside by
reason of the parcenry, and the chief lord recovered his services. This I saw
in the case of Sir Edmund the king's brother, for parceners ought not to
'murder' another's right of seignory among themselves.' The allusion can be
explained by the pedigree of Avelina, wife of Edmund of Cornwall, which will be
found in Calend. Genealog. i. p. lxvii.

their sister, holding without homage until the third heir has [p. 276] inherited[1]. Britton knows that the lord can not be compelled to take the homage of any but the eldest daughter, and that, when this has been done, he can and must look to that sister for the whole of his services; but Britton advises the lord to accept the homage of all, for should he not do so, he may find some difficulty in getting wardships and marriages in the younger lines[2]. The lords from this time forward had their choice between two courses. As a matter of fact they took Britton's advice, followed the king's example and exacted homage from all the sisters. Very soon, if we are not mistaken, the old law of parage began to fall into oblivion[3].

The lord's interest in primogeniture. The lesson that we learn from this episode is that the lord's interest has been powerful to shape our law of inheritance. At one time it looks as if even among women there would be what we may call an external primogeniture, so that the eldest of the daughters would be the only representative of the fee in the eyes of the lord and of the feudal courts. Had this principle been consistently applied, the rights of the younger daughters might have become merely moral rights. But in the thirteenth century wardships and marriages were of greater importance than knight's service and scutage, and first the king and then the other lords perceived that they had most to gain by taking the homage of all the sisters.

Inheritance of villein land. It is by no means impossible that the spread of primogeniture to tenements that were hardly military save in name, and then to tenements that were not military even in name, was made the easier by the prevalence of 'impartible succession' among the holders of villein tenements. We have already said that in the thirteenth century such tenements often pass from ancestor to heir[4]. There is a custom of inheritance which is known to the manorial court and maintained against all but the lord. That custom seems generally to point to one person and one only as entitled to succeed to the dead man's tenement. In a manorial extent it is rare to find the names of two brothers or even of two sisters entered as those of the tenants of a [p. 277]

---

[1] Bracton, f. 78 and the cases in the Note Book cited above.

[2] Britton, ii. 29, 40.

[3] So in France Philip Augustus tried to suppress parage tenure: Warnkönig, Französ. Geschichte, ii. 456.

[4] See above, vol. i. p. 379.

tenement[1]. On the other hand, it is very common to find that the tenant is a woman. Often she is a widow, and it is clear that she is holding the virgate of a dead husband. But putting the widow out of the case, then, if there were several sons, either the eldest or the youngest seems usually to have succeeded to his father to the exclusion of his brothers. In later days very many copyholds follow the primogenitary rules of the common law, and we can not think that those rules have been thrust upon them in recent days, though no doubt the courts have required strict proof of abnormal customs. We imagine therefore that from a remote time many villein tenements have descended in a primogenitary course. On the other hand, it is certain that a scheme which gave the land to the youngest son was common.

A mere accident—for we think that it was no better—has given the name 'borough English' to this custom of ultimogeniture. In the Norman days a new French borough grew up beside the old English borough of Nottingham. A famous case of 1327 drew the attention of lawyers to the fact that while the burgages of the 'burgh Francoys' descended to the eldest son, those of the 'burgh Engloys' descended to the youngest[2]. It was natural for the lawyers to find a name for the custom in the circumstances of this case, to call it the custom of the borough English, or the custom of borough English, for such a custom came before them but rarely[3]. Without saying that it never ruled the descent of tenements held by the free socage of the common law, we seem fully entitled to say that, if we put on one side what in the thirteenth century were distinguished from socage as being burgage tenures, and if we also put on one side the 'sokemanry' of the ancient demesne, then a freehold tenement descending to the youngest son was an exceedingly rare phenomenon; and in 1327 the Westminster courts had as yet had little to do with the inheritance of burgages and sokemanries. The true home of ultimogeniture is the villein tenement; among villein tenements it has widely prevailed; in Bracton's day its appearance raised

Ultimogeniture.

[p. 278]

---

[1] Among such manorial plea rolls as have been printed we have observed no instance even of two women claiming to be co-heirs of a villein tenement.

[2] Y. B. 1 Edw. III. f. 12 (Pasch. pl. 38). See Elton, Origins of English History, 179.

[3] Litt. sec. 165, 211.

a presumption that the tenements which it governed were not free[1].

Origin of ultimo-geniture.

It is hardly to be explained without reference to the lord's interest and the lord's will. But what has thus to be explained is not really the preference of the youngest son, but the impartible inheritance. If once we grant that the tenement is not to be divided, because the lord will have but one tenant, then in truth the preference of the youngest is quite as natural as the preference of the eldest son. Perhaps if the lord had merely to pursue his own interest he would as a general rule choose the first-born, for the first-born is the most likely of all the sons to be of full age at the time of his father's death. Were there military service to be done, there would be good reason for selecting him. But if we look at the matter from the tenant's point of view, there is something to be said in favour of the youngest son. If the eldest son took the tenement, he might marry and beget a new family while his brothers were still unable to earn a livelihood. Give it to the youngest, and the brothers may all dwell together until all can labour. Add to this—and it will count for something—that the youngest is the son most likely to be found in the house at his father's death; he will be at the hearth; he is the fireside child. The ancient customs of free tenements will sometimes respect this idea: the land is to be equally divided among the sons, but the house, or, if not the house, at least the hearth, is given to the youngest. Perhaps we may see in this a trace of an ancient religion of which the hearth was the centre. If then

---

[1] Note Book, pl. 794, 1005, 1062. As a fair selection of copyhold customs, which have been reduced to writing in comparatively modern times, we may take those collected in Watkins, Copyholds (3rd ed.), ii. p. 228 fol. Dymock, Gloucestershire: no inheritance beyond heirs of the body. Yetminster, Dorset: widow has rights but there is no true inheritance. Weardale, Durham: eldest son, and failing sons, daughters jointly. Mayfield, Sussex: yard-lands to youngest son, and failing sons, youngest daughter; assart lands to eldest son, or failing sons, eldest daughter. Framfield, Sussex: the like; primogeniture or, as the case may be, ultimogeniture prevails even when the descent is to remote relations. Stepney, Middlesex: partible between sons and, failing sons, between daughters; partible between remoter kinsfolk of equal degree, whether male or female. Cheltenham, Gloucestershire: youngest son and, failing sons, youngest daughter. Taunton, Somerset: widow inherits in fee from her husband to the exclusion of children. Robinson, Gavelkind (last chapter), gives a list of places, mostly in the south-east of England, where 'borough English' has prevailed in modern times. That an eldest or youngest daughter should, in default of sons, take the whole land was not uncommon.

[p. 279] we suppose a lord insisting on the rule, 'One tenement, one tenant,' and yet willing to listen to old analogies or to the voice of what seems to be 'natural equity,' it is not at all improbable that, with the general approval of his tenantry, he will allow the inheritance to fall to the youngest son.

A good illustration of the conflicting principles which will shape a scheme of descent among peasant holders is afforded by a verdict given in 1224 about the custom which prevailed in the 'ancient demesne' manors of Bray and Cookham[1]:— The jurors have always seen this custom, 'that if any tenant has three or four daughters and all of them are married outside their father's tenement, save one, who remains at the hearth[2], she who remains at the hearth shall have the whole land of her father, and her sisters shall recover no part thereof; but if there are two or three or more daughters and all of them are married outside their father's tenement with his chattels, whether this be so before or after his death, the eldest daughter shall have the whole tenement and her sisters no part; and if the daughters are married after their father's death with his chattels, and this without protest, and one of them remains at the hearth, she at the hearth shall retain the whole tenement as aforesaid[3].' Subject to the rule that the tenement must not be partitioned, we seem to see here an attempt to do what is equitable. If really there is no difference between the daughters—no such difference as can be expressed in general terms by a rude rule of law—then we fall back upon primogeniture; but if the other daughters have been married off, the one who is left at the hearth is the natural

Impartible peasant holdings.

---

[1] Note Book, pl. 951, 988. See also Placit. Abbrev. p. 233 (Berk.).

[2] The words are *in atrio*; Bracton, f. 267 b, uses them as an equivalent for *in astro*: 'ambo reperiuntur in atrio sive in astro.'

[3] Co. Lit. 140 b: 'Within the manor of B. [Bray] in the county of Berks, there is such a custom, that if a man have divers daughters, and no son, and dieth, the eldest daughter shall only inherit; and if he have no daughters, but sisters, the eldest sister by the custom shall inherit and sometimes the youngest.' In two Sussex manors we find the yard-lands (the old original villein tenements) governed by ultimogeniture even among daughters, while the assart lands (lands brought into cultivation at a later time) are governed by an equally strict primogeniture; but (and this is very instructive) if a tenant has lands of both kinds, they must all go together either to the eldest or to the youngest; the tenement that he acquired first will carry with it the other tenement. Watkins, Copyholds (3rd ed.), ii. pp. 282, 297; Elton, Origins of English History, p. 187.

heir[1]. But already in the thirteenth century ultimogeniture [p. 280] was becoming unpopular: Simon de Montfort granting a charter of liberties to his burgesses at Leicester abolished it. The reason that he gave is curious:—the borough was being brought to naught by the default and debility of heirs[2]. By the common assent and will of all the burgesses he established primogeniture among them. We may believe that what moved the burgesses was not so much any ill effects occasioned by the old mode of inheritance as the bad repute into which it had fallen. It was the rule for villeins, explicable only by the will of the lord. The burgesses of Leicester mean to be free burgesses and to enjoy what is by this time regarded as the natural law for free men.

Causes of ultimo- geniture.

We would not suggest that in no case can a custom of ultimogeniture have arisen save under the pressure of seignorial power. In a newly conquered country where land is very plentiful, the elder sons may be able to obtain homes of their own and, they being provided for, the father's lands may pass to the fireside child; and again there may conceivably have been a time when the pressure which made for impartible succession was rather communal than seignorial. But as a matter of fact, whether we look to England or to other European countries, we shall hardly find ultimogeniture save where some lord has been able to dictate a rule of inheritance to dependent peasants[3]. It seems to have been so in medieval Germany. The common [p. 281]

---

[1] The verdict is a good typical verdict about a customary mode of descent. It leaves many cases unprovided for. In the imperfection of all ancient state- ments of the rules of inheritance to copyholds our common law has found an opportunity for spreading abroad its own rules. Thus jurors state in the custumal that a youngest son excludes his fellows, but say nothing of a descent to brothers, uncles, cousins. Hence perhaps the not uncommon result that in modern times there is ultimogeniture among sons, primogeniture among brothers. But the reason for giving the land to a youngest son hardly extends to the case of a youngest brother. He is not so likely to be found at the dead man's fire- side.

[2] Jeaffreson, Index to the Leicester MSS. p. 66: 'propter defectum heredum et debilitatem eorum iam multo tempore [villa] fere ad occasum declinavit et ruinam.' This of course can not refer to a 'default' of heirs in the ordinary sense of that term. What is suggested is that the heirs are weaklings.

[3] We here speak of a rule which gives the whole land to the youngest son. Rules which divide the land equally among the sons but reserve 'the hearth' or house for the eldest or youngest are quite a different matter and may perhaps have their origin in a religious cult of the hearth; see Elton, Origins of English History, ch. viii.

land law divides the land among all the sons, giving perhaps
to the eldest, perhaps to the youngest a slight preference[1];
the noble fief will often pass undivided to the first-born; the
tenement of the peasant will go as a whole either to his
eldest or to his youngest son, and as a matter of geographical
distribution the primogenitary will be intermingled with the
ultimogenitary customs:—'the peasant,' says a proverb, 'has
only one child[2].' For all this, however, we are not entitled
to draw from ultimogeniture any sweeping conclusions as to
the large number of slaves or serfs that there must have
been in a remote past. The force which gives the peasant's
tenement to his youngest or his eldest son is essentially the
same force which, in one country with greater in another with
less success, contends for the impartibility of the military fee.
Somehow or another it has come about that there is a lord
with power to say 'This land must not be divided.' The
persons to whom he says this may be slaves, or the progeny of
slaves, who are but just acquiring an inheritable hold upon the
land; they may be mighty barons who have constrained him
much against his will to grant them 'loans' of land; they may
be free landowners over whom he has acquired jurisdictional
powers, which he is slowly converting into proprietary rights.

The representative principle—the principle which allows *Represen*
the children or remoter descendants of a dead person to stand *tation in*
in that person's stead in a scheme of inheritance—is one which *ance.*
in England and elsewhere slowly comes to the front. Our fully
developed common law adopts it in all its breadth and permits
it to override the preference for the male sex. The daughters,
grand-daughters and other female descendants of an eldest son
who died in his father's lifetime will exclude that father's
second son. In the twelfth century, however, this principle was
still struggling for recognition. In all probability neither the
old English nor the old Frankish law would have allowed
[p. 282] grandsons to share an inheritance with sons[3]. The spread of
primogeniture raised the problem in a somewhat new shape.

---

[1] A rule which gives the father's house to the youngest son seems to have been
very common in Germany. See Stobbe, *Privatrecht*, iv. 40; he cites a Frisian
rule which, like the Kentish rule, gives the youngest son the hearth, 'den Herd.'

[2] Stobbe, *op. cit.*, iv. 384. Ultimogeniture has been found in every quarter
of Germany, from Switzerland to Holstein, and from Bohemia to the Rhine.
See also Elton, *op. cit.*, 190.

[3] Stobbe, *Privatrecht*, iv. 94; Schröder, D. R. G., 323.

In Glanvill's day the king's court was hesitating about a case that must have been common, namely, a contest between the younger son and his nephew, the son of his dead elder brother[1]. In some cases the problem can be evaded. If, to use Glanvill's phrase, *A* who is tenant of the land 'forisfamiliates' his eldest son by providing him with a tenement for himself, this may prevent that son's son from claiming to inherit before *A*'s younger sons. On the other hand, the tenant by persuading his lord to take in advance the homage of his eldest son may secure the preference of that son's issue. If, however, there are in the case no such facts as these,—if the question between uncle and nephew is neatly raised,—then we must fall back upon the maxim *Melior est conditio possidentis*; he who is the first to get seisin can keep it.

Influence of John's accession.

Some ten years afterwards the realm of England together with duchies and counties in France was a vacant inheritance lying between John and Arthur. John's coronation and reign in England might have become a formidable precedent in favour of the uncle, had his reign been aught but a miserable failure. It might well seem, however, that a judgment of God had been given against him[2]. Had not Glanvill's nephew told him that he was not king by hereditary right[3]? The lesson that Englishmen were likely to learn from his loss of Normandy and Anjou was that hereditary right ought not to be disregarded, and that the representative principle was part of the scheme of hereditary right. Neglect of that principle had exposed England to a French invasion and had given a king of the French some plausible excuse for pretending that he ought to be king of England also[4].

[1] Glanvill, vii. 3.

[2] Très ancien coutumier, p. 13. The rule here laid down favours the son against the grandson. Then it is added that in the time of war, under our Richard I., the son of the dead son began to exclude the daughters. A later gloss treats the exclusion of the nephew by the uncle as an abuse introduced by John; but this of course is a perversion of the story. Brunner, Erbfolgesystem, p. 43.

[3] Mat. Par. Chron. Maj. ii. 454; Foedera, i. 140.

[4] The French claim was this:—Representation of dead parents is inadmissible. At Richard's death there were but two children of Henry II. still alive, (1) John, who has been adjudged to have forfeited his lands for treason, and (2) Eleanor, wife of Alfonso of Castile, whose rights have come to Louis (afterwards King Louis VIII.) either by a conveyance, or in right of his wife Blanche, daughter of Eleanor, since Eleanor's other children (the King of

So the representative principle grew in favour.   Bracton *Casus Regis.* obviously thinks that as a general rule it is the just principle, though he shows some reluctance, which has deep and ancient roots, to apply it to a case in which the uncle is, and the nephew is not, found seated at the dead man's hearth.   As to the law of the king's court it is still this, that if the uncle is, and the nephew is not, an *astrier*[1], a 'hearth-heir,' at the moment of the ancestor's death, or if, the tenement having been left vacant, the uncle is the first to obtain seisin of it, the nephew must not have recourse to self-help, nor has he any action by which he can obtain a judgment.   The possessory *mort d'ancestor* will not lie between kinsmen who are so nearly related[2], while if the nephew brings a proprietary action, the king's court will keep judgment in suspense.   It will give no judgment against the nephew; he really is the rightful heir; but a precedent stands in his way; it is the *casus Regis*; and 'so long as that case endures' no judgment can be given against the uncle[3].   The inference has been drawn[4] that Bracton wrote the passages which deal with this matter before the death of Arthur's sister, Eleanor of Britanny, which happened in 1241[5].   Henry III. kept that unfortunate lady in captivity, and took good care that she should never marry. This inference, however, does not seem necessary.   For some years after Eleanor's death Henry may have been unwilling to admit that there ever had been any flaw in his hereditary title[6].   At any rate the records of the earlier years of his reign seem fully to bear out what Bracton says[7].   On the other hand,

Castile and the Queen of Leon) have waived their claims.   Foedera, i. 140; Mat. Par. Chron. Maj. ii. 660.

[1] This term occurs as late as 1304: Y. B. 32–3 Edw. I. 271.

[2] There is no assize on the death of a grandfather.   This is a strong proof of the novelty of the representative principle.

[3] Bracton, f. 64 b, 267 b, 268, 282, 327 b.

[4] Brinton Cox, Translation of Güterbock's Henricus de Bracton, p. 28.

[5] Mat. Par. Chron. Maj. iv. 163, 175.

[6] The compiler of the 'revised Glanvill' of the Cambridge Library notices the *casus Regis*: Harvard Law Review, vi. 19.

[7] Select Civil Pleas (Selden Soc.), pl. 194 (A.D. 1201): nephew out of possession sues uncle in possession; the case is adjourned *sine die* 'quia iudicium pendet ex voluntate domini Regis.'   For Henry's reign see Note Book, pl. 90, 230, 892, 968, 982, 1185, 1830.   So late as 1246 jurors refuse to give an opinion as to whether uncle or nephew is heir, but leave this to the king: Calend. Geneal. i. pp. 4, 10.

from the Edwardian law books the *casus Regis* has disappeared. [p. 284]
The nephew can now recover the land from the uncle by writ
of right although the uncle was the first to get seisin. After
Bracton's day there was nothing that was regarded as a change
in the law; but at some moment or another an impediment
which had obstructed the due administration of the law was
removed, and thus, at what must be called an early date, the
principle of representation prevailed in England and dominated
our whole law of inheritance. In the suit for the crown of
Scotland we can see that Bruce, though he stood one step
nearer to the common ancestor, was sadly at a loss for
arguments which should win him precedence over Balliol, the
representative of an older line. He had to go to a remote
age and remote climes, to Spain and Savoy and the days of
Kenneth MacAlpin; all the obvious analogies were by this
time in favour of representation[1].

The exclusion of ascendants.

We must now turn to the rules which govern the inheritance when the dead man has left no descendants, and we
at once come upon the curious doctrine that the ascendants
are incapable of inheriting. Even though I leave no other
kinsfolk, neither my father, nor my mother, nor any remoter
ancestor can be my heir; my land will escheat to the lord.
To find an explanation for this rule is by no means easy.
Already Bracton seems to be puzzled by it, for he has recourse
to a metaphor. An inheritance is said to 'descend'; it is a
heavy body which falls downwards; it can not fall upwards.
This is one of those would-be explanations which are mere
apologies for an existing rule whose origin is obscure. Nor
is the metaphor apt. We can not say that the inheritance
always descends, for in the language of Bracton's time it is
capable of 'resorting,' of bounding back. My land can not
ascend to my father, but it can resort to my father's brother.
Thus we are driven to say that, though the heavy body may
rebound, it never rebounds along a perpendicular line. These
legal physics however are but after-thoughts[2].

<hr />

[1] Foedera, i. 778.

[2] Bracton, f. 62 b: 'Descendit itaque ius, quasi ponderosum quid cadens
deorsum, recta linea vel transversali, et nunquam reascendit ea via qua descendit
post mortem antecessorum.' When the inheritance went to a collateral, *e.g.* an
uncle, it was usual to say in pleading that the right 'resorted,' sometimes
'reverted'; it did not 'descend.'

[p. 285] There can be little doubt that the phenomenon now before This exclu- us is in some sort and in some measure the work of feudalism. sion not primitive. This at all events seems plain, that we can not treat the exclusion of ascendants as primitive. Several of the folk-laws give the father and mother a prominent place in the scheme of inheritance[1]. The passage from the Ripuarian law which the author of our *Leges Henrici* appropriated says[2]:—' If a man dies without children, his father or mother succeeds to his inheritance'; the brother and the sister are postponed to the parents. On the other hand, there is much to show that in many parts of Europe the process which made *beneficia* hereditary stopped for a while at the point at which the vassal's descendants, but no other kinsfolk, could claim the precarious inheritance[3]. What we have now to discuss, however, is not an exclusion of ascendants and collaterals, it is the admission of collaterals and the exclusion of ascendants.

An ingenious theory about this matter has been made Black- popular by Blackstone[4]. It is said that the admission of stone's explana- collaterals took place in the following fashion. Originally the tion. first feudatory, the man who has taken a *feodum novum*, could transmit an inheritance in it only to his descendants. When, however, it had passed to one of his issue, let us say a son, and that son died without issue, then there were some collaterals who might be admitted to the inheritance of this *feodum antiquum*. The restriction was that the fief was not to go to any one who was not a descendant of the original vassal, 'the first purchaser' of our English law; but among such descendants there might be collateral inheritance. Thus suppose that Adam is the first purchaser, that he leaves two sons, Bertram and Clement, that Bertram inherits the fief and dies without issue; then Clement can inherit; or, if we suppose that Bertram leaves issue, then on any future failure of his issue, Clement or Clement's issue can inherit. In such a scheme of course there is no place for inheritance by an ascendant. [p. 286] Then we are told that the next advance was to treat the *feodum novum*, the newly granted fief, as though it were a

---

[1] Stobbe, Privatrecht, v. 84-5. It is observable that Tacitus (cap. 20) mentions the *fratres*, *patrui* and *avunculi* and not the parents; but we dare not see any direct connexion between this text and our English rule.

[2] Leg. Henr. c. 70, § 20.   [3] Stobbe, Privatrecht, v. 321-2, 326-7.

[4] Comm. ii. 208-212.

feodum antiquum, a fief that by fiction of law had descended to the dead man from some ancestor. Thus Adam is enfeoffed and dies without issue; any collateral kinsman of his can inherit from him, because every collateral kinsman of his must be the descendant of some person who can be regarded by fiction of law as the first purchaser of the fief. On the other hand, none of Adam's lineal ancestors can inherit. By fiction the land came to him down some line of ancestry; we can not tell down which line it descended; we must suppose (our fiction requires this) that the ancestors in that line must be dead; therefore we have to act as though all of Adam's ancestors were dead, and therefore we exclude them from the inheritance.

Failure of the explanation. That something of this kind happened in some countries of Europe, in particular Lombardy, may be true[1]. That it happened in England or in Normandy we have no direct evidence, and indeed Norman law of the thirteenth century admitted the ascendants, though it postponed each ascendant to his or her own issue[2]. But at any rate we can not make this story explain the English law of Bracton's day. Adam is enfeoffed and dies without issue. His father can not inherit; but his elder brother can inherit, and yet the fiction that the *feodum novum* is a *feodum antiquum* would afford as good a reason for excluding an elder brother as for excluding a father. In our law it would be impossible for the younger of two brothers to acquire a *feodum antiquum* if his elder brother were still living[3]. We have not, however, for England, nor have we for Normandy, any proof that the process which converted the 'benefice' into a hereditary 'feud' made any distinct pause at the moment when it had admitted the descendants of the dead vassal. We have not for England, nor have we for Normandy, any proof that the collaterals gained their right to inherit under cover of a fiction. The terms which our modern feudists have employed, *feodum antiquum, feodum novum* are not technical terms of our [p. 287]

---

[1] 2 Feud. 50: 'Successionis feudi talis est natura, quod ascendentes non succedunt, verbi gratia pater filio.' In modern countries which have 'received' the Lombard law as a law for fiefs, ascendants have as a general rule been excluded; Stobbe, Privatrecht, v. 344.

[2] Somma, p. 77; Ancienne coutume, c. 25 (ed. de Gruchy, p. 79)

[3] This objection has often been urged against Blackstone's argument, for instance, by his editor Christian; Comm. ii. 212

English law; they were brought hither from a remote country[1]. We can not be certain that Norman law had ever excluded the ascendants; it did not exclude them in the thirteenth century. Dark as are the doings of the author of the *Leges Henrici*, we can hardly believe that he was at pains to copy from so distant a source as the law of the Ripuarian Franks a passage which flatly contradicted what already was a settled rule in this country, while it is impossible to suppose that in this instance he is maintaining an old English rule against Norman innovations[2]. On the whole, remembering that the Conquest must have thrown the law of inheritance into confusion, that the king had many a word to say about the inheritance of the great fees, that the court of Henry II. had many an opportunity of making rules for itself without much regard for ancient custom, we are inclined to look for some explanation of the exclusion of ascendants other than that which has been fashionable in England.

Another explanation has been suggested[3]. It introduces us to a curious rule which deserves discussion for its own sake, the rule, namely, that the same person can never at the same time be both lord and heir of the same tenement.

The rule as to lord and heir.

Glanvill tells us that certain difficult questions are often raised by gifts which fathers make to their sons[4]. We may well believe that this is so, for in England the primogenitary rule is just now taking its comprehensive and absolute shape, and a father must in his lifetime provide for his younger sons, if he wishes them to be provided for at all. Glanvill then supposes that a father, whom we will call *O*, has three sons whom in order of their birth we will call *A, B,* and *C*. With

The question in Glanvill.

---

[1] For a while in the last century the writings of Spelman, Wright, Gilbert and Blackstone had almost succeeded in bringing about what the Germans would call an academic 'reception' of the Lombard *Libri Feudorum*; and this process went much further in Scotland. The Lombard law of feuds was regarded at this time as the model and orthodox law of feuds. But Milan is a long way from Westminster and even from Rouen, and France rather than Italy is the feud's original home.

[2] Blackstone, Comm. ii. 211: 'Our Henry the first indeed, among other restorations of the old Saxon laws, restored the right of succession in the ascending line.' By borrowing a text of Frankish law?

[3] Brunner, Erbfolgesystem, p. 23. In some respects Brunner adopts more of Blackstone's explanation than we shall adopt in the following paragraphs.

[4] Glanvill, vii. 1.

the consent of A his apparent heir, O makes a feoffment to B^1. [p. 288] Then B dies without issue, leaving O, A and C alive. Who is to inherit? This is a knotty problem which taxes the wisdom of our wisest lawyers[2]. Glanvill distinctly supposes that O, the father, will claim that the land is to come to him[3]. But A urges that O is already the lord of the land and can not be both lord and heir. Then C appears and argues that the same objection can be urged against A; for A is heir apparent of the seignory, and, if now he be allowed to inherit the land in demesne, then, on O's death, he will be both lord and heir. Glanvill thinks that at any rate the claim of O must be rejected. He can not possibly hold the land, for he can not be both lord and heir; nor, when homage has been done, will land ever revert to the feoffor, if the feoffee has any heir however remote. Besides (says Glanvill, who brings in this physical or metaphysical consideration as an after-thought) in the course of nature an inheritance descends and never ascends[4]. Then the question between A and C must be argued. Glanvill is for allowing A to inherit at present; but if hereafter O dies and the seignory descends to A, he will not be able to retain both the seignory and the tenancy, for he must not be both lord and heir. Having become lord, he must give up the land to C.

Problems occasioned by the rule about lord and heir.
On our earliest plea rolls we may see this quaint doctrine giving rise to all manner of difficulties[5]. Obviously it is capable of doing this. For example, if in the case that has just been put we suppose that at O's death A has a son X, then there will be the question whether A, now that he has become lord, must give up the land to his own son X or to his brother C. In the former event, if A leaves at his death two sons X and Y, we shall once more have a problem to solve. We have undertaken to prevent the seignory and the tenancy

---

[1] Glanvill, vii. 1: 'cum consensu heredis sui, ne super hoc fieret contentio.'

[2] Ibid.: 'Magna quidem iuris dubitatio et virorum iuris regni peritorum disceptatio et contentio super tali casu in curia domini Regis evenit vel evenire potest.'

[3] Ibid.: 'pater enim seisinam defuncti filii sui sibi retinere contendit.'

[4] Ibid.: 'Praeterea terra ista quae sic donata est sicut alia quaelibet hereditas naturaliter quidem ad heredes hereditabiliter descendit, nunquam autem naturaliter ascendit.'

[5] Curia Regis Rolls (Pipe Roll Soc.), i. 21; Select Civil Pleas (Selden Soc.), pl. 139; Note Book, pl. 61, 564, 637, 774, 949, 1244, 1694, 1857; Calend. Geneal. p. 146; Somersetshire Pleas, pl. 592.

[p. 289] remaining in one and the same hand, and yet the common rules of inheritance are always bringing them together[1].

Glanvill in his treatment of this theme supposes that the father (*O*) has taken the homage of his son (*B*). Bracton lays stress upon this condition[2]. Only when homage has been done are we to apply the rule which excludes the lord from the inheritance. This is at the bottom of one of the peculiarities of the 'estate in frankmarriage[3].' When a father makes a provision for a daughter, he intends that if the daughter has no issue or if her issue fails—at all events if this failure occurs in the course of a few generations—the land shall come back to him or to his heir. Therefore no homage is done for the estate in frankmarriage until the daughter's third heir has entered, for were homage once done, there would be a danger that the land would never come back to the father or to his heir[4]. Here again is a reason why in parage tenure a younger sister and her heirs do no homage to the elder sister until the younger sister's third heir has entered[5]. Were homage once done, the younger sister's share could never come to her elder sister[6]. Why either in the case of frankmarriage or in that of parage the entry of the third heir should make a difference it is not easy to see. Perhaps it is presumed that, if the land has thrice descended down the line of which the daughter is the starting point, there is no reason to fear that her issue will fail. Perhaps, however, we have here some relics of an old system of inheritance which, could we understand it, would show the connexion between several puzzling rules[7].

Effect of homage.

---

[1] Bracton, f. 65 b, 66.   [2] Bracton, f. 22 b, 23, 65 b, 277.

[3] See above, vol. ii. p. 17.

[4] Bracton, f. 22 b, 23; Note Book, pl. 61. This doctrine is made obscure by the haziness of the line which divides 'reversion' from 'escheat.' See above, vol. ii. p. 23.

[5] See above, vol. ii. p. 276.

[6] Stat. Hibern. de Coheredibus (Statutes, i. p. 5).

[7] There is a good deal of evidence which hints that in old times when a partible inheritance fell to several parceners and one of them died and his share passed to the others, this was regarded not as a case of inheritance, but as a case of accruer. (See Nichols, Britton, ii. 316.) So long as the land is held by very close kinsmen there is no 'inheriting' between them. Only when the parceners are beyond a certain distance (*e.g.* the third or fourth degree) from the common stock does any true inheriting begin. We may suspect that some such idea is the root of the 'third heir rules' about *paragia* and *maritagia*; but, if so, it lies deep down and has been hidden away beneath more modern law; it

But whence this rule that excludes the lord from the [p. 290] inheritance? Why can not the same man be both lord and heir, or (to put the question in a better shape) why should not the lord inherit and the seignory become extinct? Have we here to deal merely with one of those metaphysical difficulties which lawyers sometimes create for themselves, or have we to deal with a rule that has a purpose? On the one hand, it may be said that the kernel of the whole matter is this, that the seignory, the homage, is regarded as a thing and that lawyers can not readily conceive its annihilation[1]. Such an explanation would be more probable had we before us a doctrine of the fifteenth century; in the twelfth our law had hardly entered the metaphysical stage. On the whole we are inclined to see here a struggle against the effects of primogeniture. If under this novel principle the younger sons are to have anything, it must be given them by their father in his lifetime:—the law of the royal court has decreed it. But the voice of natural justice can be heard crying as of old for as much equality among the sons as the interests of the king and of the state will permit. At all events it is not fair that one son should take the whole of the land that his father has not given away, and also come in by some accident to the land that was given—and it could hardly have been given without his consent—to one of his younger brothers. He ought not to have it so long as there is any younger brother to claim it:—enough for him that he will get homage and service; he should not ask for more. The case is not like that in which a father provides a marriage portion for a daughter. That is an old case. In the days when the inheritance was divisible among sons that case had to be met. Without the concurrence of his sons a father might give his daughter a reasonable *maritagium*[2]; but if the daughter's issue failed, then the land was to come back to her father or her brothers. The primogenitary rule which is now being enforced in all its simplicity has raised a new case. The father who enfeoffs a younger son in return for homage is (probably with his [p. 291]

can only be natural in a time when it is common that two generations will pass away before an ancestral estate undergoes a physical partition.

[1] Hale, Common Law (6th ed.), pp. 314–5, seems to treat the rule as purely irrational.

[2] Glanvill, vii. 1; see above, vol. ii. p. 15.

eldest son's consent) contending against the primogenitary rule. He is 'forisfamiliating' the younger son; he is in a possible case depriving that younger son's sons of their chance of inheriting from their grandfather[1]. We ought not to allow the eldest son to get back the land of which he has, with his own consent, been deprived by his father[2].

It is difficult for us to express this vague feeling in precise terms; but the difficulty is not of our making. In Glanvill's day it was puzzling the wisest heads in the king's court[3]. In Bracton's day there had been a great change. Men had been accommodating themselves to primogeniture. The father now freely disposes of his land without the consent of his eldest son. Often when he enfeoffs a younger son he does not take homage, and does not take it just because he desires that on failure of that son's issue his eldest son shall have the land[4]. The rule that, if homage has intervened, a lord can not inherit from his man is still in force; but it now looks like a capricious, inexplicable rule, and the judges seem to be showing it little favour[5]. The statute of 1290 which put a stop to subinfeudation soon made the whole doctrine obsolete. Thenceforward if a father enfeoffed a son in fee simple, there would be no homage, no tenure, between the feoffor and the feoffee[6].

The leaning towards equality.

We may seem to have digressed far from our original theme, the exclusion of ascendants from the inheritance; but it is a serious question whether that exclusion is not the outcome of the rule about lord and heir. Glanvill supposes a father to come forward and claim the tenement of which he enfeoffed a son who has died without issue. The father is sent empty away and is told that he must not be both lord

The exclusion of the lord and the exclusion of the ascendant.

---

[1] Glanvill, vii. 3. My younger son will be preferred to the children of my 'forisfamiliated' elder son.

[2] When Henry II.'s son Geoffrey introduced primogeniture into Britanny, he introduced along with it the rule that the elder brother is not to inherit from the younger land for which the younger has done homage to the elder; Warnkönig, Französ. Geschichte, i. Urkund. p. 27. We have here an equitable temperament of primogeniture.

[3] Glanvill, vii. 1. [4] Bracton, f. 277.

[5] Bracton, f. 277; Note Book, pl. 564, 1857.

[6] Stat. 18 Edw. I., *Quia emptores.* The rule appears in 13 Edw. I. Fitz. Abr. *Avowre*, pl. 235, and in Fleta, p. 371. After this it dies of inanition. It has never been repealed.

and heir. Would it not have been simpler to tell him that [p. 292] an elementary rule of the law of inheritance excludes all direct ancestors of the dead man? A remark about the course of nature, which does not permit inheritances to ascend, is thrown in, but it fills a secondary place; it may express a generalization which is gradually taking shape.

Exclusion of the lord leads to exclusion of the father. On the whole there are not many cases in which a man can put in any plausible claim to inherit from a dead son. If the son acquired the land by inheritance from any paternal ancestor, there can be no talk of the father inheriting from the son, for the father must be already dead. If the son acquired the land by inheritance from his mother or any maternal ancestor, there can be no talk of the father inheriting, for, as we shall see hereafter, a strict rule prevents maternal lands from falling to the paternal kinsfolk. And now we have decided that if the son comes to the land by the gift of his father, his father is not to be heir as well as lord. We have thus exhausted all the common cases in which a boy is likely to acquire land. The case in which a man dies without issue in his father's lifetime leaving land which he did not acquire by inheritance, nor yet by the gift of his father, nor yet by the gift of any one whose heir the father is,—this in the twelfth century is a rare case. It is one which the king's judges engaged in their task of rapid simplification will be apt to neglect, especially as they find the rule about lord and heir an unmanageable rule. And so we come to the principle that excludes the direct ancestors, and the only apology that can be offered for it is that heavy bodies never bound upwards in a perpendicular line.

Suggested explanation of the exclusion of ascendants. This explanation, it must be frankly owned, has in it some guesswork; but before it is rejected we must call attention to two facts. In the year 1195, unless a plea roll misleads us, a man did bring an assize of mort d'ancestor on the death of his son, and the defendant answered, not that fathers do not inherit from sons, but that the plaintiff was his villein[1]. We know of no other case of the same kind and should be much surprised to find one during the next hundred years. On the other hand, after just a hundred years we should not be

---

[1] Curia Regis Rolls (Pipe Roll Soc.), i. 133. It is possible that the scribe of this record wrote *filius* by mistake for *pater*, and, if so, the case is deprived of all its curiosity.

[p. 293] surprised to find in some solitary instance a father putting in a claim. Britton, with Bracton's text before him, deliberately and more than once asserted that the father can inherit from the son[1]. He would postpone the father to all his own descendants but would admit him after them. What apology have we to offer for Britton? Perhaps this:—He was writing when the statute of 1290 had just been made; he shows himself uncertain as to its precise effect; but he knows that it will make great changes[2]. One of these changes will be that it will deprive the old rule about lord and heir of any material to work upon. Henceforward if a father enfeoffs a son in fee simple, the son will not be the father's tenant. Why then should not the father inherit? Has not the only rational impediment to his succession been removed? But by this time the rule was too well rooted to be blown down by a side wind. The father was excluded until 1833[3].

Lastly, before our suggestion is condemned, we would ask that a law of inheritance very closely akin to our own should be examined. Scottish law, like Norman law, did not exclude the lineal ancestor; it admitted him so soon as his own issue was exhausted. But Scottish law had some rules very strange in the eyes of a Southron which had the effect, if not the object, of tempering the universal dominion of primogeniture. The youngest of three brothers purchases land and dies without issue; it is the middle, not the eldest, brother who inherits from him. It is not fair that the eldest should have everything[4]. *The ascendants in Scottish law.*

The canons which regulate the course of inheritance among the collateral kinsfolk of the dead man are worthy of observation. Our English law has been brought to bear upon a brisk controversy that has been carried on in Germany. What was the main principle of the old Germanic scheme of in- [p. 294] heritance? Was it a 'gradual' or a 'parentelic' scheme? *Inheritance of collaterals*

---

[1] Britton, ii. 319, 325.   [2] Nichols, Britton, i. p. xxv.

[3] Stat. 3–4 Will. IV. c. 106, sec. 6.

[4] Stat. Robert III. Acts of Parliament, i. p. 575; Ibid. pp. 639, 730; McDouall, Institutes, ii. 297; Bell, Principles of the Law of Scotland, § 1662–72. The *immediate* younger brother was heir of line and the *immediate* elder (not the eldest) brother was heir of conquest. The exclusion of ascendants was by no means unknown outside England; on the contrary it seems to have prevailed until quite recent times in large parts of Austria, Tyrol and neighbouring lands: Wasserschleben, Prinzip der Erbenfolge (1870), p. 35 ff. We do not profess to explain this phenomenon wherever it is found; we have spoken only of England.

Proximity of kinship may be reckoned in divers ways. The calculus which will seem the most natural to us in modern time is a 'gradual' calculus. Each act of generation makes a degree, and we count the number of degrees that lie between the *propositus* and the various claimants. It is probable that any system of inheritance with which we have to deal will prefer the descendants of the dead man to all other claimants; we will therefore leave them out of account. This done, we find in the first degree the dead man's parents; in the second his grandparents, brothers and sisters; in the third his great-grandparents, uncles, aunts, nephews, nieces; in the fourth his great-great-grandparents, great uncles, great aunts, first cousins, great-nephews, great-nieces; and so forth. Our English law of inheritance has a very different scheme. In order to explain it we had better make use of a term to which modern disputants have given a technical meaning, the term *parentela*. By a person's *parentela* is meant the sum of those persons who trace their blood from him. My issue are my *parentela*, my father's issue are his *parentela*. Now in our English scheme the various *parentelae* are successively called to the inheritance in the order of their proximity to the dead man. My father's *parentela* is nearer to me than my grandfather's. Every person who is in my father's *parentela* is nearer to me than any person who can only claim kinship through some ancestor remoter from me than my father. For a moment and for the sake of simplicity we may speak as if there were but one ascendant line, as if the dead man had but one parent, one grandparent and so forth, and we will call these progenitors father, grandfather and the like. The rule then becomes this: Exhaust the dead man's *parentela*; next exhaust his father's *parentela*; next his grandfather's; next his great-grandfather's. We see the family tree in some such shape as that pictured on the next page.

The remotest kinsman who stands in Parentela I. is a nearer heir than the nearest kinsman of Parentela II. Between persons who stand in different *parentelae* there can be no competition. In a purely gradual scheme my great-great-grandfather, my great uncle, my first cousin and my great-nephew are equally close to me. In a parentelic scheme my great-nephew, since he springs from my father, is nearer to me than my first cousin. We have here, it is said, not a 'gradual'

[p. 295]

but a 'lineal-gradual' scheme. Within each *parentela* or line
of issue the 'grade' is of importance; but no computation of

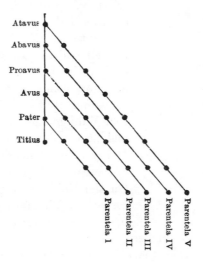

grades must induce us to jump from a nearer to a remoter
line so long as the nearer line has any representative[1].

We have preferred to state the matter in this abstract, and The
in England unfamiliar, fashion rather than to repeat the rules parentelic scheme.
that have been admirably expounded by Hale and Blackstone.
English, Scottish and Norman law seem to afford the best
specimens of the parentelic scheme. Whether this scheme is
of extremely ancient date, or whether it is the outcome of
feudalism, is a controverted question which cannot be decided
by our English books and records. We can only say that in
the thirteenth century it seems to be among Englishmen the
only conceivable scheme. Our text-writers accept it as obvious,
and this although they will copy from the civilians an elaborate
Arbor Consanguinitatis and hardly know that the English law
is radically different from the Roman[2].

---

[1] A sketch of the controversy to which we have referred will be found in
Stobbe, Privatrecht, v. 79. Modern opinion seems to be inclining to the belief
that the parentelic scheme was ancient and general; see Heusler, Institutionen,
ii. 586, and Brunner, Erbfolgesystem.

[2] The works of both Bracton and Fleta ought to have in them *arbores*
borrowed from the civilians; such trees are found in several MSS. of Bracton's
book. The *arbor* is given in Nichols's edition of Britton, ii. 321. The use of
these trees is apt to perplex the writer's exposition of English law. Still the
parentelic scheme comes out clearly enough in Bracton, f. 64 b; Fleta, p. 373;

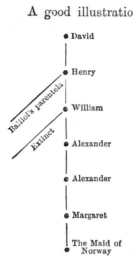

A good illustration is afforded by the careful pleadings of [p.296]
John Balliol in the great suit for the
crown of Scotland. He traced the
downward descent of the crown from
David to the Maid of Norway. He
himself had to go back to Henry, earl
of Huntingdon, in order to find an
ancestor common to him and the
proposita. But he had to face the fact
that William the Lion left daughters,
and he could not get so far back as
Henry without alleging that the lines
of these daughters had become extinct.
On the Maiden's death 'the right resorted' to William's *parentela,* but it
found that *parentela* empty and so
had to go back further[1].

Rules for
collaterals
of the same
parentela.

We have said that the *parentelae* or stocks are to be
exhausted one by one. The method of exhausting them is
that in accordance with which the descendants of the dead
man are first exhausted. We must apply our six rules:—
(1) A living descendant excludes his or her own descendants.
(2) A dead descendant is represented by his or her own
descendants[2]. (3) Males exclude females of equal degree.
(4) Among males of equal degree only the eldest inherits.
(5) Females of equal degree inherit together. (6) The rule
that a dead descendant is represented by his or her descendants
overrides the preference for the male sex.

Choice
among the
ascending
lines.

But we have as yet been treating the problem as though
it were much simpler than really it is. The dead man does
not stand at the end of a single line of ancestors. He must
have had two parents, four grandparents, and so forth. Along
which of the lines which met in him are we to move in search
of those *parentelae* which are to be called to the inheritance ? [p.297]
Our medieval lawyers, copying the pictures drawn by canonists

Britton, ii. 325. For examples, see Y. B. 21-2 Edw. I. p. 37 ; 32-3 Edw. I.
p. 17.

[1] Foedera, i. 776–8. Several of the competitors professed that they stood in
a lower *parentela* than that represented by Balliol, Bruce and Hastings ; but
their claims seem to have been stained by illegitimacy and were withdrawn.

[2] The application of this principle gave Balliol the victory over Bruce.

and civilians, are guilty of the same unjustifiable simplification
with which we can be charged.   They represent 'the ascending
line' as a single line.   In the first 'cell' in it they write 'pater,
mater,' in the second 'avus, avia,' in the third 'proavus, proavia'
and so on, apparently forgetting that every person has four
grandparents, and that the English system is not one which
can treat these four as sharing a single 'cell.'   More instructive
would it have been had they drawn their picture thus :—

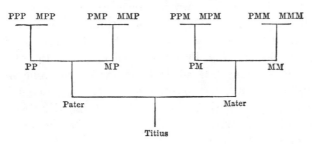

Had they done this, they might have left us some clear
principle for directing our choice between the various ascendant
lines and have solved some problems which were still open in
the nineteenth century.

As it is, we can see the rule that the heir must be one who
is related by blood kinship not only to the *propositus* but to
the purchaser.   By 'purchaser' is here meant the person who
last acquired the estate otherwise than by inheritance.   Now
if the person whose heir we are seeking was himself the
purchaser, our rule will admit every blood kinsman or kinswoman of his.   But if he was not the purchaser, then our choice
will be restricted.   Suppose that his father was the purchaser,
no one can be admitted who is not related by blood to that
father.   Suppose that his mother was the purchaser, any one
who takes the inheritance must be related by blood to her.
Suppose that his father's mother was the purchaser, a successful
claimant must be her blood kinsman.   We have here the
rule which in foreign books is expressed by the proverb *Paterna
paternis, materna maternis*[1].   Our English law does not merely
postpone the *materni* or, as the case may be, the *paterni*; it
absolutely excludes them.   My father's brother can not inherit

(marginal note:) Paterna paternis. Materna maternis.

(marginal note, left:) [p. 298]

---

[1] Abroad this return of the inheritance to the side whence it came was
known as *ius revolutionis, ius recadentiae, Fallrecht*; Stobbe, Privatrecht, **v.**
p. 105 ; Heusler, Institutionen, ii. 527.   It is a widely distributed phenomenon.

from me land that descended to me from my mother; my father's father's brother can not inherit from me land that descended to me from my father's mother. So far as we can see, this rule was in force in the thirteenth century. Attempts have been made to represent it as a specifically feudal rule, one which takes us back to a time when only the descendants of the original vassal could inherit; but such attempts seem to be unnecessary; a rule whose main effect is that of keeping a woman's land in her own family is not unnatural and may well be very ancient[1]. We see its naturalness when we apply it to the descent of a kingdom. When the Maid of Norway died, her father, king Eric, put in a claim to the throne of Scotland and sent learned Italian lawyers to argue his case in Edward's court; but no one seems to have taken him or his claim very seriously[2]. The ascending line along which the inheritance must return should obviously be the line of the Scottish kings; it is not to be tolerated that one who has no drop of their blood in his veins should fill their place. In the thirteenth century no wide gulf could be fixed between the inheritance of a kingdom and other impartible inheritances. John Balliol argued on the expressed assumption that the rules applicable to baronies were applicable to his case. If therefore at a later day we find the law of Scotland not merely rejecting the rule *Materna maternis*, but absolutely excluding all *materni* even when the inheritance has come from their side[3], we may suspect that it is no true witness to the ideas of the thirteenth century, and take to heart the lesson that a system that looks exceedingly 'agnatic' and that refuses to trace inheritable blood through a female, except in the descending line, is not of necessity very old. Those rules of inheritance which deal with unusual cases are often the outcome of no recondite causes, but of some superficial whim.

Choice among the admissible stocks.　　The rule *Paterna paternis, materna maternis* may exclude [p. 299] from our view certain of those ascending lines which go upwards from our *propositus*; it will not enable us to make a choice

---

[1] The common form which prevails now-a-days when a bride's personal property is to be settled, bears witness to this desire that, if there be no children of the marriage, the wife's property shall in certain events come back to her own kinsfolk.

[2] Rishanger, Chronicle (Rolls Ser.), pp. 132, 269, 358.

[3] Bell, Principles of the Law of Scotland, 9th ed. p. 1021, § 1665.

between the lines that are not thus excluded. Thus suppose that the person whose heir is wanted was himself the purchaser of the land, none of his kinsmen are excluded and we have to choose between many ascending lines. We think it certain that in the thirteenth century, as in later times, the line first chosen was that which we may call agnatic, the line, that is, in which there is an unbroken succession of male ancestors, and that, so long as there was any one who could trace his blood from a member of that line, no other person could inherit. Such a rule is a natural part of a system which postpones females to males. Just as the inheritance will go down from father to son so long as the male line is unbroken, so when we look upwards we first look along the male line. The remotest person in the remotest *parentela* which comes down from an ancestor who stands in that line is preferable to the nearest person in the nearest *parentela* which has some other starting point[1].

Beyond this all is dark. We gravely doubt whether during the middle ages any clear canons were established to regulate the order of succession between those *parentelae* which could trace their kinship to the *propositus* only through some female ancestor of his. That 'the male blood is more worthy than the female' was indubitable; Adam was created before Eve, but a definite calculus which should balance worthiness of blood against proximity of degree was wanting. Our lawyers were not at pains to draw pictures of their own; they transplanted the trees of the Romanists, and those trees could not take firm root in English soil. In Elizabeth's day an exceedingly simple problem was treated as an open question for which the Year Books provided no obvious solution. A man purchases land and dies without issue; who shall inherit from him, his mother's brother or a cousin who is his father's mother's [p. 300] father's son's son[3]? When this question had been decided in favour of the claimant who was of kin to the father of the

No clear principles are found.

---

[1] It is difficult to prove even this from the text-books. Glanvill, vii. 3, 4, Bracton, ff. 67–9, Fleta, pp. 372–5, Britton, ii. p. 324, are apt to speak as though in ascending we might cross from line to line in order to find the nearest ancestor, so that, *e.g.* we might prefer the father's mother's *parentela* to the father's father's father's *parentela*. But this we think due to the inadequate *arbores* that they had in their minds.

[2] *Clere* v. *Brooke*, Plowden, 442. The principal Year Book cases are 39 Edw. III. f. 29; 49 Edw. III. f. 11; 49 Ass. f. 316; 12 Edw. IV. f. 14.

propositus, it still left open a question about the order of precedence among the female ancestors upon the father's side, a question which was warmly debated and never really settled until a statute of 1833 rounded off our law of inheritance by declaring that the mother of the more remote male paternal ancestor is preferable to the mother of a less remote male paternal ancestor[1]. That in an age which allowed no testamentary disposition of freehold lands cases never happened which raised such problems as these is hardly to be believed; but, to all seeming, they did not happen with sufficient frequency to generate a body of established doctrine[2].

Place of the half-blood in the classical common law.

Our law's treatment of 'the half-blood' has been a favourite theme for historical speculators. We have been sent for its origin back to a time when 'feuds' were not yet hereditary; we have been sent to 'the agnatic family[3].' As a matter of fact we do not believe that the phenomenon which has to be explained is very ancient. It is this:—Our common law utterly excludes 'the half-blood.' No one who is connected with the *propositus* only by the half-blood can inherit from him. A man buys land and dies without issue; his half-brother, whether consanguineous or uterine, can not inherit from him. If there is no kinsman or kinswoman of the whole blood forthcoming, the land will escheat to the lord. Of course all the descendants of a man or a woman are of kin to him or to her by the whole blood. A man leaves a daughter by his first wife, a son by his second wife; his son inherits from him. A man leaves no sons and no issue of sons, but five daughters, two by his first wife and three by his second wife; they will all inherit from him together and take equal shares. Any question about the half-blood can only arise when this man [p. 301] has ceased to be and one of his descendants has become the *propositus,* and no one of them, according to our law, will become the *propositus* until he obtains an actual seisin of the

---

[1] Stat. 3–4 Will. IV. c. 106. sec. 8. Hale, Common Law, 6th ed. p. 328, had taken one side in the dispute, Blackstone, Comm. ii. 238, the other. Blackstone's departure from Hale's rule gave rise to controversy of a kind that has been very rare in England, the academic discussion of a point of law that is of no practical importance.

[2] After looking through a large number of records of the thirteenth century we are much struck by the extreme rarity of cases in which any of the more recondite rules of inheritance are called into play.

[3] Blackstone, Comm. ii. 288; Maine, Ancient Law, ch. **v.**

land. A man leaves a son and a daughter by a first wife, and a son by a second wife. His eldest son inherits and is entitled to seisin. If however he dies without issue before he has obtained seisin, then his father is still the *propositus*. That father has a daughter and a son. The son inherits before the daughter. He is not inheriting from his half-brother; he is inheriting from his father. On the other hand, if the elder son acquires seisin, all is altered. When he dies without issue he is the *propositus*. We have now to choose between a sister by the whole blood and a half-brother, and we hold, not merely that the sister is to be preferred, but that the land shall sooner escheat to the lord than go to the half-brother. *Possessio fratris de feodo simplici facit sororem esse heredem*; the entry of the eldest son has made his sister heir[1].

Now it seems clear that the law of Bracton's day had not yet taken this puzzling shape. Bracton holds that the half-blood can inherit, though it is postponed to the whole blood. *The half-blood in earlier times.* First we take the case in which a man purchases land and dies without issue, leaving a sister of the whole blood and a brother of the half-blood. The sister will inherit to the exclusion of her brother; but after her death and the failure of her heirs the brother will inherit; he is merely postponed, not excluded for good and all[2]. Next we take the case in which a man inherits land from his father and then dies without issue, leaving a sister of the whole blood and a consanguineous half-brother. Now some were for holding that the half-brother should in this case be preferred to the sister, and Bracton, though his mind may have fluctuated, probably shared this opinion. The distinction which turns on the question whether the eldest son has acquired seisin seems to be only just coming to the front[3]. Fleta and Britton agree that if a man purchases land and dies without issue, his sister by the whole blood will [p. 302] be preferred to the half-brother[4]. They do not affirm, as Bracton does, that in this case if there is no brother or sister of the whole blood, a brother or sister of the half-blood will be

---

[1] Litt. sec. 7, 8. The law was altered in 1833.

[2] Bracton, f. 66 b.

[3] Bracton, f. 65, 65 b. The text in its present condition looks as if Bracton had changed his mind and added a note contradicting what he had already written.

[4] Fleta, p. 371 ; Britton, ii. 318.

admitted; but neither do they deny this. As to the case in which the *propositus* has inherited land from his father, Fleta is for preferring the consanguineous half-brother to the sister of the whole blood, and this without reference to seisin[1]; Britton is for preferring the sister by the whole blood, and this without reference to seisin[2]. What is more, Britton holds that if a man has two wives and a son by each, one of those sons can inherit from his half-brother land that had descended to that half-brother from his mother; in other words, that I may on the death of my half-brother inherit land which belonged to my stepmother, though here of course I am not of the blood of the purchaser[3].

Fluctua-
tions in
practice. These are not speculative fancies. If we turn to the records of the time, we shall see much uncertainty; we shall see claims brought into court which the common law of a later day would not have tolerated for an instant, and juries declining to solve the simplest problems[4]. Even Britton's doctrine that through my half-brother I can acquire the land of my stepfather or stepmother, does not seem ridiculous[5]. In Edward I.'s reign the law seems to be setting its face against the claims of the half-blood; but even in Edward II.'s there is a great deal more doubt and disputation than we might have expected[6]. It is clear that a sister will inherit from her brother of the whole blood a tenement that he purchased, and exclude a brother by the half-blood; but that the brother of the half-blood is utterly incapable of taking such a tenement is not plain. When the tenement has descended from father or mother to the eldest son, the lawyers are beginning to make every thing turn on [p. 303] seisin; but they have not yet fully established the dogma that, if once that eldest son is seised, his half-brother will be incapable of inheriting from him.

---

[1] Fleta, p. 371.

[2] Britton, ii. 316.

[3] Britton, ii. 319. See also Scots Acts of Parl. i. 731–2, 638.

[4] Select Civil Pleas (Selden Soc.), pl. 1; Note Book, pl. 32, 44, 833–4, 855, 1128; Placit. Abbrev. p. 153; Calend. Geneal. pp. 31, 282; Y. B. 21–2 Edw. I. p. 552; Y. B. 32–3 Edw. I. p. 445.

[5] Note Book, pl. 1128; Y. B. 21–2 Edw. I. p. 552; Y. B. 32–3 Edw. I. p. 445. In this last case it seems to be thought that a uterine half-sister can inherit land which descended to the *propositus* from his father.

[6] Y. B. Mich. 5 Edw. II. f. 147; Mich. 12 Edw. II. f. 380; Mich. 19 Edw. II. f. 628.

Our persuasion is that the absolute exclusion of the half-blood, to which our law was in course of time committed, is neither a very ancient nor a very deep-seated phenomenon, that it tells us nothing of the original constitution of feuds nor of the agnatic family. In truth the problem that is put before us when there is talk of admitting the half-blood is difficult and our solution of it is likely to be capricious. We can not say now-a-days that there is any obviously proper place for the half-blood in a scheme of inheritance, especially in our 'parentelic' scheme[1]. The lawyers of the thirteenth and fourteenth centuries had no ready solution, and we strongly suspect that the rule that was ultimately established had its origin in a few precedents. About such a matter it is desirable that there shall be a clear rule; the import of the rule is of no great moment. Our rule was one eminently favourable to the king; it gave him escheats; we are not sure that any profounder explanation of it would be true[2].

Exclusion of the half-blood is modern.

[1] Stobbe, Privatrecht, v. 116. German and French customs afford a rich variety of rules. That the half-blood should be on an equality with the whole blood was rare; sometimes it took a smaller share; sometimes it was postponed; but the manner of postponing it varied from custom to custom. See also Heusler, Institutionen, ii. 612. In 1279 it is alleged as a custom of Newcastle that the mother's inheritance will go to daughters by a first marriage in preference to a son by a second marriage: Northumberland Assize Rolls, p. 295. Such a custom, which has its parallel in Germany (Stobbe, p. 101), should warn us that the rules of the common law were not the only rules that seemed natural to Englishmen. See also Scots Acts of Parl. i. 337.

[2] Maine, Ancient Law, ch. v.: 'In Agnation too is to be sought the explanation of that extraordinary rule of English Law, only recently repealed, which prohibited brothers of the half-blood from succeeding to one another's lands. In the Customs of Normandy, the rule applies to *uterine* brothers only, that is to brothers by the same mother but not by the same father; and limited in this way, it is a strict deduction from the system of Agnation, under which uterine brothers are no relations at all to one another. When it was transplanted to England, the English judges, who had no clue to its principle, interpreted it as a general prohibition against the succession of the half-blood.' We have not been able to find any text of Norman Law which excludes the uterine but admits the consanguineous brother. The Grand Coutumier, c. 25 B, admits the consanguineous brother when the inheritance has descended from the father and the uterine brother when the inheritance has descended from the mother. As to land purchased by the *propositus*, we can see no words which declare the uterine brother incapable of inheriting. See Brunner, Erbfolgesystem, p. 44. In the later custom (Art. 312) the uterine and consanguineous brothers can claim a share with the brothers of the whole blood. The strongholds of the distinction between the consanguineous and the uterine half-blood seem to be the Lombard law of feuds and the Scottish law. In the Libri

When an inheritance falls to the daughters of the dead man, [p. 304] each of these 'parceners' (*participes*) is conceived as having a certain aliquot share in the as yet undivided land[1]. This share is her 'purparty' (*propars*); it will obey the ordinary rules of inheritance; it will descend to her issue, and, on failure of her issue, it will resort to her sisters or their descendants. We may, as already noticed[2], see traces of an older scheme which would admit a right of accruer between sisters and the near descendants of sisters; but this was fast disappearing[3]. Once more we see the representative principle brought into play; the distribution of shares between the descendants of dead daughters is *per stirpes* not *per capita*. If we suppose the only issue of the *propositus* living at his death to be the two grand-daughters that have sprung from one of his daughters and the three that have sprung from another, the inheritance must first be halved, and then one half of it will be halved again, while the other half will be divided into thirds. It would be a great mistake to suppose that our male-preferring and primogenitary system succeeded in keeping almost all of the great inherit- ances as unbroken wholes. Glanvill's own lands passed to three [p. 305] daughters. Twice within a few years the inheritance of an Earl of Chester 'fell among the spindles.' The inheritance of William Marshall the regent was soon split into thirty-fifths.

Feudorum such a distinction is in its proper place and this without any reference to agnatic families. Except as an anomaly, no fief can descend to a woman or through a woman, for fiefs are the estates of a military class; and since it can not descend through a woman, it can not pass to an uterine brother. Scottish law postponed the consanguineous half-brother, and it utterly excluded the uterine half-brother, even when the land had descended from his mother. But we should like to see a proof that this is not due to the powerful influence which the Libri Feudorum exercised over the Scottish lawyers of the sixteenth and later centuries. Here in England and in the year 1234 it was argued that a uterine brother should exclude a sister of the whole blood from land which had descended to the *propositus* from his mother (Note Book, pl. 855). When this was possible men were very far from 'agnation.' Again, for some time before 1855, Scottish law utterly excluded the mother and maternal kinsfolk even from the succession to movables; but it seems to be very doubtful whether this exclusion was ancient: Robertson, Law of Personal Succession, p. 380.

[1] Bracton, f. 373 b.

[2] See above, vol. ii. p. 291, note 7.

[3] So late as 1325 it is said that if a man dies leaving several daughters by different wives, and these daughters divide the inheritance, and one of them dies without issue, her share will go to her sisters of the half-blood as well as to her sisters of the whole blood: Y. B. 19 Edw. II. f. 628. See Britton, ii. 73 *note*.

for one of his five daughters was represented by seven daughters[1]. For a male to get a share ' by distaff right[2] ' was by no means uncommon.   But generally when an estate, at all events when a great estate, became partible, it was soon physically partitioned.   Any one of the parceners could demand a partition, and the days were past when a family would keep together after the death of its head.   The young heiress did not long remain unespoused ; her marriage was disposed of at the earliest possible moment ; the rich widow generally found another husband, though the church would not bless her second union ; it is rare therefore to find that any large mass of land long remains in the hands of a *feme sole.*

Germanic law seems to have set a limit to blood relationship, or ' sib-ship.'   An inheritance can not be claimed by one who does not stand within a certain degree, or rather, a certain ' joint ' or generation, the fifth, the sixth or the seventh.   The family was pictured not as a scale with degrees, nor as a tree with branches, but as a human body with joints.   The parents, according to one scheme, stand in the head, brothers in the neck, first cousins at the shoulders, second cousins at the elbows, third cousins at the wrists, fourth, fifth and sixth cousins at the finger-joints ; here the sib ends ; seventh cousins would be ' nail cousins ' and there would be no legal relationship between them[3].   We may see traces of this idea in England and in Normandy[4].   The Norman custom held that the line of consanguinity did not extend beyond the seventh degree[5]. Bracton refuses to draw the ascending line beyond the *tritavus,* the sixth ancestor of the *propositus* ; beyond this point memory will not go[6].   However, the rules for the limitation of actions

Limits of inheritance.

[p. 306]

---

[1] Stapleton, Liber de Antiquis Legibus (Camden Soc.), p. xix.   The annual value of a thirty-fifth share was reckoned at £217.

[2] Winchcombe Landboc, i. 131–3 : ' iure coli.'

[3] Heusler, Institutionen, ii. 591–3 ; Stobbe, Privatrecht, v. 67–9 : Schröder, D. R. G., 324.   The whole ' family ' which consists of parents and children stands ' within the first joint,' so that the reckoning by joints begins with first cousins. But a great deal is very obscure.

[4] An allusion to some such idea occurs in the Anglo-Saxon tract on Wergild: Schmid, App. vii.   A certain payment is made only to those near relations of the slain who are within the joint (*binnan cneówe ; infra genu*).   In Leg. Hen. 70, § 20, the inheritance descends to males *in quintum geniculum* ; but this is old Ripuarian law.

[5] Somma, p. 77 ; Ancienne coutume, c. 25 ; Brunner, Erbfolgesystem, p. 44.

[6] Bracton, f. 67 ; Brunner, *op. cit.,* p. 18.

that were in force in Bracton's day would in any ordinary case
have made it impossible for even a fifth cousin to bring an
action for an inheritance, for a demandant was obliged to allege
that the common ancestor who connected him with the *propositus* had been seised since the coronation of Henry II.[1] The
rule therefore against ascending beyond the *tritavus* fell into
oblivion[2], and then, owing to the spasmodic nature of our
statutes of limitation, it becomes theoretically possible for a
man to claim an inheritance from any kinsman however remote.

Restriction
of aliena-
tion in
favour
of the
expectant
heir.   We turn to speak of an important episode which is
intimately connected with the spread of primogeniture.   In
the thirteenth century the tenant in fee simple has a perfect
right to disappoint his expectant heirs by conveying away the
whole of his land by act *inter vivos*. Our law is grasping the
maxim *Nemo est heres viventis*. Glanvill wrote just in time,
though only just in time, to describe an older state of things[3].

Glanvill's
rules.   Several distinctions must be taken. We must distinguish
between military tenure and free socage; between land that
has come to the dead man by descent ('heritage') and land
that he has otherwise acquired ('conquest'); between the
various purposes for which an alienation is made[4]. Without
his expectant heir's consent the tenant may give reasonable
marriage portions to his daughters, may bestow something on
retainers by way of reward, and give something to the church.
His power over his conquest is greater than his power over
his heritage; but if he has only conquest he must not give the
whole away; he must not utterly disinherit the expectant heir.
Curiously enough, as it may seem to us, he has a much greater [p. 307]
power of providing for daughters, churches and strangers than
of providing for his own sons. Without the consent of his eldest
son he can 'hardly' give any part of his heritage to a younger
son[5]. The bastard therefore is better off than the legitimate

---

[1] Bracton, f. 372 b. Not only must you take as your *propositus* one who
died seised within the appointed period, but you may not 'resort' to one who
died beyond that period.

[2] Britton, ii. 324.

[3] Glanvill, vii. 1.

[4] Glanvill contrasts *hereditas* with *quaestus*. In borrowing from beyond the
Tweed the words *heritage* and *conquest* we show that in England the distinction
soon became unimportant. To express it we have no terms of our own less
cumbrous than 'lands which have come to a person by inheritance,' 'lands that
have come to him by purchase.'

[5] Glanvill, vii. 1: 'non poterit *de facili*......donare.'

younger son. Glanvill confesses that this is a paradox; but
it is law. As to the man who holds partible socage, he can
give nothing, be it heritage, be it conquest, to any son, beyond
the share that would fall to that son by inheritance. Glanvill,
however, is far from defining an exact rule for every possible
case; he nowhere tells us in terms of arithmetic what is that
reasonable portion which the father may freely alienate. We
can see however that one main restraint has been the deeply
rooted sentiment that a father ought not to give one of his
sons a preference over the others; they are equals and should
be treated as equals[1]. In the case of partible socage land this
sentiment still governs; but the introduction of primogeniture
has raised a new problem. When Glanvill is writing, the court
is endeavouring to put the eldest son in the advantageous
position that is occupied by each of the sokeman's expectant
heirs; without his consent he should not be deprived by any
gift made to his brothers of that which was to come to him
upon his father's death. But under the new law what was
to have come to him at his father's death was the whole of
his father's land. Are we then to secure all this for him, and
that too in the name of a rule which has heretofore made for
equality among sons? If so, then we come to the paradox that
it is better to be a bastard than a legitimate younger son.
This could not long be tolerated. Free alienation without the
heir's consent will come in the wake of primogeniture. These
two characteristics which distinguish our English law from her
nearest of kin, the French customs, are closely connected.

The charters of the twelfth century afford numerous *The heir's*
examples of expectant heirs joining in the gifts of their *consent.*
ancestors. Occasionally the giver may explain that he has not
obtained his heir's concurrence, because he is disposing not of
heritage but of conquest[2]; but very often one heir or several
[p. 308] heirs are said to take part in the gift. To all seeming the
necessity for the heir's concurrence was not confined to the
common case in which the donor had a son. Walter Espec's
foundation of Kirkham Abbey was confirmed by his nine

---

[1] *Somma*, p. 114; *Ancienne coutume*, c. 36: 'Cum pater plures habeat
filios, unum meliorem altero de hereditate sua non potest facere.'

[2] Somner, *Gavelkind*, p. 40: Charter of 1204: 'et quia praedicta terra de
libero catallo et proprio perquisito meo fuit, et non de aliqua hereditate
parentum meorum.'

nephews, the sons of his three sisters[1]; and the consent of the donor's daughters is sometimes mentioned[2]. It would seem too that it was not enough that the heir apparent, the donor's eldest son, should give his consent. If he consented, he could not afterwards complain; but if he died before his father, his consent would not bar his brothers, perhaps not his sons. Therefore the prudent donee procures the concurrence of as many of the donor's near kinsfolk as can be induced to approve the gift[3]. Daughters consent though the donor has sons who also consent[4]. In a gift to Winchcombe three of the donor's sons give a sworn consent, and further swear that they will if possible obtain the consent of a fourth son, should he return to the king's peace[5]. The Abbey of Meaux could not get the consent of the donor's eldest brother, but it took the consents of his other brothers and 'all his other kinsfolk'; the eldest brother died in the donor's lifetime and his sons brought a suit for the land, which the monks were glad to compromise[6]. Well worthy of notice are the cases, not very uncommon, in which little children are made to approve their father's pious gifts; worthy of notice, because an attempt seems made to bind them by receipt of a *quid pro quo*. At Abingdon the monks, fearing that the heir might afterwards dispute the donation, gave him twelve pence and a handsome leather belt[7]. At Ramsey two *infantes* receive five shillings apiece, an *infantulus* a shilling, and a baby held in its mother's arms twenty pence[8]; so at Chartres four pence are put into the hands of a [p. 309] child who is too young to speak[9]; and so, to return to England, the monks of Winchcombe who are taking a conveyance from a woman before the king's justices at Gloucester, besides making a substantial payment to her, give six pence to her

---

[1] Monasticon, vi. 209; see also the foundation charter of Rievaulx: Cart. Riev. p. 21.

[2] Cart. Glouc. i. 367.

[3] It is quite common to find several sons or brothers joining in the gift. See *e.g.* Madox, Formulare, p. 4, the donor's wife, two sons, two brothers and one grandson or nephew (*nepos*) declare their consent.

[4] Cart. Rams. i. 132, 139.

[5] Winchcombe Landboc, i. 35.

[6] Chron. de Melsa, i. 313.

[7] Hist. Abingd. ii. 202: 'zonam ei cervinam optimam dedit et nummos xii.'

[8] Cart. Rams. i. 137, 139, 145.

[9] Cart. de S. Père de Chartres (Documents inédits), ii. p. 576.

son and six pence to each of her three daughters[1]. In some
charters the heirs are put before us not merely as assenting
to, but as joining in the gift; it is a gift by a man and his
heirs; in other cases the heirs are named among the witnesses
of the deed. What ceremony was observed upon these occasions
we cannot tell, but when the heirs are spoken of as giving the
land, it is by no means impossible that the symbolic turf, twig
or charter was delivered to the donee by the 'joint hands' of
all the givers[2].

Unfortunately when in 1194 the rolls of the king's court
begin their tale, it is too late for them to tell us much about
this matter[3]. However in 1200 Elyas Croc gave the king
thirty marks and a palfrey to have a judgment of the court
as to whether a gift made by his father Matthew was valid.
Matthew had given to his own younger brother, the uncle of
Elyas, a knight's fee which, so Elyas asserted, was the head
of the honour and barony[4]. Whether Elyas got a judgment
or no we can not say; but this looks like an extreme case;
the father had been giving away the ancestral mansion. So
late as 1225 a son vainly tries to get back a tenement which
his father has alienated, and plaintively asks whether his
father could give away all the land that he held by military
tenure without retaining any service for himself and his heirs:
—but it is unavailing[5]. Bracton knows nothing of—or rather,
having Glanvill's book before him, deliberately ignores—the old
restraint: it is too obsolete to be worth a word. The phrase
'and his heirs' in a charter of feoffment gives nothing to an
heir apparent[6].

Disappearance of the restriction.

The change, if we consider its great importance, seems to
have been effected rapidly, even suddenly. The earliest plea
rolls have hardly anything to say of rules which, however
indefinite, were law in 1188. We seem to see here, as already

Causes of the change

p. 310]

---

[1] Winchcombe Landboc, i. 180.

[2] Cart. Glouc. i. 205, 235, 296; Cart. Riev. p. 52. See the cross on the
charter made by the heir in Brinkburn Cart. pp. 1, 2.

[3] A few pertinent stories are found in chronicles. Hist. Abingd. ii. 205-6
(early Henry II.): apparent heirs try ineffectually to stop a gift being made to
the church; this gives rise to proceedings in the hallmoot, where they fail.
Chron. de Melsa, i. 103, 231-2, 289-90-91 (temp. John): an heiress recovers
land given by her ancestor; the monks complain of favouritism.

[4] Oblate Rolls (ed. Hardy), p. 87.

[5] Note Book, pl. 1054.　　　　[6] Bracton, f. 17.

suggested, the complement of that new and stringent primogeniture which the king's court had begun to enforce. The
object of the restraint in time past had not been solely, perhaps
not mainly, the retention of land 'in a family'; it had secured
an equal division of land among sons, or as equal a division as
the impartibility of the knight's fee would permit. It became
useless, inappropriate, unbearable, when the eldest son was to
have the whole inheritance. No great harm would be done
to the feudal lords, at all events to the king, by abolishing it.
They had, or they meant to have, some control over the alienations made by their tenants[1], more control than they could
have had under a law which partitioned the inheritance.

Rebutting
effect of a
warranty.
The material cause of the great change we may find in
such considerations as these; but it must have been effected
by some machinery of legal reasoning, and we may suspect
that the engine which did the work was one that was often to
show its potency in after centuries—'the rebutting effect of
a warranty.' Alan alienates land to William; Alan declares
that he and his heirs will warrant that land to William and
his heirs. Alan being dead, Baldwin, who is his son and heir,
brings suit against William, urging that Alan was not the
owner of the land, but that it really belonged to Alan's wife
and Baldwin's mother, or urging that Alan was a mere tenant
for life and that Baldwin was the remainderman. William
meets the claim thus:—'See here the charter of Alan your
father, whose heir you are. He undertook that he and his
heirs would warrant this land to me and mine. If a stranger
impleaded me, you would be the very person whom I should
vouch to warrant me. With what face then can you claim the
land?' Baldwin is rebutted from the claim by his ancestor's
warranty. It is a curious and a troublesome doctrine which
hereafter will give rise to many a nice distinction. A man is
debarred, rebutted, from claiming land because the burden of
a warranty given by one of his ancestors has fallen upon him.
In later days, already when Bracton was writing, this doctrine
no longer came into play when a tenant in fee simple had
alienated his land; for in such a case the heir had no right to [p. 311]
the land, no claim which must be rebutted. It only came into
play when the alienator and warrantor had been doing something that he had no business to do, when a husband had been

[1] See above, vol. i. p. 332.

alienating his wife's land, or a tenant for life had made a feoffment in fee. But we may suspect that this doctrine performed its first exploit when it enabled the tenant in fee simple to disappoint his expectant heirs by giving a warranty which would rebut and cancel their claims upon the alienated land[1].

Be this as it may, our law about the year 1200 performed very swiftly an operation that elsewhere was but slowly accomplished. Abroad, as a general rule, the right of the expectant heir gradually assumed the shape of the *retrait lignager*. A landowner must not alienate his land without the consent of his expectant heirs unless it be a case of necessity, and even in a case of necessity the heirs must have an opportunity of purchasing. If this be not given them, then within some fixed period—often it is year and day—they can claim the land from the purchaser on tendering him the price that he paid[2]. The conception of a case of necessity may be widened indefinitely; but for centuries the seller's kinsmen enjoy this *ius retractus*. Norman law[3] and Angevin law[4] took this turn, and we can see from our own borough customs that it was a turn which our own law might easily have taken[5]. But above our law at the critical moment stood a high-handed court of professional justices who were all for extreme simplicity and who could abolish a whole chapter of ancient jurisprudence by two or three bold decisions.

A great and sudden change.

---

[1] See *e.g.* Note Book, pl. 224: *A* claims land from *X*; *X* pleads a feoffment made to him by an ancestor of *A*, and says that *A* is bound to warrant that gift. See also pl. 1685. Were it fully established that a tenant in fee simple could alienate without his heir's consent, a reliance on warranty would be needless. Blackstone, Comment. ii. 301, says that express warranties were introduced 'in order to evade the strictness of the feodal doctrine of non-alienation without the consent of the heir.' This, though the word 'feodal' is out of place, we believe to be true. The clause of warranty becomes a normal part of the charter of feoffment about the year 1200.

[2] For Germany, see Heusler, Institutionen, ii. 60.

[3] Somma, p. 300; Ancienne coutume, c. 118 (ed. de Gruchy, p. 295).

[4] Viollet, Établissements, i. 120.

[5] See above in our section on The Boroughs. A right of pre-emption, so archaic as to be a tribal rather than a family right, still exists in Montenegro: Code Général des Biens, tr. Dareste et Rivière, Paris 1892, art. 47–56.

§ 3. *The Last Will.*

The germs of the last will.

We may believe that, even in the first days of English [p. 312 Christianity, the church was teaching that the dying man was in duty bound to make such atonement as was possible for the wrongs that he had done and to devote to the relief of the poor and other pious works a portion of the wealth that he was leaving behind him. There is a curious story in Bede's history which may prove somewhat more than this. A certain householder in the realm of Northumbria died one evening but returned to life the next morning. He arose and went into the village church, and, after remaining for a while in prayer, he divided all his substance into three parts; one of these he gave to his wife, another to his sons, the third he reserved to himself, and forthwith he distributed it among the poor. Shortly afterwards he entered the abbey of Melrose[1]. Now certainly this man behaved as though he conceived his property to consist of 'wife's part,' 'bairns' part' and 'dead's part,' and it is a remarkable coincidence that this tale should be told of a Northumbrian, for in after days it was in Scotland and the northern shires of England that the custom which secured an aliquot share to the wife, an aliquot share to the children, and left the dying man free to dispose of the residue of his goods, struck its deepest roots. We might be wrong however in drawing any wide inference from this isolated story, the only tale of the kind that comes to us from these very ancient times, and at all events we are not entitled to say that this man made a testament. To all seeming his pious gift was irrevocable and took effect immediately.

What is a will?

From the middle of the ninth century we begin to get documents which are often spoken of as Anglo-Saxon wills or testaments[2]. Before using these terms, it will be well for us to say a few words about their meaning, and, though we allow

---

[1] Beda, Hist. Eccl., lib. v. cap. 12. See Baedae Opera, ed. Plummer, ii. 295. The English translation describes his act thus: 'and sona æfter ðon ealle his æhto on ðreo todælde, ænne dæl he his wife sealde, oþerne his bearnum, ðone ðriddan ðe *him gelamp* he instæpe ðearfum gedælde.'

[2] These documents are conveniently collected by Thorpe, Diplomatarium, pp. 459-601. Their nature is discussed by Brunner, Geschichte der Urkunde, i. 199; Hübner, Donationes post obitum (Gierke's Untersuchungen, No. xxvi.).

[p. 313] to them their largest scope, we ought, it would seem, to insist that a will or testament should have at least one of three qualities. In the first place, it should be a revocable instrument. Secondly, it should be an ambulatory instrument. By this we mean that it should be capable of bestowing (though in any given instance it need not necessarily bestow) property which does not belong to the testator when he makes his will, but which does belong to him at the moment of his death. For the third quality that we would describe we have no technical term; but perhaps we may be suffered to call it the 'hereditative' quality of the testament; it can make an heir, or (since our own history forbids us to use the term *heir* in this context) it can make a representative of the testator.

This matter may be made the clearer by a short digression through a later age. In the twelfth century it became plain that the Englishman had no power to give freehold land by his will, unless some local custom authorized him to do so. A statute of 1540[1], which was explained and extended by later statutes[2], enabled any person who should 'have' any lands as tenant in fee simple to 'give, dispose, will and devise' the same 'by his last will and testament in writing.' Nevertheless, we find the courts holding—and apparently they were but following a rule which had long been applied to those wills of land that were sanctioned by local custom[3]—that a will of freehold lands is no ambulatory instrument. The statute, they hold, does but empower a man to give by will what he 'has' when he makes the will. And such was our law until 1837[4]. Now this piece of history will dispose us to believe that our ancestors, in times not very remote from our own, found great difficulty in conceiving that a man can give by his will what does not belong to him when he makes that will. Our common lawyers would not allow that a statute had surmounted this difficulty, and this although for a long time past the will of chattels, which was under the care of the canonists, had been [p. 314] an ambulatory instrument. Still the statutory will of freehold land was a revocable instrument; it did nothing at all until

Ambulatory quality of a will.

---

[1] Stat. 32 Hen. VIII. c. 1.

[2] Stat. 34–5 Henry VIII. c. 5; 12 Car. II. c. 24. In this context we need not speak of the partial restriction on a will of land held by knight's service which prevailed between 1540 and 1660.

[3] Y. B. 39 Hen. VI. f. 18 (Mich. pl. 23).

[4] Stat. 7 Will. IV. and 1 Vic. c. 26, sec. 3.

its maker died; it did not impede him from selling or giving away the lands that were mentioned in it; and it was always called 'a last will and testament.'

Then again the 'hereditative' quality of the will comes to the front but very slowly. We are not here speaking about the use of words. In England it is as true to-day as it was in the time of Glanvill that only God, not man, can make an heir, for the term *heir* we still reserve as of old for the person who succeeds to land *ab intestato*. But, to come to a more important matter, though at the present day it is possible for the Englishman by his will to transmit the whole of his *persona*, the whole of his fortune 'active and passive,' to a single person—as when he writes 'I give all my real and personal estate to my wife and appoint her my sole executrix'— he can make a complete will without doing this. He may leave Blackacre to John, Whiteacre to Thomas, Greenacre to William, and so forth; there will then be no one person representing the whole of his fortune, the whole mass of those rights and duties which were once his and continue to exist though he is dead, nor will there be any group of persons who jointly represent him or his fortune. John, William, and Thomas do not jointly represent him even as regards the rights that he had in his land. John, for example, has nothing whatever to do with Whiteacre or Greenacre. We find this a tolerable state of things even in the nineteenth century[1]. For a long time past the executor, or the group of executors, has represented the testator as regards that part of his fortune which is called his 'personalty'; but of this representation also we shall see the beginnings in the thirteenth century. What of the ninth?

Nothing is plainer than that the so-called Anglo-Saxon will is not the Roman testament. The use of writing is Roman, and a vague idea that in some way or another a man can by written or spoken words determine what shall be done after his death with the goods that he leaves behind, comes as a legacy from the old world to the new; but the connexion between the Anglo-Saxon will and the Roman testament is exceedingly remote. We have no one instance of an Englishman endeavouring to institute a *heres* in the Roman sense of that term. That term was in use among the clerks, but it [p. 315]

*Heredita-
tive wills.*

*The Anglo-
Saxon will.*

---

[1] A great change is being made by the Land Transfer Act, 1897.

could be applied to one who in no sense bore the whole *persona* of a dead man, it could be applied to a devisee, as we should call him, who became entitled to a single piece of the testator's land[1]. The word *testamentum* was laxly used; almost any instrument might be called a testament; the ordinary land-book which witnessed a conveyance by one living man to another living man was a testament[2]. The Anglo-Saxon 'will,' or *cwiðe* as it calls itself, seems to have grown up on English soil, and the Roman testament has had little to do with its development.

The most important of its ingredients we shall call 'the post obit gift.' A man wishes to give land to a church, but at the same time he wishes to enjoy that land so long as he lives. A 'book' is drawn up in which he says, 'I give (or, I deliver) the land after my death[3].' Now this book can not fairly be called a will. To all seeming it is neither revocable, nor ambulatory, nor yet is it hereditative. At this moment the testator gives a specific plot of land to a church; he makes the gift for good and all; but the church is not to have possession until after he is dead. Men do not seem to see the ambiguity of this phrase, 'Dono post obitum meum,' or to apply the dilemma, 'Either you give at this moment, in which case you cease to have any right in the land, or else you only promise to give, in which case the promisee acquires at most the benefit of an obligation.' Occasionally, but rarely, the donor says something that we may construe as a reservation of an usufruct or life estate[4]; but generally this seems to be thought quite unnecessary; 'I give after my death,' is plain enough[5].

The post obit gift.

---

[1] The royal land-book often says that the donee may at his death leave or give the land to anyone, or to any *heres*, whom he chooses. It seems plain that the person whom he chooses will be his *heres* for that particular piece of land. Apparently the English word which *heres* represented had this same meaning. Thus if Bishop Oswald gives land to Æthelmær for three lives, so that he shall have it for his day, 'and æfter his dæge twam erfeweardan ðam ðe him leofest sy,' any person to whom the donee leaves the land is his *yrfeweard* so far as that plot of ground is concerned. See Cod. Dipl. 675 (iii. 255).

[2] See *e.g.* Cod. Dipl. 90 (i. 108). So also on the continent almost any legal instrument may be called a *testamentum*. Thus a deed of sale is *testamentum venditionis*. Ducange, s.v. *testamentum*.

[3] See *e.g.* Cod. Dipl. i. pp. 133, 216-7, 290.

[4] See *e.g.* Thorpe, Diplomatarium, p. 518.

[5] Thorpe, p. 492: 'Ceolwin makes known by this writing that she gives the land at Alton......she gives it after her day to the convent at Winchester.'

[p. 316]

The post obit gift and the royal land-book.

At a later time such a gift has become impossible, because the courts insist that there can not be a gift without a livery of seisin. You can not give and keep. The desired transaction, if it is to be effected at all, must involve two feoffments. You must enfeoff the church in fee and be re-enfeoffed as its tenant for life. That laxer notions about seisin should have prevailed in earlier times may seem strange, but is a well-attested fact[1]. In part we ascribe it to the influence of those royal land-books which bear the crosses of the bishops and the anathema of the church. The book that the lay holder of bookland possesses authorizes him in express terms to give that land in his lifetime or after his death to whomsoever he pleases, or to whatsoever 'heir' he pleases. The pious recitals in the book tell us that one of the objects of these words is that the donee may have wherewithal to redeem his soul and benefit the churches. The holder of bookland when he makes his post obit gift is, to use a modern but not inappropriate phrase, 'executing a power of appointment' given to him by an authoritative privilege, he is doing what he is empowered to do by the *forma doni*. And as he can give his land after his death, so he can burden his land with the payment of a rent which is only to become current at his death. He can combine these forms. He may give the land to his wife for her life, she paying a rent to the monks at Winchester, and declare that on her death the land itself is to go to the New Minster[2]. He may declare that one thing is to happen if he dies without a son and another thing if he has a son[3]. He can make contingent and conditional gifts[4]. All this he can do, at all events with the king's consent, for a full liberty of alienation *post obitum suum* is secured to him by his land-book.

The death-bed distribution.

But there is a second ingredient in the will, namely, the death-bed confession with its accompanying effort to wipe out past sin. Already in the eighth century the dying man's last words, his *verba novissima*, are to be respected. In the dialogue ascribed to Egbert, Archbishop of York, the question is put, 'Can a priest or deacon be witness of the *verba novissima* which dying men utter about their property?' The answer

---

[1] See above, p. 92.   [2] Thorpe, p. 495 (Wulfgar).
[3] Thorpe, p. 483 (Ælfred the ealdorman); p. 506 (Ælfgar).
[4] Ibid., p. 470 (Abba).

is, 'Let him take with him one or two, so that in the mouth
[p. 317] of two or three witnesses every word may be established, for
perchance the avarice of the kinsfolk of the dead would contradict what was said by the clergy, were there but one priest
or deacon present[1].' We have here something different from
those post obit gifts of which we have already spoken. A man
may make a post obit gift though he expects to live many
years; but those last words which we find the church protecting are essentially words spoken by one who knows himself
to be passing away. And we seem to see that they are as
a rule spoken, not written, words; they form part (we may
almost say this) of the religious service that is being performed
at the death-bed. How much power they have we know not.
Some portion of his chattels, no doubt, the dying man may
give to pious uses, and perhaps his last words may convey the
title to his bookland :—his 'avaricious' kinsfolk (so they are
called by the clergy) are watching him narrowly[2]. But further,
there is much in future history, much in continental history,
to suggest that even here we have to deal with gifts which
are thought of as gifts *inter vivos*. The sick man distributes,
divides, 'devises,' a portion of his chattels[3]. He makes that
portion over to his confessor for the good of his soul; he makes
what—regard being had to the imminence of death—is a
sufficient delivery of them to the man who is to execute his
last will. The questions that we wish to ask—Are his words revocable and are they ambulatory?—are not practical questions.
Not in one case in a thousand does a man live many hours
after he has received the last sacrament. The germ of
executorship seems to be here. The dying man hands over
some of his goods to one who is to distribute them for the
good of his soul.

Then these two institutions 'the post obit gift' and 'the
last words' seem to coalesce in the written *cwiðe* of the ninth,
tenth and eleventh centuries. At first sight it seems to have
many of the characteristics of a true will. For one thing, it
is an exceedingly formless instrument; it is almost always

The
written
cwiðe.

---

[1] Dialogus Ecgberti, Haddan and Stubbs, Councils, iii. 404.

[2] The case of Eanwene, Cod. Dipl. iv. p. 54, Thorpe, p. 336, is sometimes
cited as involving a nuncupatory will of land. But apparently the *quasi*
testatrix is still living when the shire moot establishes the gift that she has
made.

[3] The *devisare* of later records slowly branches off from *dividere*.

written in the vulgar tongue, not in Latin, even though it [p. 318]
comes from a bishop. It calls itself a *cwiðe*, that is a saying,
a *dictum*; it is its maker's *nihsta cwiðe*[1]; it contains in advance
(if we may so speak) his *verba novissima*. He gives his various
lands specifically, providing for his kinsfolk, remembering his
dependants, freeing some of his slaves and bestowing lands
and rents upon various churches. He also makes gifts of
specific chattels, his precious swords, cups and vestments are
distributed. He says how many swine are to go with this
piece of land and how many with that. He sometimes gives
what we should describe as pecuniary legacies. Distinct traces
of those qualities which we have called ambulatoriness and
revocability are very rare. Occasionally however we see residuary gifts of chattels and of lands[2]. King Alfred tells us
that in the past when he had more money and more kinsmen,
he had executed divers writings and entrusted them to divers
men. He adds that he has burned as many of the old writings
as he could find, and declares that if any of them still exist
they are to be deemed void[3]. But it is never safe for us to
assume that every man can do what a king does with the
counsel of his wise men. Lastly, the testator—though this
is not very common—says something about debts that are
owed to him or by him, and which are not to perish at his
death[4].

The right
to be-
queath.
But, though all this be so, we can not think that an instrument bearing a truly testamentary character had obtained
a well-recognized place in the Anglo-Saxon folk-law. With
hardly an exception these wills are the wills of very great
people, kings, queens, king's sons, bishops, ealdormen, king's
thegns. In the second place, it is plain that in many cases the
king's consent must be obtained if the will is to be valid, if
the *cwiðe* is to 'stand.' That consent is purchased by a
handsome heriot. Sometimes the *cwiðe* takes the form of a

---

[1] Thorpe, p. 500 = Cod. Dipl. no. 492.

[2] Thorpe, p. 527 = Cod. Dipl. no. 593: Ælfheah, after disposing specifically
of various lands, gives to his wife, if she survives him, 'all the other lands which
I leave.' See also pp. 554, 585 (Wulf). It must be remembered however that (as
the history of our law between 1540 and 1837 proves) we can not argue from a
residuary gift to the ambulatory character of the instrument.

[3] Thorpe, p. 490.

[4] Thorpe, p. 550–1 (Archbishop Ælfric); p. 561 (Æthelstan the ætheling);
p. 568 (Bishop Ælfric) = Cod. Dipl. nos. 716, 722, 759.

supplicatory letter addressed to the king.   In the third place,
[p. 319] an appeal is made to ecclesiastical sanctions; a bishop sets his
cross to the will; the torments of hell are denounced against
those who infringe it.   Then again, even in the eleventh century, it seems to be quite common that the *cwiðe* should be
executed in duplicate or triplicate, and that one copy of it
should be at once handed over to that monastery which is the
principal donee, and this may make us doubt whether it is a
revocable instrument[1].   In some cases the will shades off into
a family settlement[2].   Often it is clear enough that the testator is not disposing of all his property.   He merely tries to
impose charges in favour of the churches on those unnamed
men who will succeed to his land.

On the whole it seems to us that we have here to deal with
a practice which has sprung up among the great, a practice
which is ill-defined because it is the outcome of *privilegia*.   As
to the common folk, we may perhaps believe that the land-
holder, if and when he can give away his land at all, may make
a post obit gift of it which will reduce him to the position of a
tenant for life, and that every man, even when his last hour
has come, may distribute some part of his goods for the efface-
ment of his sins and the repose of his soul.   This distribution
we strongly suspect of being in theory a gift *inter vivos*.   The
goods are handed over to those who are to divide them.   In
the written *cwiðe* of the great man, it is true, we do not at
first sight see anything that looks like either a delivery *inter
vivos* or the appointment of an executor.   At first sight the
dead man's estate seems expected to divide itself.   Then, however, we observe that the will begins with a prayer that the
king will uphold it.   May we not say that the king is the
executor of these wills?   In a few instances we find something
more definite.   'Now I pray Bishop Ælfstan that he protect
my widow and the things that I leave to her......and that he
aid that all the things may stand which I have bequeathed[3]'—
'And be Bishop Ælfric and Tofig the Proud and Thrunni
guardians of this *cwiðe*[4].'   When among the great the practice

*Wills and
death-bed
gifts.*

---

[1] Some specimens of these 'chirographed' wills are given in Brit. Mus.
Facsimiles, vol. IV.   Apparently they are not signed either by the testator or by
any witnesses.

[2] Thorpe, pp. 468, 479, 500.   [3] Thorpe, p. 517.

[4] Thorpe, p. 566 = Cod. Dipl. no. 970: 'And be Alfric biscop and Tofi Prude
and Ðrunni ðese quides mundes hureðinge ðat it no man awende.'

of uttering one's last words in advance while one is still whole [p. 320] and strong becomes established, the goods are no longer handed over when the words are uttered and the *cwiðe* is becoming an ambulatory instrument; but still some person is named who is to effect that distribution which is to be made at the testator's death. A well-known text in the Epistle to the Hebrews, a text far better known than anything in the Institutes, says that a testament is of no effect until the testator's death; but even at the call of an inspired writer men were not able to accept this doctrine all at once[1].

Intestacy in Cnut's day.

Already in Cnut's day it was unusual for a man to die without 'last words,' and it was necessary for the king to combat, or perhaps to renounce, the notion that the man who has said no last words has proved himself a sinner. 'If any one leaves this world without a *cwiðe*, be this due to his negligence or to sudden death, then let the lord take naught from the property, save his right heriot; and let the property be distributed according to his (the lord's) direction and according to law among the wife and children and nearest kinsfolk, to each the proper share[2].' Some lords, we may suspect, perhaps some episcopal and abbatial lords, had already been saying that if a man leaves the world without taking care of his soul, his lord, or the church, ought to do for him what he should have done for himself. But the time had not come when this doctrine would prevail.

The lord and the *cwiðe*.

The law that we have just cited seems to assume, not only that every man will have a lord, but that every man will have a lord with a court, and that by this lord's hand his goods, perhaps also his lands, will be divided among his kinsfolk, the 'right heriot' having been first taken. The heriot gives an occasion for what we may call a magisterial, though it is also a seignorial, intervention between the dead man and his heirs. Another such occasion is afforded by the soul-scot or mortuary. The dead man's parish church has a legal claim to a payment when he is buried[3]. At least in later days, it generally claims

---

[1] Paulus ad Hebraeos, ix. 16, 17: 'Ubi enim testamentum est, mors necesse est intercedat testatoris. Testamentum enim in mortuis confirmatum est. Alioquin nondum valet, dum vivit qui testatus est.' See Hist. Rames. c. 26 (Gale, p. 406).

[2] Cnut, ii. 70.

[3] See the passages collected in Schmid, Glossar. s. v. *sáwl sceat*.

[p. 321] the best, or the second best, beast or other chattel; very commonly the testator provides for his mortuary in his will. Not unfrequently it happens that a monastery can demand both soul-scot and heriot. But though the lord is thus tempted to intervene, it does not seem likely that Anglo-Saxon law knew anything either of the probate of wills or of any legal proceeding that must of necessity take place when there has been an intestacy, anything like the 'grant of administration.'

We may doubt whether the Normans brought with them to England any new ideas about these matters. They knew the post obit gift of land. It was possible for a man to say in a charter, 'I have given this land after my death,' or 'I have given it after the deaths of myself and my wife,' or 'I have given the whole of it after my death if I leave no issue of my body, but half of it if I leave issue[1].' In all probability they knew the death-bed distribution of chattels. But that they had either accepted or rejected anything that could be accurately called a testament we do not know. Norman law.

In England after the Conquest there was no sudden change. A man could still make a post obit gift of land and sometimes made it with impressive solemnity. Thus in a charter which comes from the early years of the twelfth century we read— 'And thereupon in the same chapter the said Wulfgeat after his death for the weal of his soul gave to the church of Ramsey ten acres of his own land. And after the chapter was at an end the monks together with the said Wulfgeat came together into the new church, and there when, as the custom was after a chapter, the prayers for the dead had been finished, the said Wulfgeat made a gift of the said land upon the portable altar dedicated to the Holy Trinity by a rod which we still have in our keeping[2].' Occasionally in such cases it was thought well that the donor should put himself under the obligation of paying a small rent to the abbey while he lived[3], but there was no necessity for a duplex process of feoffment and refeoffment, which would imply an analysis of the post obit gift such as men had not yet made. The will under the Norman kings.

---

[1] Cartulaire de l'abbaye de la S. Trinité du Mont de Rouen (Documents inédits), i. 429.

[2] Cart. Rams. ii. 262. The mention of the prayers for the dead suggests that by way of fiction Wulfgeat is supposed to he making the gift 'post obitum suum.'   [3] Ibid. i. 133.

Post obit
gifts of
chattels.

The vague conception that prevailed as to the nature of [p. 322]
these transactions can be illustrated by certain dealings which
are characteristic of the Norman age.   We hardly know how to
describe them.   The result of them is to be that after a certain
person's death a church will take the whole, or some aliquot
share, of his chattels.   If we call them testaments, we say too
much ; if we call them present gifts, we say too much ; if we call
them covenants to give, again we say too much.   Occasionally
the language of contract may be employed.   For example, a
conventio is made between the Abbot of Burton and Orm of
Darlaston ; the Abbot gives land to Orm, and Orm and his son
agree that upon their deaths their bodies shall be carried to
Burton, and with their bodies is to go thither the whole of
their *pecunia* whatsoever and wheresoever it may be[1].   Or
land may be given by the monks 'upon this convention,' that
when the feoffee is dead he shall cause himself to be carried
to the monastery for burial with his whole *pecunia*[2].   Or one
who holds land of a convent may endeavour to bind his heirs
for all time to leave the third part of their chattels 'by way
of relief' to the house of Stanlaw[3].   So we are told that Earl
Hugh and his barons, when they founded the abbey at Chester,
ordained that all the barons and knights should give to God
and St Werburgh their bodies after death and the third part
of their whole substance ; and they ordained this not only for
the barons and knights, but also for their burgesses and other
free men[4].   Such a transaction as this, in which the gift shades
off into a law for the palatinate, is of great importance when
we trace the growing claims of the church to distribute for
pious uses the chattels of dead persons ; but for the moment
we are discussing the post obit gift, and, though words of
covenant may sometimes be used, we seem to see that the
transaction is conceived to be a present gift.   'He gave himself
to the church so that, should he wish to become a monk, he

[1] Cart. Burton, p. 35 : 'Debet autem cum eis afferri et tota pars eorum
pecuniae quantacunque habuerint et in omnibus rebus et in omnibus locis.'

[2] Cart. Burton, p. 30 : 'cum autem mortuus fuerit, deferre ad nos se faciet
cum tota pecunia sua ad sepeliendum.'

[3] Whalley Coucher, i. 155.

[4] Monasticon, ii. 386.   'Insuper constituerunt ut singuli barones et milites
darent Deo et S. Werburgae post obitum suum sua corpora et tertiam partem
totius substantiae suae.   Et non solum haec constituerunt de baronibus et
militibus sed etiam de burgensibus et aliis hominibus liberis suis.'

[p. 323] would enter religion in no other place, and, in case he should die a layman in England, he should be buried here with a third of the whole *pecunia* which he should have in England[1].' When Earl Gilbert of Lincoln says in a charter, 'Know ye that for the redemption of my sins, and for the special love that I have for the church of St Mary of Bridlington, I have delivered myself (*mancipavi me ipsum*) to the said church, to the intent that wherever I may bring my life to a close I may receive a place of burial in the said church[2],' if we were to translate his curious words into modern terms, we might perhaps say that he is making an irrevocable will of his personalty for the behoof of his favourite church; still he thinks that he is making a present gift.   Even in 1240 a man will say, 'Know that I have given and confirmed by this charter to God and St German of Selby all the lands that I now have or shall hereafter acquire, and one half of the chattels that I shall acquire during my life, to be received by the monks after my death[3].'

We have now to watch a complicated set of interdependent changes, which took place during the twelfth and thirteenth centuries, and which gradually established a definite law.   In the first place we will describe in a summary fashion the various movements. Evolution of definite law.

(1)   The king's court condemns the post obit gift of land and every dealing with land that is of a testamentary character; but it spares the customs of the boroughs and allows certain novel interests in land to be treated as chattels.

(2)   By evolving a rigorously primogenitary scheme for the inheritance of land, it destroys all such unity as there has ever been in the law of succession.   Henceforth the 'heir' as such will have nothing to do with the chattels of the dead man, and these become a prey for the ecclesiastical tribunals.

(3)   The church asserts a right to protect and execute the last will of the dead man.   In her hands this last will (which now can only deal with chattels) gradually assumes

---

[1] Hist. Abingd. ii. 124.   Similar arrangements, Ibid. 130, 168.

[2] Monasticon, vi. (1) 288 : 'mancipavi me ipsum eidem ecclesiae, ea videlicet ratione ut ubicunque vivendi finem fecero in monasterio Bridlintonensi locum sepulturae accipiam.'

[3] Selby Coucher Book, i. 204.   As to these post obit gifts of the whole or an aliquot share of the goods that the giver will leave at his death, see Heusler, Institutionen, ii. 630–642.

under foreign influence a truly testamentary character, and [p. 324] the executor of it gradually becomes the 'personal representative' of the dead man, but has nothing to do with freehold estates.

(4)　The horror of intestacy increases. The church asserts a right (it is also a duty) of administering the dead man's goods for the repose of his soul. The old law which would have given the intestate's goods to his kinsfolk, being now weakened by the development of the rule which gives all the land to the eldest son, disappears, or holds but a precarious position at the will of the church.

Of these four movements we must speak in turn, though they affect each other.

Feudalism and wills of land. The common belief that before the Conquest the land-holder could give his land by will, and that this power was taken from him at a blow by the 'feudalism' which came from France, we can not accept. The post obit gift of land—and this we believe to have been all that had been sanctioned by the ordinary law of unconquered England—did not disappear until late in the twelfth century; it had been well enough known in Normandy; and the force that destroyed it in England can not properly be called feudal.

Post obit gifts of land. From the point of view of the feudal lord a post obit gift is not much more objectionable than an out and out gift. We can not in mere feudalism find any reason why the landholder should not make a post obit gift with the consent of his lord, and without the consent of his lord it is very doubtful whether he can make a gift at all[1]. And so there need be nothing to surprise us in the following story. That great man Eudo the Dapifer was lying on his death-bed in Normandy, and, having received absolution, he made a division, or 'devise' as we say, of all his property in the presence and with the advice and consent of King Henry I. And he commanded his folk, appealing to the fealty which they owed him, to carry his body to the abbey which he had built at Colchester. And with his body he bequeathed to that house the manor of Brightlingsea and a hundred pounds of money and his gold ring. He also gave a cup and his horse and his mule; but these the abbot had to surrender to the king in order that he might obtain a concession

---

[1] See above, vol. i. p. 343.

[p. 325] of the said manor: in order (to use the old phrase) that the *cwiðe* might stand[1].

We are told by a plaintive monk that a few years after Glanvill's book was written, some new rule was put in force at the instance of Geoffrey Fitz Peter, one of Glanvill's successors in the justiciarship, so as to invalidate a gift which William de Mandeville, Earl of Essex, had made on his death-bed to Walden Abbey. The ministers of the devil had of late years established a law which until then had never been heard of, to the effect that 'no one, even though he be one of the great, when he is confined to his bed by sickness, can bequeath by his last will any of the lands or tenements that he has possessed, or grant them to those men of religion whom he loves above all others[2].' We may well believe that there is some truth in this story, and that just at the time when Glanvill was writing and the last of the Mandeville earls was dying, the newly reformed king's court was for the first time setting its face sternly against the ancient post obit gift of land.

Condemnation of the post obit gift.

The reasons for this determination are not far to seek, for Glanvill was at pains to explain them at some length. In one place he says that only God can make an heir, not man[3]. This remark takes us back to the 'nullum testamentum' of Tacitus; but it is thrown out by the way, for of any institution of an

The law in Glanvill.

---

[1] Monast. iv. 608: 'Ipse vero...rerum omnium suarum fecit divisionem, praesente et adhortante atque concedente rege Henrico. Praecepit etiam suis omnibus, contestans fidem quam ei debebant, ut suum corpus ad abbatiam suam quam Colecestriae construxerat deferrent. Delegavit etiam cum suo corpore ad illum locum manerium Bryhtlyngeseie et centum libras denariorum, anulum etiam suum aureum......Praeterea cyphum suum......equum etiam suum et mulum; quae tamen omnia Gilebertus Abbas......regi Henrico remisit ut impetraret ab eo concessionem praedicti manerii; et beneficium regium in hoc impetratum est.' The source from which this story comes is not first-rate, but had a writer of a later time wished to forge a title for the house, he would have told some lie more probable than one which makes land pass by a last will. Whether Eudo had kinsfolk or no, seems uncertain; see Round, Geoffrey de Mandeville, p. 173.

[2] Monast. iv. 147: 'Novi igitur recentesque venerunt qui hanc inauditam a saeculo legem a ministris Zabuli noviter inventam statuere decreverunt. Ne aliquis quamvis magnus lecto prae infirmitate receptus in extrema voluntate quicquam de terris vel tenementis iam ante possessis alicui liceat legare, nec etiam viris religiosis prae aliis dilectis conferre.' Earl William died in 1189: had he lived a little longer, he also would have been justiciar along with Hugh de Puiset; see Round, Geoffrey de Mandeville, p. 243.

[3] Glanvill, vii. 1.

heir in the Roman sense there never had been any talk in [p. 326] England, unless some new ideas had of late flown hither from Bologna and threatened to convert the old post obit gift into a true testament[1]. But in another passage we have earnest argument. 'As a general rule, every one in his life-time may freely give away to whomsoever he pleases a reasonable part of his land. But hitherto this has not been allowed to any one who is at death's door, for there might be an immoderate dissipation of the inheritance if this were permitted to one who in the agony of approaching death has, as is not unfrequently the case, lost both his memory and his reason; and thus it may be presumed that one who when sick unto death has begun to do, what he never did while in sound health, namely, to distribute his land, is moved to this rather by his agony than by a deliberate mind. However, such a gift will hold good if made with the heir's consent and confirmed by him[2].'

Testamentary gifts abolished in the interest of the heir. And so the gift of land by a last will stood condemned; not because it infringes any feudal rule, for in this context Glanvill says no word of the lord's interests, but because it is a death-bed gift, wrung from a man in his agony. In the interest of honesty, in the interest of the lay state, a boundary must be maintained against ecclesiastical greed and the other-worldliness of dying men. And that famous text was by this time ringing in the ears of all lawyers—'Traditionibus et usucapionibus dominia rerum, non nudis pactis transferuntur[3].' Rejecting the laxer practices of an earlier time, rejecting the symbolic delivery of land by glove or rod or charter[4], they were demanding a real

---

[1] In a very vague sense there has sometimes been in the Norman time some talk about making an heir. Hist. Abingd. ii. 130 (temp. Hen. I.): a tenant of the abbey covenants that he will make no heir to his land and will endow no wife thereof, but that after his death he will demise it to the abbey. This seems a confession that he is but tenant for life. Cart. Whitby, ii. 680 (early twelfth century): Nigel de Albini writes to his brother William—I have instituted you heir of my honour and all my property, in order that you may confirm the restorations of lands that I have made to divers churches and to men whom I had disinherited.

[2] Glanvill, vii. 1: 'In extremis tamen agenti non est hoc cuiquam hactenus permissum.' The *hactenus*, which we translate as *hitherto*, seems to tell us that the doctrine is not as yet very firmly established, nor utterly beyond argument. On the other hand, it does not tell us that an old, strict rule against death-bed gifts is being now called in question for the first time. Glanvill is speaking of the practice of the king's court, and the king's court of his day was but just beginning to be an ordinary tribunal with definite doctrines.

[3] Cod. 2. 3. 20; Bracton, f. 38 b, 41.   [4] See above, p. 89.

[p. 327] delivery of a real seisin. They were all for publicity; their new instrument for eliciting the truth, the jury, would tell them only of public acts. And so the old post obit gift perished. It was a gift without a transfer of possession. Henceforth if a tenant in fee would become tenant for life, there must be feoffment and refeoffment, two distinct transactions, two real transfers of a real seisin. The justices were fighting, not so much against a Roman testament, as against the post obit gift. They had the heir's interest at heart, not the lord's. Even the lord's licence would not enable the tenant to disinherit his heir by a 'devise' or a post obit gift. And these justices owed the heir something. They were on the point of holding that he had no right in the land so long as his ancestor lived. In their bold, rapid way they made a compromise.

As a matter of fact, during the thirteenth century men not unfrequently professed to dispose of their lands by their last wills or by charters executed on their death-beds. It is a common story in monastic annals that so and so bequeathed (*legavit*) land to our church and that his heir confirmed the bequest[1]. The monks hurried off from the side of the dying man to take seisin of some piece of his land; they trusted, and not in vain, that they would be able to get a confirmation out of the heir; 'a father's curse' was a potent argument[2]. But as a matter of law no validity was ascribed to these legacies or imperfect gifts. What had happened, when analyzed by the lawyer, was either that the heir had made a feoffment, or that the monks having already taken seisin, he had released his right to them, and such a release would have been just as effectual if there had been no will in their favour, and if they had been—as in strictness of law they really were—mere interlopers. We have seen that for a short while in the middle of the thirteenth century it seemed very likely that a power to leave land by will would be introduced by that effective engine

Attempts to devise land.

---

[1] See *e.g.* Winchcomb Landboc, i. 156–9: Liana of Hatherley at her death bequeathed (*legavit*) all her land at Hatherley to our infirmary; her brother and heir granted and confirmed (*concessit et confirmavit*) what she had previously given (*dedit*).

[2] Damnatory clauses are occasionally found in charters of this age; *e.g.* Monasticon, v. 662, Bertram de Verdon: 'et prohibeo ex parte Dei et mea ne quis heredum meorum huic donationi meae contraire vel eam in aliquo perturbare praesumat.'

the *forma doni*.   The court hesitated for a while and then once [p. 328] more it hardened its heart: land was not, and even the *forma doni* could not make it, bequeathable[1].

Devisable burgages.

Already in Glanvill's day the burgage tenement was a recognised exception from the general rule.   We are told that the assize of mort d'ancestor will not lie for such a tenement because there is another assize which has been established for the profit of the realm[2].   These words apparently refer us to some ordinance of Henry II. which we have not yet recovered, but which may still be lurking in the archives of our boroughs. In the thirteenth century it was well-known law that under custom a burgage might be given by testament; but apparently the limits of this rule varied from town to town.   Bracton seems to have been at one time inclined to hold that the burgage could be given by will when, but only when, it was comparable to a chattel, having been purchased by the testator and therefore being an article of commerce.   However, while Bracton was writing the citizens of London and of Oxford came to the opinion that, even if the testator had inherited his burgage, he might bequeath it[3].   In course of time this doctrine prevailed in very many boroughs, and if we may judge from wills of the fourteenth century, the term 'borough' must in this context have borne its widest meaning.   We may believe, however, that in the past a line had been drawn between the purchased and the inherited tenement; it is just in the boroughs that we find what foreign lawyers know as the *retrait lignager*, the right of the expectant heir to redeem the family land that his ancestor has alienated[4].

Probate of burgage wills.

If, as Bracton thought, the burgage could be bequeathed because it was a '*quasi* chattel,' the inference might be drawn that such a bequest would fall, like other bequests, within the domain of the ecclesiastical courts.   This inference Bracton drew[5]; but the boroughs resisted it and at length succeeded in establishing the principle that the bishop had nothing to do

[1] See above, p. 26.

[2] Glanvill, xiii. 11.

[3] Bracton, f. 407 b, 409 b, 272 (a passage distorted by interpolation) ; Note Book, pl. 11.   See also the note to Britton, i. 174.

[4] See above in our section on The Boroughs.

[5] Bracton, f. 407 b, 409 b; Note Book, pl. 11 ; Plac. Abbrev. (19 Ed. I.) pp. 284–5; O. W. Holmes, L. Q. R. i. 165.

[p. 329] with the will, in so far as it was a gift of a burgage tenement[1]. In course of time some at least of the larger boroughs established registers of the wills that dealt with such tenements. The will had to be produced before the borough court and enrolled[2]; some towns were also requiring the enrolment of conveyances. Occasionally in the fourteenth century the burgher would execute two documents, a formal 'testament' dealing with his movables, and a less formal 'last will' which bestowed his tenements; but we see no more than a slight tendency to contrast these two terms[3]. It is before the borough court, not before the king's court, that the man must go who desires to claim a tenement that has been bequeathed to him but is being withheld. However, to meet his case writs are devised which enjoin the officers of the borough to do him justice; from their first words they are known as writs *Ex gravi querela*[4]; but they seem hardly to belong to the period which is now before us.

That the 'marriage,' the 'wardship' and the 'term of years,' are *quasi* chattels for testamentary purposes is a doctrine which seems to have grown up rapidly in the first half of the thirteenth century. We have already endeavoured to explain it by saying that these things are regarded as investments of money[5]. In this instance free play was given to the doctrine which likened them to movables; the legacy of a term of years, like the legacy of a horse or of ten pounds, was a matter for the spiritual tribunal, and it became settled law that the testator's 'chattels real' pass to his executors. The chattel real.

In the course of the twelfth century our primogenitary scheme for the descent of land was established in all its rigour. It then became absolutely impossible that one system of succession should serve both for land and for chattels. We have indeed argued before now that in all probability our old law had never known the unity of the Roman *hereditas*, but The church and the testament.

---

[1] Liber de Antiq. Legib. pp. 41, 106. Already in 1268 the London citizens asserted that the burgage will should be proved in the hustings, and the king took their side in a dispute with the representative of the bishop. See also Letters from Northern Registers, pp. 71–2.

[2] In London this goes back at least as far as 1258: Sharpe, Calendar of Hustings Wills.

[3] Sharpe, Calendar of Hustings Wills, pp. xxv, xxxi; Furnivall, Fifty English Wills, pp. 22, 24, 37, 43, 55, 68.

[4] Reg. Brev. Orig. f. 244 b.　　　　　[5] See above, p. 116.

may from the first have had one rule for land, another for [p. 330]
chattels, one for a man's armour, another for a woman's
trinkets.　But in the twelfth century, just when there seems
a chance that at the call of Roman law our lawyers will begin
to treat the inheritance as a single mass, they raise an insuperable barrier between land and chattels by giving all the
land to the eldest son.　Henceforward that good word *heir* has
a very definite and narrow meaning.　What is to become of the
chattels?　They do not pass to the heir; they are not inherited.　While the temporal law is hesitating, ecclesiastical
law steps in.

Progress of ecclesiastical claims.　For ages past the church had been asserting a right, which
was recognized by imperial constitutions, to supervise those
legacies that are devoted to pious uses.　The bishop, or, failing
him, the metropolitan, was bound to see that the legacy was
paid and properly applied, and might have to appoint the
persons who were to administer the funds that were thus
devoted to the service of God and works of mercy[1].　Among
the barbarians, where in the past there had been *nullum testamentum*, the pious gifts were apt to be the very essence of the
testament.　The testator was not dissatisfied with the law of
intestate succession, but he wished in his last hour to do some
good and to save his soul.　Thus the right and duty of looking
after the pious gifts tended to become a jurisdiction in all testamentary causes.　The last will as such was to be protected by
the anathema[2].

Jurisdiction over testaments.　We may believe that for some time after the Conqueror had
made his concession to the church, the clergy would have been
satisfied if testamentary causes had been regarded as 'mixed,'
that is, as causes which might come indifferently before the
lay or the spiritual tribunal.　Elsewhere they had to be
content with this.　Our Norman kings did not renounce any
such testamentary jurisdiction as was then existing.　The king
was prepared as of old to enforce the *cwiðe*.　Henry I. in his
coronation charter says[3]—'If any of my barons or men falls ill,
I concede the disposition that he makes of his fortune (*pecunia*);

---

[1] Cod. Iust. 1. 3. 45.

[2] On the whole of this subject see Selden's learned tract on the Original of
Ecclesiastical Jurisdiction of Testaments (Collected Works, ed. 1726, vol. iii.
p. 1665).

[3] Carta Hen. I. c. 7.

[p. 331] and if he meets a sudden death by arms or sickness and makes no disposition, his wife, children or liege men[1] may divide his fortune (*pecunia*) for the good of his soul, as they shall think best.' The king, and now in general terms, grants that his baron's *cwiðe* shall 'stand,' and in dealing with a case of intestacy says nothing of the bishop, though we notice that already the intestate's goods are no longer inherited; they are distributed for the good of the dead man's soul[2].

It is well worthy of remark that Henry II. and Becket, though they sought for causes of dispute, did not quarrel about the testament. Quietly the judges of the royal court, many of whom were bishops or archdeacons, allowed the testament to fall to the share of the ecclesiastical forum. They were arranging a *concordat*; the ablest among them were churchmen. About many matters, and those perhaps which seemed the most important, they showed themselves to be strong royalists; in particular they asserted, to the peril of their souls, that the church courts had nothing to do with the advowson. But as regards the testament, they were willing to make a compromise. The spiritual courts might take it as their own, provided always that there were to be no testamentary gifts of land. This concession might well seem wise. Under the influence of Roman law men were beginning to have new ideas about the testament; it was becoming a true testament, no mere post obit donation or death-bed distribution. The canonist, being also a Romanist, had a doctrine of testaments; the English law had nothing that deserved so grand a name.

Victory of the church courts.

The concession was gradually made. Glanvill knows an action begun by royal writ by which a legatee can demand the execution of a dead man's will. The sheriff is commanded to uphold, for example, the 'reasonable devise' which the dead man made to the Hospitallers, if they can prove that such a devise was made. However, if in this action the defendant denied that the testament was duly executed, or that it contained the legacy in question, then the plea went to the court Christian,
[p. 332] for a plea of testament belonged to the ecclesiastical judge.

The lay courts and the last will.

---

[1] *Aut legitimi homines.* Even if the original has *legitimi* not *ligii*, we seem to be justified in rendering the phrase by *liege men.*

[2] Also it is to be noted that the king makes no promise as to what will happen if a man, who has had fair warning of approaching death, refuses to make a will and so dies desperate.

For a short time therefore it seems as if the function of the spiritual forum would be merely that of certifying the royal court that the dead man made a valid will in such and such words, or that his supposed will was invalid in whole or in part. But this was only a transitional scheme. The writs to the sheriff bidding him uphold a testament or devise have dropped out of the chancery register at the beginning of Henry III.'s reign. Thenceforth the legatee's action for his legacy was an action in the court Christian and the will was sanctioned only by spiritual censures, though of course there was imprisonment in the background[1].

The will with executors.
Meanwhile the type of will that had begun to prevail in England was the will with executors. One of the earliest documents of this kind that have come down to us is the will of Henry II.[2]. It takes the form of a letter patent addressed to all his subjects on both sides of the sea. It announces that at Waltham in the year 1182 in the presence of ten witnesses (among whom we see Ranulf Glanvill) the king made, not indeed his testament, but his division or devise (*divisam suam*) of a certain part of his fortune. He gives sums of money to the Templars and Hospitallers, he gives 5000 marks to be divided among the religious houses of England 'by the hand and view' of six English bishops and Glanvill his justiciar; he gives 3000 marks to be divided among the religious houses of Normandy by the hand and view of the five Norman bishops, 1000 marks to be divided by the hand and view of the bishops of le Mans and Angers among the religious houses of Maine and Anjou; he gives other sums to be expended in providing marriages for poor free women in his various dominions; he charges his sons to observe this distribution; he invokes God's curse upon all who infringe it; he announces that the pope has confirmed this 'devise' and has sanctioned it with the anathema. We notice that this exceedingly solemn document, which no doubt was the very best that the English chancery could produce, did not call itself [p. 333]

---

[1] Glanvill, vii. 6, 7; xii. 17, 20. As to the Register, see Harv. L. R. iii. 168. Already the ancient Irish Register contains a writ prohibiting the ecclesiastical court from entertaining a plea of chattels, 'quae non sunt de testamento vel matrimonio': Ibid. 114. Such writs are common on early rolls of Henry III.; they imply that the legatee can go to the court Christian.

[2] Foedera, i. 47.

a testament, did not use the terms *do, lego,* did not even use the term *executor.* It contained no residuary gift, no single legacy that was not given to pious uses[1]. Still here indubitably we see executors, one set of executors for England, another for Normandy, another for Maine and Anjou; all of them, save Glanvill, are of episcopal rank. Then in Glanvill's book we find the *testamentum* and the *executor.* 'A testament should be made in the presence of two or three lawful men, clerks or laymen, who are such that they can be competent witnesses (*testes idonei*). The executors of the testament should be those whom the testator has chosen and charged with this business; but, if he has named no one, then his kinsmen and relations may assume the duty[2].'

Who is the executor and whence does he come? This is not a question that can be answered out of English documents, though, as already said, we may strongly suspect that, under some name or another (perhaps as *mund* of a *cwiðe*) he has been known in England for several centuries. That he does not come out of the classical Roman law is patent; it is only late in the day, and only perhaps in England and Scotland, that he begins to look at all like an instituted *heres*; yet under one name or another (*executor* gradually prevails) he has been known in many, if not all, parts of Western Europe, notably in France. There seems to be now but little doubt that we can pursue his history back to a time when, despite Roman influence, the transaction in which he takes a part is not in our eyes a testamentary act. The dying man made over some portion of his lands or goods to some friend who would carry out his last wishes. The gift took effect at once and was accompanied by what was at first in fact, afterwards in theory, a delivery of possession. The church developed this rude institution. It compelled the trustee, who very often was of the clergy, to perform the trust, which almost always was a trust for the religious or the poor. Then under the influence of renascent Roman law the 'last division' or 'devise' began to bear a testamentary character. The devise might be made [p. 334] by one who hoped that he had many years to live (in 1182

Origin of the executor

---

[1] Abp Theobald appoints four executors, though he does not call them by this name; they are to divide his goods among the poor according to instructions that they have received: Jo. Sarisb. epist. 57 (ed. Giles, i. 60).

[2] Glanvill, vii. 6.

Henry II. was going abroad, but he did not mean to die); it was revocable, it was ambulatory; there was no longer, even in fiction, a present transfer of possession. But the executor kept a place in the scheme; he was very useful; he was the church's lever[1].

The executor in England and elsewhere.

On the mainland and in the common law of the cosmopolitan church, as testamentary freedom grows, the executor's main duty becomes that of compelling the *heres* or *heredes* to pay the legacies. The testator's *persona* will be represented by the heir. This representation will become more and more complete as Roman law has its way, and old differences between the destiny of lands and the destiny of goods disappear. But the executor is an useful person who may intervene between the heir and the legatees; he is bound to see that the legacies are paid. If the heir is negligent, the executor steps in, collects the debts and so forth. Some canonists hold that he can sue the testator's debtors. While the heir has an *actio directa*, they will concede to the executor an *actio utilis*. He is a favourite with them; he is their instrument, for a *heres* is but too plainly the creature of temporal law, and the church can not claim as her own the whole province of inheritance[2]. But here in England a somewhat different division of labour was made in the course of time; the executor had nothing to do with the dead man's land, the heir had nothing to do with the chattels, and gradually the executor became the 'personal representative' of the testator. The whole of the testator's fortune passed to his executor, except the freeholds, and, for the purpose of a general theory of representation, this exception ceased to be of any cardinal importance as time went on, since the ordinary creditors of the dead man would have no claim against his freeholds. Finally, [p. 335]

---

[1] Holmes, L. Q. R. i. 164; Palumbo, Testamento Romano e Testamento Langobardo, ch. x.; Heusler, Institutionen, ii. 652; Le Fort, Les exécuteurs testamentaires, Geneva, 1878; Pertile, Storia del Diritto Italiano, iv. 31. There seems no doubt that the testamentary executor is in origin a Germanic *Salmann*. The term *executores* slowly prevails over many rivals such as *gardiatores, erogatores, testamentarii, procuratores, dispensatores,* and so forth. Simon de Montfort appointed, not an executor, but an attorney.

[2] As to the position of the continental executor in the thirteenth century, see Durantis, Speculum, Lib. ii. Partic. ii. § 13 (ed. Basiliae, 1624, vol. i. p. 690). He keeps a place in some of the modern codes; but it is never that prominent place which English law awards him.

at the end of the middle ages the civilian in his converse with
the English lawyer will say that the *heres* of Roman law is
called in England the executor[1].

Postponing for a while the few words that must be said The medieval will.
about this process, we may look at the medieval will and may
regret that but too few specimens of the wills made in the
thirteenth century have been published; from the fourteenth
we have an ampler supply[2]. It is plain that the church
has succeeded in reducing the testamentary formalities to a
minimum. This has happened all the world over. The dread
of intestacy induces us to hear a nuncupative testament in a
few hardly audible words uttered in the last agony, to see a
testament in the feeble gesture which responds to the skilful
question of the confessor, and that happy text about 'two
or three witnesses' enables us to neglect the Institutes of
Justinian[3]. At the other end of the scale we see the solemn
notarial instrument which contains the last will of some rich
and provident prelate or magnate who desires the utmost
'authenticity' for a document which will perhaps be produced
in foreign courts[4]. Between these poles lies the common form,
the written will sealed by the testator in the presence of several
witnesses[5].

In the thirteenth century it is usually in Latin; but Simon Its phrases.
de Montfort made his will in French—it is in the handwriting
of his son Henry[6]. French wills became commoner and in the
second half of the fourteenth century English wills begin to
appear[7]. If in Latin, the document usually calls itself a

---

[1] Doctor and Student (ed. 1668), i. c. 19 : 'the heir which in the Laws of
England is called an executor.'

[2] Testamenta Eboracensia (Surtees Soc.); Durham Wills (Surtees Soc.);
Sharpe, Calendar of London Wills ; Furnivall, Fifty English Wills. An effort
should be made to collect the wills of the thirteenth century. A cautious use
will here be made of the wills of a somewhat later age.

[3] Test. Ebor. i. 21: a knight before going to the war makes a nuncupative
will in church (1346). Peckham's Register, i. 256 ; Test. Ebor. i. 74. But the
nuncupative will was not very common in the fourteenth century.

[4] Test. Ebor. i. 13, 24, 31, 235 (John of Gaunt).

[5] The general rule of the canon law seems to have been that a will could be
sufficiently attested by the parish priest and two other witnesses, but that two
witnesses without the parish priest would suffice if the testator was leaving his
goods to pious uses. See c. 10. 11. X. 3. 26; Durantis, Speculum (ed. 1624),
p. 679.

[6] Bémont, Simon de Montfort, 328.

[7] Test. Ebor. i. 185 (1383) ; Furnivall, Fifty English Wills.

testament—*Ego A. B. condo testamentum meum* is a common [p. 336] phrase—in French or English it will call itself a testament or a devise or a last will; one may still occasionally speak of it as a 'book[1],' or a 'wytword[2].' Sometimes we see side by side the Latin testament which constitutes executors, and a last will which in the vulgar tongue disposes of burgage tenements; but no strict usage distinguishes between these terms. Sometimes a testator is made by his legal adviser to express a wish that if his testament can not take effect as a testament, it may be deemed a codicil; but this is a trait of unusual and unpractical erudition. Of course there is no institution of an heir and there is no disheriting clause. In Latin 'do, lego' are the proper words of gift; in French 'jeo devis'; in English 'I bequeath,' or 'I wyte.' The modern convention which sets apart 'devise' for 'realty' and 'bequeath' for 'personalty' is modern; in the middle ages the English word, which takes us back to the old *cwiðe*, is the equivalent of the French word.

Its sub-stance. Though damnatory or minatory clauses are now less common than they were, the will is still a religious instrument made in the name of the Father, Son and Holy Ghost. The testator's first thought is not of the transmission of an *hereditas*, but of the future welfare of his immortal soul and his mortal body. His soul he bequeaths to God, the Virgin and the saints; his body to a certain church. Along with his body he gives his mortuary, or his 'principal' (*principale*), or corspresent[3]; one of the best chattels that he has; often, if he is a knight, it will be his war-horse[4]. Both Glanvill and Bracton have protested that neither heriot nor corspresent is demanded by general law, though custom may exact it[5]. Elaborate instructions will sometimes be given for the burial; about the tapers that are to burn around the bier, and the funeral feast. For a while testators desire splendid ceremonies; later on they begin to set their faces against idle pomp. Then will come the pecuniary and specific legacies. Many will be given to pious uses; the four orders of friars are rarely forgotten by a well-to-do testator; a bequest for the repair of bridges is

---

[1] Furnivall, p. 27. [2] Test. Ebor. i. 186.

[3] Test. Ebor. i. 185.

[4] Test. Ebor. i. 264: 'pro mortuario suo meliorem equum suum cum armatura secundum consuetudinem patriae.'

[5] Glanvill, vii. 5; Bracton, f. 60.

[p. 337] deemed a pious and laudable bequest; rarely are villeins freed[1], but sometimes their arrears of rent are forgiven or their chattels are restored to them[2]. The medieval will is characterized by the large number of its specific bequests. The horses are given away one by one; so are the jewels; so are the beds and quilts, the pots and pans. The civilian or canonist names his precious books[3]; the treasured manuscript of the statutes, or of Bracton, or of Britton[4], the French romance, the English poem[5] is handed on to one who will love it. Attempts are even made to 'settle' specific chattels[6]; the Corpus Iuris finds itself entailed or subjected to a series of fidei-commissary substitutions[7]. On the other hand, the testator has no 'stocks, funds and securities' to dispose of; he says nothing, or very little, of the debts that are owed to him, while of the debts that he owes he says nothing or merely desires that they be paid.

Pro salute animae. The earliest wills rarely contain residuary or universal gifts[8]. In part this may be due to the fact that the testator has exhausted his whole estate by the specific and pecuniary legacies. But often he seems to be trusting that whatever he has not given away will be used by his executors for the good of his soul. When he does make a residuary gift, he frequently makes it in favour of his executors and bids them expend it for his benefit. This we must remember when we speak of the treatment of intestates. As time goes on we find

---

[1] Test. Ebor. i. 245: 'item lego W. B. pro suo bono servicio 13s. 4d. et facio eum liberum ab omni bondagio seu servicio bondagii' (1401). Such a devise would seldom be binding on the heir.

[2] Ibid. 350: 'item volo quod bona, sive catalla, aliquorum nativorum meorum, quos (sic) recepi in custodiam post decessionem eorundem, in commodum filiorum suorum nondum soluta, solvantur eisdem filiis sine aliqua diminucione' (1407).

[3] Ibid. 69, 168, 364–371.

[4] Ibid. 12: 'librum de statutis et omnes alios meos libros de lege terrae' (1345). Ibid. 101–2: Thomas Farnylaw, chancellor of York, leaves to Merton College 'Brakton de iuribus Angliae' (1378). Ibid. 209: 'unum Britonem' (1396); but this *Brito* may be the grammarian.

[5] Ibid. 209: 'unum librum vocatum Pers plewman' (1396).

[6] Ibid. 251: a bed given to testator's son and the heirs of his body; when they fail it is to be sold.

[7] Ibid. 168: the book is never to be alienated so long as any of the testator's issue desire to study law (1393).

[8] See the earliest specimens in Madox, Formulare. Some of the oldest precedents for wills have no residuary gifts; L. Q. R. vii. 66.

many wills which bestow the greater part of the dead man's [p. 338] fortune upon his wife and children; the wife in particular is well provided for; but the earlier the will, the more prominent is the testator's other-worldliness. His wife and children, as we shall hereafter see, have portions secured to them by law; what remains is, to use an expressive term, 'the dead's part'; it still belongs to the dead, who may be in sore need of those pardons for past wrongs and those prayers for repose which can be secured by a judicious expenditure of money.

Some usual clauses.

We see a trace of a past history when the executors are also the witnesses of the will and set their seals to it in the testator's presence[1]. Also we observe that a will is usually proved within a few days after its execution. Very often a man makes no will until he feels that death is near. A common form tells us that he is 'sick in body' though 'whole in mind.' The old connexion between the last will and the last confession has not been severed. But by this time the will is revocable and ambulatory, and occasionally a man will provide for some of the various chances that may happen between the act of testation and the hour of death. Codicils are uncommon, but at the beginning of the fifteenth century a bishop of Durham made nine[2]. It is not unknown that a man will appoint his wife to be his sole executor. Simon de Montfort does this; his wife is to be his attorney, and, if she dies before his will is performed, his son is to take her place[3]. Usually there are several, sometimes many, executors; John of Gaunt appointed seventeen[4]. Not unfrequently the testator, besides appointing executors, names certain 'supervisors' or 'coadjutors'; sometimes they will be learned or powerful friends; they are requested to aid and advise the executors. The bishop of Lincoln and Friar Adam Marsh are to give their counsel to Earl Simon's widow[5]. Now and again the executors are relieved from the duty of rendering accounts[6]. Elaborate clauses are rare; the funeral ceremonies are more carefully prescribed than is any other matter; but skilled forethought is sometimes shown by a direction for the 'defalcation' or abatement of legacies if the estate be insufficient to pay them

---

[1] L. Q. R. vii. 66.　　　　　　　　　　[2] Test. Ebor. i. 306.
[3] Bémont, Simon de Montfort, 328.　　[4] Test. Ebor. i. 234.
[5] Bémont, l. c.　　　　　　　　　　　　[6] Test. Ebor. i. 95, 126, 178.

[p. 339] in full, and by provisions as to 'lapsed' legacies[1]. A well-to-do gentleman may often have a town house to leave by his will. Before the end of the fourteenth century he will have land held for him by 'feoffees to uses,' and a new period in the history of English land law will be opening[2].

Among the common lawyers of a later day it was a pious *Probate.* opinion that in some indefinitely remote age wills were proved in the lay courts[3]. Now, as already said, it seems probable that not until the age of Glanvill did the courts Christian succeed in establishing an exclusive right to pronounce on the validity of the will, and (as the canonists of a later time had to admit) this right as an exclusive right was not given to them by any of those broad principles of ecclesiastical law for which a catholic validity could be claimed[4]. On the other hand, we may well doubt whether any such procedure as that which we call the probate of a will was known in England before the time when the jurisdiction over testaments had been conceded to the church. We have here two distinct things: (i) competence to decide whether a will is valid, whenever litigants raise that question; (ii) a procedure, often a non-contentious procedure, for establishing once and for all the validity of a will, which is implicated with a procedure for protecting the dead man's estate and compelling his executors to do their duty. The early history of probate lies outside England, and it is not for us to say whether some slender thread of texts traversing the dark ages connects it directly with the Roman process of insinuation, aperture and publication. In England we do not see it until the thirteenth century has dawned, and by that time testamentary jurisdiction belongs, and belongs exclusively, to the spiritual courts[5]. In much later days it has been known that the lord of a manor will assert that the wills of his tenants can be proved in his court; but in these cases we

---

[1] Test. Ebor. i. 170 'abatement'; 171 'lapse'; 312, the opinion of a majority of the executors is to prevail.

[2] Ibid. 115 : William Lord Latimer in 1381 devises land held by feoffees.

[3] Fitz. Abr. *Testament*, pl. 4; Y. B. 11 Hen. VII. f. 12; *Hensloe's Case*, 9 Coke's Rep. 37 b; and (*e.g.*) *Marriot* v. *Marriot*, 1 Strange, 666.

[4] Selden, *op. cit.* p. 1672. Lyndwood knew of no authoritative act that gave the right. Selden surmises that it was granted 'by parliament' in John's time. We gravely doubt whether such a grant was ever made.

[5] Selden, *op. cit.* p. 1671: 'I could never see an express probate in any particular case elder than about Henry III.'

ought to demand some proof that the manors in question have never been in the hands of any of those religious orders which [p. 340] enjoyed peculiar privileges. Pope Alexander IV. bestowed on the Cistercians in England the right to grant probate of the wills of their tenants and farmers, and thus exempted their manors from the 'ordinary' jurisdiction[1]. Therefore what at first sight looks like a relic of a lay jurisdiction may easily turn out to be the outcome of papal power.

Preroga-
tive
probate. To this we may add that, even at the end of the thirteenth century, some elementary questions in the law of probate were as yet unanswered. Granted that the bishop in whose diocese the goods of the dead man lie is normally the judge who should grant probate of his will,—what of the case in which the dead man has goods in divers dioceses? Does this case fall within the cognizance of the archbishop? And what if that archbishop be no mere metropolitan, but a primate with legatine powers? About this matter there were constant disputes between the archbishop of Canterbury and his suffragans. We sometimes speak of the feudal pyramid of lords and vassals as a 'hierarchy'; it is equally true that the ecclesiastical hierarchy is a seignorial pyramid. The question whether the overlord has any direct power over the vassals of his vassals has its counterpart in the question whether the metropolitan has any direct power over the 'subjects' of his suffragans, and as the king has often to insist that he is no mere overlord but a crowned and anointed king, so the archbishop of Canterbury has often to insist that he is no mere metropolitan but primate and legate. Archbishop Peckham asserted, and excommunicated a bishop of Hereford for denying, that the testamentary jurisdiction of Canterbury extended to all cases in which the dead man had goods in more than one of the dioceses of the province[2]. The compromise which compelled an executor to seek a 'prerogative' probate in the archbishop's court only if the testator had goods worth more than five pounds in each of two dioceses, is not very ancient[3].

Control
over
executors. In the thirteenth century it was settled law that the executors, unless they were going to renounce the duties which the testator had endeavoured to cast upon them, ought to

---

[1] Chron. de Melsa, ii. 121–2. [2] Peckham's Register, i. 335, 382; ii. 566.
[3] Lyndwood, p. 174, de testam. c. *statutum bonae*, gl. ad v. *laicis*, is very uncertain as to the minimum of *bona notabilia*.

prove his will in the proper court.　That court was the court
[p. 341] of the judge ordinary, who was in the normal case the bishop of
the diocese.　Having established the will, they swore that they
would duly administer the estate of the dead man and they
became bound to exhibit an inventory of his goods and to
account for their dealings.　Before the beginning of Edward I.'s
reign the ecclesiastical court seems to have evolved a regular
procedure for the control of executors.　If they were guilty
of negligence or misconduct, the ordinary could set them aside
and commit the administration of the estate to others[1].　On
the other hand, if an executor was acting properly, the ordinary
could not set him aside.　Archbishop Peckham apologized to
that great common lawyer Ralph Hengham, who was executor of
the bishop of Ely :—'I understood that you had renounced the
executorship; if that was a mistake, I pray you to resume your
duties, for there is no one in England who will make a better
executor than you[2].'　In a mandate which has a curiously
modern look the same archbishop orders that advertisements
shall be issued calling on all the creditors of the late bishop
of Exeter to appear within a certain period, about six weeks,
and telling them that if they do not send in their claims within
that time, they will have to show a reasonable cause for their
delay or go unpaid[3].

It is a long time before the executor becomes a prominent
figure in the lay courts.　There is little to be read of him in
Bracton's treatise or in the great collection of cases upon which
that treatise is founded.　Still it was the action of the lay
courts which in the end made him the 'personal representative'
of the testator.　The question—'What debts owed by, or to,
the testator continue to be due after his death and who can sue
or be sued in respect of them?' became (though there was some
quarrelling over this matter) a question for the temporal, not
for the ecclesiastical, forum.　In approaching it we have to
remember that for a long time such debts were few.　Pecuniary
claims which have their origin in damage done by or to the
testator would not be available after his death.　It is very
probable that claims which we should consider to be of a purely
contractual nature were only available against the dead man's
successor if the dead man had expressly bound his successor to
pay them, and were only available for the dead man's successor

The executor in temporal courts.

---

[1] Peckham's Register, i. 110.　　[2] Ibid. ii. 655.　　[3] Ibid. i. 305.

if the debtor had bound himself to pay to the successor in case the creditor died while the debt was still outstanding. In the [p. 342] foregoing sentence we have used the vague word *successor* so as to leave open the question whether that successor would be the heir or the executor. But clearly in the past it had been for the heir to pay and to receive debts. Probably our law, as it gradually felt the need of some successor who would sue and be sued in the dead man's stead, was on the point of deciding for good and all that this successor was to be found in the dead man's heir or heirs, when the formulation and extension of its primogenitary system of inheritance and the concession to the church of an exclusive jurisdiction over the testament arrested the process which would have given to inheritance the character of an universal succession. For a while all was uncertain. Clearly if the heir is to have no benefit out of the dead man's chattels, he can not long remain the person, or the one person, bound to pay his ancestor's debts, nor will it be his place to sue for money due to his ancestor, for this money should form part of the wealth that is governed by the testament. And yet it is not easy to deny that the heir is the natural representative of the dead man. Whatever influence Roman law could exercise tended to make him a full and complete representative of his ancestor, and the catholic canon law had not attempted to put the executor in the heir's place. English law therefore had to solve without assistance from abroad the difficult problem that it had raised.

Executor and heir in Glanvill. In Glanvill's book it is the heir who must pay the dead man's debts. A man, he says, who is burdened with debts can not dispose of his property (except by devoting it to the payment of debts) unless this be with the consent of his heir, and, if his property is insufficient for the payment of his debts, then the heir is bound to make good the deficiency out of his own property[1]. The scheme that for the moment is prevailing or likely to prevail is this:—the heir takes possession of lands [p. 343]

---

[1] Glanvill, vii. 8: ' Si vero fuerit debitis oneratus is qui testamentum facere proponit, nihil de rebus suis (extra debitorum acquietationem) praeter sui heredis consensum disponere potest. Verum si post debitorum acquietationem aliquid residuum fuerit, tunc id quidem in tres partes dividetur modo praedicto, et de tertia parte suum, ut dictum est, faciat testamentum. Si vero non sufficiunt res defuncti ad debita persolvenda, tunc quidem heres ipse defectum ipsum de suo tenetur adimplere: ita dico si habuerit etatem heres ipse.' Dialog. de Scac. ii. 18: 'legitimus heres pro debito patris conveniendus est.'

and chattels; he pays the debts, using the chattels as the first fund for this purpose; if they are not exhausted in the process, he makes over the residue to the executors; if all the chattels are swallowed up by debts and there are debts still due, the heir must pay them, and his liability is not limited by the value of the inheritance that has descended to him. This last trait should not surprise us. If ancient law finds great difficulty in holding that one man is bound to pay the debt incurred by another, it finds an equal difficulty in setting any bounds to such a liability when it exists.

According to Bracton it is the heir, not the executor, whom the creditor ought to sue[1]. By this time the heir's legal liability is limited to the amount of the dead man's property; but even in Bracton's eyes his moral liability is unlimited[2]. No doubt the dead man's chattels are the primary fund for the payment of debts. The Great Charter has striven to restrain the king's high-handed power of seizing the lands of his living and dead creditors; even the prerogative processes of the exchequer should spare the land while chattels can be found[3]. Still it is the heir's duty to pay debts; when debts have been paid, then the executor will claim and distribute the remaining chattels. And so in actual practice we see the heir sued for debts which are in no way connected with land; he sometimes seems to be sued even when there is no written covenant that expressly binds him to pay[4]. But from time to time we hear it doubted whether the creditor can not attack the executor. The opinion gains ground that he may do so, if, but only if, the testator has enjoined his executor to pay the debt. In such

Executor and heir in Bracton.

[1] Bracton, f. 407 b: 'Et sicut dantur [actiones] heredibus contra debitores et non executoribus, ita dantur actiones creditoribus contra heredes et non contra executores.'

[2] Bracton, f. 61: 'inhumanum esset si debita parentum insoluta remanerent.' See O. W. Holmes, Executors, Harv. L. R. ix. 42. Mr Justice Holmes is probably right in holding that when it had been decided that the dead man's chattels pass to his executor, the law conceived that the property in those goods was simply in the executor. His liability to the dead man's creditors may be limited by the value of those goods, but the goods are his. In other words, the law did not distinguish what he held as executor from what he held in his own right.

[3] Charter, 1215, cc. 9, 26.

[4] Note Book, pl. 1543: Debt against the heir of a surety (*plegius*); no written instrument mentioned. Ibid. pl. 1693: Debt against the heir for cloth sold to the ancestor; no written instrument or tally; suit tendered; the suitors know nothing of the matter and the action is dismissed.

a case the debt can be regarded as a legacy bequeathed to the creditor; the creditor can sue for it in the ecclesiastical court, and the king's justices should not prevent him from going there; [p. 344 his action may fairly be called a testamentary cause[1]. But the jealousy of the justices was aroused, and it was becoming plain that, if the creditor is to sue the executor at all, he must have an action in the temporal court.

The collection of debts.

Turning from the passive to the active side of representation, we find that in Bracton's day it is the heir, not the executor, who sues for the debts that were due to the dead man. There is here a difficulty to be surmounted. A man can not assign or give to another a mere right of action; how then can he bequeath a right of action, and, unless he can bequeath it, how can it pass to his executor? 'Actions,' says Bracton, 'can not be bequeathed[2].' But both theory and practice were beginning to allow that if the testator had recovered judgment against the debtor in his lifetime, or if (for this was really the same thing) the debtor had by way of recognizance confessed the debt in court—we see here one of the reasons why recognizances became fashionable—then the debt could be bequeathed. It was no longer a mere action; it already formed part of the creditor's property, of his goods and chattels[3]. The courts were yielding to the pressure of necessity. For one thing, it is a roundabout scheme that would compel the heir to collect money in order that he might pay it to an executor who would divide it among the legatees. For another thing, if the secular courts will not give the executor an action against debtors, the ecclesiastical courts will do this and will have plausible reasons for doing it. In the early years of Edward I. it was still very doubtful whether they would not succeed in their endeavour. The clergy complained that the spiritual tribunals were prevented from entertaining the executor's suit against

---

[1] Note Book, pl. 162: Writ of prohibition obtained by executors who have been sued by a creditor in the court Christian; the creditor pleads that the testament bade the executors pay this debt; the executors reply that this is not true and prove their assertion by producing the testament; the prohibition is upheld and the creditor is amerced. The annotator (see Bracton, f. 407 b) thinks that the decision would have been otherwise if the testator had mentioned this debt in his will or if judgment had been obtained against him in his lifetime.

[2] Bracton, f. 407 b.

[3] Bracton, f. 407 b: 'quia huiusmodi pecunia inter bona testatoris connumeratur et pertinet ad executores.' Note Book, pl. 550, 810.

the debtor, even when the debt was required for the payment
[p. 345] of legacies. The king's advisers replied that this matter was
not yet finally decided; they remarked however that the
executor should be in no better position than that which his
testator had occupied, and hinted that the task of proving a
debt before ecclesiastical judges was all too easy[1].

A change as momentous as any that a statute could make *The
executor as*
was made without statute and very quietly. Early in Edward I.'s *'personal*
reign the chancery had framed and the king's court had upheld *representative.'*
a writ of debt for executors and a writ of debt against executors[2].
In the Year Books of that reign the executor is coming to the
front, though many an elementary question about his powers
is still open. Much remains to be done. Our English lawyers
are not starting with the general proposition that the executor
represents the testator and thence deducing now one consequence and now another; rather they are being driven towards
this general proposition by the stress of particular cases. In
Edward's reign the executor had the action of debt; a statute
gave him the action of account[3]; but a statute of 1330 was
required in order that he might have an action of trespass
against one who in the testator's lifetime carried off the
testator's goods[4]. And so as regards the passive side of the
representation:—before the end of the thirteenth century the
executor could be sued by a creditor of the testator who had
sealed writing to show for the debt; and the heir could only be
sued when there was a sealed writing which expressly purported
to bind him; but every bond or covenant did, as a matter of
fact, unless it were very badly drawn, purport to bind the heir,
and very often an action against the heir would be more

---

[1] Raine, Letters from Northern Registers, p. 71: undated Articuli Cleri; it
is feared by the laity that in the court Christian a debt can be proved 'per
duos testes minus idoneos,' whereas in a temporal court a defendant can wage
his law.

[2] Debt by executors: Y. B. 20–1 Edw. I. 375; 21–2 Edw. I. 258, 598;
33–5 Edw. I. 62, 294. Debt against executors: 30–1 Edw. I. 238. Fleta, p. 126,
who seems to be troubled by Bracton's text, ends his discussion with this
sentence:—'*permissum* est tamen quod executores agant ad solutionem in foro
saeculari *aliquando.*'

[3] Stat. West. II. c. 23. A Register of Writs from the early years of
Edward I. tells us that the heir can not have a writ of account, that some say
that the executor can have it, but more properly the suit, being testamentary,
belongs to the court Christian. See Harv. L. R. iii. 214.

[4] Stat. 4 Edw. III. c. 5.

profitable than an action against the executor. It is not until
the fifteenth century discovers a new action which will enforce [p. 346]
contractual claims, the action of *assumpsit,* that the executor
begins to represent the testator in a more general sense than
that in which the heir represents him. Until our own time the
executor has nothing to do with the testator's freehold. Even
when statutes enable the tenant in fee simple to give his land
by will, the executor will have nothing to do with the land,
which will pass straight from testator to devisee as it passes
straight from ancestor to heir. Still in the early years of
Edward I. the king's justices had taken the great step; they
had thrown open the doors of their court to the executor. He
could there sue the debtors, he could there be sued by the
creditors. Such suits were not 'testamentary causes.' As of
old, it was for the spiritual judge to pronounce for or against
a will, and the legatee who wanted his legacy went to the
ecclesiastical court; but the relation between the executors on
the one hand and the debtors or creditors on the other had
become a matter for the temporal lawyers, and every change in
the law which extended the number of pecuniary claims that
were not extinguished by death made the executor more and
more completely the representative of the testator.

Restraints
on testa-
mentary
power.

We have been speaking as though a man might by his will
dispose of all his chattels. But in all probability it was only
the man who left neither wife nor child who could do this.
We have every reason to believe that the general law of the
thirteenth century sanctioned some such scheme as that which
obtained in the province of York until the year 1692 and which
obtains in Scotland at this present time. If a testator leaves
neither wife nor child, he can give away the whole of his
movable goods. If he leaves wife but no child, or child but
no wife, his goods must, after his debts have been paid, be
divided into two halves; one of these can be disposed of by his
will, it is 'the dead's part,' the other belongs to the widow, or
(as the case may be) to the child or children. If he leaves both
wife and child, then the division is tripartite; the wife takes a
share, the child or children a share, while the remaining third
is governed by the will; we have 'wife's part,' 'bairns' part,'
and 'dead's part.' Among themselves children take equal
shares; the son is not preferred to the daughter; but the heir
gets no share unless he will collate the inheritance that has

[p. 347] descended to him, and every child who has been 'advanced' by the testator must bring back the advancement into hotchpot before claiming a bairn's right.

In the seventeenth century this scheme prevailed through-out the northern province; a similar scheme prevailed in the city of London and, it may be, in some other towns; but by this time the general rule throughout the province of Canterbury denied to the wife and children any 'legitimate part' or 'legitim' and allowed the testator to dispose of his whole fortune.

History of legitim.

Now it is fairly certain that in the twelfth and thirteenth centuries some such scheme as that which we have here described was in force all England over. How much further back we can carry it is very doubtful. It at once brings to our mind Bede's story of the Northumbrian who rose from the dead and divided his property into three shares, reserving one for himself, while one was made over to his wife and another to his children. But four dark centuries divide Bede from Glanvill. No Anglo-Saxon testator whose *cwiðe* has come down to us takes any notice of the restrictions which this scheme would impose upon him were it in force; but he does not always endeavour to dispose of his whole fortune, and the earnestness with which he prays that his will may stand seems to show that he is relying on privilege rather than on common law. The substantial agreement between the law of Scotland and the custom of the province of York goes to prove that this plan of dealing with the dead man's goods has very ancient roots, while we have seen no proof that it ever prevailed in Normandy[1]. It is intimately connected, as we shall see in another chapter, with a law of husband and wife which is apt to issue in the doctrine that husband and wife have their goods in common. All Europe over, the new power of testation had to come to terms with the ancient rights of the wife, the children and the other kinsfolk. The compromises were many and intricate and one of these compromises is the scheme that is now before us. We must remember that the great solvent of ancient rules, Roman law, even in the shape that it wore in the Institutes, did not claim for the testator that unlimited

Legitim in cent. xii. xiii.

---

[1] However, Dr Brunner, Zeitschrift der Savigny-Stiftung, Germ. Abt. xvii. 134, thinks that it came to us from Normandy.

power of doing what he likes with his own which Englishmen
have now enjoyed for several centuries.

Our first definite tidings come from Glanvill. 'If a man in
his infirmity desires to make a testament, then, if he is not
burdened with debts, all his movables are to be divided into [p. 348]
three shares, whereof one belongs to his heir, another to his
wife, while a third is reserved to himself, and over this he has
free power; but if he dies without leaving a wife, then one-half
is reserved for him[1].' We notice that one share is reserved,
not to the children, but to the heir. This we take to be a relic
of the law as it stood before primogeniture had assumed its
acute English form. If for a while the king's court endeavoured
to secure for the heir not only all the land but also a third of
the chattels, it must have soon abandoned the attempt. The
charter of 1215 recognized that the wife and children could
claim shares in the dead man's goods. It does this incidentally; it is dealing with the king's power of exacting a debt
due from a dead tenant in chief:—'If nothing be due to us,
then all the chattels fall to the dead man, saving to his wife
and children (*pueris*) their reasonable shares[2].' This clause
appears in all the later versions of the charter[3].

Bracton speaks at some length:—When the debts have
been paid, the residue is to be divided into three parts, whereof
one is to be left to the children (*pueris*), another to the wife if
she be living, while over the third the testator has free power.
If he has no children (*liberos*) then a half is reserved for the
dead, a half for the wife. If he leaves children but no wife,
then half for the dead, half for the children. If there are neither
wife nor children, the whole will remain to the dead. These,
says Bracton, are the general rules which hold good unless
overridden by the custom of some city, borough or town. He
then tells us that in London the widow will get no more than
her dower, while the children are dependent on their father's
bounty. And this, he argues, ought to be so in a city, for
a citizen will hardly amass wealth if he is bound to leave it
to an ill-deserving wife or to idle and uninstructed children[4].
Curiously enough, however, it was just among the citizens of

---

[1] Glanvill, vii. 5.   [2] Charter, 1215, c. 26.   [3] Bémont, Chartes, p. 53.
[4] Bracton, f. 60 b, 61.   Fleta, pp. 124–5, copies.   It is fairly certain that by
pueri both the charter and Bracton mean, not sons, but children.   See above,
p. 267 note 3.

London that the old rules took deep root. They prevailed there until long after they had ceased to be the general law [p. 349] of the southern province; they prevailed there until 1724, a standing caution to all who would write history *a priori*[1].

As to the law of the thirteenth century there can therefore be little doubt, though some of its details may be obscure. A few words however must be said of its subsequent fate.

A meagre stream of cases running through the Year Books enables us to say that throughout the fourteenth and fifteenth centuries actions were occasionally brought by the widow and by the children claiming their legitim, their reasonable part of goods, against the executors of the dead man. We can see also that throughout this period the origin of their right was a disputed matter. Some held that the action was given by the Great Charter, and that the writ should make mention of its statutory origin. Others held that, as the Charter mentioned this right but incidentally and by exceptive words, the action could not be statutory:—'an exception out of a statute is no statute[2].' Sometimes the writ rehearsed a 'common custom of the realm.' To this exception was taken on the ground that a common custom of the realm must be common law, and that matter of law should not be stated in such a way as to invite the plea 'No such custom.' Often the writ spoke of the custom of a county or of a vill; but at times there were those who denied that such a custom would be good. In 1366 it is said that the lords in parliament will not allow that this action can be maintained by any common custom or law of this realm[3]. At the end of the period we find Fitzherbert opining that the legitim was given by the common law of the realm; but the writs on which he comments refer to the customs of particular counties[4].

Later history of legitim.

---

[1] Stat. 11 Geo. I. c. 18. sec. 17: 'And to the intent that persons of wealth and ability, who exercise the business of merchandize, and other laudable employments within the said city, may not be discouraged from becoming members of the same, by reason of the custom restraining the citizens and freemen thereof from disposing of their personal estates by their last wills and testaments.......'

[2] Reg. Brev. Orig. 142 b.　　　　[3] Y. B. 40 Edw. III. f. 38 (Mich. pl. 12).

[4] The main authorities are Fitz. Abr. *Detinue*, pl. 60 (34 Edw. I. *not* Edw. II. as is plain from the judges' names), 'usage del pais'; Y.B. 1 Edw. II. f. 9, 'usage de pais'; Y. B. 7 Edw. II. f. 215, writ on the Great Charter; Y. B. 17 Edw. II. f. 536, 'per consuetudinem regni'; the writ is abated; the justices altogether deny the custom and suggest a different interpretation of the charter;

[p. 350]

The king's court and legitim.

Now there is one conclusion to which we must be brought by this tenuous line of discrepant authorities. The matter before us is no rarity. It is no uncommon thing for a man to leave a wife or a child living at his death. The distribution of his goods will not always be a straightforward affair if a legitim is claimed. There are abundant possibilities of litigation. The question whether a child has been 'advanced,' the question whether the widow or a child is put to election between benefits given by the will and rights arising outside the will, such questions will often emerge and will sometimes be difficult. Why do not our Year Books teem with them? How is it that, after some search, we can not produce from the records of the thirteenth century one case of a wife or child claiming legitim in the king's court? How does it happen that at one moment the justices at Westminster raise no objection to the writ and at the next assert that it is contrary to law? The answer probably is that the question whether the widow or child has an action in the king's court is of but little moment. The ecclesiastical courts are seised of this matter and know all about it. On a testator's death his executor takes possession of the whole of his goods. He is bound to do this, for he has to pay the debts. The claim for legitim is therefore a claim against the executor, against one who is held accountable in the ecclesiastical court for a due administration of the dead man's goods and chattels. It is therefore in the ecclesiastical courts that the demand for legitim should be urged and all questions about it should be settled. An action in the temporal court would, at least in the ordinary case, be a luxury.

Legitim in the ecclesiastical courts.

Therefore this somewhat important piece of English history will not be understood until whatever records there may be of the ecclesiastical courts have been published. The local customs which regulated the distribution of movable goods must, so it seems to us, have been for the more part the

---

Fitz. Abr. *Dette*, pl. 156 (3 Edw. III., It. North.), custom of county of Northampton; Y. B. 17 Edw. III. f. 9 (Hil. pl. 29), custom of the realm; Y. B. 30 Edw. III. f. 25, consuetudo totius regni; Y. B. 39 Edw. III. f. 6; Y. B. 40 Edw. III. f. 38 (Mich. pl. 13), custom of a vill; Y. B. 21 Hen. VI. f. 1; Y. B. 28 Hen. VI. f. 4 (Mich. pl. 20), custom of a county; Fitz. Abr. *Respond.* pl. 95 (Mich. 30 Hen. VI.), 'par lusage'; Y. B. 7 Edw. IV. f. 21 (Mich. pl. 23); Reg. Brev. Orig. f. 142 b, custom of Berkshire; Fitz. Nat. Brev. f. 122. See also Co. Lit. 176 b; Somner, Gavelkind, 91; Blackstone, Comm. ii. 492.

customs of provinces, dioceses and peculiars, rather than the
[p. 351] customs of counties or of vills.   When we are told in a Year
Book or in the Register of Writs that the custom of Berkshire
secures the children a legitim, this must, we take it, be the
temporal side of an ecclesiastical fact.   Our interest, therefore,
will be centered in the two metropolitical courts, which by
virtue of their doctrine about *bona notabilia* were drawing to
themselves the wills of all wealthy persons and attracting all
the famous advocates.   We know that until 1692 the old rule
was maintained throughout the province of York[1]; and we may
read in the pages of Henry Swinburne, 'sometime judge of the
prerogative court of York,' a great deal about its application;
for example, we may see some settled rules of the court as to
what is to be deemed an advancement of a child[2].   Long before
this, however, the court of the southern province must have
chosen a different path and refused a legitim save when a local
custom demanded it.   How and when this happened we can
not at present say.   In 1342 the provincial constitutions of
Archbishop Stratford condemn those who on their death-beds
make gifts *inter vivos* for the purpose of defrauding the church
of mortuaries, the creditors of debts, or their wives and children
of the portions that belong to them 'by custom and law[3].'   A
century later Lyndwood, official of the court of Canterbury,
having to comment on the words 'the portion belonging to the
deceased,' sends us to the custom of the place to learn what
that portion is.   He mentions but one custom by way of
example:—it is the well-known scheme of which we have been
speaking[4].

Allusions to this method of division are not uncommonly Legitim
in wills.

---

[1] Stat. 4 Will. and Mar. c. 2.

[2] Swinburne, Testaments (ed. 1640), p. 191 ff.   Some use seems to have
been made of a treatise on Legitim by the civilian Claude Battandier; but in
the main Swinburne appears to be stating the practice of his own court.

[3] Wilkins, Concilia, ii. p. 706, cc. 8, 9: 'liberorum et suarum uxorum, qui
et quae tam de iure quam de consuetudine certam quotam dictorum bonorum
habere deberent.'   And again—'uxoresque et liberi coniugatorum suis porti-
onibus de consuetudine vel de iure ipsis debitis irrecuperabiliter defraudantur.'

[4] Lyndwood, Prov. lib. iii. tit. 13. gl. ad v. *defunctum* (ed. 1679, p. 178).   It
may be inferred from Smith, Repub. Angl. lib. 3, c. 7; Co. Lit. 176 b; Somner,
Gavelkind (1660), p. 99, that in Elizabeth's day the courts of the southern
province were no longer enforcing the old rule, except as a very exceptional
local custom.   The tripartite division had prevailed at Sandwich: Lyon, Dover,
ii. 308.

found in wills. A few examples may be given. 'All the
residue of all the goods that pertain to my share (*partem meam
contingencium*) I leave to Margery my wife[1].' 'I desire to make
my testament of my proper goods, and that Elizabeth my wife [p. 352]
shall have the share of goods that belongs to her by law or
laudable custom[2].' 'I give to my wife Joan in respect of her
share of all our goods, all the utensils of our house, and all the
bed furniture and the horses…. And I will that all the legacies
given to my wife shall be valid if she after my death in no
wise impedes my testament[3].' 'I bequeath to my two children
John and Thomas in respect of the rateable portion of goods
falling to them, to each of them seven marks sterling[4].' 'And
all the residue of my goods not hereinbefore bequeathed which
belong to my share, I will to be expended in masses for my
soul,…and I give to my wife Alice the whole of my share of
our six spoons for her own use[5].' 'Also I well that Antone
my sonne and Betress my dowghter have their barne parts of
my goodes after the lawe and custome of the cuntre[6]'……
'which I well that she have besyde her barne parte of goodes[7].'
Such allusions, however, are not so common as we might expect
them to be, did we not remember, first that when a man
disposes of 'all the residue of his goods' he may well be
speaking only of that share which he can effectually bequeath,
secondly that the testator is often making an ampler provision
for his wife and children than the law would give them if they
disputed his testament, and thirdly that children may lose all
claim to a reasonable part if their father 'advances' them
during his lifetime. Sometimes the testator will profess to
bequeath his own 'dead's part' to himself:—'Also y bequethe
my goodes in twey partyes, that ys for [to] seie, half to me,
and the tother haluyndel to Watkin my sone and to Kateryne
my dowter[8].' In 1313 a bishop spoke of the scheme that we
have been discussing, as 'the custom of the realm of England,'
and 'the custom of the English church'; but he was bishop
of Durham[9].

---

[1] Testamenta Eboracensia, vol. i. p. 3.   [2] Ibid. p. 97.
[3] Ibid. p. 139.   [4] Ibid. p. 191.
[5] Ibid. p. 197.   See also pp. 213, 250, 287.
[6] Durham Wills and Inventories, i. 113.   [7] Ibid. 124.
[8] Furnivall, Fifty English Wills, p. 1.
[9] Regist. Palat. Dunelm. i. 369, 385.

We may doubt whether there was at any time among lawyers, among ecclesiastics, or among Englishmen in general, any strong feeling for or against the old rule. At one moment [p. 353] in Edward II.'s reign some of the judges seem to dislike it. One of them, after giving a sophistical explanation of the words of the Charter, said that there is nothing either in that document or in the common law which restrains a father from devising his own goods as he pleases[1]. Again, in Edward III.'s day 'the lords in parliament' will not, we are told, allow this custom[2]. But at times during the fourteenth century the mere fact that the ecclesiastical courts were doing something was sufficient to convince royal justices and lay lords that something wrong was being done. Then, on the other hand, the canonist himself was not deeply interested in the maintenance of the old restraints. He could not regard them as outlines of the church's *ius commune*; at best they could be but customs of English dioceses or provinces. His training in Roman law might indeed teach him that the claims of children should set limits to a father's testamentary power; but 'wife's part,' 'bairns' part' and 'dead's part' can not be found in the Institutes; besides, the church had legacies to gain by ignoring the old rules. Our English law seems to slip unconsciously into the decision of a very important and debatable question. Curiously enough the Act of 1692, which enables the inhabitant of the northern province to bequeath all his goods away from his family, was professedly passed in the interest of his younger children[3]. To the modern Englishman our modern law, which allows the father to leave his children penniless, may seem so obvious that he will be apt to think it deep-rooted in our national character. But national character and national law react upon each other, and law is sometimes the outcome of what we must call accidents. Had our temporal lawyers of the thirteenth century cared more than they

[1] Y. B. 7 Edw. II. f. 536. It is suggested that the words of the Charter refer to the goods of a child which have come into the father's hands, not to the father's own goods (!).

[2] Y. B. 40 Edw. III. f. 38.

[3] Stat. 4 & 5 Will. and Mary, c. 2: 'whereby many persons are disabled from making sufficient provision for their younger children.' The complaint seems to be that the provincial custom secures for a widow more than she ought to have. A jointure does not prevent her from claiming her wife's part; enough therefore is not left for the younger children.

did about the law of chattels, wife's part, bairns' part and dead's part might at this day be known south of the Tweed.

§ 4.   *Intestacy*[1].

Horror of intestacy. During the two centuries which followed the Norman [p. 354] Conquest an intense and holy horror of intestacy took possession of men's minds. We have already seen how Cnut was compelled to say that if a man dies intestate, the lord is to take no more than his rightful heriot and is to divide the dead man's property between his wife, children and near kinsmen[2]. We have also seen how Henry I. promised that if one of his barons died without a will, the wife, children and liege men of the intestate might divide his property for the good of his soul as they should think best[3]. There has already been a change. The goods of the intestate are no longer—we may almost say it—inherited by his nearest of kin; they are to be distributed for the good of his soul, though this distribution is to be effected by the hands of those who are allied to him by blood or homage. If the *Leis Williame* say that the goods of the intestate are to be divided among his children, we may suspect them of struggling against the spirit of the age; perhaps they are appealing to Roman law[4]. According to a doctrine that was rapidly gaining ground, the man who dies intestate dies unconfessed, and the man who dies unconfessed—it were better not to end the sentence; God's mercy is infinite; but we can not bury the intestate in consecrated soil. It would seem that in Glanvill's day the lords were pressing their claim to seize the goods of such of their men as died intestate[5]. In the Charter of 1215 there is a clause which says: 'If any free man dies intestate, his chattels shall be distributed by the hands of his next kinsfolk and friends under the supervision of the church, saving to every one the debts owed to him by the dead

---

[1] Once for all we must refer our readers to Selden's tract on The Disposition of Intestates' Goods (Collected Works, vol. iii. p. 1677).

[2] Cnut, ii. 70.   [3] Coronation Charter, c. 7.

[4] Leg. Will. i. 34; see above, vol. i. p. 103; vol. ii. p. 267.

[5] Glanvill, vii. 16.   Pipe Roll, 18 Hen. II. 133: the custodians of the abbey of Battle account at the exchequer for the goods of the abbot's bailiff, who died intestate.

man[1].' The church now asserts a right to supervise the process
of distribution. But this clause was omitted from the Charter
of 1216 and was never again enacted. Why was it omitted?
Having regard to the character of the other omissions, we may
guess that it was withdrawn by Henry's counsellors in the
interest of their infant king. The thought may have crossed
their minds (and John may at times have put this thought into
[p. 355] practice) that intestacy is a cause of forfeiture. But this
clause, though it was deliberately withdrawn, seems to have
settled the law.

Bracton in words which recall those of Cnut and of Henry I. Bracton on
says: 'If a free man dies intestate and suddenly, his lord should intestacy.
in no wise meddle with his goods, save in so far as this is
necessary in order that he may get what is his, namely, his
heriot, but the administration of the dead man's goods belongs
to his friends and to the church, for the man who dies intestate
does not deserve a punishment[2].' No, intestacy—at all events
if occasioned by sudden death—is not an offence or a cause of
forfeiture, still it is a cause for grave alarm, and a reason why
all should be done that can be done for a soul that is in
jeopardy. And who so fit to decide what can be done as the
bishop of the diocese?

Many points are illustrated by a story which Jocelin of Stories of
Brakeland has told in his spirited way. In the year 1197 intestacy.
Hamo Blund, one of the richest men of the town of Bury
St Edmunds, was at the point of death, and would hardly be
persuaded to make any testament. At length, when nobody
but his brother, his wife and the chaplain could hear, he made
a testament to the paltry amount of three marks. And when
after his death the abbot heard this, he summoned those three
persons before him and sharply reproved them, because the
brother, who was heir, and the wife, wishing to have all, would
not allow any one to have access to the sick man. And then
in their presence the abbot said: 'I was his bishop and had the
cure of his soul, and, lest his ignorance should imperil me, his
priest and confessor,—for not being present I could not counsel
him—I will now do my duty, albeit at the eleventh hour. I
order that all his chattels and the debts due to him, which it is
said are worth two hundred marks, be set down in writing and
that one share be given to the heir, and another to the wife, and

---

[1] Charter, 1215, c. 27.   [2] Bracton, f. 60 b.

a third to his poor cousins and other poor folk. As to his horse which was led before the bier and offered to St Edmund, I order that it be remitted and returned, for it is not fit that our church be polluted by the gift of one who died intestate, and who is commonly accused of having habitually lent his money at usury. By the face of God! if anything of this sort happens again in my days, the delinquent shall not be buried in the [p. 356] churchyard.' When they heard this they retired in confusion.— Thus did abbot Samson, to the delight of Jocelin[1].

Soon after this there were malicious men who did not scruple to assert that Archbishop Hubert, who had been chief justiciar, had died intestate. A friendly chronicler has warmly rebutted this hideous accusation[2]. In Henry III.'s reign the monks of St Alban's believed that an enemy of theirs, Adam Fitzwilliam, a justice of the Bench, had died intestate. True that his friend and colleague, William of Culworth, had gone before the bishop of London and affirmed that Adam made a will of which he, William, was the 'procurator and executor'; but this, said the monks, was a pious lie[3]. A pious lie—for William was striving to defend his companion's fair fame against the damning charge of intestacy. Of another enemy of St Alban, the terrible Fawkes of Breauté, it is written that he was poisoned; that having gone to bed after supper, he was found dead, black, stinking and intestate[4].

In Edward I.'s time a man was attacked by robbers and he was found by the neighbours at the point of death; he died before a priest could be brought to him; he was buried in the high road. Archbishop Peckham took a merciful view of the case:—It is said that the poor wretch asked for a priest; if this can be proved, let his body be exhumed and buried in Christian fashion, for he did what he could towards making a testament[5]. Then the rector of Ightham died suddenly. Peckham, with a hope that all might yet be well, bade his official, his commissary, and the rector of another parish take possession of the dead

---

[1] Jocelin (Camd. Soc.), p. 67.

[2] Ralph of Coggeshall, p. 159: 'Sed absit, absit procul hoc, et in orbe remoto abscondat fortuna malum, ut qui testamentorum ab aliis conditorum fidelis extitit executor, intestatus decessisset!'

[3] Gesta Abbatum, i. 329. The important phrase is *pie mentiens*.

[4] Mat. Par. Chron. Maj. iii. 121.

[5] Peckham's Register, i. 39: 'cum sacerdotem cui confiteretur petierit, et sicut poterit in tali articulo, condiderit testamentum.'

man's goods.   His debts were to be paid, and then the residue
was to be disposed of according to the archbishop's orders for
the benefit of the departed[1].

[p. 357]   The pope would have liked to take the goods of all intestate
clerks.   In 1246 there had been some scandalous cases.   Three
English archdeacons, rich men, had died intestate.   Thereupon
the bishop of Rome decreed that the goods of all intestate
clerks should be converted to his use.   He did more than this,
for he declared that the mere appointment of an 'expressor and
executor' would not save the clerk's goods from being swallowed
in what Matthew Paris calls 'the papal Charybdis'—a testator
must express his own will, and not leave it to be expressed by
an expressor and executor.   But this was going too far; the
king protested and the edict was withdrawn[2].   This same pope,
that great canonist Innocent IV., had stated that in Britain
the custom was that one-third—this means the dead's part—
of the goods of the intestate, belonged to the church and the
poor[3].   In 1284 Edward I. begged a grant of the goods of
intestates from Pope Martin IV., and met with a refusal[4].

These stories may be enough to illustrate the prevailing Desperation in Normandy
opinion about intestacy.   It was not confined to England.
What is more peculiar to England is that the prelates firmly
established, as against the king and the lay lords, their right to
distribute the goods of the intestate for the weal of his soul.
It was otherwise in some parts of France, notably in Normandy.
The man who had fair warning that death was approaching, the
man who lay in bed for several days, and yet made no will and
confession, was deemed to die 'desperate,' and the goods of the
desperate, like the goods of the suicide, were forfeited to the
duke.   The church was entitled to nothing, as it had done
nothing for his soul[5].   The bishop of Llandaff complained to
Edward I. that the magnates in his diocese would not permit

---

[1] Peckham's Register, iii. 874 (A.D. 1285): 'Sed de bonis huiusmodi quae
reliquit, ipsius si quae sint debita persolvantur, et residuum dispositioni et
ordinationi nostrae pro anima eiusdem integraliter reservetur.'

[2] Mat. Par. Chron. Maj. iv. 552, 604.

[3] Innocentius, Commentaria, X. 5. 3. 42: 'ut sicut Venetiis solvitur in
morte decima mobilium, in Britannia tertia, in opus ecclesiae et pauperum
dispensanda.'

[4] Calendar of Papal Registers, i. 473.

[5] Somma, p. 56; Ancienne coutume, c. 21.   See Ducange, s. v. *intestatus*,
where a great store of illustrations is collected.

him to administer the goods of intestates, and the king replied that he would not interfere with the custom of the country[1].

The bishop and the kinsfolk. However, in the thirteenth century it became well settled law in England that the goods of the intestate are at the disposal of the judge ordinary, though in Bracton's text we may [p. 358] still hear the claim of the kinsfolk or 'friends' of the dead to take some part in the work of administration[2]. No doubt in practice this claim was often respected. The bishop would not make the division with his own hands, and in many cases those who were near and dear to the intestate might be trusted to do what was best for him. Again, the list of those works of piety and mercy which might benefit his soul was long and liberal, and, if it comprised the purchase of prayers, it comprised also the relief of the poor, and more especially of poor relations. But still the claim of his kinsfolk is no longer a claim to inherit. In 1268 it was necessary for a legatine council to remind the prelates that they were but trustees in this matter and were not to treat the goods of intestates as their own[3].

Intestate succession. When we look at this strange law we ought to remember two things. In the first place, intestacy was rare. It was easy to make a will; easy to make some sign of assent when the confessor asked you to trust him as your expressor and executor[4].

---

[1] Memor. de Parl. 33 Edw. I. (ed. Maitland), p. 73. Selden, *op. cit.*, p. 1681, resists, and as we think rightly, the opinion that the King of England was at one time entitled to the goods of intestates; but the clauses in the charters of 1100 and 1215, to say nothing of Cnut's law and the texts of Glanvill and Bracton, seem to show that there had (to say the least) been a grave danger of 'desperate' death being treated as a cause of forfeiture. Prynne, Records, vol. iii. *passim*, regards the action of the prelates as a shameless usurpation.

[2] Bracton, f. 60 b. There were towns, *e.g.* Sandwich, in which the municipal authorities claimed the right to administer the intestate's goods. See Lyon, Dover, ii. 308.

[3] Constit. Ottoboni, *Cum mortis incerta.* This constitution, after reciting that a sudden death often deprives a man of the power of making a testament, and that in such a case humanity distributes his goods for pious uses, so that they may intercede for him on high, proceeds to say that in past time a provision about this matter was made by the English prelates with the king's consent, and to declare that the prelates are not to occupy the goods of the dead contrary to that provision. What was that provision? John de Athona did not know and plunged into a marvellous anachronism. Selden thinks that the clause in the charter of 1215 was intended. We can offer no better explanation.

[4] Selden, p. 1682, speaks as though intestacy were common; but the chroniclers treat it as a scandal.

In the second place, it was only 'the dead's part' that fell to the ordinary, though the wife and children (if any there were) had by this time to take their shares from his hand.

In 1285 a statute declared that thenceforth the ordinary should be bound to pay the debts of the intestate in the same manner as that in which executors were bound to pay the debts [p. 359] of the testator[1]. The king's court was just beginning to give the creditor of a testator an action against the executor, and the purpose of the statute seems to be that the creditor of an intestate shall have a similar action against the ordinary. The executor is beginning to appear as the personal representative of the testator; the ordinary—or some administrator to whom he has delegated his duties—must appear as the personal representative of the intestate. In 1357 another statute will bid the ordinary commit the work of administration to 'the next and most lawful friends' of the dead, and will give actions of debt to and against these 'administrators[2].'

The administrator.

How far the bishops in their dealings with the kinsfolk of the dead man were guided by the table of consanguinity we can not say. In the end there was what a foreigner might describe as a partial 'reception' of Roman law as defined in the Novels of Justinian. But this seems to have taken place in much later days than those of which we are speaking. We must remember that the canonist, though his training in Roman law might incline him to treat it as written reason and to give it the benefit of every doubt, had no law of intestate succession that was his own. The catholic church had never presumed to dictate a scheme of inheritance to the world at large. Such rules as we can recover concerning the bairns' part tend to show that during the middle ages the Roman system was not observed in England. The bairns' part was strictly confined to children; no right of representation was admitted; no child of a dead child could claim a share in it[3].

The next of kin.

---

[1] Stat. West. II. c. 19.

[2] Stat. 31 Edw. III. Stat. 1, c. 11. English lawyers appropriate the term *administrator* to the representative of an intestate, reserving *executor* for the representative of a testator. In the works of the canonists our administrator appears as an *executor dative*, our executor as an *executor testamentary*. The Statute of Edward III. had the effect of introducing *administrator* as a technical term; in Y. B. 38 Edward III. f. 21, it is said that formerly the administrator when sued had been called *executor*. See Selden, *op. cit.* p. 1685.

[3] Swinburne, Testaments (ed. 1640), p. 194. So in Scotland in the

Letters of
admini-
stration.
But, to return to the law of intestate succession as it was in earlier days, we shall see it well illustrated by a document issued by a bishop of Durham in 1313, the earliest specimen of 'letters of administration' that has come under our notice. He addresses Margaret the widow of Robert Haunsard, knight, and William and John Walworth. Confiding in their fidelity, he commits to them the administration of the goods of Robert Haunsard, who has died intestate. They are to exhibit a true inventory, to satisfy creditors, and to certify the bishop's official as to the names of the creditors and the amount of the [p. 360] debts. The residue, if any, of the goods they are to divide into three parts, assigning one to the dead man, one to his widow Margaret, and one to the children 'according to the custom of the realm of England.' The dead's part they are to distribute for the good of his soul in such pious works as they shall think best according to God and good conscience, and of their administration they are to render account to the bishop or his commissaries. The bairns' part they are to retain as curators and guardians until the children are of full age. If any one impleads the bishop concerning the goods, they are to defend the action and keep the bishop indemnified[1]. Such were 'letters of administration' in the first years of the fourteenth century.

Separation
of chattels
from
lands.
To a student of economic history a system of inheritance which studiously separates the chattels from the land may seem but little suited to an age in which agriculture was almost the only process productive of wealth. The heir, it may seem, is destined to inherit bare acres, while the capital which has made them fertile goes to others. Nor in the generality of medieval wills do we find the testator favouring his heir; if he has several sons he will probably bestow equal benefits upon them. Again, at least in later law, the heir could claim no bairn's part of the chattels[2]. But when we look into the

---

nineteenth century: Fraser, Husband and Wife, ii. 994. Indeed the Scottish law of intestate succession to movables has been marvellously unlike that settled by Nov. 118. It has been at once agnatic (refusing to trace through a female ancestor) and parentelic: Fraser, ii. 1072.

[1] Regist. Palat. Dunelm. i. 369. In 1343 the Commons pray that the person to whom the ordinary commits the affairs of the intestate may have an action against creditors. The king answers that the bishop must have it, as he is responsible to others; Rot. Parl. ii. 142. See Selden, *op. cit.*, p. 1685.

[2] Swinburne, Testaments (ed. 1640), p. 196.

matter we see that a great deal of the agricultural capital is
'realty' and descends to the heir.   For this purpose the villeins
are annexed to the soil; they can not be severed from it by
testament[1]; their ploughs, oxen and other chattels are at the
heir's service.   Even if there is no personal unfreedom in the
case, what descends to the heir of a well-to-do gentleman is no
bare tract of land, but that complex known as a manor, which
includes the right to exact labour services from numerous
tenants.   The stock on the demesne land the heir will not
inherit; he will often purchase it from the executors; still he
will not inherit a mere tract of soil.

[p. 361]   Again, there are many traces of local customs which under
the name of 'principals' or 'heir-looms' will give him various
chattels, not merely his ancestor's sword and hauberk, but the
best chattels of every different kind, the best horse (if the
church does not take it) and the best ox, the best chair and
the best table, the best pan and the best pot.   The local
customs which secure him these things may well be of ancient
date, and their origin deserves investigation[2].

Heir-
looms

It is in the province of inheritance that our medieval law Review
made its worst mistakes.   They were natural mistakes.   There
was much to be said for the simple plan of giving all the land
to the eldest son.   There was much to be said for allowing the
courts of the church to assume a jurisdiction, even an exclusive
jurisdiction, in testamentary causes.   We can hardly blame our
ancestors for their dread of intestacy without attacking their
religious beliefs.   But the consequences have been evil.   We
rue them at the present day, and shall rue them so long as
there is talk of real and personal property.

---

[1] Britton, i. 197–8.

[2] Test. Ebor. i. 287: 'Item volo et firmiter praecipio H. B. filio meo super
benedictione mea quod non vendicet nec calumpnietur aliqua principalia infra
manerium meum de A., nec alibi, quia ego nulla habui de parentibus meis.'
See also Durham Wills (Surtees Soc.), i. 59.   In Edward III.'s reign the
custom of an Oxfordshire hundred is declared to be that the heir shall have as
principalia or heir-looms the best cart, the best plough, the best cup and so on
of every kind of chattels: Co. Lit. 18 b; Elton, Origins of English History (2nd
ed.), pp. 197–8.

CHAPTER VII.

FAMILY LAW.

§ 1. *Marriage.*

Antiquities
of marriage
law. THE nature of the ancient Germanic marriage has in our [p. 362]
own day been the theme of lively debates[1]. The want of any
first-rate evidence as to what went on in the days of heathenry
leaves a large field open for the construction of ingenious
theories. We can not find any fixed starting point for our
speculations, so completely has the old text, whatever it was,
been glossed and distorted by Christianity. It is said with
some show of truth that in the earliest Teutonic laws we may
see many traces of 'marriage by capture[2].' The 'rape-marriage,'
if such we may call it, is a punishable offence; but still it is a
marriage, as we find it also in the Hindu law-books. The
usual and lawful marriage, however, is a 'sale-marriage'; in
consideration of money paid down, the bride is handed over
to the bridegroom. The 'bride-sale' of which Tacitus tells us[3]
was no sale of a chattel. It was different from the sale of a
slave girl; it was a sale of the *mund*, the protectorship, over the
woman. An honourable position as her husband's consort and
yoke-fellow was assured to her by solemn contract. This need
not imply that the woman herself had any choice in the matter.
Even Cnut had to forbid that a woman should be sold to a man

---

[1] The controversy began with Sohm's Recht der Eheschliessung, which
called forth many replies. Friedberg's Recht der Eheschliessung contains
much curious matter concerning English marriages. In the Essays on Anglo-
Saxon Law, p. 163, Mr E. Young applied Sohm's theory to England, but not
without some modifications.

[2] Dargun, Mutterrecht und Raubehe; Heusler, Institutionen, ii. 277.

[3] Germania, c. 18. But unfortunately Tacitus has an eye to edification.

[p. 363] whom she disliked[1].   But, as already said, we can not be very certain that in England the wife had ever passed completely into the hand of her husband.   He became her 'elder[2]'—her *senior*, her *seigneur*, we may say,—and her lord; but the bond between her and her blood kinsmen was not broken; they, not he, had to pay for her misdeeds and received her *wergild*[3].   It seems by no means impossible that for a while the husband's power over his wife increased rather than diminished.   And when light begins to fall upon the Anglo-Saxon betrothal, it is not a cash transaction by which the bride's kinsmen receive a price in return for rights over their kinswoman; rather we must say that the bridegroom covenants with them that he will make a settlement upon his future wife.   He declares, and he gives security for, the morning-gift which she shall receive if she 'chooses his will' and the dower that she shall enjoy if she outlives him[4].   Though no doubt her kinsmen may make a profit out of the bargain, as fathers and feudal lords will in much later times, the more essential matter is that they should stipulate on her behalf for an honourable treatment as wife and widow.   Phrases and ceremonies which belong to this old time will long be preserved in that curious cabinet of antiquities, the marriage ritual of the English church.

Whether the marriage begins with the betrothal, or with the delivery of the bride to the bridegroom, or with their physical union, is one of the many doubtful questions.   For one thing, we can not be certain that a betrothal, a transaction between the bridegroom and the woman's father or other protector was essential to a valid marriage; we have to reckon with the possibility—and it is somewhat more than a possibility—of marriage by capture[5].   If the woman consented to the abduction, then, according to the theory which the Christian church was gradually formulating, there would be all the essentials of a valid marriage, the consent to be husband and wife and the sexual union.   When there had been a solemn betrothal it is likely that the bridegroom thereby acquired

What is the act of marriage?

---

[1] Cnut, II. 74.   [2] Ine, 57.   [3] See above, vol. ii. p. 243.

[4] Schmid, App. VI.   For an earlier time see Æthelb. 77; Ine, 31.

[5] Æthelb. 82 (according to Liebermann's translation): 'If a man forcibly abducts a maiden, let him pay 50 shillings to him to whom she belongs and then buy the consent of him to whom she belongs.'   There is no talk of giving her back, but a *bót* must be paid and the *mund* must be purchased.

some rights over the bride which were good against third [p. 364] persons, and that any one who carried her off would have had to pay a *bót* to him[1]. On the other hand, it seems too much to say that the betrothal was the marriage. If either party refused to perform his contract, he could only be compelled to pay money; in the one case the bridegroom lost what he had paid by way of bride-price; in the other he received back that price augmented by one-third:—such was the rule enforced by the church, and the church held that the parents of the espoused girl might give her to another man, if she obstinately refused the man to whom she had been betrothed[2].

Growth of the ecclesiastical jurisdiction. Already in the seventh century and here in England the church was making her voice heard about these matters. Her warfare against the sins of the flesh gave her an interest in marriage and all that concerned marriage. Especially earnest was she in her attempt to define the 'prohibited degrees' and prevent incestuous unions. This was a matter about which the first missionaries had consulted the pope, who told them not to be too severe with their new converts. A little later Archbishop Theodore was able to lay down numerous rules touching marriage and divorce[3]. Many of these are rules which could only be enforced by penances, but some are rules which go to the legitimacy or illegitimacy of an union, and we have every reason to suppose that the state accepted them. In some cases, more especially when they deal with divorce, they seem to be temporizing rules; they make concessions to old Germanic custom and do not maintain the indissolubility of marriage with that rigour which the teaching of the Christian fathers might have led us to expect[4]. Fresh incursions of heathen Danes must have retarded the evolution of a marriage law such as the church could approve. At all events in Normandy the great men contract with their *uxores Danicae* unions of an equivocal kind which the church condemns. The wife is not of equal rank with her husband; there has been no solemn betrothal; the children will not inherit their father's land; the wife will have to be content with the morning-gift [p. 365]

---

[1] Æthelb. 83.

[2] Theodore's Penitential, ii. xii. 33, 34 (Haddan and Stubbs, iii. 201). This passes into the Pseudo-Theodore printed by the Record Commission, Ancient Laws, ii. 11.

[3] Haddan and Stubbs, iii. 21.　　　　　[4] Ibid. 201.

which her husband makes after the bridal night; but, for all
this, there is a marriage: something that we dare not call mere
concubinage[1]. That eminently Christian king Cnut legislated
about marriage in an ecclesiastical spirit. The adulterous wife,
unless her offence be public, is to be handed over to the bishop
for judgment. The adulterous husband is to be denied every
Christian right until he satisfies the bishop[2]. The bishop is
becoming the judge of these sinners, and the judge who
punishes adultery must take cognizance of marriage.

When the Conqueror had paid the debt that he owed to
Rome by a definite separation of the spiritual from the lay
tribunals, it can not have remained long in doubt that the
former would claim the whole province of marriage law as their
own. In all probability this claim was not suddenly pressed;
the *Leges Henrici* endeavour to state the old law about
adultery; the man's fine goes to the king, the woman's to
the bishop[3]; but everywhere the church was beginning to
urge that claim, and the canonists were constructing an elaborate jurisprudence of marriage. By the middle of the twelfth
century, by the time when Gratian was compiling his con-
cordance of discordant canons, it was law in England that
marriage appertained to the spiritual forum. Richard de
Anesty's memorable law-suit was the outcome of a divorce
pronounced in or about 1143 under the authority of a papal
rescript, and seemingly one which illustrated what was to be a
characteristic doctrine of the canon law: a marriage solemnly
celebrated in church, a marriage of which a child had been
born, was set aside as null in favour of an earlier marriage
constituted by a mere exchange of consenting words[4]. Soon
after this Glanvill acknowledged that the ecclesiastical court
had an exclusive cognizance of the question whether or no
there had been a marriage, and the king's court, with a
profession of its own inability to deal with that question, was
habitually asking the bishops to decide whether or no a litigant
[p. 366] was legitimate[5]. Thenceforth the marriage law of England was

*Matrimo-
nial juris-
diction in
England.*

---

[1] As to these Danish marriages, see Freeman, Norman Conquest, 2nd ed. i.
612; Brunner, Die uneheliche Vaterschaft, Zeitschrift der Savigny-Stiftung,
Germ. Abt. xvii. 1. 19.

[2] Cnut, ii. 53, 54.   [3] Leg. Hen. 11, § 5; cf. D. B. i. 1.

[4] See above, vol. i. p. 158, Letters of John of Salisbury (ed. Giles), i. 124.

[5] Glanvill, vii. 13, 14; Select Civil Pleas (Selden Soc.), pl. 15, 92, 109.

the canon law. A few words about its main rules must be said, though we cannot pretend to expound them at length.

According to the doctrine that prevailed for a while, there was no marriage until man and woman had become one flesh. In strictness of law all that was essential was this physical union accompanied by the intent to be thenceforth husband and wife. All that preceded this could be no more than an espousal (*desponsatio*) and the relationship between the spouses was one which was dissoluble; in particular it was dissolved if either of them contracted a perfected marriage with a third person. However, in the course of the twelfth century, when the classical canon law was taking shape, a new distinction came to the front. Espousals were of two kinds: *sponsalia per verba de futuro*, which take place if man and woman promise each other that they will hereafter become husband and wife; *sponsalia per verba de praesenti*, which take place if they declare that they take each other as husband and wife now, at this very moment. It is thenceforth the established doctrine that a transaction of the latter kind (*sponsalia per verba de prae-senti*) creates a bond which is hardly to be dissolved; in particular, it is not dissolved though one of the spouses goes through the ceremony of marriage and is physically united with another person. The espousal 'by words of the present tense' constitutes a marriage (*matrimonium*), at all events an initiate marriage; the spouses are *coniuges*; the relationship between them is almost as indisseverable as if it had already become a consummate marriage. Not quite so indisseverable however; a spouse may free himself or herself from the un-consummated marriage by entering religion[1], and such a marriage is within the papal power of dispensation. Even at the present day the technical terms that are in use among us recall the older doctrine, for a marriage that is not yet 'consummated' should, were we nice in our use of words, be no marriage at all. As to *sponsalia per verba de futuro*, the doctrine of the canonists was that sexual intercourse if preceded by such espousals was a marriage; a presumption of law explained the *carnalis copula* by the foregoing promise to marry. The scheme at which they thus arrived was certainly [p. 367] no masterpiece of human wisdom. Of all people in the world

---

[1] See the English case, c. 16. X. 4. 1. The Council of Trent pronounced the anathema against those who deny this. Conc. Trident. de Sacr. Matr. c. 6.

lovers are the least likely to distinguish precisely between the present and the future tenses.   In the middle ages marriages, or what looked like marriages, were exceedingly insecure.   The union which had existed for many years between man and woman might with fatal ease be proved adulterous, and there would be hard swearing on both sides about 'I will' and 'I do.' It is interesting to notice that a powerful protest against this doctrine was made by the legist Vacarius.   He argued that there could be no marriage without a *traditio*, the self-delivery of man to woman and woman to man.   But he could not prevail[1].

The one contract which, to our thinking, should certainly be formal, had been made the most formless of all contracts.   It is true that from a very early time the church had insisted that Christian spouses should seek a blessing for their union, should acknowledge their contract publicly and in face of the church. The ceremonies required by temporal law, Jewish, Roman or Germanic, were to be observed, and a new religious colour was given to those rites; the veil and the ring were sanctified.   In the little Anglo-Saxon tract which describes a betrothal—without any good warrant it has been treated as belonging to the laws of King Edmund—we see the mass priest present; but the part that is assigned to him is subordinate.   After we have read how a solemn treaty is made between the bridegroom and the kinsmen of the bride, we read how at the delivery, the tradition, of the woman, a mass priest should be present, and confirm the union with God's blessing[2].   But the variety of the

No ceremony requisite.

---

[1] The story told in this paragraph is that which is told at great length by Freisen, Geschichte des canonischen Eherechts. See also, Esmein, Le mariage en droit canonique, i. 95–137.   How it came about that the church laid so much stress on the physical union is a grave question.   Freisen sees here the influence of Jewish tradition.   It now seems fairly clear that even Gratian saw no marriage, no indissoluble bond, no *matrimonium perfectum*, where there had been no *carnalis copula*.   The change seems in a great measure due to the influence of Peter Lombard and represents a victory of Parisian theology over Bolognese jurisprudence.   For the tract of Vacarius, see L. Q. R. xiii. 133, 270. A desire to prove that the union between St Mary and St Joseph was a perfect marriage helped the newer doctrine.   One of the epoch-making decretals relates to an English case and will be given below, p. 371.   The English canonist John de Athona in his gloss on Ottobon's constitution *Coniugale foedus* says, 'Matrimonii consummatio ad matrimonium multos addit effectus'; it makes the marriage indissoluble by profession and by dispensation; also it is of sacramental importance.

[2] Be wifmannes beweddunge, Schmid, Gesetze, App. vi.

marriage customs current among the Christian nations prevented the church from singling out any one rite as essential. From drastic legislation she was withstrained by the fear that [p. 368] she would thereby multiply sins. It was not well that there should be marriages contracted in secret and unblessed by God; still, better these than concubinage and unions dissoluble at will. And so, though at times she seemed to be on the point of decreeing that the marriage contracted without a due observance of religious ceremonies is no marriage at all, she held her hand[1]. For example, soon after the Norman Conquest Lanfranc issued a constitution condemning in strong words him who gives away his daughter or kinswoman without a priestly benediction. He says that the parties to such an union are fornicators; but it is very doubtful whether he says or means that the union is no indissoluble marriage[2]. At all events in the twelfth century, though the various churches have by this time evolved marriage rituals—rituals which have borrowed many a phrase and symbol from ancient Germanic custom—it becomes clear that the formless, the unblessed, marriage, is a marriage. In 1200 Archbishop Hubert Walter, with a salvo for the honour and privilege of the Roman church, published in a council at Lambeth a constitution which declared that no marriage was to be celebrated until after a triple publication of the church's ban. No persons were to be married save publicly in the face of the church and in the presence of a priest. Persons who married in other fashion were not to be admitted into a church without the bishop's licence[3]. At the Lateran council of 1215 Innocent III. extended over the whole of western Christendom the custom that had hitherto obtained in some countries of 'publishing the banns of marriage,' that is, of calling upon all and singular to declare any cause or just

---

[1] Freisen, *op. cit.* 120–151; Esmein, *op. cit.* i. 178–187.

[2] Parker printed this canon from a MS. belonging to the church of Worcester in Antiquitates Britannicae Ecclesiae (ed. Hanoviae, 1605), p. 114; it was copied from Parker's book by Spelman and Wilkins. Lanfranc is made to decree 'ut nullus filiam suam vel cognatam det alicui absque benedictione sacerdotali; si aliter fecerit, non ut legitimum coniugium sed ut fornicatorium iudicabitur.' He does not say that the union will be mere fornication; he says that it will be *coniugium fornicatorium*, an unlawful and fornicatory marriage. Lanfranc's words recall those of the Pseudo-Isidorian Evaristus, which appear in c. 1. C. 30. q. 5; as to this see Freisen, *op. cit.* p. 139.

[3] Hoveden, iv. 135.

impediment that could be urged against the proposed union.
From that time forward a marriage with banns had certain
[p. 369] legal advantages over a marriage without banns, which can
only be explained below when we speak of 'putative' marriages. But still the formless, the unblessed, marriage is a
marriage[1].

It is thus that Alexander III. writes to the Bishop of Decretal of
Alexander
Norwich[2]:—'We understand from your letter that a certain III.
man and woman at the command of their lord mutually
received each other, no priest being present, and no such
ceremony being performed as the English church is wont to
employ, and then that before any physical union, another man
solemnly married the said woman and knew her. We answer
that if the first man and the woman received each other by
mutual consent directed to time present, saying the one to the
other, 'I receive you as mine (*meum*),' and 'I receive you as
mine (*meam*),' then, albeit there was no such ceremony as
aforesaid, and albeit there was no carnal knowledge, the woman
ought to be restored to the first man, for after such a consent
she could not and ought not to marry another. If however
there was no such consent by such words as aforesaid, and no
sexual union preceded by a consent *de futuro*, then the woman
must be left to the second man who subsequently received her
and knew her, and she must be absolved from the suit of the
first man ; and if he has given faith or sworn an oath [to marry
the woman], then a penance must be set him for the breach of
his faith or of his oath. But in case either of the parties shall
have appealed, then, unless an appeal is excluded by the terms
of the commission, you are to defer to that appeal[3].'

We have given this decretal at length, for it shows how
complete was the sway that the catholic canon law wielded
in the England of Henry II.'s time, and it also briefly sums

---

[1] c. 3. X. 4. 3. This seems the origin of the belief that Innocent III. 'was
the first who ordained the celebration of marriage in the church.' This belief
is stated by Blackstone, Comment. i. 439, and was in his time traditional
among English lawyers. Apparently it can be traced to Dr Goldingham, a
civilian who was consulted in the case of *Bunting* v. *Lepingwell* (Moore's
Reports, 169). See Friedberg, Recht der Eheschliessung, 314.

[2] Compilatio Prima, lib. 4, tit. 4, c. 6 (Friedberg, Quinque Compilationes,
p. 47).

[3] Another decretal which Alexander III. sent to England contains an
elaborate statement of general doctrine; c. 2. X. 4. 16.

up that law's doctrine of marriage. A strong case is put. On the one hand stands the bare consent *per verba de praesenti*, unhallowed and unconsummated, on the other a solemn and a [p. 370] consummated union. The formless interchange of words prevails over the combined force of ecclesiastical ceremony and sexual intercourse.

Law of marriage in England.

And now we have to say that in the year 1843 in our highest court of law three learned lords maintained the thesis that by the ecclesiastical and the common law of England the presence of an ordained clergyman was from the remotest period onward essential to the formation of a valid marriage. An accident gave their opinion the victory over that of three other equally learned lords, and every English court may now-a-days be bound to adopt the doctrine that thus prevailed. It is hardly likely that the question will ever again be of any practical importance, and we are therefore the freer to say that if the victorious cause pleased the lords, it is the vanquished cause that will please the historian of the middle ages[1].

Law of English ecclesiastical courts.

But we must distinguish between the ecclesiastical and the temporal law. As regards the former, no one doubts what, at all events from the middle years of the twelfth century until the Council of Trent, was the law of the catholic church :—for the formation of a valid marriage no religious ceremony, no presence of a priest or 'ordained clergyman,' is necessary. Clandestine unions, unblessed unions, are prohibited; *fieri non debent*; the husband and wife who have intercourse with each other before the church has blessed their marriage, sin and should be put to penance; they will be compelled by spiritual

---

[1] We refer to the famous case of *The Queen* v. *Millis*, 10 Clark and Finelly, 534, which was followed by *Beamish* v. *Beamish*, 9 House of Lords Cases, 274. The Irish Court of King's Bench was equally divided. In the House of Lords, after the opinion of the English judges had been given against the validity of a marriage at which no clergyman had been present, Lords Lyndhurst, Cottenham and Abinger were for holding the marriage void, while Lords Brougham, Denman and Campbell were in favour of its validity. Owing to the form in which the question came before the House, the result of the division was that the marriage was held to be void. Among the pamphlets evoked by this case two tracts by Sir John Stoddart deserve special mention. He argues with great force against the historical theory to which our law seems to be committed. In this he has been followed by Dr Emil Friedberg, whose Recht der Eheschliessung contains a minute discussion of English law. See also a paper by Sir H. W. Elphinstone in L. Q. R. v. 44. But the very learned opinion given by Willes J. in *Beamish* v. *Beamish* is the best criticism of the victorious doctrine.

censures to celebrate their marriage before the face of the church; but they were married already when they exchanged a consent *per verba de praesenti,* or became one flesh after ex-
[p. 371] changing a consent *per verba de futuro.* It was contended, however, that in this matter the English church had held aloof from the church catholic and Roman. No proof of this improbable contention was forthcoming, save such as was to be found in what was called a law of King Edmund and in that constitution of Archbishop Lanfranc which we have already mentioned[1]. Of these it is enough to say, first, that the so-called law of Edmund, which however is not a law, is far from declaring that there can be no marriage without a mass priest; secondly, that in all probability Lanfranc's canon neither says this nor means this; and thirdly, that both documents come from too remote a date to be of any importance when the question is as to the ecclesiastical law which prevailed in England from the middle of the twelfth century onwards. On the other hand, we have the clearest proof that at that time the law of the catholic and Roman church was being enforced in England. We have this not only in the decretal of Alexander III. which has been set forth above[2], but also in the many appeals about matrimonial matters that were being taken from England to Rome. It would have been as impossible for the courts Christian of this country to maintain about this vital point a schismatical law of their own as it would now be for a judge of the High Court to persistently disregard the decisions of the House of Lords: there would have been an appeal from every sentence, and reversal would have been a matter of course. And then, had this state of things existed even for a few years, surely some English prelate or canonist would have been at pains to state our insular law. No one did anything of the kind. To say that the English church received or adopted the catholic law of marriage would be untrue; her rulers never conceived that they were free to pick and choose their law. We have been asked to suppose that for several centuries our church was infected with heretical

---

[1] See above, pp. 369, 370.

[2] This decretal was cited by Willes J. in *Beamish* v. *Beamish,* 9 H. L. C. 308; it was known to him through Pothier. Unfortunately it came too late. Willes J. further remarked (p. 310) that Lanfranc's canon is but the epitome of an old decretal.

pravity about the essence of one of the Christian sacraments, and that no one thought this worthy of notice. And an odd form of pravity it was. She did not require a sacerdotal benediction; she did not require (as the Council of Trent very wisely did) the testimony of the parish priest; she did not [p. 372] require a ceremony in church; she required the 'presence' of an 'ordained clergyman[1].'

The temporal law and marriage. As to our temporal law, from the middle of the twelfth century onwards it had no doctrine of marriage, for it never had to say in so many words whether a valid marriage had been contracted. Adultery was not, bigamy was not, incest was not, a temporal crime. On the other hand, it had often to say whether a woman was entitled to dower, whether a child was entitled to inherit. About these matters it was free to make what rules it pleased. It was in no wise bound to hold that every widow was entitled to dower, or that every child whom the law of the church pronounced legitimate was capable of inheriting. The question, 'Was this a marriage or no?' might come before it incidentally. When this happened, that question was sent for decision to an ecclesiastical court, and the answer would be one of the premises on which the lay court would found some judgment about dower, inheritance or the like; but only one of the premises.

Marriage and the law of dower. Now the king's justices, though many of them were ecclesiastics, seem to have felt instinctively that the canonists were going astray and with formlessness were bringing in a mischievous uncertainty[2]. The result is curious, for at first sight the lay tribunal seems to be rigidly requiring a religious ceremony which in the eyes of the church is unessential. No woman can claim dower unless she has been endowed at the church door. That is Bracton's rule, and it is well borne out by the case-law of his time[3]. The woman's marriage may be indisputable, but she is to have no dower if she was not endowed at the church door. We soon see, however, that

---

[1] John de Athona in his gloss on Otho's constitution *Innotuit*, says 'petens restitutionem uxoris non auditur de iure ubi matrimonium est contractum clandestine, scilicet, bannis non editis.' Here, however, he is referring to the possessory restitution, the *actio spolii*, of which hereafter. He knew well enough that there may be a valid marriage without any solemnities; see the gloss on Ottobon's constitution *Coniugale*.

[2] See Friedberg, Recht der Eheschliessung, p. 56.

[3] Bracton, f. 302–4; Note Book, pl. 891, 1669, 1718, 1875.

what our justices are demanding is, not a religious rite, nor 'the presence of an ordained clergyman,' but publicity. We see this very plainly when Bracton tells us that the endowment can and must be made at the church door even during an [p. 373] interdict when the bridal mass can not be celebrated[1]. It is usual to go to church when one is to be married; all decent persons do this and all persons are required to do it by ecclesiastical law. The temporal law seizes hold of this fact. Marriages contracted elsewhere may be valid enough, but only at the church door can a bride be endowed. There is a special reason for this requirement. The common contrast to the church-door marriage is the death-bed marriage[2]. At the instance of the priest and with the fear of death before him, the sinner 'makes an honest woman' of his mistress. This may do well enough for the church and may, one hopes, profit his soul in another world, but it must give no rights in English soil[3]. The justices who demanded an endowment at the church door were the justices who set their faces against testamentary gifts of land, and strenuously endeavoured to make livery of seisin mean a real change of possession. The acts which give rights in land should be public, notorious acts. It is easy, however, to slip from the proposition that no woman can claim dower unless she has been endowed at the church door, into the proposition that, so far as concerns the exaction of dower, no marriage is valid unless it is contracted before the face of the church. Both propositions mean the same thing, and Bracton adopts now the one and now the other[4].

If, however, we can not argue that a woman was not married because she can not claim dower, still less can we argue that an union is a marriage because the issue of it will,—or is not a marriage because the issue of it will not,—be capable of inheriting English land. The canon law itself admits that this may well be the case. It holds many children to be legitimate who are not the offspring of a lawful wedlock. To say nothing here of its doctrine about the retroactive force of marriage, about legitimation *per subsequens matrimonium*, it knows the so-called 'putative marriage.' Certain of the impediments to marriage that were maintained by the canon law did not prevent

Marriage and the law of inheritance.

---

[1] Bracton, f. 305, 419 b.
[2] Bracton, f. 92; Note Book, pl. 891, 1669, 1718, 1875.
[3] Note Book, pl. 1669, 1875.   [4] Bracton, f. 304.

the children of the union from being legitimate, if that union had been solemnized with the rites of the church, and if at the time when the children were begotten both or one of their parents were ignorant of the fact which constituted the impediment. Among such impediments was consanguinity. A man [p. 374] goes through the ceremony of marriage with his cousin. So long as either of them is ignorant of the kinship between them, the children that are born to them are legitimate. There is here no real marriage; but there is a putative marriage. The disabilities annexed to bastardy are regarded by the canonists as a punishment inflicted on offending parents, and in a case in which there has been a marriage ceremony duly solemnized with all the rites of the church, including the publication of banns[1], and one at least of the parties has been acting *bona fide*, that is, has been ignorant of the impediment, their unlawful intercourse, for such in strictness it has been, is not to be punished by the bastardy of their children. It was long before the canonists worked out to the full their theory about these putative marriages. Some would have held that if there was good faith in the one consort and guilty knowledge in the other, the child might be legitimate as regards one of his parents, illegitimate as regards the other. Others held that such lopsided legitimacy was impossible[2].

Putative marriages.

Bracton knew this learning and wrote it down as an indubitable part of English law. In a passage which he borrowed from the canonist Tancred, he holds that there can be a putative marriage and legitimate offspring even when the union is invalid owing to the existence of a previous marriage. 'If a woman in good faith marries a man who is already married, believing him to be unmarried, and has children by him, such children will be adjudged legitimate and capable of inheriting[3].' The canon law, however, may in this instance have been somewhat too subtle for our temporal tribunals; they were not given to troubling themselves much about so invisible an element as *bona fides*[4]. A contemporary of Bracton lays

---

[1] c. 3. X. 4. 3.

[2] Freisen, *op. cit.* pp. 857–862; Esmein, *op. cit.* ii. 33–7.

[3] Bracton, f. 63. Bracton begins by copying a passage from Tancred (ed. Wunderlich, p. 104). He then adopts c. 3. X. 4. 3 (a canon of the Lateran council of 1215) and then c. 2. X. 4. 17, a decretal of Alexander III. See Bracton and Azo, p. 221, where the texts are compared.

[4] See Bliss, Calendar of Papal Registers, i. 254. In 1248 Innocent IV.

down the law in much ruder shape. 'If a woman is divorced for kinship, or fornication, or blasphemy (as says Augustine the Great) she can not claim dower, but her children can inherit both from their father and from their mother according to the law of the realm. But if the wife is separated from her husband on the ground that he previously contracted marriage with some other woman by words of present time, then her children can not be legitimate, nor can they succeed to their father, nor to their mother, according to the law of the realm[1].' So late as 1337 English lawyers still maintained that the issue of a *de facto* marriage, which was invalid because of the consanguinity of the parties, were not bastards if born before divorce[2]. At a little later time, having lost touch with the canon law, they developed a theory of their own which was far less favourable to the issue of putative marriages than the law of the church had been[3]. This, however, lies in the future. Here we are only concerned to notice that in the thirteenth century, according to the law of the church and the law of the land, we can not argue that because a child is legitimate and can inherit, therefore his parents were husband and wife.

However, we believe that at this time our temporal courts were at one with our spiritual courts about legitimacy and the capacity to inherit; that if the church said, 'This child is legitimate,' the state said, 'It is capable of inheriting'; and that if the church said, 'This child is illegitimate,' the state said, 'It is incapable of inheriting.' To this agreement between church and state there was the one well-known exception:—our temporal courts would not allow to marriage any retroactive power; the bastard remained incapable of inheriting land even though his parents had become husband and wife and thereby made him capable of receiving holy orders and, in all probability,

Acceptance of canonical rules.

p. 375]

---

decides an English case on this point of good faith. This is one of the many instances which shows how impossible it would have been for the English church to have dissented from the Roman about matrimonial causes.

[1] From a Cambridge MS. of Glanvill; see Harv. L. R. vi. 11. Glanvill's doctrine (vi. 17) was that a divorce for consanguinity deprives the wife of dower, but leaves the issue legitimate.

[2] Y. B. 11–12 Edw. III. ed. Pike, p. 481.

[3] Pike, Year Book, 11–12 Edw. III. pp. xx–xxii. The ultimate theory of English lawyers took no heed of good or bad faith and made the legitimacy of the children depend on the fact that their parents while living were never divorced.

of taking a share in the movable goods of his parents[1]. The general rule, to which this was the exception, was implied [p. 376] in the procedure of the temporal courts. If a question about the existence of a marriage was raised in such a court, that question was sent for trial to the spiritual court, and the writ that sent it thither expressly said that such questions were not within the cognizance of the temporal forum[2]. If, on the other hand, the existence of a marriage was admitted, but one of the parties relied on the fact that his adversary was born before that marriage, then there was no question for the spiritual court, and, at least after the celebrated dispute in the Merton parliament, no opportunity was given to it of enforcing its rule about the force of the *subsequens matrimonium* :—the question 'Born before marriage or no' went to a jury as a question of fact[3]. But about all other matters the church could have, and apparently had, her way. She could maintain all her *impedimenta dirimentia*, the impediment of holy orders, the impediments of consanguinity and affinity. 'You are a bastard, for your father was a deacon':—that was a good plea in the king's court[4], and the king's court did nothing to narrow the mischievous latitude of the prohibited degrees. The bishop's certificate was conclusive. It was treated as a judgment *in rem.* If at any future time the same question about the existence of the marriage is raised, the certificate will answer it, and answer it indisputably, unless some charge of fraud or collusion can be made[5]. As to the particular point that has

---

[1] We know of no text that proves that the bastard legitimated by the marriage of his parents could succeed to a 'bairn's part' of the father's goods. But it seems quite certain that the church courts must have tried to enforce their own theory within a sphere that was their own, and we doubt very much whether the king's court would have prohibited them from so doing. Of the 'bairn's part,' we spoke above; see vol. ii. pp. 348–356.

[2] Glanvill, vii. 14: 'ad curiam meam non spectat agnoscere de bastardia.' In and after Bracton's day (f. 419 b) the language of the writ is rather more guarded, owing to the emergence of the controversy about the *subsequens matrimonium.*

[3] Before the day at Merton the issue of special bastardy was sometimes sent to the bishop: Note Book, pl. 290. Bracton argues at length, f. 416–20, that the king still has the right to compel the bishop to answer the obnoxious question. His argument seems to be founded on a perversion of history; see Note Book, vol. i. p. 104.

[4] Select Civil Pleas (Selden Soc.), pl. 205.

[5] Bracton, f. 420: Y. B. 34–5 Edw. I. p. 64. It would seem as if cases were sometimes sent even to foreign prelates: ibid. p. 184.

been disputed, we have Bracton's word that a marriage which
was not contracted *in facie ecclesiae*, though it can not give the
wife a claim to dower, may well be a good enough marriage so
[p. 377] far as regards the legitimacy of the children[1]. A case which
had occurred shortly before he wrote his treatise shows us that
he had good warrant for his assertion.

In or about 1254 died one William de Cardunville, a tenant
in chief of the crown. In the usual course an *inquisitio post
mortem* was held for the purpose of finding his heir. The
jurors told the following story :—William solemnly and at the
church door espoused one Alice and they lived together as
husband and wife for sixteen years. He had several sons and
daughters by her; one of them is still alive; his name is Richard
and he is four years old. After this there came a woman
called Joan, whom William had carnally known a long time
ago, and on whom he had begotten a son called Richard, and
she demanded William as her husband in the court Christian,
relying on an affidation that had taken place between them;
and she, having proved her case, was adjudged to him by the
sentence of the court and a divorce was solemnly celebrated
between him and Alice. And so William and Joan lived
together for a year and more. But, said the jurors,—sensible
laymen that they were—we doubt which of the two Richards
is heir, whether Richard son of Joan, who is twenty-four years
old, or Richard son of Alice, who is four years old, for Joan was
never solemnly married at the door of the church, and we
say that, if neither of them is heir, then William's brother
will inherit. When this verdict came into the chancery, the
attention of the royal officers must have been pointedly drawn
to the question that we have been discussing, and, had they
thought only of their master's interests, they would have
decided in favour of Alice's son and so secured a long wardship
for the king; but, true to the law of the church and the law of
the land, they ordered that Joan's son should have seisin of his

(margin note: No ceremony necessary.)

---

[1] Bracton, f. 304: 'Et ita poterit esse matrimonium legitimum, quoad
hereditatis successionem, ubicunque contractum fuerit, dum tamen probatum,
et illegitimum quoad dotis exactionem, nisi fuerit in facie ecclesiae contractum.'
On f. 92 he speaks with less certain sound about the capacity to inherit of the
issue of a clandestine marriage; but the word *clandestine* had several distinct
meanings; see below, p. 385, note 1. See also Fleta, 340, 353; Britton, ii.
236, 266.

father's land: in other words, they preferred the unsolemnized to the solemnized marriage[1].

Recognition of *de facto* marriages. At the same time we must notice that occasionally the [p. 378] temporal court gives something which at first sight looks like a judgment touching the validity of a marriage without sending any question to the court Christian. It is very possible that in a possessory action the jurors will give some special verdict about the birth of one of the parties or of a third person, and by so doing will throw upon the justices the duty of deciding whether, the facts being as stated by the jurors, that person is to be treated as heir for possessory purposes. In such a case the justices' decision seems to be provisional. The action itself is possessory; it can not, as the phrase goes, 'bind the right'; the defeated litigant will have another opportunity of urging his proprietary claims and, it may be, of proving that, though he has been treated as a bastard by jurors and justices, he really is legitimate. Now, when a question about a marriage arises in a possessory action, it must be dealt with in what we may call a possessory spirit, and, as we have to get our facts from juries, it is necessary that we should lay stress on those things, and those only, which are done formally and in public. If man and woman have gone through the ceremony of marriage at the church door, we may say that we have here a *de facto* marriage, an union which stands to a valid marriage in somewhat the same relation as that in which possession stands to ownership. On the other hand, if there has been no ceremony, we can not in the thirteenth century say that there is a *de facto* marriage; mere concubinage is far too common to allow us to presume a marriage wherever there is a long-continued cohabitation. But a religious ceremony is a different thing; it is definite and public; we can trust the jurors to know all about it; we can make it the basis of our judgments whenever the validity of the union has not been put in issue in such a fashion that the decision of an ecclesiastical court must be awaited. A strong objection is felt to the admission of a plea of bastardy in a possessory action, at all events when the

---

[1] Calendarium Genealogicum, i. 57: Excerpta e Rot. Fin. ii. 182. Both sons were named Richard. The writ of livery is in favour of Richard 'the first-begotten son and heir' of William. It is clear that this Richard is Joan's son, for the other Richard was but four years old and would not have been entitled to a livery even if he had been the heir.

question lies between those who as a matter of fact are brothers or cousins. Such a plea is in some sort petitory or droiturel; it goes beyond matter of fact; 'it touches the right[1].'

[p. 379]

The canonists themselves, having made marriages all too easy, and valid marriages all too difficult, had been driven into a doctrine of possessory marriage. In the canon law each spouse has an action against the other spouse in which he or she can demand the prestation of conjugal duties. Such an action may be petitory, or, as our English lawyers would have said, 'droiturel'; the canonists will even call it *vindicatio rei*. But in such an action the plaintiff must be prepared to prove that there is a valid marriage, and the defendant may rely on any of those 'diriment impediments,' of which there are but too many ready to the hand of any one who would escape from the marital bond. So a possessory action (*actio spolii*) also is given, and in this the defendant will not be allowed to set up pleas which dispute, not the existence of a *de facto* marriage, but its validity. On the other hand, in this possessory action the plaintiff must prove a marriage celebrated in face of the church. The *de facto* marriage on which the canon law will bestow a possessory protection is a marriage which has been duly solemnized and which therefore appears to the church as valid until it has been proved to be void[2]. Our English lawyers accept this doctrine and apply it to disputes about inheritance. Those marriages and only those which have been celebrated at the church door are marriages for the purpose of possessory actions. Hereafter in a droiturel action, when the bishop's certificate is demanded, such a marriage may be stigmatized as void, and on the other hand an unsolemnized

The marital possessorium.

---

[1] Bracton, f. 418 b; Y. B. 32–3 Edw. I. pp. 62, 74; 33–5 Edw. I. p. 118. The phrase '*de facto* marriage' is none of our making; it is used by Bracton, f. 303, and Coke, Lit. 33 a, b. The French parlement seems to have behaved in the same manner as our own royal court. 'Le Parlement, tout en reconnaissant bien que les officiers royaux ne pourraient pas apprécier la validité des mariages, déclara qu'ils pourraient constater la possession d'état et s'informer si en fait il y avait eu union régulière; d'où l'on déduisit qu'ils étaient compétents pour trancher au possessoire les questions matrimoniales, et même au pétitoire, si les parties ne proposaient pas d'exception.' Langlois, Philippe le Hardi, 272.

[2] Esmein, *op. cit.* ii. 16. See above, vol. ii. p. 147, as to the application of the notion of possession to marital relationships. An interesting letter by Abp Peckham (Register, iii. 940) insists on the difference between the *possessorium* and the *petitorium*.

marriage may be established; but meanwhile we are dealing only with externals, and the ceremony at the church door assures us that the man and woman regarded their union, or desired that it should be regarded, as no mere concubinage but as marriage.

Reluctance to bastardize the dead.

Again, if a question is raised about the legitimacy of one who is already dead, this question is not sent to the bishop, but goes to a jury. The charge of bastardy imports some disgrace, and it can not be made in a direct way against one who is not alive to answer it; still of course some inquiry about [p. 380] his birth may be necessary in order that we may settle the rights of other persons[1]. That inquiry will be made of a jury; but it will be made by those who openly express themselves unwilling 'to bastardize the dead.' This unwillingness at length hardened into a positive rule of law. If a bastard enters on his father's land as his father's heir and remains in untroubled seisin all his life, and then the heir of this bastard's body enters, this heir will have a title unimpeachable by the right heir of the original tenant. Such at all events will be the case between the *bastard eigné* and the *mulier puisné*: that is to say, if Alan has a bastard son Baldwin by Maud, and then marries Maud and has by her a legitimate son Clement, and if on Alan's death Baldwin enters as heir and remains seised for the rest of his life and then his son Bernard enters, Bernard will have an unimpeachable title; Clement will have lost the land for good and all[2]. It must be remembered that our medieval law did not consistently regard the bastard as *filius nullius*, though such phrases as 'You are a son of the people' might be thrown about in court[3]. The bastards with whom the land law had to deal were for the more part the issue of

---

[1] Bracton, f. 420 b; Y. B. 20–1 Edw. I. p. 193.

[2] Lit. sec. 399, 400; Co. Lit. 244; Bl. Comm. ii. 248. The oldest form of the rule seems to be very broad. Placit. Abbrev. p. 195 (6 Edw. I.): 'et inauditum est et ius [*corr.* iuri] dissonum quod aliquis qui per successionem hereditariam pacifice tenuit hereditatem toto tempore suo bastardetur post mortem suam.' Fitzherbert, Abr. *Bastardy*, pl. 28: 'nec iustum est aliquando [*corr.* aliquem] mortuum facere bastardum qui toto tempore suo tenebatur pro legitimo.' Littleton is in favour of applying the rule only where bastard and mulier have the same mother as well as the same father; but this was not quite certain even in his day. Our lawyers seem to have come to the odd word *mulier* by calling a legitimate son a *filius mulieratus*.

[3] Y. B. 32–3 Edw. I. 251: 'Jeo le face fiz al poelple.'

permanent unions. And so the bastard who enters as his father's heir must be distinguished from the mere interloper. After all, he is his father's 'natural' son, and we hardly go too far in saying that he has a 'natural' right to inherit: the rules that exclude him from the inheritance are rules of positive institution. And so, if he enters and continues seised until he can no longer answer the charge of bastardy, we must treat him as one who inherited rightfully.

For these reasons the decisions of lay tribunals which seem to establish or assume the validity or invalidity of a marriage should be examined with extreme caution. Just because there [p. 381] is another tribunal which can go to the heart of the matter, the king's justices are and must be content to look only at the outside, and thus they lay great stress on the performance or non-performance of the public marriage rite. Sometimes they expressly say that they are looking only at the outside, and that what concerns them is not marriage but the reputation of marriage. They ask the jurors not whether a dead man was a bastard, but whether he was reputed a bastard in his lifetime[1]. When a woman confronted by her deed, pleads that she was *coverte* when she sealed it, they hold that 'No one knew of your coverture' is a good reply[2]. It is with *de facto* marriages that they are concerned; questions *de iure* they leave to the church.

Temporal courts and possessory marriage.

It was, we believe, a neglect of this distinction which in 1843 led some of our greatest lawyers astray,—a very natural neglect, for the doctrine of possessory marriages looks strange in the nineteenth century. They had before them some old cases in which to a first glance the court seems to have denied the validity of a marriage that had not been celebrated in church. By far the strongest of these came from the year 1306. William brought an assize of novel disseisin against Peter. Peter pleaded that one John died seised in fee and that he (Peter) entered as brother and heir without disseisin. William replied that on John's death, he (William) entered as son and heir and was seised until he was ejected by Peter. The jurors gave a special verdict. John being ill in bed espoused (at the instance of the vicar of Plumstead) his concubine Katharine; the usual words were said but no mass was celebrated. John and Katharine thenceforth lived as husband and wife and

Del Heith's case.

[1] Y. B. 30–1 Edw. I. p. 291. [2] Y. B. 21–2 Edw. I. p. 426.

Katharine bore to John a child, namely, William. The jurors were asked whether after John's recovery any espousals were celebrated; they answered, No. They further found that on John's death his brother Peter entered as heir and was seised for fifteen days, that William then ejected Peter and was seised for five weeks, and that Peter then ejected William. The judgment follows:—And because it is found that John never espoused Katharine *in facie ecclesiae*, whence it follows that William can claim no right in the said tenement by hereditary descent from John, therefore it is considered that Peter may go without day and that William do take nothing by this assize, [p. 382] but be in mercy for his false claim[1].

Ceremony required for establishment of a possessory marriage.

Now for a moment this may seem to decide that a marriage which has not been solemnized in church is no valid marriage. We believe that it merely decides that such a marriage is no marriage for purely possessory purposes. William, after failing in the assize, was quite free to bring a writ of right against Peter. If he had done so, the question whether the marriage was valid or no would have been sent to the bishop, and we have no doubt that he would have certified in favour of its validity. The application to marital relationships of the doctrine of possession, and the requirement of a public ecclesiastical ceremony for the constitution of a marriage which shall deserve possessory protection, though no such ceremony is required for a true and 'droiturel' marriage—all this is so very quaint that no wonder it has deceived some learned judges; but all the world over it was part of medieval law and a natural outcome of a system that made the form of marriage fatally simple, while it heaped up impediments in the way of valid unions.

---

[1] This is *Del Heith's Case*, which was known to the lords only through a note in a Harleian MS. of no authority. We have found the record; De Banco Roll, Trin. 34 Edw. I. (No. 161), m. 203. The reference usually given is false. *Foxcroft's* [corr. *Foxcote's*] *Case*, which stands on De Banco Roll, Pasch. 10 Edw. I. (No. 45), m. 23, is not even in appearance so decisive, since there the party who failed had committed himself to proving a marriage in church. As to this case see Revised Reports, vol. ix. p. vii. It was an action of cosinage against a lord claiming by escheat, a purely possessory cause. The bedside marriage was contracted, not merely in 'the presence of an ordained clergyman,' but in that of a consecrated bishop; but this was insufficient for possessory purposes according to English law and canon law. We must thank Mr Baildon for helping us to find these records.

From what has been already said it follows that a marriage Unprov-
able mar-
riages. might easily exist and yet be unprovable. We can not here speak of the canonical theory of proof, but it was somewhat rigorous, requiring in general two unexceptionable witnesses. If *A* and *B* contracted an absolutely secret marriage—and this they could do by the exchange of a few words—that marriage was for practical purposes dissoluble at will. If, while *B* was living, *A* went through the form of contracting a public marriage with *C*, this second marriage was treated as valid, and neither *A*, nor *B*, nor both together could prove the validity of their clandestine union : *Clandestinum manifesto non prae-* [p. 383] *iudicat.* Thus the ecclesiastical judge *in foro externo* might have to compel a man and woman to live together in what their confessors would describe as a continuous adultery[1].

'It is better to marry than to burn':—few texts have done The
idea of
marriage. more harm than this. In the eyes of the medieval church marriage was a sacrament; still it was only a remedy for con-cupiscence. The generality of men and women must marry or they will do worse; therefore marriage must be made easy ; but the very pure hold aloof from it as from a defilement. The law that springs from this source is not pleasant to read[2].

Reckless of mundane consequences, the church, while she Impedi-
ments to
marriage. treated marriage as a formless contract, multiplied impediments which made the formation of a valid marriage a matter of

---

[1] Esmein, *op. cit.* i. 189–191, ii. 128 : Hostiensis says 'Nam in iudicio animae consuletur eis ut non reddant debitum contra conscientiam: in foro autem iudiciali excommunicabuntur nisi reddant ; tolerent ergo excommuni-cationem.' The maxim ' Clandestinum manifesto non praeiudicat' might lead us astray. There are various degrees of clandestinity which must be dis-tinguished. The marriage may be (1) absolutely secret and unprovable : this is the case to which our rule refers. But a marriage may also be called clandestine (2) because, though valid and provable, it has not been solemnized *in facie ecclesiae*, or even (3) because, though thus solemnized, it was not preceded by the publication of banns. Clandestinity of the second and third kinds might have certain evil consequences, for after 1215 there can be no 'putative marriage' which is clandestine in the second, or perhaps—but this was disputable—in the third sense. See Esmein, *op. cit.* i. 182–3.

[2] Esmein, *op. cit.* i. 84: 'Enfin, le mariage étant conçu comme un remède à la concupiscence, le droit canonique sanctionnait, avec une énergie toute particulière, l'obligation du devoir conjugal, non seulement dans le *forum internum*, mais encore devant le *forum externum*. De là toute une série de règles que les canonistes du moyen âge exposaient avec une précision minutieuse et une innocente impudeur, et qu'il est parfois assez difficile de rappeler, aujourd'hui que les mœurs ont changé et que l'on n'écrit plus en latin.'

chance. The most important of these obstacles were those which consisted of some consanguinity or affinity between the parties. The exuberant learning which enveloped the table of prohibited degrees we must not explore, still a little should be said about its main rules.

Consan-
guinity.

　　The blood-relationship which exists between two persons may be computed in several different fashions. To us the simplest will be the Roman :—In order to discover the degree of consanguinity which exists between two persons, A and X, we must count the acts of generation which divide the one from the other. If the one is the other's ancestor in blood the task is easy :—I am in the first degree from my father and mother, the second from my grandparents. But suppose that [p. 384] A and X are collateral relations, then our rule is this—Count the steps, the acts of generation, which lie between each of them and their nearest common ancestor, and then add together these two numbers. Father and son are in the first degree, brother and brother in the second, uncle and nephew in the third, first cousins in the fourth. But, though this mode of computation may seem the most natural to us, it was not the most natural to our remote ancestors. If we look at the case from the standpoint of the common ancestor, we can say that all his children are in the first generation or degree, all his grandchildren in the second, all his great-grandchildren in the third; and, if we hold to this mode of speech, then we shall say that a marriage between first cousins is a marriage between persons who are in the second, not the fourth, degree. It is also probable that the ancient Germans knew yet another calculus of kinship, which was bound up with their law of inheritance. Within the household composed of a father and children there was no degree; this household was regarded for this purpose as an unit, and only when, in default of children, the inheritance fell to remoter kinsmen, was there any need to count the grades of 'sibship.' Thus first cousins are in the first degree of sibship; second cousins in the second. Now what with the Roman method and the German method, what with now an exclusion and now an inclusion of one or of both of the related persons, it was long before the church established an uniform fashion of interpreting her own prohibitions, the so-called 'canonical computation.' In order to explain this, we will suppose for a moment that the prohibitive law reaches

its utmost limit when it forbids a marriage in the fourth degree.
We count downwards from the common ancestor, so that
brothers are in the first degree, first cousins in the second,
third cousins in the fourth. If then the two persons who are
before us stand at an equal distance from their common
ancestor, we have no difficulty in applying this method. We
have two equal lines, and it matters not whether we count the
number of grades in the one or in the other. To meet the
more difficult case in which the two lines are unequal, another
rule was slowly evolved:—Measure the longer line[1]. A prohi-
[p. 385] bition of marriages within x degrees will not prevent a marriage
between two persons one of whom stands more than x degrees
away from the common ancestor. A prohibition of marriage
in the first degree would not, but a prohibition of marriage
within the second degree would, condemn a marriage between
uncle and niece[2].

The rule to which the church ultimately came was that
defined by Innocent III. at the Lateran council of 1215, namely
that marriages within the fourth degree of consanguinity are
null[3]. Before that decree, the received doctrine was—and it
was received in England as well as elsewhere[4]—that marriage
within the seventh degree of the canonical computation was
forbidden, but that kinship in the sixth or seventh degree was
only *impedimentum impediens,* a cause which would render a
marriage sinful, not *impedimentum dirimens,* a cause which
would render a marriage null. Laxer rules had for a while
been accepted; but to this result the canonists had slowly
come. The seventh degree seems to have been chosen by
rigorous theorists who would have forbidden a marriage between
kinsfolk however remote, for it seems to have been a common
rule among the German nations that for the purposes of inheritance kinship could not be traced beyond the seventh (it may
also be called the sixth and even the fifth[5]) generation; and so
to prohibit marriage within seven degrees was to prohibit it

Prohibited degrees.

---

[1] c. 9. X. 4. 14.

[2] For the history of this matter, see Freisen, *op. cit.* pp. 371–439. The
various modes of counting kinship are elaborately discussed by Ficker,
Untersuchungen zur Erbenfolge, vol. i. The German scheme is described by
Heusler, Institutionen, ii. 587.

[3] c. 8. X. 4. 14.

[4] Canons of 1075, 1102, 1127; Johnson, Canons, ii. pp. 14, 27, 36.

[5] Heusler, *op. cit.* ii. 591.

among all persons who for any legal purpose could claim blood-relationship with each other. All manner of fanciful analogies, however, could be found for the choice of this holy number. Were there not seven days of the week and seven ages of the world, seven gifts of the spirit and seven deadly sins? Ultimately the allegorical mind of the ecclesiastical lawyer had to be content with the reflection that, though all this might be so, there were but four elements and but four humours[1].

Affinity.

Then with relentless logic the church had been pressing home the axiom that the sexual union makes man and woman one flesh. All my wife's or my mistress's blood kinswomen are connected with me by way of affinity. I am related to her [p. 386] sister in the first degree, to her first cousin in the second, to her second cousin in the third, and the doctrine of the twelfth century is that I may not marry in the seventh degree of this affinity. This is affinity of the first genus. But if I and my wife are really one, it follows that I must be related by way of affinity to the wives of her kinsmen. This is the second genus of affinity. To the wife of my wife's brother I am related in the first degree of this second genus of affinity; to the wife of my wife's first cousin in the second degree of this second genus, and so forth. But we can not stop here; for we can apply our axiom over and over again. My wife's blood relations are *affines* to me in the first genus; my wife's *affines* of the first genus are *affines* to me in the second genus; my wife's *affines* of the second genus are my *affines* of the third. I may not marry my wife's sister's husband's wife, for we stand to each other in the first degree of this third genus of affinity. The general opinion of the twelfth century seems to have been that while the prohibition of marriage extended to the seventh degree of the first genus, it extended only to the fourth degree of the second genus, and only to the second degree of the third genus[2]. But the law was often a dead letter. The council of 1215, which confined the impediment of consanguinity within the first four degrees, put the same boundary to the impediment of affinity of the first genus, while it decreed that affinity of the second or third genus might for the future

---

[1] Freisen, *op. cit.* p. 401.

[2] Freisen, *op. cit.* pp. 474–489; Esmein, *op. cit.* i. 374–383; Friedberg, Lehrbuch des Kirchenrechts, ed. 4, p. 386, where some diagrams will be found.

be disregarded[1]. Even when confined within this compass, the doctrine of affinity could do a great deal of harm, for we have to remember that the efficient cause of affinity is not marriage but sexual intercourse[2]. Then a 'quasi affinity' was established by a mere espousal *per verba de futuro,* and another and a very secret cause for the dissolution of *de facto* marriages was thus invented[3]. Then again, regard must be had to spiritual kinship, [p. 387] to 'godsib[4].' Baptism is a new birth; the godson may marry neither his godmother nor his godmother's daughter. Behind these intricate rules there is no deep policy, there is no strong religious feeling; they are the idle ingenuities of men who are amusing themselves by inventing a game of skill which is to be played with neatly drawn tables of affinity and doggerel hexameters. The men and women who are the pawns in this game may, if they be rich enough, evade some of the forfeits by obtaining papal dispensations; but then there must be another set of rules marking off the dispensable from the indispensable impediments[5]. When we weigh the merits of the medieval church and have remembered all her good deeds, we have to put into the other scale as a weighty counterpoise the incalculable harm done by a marriage law which was a maze of flighty fancies and misapplied logic.

After some hesitation the church ruled that, however young the bridegroom and bride might be, the consent of their parents or guardians was not necessary to make the marriage valid. If the parties had not reached the age at which they were deemed capable of a rational consent, they could not marry; if on the other hand they had reached that age, their marriage would be valid though the consent of their parents or guardians had not been asked or had been refused. Our English temporal law, though it regarded 'wardship and marriage' as a valuable piece of property, seems to have acquiesced in this doctrine. A case

Marriage of infants.

---

[1] c. 8. X. 4. 14.

[2] Coke, 2nd Inst. 684, tells of one Roger Donington whose marriage was null because before it he had committed fornication with the third cousin of his future wife.

[3] Freisen, *op. cit.* pp. 497–507.

[4] Ibid. pp. 507–555. At a very early time we find even the temporal law of wergild taking note of godsib; Leg. Ine, c. 76 (Liebermann, Gesetze, p. 123), where a 'bishop's-son' means a 'confirmation son'; see Haddan and Stubbs, Councils, iii. p. 219.

[5] For papal dispensations sent to England, see Bliss, Calendar of Papal Registers, vol. i., Index.

from 1224 suggests that a woman who married an infant ward
without his guardian's consent would not be entitled to dower[1]:
but a denial of dower would be no denial of the marriage, and
our law discovered other means of punishing the ward who
married without the consent of the guardian in chivalry or
rejected a 'convenable marriage' which he tendered[2]. A statute
of 1267 forbad the guardian in socage to make a profit for himself out of the marriage of his ward[3].

Age of the parties.

At the age of seven years a child was capable of consent, but
the marriage remained voidable so long as either of the parties
to it was below the age at which it could be consummated. A
presumption fixed this age at fourteen years for boys and twelve [p. 388]
for girls. In case only one of the parties was below that age,
the marriage could be avoided by that party but was binding
on the other. So far as we can see, this doctrine was accepted
by our temporal courts. Thomas of Bayeux had espoused Elena
de Morville *per verba de praesenti* with the consent of her
father, and shortly afterwards a marriage was celebrated in
church between them. Then her father died and this left her
in ward to the king. 'And' said the king's court 'whereas the
said Elena is under age, and, when she comes of age, she will
be able to consent to or dissent from the marriage, and whereas
the marriage does not bind her while she is under age, although
it is binding on Thomas, who is of full age, therefore the said
Elena remains in ward to the king until she is of age, that she
may then consent or dissent[4].' So the daughter of Ralph of
Killingthorpe is taken away from the man who has espoused
her and handed over to her guardian in order that she may
have an opportunity of dissenting from the marriage when she
is twelve years old[5]. Ultimately our common lawyers held
that a wife could claim dower if at her husband's death she was
nine years old, though the marriage in such a case was one that
she could have avoided if she had lived to the age of twelve[6];
but we seem to see this rule growing out of an earlier practice
which, in accordance with the canon law, would have made all
turn on the question of fact, whether or no she had attained
an age at which it was possible for her to consummate the

---

[1] Note Book, pl. 965, 1098.
[2] Stat. Merton, c. 6, 7; Stat. Westm. I. c. 22.　　　[3] Stat. Marlb. c. 17.
[4] Note Book, pl. 1267.
[5] Excerpta e Rot. Fin. i. 228.　　　[6] Littleton, sec. 36; Co. Lit. 33 a.

marriage[1]:—*car au coucher ensemble gaigne femme sa douaire selon la coustume de Normendie*[2].   It is possible, however, that the temporal courts did not pay much attention to the canonical doctrine that the espousals of children under the age of seven years were merely void.   Coke tells us that the nine years old widow shall have her dower 'of what age soever her husband be, albeit he were but four years old[3],' and certain it is that [p. 389] the betrothal of babies was not consistently treated as a nullity. In Henry III.'s day a marriage between a boy of four or five years and a girl who was no older seems capable of ratification[4], and as a matter of fact parents and guardians often betrothed, or attempted to betroth, children who were less than seven years old[5].   Even the church could say no more than that babies in the cradle were not to be given in marriage, except under the pressure of some urgent need, such as the desire for peace[6].   A treaty of peace often involved an attempt to bind the will of a very small child, and such treaties were made, not only among princes, but among men of humbler degree, who thus patched up their quarrels or compromised their law-suits. The rigour of our feudal law afforded another reason for such transactions; a father took the earliest opportunity of marrying his child in order that the right of marriage might not fall to the lord.

The biographer of St Hugh of Lincoln has told a story which should be here retold.   In Lincolnshire there lived a knight, Thomas of Saleby.   He was aged and childless and it seemed that on his death his land must pass to his brother

Marriage of young children.

---

[1] Bracton, f. 92: 'dummodo possit dotem promereri et virum sustinere'; Fitzherbert, Abr. tit. *Dower* pl. 172; Y. B. Edw. II. f. 78, 221, 378. The question takes this shape—At what age can a woman earn or 'deserve' her dower?   In place of the presumption of the canonist that the marriage will not be consummated until she is twelve years old, our common lawyers gradually adopt the rule that she can deserve dower when nine years old.   The canonical presumption was rebuttable: Freisen, *op. cit.* p. 328.

[2] Ancienne coutume, c. 101, ed. de Gruchy, p. 250; Somma, p. 255.

[3] Co. Litt. 33 a.

[4] See the curious but mutilated record in Calend. Genealog. i. 184.

[5] See *e.g.* Note Book, pl. 349, 696.

[6] c. un. C. 30. q. 2; c. 2. X. 4. 2.   This canon, which Gratian ascribes to Pope Nicholas, appears in the English canons of 1175 and 1236; Johnson, Canons, pp. 64, 141; it passes thence into Lyndwood's Provinciale.   The saving clause is 'nisi forte aliqua urgentissima necessitate interveniente, utpote pro bono pacis, talis coniunctio toleretur.'

William. But his wife thought otherwise, took to her bed and gave out that she had borne a daughter. In truth this child, Grace, was the child of a villager's wife. The neighbours did not believe the tale and it came to the ears of Bishop Hugh, who sent for the husband and threatened him with excommunication if he kept the child as his own. But the knight, who feared his wife more than he feared God, would not obey the bishop's command and therefore died a sudden death. The wife persisted in her wickedness, and the king gave the supposititious heiress to Adam Neville, the chief forester's brother. When she was but four years old, Adam proposed to marry her. The bishop forbad the marriage, but, whilst the bishop was in Normandy, the marriage was solemnized by a priest. On his return the bishop suspended the priest from office and benefice, and excommunicated all who had taken part in the ceremony. Then, first the hand-maid of the widow, and then [p. 390] the widow herself, confessed the fraud. The bishop used all his power to prevent it from taking effect. But Adam Neville would not give way and made confident appeal to English law. Thomas of Saleby had received Grace as legitimate, therefore she was legitimate. The bishop while in England was strong enough to prevent a judgment being given in Adam's favour. But once more he had to go to Normandy. Adam then pressed forward his suit and seemed on the eve of winning, when once more a sudden death prevented this triumph of villainy. But neither Grace nor the rightful heir profited by his death. King John sold Grace to his chamberlain Norman for two hundred marks, and, when Norman died, the king sold the poor girl once more for three hundred marks to the third and worst of all her husbands, Brian de Lisle. In the end she died childless and the inheritance at length fell to the rightful heir[1].

Divorce.

A valid marriage when once contracted could rarely be dissolved. It is highly probable that among the German nations, so long as they were heathen, the husband and wife could dissolve the marriage by mutual consent, also that the husband could put away his wife if she was sterile or guilty of conjugal infidelity or some other offences and could marry

---

[1] Magna Vita S. Hugonis, 170–7. The main facts seem to be fully borne out by records.

another woman[1]. The dooms of our own Æthelbert, Christian though they be, suggest that the marriage might be dissolved at the will of both, or even at the will of one of the parties to it[2]. And though the churches, especially the Roman church, had from an early time been maintaining the indissolubility of marriage, they were compelled to temporize[3]. The Anglo-Saxon and Frankish penitentials allow a divorce *a vinculo matrimonii* in various cases :—if the wife is guilty of adultery, the husband may divorce her and marry another and even she may marry after five years of penance; if the wife deserts her husband, he may after five years and with the bishop's consent marry another; if the wife is carried into captivity, the husband may marry another, 'it is better to do so than to fornicate[4].' [p. 391] But stricter doctrines have prevailed before the church obtains her control over the whole law of marriage and divorce.

We must set on one side the numerous causes—we have mentioned a few—which prevent the contraction of a valid marriage, the so-called *impedimenta dirimentia*[5]. Where one of these exists there is no marriage. A court pronouncing that no marriage has ever existed is sometimes said to pronounce a divorce *a vinculo matrimonii*; it declares that the union, if continued, will be what it has been in the past, an unlawful union. But, putting aside these cases in which the court proclaims the nullity of an apparent marriage, we find that a valid marriage is almost indissoluble. There seems to be but one exception and one that would not be of great importance in England. We have to suppose a marriage between two infidels and that one of them is converted to

Divorce
from bed
and board.

---

[1] Freisen, *op. cit.* pp. 778–780; Heusler, Institutionen, ii. 291; Brunner, Zeitschrift der Savigny-Stiftung, Germ. Abt., xvi. 105.

[2] Æthelb. 79, 80, 81 ; Liebermann, Gesetze, p. 8.

[3] Freisen, *op. cit.* pp. 785–790.

[4] Theodore's Penitential (Haddan and Stubbs, Councils, iii. 199–201).

[5] Owing to the fact that the church had but slowly made up her mind to know no such thing as a divorce in our acceptation of that term (*i.e.* the dissolution of a valid marriage) the term *divortium* is currently used to signify two very different things, namely (1) the *divortium quoad torum*, which is the equivalent of our 'judicial separation,' and (2) what is very often called the *divortium quoad vinculum* but is really a declaration of nullity. The persistence of the word *divortium* in the latter case is a trace of an older state of affairs (Esmein, *op. cit.* ii. 85), but in medieval practice the decree of nullity often served the purpose of a true divorce; spouses who had quarrelled began to investigate their pedigrees and were unlucky if they could discover no *impedimentum dirimens*.

Christianity. In such a case the Christian is not bound to cohabit with the infidel consort, and if the infidel chooses to go off, the marriage can be dissolved and the Christian will be free to marry again. Out of the words of St Paul the church had defined a *privilegium Paulinum* for the Christian who found himself mated to an infidel[1]. It is probable that in their dealings with Jews the English courts accorded this privilege to the faithful. In 1234 a Jewish widow was refused her dower on the ground that her husband had been converted and that she had refused to adhere to him and be converted with him[2]. An Essex jury even doubted whether if two Jews married under the *Lex Judaica* but afterwards turned to the *Lex Christiana* and then had a son, that son could be legiti- [r 392] mate[3]. This, however, was a rare exception to a general rule, and for the rest the only divorce known to the church was that *a mensa et toro* which, while it discharged the husband and wife from the duty of living together, left them husband and wife. Such a divorce could be granted only 'for the cause of fornication,' but this term had a somewhat wider meaning than it now conveys to us[4].

Divorce and the temporal law.

Our temporal law had little to say about these matters. Ultimately the common lawyers came to the doctrine that while the divorce *a vinculo matrimonii* did, the divorce *a mensa et toro* did not deprive the widow of her dower, even though she were the guilty person[5]. But we have good cause to doubt the antiquity of the last part of this doctrine. Glanvill distinctly says that the woman divorced for her misconduct can claim no dower[6]. Bracton does not speak so plainly, but says that she can have no dower if the marriage be dissolved for any cause[7]. However, in Edward III.'s day we hear the

---

[1] Freisen, *op. cit.* § 69, 70. A generation ago very similar difficulties became pressing in British India. See Sir H. Maine's speech on the Re-marriage of Native Converts (Memoir and Speeches and Minutes, Lond. 1892, p. 130).

[2] Tovey, Anglia Judaica, p. 84; Co. Lit. 31 b, 32 a.

[3] Calend. Geneal. ii. 563.

[4] Freisen, *op. cit.* p. 836; Esmein, *op. cit.* ii. 92. Some writers were for admitting a spiritual fornication, an elastic crime which might include heresy and many other offences.

[5] Co. Lit. 32 a, 33 b, 235 a.

[6] Glanvill, vi. 17; and so in the revised Glanvill of the Cambridge MS.: Harv. L. R., vi. 11; Somma, p. 254.

[7] Bracton, f. 92, 304. Britton, ii. 264, seems to think that a separation from bed and board would deprive the woman of dower. In the recorded cases

opinion that in an action for dower the widow's opponent must say, not 'You have been divorced,' but 'You were never joined in lawful matrimony.' This plea would not be competent to one who was relying on a divorce for adultery; it would be competent however to one who desired to prove that the *de facto* marriage had been set aside on the score of precontract, affinity or other diriment impediment, since in such a case the bishop would certify that there never had been a lawful marriage[1]. Meanwhile, however, a statute of Edward I. expressly punished with loss of dower the woman who eloped and abode with her adulterer, unless her husband, without being coerced thereto by the church, took her back again and 'reconciled [p. 393] her[2].' This made adultery when coupled with elopement a matter about which temporal courts and juries had to inquire. It gave rise to a case[3] which we will cite at length, not only because it illustrates the marital morality of the time and the relation between the lay and the spiritual tribunals, but also because we can thus set forth the most elaborately reasoned judgment of the king's court that has come to us from Edward I.'s day.

In 1302 William Paynel and Margaret his wife petitioned the king for the dower that was due to her as widow of her first husband John de Camoys. The king's advocate pleaded according to the statute that Margaret had eloped and committed adultery with William Paynel. In answer William and Margaret relied on a solemn charter whereby John had 'given, granted, released and quit-claimed' the said Margaret his wife to the said William. They also produced certificates from the Archbishop of Canterbury and the Bishop of Chichester attesting that they, William and Margaret, had been charged with adultery in the court Christian and that they had successfully met this charge by compurgation, Margaret's oath-helpers being married and unmarried ladies, including a prioress. They also professed themselves ready to submit to a jury the question whether or no they had committed adultery. But the king's court delivered this judgment:—'Whereas William and

A wife conveyed.

it is often difficult to see whether the divorce that is pleaded is a dissolution of marriage; *e.g.* Note Book, pl. 690. It is believed however that *divortium*, standing by itself, generally points to a divorce *a vinculo*, *e.g.* in Lit. sec. 380.

[1] Y. B. 10 Edw. III. f. 35 (Trin. pl. 24).

[2] Stat. West. II. c. 34; Second Inst. 433.

[3] Rot. Parl. i. 140 (A.D. 1302).

Margaret can not deny that Margaret in the life-time of her husband John went off and abode with William, altogether relinquishing her husband John, as plainly appears because she never in the life-time of her said husband raised any objection, and raises none now, either in her own person or by another in any manner whatsoever, but by way of making plain her original and spontaneous intention and continuing the affection which in her husband's life-time she conceived for the said William, she has since John's death allowed herself to be married to the said William; And whereas William and Margaret say and show nothing to prove that the said John in his life-time ever received her back as reconciled; And whereas it appears by the said writing which they have produced that the said Margaret was granted to the said William by the demise and delivery of the said John to remain with William for ever; And whereas it is not needful for the king's court to [p. 394] betake itself to an inquest by the country about such matters as the parties can not deny and which manifestly appear to the court, or about such matters as the parties have urged or admitted in pleading; And whereas it is more probable and to be more readily presumed in the king's court and in every other that, if a man's wife in the life-time of her husband, of her own free will without objection or refusal, abides with another man, she is lying in adultery rather than in any due or lawful fashion, and this more especially when there follows so clear a declaration of her original intent as this, namely, that when her husband is dead she marries that other man:—Therefore it seems to the court that in the face of so many and such manifest evidences, presumptions and proofs, and the admissions of William and Margaret, there is no need to proceed to an inquest by the country in the form offered by them, and that for the reasons aforesaid Margaret by the form of the said statute ought not to be admitted or heard to demand her dower: And therefore it is considered that William and Margaret do take nothing by their petition but be in mercy for their false claim.' After reading this judgment it is difficult to believe that the ecclesiastical courts were preeminently fit to administer the law of marriage and divorce.

Bastardy.   Having been compelled to speak of bastardy, we must say a little more about it. In our English law bastardy can not be called a status or condition. The bastard can not inherit from

his parents or from any one else, but this seems to be the only
temporal consequence of his illegitimate birth. He is a free
and lawful man; indeed, as we have said above, our law is
coming to the odd conclusion that the bastard must always be
a free man even though both of his parents are bond[1]. In all
respects he is the equal of any other free and lawful man, so far
as the temporal law is concerned. This is well worthy of notice,
for in French and German customs of the thirteenth century
bastardy is often a source of many disabilities, and sometimes
the bastard is reckoned among the 'rightless[2].' It is said, how-
[p. 395] ever, that this harsh treatment of him is not of very ancient
date[3]; under the influence of the church, which excludes him
from office and honour, his lot has changed for the worse; and
it well may be that the divergence of English from continental
law is due to no deeper cause than the subjection of England
to kings who proudly traced their descent from a mighty
bastard.

Our law therefore has no need to distinguish between   Mantle
various sorts of illegitimate children. A child is either a   children.
legitimate child or a bastard. The child who is born of an
unmarried woman is a bastard and nothing can make him
legitimate. In the sharp controversy over this principle which
preceded the famous scene at Merton[4], the champion of what
we may call the high-church party alleged that old English
custom was in accord with the law of the church as defined
by Alexander III. Probably there was some truth in this
assertion. It is not unlikely that old custom, though it would
not have held that the marriage in itself had any retroactive
effect, allowed the parents on the occasion of their marriage to
legitimate the already existing offspring of their union. The
children were placed under the cloak which was spread over
their parents during the marriage ceremony, and became
'mantle children[5].' We hear of this practice in Germany and

---

[1] See above, vol. i. p. 423.

[2] Thus in Beaumanoir, c. 63, § 2, the bastard is not a *franc home* and can
not do battle with a *franc home*; nor can he be a witness in a criminal cause
against a *franc home*: c. 39, § 32; c. 40, § 37. In some parts of Germany the
bastard was *rechtlos*: Heusler, Institutionen, i. 193.

[3] Heusler, *op. cit.* ii. 434; Brunner, Zeitschrift der Savigny-Stiftung, Germ.
Abt. xvii. 1 ff.

[4] Note Book, vol. i. p. 104.

[5] This is what Grosseteste says in his letter to Raleigh: Epistolae, p. 89:

France and Normandy; but we have here rather an act of adoption than a true legitimation *per subsequens matrimonium*, and it would not have fully satisfied the church[1]. This practice the king's court of Henry II.'s day had rejected, and in Henry III.'s it refused to retreat from its precedents.

Presump-
tive pa-
ternity.

On the other hand, we may almost say that every child born to a married woman is in law the legitimate child of her husband. Our law shows a strong repugnance to any inquiry into the paternity of such a child. The presumption of the [p. 396] husband's paternity is not absolute, but it is hardly to be rebutted[2]. In Edward I.'s reign Hengham J. tells this story: 'I remember a case in which a damsel brought an assize of *mort d'ancestor* on the death of her father. The tenant said that she was not next heir. The assize came and said that the [alleged] father after that he had married the mother went beyond seas and abode there three years; and then, when he came home, he found the plaintiff who had not been born more than a month before his return. And so the men of the assize said openly that she was not his heir, for she was not his daughter. All the same, the justices awarded that she should recover the land, for the privities of husband and wife are not to be known, and he might have come by night and engendered the plaintiff[3].' In this case even the rule that the presumption might be rebutted by a proof of absence beyond the four seas seems to have been disregarded. But further, we may see a strong inclination to treat as legitimate any child whom the husband has down to his death accepted as his own and his wife's child, even though proof be forthcoming that it is neither the one nor the other. This inclination of the courts is illustrated by that story about St Hugh of Lincoln which we have told above. Grace was treated as the legitimate daughter of Thomas of Saleby, even though it was demonstrable that she

---

'unde in signum legitimationis, nati ante matrimonium consueverunt poni sub pallio super parentes eorum extento in matrimonii solemnizatione.'

[1] For the *Mantel-Kinder* of Germany see Schröder, D. R. G., 712. Beaumanoir, c. 18, § 24: 'et est li fix mis desoz le drap avec le pere et avec la mere.' For Normandy, Will. Gemet. lib. 8, cap. 36 (Duchesne, Scriptores, 311–12): Duke Richard espouses Gunnora 'in Christian fashion' and the children are covered with the mantle. Selden, Diss. ad Fletam, p. 538, says that this ceremony was observed when the children of John of Gaunt and Catherine Swinford were legitimated by parliament.

[2] Bracton, f. 63 b, 278, 278 b.   [3] Y. B. 32–3 Edw. I. p. 63.

was neither his daughter nor his wife's daughter[1]. Indeed, as Bracton sees, our law in such a case went far towards permitting something that was very like adoption[2]. However, this really is no more than the result of a very strong presumption—a presumption which absolves the court from difficult inquiries—and from the time when it rejects the claims of the 'mantle-children' onwards to our own day, we have no adoption in England. Then, on the other hand, when the husband was dead, our law was quick to suspect a fraud on the part of the widow who gave herself out to be with child. At the instance of the apparent heir or of the lord it would send good and lawful matrons to examine her[3].

§ 2. *Husband and Wife.*

[p. 397] A first glance at the province of law which English lawyers know as that of Husband and Wife, and which their predecessors called that of 'Baron et Feme' will, if we do not confine our view within the limits of our own system, amaze and bewilder us[4]. At the end of the middle ages we see a perplexed variety of incongruous customs for which it is very difficult to account. Their original elements should, so we may think, be simple and uniform. For the more part we should be able to trace them back to ancient Germanic usages, since the Roman law of husband and wife with its 'dotal system,' though it has all along maintained its hold over certain districts, notably the south of France, and has occasionally conquered or reconquered other territories, has kept itself aloof and refused to mix with alien customs. However, the number of schemes of marital property law seems almost infinite, and we can not explain the prevalence of a particular scheme by the operation of any of those great events of which our historians tell us. There would be two neighbouring villages

Varieties in the law of husband and wife.

---

[1] See above, p. 391.

[2] Bracton, f. 63 b. See the curious cases in the Note Book, pl. 247, 303, 1229.

[3] Bracton, f. 69–71; Note Book, pl. 137, 198, 1503, 1605.

[4] Stobbe, Privatrecht, vol. iv.; Schröder, Eheliche Güterrecht; Schröder, D. R. G., 299, 700; Olivecrona, La communauté des biens entre époux, Revue historique de droit français et étranger, vol. xi. (1865), 169, 248, 354.

in Germany; they would be inhabited by men of the same race, religion and language, who for centuries past had been subject to the same economic conditions, and yet they would have very different rules for the governance of the commonest of all human relationships[1]. Even within our own island we find a curious problem. English law has gone one way, Scottish law another, and in this instance it is no Romanism that has made the difference. Scottish law has believed, or tried to believe, in a 'community of goods' between husband and wife, which English law has decisively rejected.

Explanation of varieties.

Probably upon further examination we should find that, underneath all this superficial variety, there was during the middle ages a substantial uniformity about some main matters of practical importance, especially about those things that a husband and wife respectively can and can not do while the [p. 398] marriage between them exists. A man marries a woman; we may postpone as academic such questions as whether each of them remains the owner of what he or she has heretofore owned, whether each remains capable of acquiring ownership, whether (on the other hand) the property or some part of the property of each of them becomes the property of both of them. Such questions will become important so soon as the marriage is at an end; but in the meanwhile the husband has everywhere a very large power of dealing as he pleases with the whole mass of property, a power however which is commonly limited by rules which forbid him to alienate without his wife's consent the immovables which are his or hers or theirs. When the marriage is at an end, we must be prepared with some scheme for the distribution of this mass. The question 'His, hers or theirs?' then becomes an interesting, practical question. Many different answers may be given to it; but history seems to show that even here the practical rules are less various than the theoretical explanations that are given of them.

Community of goods.

In the middle ages the idea of a 'community of goods' between husband and wife springs up in many parts of Europe from Iceland to Portugal, though only the first rudiments of it have been discovered in the age of the 'folk laws.' Sometimes the whole property of husband and wife, whether acquired

---

[1] It is said that in Würtemberg the number of the systems of succession between husband and wife might by a neglect of the minor differences be reduced to sixteen. Stobbe, *op. cit.* p. 75.

before or after the marriage, falls into this community; sometimes it is only the 'conquests' of husband and wife—that
is to say, the property which has been acquired during the
marriage—which forms the common stock; sometimes that
common stock comprises the movables acquired before the
marriage as well as the movable and immovable 'conquests.'
But granted that there is this common stock, jurists have
often found difficulty in deciding who, when analysis has been
carried to the uttermost, is really the owner of it. Some—
and they are likely to have the sympathies of English lawyers
with them—have maintained that during the marriage the
ownership of it is in truth with the husband, so large are
his powers while the marriage lasts of doing what he pleases[1].
Others will make the husband and wife co-owners, each of
them being entitled to an aliquot share of the undivided mass[2].
[p. 399] Others again will postulate a juristic person to bear the ownership, some kind of corporation of which the husband and wife
are the two members[3]. An idea very like our own 'tenancy by
entireties' has occurred to one school of expositors[4]. Another
deems the relation between husband and wife so unique that it
condemns as useless all attempts to employ any of the ordinary
categories of the law, such as 'partnership' or 'co-ownership.'
But then it would be a mistake to think that these conflicting
opinions remain fruitless. Called in to explain the large
rules, they generate the small rules, especially those rules of
comparatively modern origin which deal with the claims of
creditors; and so the customs go on diverging from each other.
The history of Scottish law in the nineteenth century shows
us an instructive phenomenon. The actual rules were well
settled, as we should expect them to be in a prosperous and
peaceful country, and yet it has been possible for learned
lawyers to debate the apparently elementary question whether
the law of Scotland knows, or has ever known, a community of
goods between husband and wife[5].

---

[1] Stobbe, p. 217.   [2] Stobbe, p. 219.

[3] Stobbe, p. 222.

[4] Stobbe, p. 226. An old writer holds that each of the two spouses can say
'Totum patrimonium meum est.'

[5] Fraser, Law of Husband and Wife (ed. 1876), pp. 648–678, maintains that
the idea of a *communio bonorum* does not appear in Scotland until late in the
seventeenth century, that it is imported from France by lawyers educated in the
French universities, and that it has never really fitted the Scottish law.

Our own law at an early time took a decisive step. It rejected the idea of community. So did its sister the law of Normandy, differing in this respect from almost every custom of the northern half of France[1]. To explain this by any ethnical theory would be difficult. We can not put it down to the Norsemen, for Scandinavian law in its own home often came to a doctrine of community. We can not say that in this instance a Saxon element successfully resisted the invasion of Norse and Frankish ideas, for thus we should not account for the law of Normandy. Besides, though the classical law of Saxony, the law of the *Sachsenspiegel*, rejects the community of goods, it is not very near to our common law. It is also to be noted that the author of the *Leges Henrici* stole from the *Lex Ribuaria* a passage which is generally regarded as one of the oldest testimonies that we have to the growth of a community of conquests among the Franks: apparently he knew of nothing [p. 400] English to set against this[2]. Lastly, it can be shown that for a while our English law hesitated over some important questions, and was at one time very near to a system which a little lawyerly ingenuity might have represented as a system of community.

Misdoubting the possibility of ethnical explanations, we must, if we would discuss the leading peculiarities of our insular law, keep a few great facts before our minds. In the first place, we have to remember that about the year 1200 our property law was cut in twain. The whole province of succession to movables was made over to the tribunals of the church. In the second place, we are told that in France the system of community first became definite in the lower strata of society: there was community of goods between the *roturier* and his wife while as yet there was none among the gentry[3]. We have often had occasion to remark that here in England the law for the great becomes the law for all. As we shall see below, the one great middle-class custom that our common law spared, the custom of the Kentish gavelkinders, might with some ease have been pictured as a system of community. But in England, with its centralized justice, the habits of the great folk are more important than the habits of the small. This has been so even

---

[1] Olivecrona, *op. cit.* p. 287.

[2] Leg. Hen. 70, § 22. This is a modified version of Lex Rib. c. 37.

[3] Olivecrona, *op. cit.* p. 286.

in recent days.   Modern statutes have now given to every married woman a power of dealing freely with her property, and this was first evolved among the rich by means of marriage settlements.

Another preliminary remark should be made.   A system of community need not be a system of equality.   We do not mean merely that during the marriage the husband may and, at least in the middle ages, will have an almost unlimited power of dealing with the common fund; we mean also that there is no reason why the fund when it has to be divided should be divided in equal shares.   Many schemes of division are found. In particular, it is common that the husband should take two-thirds, the wife one-third. *Community and equality.*

Lastly, we ought not to enter upon our investigation until we have protested against the common assumption that in this region a great generalization must needs be possible, and that from the age of savagery until the present age every change in marital law has been favourable to the wife.   As yet we know far too little to justify an adoption of this commodious theory. We can not be certain that for long centuries the presiding tendency was not one which was separating the wife from her blood kinsmen, teaching her to 'forget her own people and her father's house' and bringing her and her goods more completely under her husband's dominion.   On the extreme verge of our legal history we seem to see the wife of Æthelbert's day leaving her husband of her own free will and carrying off her children and half the goods[1].   In the thirteenth century we shall see that the law when it changes does not always change in favour of the wife. *Law and progress.*

[p. 401]

The final shape that our common law took may be roughly described in a few sentences—this is not the place for an elaborate account of it :— *Final form of the common law.*

1.   In the lands of which the wife is tenant in fee, whether they belonged to her at the date of the marriage or came to her during the marriage, the husband has an estate which will *Wife's land.*

---

[1] Æthelb. 78–81.   There is a remarkable entry in D. B. i. 373 which seems to show something like a separate estate.   The jurors say of a certain Asa ' ipsa habuit terram suam separatam et liberam a dominatu et potestate Bernulfi mariti sui, etiam cum simul essent, ita ut ipse de ea nec donationem, nec venditionem facere, nec foris-facere posset.   Post eorum vero separationem, ipsa cum omni terra sua recessit, et eam ut domina possedit.'

endure during the marriage, and this he can alienate without her concurrence. If a child is born of the marriage, thenceforth the husband as 'tenant by the curtesy' has an estate which will endure for the whole of his life, and this he can alienate without the wife's concurrence. The husband by himself has no greater power of alienation than is here stated; he can not confer an estate which will endure after the end of the marriage or (as the case may be) after his own death. The wife has during the marriage no power to alienate her land without her husband's concurrence. The only process whereby the fee can be alienated is a 'fine' to which both husband and wife are parties and to which she gives her assent after a separate examination.

Husband's land. 2. A widow is entitled to enjoy for her life under the name of dower one-third of any land of which the husband was seised in fee at any time during the marriage. The result of this is that during the marriage the husband can not alienate his own land so as to bar his wife's right of dower, unless this is done with her concurrence, and her concurrence is ineffectual unless the conveyance is made by 'fine[1].'

Wife's chattels. 3. Our law institutes no community even of movables [p. 402] between husband and wife. Whatever movables the wife has at the date of the marriage, become the husband's, and the husband is entitled to take possession of and thereby to make his own whatever movables she becomes entitled to during the marriage, and without her concurrence he can sue for all debts that are due to her. On his death, however, she becomes entitled to all movables and debts that are outstanding, or (as the phrase goes) have not been 'reduced into possession.' What the husband gets possession of is simply his; he can freely dispose of it *inter vivos* or by will. In the main for this purpose, as for other purposes, a 'term of years' is treated as a chattel, but under an exceptional rule the husband, though he can alienate his wife's 'chattel real' *inter vivos*, can not dispose of it by his will. If he has not alienated it *inter vivos*, it will be hers if she survives him. If he survives her, he is entitled to her 'chattels real' and is also entitled to be made the administrator of her estate. In that capacity he has a right to whatever movables or debts have not yet been 'reduced into

---

[1] This inconvenience was evaded in modern conveyancing by a device of extreme ingenuity, finally perfected only in the eighteenth century.

possession' and, when debts have been paid, he keeps these goods as his own. If she dies in his lifetime, she can have no other intestate successor. Without his consent she can make no will, and any consent that he may have given is revocable at any time before the will is proved.

4. Our common law—but we have seen that this rule is not very old—assured no share of the husband's personalty to the widow. He can, even by his will, give all of it away from her except her necessary clothes, and with that exception his creditors can take all of it. A further exception, of which there is not much to be read, is made of jewels, trinkets and ornaments of the person, under the name of *paraphernalia*. The husband may sell or give these away in his lifetime, and even after his death they may be taken for his debts; but he can not give them away by will. If the husband dies during the wife's life and dies intestate, she is entitled to a third, or if there be no living descendant of the husband, to one-half of his personalty. But this is a case of pure intestate succession; she only has a share of what is left after payment of her husband's debts. Husband's chattels.

5. During the marriage the husband is in effect liable to the whole extent of his property for debts incurred or wrongs committed by his wife before the marriage, also for wrongs committed during the marriage. The action is against him and her as co-defendants. If the marriage is dissolved by his death, she is liable, his estate is not. If the marriage is dissolved by her death, he is liable as her administrator, but only to the extent of the property that he takes in that character. Husband's liability.

[p. 403]

6. During the marriage the wife can not contract on her own behalf. She can contract as her husband's agent, and has a certain power of pledging his credit in the purchase of necessaries. At the end of the middle ages it is very doubtful how far this power is to be explained by an 'implied agency.' The tendency of more recent times has been to allow her no power that can not be thus explained, except in the exceptional case of desertion. Wife's contracts.

Having thus indicated the goal, we may now turn back to the twelfth and thirteenth centuries. If we look for any one thought which governs the whole of this province of law, we shall hardly find it. In particular we must be on our guard Law in cent. xiii. Its general idea.

against the common belief that the ruling principle is that
which sees an 'unity of person' between husband and wife.
This is a principle which suggests itself from time to time; it
has the warrant of holy writ; it will serve to round a paragraph,
and may now and again lead us out of or into a difficulty; but
a consistently operative principle it can not be. We do not
treat the wife as a thing or as somewhat that is neither thing
nor person; we treat her as a person. Thus Bracton tells us
that if either the husband without the wife, or the wife without
the husband, brings an action for the wife's land, the defendant
can take exception to this 'for they are *quasi* one person,
for they are one flesh and one blood.' But this impracticable proposition is followed by a real working principle:—
'for the thing is the wife's own and the husband is guardian
as being the head of the wife[1].' The husband is the wife's
guardian:—that we believe to be the fundamental principle;
and it explains a great deal, when we remember that guardianship is a profitable right. As we shall see below, the husband's
rights in the wife's lands can be regarded as an exaggerated
guardianship. The wife's subjection to her husband is often
insisted on; she is 'wholly within his power,' she is bound to
obey him in all that is not contrary to the law of God[2]; she and
all her property ought to be at his disposal; she is 'under the [p. 404]
rod[3].' The habit into which our lawyers fall of speaking of
every husband and wife as 'baron et feme[4]' is probably due to
the fact that the king's court has for the more part been
conversant with the affairs of gentle-folk. The wife of a
magnate, perhaps the wife of a knight, would naturally speak of
her husband as 'mon baron.' The wife of a man of humbler
station would hardly have done this; but still it is likely that
she would call him her lord, perhaps in English her elder[5].

---

[1] Bracton, f. 429 b.   [2] Glanvill, vi. 3.

[3] Bracton, f. 414: Husband and wife produce a forged charter; he is hanged,
she, whether a partner in his crime or no, is set free 'quia fuit sub virga viri
sui.' Note Book, pl. 1685: The deed of a married woman is of no avail, 'quia
hoc fecit tempore *A* de *B* viri sui dum fuit sub virga.' Sharpe's Calendar of
London Wills, i. 105: feme coverte can not devise land, for she is 'sub virga.'

[4] See *e.g.* Britton, i. 223, 227.

[5] Ine, 57. The etymological connexion between *baron* and *vir* we are not
disputing, but that was in the twelfth century a very remote fact, and we can
not easily believe that the ordinary Englishman, even when he spoke French,
called himself his wife's *baron*. In the law Latin of that time *baro* is rarely, if
ever, used in the sense of husband.

The disabilities of the woman who is *coverte de baron*—a curious phrase which we find in use so soon as we get documents written in French[1]—are often contrasted in the charters with the liege power, the mere, unconditional power, the 'liege poustie' as the Scots say, of the widow or the maid to do what she likes with her own[2]. The formula of a common writ tells us that during her husband's lifetime the wife can not oppose his will (*cui ipsa in vita sua contradicere non potuit*). But for all this, we can not, even within the sphere of property law, explain the marital relationship as being simply the subjection of the wife to her husband's will. He constantly needs her concurrence, and the law takes care that she shall have an opportunity of freely refusing her assent to his acts. To this [p. 405] we must add that, as we shall see hereafter, there is a latent idea of a community between husband and wife which can not easily be suppressed.

The lamentable acquisition by the ecclesiastical courts of the whole law of succession to movables prevents our common lawyers from having any one consistent theory of the relation between husband and wife. The law falls into two segments. We must attend in the first place to that portion of it which is fully illustrated by records of the king's court.

Divorce of personalty from realty.

We will suppose the wife to be at the time of the marriage entitled to land in fee simple or to become so entitled by inheritance, gift or otherwise during the marriage. Her husband thereupon becomes entitled to take the fruits and profits of the land during the marriage, and this right he can alienate to another. If a child is born of the marriage this enlarges the husband's right. He forthwith becomes entitled to enjoy the land during the whole of his life, and this right he

The wife's land.

---

[1] Y. B. 21–2 Edw. I. 151: 'ele fut covert de baron.' Y. B. 30–1 Edw. I. 133: 'ele fut coverte.' This term, rarely found in the law Latin but common in the law French of this age, seems to point, at least primarily, to the sexual union, and does not imply protection. See Ducange, s. v. *cooperire.*

[2] Note Book, pl. 671: 'in ligia potestate sua cartam fecit':—pl. 679: 'in legitima viduitate sua':—pl. 1277: 'in ligia potestate et viduitate sua':— pl. 1929: 'in ligia viduitate sua.' Cart. Glouc. i. 299: 'Ego Margeria...... tempore quo fui mei iuris et domina mei.' Northumberland Assize Rolls, p. 290: 'in propria et pura virginitate sua.' In course of time in this as in other contexts the word *ligius* is misunderstood and confused with *legalis, legitimus,* etc. In German *ledig* is still used in this context, *e.g.* Schröder, D. R. G. 312: 'die überlebende Frau so lange sie ledig blieb' = 'in ligia viduitate sua.'

can alienate to another. For all this, neither before nor after the birth of a child, is he conceived as being solely seised, or as having a right to be solely seised, of that land so long as the marriage endures. Unless the seisin is with some third person, then 'husband and wife are seised in right of the wife.' If the seisin is being wrongfully withheld, then the action for the recovery of the land is given to the husband and the wife; neither of them can sue without the other[1]. And so it is against the husband and the wife that an action must be brought to recover land which they are holding in the right of the wife. An instructive little doubt has occurred as to what a husband should do in such a case if he is sued without his wife. Some hold that he should plead in abatement of the writ, and this opinion wins the day; but others hold, and the common practice has been, that he should vouch his wife as a warrantor, thus treating her as an independent person whose voice should be heard[2]. When we read that a husband vouches his wife to warranty, and that she comes and warrants him and pleads her title, we must take our record to mean what it says:—the married woman appears in court and speaks there (though perhaps through the mouth of a professional pleader) words which are fateful for herself, her husband and her land. [p. 406] When the wife does not appear in person she appears by attorney. She is at liberty to appoint her husband to be her attorney; but she is at liberty to appoint a third person, and, as the appointment is made in court, she has a chance of acting freely. But further—amazing though this may seem to us—the husband sometimes appoints his wife to be his attorney[3].

Husband and wife in court.

In litigation concerning the wife's land it was essential that both husband and wife should be before the court in person or by attorney, and the default of one of them was equivalent to the default of both[4]. A statute of 1285 enabled a wife whose husband was making default, to raise her voice in court and plead in defence of her title[5]. At a much earlier time we see

[1] Bracton, f. 429 b.

[2] Bracton, f. 381, 416; Fleta, p. 408; Select Civil Pleas, pl. 233; Note Book, pl. 124, 1302, 1466, 1508, 1510.

[3] Select Civil Pleas, pl. 155; Note Book, pl. 342, 1361, 1507.

[4] Bracton, f. 370; Fleta, p. 399.

[5] Stat. West. II. c. 3; Second Institute, 341.

that royal equity, at least when stimulated by money, is capable of protecting a woman against the fraudulent default of her husband. In 1210 Henry brings an action for land against Nicholas and his wife Hawise. Nicholas does not appear; but Hawise does and explains Nicholas's default by saying that he is colluding with, and has received money from, Henry, and that she is thus being cheated out of her inheritance. King John moved by pity and by the advice of his council allowed her to put herself upon a grand assize, and it is but fair to the memory of that prince to add that the sums offered to him by both sides were equal[1]. In 1210 therefore it was a fraud for a husband to alienate his wife's lands under cover of litigation, and, if there was to be a collusive use of litigious processes, the husband might meet his match, for he would lose possession of her land if in an action against him and her for its recovery she would neither appear nor appoint an attorney[2].

That the husband has a right to exclude the wife from the enjoyment of her land would not have been admitted. If he does this, she has no action in the lay court. None is necessary; she will have recourse to the ecclesiastical court, which is only too ready to regulate the most intimate relations between [p. 407] married people. When she has obtained a sentence directing her husband to receive and treat her as his wife, the king's court, says Bracton, will know how to provide that she shall share the benefit of her tenement[3]. It will keep the husband in gaol until he obeys the sentence of the church; in John's day a man is in gaol for 'contemning' his wife[4]. In this respect there seems to be equality before the law. If the wife drives the husband out of her tenement, or even out of his tenement, it seems very doubtful whether he has an action in the lay court, unless the wife has eloped with an adulterer[5]. *Husband's rights in wife's land.*

But it may be said that the husband can deprive his wife of the enjoyment of her land by alienating it, and that his alienation of it will be valid, at least so long as the marriage *Alienation of wife's land.*

---

[1] Placit. Abbrev. 63, 66 (Staff.).   [2] Y. B. 20-21 Edw. I. p. 99.

[3] Bracton, f. 166 b: 'et si opus fuerit dominus Rex ad supplicationem ordinarii in tenemento communicando quod suum fuerit exequatur.'

[4] Placit. Abbrev. p. 67: 'captus pro contumacia sua eo quod contempsit uxorem suam.'

[5] Fleta, p. 217, § 10; Britton, i. 280, 297, 315, 328. Britton supposes a writ brought by the husband and wife against the wife, in which John and Peronel are said to complain that the said Peronel has disseised the said Peronel.

lasts. That is so, but we doubt whether during the earlier part of the thirteenth century such an alienation by the husband was regarded as rightful. During the marriage she could not complain of it. From this, however, it does not follow that he was conceived as conveying to a purchaser or donee rights which belonged to him. As a matter of fact transactions in which a husband purports to convey rights which will endure only so long as the marriage endures, or only so long as he is alive, are rare. What a husband attempts to do often enough is to make a feoffment in fee simple. A writ specially designed to enable the widow to recover the land thus alienated is both in England and in Normandy one of the oldest writs, and is in constant use[1].

Conveyance by husband and wife.

But we must look at this matter of alienation more closely. The common law of a later day holds (1) that the husband by himself can give an estate which will endure during the marriage, or (if a child has been born) during the whole of his life; (2) that the wife without her husband can not alienate at all; (3) that husband and wife together can make no alienation which the husband could not have made without the wife, unless indeed they have recourse to a fine; (4) that the one effectual [p. 408] means by which the fee simple can be alienated is a fine to which both husband and wife are parties, and to which the wife has in court given her assent. If, however, we go back a little way, we shall see married women professing to convey land by feoffment with their husbands' consent; they have seals and they set their seals to charters of donation; the feoffees are religious houses and will have been careful that all legal forms were duly observed. A good and a late instance is this:—In 1223 Isabella wife of Geoffrey de Longchamp in the full county court of Gloucester executes a deed stating how with the consent of her husband, who does not execute this deed, she has given certain lands to Winchcombe Abbey. Then 'for the greater security of our house' Geoffrey at the same session of the shire-moot executes another deed. He has confirmed his wife's gift and, so far as in him lies, he grants and quit-claims (but does not give) the land to the abbey[2]. Very often when we have before us a twelfth century charter it is

---

[1] What is practically the writ of entry *cui in vita* appears at an early date. Rot. Cur. Reg. (Palgrave) i. 359; ii. 65, 168, 196.

[2] Winchcombe Landboc, i. 161-3.

difficult to say whether the land that is being given is the land of the husband or of the wife. Sometimes the husband gives with the consent of the wife; sometimes both husband and wife make the gift. Perhaps when the husband is put before us as the donor, the land is generally his, and his wife's consent is obtained in order that she may not hereafter claim dower in that land. Perhaps when the deed puts both the parties on an equality and represents both as giving or quit-claiming, the land is generally the wife's. But to both these rules there seem to be exceptions. At any rate throughout the twelfth century and into the thirteenth we habitually find married women professing to do what according to the law of a later time they could not have done effectually. Without any fine, the wife joins in or consents to her husband's disposition of her lands and of his lands. Often the price, if price there be, is said to be paid to the husband and wife jointly; sometimes a large payment is made to the husband, a small payment to the wife[1].

[p. 409]   Then we seem to see the growth of a fear that the participation of a married woman in a conveyance by her husband may be of no avail, and that should she become a widow she will dispute its validity on the ground that while her husband lived she had no will of her own. We perhaps see this when a purchaser, besides paying a substantial sum to the husband, pays a trifling sum to the wife, gives her a new gown, a brooch, a ring or the like[2]. We see it yet more clearly when she is made to pledge her faith that, should she outlive her husband, she will not dispute the deed, or when she subjects

The wife's fine.

---

[1] Examples are abundant. A few references must suffice. (1) Conveyances by husband with wife's consent: Cart. Glouc. i. 156, 167, 175, 185 (she seals), 187 (she seals), 192 (she seals), 233, 246, 319, 335 (wife's inheritance), 353, 367, 375; ii. 28, 83, 118, 162, 163, 195, 243, 252, 291 (wife's land; she seals): Cart. Riev. pp. 44, 45, 48, 53, 55, 60, 79, 84, 123 (wife's marriage portion): Cart. Rams. i. 139, 159, 160 (she seals). (2) Conveyances by husband and wife: Cart. Glouc. i. 307, 344, 378 (wife's land); ii. 48 (wife's land), 82 (wife's land), 113: Cart. Riev. pp. 62, 78, 82, 83, 93 (wife's land), 99, 114 (wife's land), 131, 235, 236, 240 (she seals), 251: Madox, Formulare, pp. 190 (joint purchase), 260, 279 (land purchased by husband).

[2] See *e.g.* Cart. Glouc. i. 378, where the husband has seven marks and the wife a cloak worth five shillings; Cart. Riev. p. 56, fifteen marks to husband and wife and a gold ring to wife; Madox, Formulare, p. 276, a mark to the husband and a buckle worth twelve pence to the wife; Reg. Malm. ii. 48, the like.

herself to the coercion of the church in case she shall strive to undo the conveyance[1].   We see it also when a charter declares that money has been paid to the husband or the husband and wife 'in their urgent necessity[2].'   There is much to suggest that the law in time past has upheld dispositions by the husband of the wife's land if he was driven to them by want.   Even in Bracton's day the court will not be inclined to inquire into the reality of the wife's assent if proofs be given that the needs of the common household demanded the conveyance[3].   Another expedient has been to obtain in open court the wife's confession that she has conveyed her land or has assented to her husband's act, for by what she says in open court she will be bound. Late in Henry II.'s reign a wife sold a house to the Abbot of Winchcombe; two marks and two loads of wheat were paid to her and six pence were paid to each of her four children; with the consent of her husband she abjured the land in the full county court of Gloucester, and then when the king's justices [p. 410] came round in their eyre she went before them and once more abjured the land; her deed was witnessed by all the justices and the whole county[4].   That a married woman when she is conveying away her land may need some protection against the dominance of her husband's will is by no means a merely modern idea.   Lombard law of the eighth century had required that the wife who was alienating her land should declare before two or three of her own kinsmen or before a judge that she had suffered no coercion, and her declaration was to be attested by a notary[5].   In Italy a regular practice of 'separate examination' had been established long before the time of which we are speaking[6].   We need not suppose that this Italian practice was

---

[1] Cart. Riev. p. 96; Reg. Malmesb. ii. 148, 240; Cart. Glouc. i. 304; Madox, Formul. pp. 85, 87.

[2] Cart. Glouc. i. 335–6; ii. 252; Cart. Burt. 48.

[3] Bracton, f. 331 b, 332.   Note Book, pl. 294 : action by widow for a shop in Winchester; plea, that she and her husband sold it in their great necessity and therefore that by the custom of the city she can not upset the sale.   The *urgens necessitas* of our deeds seems to be the *echte Not* of German law.   In some districts on the continent if the wife would not give her assent to a necessary sale of her land, the consent of the court would do as well.

[4] Winchcombe Landboc, i. 180.   The date is fixed by the names of the justices.   See Eyton, Itinerary of Henry II. p. 298.

[5] Leg. Luitprandi, c. 22 (M. G., Leges, vol. iv. pp. 117–8).

[6] This is the subject of a monograph: Rosin, Die Formvorschriften für die Veräusserungsgeschäfte der Frauen (Gierke, Untersuchungen, viii.).

transplanted into England; similar securities for the freedom of the wife are not unknown elsewhere, and the idea that the husband's guardianship of his wife is subject to and controlled by a superior guardianship exercised by her own kinsmen or by that guardian of all guardians, the king, may have come very naturally to our ancestors: it is not a very recondite idea. At any rate soon after Glanvill's day, so soon as the king's court was habitually sanctioning 'final concords,' it slowly became law that the fine levied in the king's court by husband and wife is the one process whereby the wife's land can be conveyed or her right to dower barred. The development of this rule seems to have been the outcome of judicial decisions rather than of statute or ordinance. In opposition to older and looser notions, Bracton held that a deed acknowledged before the court and enrolled on the plea roll was not fully effectual; nothing but the chirograph of a fine was safe[1].

[1] It has been usual to attribute the efficiency of the fine in these cases to the fictitious litigation of which it is the outcome, and to regard the 'separate examination' of the married woman as an afterthought. We do not think that this correctly represents the historical order of ideas. The married woman can with her husband's concurrence convey her land; but, except perhaps in case of urgent necessity, it is requisite that there should be some proof of her free action. This is secured by requiring that she shall acknowledge her gift in court. Meanwhile for other reasons the conveyance in court which purchasers wish to have in order that they may enjoy the king's preclusive ban (see above, p. 101) has taken the form of a 'fine.' Therefore the proper conveyance for a wife is a fine. Bracton, f. 321 b, 322, hesitates as to the efficiency of an enrolled deed, attributes no mysterious influence to a fine, introduces no fiction, and will not say dogmatically that by a fine and only by a fine can the conveyance be effected. Thus it came about that in London and 'many other cities, boroughs and towns' (see Stat. 34–5 Hen. VIII. c. 22) a custom arose that the wife, with the husband's concurrence, could convey land without any fictitious litigation, by a deed enrolled, she having been 'separately examined' by the mayor or some other officer. For an early record of the London custom, see Liber Albus, i. 71. See also the Cinque Ports' Custumals: Lyon, Dover, ii. 307, 354. It is also to be remembered that the two systems of marital property law which are most closely related to the English, namely, the Scottish and the Norman, do not, to all seeming, know the 'fine' as the proper conveyance for the married woman. It is by no means unrecorded that the English wife when she has come into court will refuse her consent to the fine: Note Book, pl. 419; Northumberland Assize Rolls, p. 49. Nor is it unknown that a husband who has fraudulently levied a fine of his wife's land, by producing in court another woman who personated his wife, will have to answer his wife in an action of deceit and will be sent to gaol. See a remarkable record, Coram Rege Roll, Mich. 9–10 Edw. I. (No. 64) m. 46 d, *Adam de Clothale's case.* Adam is attached to answer the king and his (Adam's) wife for this deceit; the wife claims damages.

The
husband as
guardian.

The doctrine that the husband has for his own behoof a [p. 411] definite ' estate' in the land is one which loses its sharp outlines as we trace it into our earliest records. His right begins to look like a guardianship, though of course a guardianship profitable to the guardian, as all guardianships are. Thus in pleadings we read—'He died seised of that land not in fee but as of the wardship which he had for his whole life by reason that he had a son by his wife[1]':—'And Alan confesses that the land was the inheritance of his wife and he had nothing in that land save by reason of the guardianship of his sons and the heirs of his wife[2]':—'He held that land with Isabel his wife, whose inheritance it was, so that he has nothing in the land save a guardianship of the daughters and heirs of Isabel who are under age[3].' The husband's right is brought under the category which covers the right of the feudal lord who is enjoying the land of a tenant's infant heir. The one right is vendible; so is the other. In England every right is apt to [p. 412] become vendible.

Tenancy
by the
curtesy.

We have said that so soon as a child is born of the marriage, which child would, if it lived long enough, be its mother's heir, the husband gains the right to hold the wife's land during the whole of his life. This right endures even though the wife dies leaving no issue and the inheritance falls to one of her collateral kinsmen; it endures even though the husband marries a second time. This right bears two curious names. The husband becomes tenant ' by the law of England' and tenant 'by the curtesy of England.' The latter phrase seems to be much the newer of the two. We do not read it in Latin records; it seems to make its first appearance in the French Year Books of Edward I.'s age[4]. An ingenious modern theory would teach us that curtesy or *curialitas* 'was understood to signify rather an attendance upon the lord's *court* or *curtis* (that is, being his vassal or tenant,) than to denote any

---

[1] Rot. Cur. Regis (Palgrave), ii. 65: 'utrum obiit saisitus ut de feodo an ut de warda quam habuit in tota vita sua occasione quod de ea habuit fil[ium] ut dicitur.' Ibid. 196: 'utrum idem L. obiit saisitus ut de feodo an ut de warda quam inde habuit occasione quod de ea habuit fil[ium].' Placit. Abbrev. p. 30 (Salop).

[2] Note Book, pl. 1771.

[3] Note Book, pl. 1774.

[4] Y. B. 20–1 Edw. I. 39: 'le baron tendra le heritage sa femme par la corteyse dengleterre.' Ibid. 55.

peculiar favour belonging to this island. And therefore it is laid down[1] that by having issue, the husband shall be entitled to do homage to the lord, for the wife's lands, alone: whereas, before issue had, they must both have done it together[2].' This explanation seems more ingenious than satisfactory. The rule about homage that is here laid down flatly contradicts Glanvill's text, and it is with Glanvill, as the oldest representative of English feudal theory, that we have here to reckon. He says that a woman never does homage; he says that when an heiress is married—not when she has issue—her husband is bound to do homage[3]; he says that no homage is done for the wife's marriage portion (*maritagium*)[4], and yet of this marriage portion the husband on the birth of issue becomes tenant by the law of England[5]. Again, we have never seen in any record any suggestion that before issue had been born of the marriage the husband was not entitled and bound to do suit to the lord's court; nor can we easily suppose that the lord went without a suitor where there was a childless marriage. Lastly, we have never seen the word *curialitas* or *courtesie* used to signify a [p. 413] right or a duty of going to court, unless it is so used in the phrase that is before us. It is a common enough word, and means 'civility,' 'good-breeding,' 'a favour,' 'a concession.'

For some reason or another from Glanvill's day onwards our lawyers are always laying stress upon the Englishness (if we may use that term) of this right. They are always saying that the husband holds 'according to the custom of the kingdom'; and in Bracton's day 'tenant by the law of England' (*tenens per legem Angliae*) has become a well-established phrase with a technical meaning[6]. Now if we ask what other law the lawyers of 1200 can have had in their minds by way of contrast to the law of England, we must answer—The law of Normandy. It was still common that a rich heiress should have lands on both sides the sea. We look then to Norman law, and we see that it does know a right very like the curtesy of England; the two are so much alike that it is worth a lawyer's while to contrast them. The Norman husband if a child has been born is entitled to a veufeté (*viduitas*); but he loses it if he marries

Tenancy by the law of England.'

---

[1] Lit. sec. 90; Co. Lit. 30, 67.   [2] Blackstone, Comment. ii. 126.
[3] Glanvill, ix. 1.   [4] Glanvill, ix. 2; vii. 18.   [5] Glanvill, vii. 13.
[6] Note Book, pl. 266, 291, 319, 487, 917, 1182, 1686; Bracton, f. 438.

again[1]. It is we believe just to this difference that the English lawyers are pointing when they speak with emphasis of the law of England :—'He had children by reason of whom he claims to hold the land for his whole life according to the law and custom of the kingdom' :—'According to the custom of the kingdom he ought to hold that land during his whole life[2].' Over and over again the words which restrict this law or custom to the kingdom are brought into close proximity with the words 'for his whole life.' A *viduitas* which endures beyond viduity—that is the specifically English peculiarity. Britton, who writes in French, does not yet speak of the curtesy of England, but he uses an almost equivalent phrase :—the husband, when issue has been born, holds by 'a specialty granted as law in England and Ireland[3].' It is a privilege, an exceptional rule of positive institution which can not be explained by general principles. Then, not many years after the first recorded appearance of the term 'curtesy,' the author of the Mirror asserts that this privilege was granted to husbands [p. 414] by the curtesy of Henry I.[4] No one will now trust the unsupported word of this apocryphal book, and the assertion about Henry I. may be idle enough; but we seem to be entitled to the inference that, very soon after it had become the fashion to call the husband 'tenant by the curtesy of England,' it was possible to explain this phrase by reference to some royal concession. And in truth an explanation of that kind may seem to us reasonable enough.

The law of England a courteous law.

In the first place, the right given to the husband by English law is a large, a liberal right. It comprehends the wife's lands by whatever title she may have acquired them, whether by way of inheritance or by way of marriage portion, or by any other way; it endures though there is no longer any issue of the marriage in existence; it endures though the husband has married another wife; it is given to a second husband, who can thereby keep out a son of the first marriage from his inheritance. About these points there has been

---

[1] Somma, p. 307; Ancienne coutume, c. 119 (ed. de Gruchy, p. 301). In later days the husband continues to enjoy a third of the land after a second marriage: Reformed Custom, c. 382 (Coutume de Normandie, ed. 1779, vol. i. p. 435). Brunner, Zeitschrift der Savigny-Stiftung, Germ. Abt. xvi. 98, thinks that the English rule is older than the Norman.

[2] Note Book, pl. 291, 487, 917, 1686.

[3] Britton, i. 220.

[4] Mirror (Seld. Soc.), p. 14.

controversy, but at every point the husband has been victorious. For example, in 1226 it was necessary to send a rescript to the Irish courts telling them that the second husband was to enjoy the land during his life, although there was in existence a child of full age by the first husband[1]. Some judges thought this an unreasonable extension of the right; but the king refused to legislate against it[2]. If we compare our law with its nearest of kin, we see a peculiar favour shown to the husband. Norman law deprives him of his right when he marries again; at any rate he must then give up two-thirds of the land. Scottish law gives him his 'curtesy' only in lands which his wife has inherited, not in lands which have been given to her[3]. The English lawyers know that their law is peculiar, believe that it has its origin in some 'specialty.' This being so, it is by no means unnatural that they should call it 'courteous,' or as we might say 'liberal,' law. They look at the matter from the husband's point of view; this is the popular point of view.

[p. 415] They see the curtesy of England setting a limit to the most oppressive of the feudal rights, the right of wardship. This seems the core of the matter:—the husband keeps out the feudal lord though there is an infant heir. Here in England the husband keeps out the feudal lord even though the infant heir is not the husband's child. The lawyers can not explain this, and, to be frank, we can not explain it. In a country where the seignorial right of wardship has assumed its harshest form, it is an anomaly that the husband should keep out the lord from all the wife's lands. So long as the husband lives, the lord will enjoy neither wardship nor escheat. Surely we may call such a rule as this a gracious rule.

So much as to the name. As to the substance of the right, Origin of we have as much difficulty in accounting for its wide ambit as curtesy. had the lawyers of the thirteenth century. Perhaps several ancient elements have been fused together. One of these, as already said, seems to be a profitable guardianship over wife and children. In our first plea rolls the husband is still spoken

[1] Rot. Pat. 11 Hen. III. pt. 1, m. 12 (Calendar of Irish Documents, i. p. 220).

[2] Bracton, f. 438; Note Book, pl. 487, 917, 1182, 1425, 1921, especially pl. 1182: 'Dominus Rex non vult mutare consuetudinem Angliae usitatam et optentam a multis retrotemporibus.'

[3] Fraser, Law of Husband and Wife (2nd ed.), p. 1123.

of as having but a *custodia* or a *warda* of the land. To this, so we think, points the requirement that a child capable of inheriting from the wife shall be born—born and heard to cry within the four walls. This quaint demand for a cry within the four walls is explained to us in Edward I.'s day as a demand for the testimony of males—the males who are not permitted to enter the chamber where the wife lies, but stand outside listening for the wail which will give the husband his curtesy[1]. In many systems of marital law the birth of a child, even though its speedy death follows, has important consequences for husband and wife; sometimes, for example, the 'community of goods' between husband and wife begins, not with the marriage, but with the birth of the firstborn. These rules will send back our thoughts to a time when the sterile wife may be divorced, and no marriage is stable until a child is born[2].

The widower's free bench.　In this context we must take into account a system which [p. 416] is in all probability at least as ancient as that of the common law. The gavelkind custom of Kent makes hardly any difference in this respect between husband and wife. The surviving spouse enjoys, so long as he or she remains single, one-half of the land of the dead spouse. This right, whether enjoyed by the widow or the widower, bears the name of 'free bench.' For that name also a feudal explanation has been found. The freehold suitors of the seignorial court are its free 'benchers,' and the surviving spouse is supposed to enjoy the right of representing in that court the land of the dead spouse. Granting that the suitors of a court are sometimes called its 'benchers,' we can not easily accept the proposed explanation. Outside Kent the term 'free bench' is far more commonly given to the right of the widow than to the right of the widower, and yet we can not believe that the widow sat as a bencher in the lord's court.

---

[1] Placit. Abbrev. p. 267: 'quia femina non admittitur ad aliquam inquisitionem faciendam in curia Regis, nec constare potest curiae utrum natus fuit vivus puer vel non, nisi visus esset a masculis vel auditurus [*corr.* auditus] clamare ab eisdem . . . . . eo quod non est permissum quod masculi intersint huiusmodi secretis.' It is just possible that the talk about the four walls is a relic of a different test of the infant's vitality. According to the ancient Alaman or Swabian law, a child is not reckoned to be born alive unless it can open its eyes and see the roof and the four walls. M. G., Leges, iii. 78, 115, 166.

[2] Brunner, Die Geburt eines lebenden Kindes, Zeitschrift der Savigny-Stiftung, Germ. Abt. xvi. 63 ff.

The bench in question was, we may guess, not a bench in court but a bench at the fireside[1]. The surviving spouse has in time past been allowed to remain in the house along with the children. In the days when families kept together, the right of the widower or widow to remain at the fireside may have borne a somewhat indefinite character. Especially in the case of the widower, there might be an element of guardianship in his [p. 417] right. A later age unravels the right. By way of 'free bench' the surviving spouse now has the enjoyment of one-half of the land until death or second marriage, whether there has ever been a child of the marriage or no. But in addition to this, he or she will very possibly be entitled to enjoy a profitable guardianship over the other half of the land. The law of socage land gives the wardship of the infant heirs of the dead spouse to the surviving spouse. In Kent it must have been common enough to see a widower or a widow enjoying the whole of the land left behind by the dead wife or husband[2].

Probably it is upon some such scheme as this that feudalism has played. Here in England it destroys the equality between husband and wife. On the husband's death, the widow is allowed by way of dower one-third of his land at the utmost. This she may enjoy even though she marries again, for it is not given to her as to a mother who will keep a home for her husband's heirs. The guardianship is taken from her and falls to the lord. But it is hard to take from a man the guardianship of his own children. Even the law of England is too 'courteous' for that. The widow can not do military service, the widower can. The law of military fees gives him more, much more, than ancient custom would give him. Even in the first years of the thirteenth century it is still hesitating as to how far his rights are a guardianship, and the fact that to the last he will lose the land on his wife's death unless a child has been born

Feudalism and curtesy.

---

[1] Observe how Bracton, f. 97 b, introduces the term. He has been saying that, if there is more than one house, the wife is not to be endowed of the capital messuage. Even if there is but one house, another should be erected for her on the demesne land. If however this cannot be done 'tunc de necessitate recurrendum erit ad capitale messuagium, sicut in burgagiis ad liberum bancum.' Our 'free bench' seems to have its origin in what German writers call the *Beisitz* of the widow (see Schröder, D. R. G. 312), her right to remain in the house along with the heirs, a right which in course of time generally develops into a right to the exclusive enjoyment of some share of her husband's property.

[2] Valuable materials are collected in Robinson, Gavelkind, Bk. ii. ch. i.

seems to show that at one time the element of guardianship had been prominent. But the right is soon extended beyond any limits that can be easily explained. The forces which extend it seem to be the same as those which introduce our rigorous primogeniture. If possible, the fee must remain undivided. We can not, as the Kentish gavelkinders do, give the widower a half of the wife's land. If he has the half, he must have the whole. What our law is striving for at the end of the twelfth century is the utmost simplicity. When once it has established—this is the main point—that the husband can successfully oppose the lord's claim to a wardship of the wife's infant heir, it makes a short cut through many difficulties and gives the husband, so soon as a child is born, an estate for life in the wife's land, an estate for his whole life in the whole land. The lawyers themselves can not defend this exaggeration of the right; it is an anomalous 'specialty,' a concession to husbands [p. 418] made by the courteous, but hasty, law of England[1].

Dower.

The wife's right of dower is attributed by the lawyers to a gift made by the bridegroom to the bride at the church door; but, says Glanvill, every man is bound both by ecclesiastical and by temporal law to endow his spouse at the time of the espousals[2]. He may endow her with certain specific lands, and thus constitute a *dos nominata*; but this *dos nominata* must not exceed one-third of his lands. If he names no particular lands, he is understood to endow her with one-third of the lands of which he is seised at the time of the espousals; this is a reasonable dower (*dos rationabilis*); of lands which come to him

---

[1] Glanvill, vii. 18, mentions the husband's right only in connexion with the wife's marriage portion. The so-called Statute *de tenentibus per legem Angliae* (Statutes, vol. i. p. 220), which is merely a bit of Glanvill's text and has no claim to statutory authority, does the like. We can not argue from this that the widower of Glanvill's day had no right in the lands which his wife had inherited. Rather, so it seems, Glanvill takes this for granted and puts a more extreme case. What he is concerned to say is that a husband has a right to hold *even* his wife's marriage portion if once a child of the marriage has been born, and to hold it for his whole life. The second husband (this is a climax) can hold the *maritagium* given at the first marriage even though a child of the first marriage is living. In this matter we may argue *a fortiori* from the case of the marriage portion, which has been destined to revert on a failure of the issue of the wife, to the case of the wife's inherited land. This part of Glanvill's text passed into the Regiam Maiestatem (ii. 53). Nevertheless in recent times it is only of lands inherited by the wife, not of lands given to her, that the Scottish law concedes curtesy.

[2] Glanvill, vi. 1; Bracton, f. 92.

during the marriage she can claim nothing, unless he used (as it was lawful for him to use) words which would comprise them. If the bride accepts a *dos nominata,* she can when widowed claim that and no more. Sometimes a dower of chattels or money will be constituted, and, if the bride is content to be married with a dower of this kind, she will have no right to any share of her husband's land[1].

During the thirteenth century the widow's right was extended in one direction. Some words interpolated in 1217 into the Great Charter say that there shall be assigned as her dower the third part of all the land of her husband which was his [not at the time of the marriage, but] in his lifetime, [p. 419] unless she was endowed of less at the church door[2]. Bracton's text and decisions of Bracton's time suggest that this phrase was loosely used and without any intention of changing the law laid down by Glanvill[3]. A little later, perhaps in consequence of attention directed to the words of the charter, the law was that, unless she had accepted less at the church door, the widow was entitled to a third of the lands of which the husband was seised at any time during the marriage[4]. At a yet later time it became law that she might be entitled to more, but could not be entitled to less, than this her 'common law dower.' The husband at the church door might even declare that she was to hold the whole of his lands for her dower, while the wife on the other hand, so soon as she had become a widow, might reject the *dos nominata* and claim those rights which the common law gave her[5]. This change however did not take place in the age that is before us. In the thirteenth century a third of the husband's land is the maximum dower that can be claimed in lands held by military service, and from the frequency with which a *dos nominata* is mentioned, we should gather that many widows of high station had to be content with less. On the other hand, it is common to find that the socager's widow claims a half, and this without relying on any peculiar local

The maximum dower.

---

[1] Glanvill, vi. 1, 2.

[2] Charter, 1217, c. 7. The way in which this clause was modified is best seen in Bémont, Chartes, p. 50. See also Blackstone, Comm. ii. 134.

[3] Bracton, f. 92, 93; Note Book, pl. 970, 1531.

[4] Nichols, Britton, i. p. xli; ii. 242.

[5] Littleton, secs. 39, 41. See the interesting note from a MS. of Britton, in Nichols, Britton, ii. 236.

custom[1]; indeed it would seem that at one time it was almost common law that the widow is to enjoy a moiety of the land that her husband held in socage[2]. But in this case as in other cases the aristocratic usage prevails; uniformity is secured, and dower of a moiety can only be claimed by virtue of a custom alleged and proved[3].

Assignment of dower

The common law allows the widow to enjoy the land during her whole life, and this right she can alienate to another. On the other hand, the gavelkind custom takes, and it is believed that many socage and burgage customs took, her dower from her if she married again or if she was guilty of unchastity, at all events if a bastard child was born[4]. On the death of her husband, if she had a *dos nominata,* she could at once enter on the lands that it comprised; otherwise she had to wait until her dower was 'assigned' and set out for her by metes and bounds. To 'assign' the widow's dower was the duty of the heir or of his guardian: a duty to be performed within forty days after the husband's death. During these forty days the widow had a right, sanctioned by the Great Charter, to remain in the principal house and to be maintained at the cost of the as yet undivided property; this right was known as her quarantine[5]. A fair third of the land was to be assigned to her, and she was entitled to 'a dower house' but not to the capital messuage, though if her husband held but a town house she had a right to one-third, or by custom one-half, of it, as representing her 'free bench[6].'

[p. 420]

Wife's rights during the marriage.

The nature of the wife's right while the marriage endures is not very easily described, for we seem to see the law hesitating. We must distinguish between the 'named' and the 'unnamed'

---

[1] Note Book, pl. 7 (Hereford), 124 (Norfolk), 253 (Kent), 459 (town of Nottingham), 475 (Hertford), 500 (Norfolk), 577 (town of Oxford), 591 (Norfolk), 622 (Kent), 623 (Cambridge), 642 (Norfolk, Suffolk), 721 (Norfolk), 758 (Essex), 767 (Kent), 1080 (town of Worcester), 1668 (Suffolk), 1843 (Norfolk). If we exclude the boroughs and Kent, it is chiefly from the old home of the *sokemanni* that our instances come.

[2] Bracton, f. 93. Note Book, pl. 758: 'Dicit eciam quod uxores hominum tenencium de eodem manerio recuperant et habent nomine dotis semper terciam partem sicut de libero feodo et non medietatem sicut de soccagio.'

[3] Littleton, sec. 37.

[4] The early cases are collected in Robinson, Gavelkind, Bk. ii. ch. ii.

[5] Charter, 1215–6–7, c. 7; Bracton, f. 96. Our 'quarantine' corresponds to the German *Dreissigste,* the widow's month.

[6] Bracton, f. 97 b.

dower. In Bracton's day if a named dower has been constituted
at the church door, the woman's rights from that moment
forward seem to be true proprietary rights. If her husband
alienates the land without her consent, or even with her
consent if she has not joined in a final concord levied before
the king's justices, then (though so long as the marriage
endures she can make no complaint) she can when her husband
is dead recover that land from any one into whose hands
it has come. The tenant whom she sues will immediately
or mediately vouch her husband's heir, and he in all probability will be bound to warrant his ancestor's gift, and,
failing to satisfy this duty, will have to make compensation
[p. 421] to the evicted tenant out of the ancestor's other lands[1]. But
this is a matter between the evicted tenant and the heir;
the dowager can evict the tenant; she is entitled to the
very lands that were set apart for her at the church door.
If, however, she has to rely, not upon a specific, but upon a
general endowment, the case stands otherwise. She demands
from her husband's feoffee one-third of the land (we will call it
Blackacre) that he holds under the feoffment. The feoffee
vouches the heir, and the widow is bound to bring the heir
before the court, for the heir is the warrantor of the widow's
dower. The heir, we will suppose, has no defence to set up
against the widow's claim; he can not say, for example, that she
is already sufficiently endowed. Now the widow is not precisely
entitled to a third of Blackacre; she is entitled to a third of
her husband's lands. If therefore the heir confesses that other
lands have come to him out of which he can sufficiently endow
her, the feoffee will keep Blackacre and she will have judgment
against the heir[2]. On the other hand, if the heir has no other
lands, the widow will recover a third of Blackacre from the
feoffee, and the feoffee will have judgment against the heir;
when the widow dies, the feoffee will once more get back her
third of Blackacre[3]. The unspecified dower is therefore treated
as a charge on all the husband's lands, a charge that ought to
be satisfied primarily out of those lands which descend to the
heir, but yet one that can be enforced, if need be, against the
husband's feoffees. If, however, we go back to Glanvill, we

[1] Bracton, f. 299 b ; Fleta, p. 350-1 ; Note Book, pl. 156, 944, 1525, 1964.

[2] Bracton, f. 300; Note Book, pl. 1102, 1413.

[3] Note Book, pl. 571, 633, 1683.

shall apparently find him doubting whether, even in the case of
a specified dower, a widow ought ever to attack her husband's
feoffees, at all events if the heir has land out of which her claim
can be satisfied[1].

Alienation
by husband
of his land.

Some hesitation about this matter was not unnatural, for
our law was but slowly coming to a decision of the question
whether and how the land burdened with dower can be
effectually alienated during the marriage. The abundant
charters of the twelfth century seem to show that, according to
common opinion, the husband could not, as a general rule, bar
the wife's right without her consent, that he could bar it with
her consent, and that (though this may be less certain) her
consent might be valid though not given in court[2]. Just in
Glanvill's day the king's court was beginning to make a regular [p. 422]
practice of receiving and sanctioning 'final concords,' and in the
course of the thirteenth century the fine levied by husband and
wife after a separate examination of the wife became the one
conveyance by which dower could be barred. But, as already
said, there had very possibly been in the past, some rule which
dispensed with the wife's consent in cases of 'urgent necessity[3],'
and when Glanvill was writing there may have been in the
royal court, which was all for simplicity, some justices who,
unable to define this 'urgent necessity,' were for increasing the
husband's power and giving the wife no more than a right to a
third of what descended to the heir. These same justices were
beginning to refuse to the heir his ancient right of recalling the
land alienated by his ancestor. Why should a wife be better
treated than a son? It seems possible that the charter of 1217
when it secured to the widow a third part of those lands that
the husband held 'in his lifetime,' was a protest against a
doctrine which was in advance of the age. The common law of
dower remained for centuries an impediment to the free
alienation of land; but to make land alienable at the cost of
old family rights was the endeavour of the justices who sat in
the king's court at the end of the twelfth century. In some
boroughs, notably in Lincoln, it was law in Bracton's day that
the widow could only claim dower out of lands of which her
husband died seised. In York her claim for dower was

---

[1] Glanvill, vi. 3.

[2] References to a few of these charters are given above on p. 411.

[3] See above, p. 412.

barred by the lapse of year and day from her husband's death[1].

The husband completely represents all his lands in court, The husband in litigation. even though a 'named dower' has been constituted in them. He sues and is sued without his wife. This enables him at times to defeat his wife's claims by means of collusive actions; but the court in Bracton's day was doing what it could to suppress this fraud, for fraud it was[2], and a statute of 1285 seconded its efforts[3].

Dower is set before us by our text writers, not as a provision Dower as a gift. which the law makes for the widow, but as a provision made by [p. 423] the husband or bridegroom at the time of the marriage[4]. This treatment of it is inevitable. For one thing, there will be no dower unless the marriage is solemnized at the church door, and, as we have seen above, there well may be a valid marriage that has not been solemnized at all. For another thing, the amount of the dower is not fixed immediately by the law; the law only fixes a maximum; the husband says what dower the wife shall have, and this may be a matter of bargain between the spouses, their parents and guardians. Nevertheless we should probably go wrong if we drew the inference that dower is a new thing or that men have as a general rule been free to marry without constituting a dower. The feudal movement and the extension of feudal language have given an air of novelty to an old institution. We can not here enter on vexed questions of remote history about the various provisions made for wives and widows under the sway of Germanic law, about the perplexing words of Tacitus[5], about the relation of the dower of later times to the bride price on the one hand, and on the other to that ancient 'morning gift' which appears in every country where the German sets foot. It must be enough that very generally the widow obtains in course of time a right to

[1] Bracton, f. 309; Note Book, pl. 1889. In Scotland it became law that the husband by conveyance *inter vivos* could deprive the wife of her terce; also the Scottish wife, without any proceeding similar to a fine, might during the marriage renounce her terce: Fraser, Husband and Wife (1878), p. 1110.

[2] Bracton, f. 310.

[3] Stat. Westm. II. c. 4; Second Institute, 347.

[4] The contrary opinion had begun to prevail early in Edward II.'s day; see Nichols, Britton, ii. 236: 'and because usage of dower is become law, a wife is sufficiently endowed though her husband say nothing.'

[5] Germania, c. 18.

enjoy for her life some aliquot share, a fourth, a third, a half, of her husband's property, and this right very often becomes during the marriage a charge on the husband's land, of which he can not get rid without her consent. A less determinate right to remain at the fireside and enjoy a 'free bench' gives way to a more definite and, if the word be allowed, more individualistic provision[1]. The church, in her endeavour to bring marriages under her sway, took over from ancient custom the formula by which a dower was constituted and made it part of her ritual. Thus even our *dos rationabilis* or 'common law dower' can easily be represented as the result of the bridegroom's bounty. The wife is endowed, because the husband has said at the church door that he endows her.

Dower and the church. There seems, however, to be no sufficient reason for supposing that the right is of ecclesiastical origin[2]. At all events in some [p. 424] lands, the law of a remote age was compelled to repress, rather than to stimulate, the bridegroom's liberality[3]. This it did, partly perhaps in the interest of expectant heirs, partly in the interest of a militant state, which regarded the land as a fund for the support of warriors. But feudalism made against dower. If it is a concession that the dead man's *beneficium* should descend to his heir, it is a larger concession that a third of it should come to the hand of the widow. Here in England we have constantly to remember that the widow's right in a very common case comes into conflict with the claim of a lord who is entitled to a wardship. The widow of the sokeman or the Kentish gavelkinder is more liberally endowed than is the countess or the baron's lady, but her 'free bench' shows its ancient origin when she has to abandon it on a second marriage. Difficult as it is to construct a law of husband and wife for the days before the Conquest, we can hardly doubt that during a considerable space of time, the truly feudal age, the rights of wives and widows in the lands of their husbands were waning rather than waxing[4].

[1] Schröder, D. R. G. 312; Heusler, Institutionen, ii. 298, 326, 342.

[2] Maine, Ancient Law, ch. vii., ascribes the provision for widows to the exertions of the church.

[3] So among the Lombards and West Goths, Schröder, D. R. G. 305.

[4] Essays in A.-S. Law, 172–9. Beaumanoir, vol. i. p. 216, says that the general French law that a widow should enjoy as dower half the land that her husband had at the time of the marriage, had its origin in an ordinance of 'the good King Philip who reigned in the year 1214.' Before that time the widow

In manorial extents it is common to find a widow as the tenant of a complete villein tenement, and there seems to be much evidence of a general usage which allowed her to enjoy the whole of her husband's lands[1]. Where the lords are [p. 425] insisting on impartible succession, such a usage is by no means unnatural. In what is regarded as the normal case, the man who leaves a widow leaves infant children, and the widow is the member of the family most competent to become the lord's tenant. In a few of our copyhold customs this right of the widow has become a regular right of inheritance; she appears as her husband's heir, an exception to the very general rule that there is no inheritance between husband and wife[2].

The villein's widow.

It is only when we turn from lands to chattels that we come upon the most distinctive feature of our marital law. The marriage transfers the ownership of the bride's chattels to the husband, and whatever chattels come to the wife during the marriage belong to the husband:—these are the main rules of our fully developed common law, and at first sight we may be disposed to believe that more special rules about 'choses in action,' 'chattels real' and 'paraphernalia' are exceptional and of an origin which must in this context be called modern. However, if we patiently examine the records of the thirteenth century, we may be persuaded that there was an age in which our law had not decisively made up its mind against a community of chattels between husband and wife. We see rules which, had our lawyers so pleased, might have been represented as the outcome of this community.

The chattels of husband and wife.

We must begin by looking at what happens on the dissolution of the marriage by the death of one of the parties, for

The germs of a community.

only took what had been named at the time of the marriage. He adds the formula which in old times the priest had put into the bridegroom's mouth.—'Du doaire qui est devisés entre mes amis et les tiens, te deu.' It is probable that a similar form had been used in England. We must leave it to students of English liturgies to say at what time the vague words 'with all my worldly chattel,' or the like, made their way into our marriage service; but so far as we have observed they only appear in an age which has settled that 'common law dower' is independent of the wills of the parties and springs from the mere fact of marriage. Cf. Blackstone, Comment. ii. 134.

[1] Thus in Cart. Rams. it is the widow who pays the heriot: 'relicta eius si ipsum supervixerit, dabit pro herieto quinque solidos, et erit ab omni opere quieta per triginta dies' (i. 312). Select Pleas in Manorial Courts (Selden Soc.), pp. 44, 173.

[2] The vast manor of Taunton is the classical example; Elton, Origins of English History (2nd ed.), p. 189.

experience seems to show that the fate of the chattels at that moment is apt to exercise a retroactive influence on the theory that the law will have as to the state of things that has existed during the marriage. How much is secured for a widow, how much for a widower?—such questions as these are of practical importance to thousands of men and women. These answered, it remains for the lawyer to explain the answers; and he often has a choice between more than one explanation.

Husband's death.   The husband dies first. We have seen that in the thirteenth century a very general usage, if it is not the common law of England, assures to the wife a half, or if there is a child alive, a third of the chattels. By his will the husband can only give away his share, 'the dead's part.' Of this enough has been said[1]. [p. 426]

Wife's death.   The wife dies first. Has she been able to make a will? Bracton says that a woman who is under the power of a husband can not make a will without the consent of her husband. This is so for the sake of seemliness (*propter honestatem*). Nevertheless, he adds, it is sometimes received as law that she can make a will of that reasonable part which would have been hers if she had survived her husband, and more especially can she dispose of things that are given to her as ornaments, which things may be called her very own (*sua propria*), as for instance clothes and jewels[2]. From this we might gather that in Bracton's day it was by no means unknown that a husband would suffer a wife to dispose by will, not merely of the ornaments of her person, but of an aliquot share, a third or a half, of that mass of chattels which they had been enjoying in common. We believe that such wills were frequently made. So soon as we begin to get any large number of testamentary documents, we find among them wills of married women such as Bracton has described[3]. Four, for example, are proved at York in the year 1346[4]. Thus, Emma, who describes herself as the wife of William Paynot, makes her will and gives many specific and pecuniary legacies. Then she says, 'And the residue not bequeathed of my portion of goods I give to my husband William.' Her two sons and the vicar of the parish, not her husband, are her executors[5].

[1] See above, p. 348.   [2] Bracton, f. 60 b.
[3] Early instances: Nicolas, Testamenta Vetusta, 45; Note Book, pl. 550.
[4] Testamenta Eborac. i. pp. 21, 33, 36.
[5] Ibid. p. 36. Later instances, ibid. pp. 70, 142, 146, 240, 258, 280, 281, 282, 288, 290, 291, 338, 353.

Now when we see a husband permitting his wife to give The wife's will. him by her will specific and pecuniary legacies and an aliquot share of his own goods, we can not but feel that, in his opinion and in common opinion, those goods are hardly his own. In the middle of the fourteenth century, however, the power of a married woman to make a will is set before us as a matter in dispute between the clergy and the laity. A provincial council held at London in 1342 denounced the sentence of excommunication against those who should impede the free testation 'of villeins and other persons of servile condition or of women, [p. 427] married or unmarried, or of their own wives[1].' Two years later the commons complained in parliament that the prelates had made a constitution sanctioning the testaments of wives and villeins, and that this was against reason[2]. No more was obtained from the king by way of response than that law and reason should be done[3]. The struggle was not yet ended; but about this matter the lay courts could have the last word. They could maintain the widower against the wife's executor unless the widower had consented to probate of the will, and slowly the spiritual tribunals were brought to a reluctant admission that the wife has only such testamentary power as her husband is pleased to allow her, and that his consent can be revoked at any time before he has suffered the will to be proved[4].

The ecclesiastical lawyers themselves had not been able to The canon law. formulate a clear theory about this matter; they could find no 'community' in the Roman texts, and from those texts they

---

[1] Wilkins, Concilia, ii. 705. This reinforces a constitution of Abp. Boniface (A.D. 1261): 'Item statuimus ne quis alicuius solutae mulieris vel coniugatae, alienae vel propriae, impediat vel perturbet, seu impediri aut perturbari faciat seu procuret, iustam et consuetam testamenti liberam factionem.' See Appendix to Lyndwood, p. 20.

[2] Rot. Parl. ii. 149: 'et que neifs et femmes poent faire testament, quest contre reson.'

[3] Ibid. 150: 'le Roi voet qe ley et reson ent soient faites.'

[4] In the fifteenth century Lyndwood writes thus;—'Mirum est quod nostris diebus mariti nituntur uxores suas a testamenti factione impedire' (Provinciale, p. 173; c. *Statutum bonae*, gl. ad. v. *propriarum uxorum*). Also Broke (Abr. tit. *Devise*, pl. 34) cites a decision from so late a reign as Henry VIII.'s to prove that the husband can withdraw his consent at any time before probate is granted. But Lyndwood does not stand at the old point of view. He seems hardly to know whether the true doctrine would be that the wife can bequeath an aliquot share of goods that are held in common, or that she can bequeath paraphernalia.

began to borrow the inappropriate term *paraphernalia* to describe those goods which the wife can bequeath by her testament[1]. Even this word, however, was taken from them by the lay courts and turned to another purpose. It is not improbable that from of old the wife's clothes and ornaments had stood in a separate category apart from the general mass of chattels; that on the dissolution of the marriage she or her representatives had been able to subtract these from the [p. 428] general mass before it was divided into aliquot shares; and that similarly the husband or his representatives had been able to subtract his armour and other articles appropriate to males. Very ancient Germanic law knows special rules for the transmission of female attire; it passes from female to female[2]. This idea that the ornaments of the wife's person are specially her own seems to struggle for recognition in England[3]. In the end a small, but a very small, room is found for it. If the wife survives the husband, these things will not pass under his testament; the wife's claim upon them will prevail against his legatees, though it will not—except as regards her necessary clothing—prevail against his creditors. If she dies before him, they are his. Such are the 'paraphernalia' of our fully developed common law[4].

The husband's intestacy. We have seen our old law securing to the widow an aliquot share of chattels of which her husband can not deprive her by testamentary disposition, and we have seen it hesitating from century to century as to whether the wife can not dispose of her share by will if she dies in her husband's lifetime. One other point remains to be considered. What if the wife dies intestate? Will not the idea of a community compel us to hold that her share ought to pass, not to her husband, but to her children or other kinsmen by blood? That even this rule was not at one time very strange to our law we may infer from its appearance in the law of Scotland which was closely akin to

---

[1] Lyndwood, *loc. cit.*: 'Et sic patet quod licet in rebus dotalibus maritus sit dominus, non tamen sic in rebus paraphernalibus. Nam res paraphernales sunt propriae ipsius mulieris, etiam stante matrimonio, ut legitur et notatur C. *de pact. conven.* l. fi. et l. *hac. l.* [Cod. 5, 14, l. 8. 11] de quibus uxor libere testari potest, ut ibi innuitur.'

[2] Schröder, D. R. G. 300, 702.

[3] In the wills of married women it is common to find specific bequests of clothes and jewels.

[4] Blackstone, Comm. ii. 435.

the custom of the province of York.   In Scotland until recent times the wife's third or half has, on her death intestate in her husband's lifetime, gone, not to him, but to her own kindred[1].   In the England of the thirteenth century, however, the question would have taken this shape : When the wife dies intestate, ought one-third, or perhaps one-half, of the chattels [p. 429] to be distributed for the good of her soul ?   It seems probable, though we can not prove, that the church answered this question in the affirmative; but in this instance she would have had to play an unpopular part.   In her own interest and the interest of souls she had destroyed the old rules of intestate succession. The struggle on the wife's death would not be in England, as it might be elsewhere, a struggle between the husband and the blood kinsmen; it would be a struggle between the husband and the ordinary, in which the latter would have to demand a share of the goods that the husband had been enjoying, and this on the ground that the husband could not be trusted to do what was right for his wife's soul[2].   This is a point of some importance:—the clerical theory of intestacy was an impediment to the free development of a doctrine of 'community' between husband and wife; that theory could be pressed to a conclusion which husbands would feel to be a cruel absurdity.   We can not, however, say that a doctrine of community rigorously requires that the surviving husband must give up to some third person the share of his intestate wife.   The law of intestate succession may make the husband the one and only successor of his wife.   Our English system might have taken the form, not unknown upon the continent, of a 'community of movables' with the husband as the wife's only intestate successor[3].

---

[1] Down to 1855 Scottish law held that on the wife's death a share of the chattels, 'the wife's share of the goods in communion' (which was one-third if there was a child, one-half if there was no child of the marriage) passed under the wife's will, or in case of intestacy, passed to her children, or, failing children, to her brothers, sisters and other next of kin.   This was altered by Stat. 18–9 Vic. c. 23, sec. 6.   Fraser, Husband and Wife (ed. 1878), p. 1528.

[2] This might be well illustrated by the law about mortuaries.   In the thirteenth century the church on the death of the wife often claimed a beast from the surviving husband.   See *e.g.* Cart. Rams. i. 294: 'maritus eliget primum, et persona secundum.'   Abp. Langham, with a saving for local customs, had to withdraw this demand: 'si mulier viro superstite obierit, ad solutionem mortuarii minime coerceatur.'   See Lyndwood, Provinciale, p. 19; c. *Statutum.*   Lyndwood thought this concession unreasonable.

[3] Systems of community in which the surviving spouse is the sole heir of the

Rejection
of com-
munity.We are not contending that the law of England ever
definitely recognized a community of goods between husband
and wife.   We have, however, seen many rules as to what takes
place on the dissolution of the marriage which might easily
have been explained as the outcome of such a community, had
our temporal lawyers been free to consider and administer
them.   Unfortunately about the year 1200 they suffered the
ecclesiastical courts to drive a wedge into the law of husband [p. 430]
and wife which split it in twain.   The lay lawyer had thenceforth no immediate concern with what would happen on the
dissolution of the marriage.   He had merely to look at the
state of things that existed during the marriage.   Looking at
this, he saw only the husband's absolute power to deal with the
chattels *inter vivos*.   Had he been compelled to meditate upon
the fate which would befall this mass of goods so soon as one of
the spouses died, he might have come to a conclusion which his
foreign brethren accepted, namely, that the existence of a
community is by no means disproved by the absolute power of
the husband, who is so long as the marriage endures 'the head
of the community.'   As it was, he saw only the present, not the
future, the present unity of the mass, not its future division
into shares.   And so he said boldly that the whole mass
belonged to the husband.   'It is adjudged that the wife has
nothing of her own while her husband lives, and can make no
purchase with money of her own[1].'   'She had and could have
no chattel of her own while her husband lived[2].'   'Whatsoever
is the wife's is the husband's, and the converse is not true[3].'
'The wife has no property in chattels during the life of her
husband[4].'   'This demand supposes that the property in a
chattel may be in the wife during the life of her husband, which
the law does not allow[5].'

The rejec-
tion of a
community
and the
separation
of goods.Once more we see the lawyers of the thirteenth century
making a short cut.   A short cut it is, as all will allow who
have glanced at the many difficulties which the idea of a
'community' has to meet.   When they gave to the husband

---

dead spouse (*Alleinerbrecht des überlebenden Ehegatten*) are sometimes found;
and there are, or have been systems, in which the husband inherits the wife's
share, but the wife does not inherit the husband's.   See Stobbe, Privatrecht, iv.
243.

[1] Placit. Abbrev. p. 41, Northampton (4 John).
[2] Ibid. p. 96, Norf.   [3] Britton, i. 227.
[4] Y. B. 32–3 Edw. I. p. 186.   [5] Y. B. 33–5 Edw. I. p 313.

the ownership of the wife's chattels, they took an important step. Having taken it, they naturally set themselves against the wife's testamentary power (for how can Jane have a right to bequeath things that belong to John?) and they set themselves against every restraint of the husband's testamentary power (for why should not a man bequeath things that belong to him?), they secured for the widow nothing but the clothes upon her back. On the other hand, by basing the incapacities of the married woman rather upon the fact that she has no chattels of her own than upon the principle that she ought to [p. 431] be subject to her husband, they were leaving open the possibility that a third person should hold property upon trust for her and yet in no sort upon trust for him. In course of time this possibility became a reality, and by means of marriage settlements and courts of equity the English wife, if she belonged to the richer class, became singularly free from marital control. Modern statutes have extended this freedom to all wives. A law which was preeminently favourable to the husband has become a law that is preeminently favourable to the wife, and we do not adequately explain this result by saying that a harsh or unjust law is like to excite reaction; we ought also to say that if our modern law was to be produced, it was necessary that our medieval lawyers should reject that idea of community which came very naturally to the men of their race and of their age. We may affirm with some certainty that, had they set themselves to develop that idea, the resulting system would have taken a deep root and would have been a far stronger impediment to the 'emancipation of the married woman' than our own common law has been. Elsewhere we may see the community between husband and wife growing and thriving, resisting all the assaults of Romanism and triumphing in the modern codes. Long ago we chose our individualistic path; what its end will be we none of us know.

A few minor points have yet to be noted. It is long before *Payments to husband and wife.* our lawyers have it firmly in their minds that a payment of money to husband and wife must be exactly the same as a payment to the husband. When the husband and wife are disposing of her land by fine, it is common to record that money is paid, not to him, but to them[1]. Nor is it uncommon to record that a husband and wife pay money for a conveyance to

---

[1] Fines (ed. Hunter), i. pp. 37, 60, 82, 92, 95, etc.

them and their heirs, or to them and the heirs of the wife[1]. In early wills legacies to married women are often found; sometimes one legacy is given to the husband, another to the wife.

Conveyances to husband and wife 'and their heirs' are plenteous[2]. According to the interpretation which would have been set upon such words at a later day, the husband and wife are thereby made 'tenants by entireties' in fee simple. A tenancy by entireties has been called 'the most intimate union of ownership known to the law[3].' It has been said that while [p. 432] two joint tenants are seised *per my et per tout,* the husband and wife in such a case are seised *per tout et non per my.* The one means by which the land can be alienated during the marriage is the fine levied by husband and wife; if no such alienation be made, the survivor will become sole tenant of the whole. During the marriage the husband has in the land no share of which he can dispose. Neither of the spouses has anything; both of them have all. Some of the numerous conveyances that are made in this form at an early time may not have been intended to have this effect[4], but the doctrine of the tenancy by entireties serves to show that an intimate 'community of marital conquests' was not very far from the minds of our lawyers[5].

Another rule that grows dimmer as we trace it backwards is that which denies to the married woman all power of contracting a debt. In 1231 a woman was adjudged to pay a debt for goods bought and money borrowed by her while she was *coverte*; but stress was laid on the fact that she had quarrelled with her husband and was living apart from him[6]. In 1234 a divorced woman was sued for a debt contracted while the *de facto* marriage endured[7]. We may suspect that the treatment

---

[1] Fines (ed. Hunter), i. pp. 1, 2, 18, 23, 26, etc.

[2] Ibid. pp. 3, 18, 20, 23, 26, etc.

[3] Challis, Real Property (1892), p. 344.

[4] It may be doubted, for example, whether the scribe always saw the difference between 'to John and Joan his wife and their heirs' and 'to John and Joan his wife and the heirs of their two bodies begotten.' He might argue that the former gift is confined to those persons who are heirs of both John and Joan.

[5] Stobbe, Privatrecht, iv. p. 226. Some commentators have attempted to explain the continental community as a *condominium plurium in solidum.* One old writer says: 'sic utriusque coniugis bona confunduntur, ut quivis eorum totius patrimonii in solidum dominus sit.'

[6] Note Book, pl. 568.　　　　　　　　[7] Note Book, pl. 830.

of the wife's promise as a mere nullity belongs to the age which has become quite certain that in no sense has the wife any chattels[1]. In some towns[2] the married woman who carried on a trade could be sued for a debt that she had contracted as a trader, and this custom may well be very ancient[3]. What, [p. 433] had our law taken a different turn, might have appeared as a carefully limited power of the wife to incur on behalf of the community small debts for household goods[4], appears here as her power to 'pledge her husband's credit' for necessaries. The little that we can read about this in our oldest reports suggests that the lawyers were already regarding it as a matter of agency[5]. If the husband starved or otherwise maltreated his wife, she could go to the spiritual court, and if he was obstinate the temporal arm would interfere. In 1224 a wife obtained a writ directing the sheriff to provide her with a sufficient maintenance out of the lands of a husband who had refused to behave as a husband should and been excommunicated[6].

In order that the main import of our old law of husband and wife might be more plainly visible, we have as yet kept in the background an element which is constantly thrust upon our notice by our old books. All depends upon seisin or possession. The husband must obtain seisin of the wife's land during the coverture, otherwise when left a widower he will go without his curtesy. The wife is entitled to dower only out of the lands of which the husband is seised at some moment during the coverture. Even so the husband becomes the owner only of those chattels of the wife of which he obtains possession during the coverture. He can collect the debts due to his wife and give a good receipt for them; but, should he die before his

The influence of seisin.

---

[1] Foreign systems, which agreed with the English as to the general outlines of the law which holds good while the marriage lasts, generally allowed that the wife could incur a debt which could be enforced against her so soon as she was a widow. Stobbe, *op. cit.* iv. 87.

[2] See *e.g.* Lyon, Dover, ii. 295.   [3] Stobbe, iv. 89.

[4] Abroad there was sometimes a fixed pecuniary limit to this power; Stobbe iv. 88.

[5] Fitz. *Dette*, pl. 163 (Mich. 34 Edw. I.). This may possibly be the same case as Y. B. 33–5 Edw. I. p. 312. It is commented on in the famous *Manby v. Scott* (2 Smith's Leading Cases), a case which shows that the middle ages left behind them little law about this matter.

[6] Rot. Cl. 8 Hen. III. m. 8 (p. 592): 'qui excommunicatus est, ut dicitur, eo quod non vult ipsam lege maritali tractare.'

wife, any debt that he has not recovered will belong to her, not to his executors. Our lawyers seem hardly able to imagine that any right can come into being or be transferred unless there is a change of seisin or possession.

The personal relation-ship.

The relationship between husband and wife, in so far as it was merely personal, was more than sufficiently regulated by the ecclesiastical tribunals. To the canonist there was nothing so sacred that it might not be expressed in definite rules. The king's court would protect the life and limb of the married woman against her husband's savagery by punishing him if he [p. 434] killed or maimed her. If she went in fear of any violence exceeding a reasonable chastisement, he could be bound with sureties to keep the peace[1]; but she had no action against him, nor had he against her. If she killed him, that was petty treason.

Civil death of husband.

Of exceptional cases in which the 'disabilities of coverture' are wholly or partially removed though there is still a marriage, we as yet read very little. The church will not, at least as a general rule, permit a husband or wife to enter religion unless both of them are desirous of leaving the world; but occasionally we may see a woman suing for her land or for her dower and alleging that her husband is a monk[2]. In 1291 a case, which was treated as of great importance, decided that a wife whose husband had abjured the realm might sue for her land; after an elaborate search for precedents only one could be found[3].

§ 3. *Infancy and Guardianship.*

Paternal power in ancient times.

In the seventh century even the church was compelled to allow that in a case of necessity an English father might sell into slavery a son who was not yet seven years old. An older boy could not be sold without his consent. When he was

---

[1] Reg. Brev. Orig. f. 89. The husband's duty is thus expressed, 'quod ipse praefatam *A* bene et honeste tractabit et gubernabit, ac damnum vel malum aliquod eidem *A* de corpore suo, aliter quam ad virum suum ex causa regiminis et castigationis uxoris suae licite et rationabiliter pertinet, non faciet nec fieri procurabit.' The Norman Somma, p. 246, says that a husband may not put out his wife's eye nor break her arm, for that would not be correction.

[2] Note Book, pl. 455, 1139, 1594. Later law would not allow the wife her dower in this case: Co. Lit. 33 b; and this seems to go back as far as 32 Edw. I. Fitz. *Dowere*, 176.

[3] Rot. Parl. i. 66–7; Co. Lit. 133 a.

thirteen or fourteen years old he might sell himself[1]. From this we may gather that over his young children a father's power had been large; perhaps it had extended to the killing of a child who had not yet tasted food. It is by no means certain however that we ought to endow the English father with an enduring *patria potestas* over his full-grown sons, even when we are speaking of the days before the Conquest. On this point there have been many differences of opinion among [p. 435] those who have the best right to speak about early Germanic law[2].

That women were subject to anything that ought to be called a perpetual tutelage we do not know. Young girls might be given in marriage—or even in a case of necessity sold as slaves—against their will; but for the female as well as for the male child there came a period of majority, and the Anglo-Saxon land-books show us women receiving and making gifts, making wills, bearing witness, and coming before the courts without the intervention of any guardians[3]. The maxim of our later law that a woman can never be outlawed—a maxim that can be found also in some Scandinavian codes—may point to a time when every woman was legally subjected to the *mund* of some man, but we can not say for certain that it was a part of the old English system[4]. It is probable that the woman's life was protected by a *wergild* at least as high as that of the man of equal rank; some of the folk-laws allow her a double *wergild*, provided that she does not fight—a possibility that is not to be ignored[5]. But both as regards offences committed by, and offences committed against women, there is no perfect harmony among the ancient laws of the various Germanic tribes, and we can not safely transplant a rule from one system to another. After the Norman Conquest the woman of full age who has no husband is in England a fully competent person for all the purposes of private law; she sues and is sued, makes feoffments, seals bonds, and all this without any guardian; yet many relics

The tutelage of women.

---

[1] Theodore's Penitential (Haddan and Stubbs, iii. 202).

[2] Stobbe, Privatrecht, iv. 386; Schröder, D. R. G. 313; Heusler, Instit. ii. 435; Essays in A.-S. Law, 152–162.

[3] See *e.g.* Cod. Dipl. 82 (i. 98); 1019 (v. 58); 220 (i. 280); 323 (ii. 127); 328 (ii. 133); 499 (ii. 387 = Essays in A.-S. Law, p. 342) a woman's claim is asserted in court by a kinsman, but she does the swearing; 693 (iii. 292).

[4] Brunner, D. R. G. i. 172; Wilda, Strafrecht, 649.

[5] Brunner, D. R. G. ii. 614; Wilda, *op. cit.* 571, 648.

of a 'perpetual tutelage of women' were to be found on the continent in times near to our own[1].

Paternal power in cent. xiii. If our English law at any time knew an enduring *patria potestas* which could be likened to the Roman, that time had passed away long before the days of Bracton. The law of the thirteenth century knew, as the law of the nineteenth knows, infancy or non-age as a condition which has many legal [p. 436] consequences; the infant is subject to special disabilities and enjoys special privileges; but the legal capacity of the infant is hardly, if at all, affected by the life or death of his father, and the man or woman who is of full age is in no sort subject to paternal power. Bracton, it is true, has copied about this matter some sentences from the Institutes which he ought not to have copied; but he soon forgets them, and we easily see that they belong to an alien system[2]. Our law knows no such thing as 'emancipation,' it merely knows an attainment of full age[3].

Infancy and majority. There is more than one 'full age.' The young burgess is of full age when he can count money and measure cloth; the young sokeman when he is fifteen, the tenant by knight's service when he is twenty-one years old[4]. In past times boys and girls had soon attained full age; life was rude and there was not much to learn. That prolongation of the disabilities and privileges of infancy, which must have taken place sooner or later, has been hastened by the introduction of heavy armour. But here again we have a good instance of the manner in which the law for the gentry becomes English common law. The military tenant is kept in ward until he is twenty-one years old; the tenant in socage is out of ward six or seven years earlier. Gradually however the knightly majority is becoming the majority of the common law. We see this in Bracton's text: the tenant in socage has no guardian after he is fifteen

---

[1] Stobbe, Privatrecht, iv. 427; Viollet, Histoire du droit civil, 290.

[2] Bracton, f. 6. Bracton and Azo, p. 73.

[3] Bracton, f. 6 b: 'Item per emancipationem solvitur patria potestas; ut si quis filium suum forisfamiliaverit cum aliqua parte hereditatis suae, secundum quod antiquitus fieri solet.' This seems to be an allusion to Glanvill, vii. 3. In old times a forisfamiliated son, that is, one whom his father had enfeoffed, was excluded from the inheritance. This is already antiquated, yet Bracton can find nothing else to serve instead of an *emancipatio*.

[4] Glanvill, vii. 9; Bracton, f. 86 b; Fleta, p. 6; Britton, ii. 9. As to the phrase *cove et keye*, see Oxford Engl. Dict.

years old, but he still is for many purposes a minor; in particular, he need not answer to a writ of right[1], and it is doubtful whether, if he makes a feoffment, he may not be able to revoke it when he has attained what is by this time regarded as the normal full age, namely one and twenty years[2]. In later [p. 437] days our law drew various lines at various stages in a child's life; Coke tells us of the seven ages of a woman; but the only line of general importance is drawn at the age of one and twenty; and *infant*—the one technical word that we have as a contrast for the person of full age—stands equally well for the new-born babe and the youth who is in his twenty-first year[3].

An infant may well have proprietary rights even though his father is still alive. Boys and girls often inherit land from their mothers or maternal kinsfolk. In such case the father will usually be holding the land for his life as 'tenant by the law of England,' but the fee will belong to the child. If an adverse claimant appears, the father ought not to represent the land in the consequent litigation; he will 'pray aid' of his child, or vouch his child to warranty, and the child will come before the court as an independent person[4]. What is more, there are cases in which the father will have no right at all in the land that his infant son has inherited; the wardship of that land will belong to some lord[5]. *Proprietary rights of infants.*

An infant may be enfeoffed, and this though his father is living; he may even be enfeoffed by his father. If the child is *Infants in seisin.*

[1] Bracton, f. 274 b.

[2] Bracton, f. 275 b. Apparently a local custom is required to validate such a feoffment. See the note on Britton, i. 9.

[3] Co. Lit. 78 b: 'A woman hath seven ages for severall purposes appointed to her by law: as, seven yeares for the lord to have aid *pur file marier*; nine yeares to deserve dower; twelve yeares to consent to marriage; until fourteene yeares to be in ward; fourteene yeares to be out of ward if she attained thereunto in the life of her ancestor; sixteene yeares for to tender her marriage if she were under the age of fourteene at the death of her ancestor; and one and twenty yeares to alienate her lands, goods and chattells.'

[4] Note Book, pl. 413, 1182; Placit. Abbrev. 267 (Westmoreland). In the earliest records an 'aid prayer' is hardly distinguished from a voucher.

[5] Bracton, f. 438. Husband and wife have a son; the wife dies; the son inherits from his maternal uncle lands held by knight's service. Here the husband will have no curtesy, for he obtained no seisin in his wife's lifetime. The feudal lord takes the land. But, at all events in later days, the father, not the lord, will have the wardship of the son's body and his marriage; Lit. sec. 114.

very young there may be some difficulty about enfeoffing him; for how can he take seisin? Bracton says that in such a case the donor must appoint a *curator* for the infant; he is troubled by the Roman doctrine that children of tender years can not acquire possession[1]. In 1233 we may see a father bent on enfeoffing a younger son who is but seven years old. He receives the child's homage in the hundred court, he takes the child to the land and makes the tenants do homage to their new lord, and then he commits the land to one Master Ralph who is to keep it 'to the use' of the boy. This is a good feoffment, and after the father's death is upheld against his heir[2]. In such transactions Bracton might find some warrant for his talk about curators and tutors; it is difficult, unless some third person intervenes, for a father to cease to possess in favour of a small boy who is living in his house; but infants occasionally acquire land by feoffment, and we hear nothing of curators or tutors. Any speculative objection that there may be against the attribution to infants of an *animus possidendi*, runs counter to English habits. Indubitably an infant can acquire seisin and be seised. When all goes well the infant heir acquires seisin and is seised; the guardian is not seised of the land; the ward is seised. Indubitably also an infant can acquire seisin wrongfully; an infant disseisor is a well-known person and must answer for his wrongful act. If an infant can acquire seisin by entry on a vacant tenement or by an ejectment, why should he not acquire it by delivery?

[p. 438]

Infants as plaintiffs.

An infant can sue; he sues in his own proper person, for he can not appoint an attorney. He is not in any strict sense of the word 'represented' before the court by his guardian, even if he has one. Suppose, for example, that *A*, who held his land by knight's service of *M*, dies seised in fee leaving *B* an infant heir, and that *X* who has adverse claims takes possession of the vacant tenement; it is for *B*, not for *M*, to bring an action (assize of mort d'ancestor) against *X*. If *M* had been in possession as *B*'s guardian and had been ejected by *X* who claimed a better right to the guardianship, this would have been a different case; *M* would have had an action (*quare eiecit de custodia*) against *X*. The guardian has rights of his own which he can make good; the infant has rights of his own

---

[1] Bracton, f. 43 b; also ff. 12, 14 b. Compare Note Book, pl. 1226.

[2] Note Book, pl. 754. See also pl. 421.

which he can make good.   Often enough it happens that an infant brings an action against the person who, according to the infant's assertion, ought to be his guardian.   The lord has entered on the tenement that was left vacant by the ancestor's death and denies the rights of the infant heir.   This is a common case ; the lord sets up rights of his own and is sued by [p. 439] the infant[1].   He is sued, we say, by the infant ; the record will say so ; that is the legal theory[2].   But the infant may be a baby.   Who, we may ask, is it that as a matter of fact sets the law in motion ?   The plea roll will not say, and the court, we take it, does not care.   Some 'friend' of the infant sues out the writ and brings the child into court.   But, so far as we can see, any one may for this purpose constitute himself the infant's friend.   The action will be the infant's action, not the friend's action, and the court will see that the infant's case is properly pleaded.   It will allow a child some advantages that would be denied to a mature litigant ; it will not catch at his words[3].   Even when the infant has a guardian who is in possession of the land, an action for waste can be brought by the infant against the guardian, and, if the waste is proved, the guardianship will be forfeited[4].   Statutes of Edward I.'s day introduced a more regular procedure into the suits of infants ; if the infant could not himself obtain a writ, some 'next friend' (*prochein amy, proximus amicus*) might obtain one for him[5].   How weak the family tie had become we see when we learn that this next friend need not be a kinsman of the infant ; in course of time the judges will hold that one of their subordinate officers will be the best *prochein amy* for the good furtherance of the infant's cause[6].

[1] Bracton, f. 253 b.

[2] See *e.g.* Note Book, pl. 1477: 'Assisa venit recognitura si Matillis...mater Ricardi...fuit seisita...Et Ricardus dicit quod est infra etatem.'

[3] Note Book, pl. 1948.   An infant first vouches *A* and then vouches *B* ; 'et quia est infra etatem non occasionetur.'

[4] In some of these cases of waste we find that a named person, often the infant's mother, is said to sue the guardian.   See Note Book, pl. 485, 717, 739, 1056, 1743.   But in others, pl. 1075, 1201, 1840, the infant is said to sue.   In pl. 1840 one Milisant brings a novel disseisin against her guardian, and casually in the course of the record we read of some unnamed person 'qui pro ea loquitur.'   Bracton, f. 285, speaks of 'aliquis parens vel amicus qui de vasto sequatur pro minore.'

[5] Stat. West. I. c. 48 ; Stat. West. II. c. 15.

[6] Second Inst. 261, 390 ; Co. Lit. 135 b *note*.   The orthodox learning is that 'At common law, infants could neither sue nor defend, except by guardian ; by

Infants as
defendants.

An infant can be sued. The action is brought against him in his own name and the writ will say nothing of any guardian. Very often the record will say that the infant appears and that [p. 440] some named person who is his guardian appears with him[1]. When the action is one in which the guardian has an interest, when, for example, it will if successful take away from an infant land which the lord is enjoying as his guardian, then this guardian has a right to come into court with the infant; the infant will perhaps refuse to answer until this guardian is summoned[2]. But it is very possible that there is no guardian who has any interest in the action, and it is not impossible that the infant has no guardian at all. In these cases the court seems quite content if some person, who as a matter of fact has charge of the child, appears along with him[3]. Such a person will not always be called a guardian (*custos*), but he seems to act as a guardian *ad litem*. Sometimes however we read no word of any such person. Our record tells us that the infant is sued and that he 'comes and says' this or that by way of answer[4]. An infant must answer for his own wrongdoing, for example, a disseisin that he has perpetrated, and he may not have any guardian either in law or in fact. Now as to the 'coming,' we must take our record at its word; the infant does appear before the court. As to the 'saying,' this may be done by the mouth of a professional pleader. But the court itself watches over the interest of the infant litigant[5], and, as we shall

whom was meant, not the guardian of the infant's person and estate, but either one admitted by the court for the particular suit on the infant's personal appearance, or appointed for suits in general by the king's letters patent.' Then the Statutes of Westminster allowed a *prochein amy* to sue. 'But,' says Coke (Second Inst. 390), 'observe well our books, where many times a gardein is taken for a *prochein amy*, and a *prochein amy* for a gardein.'

[1] Note Book, pl. 43, 421, 571, 845, 968, 1083. [2] Note Book, pl. 1442.

[3] Thus Bracton, f. 247 b, supposes a *Quare impedit* brought against an infant, who has no property open to distress; 'tunc summoneatur ille in cuius manu fuerit et cuius consilio ductus quod sit et habeat [infantem coram iusticiariis] tali die.'

[4] Note Book, pl. 191: 'et idem Johannes praesens est et est infra etatem et dicit quod non debet ad cartam illam respondere.' Ibid. pl. 200: action on a fine against Richard: 'Et Ricardus venit et est infra etatem et dicit quod bene potest esse etc....Et quia Ricardus non dedicit finem....Ricardus in misericordia.' Bracton, f. 392: 'Ad finem factum respondebit quilibet minor, etsi non esset nisi unius anni.'

[5] Note Book, pl. 1958: 'set quia Alicia [*plaintiff*] est infra etatem, nec credendum est custodi suo, vel alicui eorum, cum ambo [*plaintiff and defendant*] sint infra etatem, ideo inquiratur per sacramentum iuratorum etc.'

see, proprietary actions are in general held in suspense so long as there is infancy on the one side or on the other.

We here come upon a principle fertile of difficulties and distinctions. We may state it thus:—During infancy the possessory *status quo* is to be maintained[1]. On the one hand, if the infant inherits from an ancestor who died seised as of fee, he is entitled to seisin and his seisin will be upheld during his non-age. If any one has a better title, he will not be able to recover the land from the heir until the heir is of full age. He can indeed begin an action against the infant, but infancy will be pleaded against him, and 'the parol' will 'demur' (*loquela remanebit*): that is to say, the action will remain in suspense, until the heir has attained his majority. On the other hand, if the infant inherits from an ancestor who at his death was out of seisin, then the heir so long as he is under age will not be able to make good his ancestral claim[2]. He may bring his action, but the parol will demur. And what can not be done by action must not be done by force. The *status quo* which the dead ancestor left behind him is stereotyped, whether it be to the advantage or to the detriment of the infant heir. We see once more that deep reverence for seisin which characterizes medieval law. For a period of twenty years the claim of the true owner who has lost seisin may be kept in suspense. This principle did not work very easily; it was overlaid by numerous distinctions between the various forms of action; but it was deeply rooted[3]. We see it even in the region of debt. The heir need not answer the demands of his ancestor's creditors so long as he is under age[4]. So distant from our law has been any idea of the representation of an infant by a guardian, that it will hang up a suit for many years rather than suffer it to proceed while an infant is interested in it.

No part of our old law was more disjointed and incomplete than that which deals with the guardianship of infants[5]. When

Marginal notes: Demurrer of the parol.

[p. 441]

Law of guardianship.

---

[1] This principle appears in other countries; Schröder, D. R. G. 316.

[2] Bracton, f. 274–5 b; 421 b–5 b; Note Book, vol. i. p. 95.

[3] Much of the learning is collected in *Markal's Case*, 6 Coke's Reports, 3 a.

[4] Note Book, pl. 1543: 'Et Willelmus dicit quod infra etatem est et non debet respondere de debito avi sui, et petit etatem suam. Et habet etc.' The demurrer of the parol was not abolished until 1830; Stat. 11 Geo. IV. and 1 Will. IV. c. 47, sec. 10.

[5] As to guardianship in chivalry and in socage, see above, vol. i. pp. 318–329.

it issued from the middle ages it knew some ten kinds of
guardians, and yet it had never laid down any such rule as that
there is or ought to be a guardian for every infant[1]. It had [p. 442]
been thinking almost exclusively of infant heirs, and had left
other infants to shift for themselves and to get guardians as
best they might from time to time for the purpose of litigation.
The law had not even been careful to give the father a right to
the custody of his children; on the other hand, it had given him
a right to the custody of his heir apparent, whose marriage he
was free to sell[2]. It had looked at guardianship and paternal
power merely as profitable rights, and had only sanctioned them
when they could be made profitable. A statute was required
to convert the profitable rights of the guardian in socage into a
trust to be exercised for the infant's benefit[3]; and thereupon
Britton denied that such a guardian is rightly called a guardian
since he is no better off than a servant[4]. The law, at all events
the temporal law, was not at pains to designate any permanent
guardians for children who owned no land. We may suppose
that in the common case the sisters and younger brothers of
the youthful heir dwelt with their mother in the dower house—
often she purchased the wardship of her first-born son—but we
know of no writ which would have compelled her or any one
else to maintain them, or which would have compelled them to
live with her or with any one else. Probably the ecclesiastical
courts did something to protect the interests of children by
obliging executors and administrators to retain for their use
any legacies or 'bairns' parts' to which they had become
entitled[5]. Here again the fissure in our law of property, which
deprived the temporal courts of all jurisdiction over the fate of
the dead man's chattels, did much harm[6].

[1] Co. Lit. 88 b.

[2] See *Ratcliff's Case*, 3 Co. Rep. 37, and Hargrave's note to Co. Lit. 88 b.
The writ for a father or other 'guardian by nature' against the abducer of the
child, called the child the plaintiff's *heres*, and contained the words *cuius
maritagium ad ipsum pertinet*. According to the old law there was no 'guardianship by nature' except the ancestor's guardianship of an apparent—and
perhaps of a presumptive—heir.

[3] Prov. Westm. (1259) c. 12; Stat. Marlb. (1267) c. 17; see above, vol. i.
p. 322.

[4] Britton, ii. 9. [5] See above, vol. ii. p. 362.

[6] At any rate in later times, the courts of the church tried to enforce as far
as they were able some romanesque law about tutors and curators; but they
could not interfere with a wardship. See Swinburne, Testaments (ed. 1640),
pp. 170–181; also Hargrave's note to Co. Lit. 88 b.

[p. 443] But a comprehensive law of guardianship was the less **The guardian not a curator.** necessary, because, according to our English ideas, the guardian is not a person whose consent will enable the infant to do acts which he otherwise could not have done. The general rule about the validity of the acts of an infant, to which our courts were gradually coming, was that such acts are not void, but are voidable by the infant. The case of a feoffment is typical. The infant makes a feoffment; the feoffee will enjoy the land until the feoffor or some heir of the feoffor avoids the feoffment[1]. But, be this as it may,—and by degrees our law came to an elaborate doctrine,[2]—the guardian can neither bind the infant nor help the infant to bind himself. There is no representation of the ward by the guardian, nor will the guardian's authority enable the infant to do what otherwise he could not have done.

This part of our law will seem strange to those who know **The king's guardianship.** anything of its next of kin. Here in England old family arrangements have been shattered by seignorial claims, and the king's court has felt itself so strong that it has had no need to reconstruct a comprehensive law of wardship. That the king should protect all who have no other protector, that he is the guardian above all guardians, is an idea which has become exceptionally prominent in this much governed country. The king's justices see no great reason why every infant should have a permanent guardian, because they believe that they can do full justice to infants. The proceedings of self-constituted 'next friends' can be watched, and a guardian *ad litem* can be appointed whenever there is need of one.

We have now traversed many of the fields of private law. **Review of English private law.** For a moment we may pause, and glancing back along our path we may try to describe by a few words the main characteristics of the system that we have been examining. Of course one main characteristic of English medieval law is that it is medieval. It has much in common with its sisters, more especially with its French sisters. Bracton might have travelled through France and talked with the lawyers whom he met without hearing of much that was unintelligible or very surprising. And yet English law had distinctive features. Chief among these, if we

---

[1] The writ of entry *dum fuit infra aetatem* (Reg. Brev. Orig. f. 228 b) is the infant's action.

[2] See Co. Lit. 380 b, 172 a, 308 a, etc.

are not mistaken, was a certain stern and rugged simplicity. [p. 444]
On many occasions we have spoken of its simplicity, and in so
doing we have encountered that common opinion which ascribes
all that it dislikes or cannot understand to 'the subtleties of the
Norman lawyers.' Now subtlety is the very last quality for
which we should either blame or praise the justices who under
Henry II. and his sons built up the first courses of our common
law. Those who charge them, and even their predecessors of
the Norman reigns, with subtlety are too often confusing the
work of the fifteenth century with the work of the twelfth, and
ascribing it all to 'Norman lawyers':—they might as well
attribute flamboyant tracery to architects of the Norman age.
Gladly would we have had before us a judgment passed by some
French contemporary on the law that is stated by Glanvill and
Bracton. The illustrious bailli of Clermont, Philippe de Remi,
sire de Beaumanoir, lawyer and poet, may have been in England
when he was a boy; he sang of England and English earls and
the bad French that they talked[1]. If he had come here when
he was older, when he was writing his Coutumes, what would
he have said of English law? Much would have been familiar
to him; he would have read with ease our Latin plea rolls,
hesitating now and again over some old English word such as
sochemannus; the 'Anglo-French' of our lawyers, though it
would have pained his poet's ear, was not yet so bad that he
would have needed an interpreter; hardly an idea would have
been strange to him. We are too ignorant to write his judgment for him; but some of the principles upon which he would
have commented would, so we think, have been these :—(1) In
England there can be no talk of *franc alleu,* nor of *alleu* of any
kind; (2) Every inheritable estate in land is a *feodum,* a *fief;*
(3) English *gentix hons* have no legal privileges, English counts
and barons very few; (4) The *vilain* is a *serf,* the *serf* a *vilain;*
(5) There is no *retrait lignager ;* the landowner can sell or give
without the consent of his heir; (6) Land can not be given by

---

[1] Beaumanoir, besides the Coutumes du Beauvoisis, wrote two poems, La
Manekine and Jehan et Blonde. These were published by Hermann Sucher for
the Société des anciens textes français. The editor (i. p. x.) thinks that
Beaumanoir may have been in England between 1261 and 1265, perhaps as a
page in the train of Simon de Montfort. The second of the two poems was
published by the Camden Society under the title Blonde of Oxford; the scene
is laid in England, and the earls of Oxford and Gloucester are introduced; the
latter talks bad French.

[p. 445] testament ; (7) There can be no conveyance of land without the real livery of a real seisin ; (8) The eldest son absolutely excludes his brothers from the paternal inheritance ; (9) Succession to movables, whether under a will or upon intestacy, is a matter that belongs to the courts of Holy Church ; (10) There is no community of goods, no *compaignie*, between husband and wife ; the bride's chattels become the bridegroom's. When, after dipping into foreign books, we look at all these principles together, we shall find their common quality to be, not subtlety, but what we have called a stern and rugged simplicity. They are the work of a bold high-handed court which wields the might of a strong kingship. From the men who laid down these rules, from Ranulf Glanvill, Hubert Walter and their fellows, we cannot withhold our admiration, even though we know that a premature simplicity imposed from above is apt to find its sequel in fiction and evasion and intricate subtlety ; but their work was permanent because it was very bold.

CHAPTER VIII.

CRIME AND TORT.

ON no other part of our law did the twelfth century [p. 446] stamp a more permanent impress of its heavy hand than on that which was to be the criminal law of after days. The changes that it made will at first sight seem to us immeasurable. At the end of the period we already see the broad outlines which will be visible throughout the coming ages. What lies before us is already that English criminal law which will be fortunate in its historians, for it will fall into the hands of Matthew Hale and Fitzjames Stephen. We go back but a few years, we open the *Leges Henrici,* and we are breathing a different air. We are looking at a scheme of *wer* and blood-feud, of *bót* and *wíte.* It is one of many similar schemes and is best studied as a member of a great family. To the size of that family we now-a-days can hardly set a limit. From many ages and many quarters of the globe archaeologists and travellers are bringing together materials for the history of *wer* and blood-feud, while as regards our own Teutonic race a continuous and a well-proved tale can be and has been told. We shall not here retell it, and on the other hand we shall not follow the fortunes of what we may call our new criminal law beyond its earliest days. There are admirable books at our right hand and at our left; our endeavour will be to build a bridge between them[1].

---

[1] The principal books which enable us to trace our modern law of crimes, from the later middle ages onwards, are Staundford, Les Plees de Corone; Coke, Third Institute; Hale, Pleas of the Crown (for historical purposes this is one of the very best of our legal text-books); Blackstone, Comment. vol. iv.; J. F. Stephen, History of the Criminal Law; Pike, History of Crime in England. For the old Germanic law, Wilda, Strafrecht der Germanen, is still an excellent

§ 1.   *The Ancient Law.*

[p. 447]   Of the more ancient system we shall say but little. On the eve of the Norman Conquest what we may call the criminal law of England (but it was also the law of 'torts' or civil wrongs) contained four elements which deserve attention; its past history had in the main consisted of the varying relations between them. We have to speak of outlawry, of the blood-feud, of the tariffs of *wer* and *bót* and *wíte*, of punishment in life and limb. As regards the malefactor, the community may assume one of four attitudes: it may make war upon him, it may leave him exposed to the vengeance of those whom he has wronged, it may suffer him to make atonement, it may inflict on him a determinate punishment, death, mutilation, or the like.

The old law of crime and wrong.

Though we must not speculate about a time in which there was no law, the evidence which comes to us from England and elsewhere invites us to think of a time when law was weak, and its weakness was displayed by a ready recourse to outlawry. It could not measure its blows; he who defied it was outside its sphere; he was outlaw. He who breaks the law has gone to war with the community; the community goes to war with him. It is the right and duty of every man to pursue him, to ravage his land, to burn his house, to hunt him down like a wild beast and slay him; for a wild beast he is; not merely is he a 'friendless man,' he is a wolf. Even in the thirteenth century, when outlawry had lost its exterminating character and had become an engine for compelling the contumacious to abide the judgment of the courts, this old state of things was not forgotten; *Caput gerat lupinum*—in these words the courts decreed outlawry[1]. Even in the nineteenth century the king's

Outlawry in old law.

[p. 448]   right to 'year, day and waste' of the felon's land remained as a

book; but the whole subject is now covered by Brunner, Deutsche Rechts-geschichte. Two valuable essays by the same writer on Outlawry and Responsibility for Unintentional Misdeeds are included in his Forschungen. Henderson, Verbrechen und Strafen in England, Berlin, 1890, has collected valuable materials for the Norman period of English law. Post, Bausteine für eine allgemeine Rechtswissenschaft, 1880–1, describes the nascent criminal law of many rude peoples.

[1] Select Pleas of the Crown (Selden Soc.), p. 47. Y. B. 20–1 Edw. I. p. 237: ' crié *Wolveseved.*'

memorial of the time when the decree of outlawry was a decree
of fire and sword[1].

Prominence of outlawry.   A ready recourse to outlawry is, we are told, one of the
tests by which the relative barbarousness of various bodies of
ancient law may be measured. Gradually law learns how to
inflict punishment with a discriminating hand. In this respect
some of the Scandinavian codes, though of comparatively recent
date, seem to represent an earlier stage than any to which our
Anglo-Saxon law bears witness; outlawry in them is still the
punishment for many even of the smaller deeds of violence.
Among our English forefathers, when they were first writing
down their customs, outlawry was already reserved for those
who were guilty of the worst crimes[2].

Blood-feud.   Without actively going to war with the offender, the law
may leave him unprotected against those who have suffered by
his misdeed; it may concede to them the right to revenge
themselves. The slaughter of a member of one by a member
of another kin has been the sign for a blood-feud. The
injured kin would avenge its wrong not merely on the person
of the slayer, but on his belongings. It would have life or
lives for life, for all lives were not of equal value; six ceorls
must perish to balance the death of one thegn. Whether or no
Teutonic law in general, or the Anglo-Saxon law in particular,
knew what may properly be called a legal right of blood-
feud, is a question that has been disputed. Some writers,
while not doubting that blood-feuds were vigorously prosecuted,
seem disposed to believe that within the historic time the feud
was not lawful, except when the slayer and his kinsfolk had
made default in paying the dead man's *wergild*, the statutory
sum which would atone for his death. Others regard the
establishment of these statutory sums as marking an advance,
and speak of an age when the injured kin was allowed by law
the option of taking money or taking blood. Without attempting to solve this problem, we may say that even in our
earliest laws a price is set on life, and that in Alfred's day it [p. 449]

---

[1] Brunner, Abspaltungen der Friedlosigkeit, Forschungen, p. 444; Post,
Bausteine, i. 164.

[2] When outlawry has been reduced from the level of punishment or warfare
to that of a mere 'process' against the contumacious, another movement
begins, for this 'process' is slowly extended from the bad crimes to the minor
offences, and in England it even becomes part of the machinery of purely civil
actions.

was unlawful to begin a feud until an attempt had been made to exact that sum[1]. A further advance is marked by a law of Edmund. He announces his intention of doing what in him lies towards the suppression of blood-feuds. Even the slayer himself is to have twelve months for the payment of the *wer* before he is attacked, and the feud is not to be prosecuted against his kindred unless they make his misdeed their own by harbouring him: a breach of this decree is to be a cause of outlawry[2].

A deed of homicide is thus a deed that can be paid for by money. Outlawry and blood-feud alike have been retiring before a system of pecuniary compositions, of *bót*: that is, of betterment. From the very beginning, if such a phrase be permissible, some small offences could be paid for; they were 'emendable.' The offender could buy back the peace that he had broken. To do this he had to settle not only with the injured person but also with the king: he must make *bót* to the injured and pay a *wíte* to the king[3]. A complicated tariff was elaborated. Every kind of blow or wound given to every kind of person had its price, and much of the jurisprudence of the time must have consisted of a knowledge of these pre-appointed prices. Gradually more and more offences became emendable; outlawry remained for those who would not or could not pay. Homicide, unless of a specially aggravated kind, was emendable; the *bót* for homicide was the *wergild* of the slain.

The system of compositions.

Along with this process and constantly interfering with it went on another, which we may call the institution of true punishments. Perhaps there never was a time in this country when the community did not inflict punishment upon, as distinguished from declaring outlawry against, certain criminals. To distinguish between these two acts may have been difficult. Outlawry was the capital punishment of a rude age. But the [p. 450] outlaw may at times have been reserved, even in the rudest

True punishments.

---

[1] Alfred, c. 42.

[2] Edmund, ii. 1. As to the earlier but parallel Frankish legislation, see Brunner, D. R. G. ii. 529–531; it did not meet with permanent success.

[3] Tacitus, Germ. c. 12: 'pars multae regi vel civitati, pars ipsi qui vindicatur vel propinquis eius exsolvitur.' Some of the German nations reckon the sum due to the king as a part of the whole composition, in accordance with these words of Tacitus; others, including the English, distinguish more clearly the *wíte* from the *bót*.

age, for a solemn death; he was devoted to the gods, a human sacrifice[1]. Tacitus tells us that in certain cases the Germans inflicted capital punishment by hanging, drowning or burying alive in a morass. The crimes that he mentions include those most hateful to a warlike folk, such as treason and cowardice, and also some misdeeds which may have been regarded as crimes against religion[2]. Homicide on the other hand was 'emendable' with money, or rather with horses and oxen. The influence of Christianity made for a while against punishment and in favour of 'emendation' or atonement[3]. The one punishment that can easily be inflicted by a state which has no apparatus of prisons and penitentiaries is death. The church was averse to bloodshed, and more especially to any curtailment of the time that is given to a sinner for repentance. The elaboration of the system of *bót* among the Germanic peoples is parallel to and connected with the contemporary elaboration of the ecclesiastical system of penance, which is a system of atonements. Nowhere was there a closer relation between the two than in England. Nevertheless during the best age of Anglo-Saxon law, under the kings of the West Saxon house, true afflictive punishment made progress at the expense of emendation. Æthelstan and his wise men issued decree after decree against theft[4]. But this victory was hardly maintained by his successors. During the troublous times of the Danish invasions there seems to have been some retrogression; crimes that had ceased to be emendable became emendable once more, and the protests of the church against the frequent infliction of death bore fruit in legislation. Even the reign of Cnut did not turn back this wave, and on the eve of the Conquest many bad crimes could still be paid for with money.

Kinds of punishment.

When punishment came it was severe. We read of death inflicted by hanging, beheading, burning, drowning, stoning, precipitation from rocks; we read of loss of ears, nose, upper-lip, [p. 451]

---

[1] Brunner, D. R. G. i. 173–7.

[2] Germ. c. 12: 'Licet apud concilium accusare quoque et discrimen capitis intendere. distinctio poenarum ex delicto. proditores et transfugas arboribus suspendunt, ignavos et imbelles et corpore infames coeno ac palude iniecta insuper crate mergunt. diversitas supplicii illuc respicit, tamquam scelera ostendi oporteat dum puniuntur, flagitia abscondi.'

[3] Brunner, D. R. G. ii. 609. See the Introduction to Alfred's laws, 49, § 7.

[4] See especially Æthelst. iv. 6.

hands and feet; we read of castration and flogging and sale into slavery; but the most gruesome and disgraceful of these torments were reserved for slaves[1]. Germanic law is fond of 'characteristic' punishments; it likes to take the tongue of the false accuser and the perjurer's right hand. It is humorous; it knows the use of tar and feathers. But the worst cruelties belong to a politer time.

One of the many bad features of the system of pecuniary mulcts was the introduction of a fiscal element into the administration of criminal law. Criminal jurisdiction became a source of revenue; 'pleas and forfeitures' were among the profitable rights which the king could grant to prelates and thegns. A double process was at work; on the one hand the king was becoming the supreme judge in all causes; on the other hand he was granting out jurisdiction as though it were so much land. In Cnut's day the time had come when it was necessary and possible for him to assert that certain pleas, certain crimes, were specially his own; that the cognizance and the profits of them belonged only to him or those to whom he had granted an unusual favour. We get our first list of what in later days are called the pleas of the crown. 'These are the rights which the king has over all men in Wessex, *mund-bryce* and *hámsócn, forsteal* and *flýmena-fyrmð* and *fyrd-wíte......*And in Mercia he has the same over all men. And in the Danelaw he has *fyhtwíte* and *fyrdwíte* and *griðbrice* and *hámsócn.*' Breach of the king's special peace, his *grið* or *mund* is everywhere a plea of the crown; so also are *hámsócn*, the attack on a man's house, *forsteal* or ambush, the receipt of fugitives, that is of outlaws, and neglect of military duty[2]. After all, however, this list is but a list of the pleas that are ordinarily reserved. The king can give even these away if he pleases.

Crime and revenue.

This catalogue of pleas of the crown may at first sight look comprehensive; in reality it covers but little ground. If it looks comprehensive this is because we read a modern meaning into its ancient terms. We may think that every crime can be esteemed a breach of the king's peace; but breach of the king's *grið* or *mund* had no such extensive meaning. It only covered deeds of violence done to persons, or at places, or in short seasons that were specially protected by royal power[3]. Other

Cnut's pleas of the crown.

[p. 452]

---

[1] Schmid, Gesetze, p. 656.   [2] Cnut, ii. 12–15.
[3] See Pollock, The King's Peace, Oxford Lectures, p. 68.

persons as well as the king have their *grið* or *mund*; if it is broken, compensation must be made to them. The church has its peace, or rather the churches have their peaces, for it is not all one to break the peace of a 'head-minster' and to break that of a parish church[1]. The sheriff has his peace, the lord of a soken has his peace; nay, every householder has his peace; you break his peace if you fight in his house, and, besides all the other payments that you must make to atone for your deed of violence, you must make a payment to him for the breach of his *mund*[2]. The time has not yet come when the king's peace will be eternal and cover the whole land. Still we have here an elastic notion :—if the king can bestow his peace on a privileged person by his writ of protection, can he not put all men under his peace by proclamation ?

Pleas of the crown in Domesday. There are many passages in Domesday Book which in a general way accord with this law of Cnut. King Edward, we are told in one passage, 'had three forfeitures' throughout England, breach of his peace, *forsteal*, and *hámfare*, which seems the same as *hámsócn*[3]; elsewhere we read of four 'forfeitures' which he had throughout his realm[4]; in Hereford breach of the peace, *forsteal* and *hámfare* are the reserved 'forfeitures'[5]; larceny, homicide, *hámfare* and breach of the peace are reserved in one place[6]; larceny, breach of the peace and *forsteal* in another[7]. In the land between the Ribble and the Mersey we find longer lists[8]. But there certainly were franchises in which even these specially royal pleas belonged to the lord. The [p. 453] Abbot of Battle claimed all the royal forfeitures of twenty-two hundreds as appurtenant to his manor of Wye[9]; in his enormous

---

[1] Æthelr. viii. 5; Cnut, i. 3.   [2] Ine, 6; Alf. 39; Leg. Henr. 81, §§ 3, 4.

[3] D. B. i. 252 (Shropshire): 'has iii. forisfacturas habebat in dominio rex E. in omni Anglia extra firmas.'

[4] D. B. i. 238 b (Alvestone): 'et omnes alias forisfacturas preter illas iiij. quas rex habet per totum regnum.'

[5] D. B. i. 179.   [6] D. B. i. 61 b (Cheneteberie).

[7] D. B. i. 10 b (Romenel).

[8] D. B. i. 269 b: 'praeter has vi. pace infracta, forsteal, heinfara, et pugna quae post sacramentum factum remanebat, et si constrictus iusticia prepositi alicui debitum [non?] solvebat, et si terminum a preposito datum non attendebat.' Ibid. 270: 'praeter vi. has, furtum, heinfare, forestel, pacem regis infractam, terminum fractum a preposito stabilitum, pugnam post sacramentum factum remanentem.' The *pugna quae remanet post sacramentum factum* is perhaps a blood-feud prosecuted after the oath of peace has been sworn.

[9] D. B. i. 11 b: 'De xxii hundredis pertinent isti manerio saca et soca et omnia forisfactura quae iuste pertinent regi.'

manor of Taunton the Bishop of Winchester had breach of the peace and *hámfare*[1]; the king in Worcestershire had breach of the peace, *forsteal*, *hámfare* and rape, save in the lands of Westminster Abbey[2]. In short, the pleas of the crown were few, and in many of the lands of the churches they did not belong to the king.

It is by no means certain that the Conqueror had enjoyed in Normandy more extensive pleas and forfeitures than those which he could claim in England as the successor of St Edward. In later days we find that, as the King of England has the pleas of the crown, so the Duke of Normandy has the pleas of the sword, *placita spatae, placita gladii.* When we begin to get lists of them, their number seems to be already on the increase. By a comparison of such lists we are brought to the conclusion that the *placita spatae* had once been few in number and of a nature very similar to those 'rights over all men' that Cnut reserved for himself. Assault on a highway leading to a city or ducal castle was such a plea; from such highways one had to distinguish by-ways. What Englishmen and Danes, perhaps the Normans themselves, would have called *hámsócn* or *hámfare* was such a plea, and in Normandy the sanctity of the house extended over a distance of four perches from its walls. Then in Normandy the plough was sacred; an attack upon a man while at the plough was an offence against the duke. The English *forsteal* had its Norman representative in the plotted assault, *assultus excogitatus de veteri odio, guet-apens*. Offences against the duke's money, and offences against his writs of protection, were pleas of the sword. When from Henry II.'s day we hear that homicide, mayhem, robbery, arson and rape belong to him, we may infer that the duke of the Normans, like the king of the English, has been making good some new and far-reaching claims. Within some of the franchises the [p.454] duke was reduced to three pleas, disobedience to his summons of the army, attacks on those journeying to or from his court, offences that concerned his coin[3].

Norman pleas of the sword.

---

[1] D. B. i. 87 b.   [2] D. B. i. 172.

[3] See Très Ancien Coutumier, ed. Tardif, especially cap. 15, 16, 35, 53, 58, 59, 66, 70. The frequent mention of the house, the plough and the highway as specially within the duke's protection, suggests a time when there was no general rule that homicide and all other serious deeds of violence were ducal pleas. Delisle, Bibliothèque de l'École des chartes, 3me Série, vol. iii. p. 103,

Pleas of
the crown
in the Nor-
man age. Whatever may have been the pleas and forfeitures of our Norman kings in their ancestral duchy, they seem to have made no very serious endeavour to force new law upon the conquered kingdom. They confirmed the old franchises of the churches, they suffered French counts and barons to stand in the shoes of English earls and thegns and claim the jurisdictional rights which had belonged to their dispossessed *antecessores*. In charter after charter regalia were showered on all who could buy them. This practice however must be looked at from two sides:—if on the one hand it deprives the king of rights, it implies on the other hand that such rights are his; that he does sell them proves that they are his to sell. As the lists of 'franchises' granted in the charters grow longer and more detailed, the idea is gaining ground that no justice of a punitive kind can be exercised by any, save those to whom it has been expressly and indisputably delegated; the danger that criminal justice will be claimed as a normal appurtenance of feudal lordship is being surmounted. Then our good luck ordains that the old English terms shall become unintelligible, so that a court of the Angevin period will be able to assert that they confer but lowly or impracticable rights[1].

Criminal law in Domesday. But we will leave the pleas of the crown for a time in order to consider the general character of criminal law. There are entries in Domesday Book which show us the old rules at work, but at the same time warn us that they are subject to [p. 455] local variations. We see that outlawry is still regarded as the punishment meet for some of the worst crimes. We see the classification of crimes as 'emendable' and 'unemendable.' We see signs that the line between these two great classes has fluctuated from time to time and still fluctuates as we pass from district to district. We see that many bad crimes are

says that before the thirteenth century 'les hautes justices' were rarely found in the hands of the Norman lords. In Rot. Cart. 19 is a charter of 1199 granted by John to the bishop of Lisieux, in which the king reserves 'tantummodo tria placita quae de spata vocantur...videlicet de summonicione exercitus nostri, de via curiae nostrae, et de moneta.' As to the peace of the plough, see Wilda, Strafrecht, 246; it seems to have been well enough known to the Scandinavian laws.

[1] The author of the Leges Henrici in c. 10 endeavours to collect the pleas of the crown. Already the long, disorderly list extends beyond Cnut's doom and the testimony of Domesday Book. But there has not yet been much generalization.

still emendable. A few illustrations may be given. In Berkshire he who slew a man having the king's peace forfeited his body and all his substance to the king; he who broke into a city by night paid 100 shillings to the king[1]. In Oxfordshire he who by homicide broke the king's peace given under his hand or seal forfeited his life and members to the king; if he could not be captured he was outlaw, and any one who slew him might enjoy the spoil; *hámsócn* with intent to kill or to wound or to assault brought 100 shillings to the king, while to slay a man in his own house or court caused a forfeiture of life and property to the king, with a saving for the dower of the criminal's wife[2]. At Lewes the fine for bloodshed was 7*s*. 4*d*.; that for rape or adultery 8*s*. 4*d*.; in the case of adultery both man and woman paid, the former to the king, the latter to the archbishop[3]. In Worcestershire and Shropshire wilful breach of a peace given by the king's hand was a cause of outlawry[4]; *forsteal* and *hámfare* could be paid for with 100 shillings; in Shropshire the fine for bloodshed was 40 shillings; in Worcestershire rape was not emendable. In Herefordshire breach of the king's peace was atoned for by 100 shillings, like *forsteal* and *hámfare*. In Urchinfield one could commit *hámfare* and slay the king's man without having to pay more than 120 shillings to the king, and arson seems to have cost but 20 shillings. As to the Welshmen in this district, they lived Welsh law and prosecuted the blood-feud, not only against the manslayer, but also against his kin; they ravaged the lands of their enemies so long as the dead man remained unburied; the king took a third of the spoil[5]. In Chester to break the king's peace given by his hand or writ was a crime for which 100 shillings would be accepted, unless it was aggravated by homicide and *hámfare*, in which case outlawry followed; for mere homicide the fine was 40 shillings, for mere bloodshed 10 shillings, except during sacred seasons, when it was doubled[6]. But we have given examples enough.

[p.456]

The writer of the *Leges Henrici* represents the criminal law of his time as being in the main the old law, and we have no reason to doubt the truth of what he tells us. Some crimes are emendable, some are not. Unemendable are housebreach, arson,

Criminal law in the Leges.

---

[1] D. B. i. 56 b.   [2] D. B. i. 154 b.   [3] D. B. i. 26.
[4] D. B. i. 172: 'utlaghe iudicatur'; 252, 'utlagus fiebat.'
[5] D. B. i. 179.   [6] D. B. i. 262 b.

open theft, that form of aggravated homicide which is known as open *morð*, treason against one's lord, breach of the church's or the king's hand-given peace when aggravated by homicide. These are emendable with 100 shillings: breach of the king's special peace, obstruction of the king's highway, *forsteal*, *hámsócn*, receipt of outlaws. In some other cases the criminal must pay his *wer*; in some it is doubtful whether any emendation need be accepted[1]. About homicide we have elaborate tidings. Clearly a mere wilful homicide, when there has been no treachery, no sorcery, no concealment of the corpse, no sacrilege, no breach of a royal safe-conduct, is not unemendable. It still, if not duly paid for, exposes the slayer to the vengeance of the slain man's kin. But it can be paid for. The tariff however is now very cumbrous. In the simplest case there is the *wer* of the slain, varying with his rank, to be paid to his kin; there is the *manbót* to be paid to his lord, and this varies with the lord's rank; there is the *wíte* to be paid to the king or some lord who has regalia. But in all probability the offender will have run up a yet heavier bill by breaking some *grið*; the owner of the house will claim a *griðbrice*, the owner of the soken will claim *fyhtwíte* or *blódwíte*; happy will it be for our manslayer if he has committed neither *hámsócn* nor *forsteal*[2].

Changes in the twelfth century. Now in England this elaborate system disappears with [p. 457] marvellous suddenness. For it is substituted a scheme which certainly does not err on the side of elaboration. In brief it is this:—(1) There are a few crimes with wide definitions which place life and limb in the king's mercy. (2) The other crimes are punished chiefly by discretionary money penalties which have taken the place of the old pre-appointed *wítes*, while the old pre-appointed *bót* has given way to 'damages' assessed

---

[1] Leg. Henr. 12: 'Quaedam non possunt emendari, quae sunt: husbreche, et bernet, et openthifthe, et eberemorth, et hlafordswike, et infractio pacis ecclesiae vel manus regis per homicidium. Haec emendantur c. solidis: grithebreche, stretbreche, forestel, burchbreche, hamsokna, flymonfirma.' What exactly this writer meant by *burchbreche*, it is difficult to say; see Schmid, Gesetze, s.v. *bohr-bryce*. By *open theft* is meant *hand-having* theft, *furtum manifestum*. The word *morð* seems to imply secrecy; it is homicide committed secretly, poisoning being the typical case. Then *open morð* is committed by one who is guilty of *morð* and is taken in the act. See Schmid, Gesetze, p. 633.

[2] Leg. Henr. cc. 71–94. See above, vol. i. p. 106. In Leg. Henr. 80, § 11, we see traces of a 'constructive' jurisprudence of *hámsócn*. To chase a man into a mill or a sheep-fold is *hámsócn*.

by a tribunal.   (3) Outlawry is no longer a punishment; it is mere 'process' compelling the attendance of the accused[1].

When we first begin to get judicial records the change is already complete.   We have the utmost difficulty in finding a vestige of those pre-appointed 'emendations' which, if we believe the writers of the Norman age, were still being exacted in their day.   We can only remember one of the old fixed fines that lived on.   This is the fine of sixty shillings exacted from the man who is vanquished in the judicial battle; it is the 'king's ban' of the ancient Frankish laws[2].   To this we may add that the London citizens of the thirteenth century claimed as a chartered right that none of them could be compelled to pay a higher fine than his *wer* of a hundred shillings, and the Kentish gavelkinders still spoke of a man being obliged to pay his *wer* in an almost impossible case[3]. The change is not due to a substitution of Norman for English law; we may see the pre-appointed *bót* in Normandy when we can no longer find it in England[4].   The most marvellous [p. 458] revolution however is that which occurs in the law of homicide, for not only does wilful homicide become a capital crime—this we might have expected to happen sooner or later—but the kinsfolk of the slain lose their right to a *wer* and to compensation of any sort or kind.   A modern statute was required to give the *parentes occisi* a claim for damages in an English court[5]. Yet in many parts of western Europe at a comparatively

Disappearance of wíte and bót.

---

[1] What we have called the new criminal law is stated for popular purposes in Dial. de Scac. ii. 16: 'Quisquis enim in regiam maiestatem deliquisse deprehenditur, uno trium modorum iuxta qualitatem delicti sui regi condemnatur: aut enim in universo mobili suo reus iudicatur, pro minoribus culpis; aut in omnibus immobilibus, fundis scilicet et redditibus, ut eis exheredetur; quod si pro maioribus culpis, aut pro maximis quibuscunque vel enormibus delictis, in vitam suam vel membra.'   This is too simple, but is not far from the truth, and is a marvellous contrast to the chaos of the Leges Henrici.

[2] Leg. Henr. 59, § 15; Glanvill, ii. 3; Note Book, pl. 592, 1460.   In practice sixty shillings and a penny are paid.   The penny we can not explain.   The author of the Mirror (Seld. Soc.), p. 110, who supposes that the sixty shillings go to the victor, adds a half-penny for a purse to hold the money.   For the *bannus Regis* of Frankish law, see Brunner, D. R. G. ii. 35.

[3] London charter of Hen. I. c. 7.   Liber Albus, i. 111, 115: Of pledges who do not produce a man accused of crime it is said 'iudicatur unusquisque *a sa were*, scilicet, in misericordia centum solidorum.'   Consuetudines Kantiae, Statutes, i. 225.

[4] Somma, p. 204; Ancienne coutume, c. 85, ed. de Gruchy, p. 195.

[5] Lord Campbell's Act, Stat. 9–10 Vict. c. 93.

recent time men have sued for a *wer*; nor only so, they have lawfully prosecuted the blood-feud[1].

Oppressive character of the old system.

But great as was the change, it begins to look less when we strive to picture to ourselves the practical operation of the old law. The sums of money that it had demanded were to all seeming enormous, if we have regard to the economic position of the great mass of Englishmen. In the books of the Norman age the *wer* of the mere *ceorl*, or *villanus* as he is now called, is reckoned at £4, that of the thegn, or the *homo plene nobilis* who fills the thegn's place, is £25[2]. In some cases the amount of a *wíte* seems to have been doubled or trebled by that change in the monetary system which the Conquest occasioned; Norman shillings of twelve pence were exacted instead of English shillings of four or five pence. But in other cases, in which a due allowance was made for the new mode of reckoning, the penalty was still very heavy. A *wíte* of £5 was of frequent occurrence, and to the ordinary tiller of the soil this must have meant ruin. Indeed there is good reason to believe that for a long time past the system of *bót* and *wíte* had been delusive, if not hypocritical. It outwardly reconciled the stern facts of a rough justice with a Christian reluctance to shed blood; it demanded money instead of life, but so much money that few were likely to pay it. Those who could not pay were outlawed, or sold as slaves. From the very first it was an aristocratic system; not only did it make a distinction between those who were 'dearly born[3]' and those who were cheaply born, but it widened the gulf by impoverishing the poorer folk. One unlucky blow resulting in the death of a [p. 459] thegn may have been enough to reduce a whole family of ceorls to economic dependence or even to legal slavery. When we reckon up the causes which made the bulk of the nation into tillers of the lands of lords, *bót* and *wíte* should not be forgotten. At any rate to ask the *villanus* of Henry I.'s day to pay £5 as an atonement for his crime is to condemn him to outlawry.

Then again, for a long time past there has been in the

---

[1] Günther, Wiedervergeltung, i. 207. The blood-feud seems to have lived longest in Friesland, Lower Saxony, and parts of Switzerland, where it was prosecuted even in the sixteenth century.

[2] Leg. Henr. 70, § 1; 76, § 4; Leg. Will. i. c. 8. See Schmid, Gesetze, p. 676.

[3] Ine, 34 § 1.

penal system a much larger element of 'arbitrariness' or 'discretion' than the dooms disclose to a first glance.   Dr Brunner
has shown us how very many of the pure punishments, the
'afflictive' punishments, have their root in outlawry[1].   They
are mitigations of that comprehensive penalty.   The outlaw
forfeits all, life and limb, lands and goods.   This, as law and
kingship grow stronger, puts the fate of many criminals into
the king's hands[2].   The king may take life and choose the kind
of death, or he may be content with a limb; he can insist on
banishment or abjuration of his realm or a forfeiture of chattels.
The man who has committed one of the bad crimes which have
been causes of outlawry is not regarded as having a right to
just this or that punishment.   Under the new Norman kings,
who are not very straitly bound by tradition, this principle
comes to the front, and it explains an episode which is otherwise puzzling, namely, the ease with which punishments were
changed without any ceremonious legislation.   The Conqueror
would have no one hanged; emasculation and exoculation were
to serve instead[3].   Henry I. would now take money and now
refuse it[4].   He would reintroduce the practice of hanging
thieves taken in the act[5].   Loss of hand and foot became
fashionable under Henry II.; but we are told of him that he
[p. 460] hanged homicides and exiled traitors[6].   Very slowly in the
course of the thirteenth century the penalty of death took the
place of mutilation as the punishment due for felons, and this
without legislation.   The judges of that age had in this matter
discretionary powers larger than those that their successors
would wield for many centuries, and the kings could favour

---

[1] Forschungen, 444.

[2] Wihtræd, c. 26. Already in this very ancient set of laws we read that if a
thief is taken in the act, the king may decree that he shall be put to death, or
sold over seas, or suffered to redeem himself by his *wer*. So in Ine, c. 6, if a
man fights in the king's house, it is for the king to decide whether he shall have
life or no.

[3] Laws of William (Select Charters), c. 10: 'Interdico etiam ne quis
occidatur aut suspendatur pro aliqua culpa, sed eruantur oculi, et testiculi
abscidantur.' We use too mild a word if we speak of 'blinding.' The eyes
were torn out.

[4] Will. Malmesb. Gesta Regum, ii. 487.

[5] Flor. Wig. ii. 57.

[6] Diceto, i. 434: 'homicidae suspendio punirentur, proditores damnarentur
exilio, levioribus in flagitiis deprehensi truncatione membrorum notabiles
redderentur.'

now one and now another punishment[1]. Such changes could take place easily, because a main idea of the old law had been that by the gravest, the unemendable, crimes a man 'forfeited life and member and all that he had.' It was not for him to complain if a foot was taken instead of his eyes, or if he was hanged instead of being beheaded.

§ 2. *Felony and Treason.*

Causes of the change.

We have not far to seek for political, social and economic causes which in the twelfth century were making for revolution and reconstruction in the domain of criminal law. Some of them were common to many lands, others were peculiar to England. We might speak of the relaxation of the bond of kinship which was caused by the spread of vassalage,—of the presence of numerous foreigners who had no kin but the king, —of the jostle between the various tariffs, Saxon, Scandinavian, Frankish,—of the debasement of the great bulk of the peasants under a law of villeinage which gave their lords a claim upon those chattels that might otherwise have paid for their misdeeds, —of the delimitation of the field of justice between church and state, which left the temporal power free to inflict punishment without first going through the ceremony of demanding an almost impossible atonement,—or again, of the influence of Roman law, which made for corporal pains but would leave much to the discretion of the judge,—or lastly, of a growing persuasion that the old system of pre-appointed *bót* and *wíte*, which paid no heed to the offender's wealth, was iniquitous. It is not for us to describe all these converging forces; it must be enough if we can detect the technical machinery by which [p. 461] they did their work.

How the change was effected.

The general character of this process will become plain if we here repeat the words which in Bracton's day are the almost invariable preamble of every charge of grave crime. We will suppose that Alan is going to accuse William of wounding, robbery or the like. He will say that 'Whereas the said Alan was (*a*) in the peace of God and of our lord the king, there came

---

[1] Select Pleas of the Crown (Selden Soc.), pl. 77. On a roll of 1202 it is said of a woman 'et ideo meruit mortem, sed per dispensationem eruantur ei oculi.'

the said William (*b*) feloniously as a felon (*felonessement com felon*), and (*c*) in premeditated assault' inflicted a wound on Alan, or robbed him of his chattels. Now here, if we have regard to past history, Alan accuses William not only of the crime of wounding or (as the case may be) of robbery, but of three other crimes, namely, (*a*) a breach of the king's peace, (*b*) a felony, (*c*) *forsteal*, way-laying, *guet-apens*[1].

The phrase which tells how Alan was in the peace of God and of our lord the king, though it may rapidly degenerate into a 'common form,' must have been originally used for the purpose of showing both that the crime in question was one of the reserved pleas of the crown and that it was a heinous, if not a bootless, crime. The allusion to the peace of God may be an echo of the *treuga Dei* which had at one time been enforced in Normandy, if not in England, and which, when it had attained its largest scope, comprehended many holy seasons and a long half of every week: but we do not know that it was of much importance in this country[2]. Be this as it may, the words about the king's peace have had a definite meaning; they point to a breach of the king's *griÐ* or *mund*, a crime which at all events deserves the heavy *wíte* of a hundred shillings, and which, when [p. 462] coupled with homicide, has been unemendable[3]. The manner in which the king's *griÐ* or *mund* has been extending itself, until it begins to comprehend all places within the realm, all persons who are not outlaws and every time which is not an interregnum, we must not describe at any length[4]. When the

The king's peace.

---

[1] Ancienne coutume de Normandie, c. 74 (75), ed. Gruchy, p. 177; Somma, p. 184: 'In omni enim sequela quae fit ad damnamentum membrorum debet in clamore exprimi quod illud, super quo appellatio movetur, factum est cum felonia in pace Dei et Ducis.' Bracton, f. 138, 144, 146. In early enrolments many of the appellor's phrases are omitted or represented by *etc.* We must not assume that he did not mention *felony* because this word is not on the roll.

[2] See above, vol. i. p. 75. In the Normandy of Henry I. the effect of breaking the peace of the church as well as the peace of the duke by homicide was that the bishop got nine pounds out of the forfeited chattels of the offender : Très ancien coutumier (ed. Tardif), p. 66. In England at that time the bishop in such a case may have been able to claim five pounds : Leg. Henr. 11, § 1. At a later date we find that in London assaults committed within the octaves of the three great festivals were treated as graver offences than other assaults : Munim. Gildh. i. 56.

[3] Leg. Henr. 12, §§ 1, 2; 35, § 2.

[4] See Pollock, The King's Peace, Oxford Lectures, p. 65; Liebermann, Leges Edwardi, p. 63. Select Pleas of the Crown, pl. 84: a crime committed between Richard's death and John's coronation is said to have been done 'after the

Conqueror declared that all the men whom he had brought
hither were within his peace, he was spreading abroad his
mund[1]. Precedents from the thirteenth century suggest that
in this process of generalization the king's high-way was an
useful channel. Often the appellor is supposed to say not
merely that he was in the king's peace, but also that he was on
the king's high-way when he was assaulted, and this assertion,
though it has already become a mere rhetorical ornament, has
assuredly had a past history :—appellors have been suffered or
encouraged to declare that deeds were done on the high-way
which really were done elsewhere, and the specially royal roads
are losing their prerogative[2]. Already in Glanvill's day it is
understood that an accuser can place an assault outside the
competence of the local courts by some four or five words about
the king's peace[3].

The king's
peace at
its widest.
　　But the very ease with which the king's peace spread itself
until it had become an all-embracing atmosphere prevented a
mere breach of that peace from being permanently conceived as
a crime of the highest order. Every action of trespass in the
king's court supposes such a breach ; every convicted defendant [p. 463]
in such an action must go to prison until he pays a fine to which
the law sets no limits ; and yet the day for nominal trespasses
is approaching ; a breach of the king's peace may do no perceptible harm, and accusations of that offence will be freely thrown
about in actions which are fast becoming merely civil actions.

Felony.
　　It was otherwise with *felony*. This becomes and remains a
name for the worst, the bootless crimes. Hardly a word has

peace of our lord the king, then duke of Normandy and *lord* of England, had
been sworn.'

　　[1] Laws of William (Sel. Charters), c. 3. Henry II. in his Coronation
Charter, c. 12, says, ' Pacem firmam in toto regno meo pono et teneri amodo
praecipio.'

　　[2] See *e.g.* Bracton, f. 144: ' sicut fuit in pace domini Regis in tali loco, vel
sicut ivit in pace domini Regis in chimino domini Regis.' The king's hand-
given or hanselled *grið* was also useful. Bracton, f. 138: ' et contra pacem
domini Regis ei [appellatori] datam.' Select Pleas of the Crown, pl. 104: in
1211 a wounded man obtains the king's peace from the king's serjeant; this is
mentioned as an aggravation of a subsequent attack upon him by his enemy.
In Edward III.'s day to slay a royal messenger, who according to old ideas
would have been specially within the king's *grið*, was accounted by some to be
no mere felony, but high treason: Hale, P. C. i. 81.

　　[3] Glanvill, i. 2: ' nisi accusator adiciat de pace domini Regis infracta.' For
the importance of these words see Select Pleas of the Crown, pl. 21, 31,
88, 172.

given more trouble to etymologists that the low Latin *felo*, which starting from France finds a home in many languages[1]. We are now told that Coke's guess may be right after all[2] and that 'of the many conjectures proposed, the most probable is that *fellōne-m* is a derivative of the Latin *fell-*, *fel*, gall, the original sense being one who is full of bitterness or venom,' for gall and venom were closely associated in the popular mind. When the adjective *felon* first appears it seems to mean cruel, fierce, wicked, base[3]. Occasionally we may hear in it a note of admiration, for fierceness may shade off into laudable courage[4]; but in general it is as bad a word as you can give to man or thing, and it will stand equally well for many kinds of badness, for ferocity, cowardice, craft. Now in the language of continental law it seems soon to have attached itself to one class of crimes, namely, those which consist of a breach of that trust and faith which should exist between man and lord. The age in which *felon* became a common word was the age in which the tie of vassalage was the strongest tie that bound man to man. We have seen that in England *felonia* threatened for a while to bear a narrow meaning and only to cover offences similar to those which at a later time were known as high and petty treasons[5]. But in England and in Normandy[6] something [p. 464] saved it from this fate and gave it a wider meaning. This something we shall probably find in the rule that the felon's fee should escheat to his lord. The specific effect of the 'words of felony' when they were first uttered by appellors, who were bringing charges of homicide, robbery, rape and so forth, was to provide that, whatever other punishment the

---

[1] Oxford English Dictionary, s.v. *felon*.

[2] Co. Lit. 391. Blackstone, iv. 95, speaks scornfully of Coke's endeavour, and himself favours Spelman's *fee-lon* (*pretium feodi*). In Y. B. 21-2 Edw. I. p. 355, a judge speaks as though felony and venom were connected in his mind. Henry III. tells the pope that the Bishop of Ely is behaving treasonably, 'non oblitus antiquam suae mentis et fellitam malitiam': Foedera, i. 155.

[3] The relation of the English adjective *fell* to *felon* is explained in Oxf. Dict.

[4] The editors of the Oxf. Dict. give a few instances of this use.

[5] See above, vol. i. pp. 303-5; Blackstone, Comment. iv. 96. After Leg. Henr. 43, § 7; 46, § 3; 53, § 4, one of the first occurrences of *felonia* is in Ass. Northampt. c. 1: an accused person who comes clean from the ordeal may remain in the country unless he is defamed of murder 'vel alia turpi felonia,' in which case he must abjure the realm. It would seem therefore that every robbery or the like, if already a *felonia*, is not a *turpis felonia*.

[6] See the passage from the Coutumier cited above, p. 463, note 1.

appellees might undergo, they should at all events lose their land. The magnates saw no harm in this, though in truth the extension of felony, if it might bring them some accession of wealth, was undermining their power[1].

The felonies.

At all events this word, expressive to the common ear of all that was most hateful to God and man, was soon in England and Normandy a general name for the worst, the utterly 'bootless' crimes. In later days technical learning collected around it and gave rise to complications, insomuch that to define a felony became impossible; one could do no more than enumerate the felonies. But if we place ourselves in the first years of the thirteenth century some broad statements seem possible. (i) A felony is a crime which can be prosecuted by an appeal, that is to say, by an accusation in which the accuser must as a general rule offer battle[2]. (ii) The felon's lands go to his lord or to the king and his chattels are confiscated. (iii) The felon forfeits life or member. (iv) If a man accused of felony flies, he can be outlawed. Conversely, every crime that can be prosecuted by appeal, and every crime that causes a loss of both lands and goods, and every crime for which a man shall lose life or member, and every crime for which a fugitive can be outlawed, is a felony[3].

[1] The rule that an attainder for wilful homicide or the like will always involve disherison seems not to have been fully established even in 1176. See above, vol. i. p. 457, note 4.

[2] Bracton, f. 141: 'Item nullum appellum, nisi fiat mentio de felonia facta.' Were we to begin by saying that the felonies are a species of 'indictable offences' we should mislead a student of thirteenth century law. There are several felonies that are not indictable felonies. This will become plain hereafter. See Britton, i. 98.

[3] Glanvill, xiv. 1: 'Si vero per huiusmodi legem super capitali crimine fuerit quis convictus, ex regiae dispensationis beneficio tam vitae quam membrorum suorum eius pendet iudicium, sicuti in ceteris placitis de felonia.' Bracton, f. 137: 'et si appellatus victus fuerit capitalem subibit sententiam cum exheredatione et omnium bonorum suorum amissione, et sicut esse debet in omni vel quolibet genere feloniae.' The difficulties in the way of a definition of felony are stated by Blackstone, Comment. iv. 97, and Stephen, Hist. Crim. Law, ii. 192. Blackstone says: 'Felony may be without inflicting capital punishment, as in the cases instanced of self-murder, excusable homicide, and petit larceny: and it is possible that capital punishments may be inflicted and yet the offence be no felony, as in the case of heresy by the common law...... And of the same nature was the punishment of standing mute.' Sir J. F. Stephen writes: 'It is usually said that felony means a crime which involved the punishment of forfeiture, but this definition would be too large, for it would include misprision of treason which is a misdemeanour. On the other hand, if

[p. 465]   We thus define felony by its legal effects; any definition Import of felony.
that would turn on the quality of the crime is unattainable.
We may see, however, that in Bracton's day the word imports a
certain gravity in the harm done and a certain wickedness in
the doer of it. The justices have been compelled to set limits
to the 'appeal of felony,' for sometimes not only the accuser
but the accused also will be desirous of using for the settlement
of trivial disputes a process which sanctifies a good open fight
in the presence of a distinguished company. 'Wickedly and in
felony you struck the dust from my cap'—if, says Bracton, an
appellor speaks thus, the justices must quash the appeal
although the appellee wishes to deny the charge 'by his body[1].'
[p. 466] In the department of violence to the person a line is drawn
between the wound and the bruise; 'blind blows' which
neither break bone nor draw blood are no sufficient foundation

felony is defined as a crime punishable with death, it excludes petty larceny
which was never capital, and includes piracy which was never felony.' These
objections, however, disappear if we take our stand about the year 1200, and in
accordance with the spirit of the time speak, not of 'crimes punishable with
death,' but of crimes for which a man 'forfeits life or member.' Men may lose
their ears for petty larceny (Britton, i. 61); if they are let off with minor
punishments this is regarded as an act of mercy. Possibly the petty larcener's
lands did not escheat; in later times they did not; but a freeholder of this age
was in general above the temptations of petty larceny. Of piracy the law as
yet knew nothing. Any act that would afterwards have been 'misprision of
treason' would almost certainly have been called and treated as treason. The
peine forte et dure in its inception was not regarded as a punishment; it was
mere process. Excusable homicide was sharply contrasted with felonious
homicide. If heresy was punishable with death, the English temporal courts
had nothing to do with this. As to 'self-murder,' we doubt whether the
law of 1200 called this felony. Of these points we shall speak below. We
are not concerned to exclude high or petty treason from our definition of
felony. Every treason was a felony. For this reason we say that the felon's
lands go either to the lord or—this is the case in high treason—to the king.
We believe that we are right in saying that about the year 1200 men were not
outlawed for crimes falling short of felony. The extension of outlawry to
smaller offences, in particular, trespass *contra pacem Regis*, was just taking
place in Bracton's day. He sees (f. 127 b, 441) that a minor outlawry is being
developed and that this is parallel to the minor excommunication. The
passage on f. 127 b ('Facta autem...humana') is marginal. On the whole in
the thirteenth century, though there might be some small anomalies, the gulf
between the felonies and the minor offences was broad and deep.

[1] Bracton, f. 101 b, 102. Select Pleas of the Crown, pl. 35: in 1202 the
justices refuse to hear an appeal which charges a mere trespass on land;
'appellum de pratis pastis non pertinet ad coronam Regis.' Many entries
suggest that an appeal of felony often has its origin in a dispute about
proprietary rights.

for a charge of felony[1]. But the word is also being used to signify the moral guilt which deserves a punishment of the highest order. Homicide by felony is frequently contrasted with homicide by misadventure, homicide by self-defence and homicide committed by one who is of unsound mind[2].

Premeditated
assault. In this context the word *felony* is often coupled with what will in the future be another troublesome term of art, to wit, *malice aforethought* or *malice prepense* (*malitia excogitata, praecogitata*). This has a past as well as a future history. If we look at the words which an appellor commonly uses, we shall find that, though he does not speak of premeditated malice, he does charge his adversary with a premeditated assault (*assultus praemeditatus*)[3]. Now this, we take it, is a charge of another of the old pleas of the crown; it is a charge of way-laying, of *forsteal*[4]. In the French *Leis Williame* the English *forsteal* is represented by *agwait purpensé*[5], premeditated awaiting, the *guet-apens* of modern French law. In Normandy the appellor spoke of *aguet purpensé* just where in England he spoke of *assault purpensé*[6]. The idea on which stress is being laid is becoming a little more general than it once was; a premeditated, or as we should say intentional, assault takes the place of lying in wait, lying in ambush. A [p. 467] further generalization may be seen when in the thirteenth century the chancery is beginning to contrast a homicide by misadventure, which deserves a pardon, with a homicide which has been committed *in felonia et per malitiam praecogitatam*[7].

---

[1] Bracton, f. 144 b.

[2] Britton, i. 113: 'Ou il porra dire, qe tut feist il le fet, neqedent ne le fist il mie par felonie purpensé, mes par necessité defendaunt sei...ou par mescheaunce en akune manere e sauntz felonie penser (*al.* purpensé).' See the pardons cited below, p. 480. Already in 1214 we find 'per infortunium et non per feloniam'; Select Pleas of the Crown, pl. 114. The wickedness of felony is made evident by the common phrase *nequiter et in felonia*; but, while the *in felonia* became essential and sacramental, the *nequiter* was never, so far as we are aware, an indispensable phrase. The 'special instigation of the devil' is a late ornament.

[3] Bracton, f. 138, 141 b, 144, 144 b: 'in assultu praemeditato.' Select Pleas of the Crown, pl. 88 (A.D. 1203).

[4] Schmid, Gesetze, Glossar, s.v. *forsteal*; Brunner, D. R. G. ii. 563.

[5] Leg. Will. I. c. 2. Already in D. B. i. 269 we have 'homicidium et furtum et heinfar [hámfare] praecogitata.'

[6] Somma, p. 184; Ancienne coutume, c. 74 (75), ed. Gruchy, p. 176: 'cum agueito praecogitato': 'en aguet pourpensé.'

[7] See the pardons of which instances are given below, p. 480.

The word *malitia* is more general than the word *assultus*; it is indeed a large word, equivalent perhaps to our *wrong-doing*, and a larger word than *assault* is necessary, because we may wish to state that the man who is being pardoned for an excusable homicide was guiltless, not only of an intentional assault, but of any act intended to do harm. In course of time the term *malitia* has brought many difficulties upon English lawyers. Of these we must not speak, but we believe that in this case it is rather the popular than the legal sense of the word that has changed. When it first came into use, *malitia* hardly signified a state of mind; some qualifying adjective such as *praemeditata* or *excogitata* was needed if much note was to be taken of intention or of any other psychical fact. When we first meet with *malice prepense* it seems to mean little more than intentional wrong-doing; but the somewhat weighty adjectives which are coupled with *malitia* in its commonest context—adjectives such as *excogitata* —are, if we mistake not, traces of the time when *forsteal*, *guet-apens*, waylaying, the setting of ambush, was (what few crimes were) a specially reserved plea of the crown to be emended, if indeed it was emendable, by a heavy *wíte*[1].

[1] If we are right, the *guet-apens* which in modern French law raises a mere *meurtre* to the dignity of an *assassinat*, is first cousin to the *malice aforethought* which characterizes our English *murder*; both go back to days when waylaying is a specially heinous crime and a cause for royal interference. For the French *guet-apens*, see Viollet, Établissements, i. 238. In England the course of development is this:—a charge of *forsteal* or (Leg. Will.) *agwait purpensé* becomes an ordinary part of every appeal in the form *assault purpensé*, *assultus praemeditatus*; a slight change makes this the *malitia praemeditata* (*excogitata*) of a chancery formula that is quite common before the end of Henry III.'s reign. The three terms *agait, assaut ou malice purpensé* are brought together into one phrase on the Parliament Roll for 1389; Rot. Parl. iii. 268. See Stephen, Hist. Crim. Law, iii. 41–2; but we can not think that there is any connexion between the *malitia* of this formula and the *odium et atia* of the famous writ. As to *malice* (*malitia*), this creeps into records and law-books as a vague word expressive of intentional wrong-doing; but (though it would exclude harm done by misadventure) it lays no strong emphasis on the intention, and makes no special reference to spite or hatred. See *e.g.* Bracton, f. 138 b, line 8; Note Book, pl. 687; Britton, i. 67, 83, 87, 89, 91. It was becoming common in Edward I.'s reign; but had, so it seems to us, first become prominent in the numerous pardons that were granted to those who were man-slayers by misadventure or in self-defence. As to *forsteal*, this word perdured in the practice of local courts, which had nothing to do with grave crimes, and from the sense of way-laying it passed to that of lying in wait for merchants who are bringing goods to the town so that the price of victuals is enhanced.

[p. 468]

The group of felonies.

By the process which we have endeavoured to trace a certain group of crimes, comprising homicide, mayhem, wounding, false imprisonment, arson, rape, robbery, burglary and larceny, was broadly marked off from all the minor offences. They were felonies and unemendable crimes which deserved a judgment 'of life or member;' they worked a disherison. We shall have more to say of them; but before we carry our story any further we ought to state briefly such answer as modern researches enable us to give to a general question about culpability.

Culpability in ancient law.

What is the measure of culpability that ancient law endeavours to maintain? Is it high, is it low? Do we start with the notion that a man is only answerable for those results of his actions that he has intended, and then gradually admit that he is sometimes liable for harm that he did not intend, or, on the other hand, do we begin with a rigid principle which charges him with all the evil that he has done, and then do we accept first one and then another mitigation of this rule[1]? There seems to be now little room for doubt that of these two answers the second is the truer. Law in its earliest days tries to make men answer for all the ills of an obvious kind that their deeds bring upon their fellows.

Causation in ancient law.

Guesswork perhaps would have taught us that barbarians will not trace the chain of causation beyond its nearest link, and that, for example, they will not impute one man's death to another unless that other has struck a blow which laid a corpse at his feet. All the evidence however points the other way :— I have slain a man if but for some act of mine he might perhaps be yet alive. Very instructive is a formula which was still in use in the England of the thirteenth century; one who was accused of homicide and was going to battle was expected to [p. 469] swear that he had done nothing whereby the dead man was 'further from life or nearer to death[2].' Damages which the

---

[1] See Brunner, Absichtslose Missethat, Forschungen, 487; Post, Bausteine, i. 230; Wigmore, Responsibility for Tortious Acts, Harv. L. R., vii. 315, 383, 441. Mr Wigmore has made a very full collection of early English cases bearing on this question.

[2] Leg. Hen. 90, § 11: 'quod per eum non fuerit vitae remotior morti propinquior.' Bracton, f. 141 b: 'per quod remotior esse debeat a vita et morti propinquior.' Note Book, pl. 1460: 'nec per ipsum fuit morti appropiatus nec a vita elongatus.' Munim. Gildh. i. 105: 'Iuravit...quod numquam ipsam Isabellam verberavit, unde puer, de quo fecit aborsum, propinquior fuit morti

modern English lawyer would assuredly describe as 'too remote,' were not too remote for the author of the *Leges Henrici*. At your request I accompany you when you are about your own affairs; my enemies fall upon and kill me; you must pay for my death[1]. You take me to see a wild-beast-show or that interesting spectacle a madman; beast or madman kills me; you must pay. You hang up your sword; some one else knocks it down so that it cuts me; you must pay. In none of these cases can you honestly swear that you did nothing that helped to bring about death or wound[2].

If once it be granted that a man's death was caused by the act of another, then that other is liable, no matter what may have been his intentions or his motives. To this principle our evidence directs us, though for an unmitigated application of it we may have to look to a prehistoric time. In a yet early age law begins to treat intentional as worse than unintentional homicide. In either case the *wer* is due; but in the one there can, in the other there can not, be a legitimate feud; intentional homicide must be paid for by *wíte* as well as *wer*, unintentional by *wer* without *wíte*, at all events if the slayer, not waiting for an accusation, proclaims what he has done and proves that there was misadventure[3]. We may see in curious instances a growing appreciation of moral differences which has not dared to abolish, but has tried to circumvent the ancient law. The old code of the Swabian race declares that if you are slain by the bite of my dog I must pay half your *wer*. In strictness your whole *wer* can be demanded; but if a kinsman of yours is unreasonable enough to exact this, he must submit to have the corpse of the dog hanging over his door-way until it rots and perishes[4]. A parallel passage in our own *Leges Henrici* says that if by mischance you fall from a tree upon me and kill me, then, if my kinsman must needs have vengeance, he may climb a tree and fall upon you[5]. Even when a demand for the *wer* is becoming obsolete, and the general

Absolute liability for the effects of acts.

[p. 470]

---

et remotior a vita.' Brunner, Forschungen, p. 495, gives a similar formula from the Icelandic Grágás.

[1] Leg. Hen. 88, § 9.   [2] Leg. Hen. 90, § 11.

[3] Brunner, Forschungen, 500–5.

[4] Brunner, Forschungen, 492; Lex Alaman. Mon. Germ. Leges, iii. p. 39.

[5] Leg. Hen. 90, § 7. We read of an exactly similar judgment given of late years in Abyssinia; Parkyns, Life in Abyssinia, London, 1868, pp. 366–7, cited by Günther, Wiedervergeltung, i. 13.

rule is that he who slays another must be put to death, men
are still unable to formulate a principle which will excuse any
manslayer, however morally innocent he may be, unless indeed
his act falls within one of a few narrow categories such as that
which comprises the execution of a lawful sentence. Such
manslayers as no one would wish to hang are not acquitted,
but are recommended to the 'mercy' of judges and princes, for
the *rigor iuris* holds them answerable for all the effects of their
actions[1].

Liability
for the acts
of slaves
and beasts. But the most primitive laws that have reached us seem to
point to a time when a man was responsible, not only for all
harm done by his own acts, but also for that done by the acts
of his slaves, his beasts, or—for even this we must add—the
inanimate things that belonged to him[2]. Law which demands
a 'noxal surrender' of the peccant slave or ox is already a mitigation of older law which would not have let the master off so
easily. As regards the delicts of slaves, various laws of the same
family soon begin to go different ways, for there are here many
difficult problems to be solved. However firmly we grasp
the principle that a slave is a thing, we can not help seeing that
the state may with advantage treat slaves as capable of committing crimes and suffering punishments, and when the state
has begun to punish the slave it begins to excuse the master,
provided that he will deliver the slave to justice. The same
principle can be applied with some modifications to the case of
beasts. Ancient law will sometimes put the beast to death, and
will not be quite certain that it is not inflicting punishment
upon one who has deserved it[3]. But the most startling illustra- [p. 471]
tions of its rigour occur when we see a man held liable for the
evil done by his lifeless chattels, for example, by his sword. If
his sword kills, he will have great difficulty in swearing that he
did nothing whereby the dead man was 'further from life or

---

[1] For French medieval law, see Brunner, *op. cit.* 493–4, and Esmein,
Histoire de la procédure criminelle, p. 255. Post, Bausteine, i. 233, says that
this idea, namely, that homicide by misadventure deserves pardon, still prevails
in Chinese law.

[2] Brunner, *op. cit.* 507–523.

[3] Brunner, *op. cit.* 519, and D. R. G. ii. 556. On the continent the trial
and formal punishment of beasts have been known in recent times; but there is
some dispute as to how far this is due to the sanctity attached by bibliolaters to
the archaic Hebrew Law contained in Genesis, ix. 5, and Exodus, xxi. 28–32.
See Laws of Alfred, Introduction, 21.

nearer to death.' If you hand over your sword to a smith to be
sharpened, see that you get it back 'sound,' that is to say, with
no blood-guiltiness attaching to it, for otherwise you may be
receiving a 'bane,' a slayer, into your house[1]. But let us hear
the enlightened Bracton on this matter, for old popular phrases
will sometimes crop up through his rational text. 'If a man by
misadventure is crushed or drowned or otherwise slain, let hue
and cry at once be raised; but in such a case there is no need
to make pursuit from field to field and vill to vill; for the
malefactor has been caught, to wit, the bane[2].' Yes, the malefactor, the *bana*, the slayer, has been caught; a cart, a boat, a
mill-wheel is the slayer and must now be devoted to God.

Our English law of deodands gives us a glimpse into a far
off past. In 1846[3] we still in theory maintained the rule that
any animate or inanimate thing which caused the death of a
human being should be handed over to the king and devoted
by his almoner to pious uses, 'for the appeasing' says Coke 'of
God's wrath.' In the thirteenth century the common practice
was that the thing itself was delivered to the men of the township in whose territory the death occurred, and they had to
answer for its value to the royal officers. In very early records
we sometimes find that the justices in eyre name the charitable
purpose to which the money is to be applied; thus the price of
a boat they devote 'for God's sake' to the repair of Tewkesbury
[p. 472] bridge[4], and the sister of a man who has been run over obtains
the value of the condemned cart, since she is poor and sick[5].
Horses, oxen, carts, boats, mill-wheels and cauldrons were the
commonest of deodands. In English men called the deodand

*The
deodand.*

---

[1] Laws of Alfred, 19, § 3; Leg. Henr. 87, § 2, 3; 90, § 11. Brunner,
Forschungen, 521. The Ripuarian Law, adopted in Leg. Henr. 90, § 6,
says that if a beam of mine or the like kills a man, I need not pay for
him, unless I take the 'auctor interfectionis,' this man-slaying log, into
my service.

[2] Bracton, f. 116: 'cum malefactor captus sit, scilicet *la bane.*'

[3] Stat. 9–10 Vic. c. 62. For the law of deodands, see Bracton, f. 122; Fleta,
p. 37; Britton, i. 14, 15, 39; Staundford, P. C. f. 20; Coke, Third Inst. 57;
Hale, P. C. i. 419; Stephen, Hist. Crim. Law, iii. 77.

[4] Gloucestershire Pleas, pl. 230. One record gives 'dentur deo ad pontem,'
another 'dentur ponti pro deo.'

[5] Ibid. pl. 113. In pl. 118 a man having been killed by his own cart, its
price is given to his children *pro deo.* In pl. 298 a horse is given to a poor
man who was once its owner.

the *bane,* that is, the slayer[1]. In accordance with ancient ideas this bane, we take it, would have gone to the kinsmen of the slain; the owner would have purchased his peace by a surrender of the noxal thing; but what we have said above about intestacy[2] will prepare us to see that in the thirteenth century the claim of a soul which has been hurried out of this world outweighs the claim of the dead man's kinsfolk, and in the past they will have received the bane, not as a compensation for the loss that they suffered, but rather as an object upon which their vengeance must be wreaked before the dead man will lie in peace[3]. Even therefore when, as was commonly the case, the bane was a thing that belonged to the dead man, none the less it was deodand[4].

Restriction of culpability.

The deodand may warn us that in ancient criminal law there was a sacral element which Christianity could not wholly suppress, especially when what might otherwise have been esteemed a heathenry was in harmony with some of those strange old dooms that lie embedded in the holy books of the Christian. Also it is hard for us to acquit ancient law of that unreasoning instinct that impels the civilised man to kick, or consign to eternal perdition, the chair over which he has [p. 473] stumbled[5]. But law which would not confess to sanctioning this instinct still finds grave difficulties in its way if it endeavours to detect and appreciate the psychical element in guilt and innocence. 'The thought of man shall not be tried, for the devil himself knoweth not the thought of man':—thus

---

[1] Munim. Gildh. i. 98: 'de praedicto equo, qui fuit banum praedicti garcionis.' In the A.-S. laws *bana* is the usual word for a slayer. Bracton, f. 116.

[2] See above, vol. ii. p. 356.

[3] Brunner, D. R. G. ii. 558.

[4] In the oldest records we see no attempt to distinguish the cases in which the dead man was negligent from those in which no fault could be imputed to him, and the large number of deodands collected in every eyre suggests that many horses and boats bore the guilt which should have been ascribed to beer. A drunken carter is crushed beneath the wheel of his cart; the cart, the cask of wine that was in it and the oxen that were drawing it are all deodand: Northumberland Assize Rolls, p. 96. Bracton, f. 136 b, apparently thought it an abuse to condemn as deodand a thing that had not moved; he would distinguish between the horse which throws a man and the horse off which a man stupidly tumbles, between the tree that falls and the tree against which a man is thrown. We do not see these distinctions in the practice of the courts.

[5] Holmes, Common Law, p. 11; Wigmore, Harvard Law Rev. vii. p. 317, note 8.

at the end of the middle ages spoke Brian C. J. in words that
might well be the motto for the early history of criminal law[1].
It can not go behind the visible fact. Harm is harm and should
be paid for. On the other hand, where there is no harm done,
no crime is committed; an attempt to commit a crime is no
crime[2]. We may fairly remember in our ancestors' favour that
in their day the inference that he who kills has meant to kill,
or at least to wound, was much sounder than it would be now
when, the blood-feud having been suppressed and murders being
rare, we have surrounded ourselves with lethal engines, so that
one careless act may slay its thousands. But in truth the
establishment of a reasonable standard of responsibility is a
task which can only be accomplished after many experiments.
A mean must be found between these two extremes—absolute
liability for all harm done, and liability only for harm that is
both done and intended. Even criminal law can not be satisfied
with the latter of these standards. We hang as guilty of
'wilful murder by malice aforethought' the man who killed
when he meant only to inflict some grievous bodily harm, and
we have not even yet so precisely defined the murders which
deserve death that all recommendations to the king's 'mercy'
have become unnecessary. Ancient law comes but gradually to
a distinction between civil and criminal liability and has no
large choice of penalties. The modern judge with a convicted
manslayer before him has beneath his fingers a whole gamut
of punishments ranging from life-long penal servitude to a
trivial fine. The doomsmen of old days must exact the *wer* or
let the slayer go quit. To exact half a *wer* if there was some,
but little, guilt may well have seemed an illogical compromise
[p. 474] to the straiter sort of lawmen. And as regards civil liability,
even now-a-days the rule that a man ought to pay for all the
harm that he does to his neighbours will seem equitable enough
to a first glance, and but a few years ago there were plausible, if
insufficient, grounds for the assertion that in English courts a
plea that there was neither negligence nor an intent to do harm
was no answer to an action which charged the defendant with

---

[1] Y. B. 7 Edw. IV. f. 2 (Pasch. pl. 2). So Hale, P. C. i. 429, speaking of
witchcraft: 'it cannot come under the judgment of felony, because no external
act of violence was offered whereof the common law can take notice, and secret
things belong to God.'

[2] Brunner, D. R. G. ii. 558–64.

having hurt the plaintiff's body[1]. Any such ideas as the Roman *culpa* or our modern English *negligence* are but slowly fashioned. Ancient law has made a great advance when it has held that, though a *wer* or *bót* is due, there is not that intentional wrong-doing which calls for a *wíte* or lets loose the blood-feud[2].

Mens rea.
Of course the Christian church in her penitential books, which exercised a not inconsiderable influence on the parallel tariff of *wíte* and *bót*, laid stress on the mental elements in sin. Still some of the earliest of those books set up a very high standard of liability, even *in foro conscientiae*, for remote and unintended harm[3]. This may be due in part to that nervous horror of blood which at a later time would prevent an ordained clerk from taking part in a surgical operation, but is due in part to the example set by temporal law and public opinion. We receive a shock of surprise when we meet with a maxim that has troubled our modern lawyers, namely, *Reum non facit nisi mens rea*, in the middle of the *Leges Henrici*[4] among rules which hold a man answerable for all the harm that he does, and not far off from the old proverb, *Qui inscienter peccat, scienter emendet.* But the borrowed scrap of St Augustine speaks only of perjury, and that any one should ever have thought of [p. 475] charging with perjury one who swore what he believed to be true, this will give us another glimpse into ancient law[5].

---

[1] *Stanley* v. *Powell* [1891], 1 Q. B. 86. See the cases collected by Mr Wigmore in Harvard Law Rev. vii. 456: also Pollock, Torts, 5th ed. 129 ff.

[2] Kovalevsky, Droit coutumier Ossétien, pp. 294–304, gives a most interesting account of what until lately were causes of blood-feud among these inhabitants of the Caucasus. Homicide by misadventure or in self-defence was avenged or paid for at the full price. So if *A*'s sheep were pasturing on the mountain side, and one of them dislodged a stone which killed *B*, this was just cause for a feud. If a stolen gun went off in the hands of the thief who was carrying it away and killed him, the thief's kin had a just feud against the owner of the gun (p. 295).

[3] Brunner, Forschungen, p. 504.   [4] Leg. Hen. 5, § 28.

[5] As to the *mens rea*: Coke, Third Inst. 6, gives 'Et actus non facit reum nisi mens sit rea.' Coke knew the Red Book of the Exchequer which contains the Leges Henrici where the maxim stands 'Reum non facit nisi mens rea.' The original source is S. Augustinus, Sermones, No. 180, c. 2 (Migne, Patrol. vol. 38, col. 974) : 'Ream linguam non facit nisi mens rea.' This passes into the Decretum, c. 3, C. 22, qu. 2. The author of the Leges took it from some intermediate book in which the *linguam* may possibly have disappeared. In some Year Books of the fourteenth century we find our lawyers appealing to a far more dangerous maxim, *Voluntas reputabitur pro facto.* See Coke, Third Instit. 5; Stephen, Hist. Crim. Law, ii. 222. This was we believe due to the fact that, owing to the disuse of appeals, our criminal law had become far too

In the twelfth century the resuscitated Roman law introduced some new ideas. Men began to contrast, as Glanvill
does, civil with criminal causes, to speak of *dolus* and *culpa* and
casus, and to lay stress on the psychical element in crime.
Bracton has borrowed from Azo many generalities about crimes
and punishments; he has himself looked at Code and Digest; he
has transplanted a discourse on homicide from the works of
Bernard of Pavia, a distinguished canonist[1]. Of homicide the
canonists had by this time much to say, and much that concerned Englishmen. We must remember that, according to the
clerical contention, a clerk charged with crime could be tried
only by a spiritual court, and that this contention, at least so
far as the felonies were concerned, was sanctioned by the law of
England[2]. They had therefore ample occasion for enforcing,
not merely in the confessional, but by a public and coercive
procedure their doctrine of the various shades of homicidal
guilt, and they now had the old Roman texts before them.
Some of the most renowned decretals about this matter were
addressed to English prelates and dealt with English cases[3]. In
the thirteenth century a rudely complete table had been
constructed of the various sorts of homicide; and this Bracton
lifted from the famous Bernard[4]. On the whole, the canonical
[p. 476] scheme of responsibility was by no means unduly lenient; it
fully acquitted the man who slew his fellow by misadventure, if,
but only if, his act was in itself lawful and was also done with
all due care. It could afford to define various degrees of guilt,
because it could command a scale of punishments which
stretched from perpetual incarceration to that mere disablement
from further promotion which would be the penalty of a clerk
who had been but slightly careless. For this reason in Bracton's

lenient in cases of murderous assaults which did not cause death. We must
not here discuss this matter, but we believe that the adoption, even for one
limited purpose, of this perilous saying was but a momentary aberration. Our
old law started from the other extreme:—*Factum reputabitur pro voluntate.*

[1] Bracton, f. 104 b, 105. This is partly from Azo, Summa C. (de poenis) 9,
47; but Bracton keeps his eye on Dig. 48, 19, and makes a cento of passages
from that title.

[2] See above vol. i. pp. 441 ff.

[3] cc. 6, 9, 13, X. 5, 12. The last of these canons = Calendar of Papal
Registers, ed. Bliss, i. 9.

[4] Bracton, f. 120 b. This general discussion of homicide seems to be taken
with some changes from Bernardi Papiensis Summa Decretaliun (ed. Laspeyres,
Ratisbon, 1861), p. 219. The texts are collated in Bracton and Azo, p. 225.

text we may see Bernard's doctrine of homicide floating on the surface of, and scarcely mingling with the coarser English law, which hardly knew what to do with a manslayer who was not guiltless but did not deserve to be called a felon and put to death.

The felonies. Homicide.

We may now examine one by one the felonies of Bracton's age[1].

Homicide is the crime of which there is most to be said, but the practicable English law that lies beneath the borrowed Italian trappings is rude. In a few cases homicide is absolutely justifiable and he who commits it will suffer no ill. One such case is the execution of a lawful sentence of death. Another—and this is regarded as a very similar case—is the slaying of an outlaw or a hand-having thief or other manifest felon who resists capture. Only under local custom on the wild Welsh march may one slay an outlaw who makes no resistance[2]. The furthest point to which we have seen this class of cases stretched is marked by a judgment of 1256. A lunatic chaplain had broken into a house by night; a servant of the householder struck him on the head so that he died; the justices suffered the slayer to go quit[3]. Bracton in his text would allow a man to slay a housebreaker, if to do so was a necessary act of self-defence; but in his margin he noted a case of this kind in which the slayer was pardoned by the king[4]. There was need in 1293 for a statute to say that in certain [p. 477] circumstances a forester or parker was to be acquitted of the death of a trespasser whom he was endeavouring to arrest and slew in the endeavour[5]. In 1532 there was need for a statute

When justifiable.

---

[1] Once for all we may say that of the Mirror of Justices we shall take no notice. Its account of criminal law is so full of fables and falsehoods that as an authority it is worthless.

[2] Bracton, f. 128 b.

[3] Northumberland Assize Rolls (Surtees Soc.), 94. We imagine that in this case the prisoner was fortunate. Staffordshire Collections, vol. vi. pt. 1, p. 258: in 1293 *A* and *B* by night pursue a flying thief; each mistakes the other for the malefactor; *B* wounds *A*; then *A* kills *B*; the justices send *A* back to prison to await a pardon.

[4] Bracton, f. 144 b. The words 'sicut coram rege...perdonavit mortem' are marginal in the best MS. Staffordshire Collections, iv. p. 215: in 1272 one who has beheaded a flying robber is acquitted.

[5] 21 Edw. I. st. 2 (Statutes, i. p. 111); Stephen, Hist. Crim. Law, iii. 37. In 1236 there was a controversy between the king and the magnates about the right to arrest and imprison men who were found doing wrong in parks and preserves. This is reported in Stat. Merton. c. 11. Just at that time the king had pardoned a forester of the Earl of Ferrers, who had slain a malefactor in

to say that a person who killed any one who attempted to rob him in his own house or on or near the high-way should not incur a forfeiture of his goods[1]. Altogether in our common law the sphere of justifiable homicide was very narrow, and the cases which fell within it were those which in old times would have been regarded less as cases of legitimate self-defence than as executions, for the *fur manifestus* had been *ipso facto* an outlaw[2].

The man who commits homicide by misadventure or in self-defence deserves but needs a pardon. Bracton can not conceal this from us[3], and it is plain from multitudinous records of Henry III.'s reign. If the justices have before them a man who, as a verdict declares, has done a deed of this kind, they do not acquit him, nor can they pardon him, they bid him hope for the king's mercy[4]. In a precedent book of Edward I.'s time [p. 478] a justice is supposed to address the following speech to one whose plea of self-defence has been endorsed by the verdict of a jury : 'Thomas, these good folk testify upon their oath to all that you have said. Therefore by way of judgment we say that what you did was done in self-defence; but we can not deliver you from your imprisonment without the special command of

Misadventure and self-defence.

self-defence; but the king expressly protested that this was an act of grace and not of justice. See Note Book, pl. 1216.

[1] Stat. 24 Hen. VIII. c. 5; Stephen, Hist. Crim. Law, iii. 39.

[2] Brunner, Forschungen, 458. We do not think that in the thirteenth century a homicide in self-defence would have been justifiable, even though it was perpetrated in the endeavour to prevent a felony. See Northumberland Assize Rolls, 85: a man attempting rape assaulted a woman; she drew a small knife and killed him; she fled; her father offers the justices forty shillings for a permission that she may return to the peace; they receive the fine and will speak to the king.

[3] Bracton, f. 134: 'Tenetur etiam [Rex] aliquando de gratia concedere ei vitam et membra, ut si per infortunium vel se defendendo hominem interfecerit.' Ibid. f. 104 b: 'crimen homicidii, sive sit casuale vel voluntarium, licet eandem poenam non contineant, quia in uno casu rigor, in alio misericordia.' Contrast these with the romanesque passages on f. 120 b, 136 b.

[4] The practice is illustrated by Select Pleas of the Crown (Selden Soc.), pl. 70, 114, 188; Gloucestershire Pleas, pl. 15, 53, 362; Note Book, pl. 1084, 1216; Northumberland Assize Rolls, pp. 85, 94, 98, 111, 323, 343, 348, 361–2–3; Y. B. 30–31 Edw. I. 511, 513, 529. When a presentment of homicide by misadventure is made against a man who has fled, the roll sometimes says that he may come back if he will, though his chattels are forfeited; we do not think that this dispenses him from the necessity of procuring a pardon. He has not been tried and therefore has not been acquitted.

our lord the king; therefore we will report your condition to the king's court and will procure for you his special grace[1].'

Pardons for homicide. On the patent rolls of Henry III. pardons for those who have committed homicide by misadventure, in self-defence, or while of unsound mind, are common. Their form is the following:—Whereas we have learnt by an inquest taken by so and so (sometimes it is taken by the sheriff in full county court)—*or* Whereas our justices in their eyre in such a county have informed us after an inquest taken before them—that Nicholas of Frackenham slew Roger of Mepham by misadventure and not by felony or malice aforethought—*or* that William King killed Ralph de le Grave in self-defence and not of malice aforethought, for that the said Ralph ran upon a lance that William was holding—*or* that Walter Banastre, intending to chastise his son Geoffrey, wounded him by misadventure and not by felony in the arm so that he died—*or* that Maud who is in prison for slaying her two sons killed them in a fit of madness and not by felony or malice aforethought—*or* that Alexander of Gathurst aged twelve killed Helowise daughter of John le Hey aged less than eleven by misadventure and not by felony or malice aforethought—*or* that Alan Blount imprisoned by our bailiffs of Lincoln for suspicion of robbery died from the severity of the imprisonment and not by the act of Adam Williamson—now we have pardoned to him the suit which pertains to us for the said death (*or, in appropriate cases,* the outlawry promulgated against him), and have granted him our firm peace, but so that he shall stand to right in our court if any one (*or,* if any of the kinsfolk of the slain) desires to complain against him[2].

Practice in cases of excusable homicide. From these pardons we learn that sometimes a person [p. 479] charged with homicide obtained a writ from the king ordering the sheriff, or the coroners, to take an inquest as to whether there was felony or misadventure, while at other times the justices in eyre had an accused person before them and took a similar inquest. In either case, if the jurors gave a favourable

---

[1] La Corone pledee devant justice: Camb. Univ. Libr. Mm. i. 27, f. 129.

[2] Our instances are from the unprinted Patent Rolls of 20, 30, 40 Henry III. There is generally an express statement to the effect that there was no *felonia*, or no *malitia excogitata*. Occasionally the pardon is granted at the instance of some great one; *e.g.* Rot. Pat. 40 Hen. III. m. 3, the king at the request of his daughter, the Queen of Scotland, pardons a chaplain who has committed homicide *per infortunium*.

verdict, a pardon was granted. In 1278 the procedure was reformed by the Statute of Gloucester[1]. No more writs for inquests were to be granted, but the accused was to appear before the justices and 'put himself upon the country for good and ill.' In case the jurors returned a verdict of 'misadventure' or 'self-defence,' the justices were to report the case to the king, who would, said the statute, if it pleased him, take the accused into his grace. This change had the effect of bringing all these cases under the eye of the justices and apparently of keeping in prison men who in former times might have obtained a speedier pardon. The statute is far from suggesting that these pardons were already 'pardons of course,' though such they became in a later age. In one respect however our law increased its severity. So far as we can see, the homicide who obtained a pardon on the score of misadventure or self-defence (unless he had fled on account of his deed), did not in Henry III.'s time incur that forfeiture of his chattels which was inflicted upon him in after days[2]. But very often he had fled, and this, so it seems to us, may have enabled our ever needy kings to establish forfeiture as a general accompaniment of the 'pardon of course.' According to the rigour of the law such a forfeiture might have been exacted even in the year 1828[3].

[p. 480]   A misinterpretation of the statute of Marlborough led some lawyers of a later age, among whom was Coke, to believe that before the year 1267 the man who killed another in self-defence or by misadventure was hanged[4]. Their error has been sufficiently exposed by modern writers, who however have been too loud in their exclamations over its absurdity[5]. The clause in

Liability and misadventure.

[1] Stat. Glouc. c. 9; Coke, Second Inst. 315; Stephen, Hist. Crim. Law, iii. 37. We are not persuaded by the commentators that this statute had anything to do with the writ *de odio et atia*. The writs which directed an inquest where there was alleged misadventure or alleged self-defence said nothing of *odium et atia*. But of the writ *de odio et atia* we shall speak in the next chapter.

[2] See the cases cited above on p. 479, note 4. Foster, Discourse of Homicide, ch. iv. Stephen, Hist. Crim. Law, iii. 38–40.

[3] Stat. 9 Geo. IV. c. 31, sec. 10; Stephen, Hist. Crim. Law, iii. p. 77; the old law however had fallen into desuetude. Justices allowed jurors to find a man 'not guilty,' instead of giving a special verdict about misadventure or self-defence.

[4] Y. B. 21 Edw. III. f. 17 (Hil. pl. 23); Coke, Second Inst. 148.

[5] Hale, P. C. i. 425; Foster, Discourse of Homicide, ch. iv.; Blackstone, Comment. iv. 188; Stephen, Hist. Crim. Law, iii. 42.

question dealt, not with the crime of homicide, but with the *murdrum*, the murder-fine exacted from the hundred. It declared that this was not to be levied when a death occurred by misadventure. In so doing it overruled a contrary custom of some shires which in a recent famine had become intolerable—there were so many starved corpses to be paid for[1]. This however, even when rightly interpreted, will give us food for reflection. An accidental death has been paid for by a *murdrum*, by a fine, a portion of which under the law of the Norman age went to the kindred of the dead man. Before we laugh at Coke let us look at a body of law which stands very near our own. The earliest of the Norman custumals declares in the plainest words that the man who kills his lord by misadventure must die; he will escape the torment of being 'drawn,' but he must die[2]. And what, let us ask, could an Englishman have done if about the year 1180 he had been appealed of homicide and had desired to urge that it was the result of misadventure? At that time he would have had no right to put himself upon a jury 'for good and ill,' and we see no trace of his being able to set up the misadventure by way of 'exception[3].' We believe that he must have gone to battle, and that, vanquished in [p. 481] battle, his life and members would have been in the king's mercy.

The pardon and the offended kin.

The king could not protect the man-slayer from the suit of the dead man's kin. Even when the pardon was granted on the score of misadventure, this suit was saved by express words. Proclamation was made in court inviting the kin to prosecute, but telling them that they must come at once or never[4]. What

---

[1] Bracton, f. 135; Oxford Petition of 1258, c. 21; Provisions of Westminster, c. 22; Stat. Marlb. c. 25; Maitland, Gloucestershire Pleas, p. xxx.; Chadwyck Healey, Somersetshire Pleas, p. lx.

[2] Très ancien coutumier (ed. Tardif), p. 30; 'si homo dominum suum occiderit, nisi per infortunium hoc contigerit, detractus suspendatur, et, si per infortunium, morte puniatur.'

[3] Bracton, f. 141, suggests a good many 'exceptions' that the appellee may plead; but none of them meets this case. Britton, i. 113 and Fleta, 49, allow a special plea of misadventure or self-defence.

[4] Northumberland Assize Rolls, 98 (A.D. 1256): 'Et quia dominus Rex concessit ei pacem suam dummodo ipse staret recto, sicut praedictum est, interrogatum est semel, bis, ter, si aliquis ex parentibus eiusdem Uctredi vel aliquis alius velit sequi versus eum, modo veniant, vel nunquam. Et quia non est aliquis qui versus eum velit sequi, ideo Petrus inde quietus, et conceditur ei firma pax.'

could the kin do in such a case?   They could make themselves extremely disagreeable; they could extort money.   In Henry III.'s day Mr Justice Thurkelby was consulted by a friend who had obtained a pardon, but was being appealed.   The advice that the expert lawyer gave was this:—You had better go to battle; but directly a blow is struck cry 'Craven' and produce your charter; you will not be punished, for the king has given you your life and members[1].

We do not say that the law of England was ever committed to the dogma that he who slays by misadventure must be put to death.   We take the truth to be this:—Far into the twelfth century the main theory of the law still was that an intentional homicide could be paid for by *wer* and *wíte*; but there were exceptions which devoured the rule, and, under cover of charges of felony, *guet-apens* and breach of the king's peace, intentional homicide became an unemendable crime to be punished with death or mutilation.   What to do with cases of misadventure, the law did not see.   In the past many or all of them had given occasion for a *wer*, if not for a *wíte* or a blood-feud. There was nothing for it but 'mercy'; the king himself must decide in each case whether life and limb shall be spared. Meanwhile the law of *wer*, being no longer applicable if there was felony, perished for lack of sustenance, and the *parentes occisi* were reduced to getting what they could by threats of an appeal[2].   That a man who kills another in self-defence should [p. 482] require a pardon will seem to us even more monstrous than that pardons should be needed where there has been misadventure, for the 'misadventure' of this age covers many a blameworthy act.   But the author of the *Leges Henrici*, if we read him rightly, would demand a *wer* from the self-defender[3], and our law when she puts self-defence on a par with misadventure is accompanying her French sister.   In France, as in

History of misadventure.

---

[1] La Corone pledee devant justice: Camb. Univ. Libr. Mm. i. 27, f. 124.

[2] Select Pleas of the Crown (Selden Soc.), pl. 102.   In 1208 the kinsfolk of the dead man receive the substantial sum of 40 marks; besides this, one of them is to be made a monk or canon at the expense of the offender, and the slayer is to serve seven years in the Holy Land for the good of the dead man's soul.   This treaty is sanctioned by the king and recorded on a plea roll, but probably in this case there had been wilful homicide.   Ibid. pl. 47: the king pardoning a homicide bids his justices do what they can to make peace between the slayer and the *parentes interfecti*.   But the kinsfolk no longer have a legal right to a *wer*.

[3] Leg. Hen. 80, § 7; 87, § 6.

England, throughout the later middle ages and far on into modern times the king's *lettres de grâce* were granted to those who had slain a man *per infortunium vel se defendendo*[1]. We are not dealing with an insular peculiarity.

Homicide by young children.

It is with difficulty that even a child can escape the hard law. 'Reginald aged four by misadventure slew Robert aged two; the justices granted that he might have his life and members because of his tender age[2].' A little later we hear that a child under the age of seven shall not suffer judgment in a case of homicide[3].

Limits of misadventure and self-defence.

The records of this time are so curt that we can frame no severe theory as to the boundary that divided felonious homicide from homicide by misadventure; only this we may notice, that the one word 'misadventure' (Lat. *infortunium*) does duty both in cases in which no human agency, unless it be the sufferer's own, has brought an untimely death upon him, so that there is nothing for justice to do but to exact a deodand, and also in cases in which the act of another has intervened and there is need for a pardon. Then again, in cases of the latter sort we never hear of 'negligence' or of any similar standard of liability, though just once by the way we see a boy, who frightened a horse which threw and killed its rider, sent back to gaol *pro stultitia sua*[4]. As to the limits of pardonable defence, we may guess that they were somewhat wide and that [p.483] a man might 'without felony' slay in defence of his own life or that of his wife or of his lord or of any member of his household[5]; but there could be little law about this, for all depended upon the king's 'grace.' On the other hand, anything like vengeance or the prosecution of a feud, even against the homicide, would have been sternly suppressed. There are signs that the outraged husband who found his wife in the act of adultery might no longer slay the guilty pair or either of them, but might emasculate the adulterer[6].

---

[1] Esmein, Histoire de la procédure criminelle, p. 255. See also Viollet, Établissements, i. 233.

[2] Northumberland Assize Rolls, 323.

[3] Y. B. 30–1 Edw. I. p. 511. See Wigmore, Harv. L. R. vii. 447; Hale, P. C. i. 20–9. 　　　　[4] Munim. Gildh. i. 97.

[5] To this effect Britton, i. 113.

[6] For the old law see Alfred, 42, § 7; Leg. Will. i. 35 (which may be romanizing); Leg. Henr. 82, § 8. Matthew Paris, Chron. Maj. v. 35, tells how in 1248 a case of mutilation induced Henry III. to decree as law 'ne prae-

By this time it was law, except perhaps in the Welsh Homicide unemendable.
marches[1], that if the king could not absolve a slayer from the
suit of the kinsfolk of the slain, they on the other hand could
not absolve him from the king's suit or save him from the
gallows. In 1221 a Basset was hanged after he had made his
peace with the family of the dead man,—a peace that was
ratified by a marriage and sanctioned by the sheriff—and the
dead man's widow was amerced for discontinuing her appeal[2].
Still to the end of our period an appeal rather than an indictment is the normal procedure against criminals. Some offences
are punished far more heavily when conviction has been secured
by an appeal than when the offender is arraigned at the king's
suit[3].

Every homicide that is neither justifiable nor yet excusable Murder.
as the result of misadventure or self-defence, is in Bracton's age
[p. 484] felonious; also it is conceived as having been perpetrated by
'premeditated assault' or by 'malice aforethought[4]'; also it
earns the punishment of death—usually death by hanging;
but this will be aggravated by 'drawing' if there has been
petty treason, or, in other words, if a man has slain his lord, a
servant his master, a wife her husband. If we leave out of
sight this additional torment for traitors, we may say that our
law knows but one degree of criminal homicide; it does not yet
know the line that will divide 'murder' from 'manslaughter[5].'

sumat quis, nisi pro coniuge, adulterum membris mutilare genitalibus.' See
Select Pleas of the Crown, pl. 87: in an appeal of wounds the appellee pleads
that he found the appellor in his bed room intending his shame. Rot. Cl. i.
126: in 1212 King John orders that *A* who has emasculated *B* is to have his
land restored to him, if an inquest finds that *B* committed adultery with *A*'s
wife after being forbidden to visit her.

1 Note Book, pl. 1474. 2 Gloucestershire Pleas, pl. 101.

3 Britton, i. 98: 'There are also some felonies where no other execution
follows at our suit than such as takes place in trespasses, as in mayhems,
wounds and imprisonment; and there are others where judgment of death
ensues, as well at our suit as another's, as in felonies for the death of a man,
rape, arson, robberies and others.' When Britton wrote, rape had lately
passed from the one class to the other. In Bracton's day (f. 143) there were
some who thought that if, when an appeal had been quashed, the appellee was
arraigned at the king's suit, his punishment should only be a fine.

4 This appears from the forms of pardon. See above, vol. ii. p. 480.

5 The one instance in which we have seen a trace of this line is the story
told by Thomas Wykes (Ann. Monast. iv. 233–5). In 1270 the Earl of
Warenne and Alan de la Zouche were litigating before the justices in
Westminster Hall. From words they came to blows and Warenne's retainers
grievously wounded Alan so that after a while he died. Warenne was allowed

This is somewhat strange, for from of old the Germanic peoples have commonly treated under the head of *morth* a few aggravated kinds of homicide which were unemendable crimes, while mere open and intentional slaying was emendable. The word *morth*, which was known to Normans as well as to Englishmen[1], seems to imply concealment, in particular the hiding away of the dead body[2]. But in our twelfth century a levelling process was at work; it made 'unemendable' all homicide that was regarded as worthy of heavy punishment. In Latin and French forms (*murdrum, murdre*) the old *morth* lived on, and in Glanvill's day one had still to distinguish that secret homicide which is *murdrum* from a mere *homicidium*. As the prosecutor for a *murdrum* only a near kinsman of the slain may appear, while any one connected with the slain by blood, homage or lordship may take action if there has been open homicide[3]. The point of the distinction seems to be this, that normally an [p. 485] appellor must declare that he saw the crime committed, but that, this being impossible in the case of a *murdrum*, very close kinsmen are allowed to take action without protesting that they were eye-witnesses of the deed[4]. This distinction soon dropped away, for more and more the words about eye-sight became a 'common form' which every appellor was expected to utter and

to make his peace on paying 5000 marks to the king and 2000 to the wounded man and on swearing with fifty compurgators that the deed was done 'non ex praecogitata malitia...sed ex motu iracundiae nimis accensae.' Here we already have the contrast between 'malice aforethought' and a 'sudden falling out'; but apparently we have rather an act of grace than a judicial sentence.

[1] Très ancien coutumier, p. 29: He who slays his son wilfully (*inique*) is exiled, but not put to death; but he who murders (*murdrierit*) his son is burnt. Ibid. p. 64: 'homicidium sive clam factum fuerit, quod lingua Dacorum murdrum dicitur, sive palam.'

[2] Brunner, D. R. G. ii. 627. Jostice et Plet (Documents inédits) p. 290.

[3] This point seems to have escaped the attention of commentators; it can be brought out by a few italics. Glanvill, xiv. 3: 'Duo autem sunt genera homicidii. Unum est quod dicitur murdrum, quod nullo vidente, nullo sciente clam perpetratur...ita quod mox non assequatur clamor popularis...In *huiusmodi* autem accusatione non admittitur aliquis *nisi fuerit de consanguinitate ipsius defuncti*...Est et aliud homicidium quod...dicitur simplex homicidium. In hoc etiam placito non admittitur aliquis accusator ad probationem, nisi fuerit mortuo consanguinitate coniunctus, *vel homagio, vel dominio, ita ut de morte loquatur sub visus sui testimonio.*' We see the same distinction in the Ancienne coutume de Normandie, c. 70 (69), ed. de Gruchy, 172; Somma, p. 178. The nearest kinsman can bring an appeal of murder; a vassal may bring an appeal of homicide, but must have been present at his lord's death.

[4] See Bracton, f. 125.

from which no appellor shrank ; also the vassal was slowly losing his right to bring an appeal for the death of his lord[1].

In this region therefore the old term had no further part to play. It had also, however, found a place for itself in those cases in which under the Conqueror's law[2] the hundred paid a fine when a foreigner was slain and the slayer was not produced. This fine and its cause were alike known as a *murdrum* : it was a fine occasioned by a secret homicide, a homicide secret in this sense that no one was brought to justice as its author. In every eyre of the thirteenth century numerous *murdra* were exacted and a jurisprudence of *murdra* was evolved[3]. We will notice only a few salient points[4]. The original *murdrum* was a sum of 46 marks, of which 40 went to the king, 6 to the kinsfolk of the slain[5]; but our earliest rolls show us that this must have been a crushing penalty, for the sums actually demanded are much smaller[6]; no part of them, so far as we can see, goes to the kinsfolk. Large tracts of England, chartered boroughs and other 'liberties,' were quit of the *murdrum* ; it was unknown in some of the northern counties. The odd presumption that every slain man was a foreigner had been firmly established ; the hundred had to pay unless his Englishry was proved by the testimony of his kinsfolk. In some counties a *murdrum* was exacted by custom in case of accidental death ; Bracton regarded this as an abuse, and, as already said, it was abolished[7].

This then became for a while the one and only meaning of *murder* ; but probably in the popular mind that word still stood

The murder fine.

p. 486]

Murder in later history.

---

[1] Select Pleas of the Crown, pl. 80, 89, 197, appeals for the death of a lord ; pl. 76, appeal for the death of a fellow-vassal ; pl. 121, appeal by *A* for the death of *B* whom *A* had sent on a message. Britton, i. 109, still allows the appeal to be brought by one who has done homage to, or been in the household of, the slain. In Select Pleas, pl. 29 [A.D. 1202] we seem to have a decision that even a brother of the dead man must allege that he witnessed the deed. This would over-rule Glanvill's distinction.

[2] See above, vol. i. p. 89.

[3] Bracton, f. 135. It is evident that there were many diversities of practice. Bracton, for example, would excuse the hundred if it could name, though it could not produce, the slayer. Certainly some other judges did not hold this opinion.

[4] For more, see Liebermann, Leges Edwardi, p. 108; Chadwyck Healey, Somersetshire Pleas, p. lviii.

[5] Leg. Will. III. 3 ; Leg. Will. I. 22 ; Leg. Henr. 91 ; Leg. Edw. 15, 16.

[6] Pike, History of Crime, i. 454; also *e.g.* Gloucestershire Pleas, pp. 118 ff.

[7] See above, vol. ii. p. 482.

vaguely for homicide of the very worst kind[1]. In 1340 a statute[2], which abolished the murder fine, set the word free from the purpose that it had been serving, and at a later time by a process which it is not for us here to trace 'wilful murder by malice aforethought' became the name for an aggravated kind of felonious homicide which was excluded from the benefit of clergy and was to be contrasted with the felonious but 'clergyable' crime of man-slaughter[3].

Suicide.

As to suicide Bracton seems to have had many doubts, and at one time he was for giving the name *felo de se* only to a criminal who killed himself in order to escape a worse fate. We think that the practice of exacting a forfeiture of goods in every case in which a sane man put an end to his own life was one that grew up gradually, and that thus the phrase *felonia de se* gained an ampler scope. We have seen before now that a similar forfeiture of the goods of one who died obstinately intestate was imminent for a while[4].

Wounding etc.

Of the other felonies there is much less to be said. Wound, [p. 487] mayhem, or imprisonment might be made the foundation of an appeal by the sufferer and the convicted appellee 'forfeited life and member,' that is to say, the justices might inflict the punishment of death or any other of the recognized penalties[5]. As a matter of fact the appellee seldom, if ever, lost life and seldom lost member; still we can cite a case from 1221 in which a man who had wounded another in the arm and had been defeated in the judicial combat underwent a horrible mutilation[6]. Britton holds that there should be strict retaliation—member

---

[1] In the Assize of Clarendon *murdrator* is freely used. Perhaps it here covers all felonious homicide.

[2] 14 Edw. III. st. 1, c. 4.

[3] For the later history, see Stephen, Hist. Crim. Law, iii. 40, 43–5.

[4] See above, vol. ii. p. 359. Bracton, f. 150, speaks of suicide. Some sentences in this chapter are marginal *additiones* and seem to betray a fluctuating mind. Gloucestershire Pleas, A.D. 1221, pl. 22: a case of suicide is presented; the township must answer for the chattels; but a *loquendum* is entered on the roll, which shows that the king is to be consulted. At a little later date the suicide's goods are always forfeited; Northumberland Assize Rolls, 83, 113, 338, 345. For later law, see Hale, P. C. i. 411; for Norman law, Ancienne coutume, c. 21, ed. de Gruchy, p. 56; Somma, p. 56.

[5] Bracton, f. 144–6. Observe what he says of the punishment for castration (f. 144 b): 'sequitur poena aliquando capitalis, aliquando perpetuum exilium cum omnium bonorum ademptione.'

[6] Gloucestershire Pleas of the Crown, pl. 87: 'Thomas devictus est et obcecatus et ementulatus.'

for member, wound for wound, imprisonment for imprisonment[1];
but here he is hebraizing and introducing an element that is
foreign to the law of our race[2]. Already there was room for
unpractical speculation. Appeals for wounds had not been
uncommon; but the justices seem to have taken delight in
quashing them as informal[3]. The appeal having been quashed,
they arraigned the appellee at the king's suit; if he was convicted, he suffered no worse than imprisonment and fine[4]. Also
about the middle of the thirteenth century the growth of the
action of trespass afforded the injured party an alternative and
preferable mode of procedure. Saying nothing of felony, he
would sue for damages, and Britton strongly advised him to do
[p. 488] so[5]. Thus once more instead of vengeance he could obtain, to
use the old phrase, a sufficient *bót*, but a *bót* the amount of
which was no longer fixed by law. The new procedure became
so much more popular than the old that all ' offences against the
person,' except homicide, dropped out of the list of felonies[6].
Our law, if it had once been too severe, became much too mild,
and was at times tempted to retrace its steps by aid of the
maxim that the will manifested in a murderous assault may be
taken for the deed[7]. Little learning collected round these
crimes in the age that is before us. The justices had a certain
discretion in deciding whether there was a wound sufficient to

---

[1] Britton, i. 123–4; cf. Fleta, p. 59.

[2] Brunner, D. R. G. ii. 589. Long ago King Alfred (Laws, Introduction,
c. 19) had copied the Hebraic rule from Exodus, but without intending to
enforce it. When crude retaliation appears in a medieval code, the influence of
the Bible may always be suspected. What we may call characteristic punishment, *e.g.* castration for adultery, or loss of a hand for forgery, is a very
different thing. See Günther, Idee der Wiedervergeltung (Erlangen, 1889).

[3] For appeals of mayhem or wounds, see Select Pleas of the Crown, pl. 4,
9, 11, 24, 37, 41, 54, 79, 87, 155; Gloucestershire Pleas, pl. 87, 434; Note
Book, pl. 134, 259, 346, 511, 548, 592, 943, 1084, 1697. Any one who looks
through these cases will see that little comes of a great deal of talk.

[4] Bracton, f. 144; Britton, i. 98, 123. Northumberland Assize Rolls, p. 117:
an appeal of wounding having been quashed, the appellee is arraigned and
convicted at the king's suit; 'custodiatur pro transgressione.' So Munim.
Gildh. i. 90: in 1244 three men convicted of a murderous assault are fined
but one mark, being poor. Staffordshire Collections, iv. 210: in 1272 a man
is fined a half-mark for a wound.

[5] Britton, i. 123–4. Bracton, f. 145 b, already knows the civil action for
wounds or imprisonment. See Northumberland Assize Rolls, pp. 49, 108
(A.D. 1256), for early instances.

[6] Blackstone, Comment. iv. 206, 314; Stephen, Hist. Crim. Law, iii. 108.

[7] See above, vol. ii. p. 476, note 5.

support an appeal[1]. The distinction between wound and mayhem was of procedural importance. The man who had been
maimed, that is, who had been deprived of the use of a member
which would be serviceable in a fight[2], was not bound to offer
or accept battle. In such case one or other of the parties was
sent to the ordeal, until the Lateran Council of 1215 abolished
that mode of trial; in later days the appellee had to submit to
the verdict of a jury[3]. We may gather from a case which
occurred in 1225 that a mayhem committed in self-defence was
justifiable[4]; the strict rules that were applied to homicide were
relaxed when there was no death.

Rape.

The crime which we call rape had in very old days been
hardly severed from that which we should call abduction; if it
had wronged the woman it had wronged her kinsmen also, and
they would have felt themselves seriously wronged even if she
had given her consent, and had, as we should say, eloped[5].
Traces of this feeling may be found at a late time; but rape in
the sense of *violentus concubitus* is soon treated as a crime for [p. 489]
which the woman and only the woman can bring an appeal.
Probably from the Conquest onwards it was deemed a bootless
crime if she pressed her suit[6]. Famous words have told us of
the Conqueror's severe treatment of an offence which may have
been but too common in a land overrun by foreign soldiers[7].
The characteristic punishment of castration, often coupled with
blinding, was considered appropriate to it; but a story, which
to our regret is told in a reputable chronicle, shows us Ranulf
Glanvill satisfying a private grudge by sending a man to the
gallows for abduction[8]. Bracton reserves the gravest punishment, namely blinding and castration, for cases in which the
appellor has been deflowered; in other cases some corporal

---

[1] Bracton, f. 145.

[2] Glanvill, xiv. 1; Bracton, f. 145; Britton, i. 123; Fleta, p. 58.

[3] Select Pleas of the Crown, pl. 4, 11, 24; Glanvill, xiv. 1; Bracton, f. 142 b.

[4] Note Book, pl. 1084.

[5] Brunner, D. R. G. ii. 666. For the treatment of *violentus concubitus* in A.-S. Law, see Alfred, 11, 18, 25, 26. Bracton, f. 147, in a marginal *additio* cites what he supposes to be an ancient English doom denouncing a punishment of life and member where Alfred would have been content with a 60 shilling *bôt*. We know nothing of the source whence he obtained this passage.

[6] Leg. Will. i. c. 18; Leg. Henr. 13, § 6.

[7] A.-S. Chron. vol. ii. p. 355 (A.D. 1087).

[8] Gesta Henrici (Benedict), i. 314–5; Hoveden, ii. 286.

chastisement falling short of loss of limb should be inflicted; but he looks back to a time when every rape was a capital offence[1]. Concerning these matters we can find little 'case-law.' Appeals of rape were often brought in the thirteenth century; but they were often quashed, abandoned or compromised[2]. Glanvill in a curious passage protested that the appeal must not be so used as to force a noble man or noble woman into a disparaging union[3]; but, as a matter of fact, an appeal of rape was not unfrequently the prelude to a marriage[4]. The judges seem to have thought that if the woman was satisfied, public justice might be satisfied. She could prosecute her ravisher and use 'words of felony'; but if she made no appeal and the man was arraigned at the king's suit, then [p. 490] imprisonment and fine were a sufficient punishment[5]. In 1275 the first Statute of Westminster gave the woman forty days for her appeal and fixed the punishment of an indicted ravisher at two years' imprisonment to be followed by ransom at the king's pleasure. Ten years later the second Statute of Westminster provided a judgment of life and member for all cases of rape, even though the woman was content not to sue, and thenceforward this crime fell into the ranks of those felonies which, whether prosecuted by appeal or by indictment, were punished by death[6].

[1] Bracton, f. 147–148 b. In the precedent books we find as words of common form 'abstulit ei virginitatem suam' or 'pucellagium suum.' On f. 127 b Bracton says that the man guilty of rape may even be sentenced to death if he fled for his crime.

[2] Select Pleas of the Crown, pl. 7, 96, 141, 166; Gloucestershire Pleas, pl. 4, 16, 76, 102, 155, 179, 341, 426; Northumberland Assize Rolls, pp. 92, 94, 109, 111, 122, 329.

[3] Glanvill, xiv. 6.

[4] Bracton, f. 148, with Glanvill's text before him, alters it and seems to allow that the low-born woman can force the high-born ravisher to marry her. Très ancien coutumier, p. 41. For actual cases, see Select Pleas of the Crown, pl. 7; Northumberland Assize Rolls, p. 111; Coke, Third Inst. 181. Bracton, f. 147 b, has a romantic tale about King Robert of France. Its origin we have not found.

[5] Northumberland Assize Rolls (A.D. 1256), p. 92, the ravisher is fined one mark; p. 94, a similar fine; (A.D. 1279), p. 329, a fine of four marks; Somersetshire Pleas, pl. 963: a fine of two marks.

[6] Stat. West. I. c. 13; Stat. West. II. c. 34; Britton, i. 55; Coke, Third Inst. 180, 433; Hale, P. C. i. 627; Blackstone, Comment. iv. 212. It does not seem to us correct to say that by the first of the two statutes 'the punishment for rape was mitigated.' Rape, like mayhem, wounding and false imprisonment, was in Henry III.'s day a crime which could be prosecuted by appeal with

Arson.

The crime which we call *arson* and which our ancestors called *bærnet* was mentioned by Cnut as one of the bootless crimes[1]; ancient law is wont to put it in the same class with 'manifest' theft[2]. It naturally finds a place in the list of felonies[3]. We are told that the punishment was death by burning[4], and are able to vouch a case from John's day in which this punishment was inflicted[5]; but the fully developed common law substituted the gallows for the stake. The thing that is burnt must be a 'house'; but this word has a large meaning[6]; already in 1220 we find the burning of a barn that was full of corn treated as felony[7]. This crime is of some interest as [p. 491] being one of the first in which the psychical element, the intention, becomes prominent. At a very early time men must distinguish between fires that are and fires that are not intended[8].

Burglary.

'A burglar,' says Coke, 'is by the common law a felon, that in the night breaketh and entreth into the mansion house of another, of intent to kill some reasonable creature, or to commit some other felony within the same, whether his felonious intent be executed or not[9].' Though there are ancient elements in

'words of felony,' and, if so prosecuted, it would be punished by mutilation, at least where there was defloration and the woman would make no peace. On the other hand, if the ravisher was arraigned at the king's suit, he would, like the wounder or imprisoner, be punished merely by fine and imprisonment, and we may see very small fines inflicted. The first of the two statutes gave the woman a longer time than she had previously enjoyed for her appeal, and also provided that the ravisher, if arraigned at the king's suit, should remain in prison for at least two years before making fine. The statute law is not fluctuating; the first statute is a step towards the second. See Y. B. 30–1 Edw. I. p. 499. The unprinted tract *La Corone pledee devant justice* says that blinding without emasculation was inflicted if the criminal's wife intervened in his favour.

[1] Cnut, II. 64; Leg. Henr. 12, § 1. See also Æthelst. II. 6, § 2 and Schmid, App. xiii., also Schmid, Glossar. s.v. *bærnet*.

[2] Brunner, D. R. G. ii. 657.   [3] Bracton, f. 146 b.

[4] Britton, i. 41.   [5] Gloucestershire Pleas, pl. 216.

[6] Coke, Third Inst. 67; Hale, P. C. i. 567.

[7] Select Pleas of the Crown, pl. 203. Britton, i. 41, speaks of the burning of corn as well as of the burning of houses.

[8] Brunner, D. R. G. ii. 545–6, 654. Bracton, f. 146 b, expatiates on the *mala conscientia* that is necessary for this crime; he contrasts it with *negligentia*. In early indictments malice aforethought (*malitia praecogitata*) appears; Coke, Third Inst. 66. For more of arson, see Coke, *loc. cit.*; Hale, P. C. i. 566; Blackstone, Comment. iv. 220; Stephen, Hist. Crim. Law, iii. 188.

[9] Coke, Third Inst. 63. See also Hale, P. C. i. 547; Blackstone, Comment. iv. 223; Stephen, Hist. Crim. Law, iii. 150.

this definition, it does not seem exactly to fit the crime that
the men of the thirteenth century knew as *burglaria*. Britton
gives the name of burglars to 'those who feloniously in time of
peace break churches or the houses of others, or the walls or
gates of our cities or boroughs'; he thus omits that 'by night'
which is essential in after times; he also excuses the hungry
man who enters the house of another for victuals worth less
than twelve pence[1]. Unless we are mistaken, there was no
well marked form of appeal for burglary, nor was that crime
mentioned in the Assizes of Henry II.[2] The words which
describe it first come to the front in presentments made by
jurors, and we are not satisfied that a nocturnal crime is
always indicated[3]. The old word *hámsocn* was still being used
by appellors who complained of robbery committed in their
houses[4]; it found a permanent home in the legal vocabulary of
Scotland. *Hámsocn* or *hámfare* had been a reserved plea of
the crown and a bad crime; some aggravated form of it known
[p. 492] as *húsbrice* had been stigmatized by Cnut as bootless[5]. The
thought that crimes committed at night are to be punished
more severely than similar crimes committed by day was not
far from our ancestors[6], but we can as yet give no precise
account of the genesis of burglary.

In later times robbery is regarded as an aggravated kind of Robbery.
theft[7]. In old law the two crimes are kept apart; the one is the

---

[1] Britton, i. 42.

[2] The term *in burgeria* will sometimes appear in an appeal of robbery;
Select Pleas of the Crown, pl. 122.

[3] Select Pleas of the Crown, pl. 6, 8; Gloucestershire Pleas, pl. 62, 139, 346,
362; Northumberland Assize Rolls, pp. 90–1–5–6–7 etc. If all these robberies
were nocturnal, where are the presentments of robberies perpetrated by day?

[4] Select Pleas of the Crown, pl. 60, 86.

[5] Cnut, ii. 64; Leg. Henr. 12, § 1. See Schmid, Glossar. s.v. *húsbrice*, and
Brunner, D. R. G. ii. 653. The distinction seems to be between a mere
invasio domus and an *infractura domus*. The first beginning of an attack on
a house would be *hámsocn*, e.g. if a stone were thrown at the door: Leg. Henr.
80, § 11.

[6] Brunner, ii. 646, 655. Bracton, f. 144 b, speaks of *hamsokne* in close
connexion with the *fur nocturnus*. Coke, Third Inst. 63, has two curious cases
from Edward I.'s time which speak of crimes committed *inter canem et lupum*;
we have seen the same phrase on an unprinted roll. See also Gross, Coroner's
Rolls, pp. 1, 6, 16. Ducange, s.v. *canis*, says that *entre chien et loup* means
at an hour when the wolf can not be distinguished from the dog.

[7] Coke, Third Inst. 68; Hale, P. C. i. 532; Blackstone, Comment. iv. 243;
Stephen, Hist. Crim. Law, iii. 149. See the attempted definitions in the
Cambridge gloss on Britton, i. 55.

open, the other the secret crime. There is an ethical distinction between them; theft is far more dishonourable than robbery[1]. We imagine that this difference was still felt in the thirteenth century; Bracton has to argue that the robber is a thief[2]. Appeals of robbery were common, and some of those against whom they were brought, though guilty, would hardly have been called thieves. Often enough their motive has been no desire for dishonest gain, but vengeance or the prosecution of a feud, and the horse or sword or cloak was seized in a scuffle. Again, in Glanvill's day robbery was a royal, while theft was a vicecomital plea. Many an ancient trait still clung to the action for theft; it was an *actio dupli*, in which the plaintiff might recover twice the value of what he had lost[3]. However, by this time the *robator* and the *latro*[4] were being placed in one [p. 493] class, that of 'felons.' According to Bracton, the sentence for robbery was sometimes death, sometimes mutilation[5]; a little later death by hanging was the invariable punishment[6].

Larceny.   Theft or larceny (*latrocinium*) is treated by Bracton as though it were a crime which stood in a different class from that which comprises robbery and the other felonies[7]. He seems hardly to know that 'appeal of larceny' which became fashionable at a later time, nor do we find appeals of larceny, as distinguished from robbery, on the earliest plea rolls. What he knows is the old English *actio furti*, and of this we have spoken in another place[8]. Only by slow degrees was larceny becoming

---

[1] Brunner, D. R. G. ii. 647.

[2] Bracton, f. 150 b, introducing from Instit. 4, 2, pr. the question 'Quis enim magis alienam rem invito domino contrectat quam qui vi rapit?'

[3] Glanv. i. 2; xiv. 8. Dial. de Scac. ii. 10. We see no reason for doubting the truth of Bishop Richard's account of the action for theft. The recovery of double value may for a moment look Roman; but it was known to Anglo-Saxon and to Frankish law (Brunner, D. R. G. ii. 643), and the author of the dialogue speaks of it in popular terms (*solta et persolta*) which he has to explain. The Conqueror had decreed that one who bought cattle in secret must be prepared *solvere et persolvere*, i.e. to pay double value. See Laws of William (Select Charters), c. 5.

[4] Ass. Clarend. *passim*. It is somewhat curious that *latrocinium* expels *furtum* from the technical language of the law.

[5] Bracton, f. 146 b.

[6] Britton, i. 119. In the fully developed common law robbery was a capital crime, though the thing taken was not worth a shilling; Hale, P. C. i. 532.

[7] Bracton, f. 150 b.

[8] See above, vol. ii. p. 157 ff. As to the actions open to an owner of chattels see Ames, History of Trover, Harv. L. R. vol. xi. We regret that these learned articles only come to our hands as this sheet goes to press.

a plea of the crown; hand-having larceny or manifest theft was still within the competence of the hundred courts and of such seignorial courts as enjoyed the franchise of *infangthief.* Larceny became a plea of the crown under cover of a phrase which charged the thief with breaking the king's peace; to all appearance it was the last of the great crimes to which that elastic phrase was applied. This was natural, for to say of the thief that he has broken the king's peace is to say what is hardly true until those words have acquired a non-natural meaning. However, Henry II. had comprehended larceny within the net of that new indictment-procedure which he introduced[1]. The old action of theft, which might rightly be used against an honest man, and which was, at least in some cases, an action for double value[2], was becoming obsolete, and the loser of the stolen goods might thank his stars if he was able to get them back again, so keen was the king in pursuit of 'the chattels of felons[3].' Larceny then takes its place among the felonies that are prosecuted by appeal or by indictment.

As to the thief's punishment, many old systems of law have at one time or another drawn two lines: they have distinguished between great and petty theft, and between manifest and [p. 494] non-manifest theft[4]. He who is guilty of a great and manifest theft is put to death in a summary fashion; other thieves receive a much milder punishment; they escape with *bót* and *wíte*, and the *bót* often represents the value of the stolen thing multiplied by two, three or some higher number[5]. In England both an old English and an old Frankish tradition may have conspired to draw the line between 'grand' and 'petty larceny'

Punishment of larceny.

---

[1] Ass. Clarend. *passim.*   [2] Dial. de Scac. ii. 10.

[3] See above, vol. ii. pp. 158–164; Y. B. 30–1 Edw. I. pp. 513–5, 527.

[4] It will be convenient to use the Roman term *manifest.* In England one had spoken (Cnut, ii. 64) of *open þýfð* (which exactly translates *furtum manifestum*); or one had said that the thief was captured *æt hæbbendre handa* (Æthelst. ii. 1). In the thirteenth century one said that he was *handhabende and bachberende,* that he was *seisitus de latrocinio,* or that he was taken with the *mainour (cum manuopere)* or with the *pelf (pelfra).* The learned saw substantially the same distinction in Instit. 4, 1, 3, and spoke of *furtum manifestum*; but there is here no borrowing from Roman law, which, as it stands in the Institutes, demands no more than a fourfold *bót* even in case of manifest theft.

[5] Brunner, D. R. G. ii. 637; Dareste, Études d'histoire du droit, 299. For England, see Schmid, Gesetze, Glossar. s.v. *Diebstahl* and Dial. de Scac. ii. 10.

at twelve pence[1]. Though the old dooms sometimes speak as if every 'open,' that is, manifest, theft were bootless[2], we take it that during the Norman period only a theft that was both manifest and great was absolutely beyond all hope of emendation[3]. Henry I., we are told, decreed that all thieves taken in the act should be hanged[4], and in his reign, as all know, Ralph Basset did a fine day's work in Leicestershire, for he hanged forty-four thieves, an exploit without a precedent[5]. But the punishment fluctuated between death and mutilation. In the thirteenth century manifest grand larceny was a capital crime; the sentence was often pronounced in local courts and was frequently executed by the pursuer or 'sakeber[6]' who struck off the thief's head or precipitated him from a rock into [p. 495] the sea[7]. But all grand larceny was becoming a capital crime; the distinction between the fate of the manifest and that of the non-manifest thief was becoming a matter of procedure. The one after a summary trial, that was hardly a trial at all, was put to death by hanging or in some fashion sanctioned by antique custom; the other, tried and sentenced by the king's justices, went to the gallows.

Manifest
theft.

Some would explain the difference between the treatment of 'hand-having' and that of other thieves by referring us to

[1] Brunner, D. R. G. ii. 640.

[2] Cnut. ii. 64; Leg. Hen. 12, § 1.

[3] This appears from the story of Ailward told in Materials for the Life of Becket, i. 156; Bigelow, Placita, 260; Stephen, Hist. Crim. Law, i. 78. Even the hand-having thief does not forfeit life or member if the goods are of small value.

[4] Flor. Wig. ii. 57 (A.D. 1108): 'ut si quis in furto vel latrocinio deprehensus fuisset suspenderetur.' Sir James Stephen, Hist. Crim. Law, i. 458, was mistaken when he supposed this story to rest upon Hoveden's testimony; this is noticed by Henderson, Verbrechen und Strafen, p. 15. Henry's ordinance seems to have spoken only of hand-having thieves.

[5] A.-S. Chron. vol. ii. p. 376 (A.D. 1124).

[6] See above, vol. ii. p. 160.

[7] Northumberland Assize Rolls, p. 70: 'consuetudo comitatus talis est, quod quamcito aliquis capiatur cum manuopere, statim decolletur, et ipse qui sequitur pro catallis ab ipso depridatis, habebit catalla sua pro ipso decollando.' Other case of decollation, ibid. 73, 79, 80, 84 etc. In Hengham Parva, ed. 1616, p. 80, various customary punishments are mentioned. In some sea-port towns the criminal was tied to a stake below high-water mark and left to drown. At Winchester he was mutilated, at Dover precipitated from a cliff. See Green, Town Life, i. 222. Burying alive seems to have been practised at Sandwich, Lyon, Dover, ii. 301. See also Akerman, Furca et Fossa, Archaeologia, xxxviii. 54.

an age when the state was yet too weak to interfere with the
vengeance done on those who were captured in flagrant delict,
or to an age when the punishment of the criminal was measured
less by his culpability than by the resentment of the injured
man[1]. But we doubt whether we can wholly acquit our
forefathers of the less logical idea that half-proven guilt is
proven half-guilt[2]. In 1166 Henry II., when he was introducing the indictment, or sworn communal accusation, into our
criminal procedure, declared that the thief or robber who was
taken 'in seisin' and who was of bad repute was to 'have no
law'; other men indicted of theft were to go to the ordeal
swearing that they had not to their knowledge stolen to the
value of five shillings—a fairly high sum—since the beginning
of the reign. He who was foul at the ordeal was to lose a foot;
ten years afterwards a hand also was taken[3]. A new accusatory
process was being tried, and for a while men were not certain
that it was as just or as cogent as the appeal in which the
[p. 496] accuser risked his body[4]. Even in the next century we may
find that people who had stolen what was worth more than
twelve pence were allowed to abjure the realm or suffered but
the loss of a thumb; the justices, it is plain, had a considerable
choice of punishments[5]. But the line drawn at a shillingsworth reappears and our law at length stands committed to
the rule that he who steals more than this must be hanged.

As to petty larceny, this is punished sometimes by a Petty
larceny.
whipping, sometimes by pillory or tumbrel, sometimes by loss
of an ear. One ear may be taken for a first, another for a
second offence, while the gallows awaits those who have no

[1] Maine, Ancient Law, ch. x.; Dareste, Études d'histoire du droit, 299–301.

[2] It is further to be remembered that among some barbarous folks, which
are not utterly lawless, successful theft is regarded with tolerance, if not
admiration, and gives rise to a mere claim for the restoration of the goods,
while 'manifest theft' is unsuccessful theft and exposes the thief to a beating.
See Post, Bausteine, i. 288; Kovalevsky, Droit Ossétien, p. 341.

[3] Ass. Clarend. cc. 1, 12; Ass. North. c. 1.

[4] There is an instructive parallel in the history of the canon law. The man
who is convicted, not upon an *accusatio*, but under the new *inquisitio*, is not to
suffer the full punishment. Esmein, Histoire de la procédure criminelle, p. 76;
Biener, Beiträge zur Gesch. d. Inquisitions-Processes.

[5] Note Book, pl. 1723, 1725 (A.D. 1226): a woman who had stolen a piece
of canvas was discharged because of its small value; afterwards she cut a
purse containing 3s. 6d., and, though taken with the purse, she only lost her
thumb.

more ears to lose[1]. A man who has lost an ear in honourable
warfare will sometimes obtain an explanatory charter from the
king, for it is dangerous as well as shameful to go about earless.
Under local custom the thief is sometimes forced to do the
executioner's work; his ear is nailed to a post and he may set
himself free by the use of the knife[2]. Folk are saying that
the limit of twelve pence allows a man to steal enough to keep
himself from starvation for eight days without being guilty of
a capital crime; they are also boasting, rightly or wrongly,
that the law of England is milder than that of France[3].

Definition
of larceny.
 Bracton borrowed from the Institutes a definition of theft,
but he modified it and omitted what did not suit him[4]. There
can we think be little doubt that the 'taking and carrying away,'
upon which our later law insists, had been from the first the
very core of the English idea of theft[5]. 'He stole, took and [p. 497]
carried away': this is the charge made against the thief[6].
The crime involves a violation of possession; it is an offence
against a possessor and therefore can never be committed by a
possessor[7]. For this reason it is that one can not steal 'pigeons,
fish, bees or other wild animals, found in a wild condition'; but
it is otherwise 'if they have been feloniously stolen out of
houses, or, if they are tame beasts, out of parks[8].' Some of the

---

[1] Bracton, f. 151 b; Fleta, pp. 54–6; Britton, i. 56, 61, 119. Stat. West. I.
c. 15 helps to fix the limit at a shilling; petty larceny 'que ne amonte a la
value de xii. deniers,' is a bailable offence.

[2] Green, Town Life, i. 222. [3] See the Cambridge gloss on Britton, i. 56.

[4] Bracton, f. 150 b: 'Furtum est secundum leges contrectatio rei alienae
fraudulenta cum animo furandi, invito illo domino cuius res illa fuerit.'
Instit. 4, 1, 1 from Dig. 47, 2, 1, § 3 (Paulus): 'Furtum est contrectatio rei
fraudulosa [lucri faciendi gratia] vel ipsius rei vel etiam usus eius possessionisve.'
The bracketed words are not in the Institutes. See Stephen, Hist. Crim. Law,
iii. 131.

[5] Brunner, D. R. G. ii. 638, says of the continental folk-laws that they
require an asportation (*auferre*) as essential to theft.

[6] Britton, i. 115: 'embla et prist et amena.'

[7] See above, vol. ii. pp. 157–170, where we have discussed the English *actio
furti*; also Ames, History of Trover, Harv. L. R. xi. 277, 374. Curia Regis
Rolls, No. 569, m. 31 (Norfolk eyre of 53 Hen. III.): jurors find that the
prisoner kept (*custodivit*) the sheep of *T* and sold one of the sheep of his lord;
also that another prisoner kept the sheep of *W* and of *R* and, having lost two of
R's lambs, gave *R* one of *W*'s sheep. The Court adjudges that this is not *mere
latrocinium*, but orders that the accused be imprisoned for the *transgressio*.
They make, or one of them makes, fine with one mark.

[8] Britton, i. 122. Brunner, D. R. G. ii. 639, cites the Ripuarian law, 'non
hic re possessa sed de venationibus agitur.'

decisions of a later day about 'things capable of being stolen' were probably dictated by a desire to mitigate law that had become too severe[1]. We can, for example, cite from the year 1200 a charge of stealing title-deeds[2]. In the old days slaves could be stolen, but we hear nothing of stolen villeins, and no one seems to have ever supposed that land could be stolen[3]. Bracton, as his habit is, insists on the mental factor; there must be an *animus furandi*[4]. Nevertheless, we believe that in the past any one who without due legal formalities took a chattel from another's possession ran a great risk of being treated either as a robber or as a thief[5]. Britton supposes a man going to replevy his beasts. He who has got them claims them as his own. What is to be done? The hue is to be levied and an appeal of robbery is to be begun[6]. The man who has unceremoniously taken what is his own may escape the gallows, but he loses irreparably the thing that he has taken[7]. Old law, if we may so say, did not wish to put every open taking on a par with robbery, or every secret taking on a par with theft. But how to try the thought of man? The distrainor who did not observe all the complex rules of the code of distress was lucky if he extricated his neck from the noose[8]. An old book tells us that concealing the king's chattels is equivalent to theft[9], and later writers speak of a concealment

[p. 498]

---

[1] Stephen, Hist. Crim. Law, iii. 142–5.

[2] Select Pleas of the Crown, pl. 82 (A.D. 1200): 'et cartas de terris suis in roberia asportavit.'

[3] Brunner, D. R. G. ii. 639, 648.

[4] Bracton, f. 150 b; 'sine animo furandi non committitur.'

[5] See above, vol. ii. p. 168. Y. B. 33–5 Edw. I. p. 503: 'One *R* because his rent was in arrear took his farmer's corn and carried it off and did what he pleased with it; and he was hanged for that deed.'

[6] Britton, i. 138.

[7] Britton, i. 116. Sir James Stephen, Hist. Crim. Law, iii. 133, says, 'If the appellee could prove that the horse was his own, and that he lost him, it is difficult to see why he should not keep him after retaking him.' Britton gives the reason:—'for we will that men proceed by judgment rather than by force.' One or two modern decisions have lost sight of this principle.

[8] This seems to be the point of Ailward's case, cited above, p. 496, note 3. Ailward breaks a house in the process of distraining his debtor, gets treated as a hand-having thief, is mutilated and has need of a miracle. See also p. 499, note 5.

[9] Leg. Henr. 13, § 5: 'Dominica captalia regis celata pro furto habeantur.'

of treasure trove as akin both to treason and to larceny[1]. But the king 'was prerogative[2].'

We have yet to speak of treason. In later times the crimes known to our law were classified as (1) treasons, high or petty, (2) felonies, (3) misdemeanours; and several important characteristics marked off high treason from all other crimes. For one thing, it earned a peculiarly ghastly punishment. For another, it was 'unclergyable,' while every felony was 'clergyable' unless some statute had otherwise ordained[3]. Thirdly, while the felon's land escheated to his lord, the traitor's land was forfeited to the king. This last distinction influenced the development of the law. Kings wished to extend treason at the expense of felony; the magnates resisted. A lord whose tenant had, for example, slain a king's messenger was much concerned that this offence should be felony, not treason. In the one case he would get an escheat; in the other case, far from getting an escheat, he would lose seignorial dues, unless the king took pity on him, for the king would hold the traitor's land and no one can be the king's lord[4].

These distinctions, however, become plain but slowly. It [p. 499] had indeed long been felt that hanging was too good a death for one who killed his lord. He should perish in torments to which hell-fire will seem a relief[5]. This is the origin of that 'drawing' which forms the first part of the penalty for high and petty treason. The malefactor was laid on the ground and tied to a horse which dragged him along the rough road to the gibbet. The hurdle that we afterwards hear of may be introduced of mercy; we suspect that originally it fulfilled its object by securing for the hangman a yet living body[6]. In

---

[1] Glanvill, i. 2; xiv. 2; Bracton, f. 119 b: 'quasi crimen furti.'

[2] Britton, i. 60, speaks as though cheating, *e.g.* by selling brass for gold, could be treated as felony. At present this statement is unsupported.

[3] There may be some doubt as to two crimes, (1) *insidiatio viarum et depopulatio agrorum*, (2) wilful burning of houses; Hale, P. C. ii. 333.

[4] Hale, P. C. i. 254: 'Where land comes to the crown by attainder of treason all mesne tenures of common persons are extinct; but if the king grants it out, he is *de iure* to revive the former tenure, for which a petition of right lies.'

[5] Leg. Henr. 75, § 1. The *comatio et excoriatio* is the German *Strafe zu Haut und Haar*: Brunner, D. R. G. ii. 605–6.

[6] Blackstone, Comment. iv. 92: 'Usually (by connivance at length ripened by humanity into law) a sledge or hurdle is allowed, to preserve the offender from the extreme torment of being dragged on the ground or pavement.' In

course of time the law was not content with this in the graver
cases of high treason.   It demanded drawing, hanging, dis-
embowelling, burning, beheading, quartering.   But there are
many signs that it attained the full height of its barbarity by
trying to punish one man for many capital crimes.   The famous
traitors of Edward I.'s day, David of Wales and William
Wallace, had in the sight of Englishmen committed all crimes
against God and man and were to suffer four or five different
deaths[1].

Again, a distinction between 'clergyable' and 'unclergyable'
[p. 500] crimes was not in the thirteenth century a main outline of the
criminal law.   The benefit of clergy was as yet a privilege of
ordained clerks, and was but slowly showing its impotence to
shield them from charges of high treason[2].   Lastly, if we are
not mistaken, the rule that gave the felon's land to his lord, the
traitor's to the king, was the compromise of a struggle.   It is
ignored or slurred over in the law books[3].   John, however, was
compelled to promise that after year and day the land of one
who was convicted of *felonia* should be surrendered to his lord[4].
On the other hand, the *terrae Normannorum*, the lands of the
Normans who had renounced their allegiance, and who in
English eyes were traitors, remained in the king's hand to the

Points of
difference
between
treason
and felony.

---

33 Lib. Ass. f. 200, pl. 7, the judge expressly forbids the use of an alleviating
hurdle.   Of Thomas de Trubleville executed in 1293 we are told in Ann. Wigorn.
(Ann. Monast. iv. 523) that 'super corium bovinum tractus, ne concito
moreretur...suspendebatur.'   For stories recorded by the chroniclers, see
Henderson, Verbrechen und Strafen, 16–18.   See also Select Pleas of the
Crown, pl. 179; Très ancien coutumier, p. 30.

[1] Therefore mere drawing and hanging remained the punishment for petty
treason, and for counterfeiting the coin; perhaps a counterfeitor of the great
seal could be let off with this.   See Hale, P. C. i. 187.   In 1238 a man who
attempted the king's life was drawn, hanged, beheaded, quartered; Mat. Par.
Chron. Maj. iii. 498.   According to Ann. Dunstapl. 294, David of Wales was
drawn for treason, hanged for homicide, disembowelled for sacrilege, beheaded
and quartered for compassing the king's death.   So Wallace was drawn for
treason, hanged for robbery and homicide, disembowelled for sacrilege, beheaded
as an outlaw and quartered for divers depredations.   See his sentence in Y. B.
11–12 Edw. III. (ed. Pike), p. 171, and the editor's preface, pp. xxix–xxxiv.   The
evisceration and quartering however occur already in the sentence of William de
Marisco executed in 1242; Mat. Par. Chron. Maj. iv. 196.

[2] See above, vol. i. pp. 441–7.

[3] See *e.g.* Bracton, f. 118 b; Britton, i. 40.

[4] Charter, 1215, c. 32: 'Nos non tenebimus terras illorum qui convicti
fuerint de felonia, nisi per unum annum et unum diem, et tunc reddantur
terrae dominis feodorum.'

profit of his exchequer[1]. The words of the Great Charter, to which we have just now referred, had an important effect. If there was any crime which would give the offender's land not to his lord but to the king, that crime could not be a mere *felonia*. Some term was wanted which would specify the cases in which seignorial must yield to royal claims, and though 'words of felony' were habitually used where there was a charge of high treason[2], and though men were slow to forget that every treason is a felony[3], still felony was soon contrasted with treason, and such words as *proditio, traditio, seditio* and *seductio* become prominent. Ultimately *proditio* triumphs in our law Latin and becomes a sacramental term; but *traditio, traitio*[4], *trahison, treason* triumph in French and English, while *seditio* and *seductio* gradually disappear, and *felony* no longer alludes, as once perhaps it did, to a breach of fealty[5].

Treason and the statute of 1352.

Treason has a history that is all its own. While as yet the [p. 501] felonies were being left to unenacted common law, treason became in 1352 the subject of an elaborate statute. This statute, though in all probability it preserved a great deal of the then current doctrine, became the whole law of treason for after times; every word of it was weighed, interpreted and glossed by successive generations. Our task therefore is hard if we would speak of treason as it was before the statute, for we have no unbroken stream of legal tradition to guide us[6].

---

[1] See Staundford, Prerog. Regis, c. 12; and see above, vol. i. p. 462. Most of the traitors of the twelfth century were tenants in chief or the vassals of rebellious tenants in chief, and the king could claim their lands either as king or as lord. The defection of the *Normanni* raised a new question on a large scale.

[2] Bracton, f. 119. Britton, i. 100: 'felounosement cum feloun et traytouressement cum traytre.'

[3] Coke, Third Inst. 15: 'In ancient time every treason was comprehended under the name of felony, but not *e contra*; and therefore a pardon of all felonies was sometimes allowed in case of high treason.' Hale, P. C. i. 179.

[4] Très ancien coutumier, p. 30.

[5] As to *seditio* and *seductio*, see Hale, P. C. i. 77. In MSS. of this time they seem to be used interchangeably and as though they were really but one word.

[6] 25 Edw. III. stat. 5, cap. 2. Briefly stated, the statute declares the following to be treasons:—(1) to compass or imagine the death of the king, his queen or eldest son; (2) to defile the king's wife or his eldest unmarried daughter or his eldest son's wife; (3) to levy war against the king in his realm; (4) to be adherent to his enemies, giving them aid and comfort; (5) to counterfeit the king's great or privy seal or money; (6) to bring false money into the realm; (7) to slay certain officers or justices being in their places doing their offices. See Hale, P. C. i. 87–252; Stephen, Hist. Crim. Law, ii. 248–297.

Treason is a crime which has a vague circumference, and more than one centre. In the first place, there is the centre that is to this day primarily indicated by the word *betray*. In the earliest days to which we can go back the man who aided the enemies of his own tribe was hanged; probably his death was sacrificial[1]. This element is well marked in our old books; it is the *seditio exercitus vel regni,* a betraying of the army or of the realm[2]. When our law crystallizes in the famous statute, 'adhering to the king's enemies' finds a natural place in the list of high treasons. Flight from battle stands as a capital crime in the laws of Cnut and the *Leges Henrici,* and the coward's lands go to his lord or to the king[3]. The bond of fealty is another centre. To betray one's lord was already in Alfred's day the worst of all crimes; it was the crime of Judas; he betrayed his lord[4]. Then a Roman element entered when men [p. 502] began to hear a little of the *crimen laesae maiestatis*[5]. Less emphasis was thrown upon the idea of betrayal, though such terms as *traditio, proditio, seditio* are always pointing back to this,—and plotting against the king's life or the lord's life became prominent[6]. In marked contrast to the general drift of our old criminal law, the crime was in this case found, not in a harmful result, but in the endeavour to produce it, in machination, 'compassing,' 'imagining.' The strong feudal sentiment claimed as its own this new idea; the lord's life, as well as the

---

[1] Tacitus, Germania, c. 12; Brunner, D. R. G. ii. 685–7.

[2] Glanvill, i. 2: 'ut de nece vel seditione personae domini Regis vel regni vel exercitus.' Bracton, f. 118 b: 'ad seditionem domini Regis vel exercitus sui. We believe that in these passages the best rendering for *seditio* is, not *sedition,* but *betrayal.*

[3] Cnut, ii. 77; Leg. Henr. 13, § 12. See Schmid, Gesetze, Glossar, s.v. *fyrd.*

[4] Alfred, Introduction, 49, § 7. Dante's placing of Brutus and Cassius in the same extreme of infamy is the well-known high-water mark of this doctrine; its adoption by Fra Angelico in a Last Judgment now in the Museum at Berlin shows that this was no mere private imperialist opinion of the poet's.

[5] Brunner, D. R. G. ii. 688.

[6] Æthelr. v. 30; vi. 37, mention only the king; Cnut, ii. 57, speaks also of the lord; Leg. Henr. 75, § 2. In old times the king had a *wergild*; but before we draw inferences from this we must remember both that a *wergild* was exacted when the slaying was unintentional, and that the price set on the king was no less than £240. Hardly in any case could such a sum be raised, except when the death of the king of one folk could be charged against another folk, as when Ine obtained a heavy sum from the men of Kent for the death of Mul. See A.-S. Chron. (A.D. 694), p. 66, and the note to Thorpe's translation.

king's, is to be sacred against plots or 'imaginations.' In the twelfth century another wave of Romanism was flowing. The royal lawyers began to write about *laesa maiestas*, to paint in dark colours the peculiar gravity of the crime, to draw a hard line between the king and mere lords[1]. But they could not altogether destroy the connexion between vassalship and treason; men were not yet ready to conceive a 'crime against the state.' Petty treason perpetrated against a lord was but slowly marked off from high treason perpetrated against the king; and in much later days our law still saw, or spoke as if it saw, the essence of high treason in a breach of the bond of 'ligeance[2].'

Elements of treason.

Meanwhile, in this feudal stage of its history, treason [p. 503] gathered round it and embraced some offences which can be regarded as the vilest breaches of the vassal's troth, such as adultery with the lord's wife, violation of his daughter, forgery of his seal. Glanvill and Bracton at the suggestion of civilians would like to institute a *crimen falsi*[3]. But English law was not ready for this. The only forgery that it was prepared to treat with great severity was forgery of the king's seal or of the seal of the forger's lord; and these it dealt with under the name of treason[4]. Under the same head were brought the clipping of the king's coin and the making of counterfeit

---

[1] Bracton, f. 118 b: 'est enim tam grave crimen istud quod vix permittitur heredibus quod vivant.'

[2] Bracton, having *laesa maiestas* before his eyes, says nothing of 'treason' against a lord. In one place however, f. 105, he says, 'Igne concremantur qui saluti dominorum suorum insidiaverint.' Here he is copying, but with notable omissions, from Dig. 48, 19, 28, § 11: 'Igni cremantur plerumque *servi* qui saluti dominorum suorum insidiaverint, nonnunquam etiam liberi plebeii et humiles personae.' He holds therefore that to plot against one's lord's life is a capital crime. We imagine that this crime would have been punished in England rather by drawing and hanging than by burning. See Select Pleas of the Crown, pl. 179; Très ancien coutumier, p. 30. Britton, i. 40, seems to be the first writer who talks expressly of *high* (or rather, *great*) and *petty* treasons; with him to 'procure' the death of one's lord is great treason, and one is hanged and drawn for forging one's lord's seal or committing adultery with his wife. By 1352 a change had taken place, or else a change was effected by the statute of that year; 'treason' against any one but the king is always 'petty,' and only exists where a servant (not vassal) actually kills (not compasses to kill) his master (not lord), or a wife her husband, or a clerk his prelate. See Hale, P. C. i. 378.

[3] Glanvill, xiv. 7; Bracton, f. 119 b.

[4] Britton, i. 41; Fleta, p. 32.

money[1]. The crimes of the moneyers had long been severely
punished: frequently by loss of a hand[2], under Henry II. by
various mutilations[3]. That issuing bad or clipping good money
should be a capital offence will not surprise us. The inclusion
of these offences in the class of high treasons seems due to
Roman influence[4]; they were regarded, however, not as mere
frauds fraught with grave harm to the community, but also and
chiefly as the invasion of a specially royal right which our
kings had jealously guarded, and any tampering with the
king's image and superscription on seal or coin was assimilated
to an attack upon his person.

In the statute of 1352 there is an item which every modern
reader will expect to find there. To 'levy war against our lord
the king in his realm'—this should certainly be an act of high
treason. Nevertheless we believe that this is the newest item
in the catalogue. So long as the feudal sentiment was at its
strongest, men would not have been brought to admit in perfectly general terms that the subject who levies war against the
king is a traitor. The almost slavish obedience that a vassal
owes to his lord is qualified by a condition: if a lord persistently
refuses justice to his man, the tie of fealty is broken, the man
may openly defy his lord, and, having done so, may make war
upon him[5]. Kings of England who were homagers of the
kings of France might by their own mouths have been sen-
tencing themselves to shame, and even to shameful death, had
they declared that in no case whatever could a vassal without
treason levy war upon a king in his realm. Edward III. was
the first of our kings since the Conquest who could afford to
make such a declaration, for, being in his own eyes king of
France, he owed homage to nobody. Earlier kings of England
had levied war against the kings of France in the realm of
France, and the cause of war was often enough one which

Treason by levying war.

[p. 504]

---

[1] Glanvill. xiv. 7; Bracton, f. 119 b.

[2] Æthelst. ii. 14; Æthelr. iii. 8, 16; Cnut, ii. 8; Leg. Henr. 13, § 3.

[3] Flor. Wigorn. ii. 57 (A.D. 1108); Henr. Huntingd. 246 (A.D. 1125).

[4] Cod. 9, 24, 2. The Roman idea of *maiestas* includes a religious element;
falsifying Caesar's image is a kind of sacrilege.

[5] See for Angevin law, Viollet, Établissements, i. 180. In England the high-
water mark of the purely feudal conception of treason is Stephen's conduct
after the siege of Exeter in 1136. He spared the garrison, having listened to
the plea that they had never sworn fealty to him but were the men of Baldwin
de Redvers; Gesta Stephani, 27; Henr. Huntingd. 257.

arose in France and one which would in no wise have concerned a mere king of England. Could they mete the acts of their barons by a measure other than that by which they meted their own acts? Was not the case of a Count of Britanny who was Earl of Richmond sufficiently parallel to that of a King of England who was Duke of Aquitaine? For two centuries after the Conquest, the frank, open rebellions of the great folk were treated with a clemency which, when we look back to it through intervening ages of blood, seems wonderful[1]. Henry II., for example, spared the rebels of 1173, though he had thoroughly subdued them and had been within an ace of losing his kingdom[2]. Never was there anything that we could call a proscription of defeated partizans. The Dictum of Kenilworth shines out in startling contrast to the attainders of the fifteenth century. In part perhaps we may account for this by saying, if this be true, that men became more cruel as time went on; but also we ought to see that there had been a real progress, the development of a new political idea. Treason has been becoming a crime against the state; the supreme crime against [p. 505] the state is the levying of war against it. A right, or duty, of rising against the king and compelling him to do justice can no longer be preached in the name of law; and this is well[3].

Compass of treason in cent. xiii.

Although during the thirteenth century treason may have been a vague enough crime, such stories as have come down to us do not entitle us to say that many persons, except the Jewish money-clippers[4], suffered for it. A fomenter of civic

---

[1] Are not the cases of Waltheof and William of Eu almost the only cases in which a high-born rebel loses either life or limb by judicial sentence? As to Waltheof, see above, vol. i. p. 91. In the case of William of Eu we have a rare example of a regular appeal of treason and a trial by battle. The garrison of a castle taken in flagrant delict was sometimes hanged out of hand, and the chief rebels were sometimes kept in prison even until they died, but their imprisonment was rather 'a measure of state' than the outcome of a sentence.

[2] It must be to this that Diceto refers when (see above, vol. ii. p. 461, note 6) he speaks as though mere exile were the punishment of treason.

[3] The famous passage inserted in Bracton's book, f. 34, by his own or some other hand, comes near to a declaration that it may be the right and duty of the barons to rise against the king. The change in the treatment of rebels can not be put down to the insecure titles of the Lancastrian, Yorkist and Tudor kings. Every king from the Conqueror to Henry III. had to fight against insurgents, and in many cases the insurrection was headed by his son or brother.

[4] Ann. Dunstapl. 279 (A.D. 1278): two hundred and eighty Jews hanged in London, and many elsewhere, for clipping.

sedition would sometimes be hanged in an exceedingly summary fashion: witness the fate of William Fitz Osbert in
1196[1], and of Constantine Fitz Athulf in 1222[2]. The severest
doctrine that we hear is that he who knows of a plot against
the king and does not at once reveal it is himself guilty of
treason[3]. We may see perhaps that a wide scope might be
given to the phrase which condemned those who 'imagined'
the king's death. One Peter of Wakefield was hanged for
predicting that by next Ascension-day John would no longer
be king[4]; under James I. he would have suffered a similar
punishment for a similar prophecy[5]. To declare that there
was no king's peace, as the king was among his enemies in
Wales and would never return,—this also seems treason in
John's reign[6]. It was of treason that Robert de Montfort
appealed, and by battle convicted, Henry of Essex, and though
the real charge against the royal standard-bearer was in our
eyes a charge of cowardly flight from battle, we are told in a
[p. 506] significant way by a chronicler, who had the tale from Henry's
own lips, that he was also accused of having cried aloud that
the king was slain[7]. Betraying the king's secrets to his
enemies and thus 'adhering' to them was treason under
Edward I.[8] Any one who grossly insulted the king might have
found that the law of treason was expansive. Walter de
Clifford, who in 1250 had been guilty of making a royal process-
server eat writ and wax, was, we are told, in peril of a judgment
of death and disherison, but, making humble submission,

---

[1] Palgrave, Rot. Cur. Reg. vol. i., Introduction; Stubbs, Const. Hist. i. 547;
Hoveden, iv. 6; Diceto, ii. 143; Gervase, i. 532.

[2] Mat. Par. Chron. Maj. iii. 73; Ann. Waverl. 297; Ann. Dunstapl. 79.

[3] Bracton, f. 118 b. Therefore our law needs no such crime as the 'misprision of treason' of later days. For a relevant story, see Ann. Dunstapl. 97.

[4] Mat. Par. Chron. Maj. ii. 535, 547.

[5] Compare the fate of Williams, the author of *Balaam's Ass*; Stephen, Hist.
Crim. Law, ii. 306.

[6] Select Pleas of the Crown, pl. 115.

[7] Jocelin of Brakelonde (Camd. Soc.), p. 52.

[8] Oxford City Documents, p. 204 (A.D. 1285): 'Magister Nicholaus de
Wautham contra fidelitatem suam et contra foedus suum et ligeitatem...seditiose
ut seductor se confederavit Guydoni de Monteforti et Emerico fratri suo et
Lewelino quondam principi Walliae inimico domini Regis; et venit ad curiam
domini Regis et moram in eadem curia fecit ut privatus et specialis curiae
praedictae, insidiando et explorando secreta domini Regis et ea quae...explorare
potuit...inimicis domini Regis...nuntiavit...et parti ipsorum *adhaesit.*' The
Montforts had slain Henry of Almain and Edward regarded them as deadly foes.

escaped with a heavy fine[1]. A case that was much discussed at the time, and has at intervals been discussed ever since, arose in 1305, when after a long hesitation Nicholas Segrave was declared worthy of death for having deserted the king's army in Scotland and summoned an adversary to meet him in battle before the French king's court, thus 'subjecting the realm of England to the king of France[2].' Any one who understands the relationship between Edward and Philip will understand why our king wished to secure the conviction of a baron whose conduct seemed to imply that an appeal 'for default of justice' lay from the English to the French court. The conviction having been secured, the king was merciful; Segrave was bound to render himself to prison if called upon to do so; soon afterwards he was pardoned. This is one of the very few early cases of treason which have what we can call a political interest. Even into the statute of 1352 and the controversy that preceded it we may too easily introduce modern notions. There had, we may be sure, been no debate about the legitimate limits of political agitation. The king wanted forfeitures; the lords wanted escheats. Some of the king's justices had been holding for treason mere murders and robberies—for [p. 507] example, the murder of a king's messenger—which should, so the magnates thought, bring lands to them instead of destroying their seignories[3]. A rude compromise was established[4].

---

[1] Mat. Par. Chron. Maj. v. 95. At least one similar case occurs in the early history of the Court of Chancery. By that time the notion of contempt as a distinct offence was available.

[2] Rot. Parl. i. 172; Memoranda de Parliamento, 1305, pp. lxxvi, 255. See on this Hale, P. C. i. 79; Stephen, Hist. Crim. Law, i. 147; ii. 245. The record does not expressly say that the offence was treason.

[3] See the cases from the first half of the fourteenth century in Hale, P. C. i. 76–82, and Stephen, Hist. Crim. Law, ii. 245–7.

[4] Stephen, Hist. Crim. Law, iii. 247, says, 'Probably the great importance of the Act of Edward [III.] as a protection to what we should now call political agitation and discussion, was hardly recognized till a much later time.' With this we heartily agree. But what Sir James Stephen rightly calls the 'extreme leniency of the statute' was not due altogether to the fact that in 1352 Edward was powerful, popular and secure. The gaps in the statute which were afterwards supplied by 'construction' were gaps natural to our old law. It had started from the principle that an attempt to do harm is no offence. Very early, under Roman influence, it had admitted one exception to this rule, namely, that a plot against the king's life is a crime; but for centuries it was extremely unwilling openly to extend this to plots for imprisoning or deposing or coercing the king. 'The thought of man shall not be tried.'

Ancient law has as a general rule no punishment for those who have tried to do harm but have not done it. The idea of punishment is but slowly severed from that of reparation, and where no harm is done there is none to be repaired. On the other hand, it is soon seen that harm can be done by words as well as by blows, and that if at *A*'s instigation *B* has killed *C*, then *A* is guilty of *C*'s death[1]. Anglo-Saxon law knows the *ræd-bana* as well as the *dæd-bana*, the slayer by rede as well as the slayer by deed. In Bracton's day there was a common proverb that met this case[2]. The man who has commanded or counselled a murder has committed no crime until there has been a murder; but when the murder is committed he is guilty of it. The law of homicide is wide enough to comprise not only him who gave the deadly blow and those who held the victim, but also those who 'procured, counselled, commanded or abetted' the felony. On the other hand, we already meet with the rule that the accessory can not be brought to trial until the principal has been convicted or outlawed[3]. This rule lived on into modern times, when it looked absurd enough and did much mischief[4]. It was the

[p. 508] outcome of strict medieval logic. If you convict the accessory while the principal is neither convicted nor outlawed, you beg a question that should not be begged. The law will be shamed if the principal is acquitted after the accessory has been hanged. The modes by which guilt and innocence were proved were, or had lately been, sacral and supernatural processes which could not be allowed a chance of producing self-contradictory results. What should we think of the God who suffered the principal to come clean from the ordeal after the accessory had blistered his hand? Hence a complex set of rules which permit the escape of many accessories[5].

---

[1] Brunner, D. R. G. ii. 565. Æthelr. viii. 23; Leg. Henr. 85, § 3.

[2] Bracton, f. 142: 'Dicitur enim vulgariter quod satis occidit qui praecipit.' On the other hand, f. 139: 'ubi factum nullum, ibi forcia nulla, nec praeceptum nocere debet cum iniuria non habet effectum.'

[3] Bracton, f. 128, 139; Note Book, pl. 1548.

[4] Stephen, Hist. Crim. Law, ii. 232.

[5] There are many niceties that we must pass by. Persons who, as we should say, were principals in the second degree, were said to be appealed not *de facto* but *de vi* or *de forcia*, and hence they are often spoken of as being the *vis* and the *forcia* of the chief malefactor. You can not bring them to trial by your appeal until he has been convicted or outlawed. If, as is possible, several

The accessories of whom we have been speaking are 'accessories before the fact.' Our law was beginning to give the name 'accessories after the fact' to those who 'receive, relieve, comfort or assist' the felon. Such persons deserve the same punishment that he has earned. The crime of receiving outlaws or thieves was among the oldest and was severely handled by ancient law. Often the receiver suffered the punishment that was meet for him whom he had received[1]. Under the Assizes of Henry II. the receivers of murderers, robbers and thieves incur the penalty which is ordained for murder, robbery and theft[2]. In Bracton's day it was a capital or unemendable crime to receive a felon or outlaw knowing him to be such[3]. Roman law could be cited in favour of the principle that there is a parity of guilt between the receiver and the received[4]. The same principle is applied to those who voluntarily allow a prisoner to escape; if he was guilty, they are participators in his guilt. On prisoners for crime who broke prison the law of Bracton's day was exceedingly severe; death was their punishment, even though they were innocent of the crime for which they were imprisoned and that crime was not capital[5]. A statute of 1295 mitigated this rigour by declaring that the prison-breaker should not have judgment of life or member, unless that was the judgment provided for the offence which was the cause of his incarceration[6]. Old law is apt to treat an escape from prison as a confession. What need has it of further witness[7]?

[p. 509]

---

appellors bring appeals against several appellees for one death, each appellee is charged with at least one deadly wound, 'ita quod de plaga illa mortuus esset si aliam non haberet'; Select Pleas of the Crown, pl. 197; Note Book, pl. 1460. For the later law as to accessories see Hale, P. C. i. 612–626.

[1] Brunner, D. R. G. ii. 575; Schmid, Gesetze, Glossar, s.v. *flýmena-fyrmð.*

[2] Ass. Clar. c. 1, 2: 'robator vel murdrator vel latro vel receptor eorum.'

[3] Bracton, f. 128 b.

[4] Bracton, f. 128 b: 'et ad hoc facit lex C. de iis qui latrones et maleficos occultant, l. prima [=Cod. 9, 39, 1] ubi dicitur quod eos qui se cum alieni criminis reo occultando eum sociarunt, par ipsos et reos poena expectet.' Bracton's reading of the text was not quite that which is now received and here given. Très ancien coutumier, p. 33: 'si captus fuerit fugitivus in domo alicuius, receptator omnia catalla sua amittet, ni forte membrorum vel vitae incurret periculum.' See Viollet, Établissements, i. 251.

[5] Bracton, f. 24.

[6] 23 Edw. I. ; Statutes, i. 113.

[7] See Select Pleas of the Crown, pl. 154, 155, 199, 201.

If now we glance back over the ground that we have lately traversed, we see that towards the end of the thirteenth century our law knows only some seven crimes which it treats as very grave, namely, treason, homicide, arson, rape, robbery, burglary, and grand larceny, to which we may perhaps add breach of prison. For all these the punishment is death: in general death by hanging, but for petty treason a man shall be drawn as well as hanged and a woman shall be burnt[1], while, at least in the worst cases, high treason demands a cumulation of deaths. Three other crimes, namely, wounding, mayhem and imprisonment, have been called felonies, and perhaps might be still treated as such if the injured man brought an appeal; but they are fast falling into the category of minor crimes. High treason may be somewhat elastic and it covers some forgeries, the making of counterfeit money and the clipping of coin. But we can not call this list comprehensive or cruel. Its rude leniency we shall only perceive when we have spoken of the fashion in which the minor crimes were punished.

[p. 510]

§ 3.   *The Trespasses.*

When the felonies are put on one side, we find hardly anything that can be called either a classification of punishable acts, or a general doctrine about them. In later days, as is well known, the following scheme is fashioned:—

$$
\text{Offences are punishable}
\begin{cases}
\text{Upon indictment}
\begin{cases}
\text{Treasons} \\
\text{Felonies} \\
\text{Misdemeanours}
\end{cases} \\
\text{Upon summary conviction[2].}
\end{cases}
$$

Then with the punishable offence we contrast the *tort* which gives rise to a civil action, though the tort may also be, and very often is, a punishable offence. Torts again fall into two classes, and only those which involve some violence—the violence may be exceedingly small—are known as trespasses.

In the thirteenth century we see but the germs of this

---

[1] Women were sometimes burnt for felony; Select Pleas of the Crown, pl. 191; Munim. Gildh. i. 101, a woman burnt for arson.

[2] Occasionally an offence may be punished either summarily or upon indictment.

scheme. *Trespass* (*transgressio*) is the most general term that
there is; it will cover all or almost all wrongful acts and
defaults. Every felony, says Bracton, is a trespass, though
every trespass is not a felony[1]. In a narrower sense therefore
trespass is used as a contrast to *felony*[2]. The word *misdemeanour*
belongs as a term of art to a much later age. In the past even
the gravely punishable offences have been contemplated from
the point of view of the person who has been wronged. Thus

Trespasses or
wrongful acts are
{
Felonies to be prosecuted by appeal.

Mere trespasses giving rise to actions in
which no words of felony are used[3].
}

Only by slow degrees is the procedure which begins, not with [p. 511]
the complaint of 'the party grieved,' but with a communal
accusation (indictment or presentment), becoming a prominent
part of the law's machinery. Henry II. had set it going only
against 'murderers, robbers and thieves and the receivers of
such.' In a later ordinance he spoke of arson and forgery[4].
We have already seen that there were crimes which were
treated as felonies if there was an appeal, but as trespasses if
there was only an indictment[5]. However, long before the
beginning of Edward I.'s reign, numerous offences that are
no felonies are being punished upon indictment or presentment, while many others are being punished in the course of
civil actions. We shall perhaps breathe the spirit of the age
if we say that—

Offences less than
felony are punished
{
(*a*) In civil actions.

(*b*) Upon presentment before local courts.

(*c*) Upon presentment before the king's justices.
}

[1] Bracton, f. 119 b: 'utrum scilicet sit ibi felonia vel transgressio, quia
quaelibet transgressio dici non debet felonia, quamvis e converso.'

[2] Bracton, f. 125: 'quodlibet factum non continet sub se feloniam quamvis
aliquando contineat iniuriam et transgressionem.' Britton, i. 105: 'soit
trespas ou felonie.' *Tort* again is a large, loose word. Britton, i. 77, heads
a chapter on some of the smaller offences presented in the eyres by the title
De plusours tortz. Coke, Second Inst. 170, 418, has remarked the large sense
which *trespass* bears in our oldest statutes.

[3] Even these classes, as we have seen above, are not mutually exclusive.
The wounded man has a choice between an appeal of felony and an action for
damages. Bracton often uses *actio* as a very general word capable of including
an appeal. See *e.g.* f. 103 b.

[4] Ass. Clarend. and Ass. Northampt. See above, vol. i. p. 152.

[5] See above, vol. ii. p. 485, note 3.

To this table we shall return, but meanwhile a few words Minor punishments.
must first be said of the punishments that are inflicted.
These are in the main two, namely, (i) amercement, (ii) indefinite imprisonment redeemable by fine.

Thousands of amercements are being inflicted by courts of Amercements.
all kinds. The process is this :—So soon as the offender's guilt
is proved, the court declares that he is in mercy (*in misericordia*).
If it be a royal court, he is in the king's, if it be a county court,
he is in the sheriff's, if it be a seignorial court, he is in the lord's
mercy. Thereupon, at least in the local courts, the offender
'waged' an amercement, that is to say, he found gage or pledge
for the payment of whatever sum might be set upon him when
he should have been amerced. For as yet he had not been
amerced (*amerciatus*). At the end of the session some good
and lawful men, the peers of the offender (two seem to be
enough) were sworn to 'affeer' the amercements. They set
upon each offender some fixed sum of money that he was to
pay; this sum is his amercement (*amerciamentum*)[1].

[p. 512] In the thirteenth century amercements are being inflicted History of amercement.
right and left upon men who have done very little that is
wrong. The sums that they have to pay are small, and most
men in England must have expected to be amerced at least
once a year. Therefore this punishment could not be very
terrible. Nevertheless it seems to have its origin in a heavy
penalty. We can hardly doubt that at first the declaration
that a man is in the king's or the lord's mercy implies that the
king or lord may, if he pleases, take all his goods. Henry II.'s
treasurer has told us this explicitly[2]. We have here again what
Dr Brunner calls an offshoot of outlawry[3]. In the old days of
fixed wites there were offences which put life and limb, lands
and goods 'in the king's mercy[4].' As the differentiating
process went on, there came into existence offences which put
the offender's goods in the king's mercy, but not his life, limb
or lands. Feudalism multiplied these offences. Many of the
smaller misdeeds were regarded as exhibitions of an *infidelitas*,

---

[1] This old procedure yet lives in the game of forfeits. A forfeiture (*foris-factura*) having been committed, a *wed* is given, which is afterwards redeemed
when the amercement is affeered by good and lawful children.

[2] Dial. de Scac. lib. ii. c. 16.   [3] Forschungen, 465.

[4] D. B. ii. 7: 'Quidam clericus...iudicatus est esse in misericordia regis et
de omni cessu suo et de corpore suo.'

which, however, did not amount to a *felonia*. Also the Norman kings wielded a large power of 'banning' misdeeds, that is of declaring that certain offences would bring down the king's 'full forfeiture' on the heads of the guilty, and they were not always careful to explain what this 'full forfeiture' was[1]. The Conqueror and Rufus had made free use of the notion that many of the smaller offences,—those which did not amount to *perfidia* or *scelus,*—put the whole of the offender's chattels at the king's mercy. Henry I. when he was buying the crown had to promise an abandonment of this doctrine and a return to the old English system of pre-appointed wites[2]. This promise, like many other promises, he broke, and we may be glad that he did not keep it. The amercement marks an advance in the theory and practice of punishment. A basis for arbitrary or [p. 513] 'unliquidated' wites had thus been found, and in course of time men began to see that arbitrary wites—if they be not oppressively used—are far more equitable than the old fixed penalties. Account can now be taken of the offender's wealth or poverty, of the provocation that has been given him, of all those 'circumstances of the particular case' that the rigid rules of ancient law had ignored. So the *misericordia*, when the central power is strong, begins to devour the old wites.

Restriction of amercement.

We hear of attempts to establish some fixed maximum for the amercement. Becket alleged that there was such a maximum in every county, and that the law of Kent knew no amercement higher than forty shillings[3]. In both the England and the Normandy of Glanvill's day the rule had grown up that the amercement was to be 'affeered' by the oath of lawful men[4]. The oldest Norman custumal is very instructive, for it still regards this punishment as being in strictness a forfeiture of all chattels. The function of the sworn affeerers is to declare what goods the offender has. In the case of a

---

[1] See *e.g.* Laws of William (Sel. Charters), cc. 9, 10: 'Ego prohibeo...super plenam forisfacturam meam.'

[2] Coronation Charter, c. 8: 'Si quis baronum sive hominum meorum forisfecerit, non dabit vadium in misericordia pecuniae suae, sicut faciebat tempore patris mei vel fratris mei, sed secundum modum forisfacti ita emendabit sicut emendasset retro a tempore patris mei, in tempore aliorum antecessorum meorum. Quod si perfidiae vel sceleris convictus fuerit, sicut iustum fuerit, sic emendet.' A germ of (1) treason, (2) felony, (3) misdemeanour, may be seen in (1) *perfidia*, (2) *scelus*, (3) *forisfactura*.

[3] William FitzStephen (Materials for the Life of Becket, iii.), p. 62.

[4] Glanvill, ix. 11.

knight the duke is to have all, except his arms, destrier, palfrey and rouncey, his ploughs and beasts of the plough, his seed-corn and victuals enough for a year. So too the roturier's victuals, team and arms are spared. But there also seem to be maximum amercements varying with the wrong-doer's rank; the baron will not have to pay more than a hundred pounds, nor the roturier more than five shillings[1]. Parallel to this lies the famous passage in Glanvill which saves for the amerced his 'honourable contenement[2].' Then the Great Charter decreed that all amercements were to be set or 'affeered' by good men of the neighbourhood; that earls and barons were to be amerced by their peers; that amercements should vary with the gravity of the offence; that the knight's contenement, the merchant's merchandise, the villein's wainage should escape[3]. [p. 514] The amercement became the most flexible and therefore it could be the smallest of all punishments. Threepenny amercements were common in the local courts[4].

---

[1] Très ancien coutumier, p. 45. It must be remembered that Norman money is worth much less than English money. Compare the very similar rules in Dial. de Scac. lib. ii. c. 14, as to the chattels that may not be sold for the satisfaction of a debt due to the crown.

[2] Glanvill, ix. 11; Bracton, f. 116 b. The origin and exact meaning of the term *contenement* seem to be very obscure. See Oxford Engl. Dict.

[3] Articles of the Barons, c. 9; Charter, 1215, c. 20.

[4] In the Anglo-Saxon dooms a general forfeiture of 'all that one has' begins to recur with increasing frequency as time goes on. See Schmid, Gesetze, p. 657. But this is confined to grave crimes. For 'contempts' of king or lord these dooms have a special wite, the *oferhȳrnes*, or in Leg. Henr. *overseunessa*. See Schmid's Glossary under these words. The king's *oferhȳrnes* was however the very serious mulct of 120 (Saxon) shillings. The first stages in the development of the amercement are, we imagine, rather Frankish than English; they may be found in a forfeiture of goods for the elastic offence of *infidelitas*. The 'très ancien coutumier de Normandie' is here of the utmost value. Already in Henry I.'s charter for the Londoners we have a promise that the citizen who is adjudged *in misericordia pecuniae* shall not have to pay more than his *wer* of 100 shillings. This points to heavy amercements, for £5 is a large sum. In Glanvill's day however men are always falling into the king's mercy in the course of civil actions. The transition from a loss of all chattels *exceptis excipiendis* to a very moderate amercement was much easier in the twelfth century than it would be now. If a Norman knight of that age lost all his goods, except arms, horses, ploughs, beasts of the plough, seed-corn and victuals for a year, he might still be far from ruin. At some time or another a fixed tariff 'for the amerciament of the nobility' was allowed to develop itself in England; a duke paid £10, an earl £5, and so forth. See Coke, Second Inst. 28. Nobles were amerced by their 'peers,' the barons of the exchequer.

Imprison-
ment.

The use of imprisonment as a punishment,—more especially
if it be imprisonment for a definite period fixed by the sentence,
—is a sign of advancing civilisation. Of prisons, as of places of
detention for those who are not yet condemned, we begin to
read in the tenth century, and sometimes the law requires that
a man shall be kept in gaol for forty days before his kinsfolk
may redeem him[1]. Imprisonment would have been regarded in
these old times as an useless punishment; it does not satisfy
revenge, it keeps the criminal idle, and, do what we may, it is
costly. If the man guilty of a bad offence is to be neither
killed nor mutilated, he should be sold, or forced to sell himself,
into slavery as a *wíte-þeów*, so that thus the *bót* or *wer* that is
due from him may be raised[2]. After the Conquest we hear no
more of this penal servitude, and for a while we hear little of
imprisonment as an ordinary punishment, though the Norman
kings will sometimes keep in prison rebels or enemies whom,
for one reason or another, they do not put to death. Henry II.
had to provide for the erection of a gaol in every county; but
these gaols were wanted chiefly for the detention of the [p. 515]
indicted who had not yet gone to the ordeal[3]. Detentive
imprisonment was by this time becoming common and the old
'stocks' were no longer an adequate engine. For example, the
appellor who would not prosecute his appeal was in Glanvill's
day thrown into prison to make him change his mind[4]. The
Exchequer had its prison, and already there was some classification of the inmates; some were in durance vile, others were
merely confined within the ambit of the walls[5]. Bracton speaks
as though a prison were never a place of punishment; but he
is borrowing from Ulpian, and by his time penal incarceration
was being inflicted[6].

Punitive
imprison-
ment.

In a few cases men could be sent to gaol for definite periods.
Henry II. ordained that recognitors who perjured themselves in
a grand assize should be kept in prison for a year at least[7].
Under Henry III.'s charter the punishment for a breach of
forest law was to be a year's imprisonment, after which the
malefactor had to find sureties for good behaviour or abjure

[1] Schmid, Gesetze, p. 657.　　　　　　[2] Brunner, D. R. G. ii. 594.
[3] Ass. Clarend. c. 7.　　　　　　　　　[4] Glanvill, i. 32.
[5] Dial. de Scac. lib. ii. c. 21.
[6] Bracton, f. 105 (= Dig. 48. 19. 3 § 9): 'carcer ad continendos et non ad
puniendos haberi debet.'
[7] Glanvill, ii. 19.

the realm[1]. We believe, however, that imprisonment for a
fixed term was in all cases regarded as having its origin in
some definite assize or ordinance; in other words it was not
thought of as 'a common law punishment.' The statutes of
Edward I. made a great change in this province of law; they
freely distributed short terms of imprisonment[2]. Even in these
cases, however, the imprisonment was as a general rule but
preparatory to a fine. After a year or two years the wrong-
doer might make fine; if he had no money, he was detained
for a while longer[3].

It is, however, with an indefinite imprisonment that we are Fines.
chiefly concerned. In the thirteenth century the king's justices
[p. 516] wield a wide and a 'common law' power of ordering that an
offender be kept in custody. They have an equally wide power
of discharging him upon his 'making fine with the king.' We
must observe the language of the time. In strictness they have
no power to 'impose a fine.' No tribunal of this period, unless
we are mistaken, is ever said to impose a fine. To order the
offender to pay so much money to the king—this the judge
may not do. If he did it, he would be breaking or evading the
Great Charter, for an amercement should be affeered, not by
royal justices, but by neighbours of the wrong-doer. What the
judges can do is this:—they can pronounce a sentence of imprisonment and then allow the culprit to 'make fine,' that is to
make an end (*finem facere*) of the matter by paying or finding
security for a certain sum of money. In theory the fine is a
bilateral transaction, a bargain; it is not 'imposed,' it is 'made.'
Now, so far as we can see, the justices of Henry III.'s reign
used their power of imprisonment chiefly as a means of inflicting
pecuniary penalties. The wrong-doer but rarely goes to prison
even for a moment. On the plea roll the *Custodiatur* which
sends him to gaol is followed at once by *Finem fecit per unam
marcam* (or whatever the sum may be), and then come the
names of those who are pledges for the payment. The justices
do not wish to keep him in gaol, they wish to make him pay

---

1 Forest Charter, 1217, c. 10.

2 See *e.g.* Stat. West. I. cc. 9, 13, 15, 20, 29, 31, 32.

3 As a typical case we may take Stat. West. I. c. 9. The bailiff of a
franchise who makes default in the pursuit of felons shall be imprisoned for
one year and shall then make grievous fine, and, if he has not wherewithal,
he shall be imprisoned for another year.

money. Such a system would sometimes be abused when the king desired to crush an enemy[1], but, after looking through many rolls, it seems to us that normally the fines were light, much lighter than the wites of old times[2]. The causes for fines were now very numerous, and the king preferred a power of inflicting many small penalties to that of demanding heavy sums in a few grave cases.

Other minor punish-ments. There are three or four other punishments which deserve a passing word. A complete forfeiture of all chattels is insisted on when a man 'flies for a felony,' even if he has not committed it[3]. True exile is unknown; but the criminal who has taken sanctuary abjures the realm and occasionally, by way of grace, other criminals are allowed to do the like. Now and again we [p. 517] hear of a man compelled to abjure a town[4]. Manorial courts will sometimes decree a removal from the village; probably the delinquent in such a case is a villein. In the boroughs a loss of 'liberties' or franchises is sometimes denounced against peccant burgesses; or they may have to abjure their trades or their crafts. Pillory and tumbrel seem to be reserved almost exclusively for bakers and alewives who break the assizes of bread and beer[5]. Bracton speaks of whipping[6], and it became a 'common law' punishment for misdemeanours; we do not remember a case of his time in which it was inflicted, except as an ecclesiastical penance.

Procedure against minor offences. We can now speak briefly of the offences that were punished by amercement or by imprisonment, remembering that as a general rule imprisonment really means fine. We have said that there were three main modes of procedure.

---

[1] See *e.g.* Note Book, pl. 770, where the ex-treasurer, bishop of Carlisle, is amerced at 100 marks for unlawful distraint.

[2] Northumberland Assize Rolls, 92, 94: in two cases a man convicted of rape is fined one mark (13*s.* 4*d.*) and is at once set free on finding sureties for payment. So Munim. Gildh. i. 90: three men guilty of murderous assault are fined one mark and liberated: they were poor.

[3] Bracton, f. 125. This is common on the eyre rolls.

[4] Note Book, pl. 1179: a Jew who has fornicated with a Christian woman must abjure the realm; the partner of his guilt abjured the town of Bristol. Bracton, f. 136 § 4, speaks in romanesque terms of exile; he is thinking of abjuration and of outlawry. Liber de Antiquis Legibus, p. 70: in 1260 certain barons abjured England for a year and went into exile in Ireland.

[5] Britton, i. 61: petty theft is punished by an hour of pillory. Ibid. p. 41: the forger also may be pilloried.

[6] Bracton, f. 151 b, in case of petty theft.

1. *Offences punished in the course of civil actions.* Every (1) Civil tort, nay, every cause of civil action, was a punishable offence. actions. Every vanquished defendant, even though the action was 'real' or was contractual, had earned punishment. At the least he had been guilty of an unjust detention (*pro iniusta detentione*). In the lower courts he could only be—but he would be— amerced. By the king's court he might even be imprisoned. This would be his fate if he had broken the king's peace with force and arms, if he had infringed a 'final concord' made in the king's court, if he had falsely disputed his own deed, if he had relied on a forged charter, if he had intruded on the king or disobeyed a writ of prohibition[1]. A plaintiff too might be imprisoned, if, for example, he had failed in the endeavour to reduce a free man to villeinage[2]. But every defeated plaintiff could be amerced 'for a false claim.' Incidentally too any falsehood (*falsitas*), that is, any fraudulent misuse of the [p. 518] machinery of the law, would be punished by imprisonment[3]. Then again every default in appearance brought an amercement on the defaulter and his pledges. Every mistake in pleading, every *miskenning* or *stultiloquium,* brought an amercement on the pleader if the mistake was to be retrieved[4]. A litigant who hoped to get to the end of his suit without an amercement must have been a sanguine man; for he was playing a game of forfeits[5].

2. *Offences punished upon presentment in the local courts.* (2) Presentments The process of presentment had been introduced into the local in turn courts by Henry II., but only, so it seems, for the purpose of and leet. collecting accusations of grave offences. However, in course of time many other presentments were made there. A general understanding seems to have allowed the sheriff in his 'turns' and the lords of franchises in their 'leets' to demand presentments about any matter that concerned the king's rights or his peace. 'Articles of the Turn' or 'Articles of the View of Frankpledge' were drawn up. The different copies which have

---

[1] Note Book, pl. 187, 256, 286, 351, 384, 496, 498, 566, 583, 1105. Y. B. 20–1 Edw. I. p. 41.

[2] Northumberland Assize Rolls, pp. 46–7.

[3] Note Book, pl. 10, 208, 342, 788, 980, 1443, 1633, 1946.

[4] Note Book, pl. 298; Britton, i. 101.

[5] Très ancien coutumier, p. 57, where we learn that already in the twelfth century a Norman baron compared the procedure of the duke's court to a boys' game.

come down to us, though they bear one general character, differ in many details. They leave us doubting whether any of them had received a solemn sanction from the central power[1]. In part their object is to collect accusations of felonies which will come before the king's justices; of this purpose we need say no more. But also they ask for charges of minor offences which are dealt with on the spot by a summary procedure leading to amercements. These offences are most miscellaneous. There are the minor acts of violence, brawls, affrays, bloodshed. There are some minor acts of dishonesty, such as taking other people's pigeons, or knowingly buying stolen meat or stolen clothes. There are nuisances, especially the straitening of highways—these can be summarily redressed or 'addressed.' There are those never ceasing breaches of the assizes of bread and beer.

Present-ments in seignorial courts.

As yet we know more of the seignorial courts and the [p. 519] borough courts than of courts in which the sheriff presided. In the seignorial courts the presentment was used indis-criminately as a means for punishing by amercement all the small breaches of peace and order, even abusive words, and all breaches of the manorial custom; it gave the lord a tight grip on his villein tenants. In the boroughs, as they grew in wealth and independence, the presentment might secure the punishment of the forestaller who raised the price of goods and of the cook who sold unsound victuals, it might even protect a nascent commercial policy[2]. Altogether the local tribunals seem to have been allowed a large liberty in the infliction of amercements.

(3) Pre-sentment in the eyre.

3. *Offences punishable upon presentment before the king's justices.* The justices in eyre of the thirteenth century carry with them a list of interrogatories, known as the Articles of the Eyre (*Capitula Itineris*), which are to be addressed to the local

[1] The set given in the Statutum Walliae (Stat. i. 57) seems to be the only one which comes to us from an authoritative source. See also the apocryphal Statute de Visu Franciplegii (Stat. i. 246); Fleta, p. 112; Britton, i. 179; The Court Baron (Seld. Soc.), pp. 71, 93; and see the Articles for the London Wardmotes, Munim. Gildh. i. pp. 257, 259, 337.

[2] See Leet Jurisdiction in Norwich (Selden Soc.). In London at a later day we find a tariff ordained for small breaches of the peace: for a blow with the fist, 2s. or eight days in Newgate; for drawing blood, 3s. 4d. or twelve days; for drawing a weapon, 6s. 8d. or fifteen days; for drawing blood with a weapon, 20s. or forty days: Munim. Gild. i. 475.

juries. This list grows longer and longer[1]. When we have put
on one side the questions which deal with the felonies, we still
have before us a miscellaneous mass. We find, however, three
main groups of articles. One consists of those which desire
information about the king's proprietary rights, escheats,
wardships and so forth. These do not lead to any punishment
or any trial. Information is all that is wanted; it will
hereafter be used in various ways. Another group asks for
tales about the assumption or misuse of 'franchises.' Here
again, as a general rule, information is all that is immediately
wanted. When the justices' rolls come to the king's treasury,
his advisers will consider whether writs of *Quo warranto* should
[p. 520] not be issued for the recall of liberties that have been abused[2].
A third and a large group of articles relates to the official
misdoings of royal officers, sheriffs, coroners and bailiffs. Sometimes the justices will at once declare that the offender is in
mercy or must be kept in custody. More often they seem to
be content with having got a charge which will be used against
him in an administrative, rather than in a strictly judicial
way. When, for example, he renders his accounts at Westminster he will find that all that he has extorted from the
people he owes to the king.

These three groups being exhausted, we perceive that only Misde-
by slow degrees and in a hap-hazard way do any inquiries about meanours.
ordinary and non-official crimes that are less than felonies steal
their way into the articles. A very large part of the justices'
work will indeed consist of putting in mercy men and communities guilty of a neglect of police duties. This, if we have
regard to actual results, is the main business of the eyre—
for the amount of hanging that is done is contemptible. But
the justices collect in all a very large sum from counties,
hundreds, boroughs, townships and tithings which have mis-
conducted themselves by not presenting, or not arresting

---

[1] The Articles of 1194 and 1198 are given by Hoveden, iii. 263; iv. 61.
Then see the Articles of 1227 for an eyre in the Cinque Ports, Rot. Cl. vol. ii.
p. 213, and Bracton, f. 117 b. Then see Bracton, f. 116, and Ann. Burton,
p. 330, for a later set, and Statutes, vol. i. p. 233, for a yet later. The articles
for the London eyre of 1244 are in Munim. Gildh. i. 79; those for the eyre
of 1321 are in Munim. Gildh. ii. 347; the latter are fully seven times as long
as the former and fill fifteen octavo pages.

[2] For the practice of Edward I.'s day, see Britton, i. 76. In some cases
proceedings were taken upon the presentment; in others a writ was necessary.

criminals. With the coroners' rolls and the sheriffs' rolls before them, they have a check upon the presenting jurors, and probably no single 'community' in the county will escape without amercement. There are a few offences which are specially brought to the notice of the commissioners by the articles. If bread and beer are left to humbler courts, wine and cloth are under the protection of the king's justices. But neither in the articles nor on the eyre rolls of Henry III.'s reign—and it is of that time that we are speaking—do we see any general invitation to present, or many actual presentments of, those crimes which are the typical misdemeanours of the fully developed common law.

Penal
damages.

Useful though this laborious scheme of presentments may have been,—useful because it revealed abuses, because it served as a check upon sheriffs and lords, because it reminded every man of his always neglected police duties—the law did not place much reliance upon it as an engine of punishment. We are now in the act of passing from the sphere of criminal to that [p. 521] of civil justice, and therefore let us notice that under Edward I. a favourite device of our legislators is that of giving double or treble damages to 'the party grieved.' They have little faith in 'communal accusation' or in any procedure that expects either royal officials or people in general to be active in bringing malefactors to justice. More was to be hoped from the man who had suffered. He would move if they made it worth his while. And so in a characteristically English fashion punishment was to be inflicted in the course of civil actions: it took the form of manyfold reparation, of penal and exemplary damages[1].

Actions for
damages.

But we have gone too fast. An 'action for damages' was a

---

[1] Double damages appear in a crude form in Stat. Mert. c. 6: if a male ward marries without the lord's consent, the lord may hold the land for an additional period so as to obtain twice the value of that 'marriage' of which he has been deprived. Then in Stat. West. I. cc. 15, 17, 19, 24, 26, 27, 30, 32, 35, double and treble damages are lavishly distributed. A good example of heavy punishment inflicted in a civil action is given by Stat. West. II. c. 35; an action for 'ravishment of ward' may lead to the perpetual imprisonment of the defendant. It is just possible that actions for manyfold damages were suggested by what the Institutes (4. 6. 21) say of *actiones conceptae in duplum, triplum, quadruplum*. But Bracton, f. 102, had slurred over this passage, and we believe that the general drift of the romano-canonical influence was by this time in favour of a strict separation of criminal from civil causes and an *ex officio* prosecution of crimes.

novelty. By an action for damages we mean one in which the
plaintiff seeks to obtain, not a fixed *bôt* appointed by law, but
a sum of money which the tribunal, having regard to the facts
of the particular case, will assess as a proper compensation for
the wrong that he has suffered. We repeat that this was a
novelty. We may doubt whether Glanvill ever presided at
the hearing of such an action[1].

This may for a moment seem strange. In later days we
learn to look upon the action for damages as the common law's
panacea, and we are told that the inability of the old courts to
give 'specific relief' was a chief cause for the evolution of an
'equitable jurisdiction' in the chancery. But when we look
back to the first age of royal justice we see it doing little else
than punishing crime and giving 'specific relief.' The plaintiff
who goes to the king's court and does not want vengeance,
usually goes to ask for some thing of which he is being
[p. 522] 'deforced.' This thing may be land, or services, or an advowson, or a chattel, or a certain sum of money; but in any
case it is a thing unjustly detained from him. Or, may be,
he demands that a 'final concord' or a covenant may be
observed and performed, or that an account may be rendered,
or that a nuisance may be abated, or that (for sometimes our
king's court will do curiously modern things) a forester may
be appointed to prevent a doweress from committing waste[2].
Even the feoffor who fails in his duty of warranting his
feoffee's title is not condemned to pay damages in money;
he has to give equivalent land. No one of the oldest group
of actions is an action for damages.

*Damages
and speci-
fic relief.*

Moreover, the practice of giving damages even as a supplement for specific relief is one that we may see in the first stage
of its growth. It makes its appearance in an influential quarter,
in the popular assize of novel disseisin. Glanvill's text shows
us the embryo. The writ which begins the action commands
the sheriff 'to cause the tenement to be reseised of the chattels
taken in it' by the disseisor, and 'to cause the tenement with
the chattels to be in peace' until the hearing of the cause[3]. So
the disseisee is to recover the chattels as well as the land of

*Damages
as supple-
mentary
relief.*

---

[1] Glanvill, x. 13, holds that if a thing that has been lent perishes in the
borrower's hands, he is bound to return its *rationabile pretium*. He then asks
how this is to be assessed, and gives no answer.

[2] Note Book, pl. 56; Bracton, f. 316.　　　　[3] Glanvill, xiii. 33.

which he has been dispossessed; but even this is specific relief. We further learn, however, that the disseisee can obtain the 'fruits' of the tenement from the disseisor, and we are left to imagine that, if he can not get the corn or hay itself, he may be able to get money instead[1]. In a few years all had changed; Bracton has noticed the change[2]. The sheriff was no longer expected to 'reseise the tenement' of the abstracted chattels; the recognitors in the assize were being told to estimate in money the *dampna* which the disseisee had suffered. Along with the land he now 'recovered' a sum of money assessed as a compensation for the wrong done him[3]. Long the novel disseisin remained the only action in which both land and damages could be obtained; slowly in the course of the thirteenth century our legislators multiplied the cases in which this double remedy was to be had[4].

Growth of actions for damages.
When the sacred 'freehold' was not concerned, the hands [p. 523] of the justices were freer. They could award damages as a subsidiary remedy in actions of detinue, debt and the like[5]. The assize of novel disseisin suggested to them a method of assessing pecuniary compensation: the verdict of a jury. To find the exact place at which they first crossed the narrow line which divides an action for mere damages from an action in which damages may be given as complementary to the recovery of a specific thing or specific debt would be a toilsome task[6]. Here it must suffice that one by one there came into existence actions in which the plaintiff could obtain nothing but a money compensation assessed by justices or jurors. In this context we may mention the action for *vee de naam* (*de vetito namii*) brought against a distrainor, who, though he has now given back the beasts, has been guilty of detaining them 'against gage and pledge'; also those frequent actions brought against men who have persisted in going to the ecclesiastical tribunals

---

[1] Glanvill, xiii. 38, 39.   [2] Bracton, f. 186 b § 7: 'illud hodie non observatur.'

[3] Already in 1200; Select Civil Pleas, pl. 4.

[4] Stat. Merton, c. 1, damages for the doweress, for widows are favoured persons; Stat. Marlb. c. 16, damages against the lord in the mort d'ancestor, for he is almost as guilty as a disseisor; Stat. Glouc. c. 1, a very general enactment.

[5] Some of the continental folk laws know what seems to be an established *bót* for delay in payment, which is called *dilatura*, or *wirdira*; Brunner, D. R. G., ii. 624.

[6] Select Civil Pleas, pl. 86: in 1201 we have a claim for mere damages.

after receipt of a royal prohibition[1]. But there is one all-important action which is stealing slowly to the front, the action of trespass (*de transgressione*) against those who to a plaintiff's damage have broken the king's peace with force and arms. Though early precedents may be found for it, this fertile mother of actions was only beginning her reign in the [p. 524] last years of Henry III. Her progeny throve and multiplied, until a time came when, the older forms having been neglected, an action for damages, an action which traced descent from the *breve de transgressione*, seemed to be almost the only remedy offered by the common law[2].

What did men before they had this action? What did they in Glanvill's day? For one thing, we suspect that they uttered 'words of felony' upon slight provocation. For another thing, the old action of theft could be used for the recovery of goods from an honest hand, and a two-fold *bót* could sometimes be obtained[3]. As to blows and bruises, we take it that they sued for some pre-appointed *bót* in the local courts. The king was not to be troubled with such trifles. The early disappearance from English law of the pre-appointed *bót* is remarkable. The sister-law of Normandy after Bracton's death still knew a tariff for the minor acts of violence—five shillings for a slap, eighteen for a knock-down blow, thirty-six for a wound; but this tariff, simple when compared with those of older days, apparently obtained only among the roturiers, and

The days before 'damages.'

---

[1] The writs in Glanvill, xii. 12, 15, which touch replevin suppose that the chattels are still in the distrainor's hands and the action aims at specific relief. The action (xii. 22) for impleading in court Christian may at first have aimed only at punishment. But soon we see the action against a distrainor who has given up the chattels; Note Book, pl. 477. The action on a prohibition is brought for damages; Ibid. pl. 1423. Damages can be obtained in actions of 'mesne'; Ibid. pl. 390, 506; but even here again the plaintiff is thought of as claiming specific relief, 'acquittance' from a burden. For a long time the plaintiff in an action of covenant is usually seeking possession of a tenement. On the whole we seem to be right in regarding two actions, viz. novel disseisin and trespass, as the chief, though not the only, channels by which damages spread, and the way in which damages are given in the novel disseisin as a substitute for 'fruits' recovered in specie shows that the lawyers are not blindly 'receiving' the romano-canonical procedure, but are elaborating home-grown materials.

[2] As to trespass, see above, vol. ii. pp. 108, 166. After looking through some unprinted rolls, we feel entitled to say that this action was still uncommon in 1250, but was quite common in 1272.

[3] See above, vol. ii. p. 495.

the compensation due to a knight was a suit of armour[1]. Unfortunately the records of our local courts do not begin until the influence of Westminster is supreme and its action for damages is well known throughout the country; still we should not be surprised to find that the doomsmen of the hall-moots when they assigned damages for a blow or a 'villein word' were guided by traditional and half-forgotten tariffs and thought but little of 'the circumstances of the particular case[2].'

Actions of trespass.

The writs of trespass are closely connected with the appeals [p. 525] for felony. The action of trespass is, we may say, an attenuated appeal. The charge of *felonia* is omitted; no battle is offered; but the basis of the action is a wrong done to the plaintiff in his body, his goods or his land ' by force and arms and against the king's peace.' In course of time these sonorous words will become little better than a hollow sound; there will be a trespass with force and arms if a man's body, goods or land have been unlawfully touched. From this we may gather that the court had never taken very seriously the 'arms' of the writ or fixed a minimum for the 'force' that would beget an action. Still the action was aimed at serious breaches of the king's peace, and, so far as we can see, the court in Henry III.'s reign was seldom, if ever, troubled with 'technical trespasses' or claims for 'nominal damages[3].' If we take the plaintiffs at their word,

---

[1] Somma, p. 204; Ancienne coutume, c. 85, ed. de Gruchy, p. 195. For Anjou, see Viollet, Établissements, i. 245.

[2] In Leg. Will. i. 10, a wounded man, besides the *bót* for the wound, receives a sum of money fixed by his own oath. This our French text calls *sun lecheof*. The Latin text says *lichfe quantum scilicet in curam vulneris expendit*. Schmid would make this into *líc-feoh*, body-money. But Dr Murray tells us that it is very probably *léce-feoh, léce-feoh*, the leech fee. With the Leis Williame should be compared a curious clause in the Preston custumal: Dobson and Harland, History of Preston Gild, p. 76. In the Lombard laws the wounder in addition to the price of the wound must pay *mercedes medici*, 'the doctor's bill'; Brunner, D. R. G., ii. 613; Palgrave, Commonwealth, p. cxi. In Leg. Henr. 39. 84, there are exceedingly curious passages which show that in the twelfth century the man who sued for a *bót* when he had been beaten was regarded with contempt. Some courts would in such a case exact a *wite* from the stricken as well as the striker. This is justified by a batch of proverbs: 'Ubi unus non vult, duo non certant; et omnis unlaga frater est alterius; et qui respondet stulto iuxta stultitiam suam similis est eius.' The first of these phrases means that it takes two to make a quarrel. But at any rate it is dirty to ask a *bót* for dry blows.

[3] In 1279 a man recovers six pence for a blow on the head; Northumberland Assize Rolls, p. 351.

there have been force enough and arms enough. There has been a marauding foray; a few years earlier it would have given rise to a batch of appeals for wounds and robbery[1]. Even when we have made allowance for the froth of 'common form,' we see that there are often some twenty defendants, and this tells a tale of deliberate violence, of rapine and pillage[2]. Edward I. when he introduced this action into Wales set forth in strong words its punitive and exemplary character[3].

In the days when the writ of trespass was taking a foremost *Limits of* place in the scheme of actions, the king's court had its hands *trespass.* full if it was to redress and punish the wrongs done by gentlemen who at the head of armed bands of retainers ravaged the manors of their neighbours. We must not therefore expect to find cases which indicate the limits of trespass. We may guess [p. 526] that some self-defence was permissible[4], while all self-help, unless it took the form of the timely ejectment of a disseisor, was strictly prohibited. Also we may guess that this somewhat terrible action could not have been used against those who were not to be charged with any assault on a person, entry on land or asportation of goods, but were guilty of some misfeasance while engaged in a lawful operation. In later days, slowly and with difficulty, the court gave an action against the clumsy smith who lames the horse that he is shoeing, against the stupid surgeon who poisons the wound that he should cure[5]. Such persons could not be charged with breaking the king's peace by force and arms. We may well doubt whether Bracton or any contemporary lawyer would have told them that they had committed no tort, we may perhaps doubt whether they could not have been successfully sued in some of the local courts; but the king's justices were not as yet busied with these questions, and such records of the lowlier tribunals as are in print do not hold out much encouragement to the investigator who is in search of a medieval law of negligence, though he might

---

[1] Britton, ii. 123, advises the wounded man to bring an action of trespass, though an appeal of felony is open to him.

[2] Northumberland Assize Rolls, p. 162: an action of trespass for burning a mill is brought against 128 defendants.

[3] Stat. Wall. c. xi. (Statutes, i. 66): 'Ita quod castigatio illa sit aliis in exemplum et timorem praebeat delinquendi.'

[4] Self-defence could be pleaded even in an appeal of mayhem: Note Book. pl. 1084.

[5] Ames, History of Assumpsit, Harv. L. R. ii. pp. 2–4.

find some rules, probably severe rules, about damage done by straying cattle, goring oxen, biting dogs and fire[1]. Hardly a germ is to be found of any idea which will answer to the Roman *culpa* or become our modern negligence[2].

Master's liability. In the dominance over our growing law of torts exercised by an action which came of a penal stock we may find an explanation of a debated episode of legal history, namely, the genesis of 'employer's liability[3].' In order to clear the field, we may take for granted that the man who commands a trespass, which is committed in obedience to his command, is himself a trespasser. About this our law of the thirteenth century and of much earlier [p. 527] times had no doubt whatever. From of old the 'rede-bane' had been as guilty as the 'deed-bane[4].' What is done by a man's command may be imputed to him as though it were his own act. From the grave crimes we may argue *a fortiori* to the minor offences, though the law in all cases observed that strict rule of logic which required that a principal should be convicted or outlawed before an accessory was put on his trial[5]. All this, however, lies beside our present mark, for we would raise the question as to the liability of superiors for torts which they have not commanded but which have been committed by their inferiors.

Recent history of master's liability. Now it would seem that our present doctrine about the liability of a master for a tort committed by a servant who was 'acting within the scope of his employment' can hardly be traced in any definite shape beyond the Revolution of 1688[6]. Before that date there lie several centuries, comprising the age

---

[1] As to these matters, see Wigmore, Responsibility for Tortious Actions, Harv. L. R. vii. 315, 383, 441. As to fire, see the Chester custom in Domesday Book, i. 262 b: 'Si ignis civitatem comburebat, de cuius domo exibat emendabat per iij. oras denariorum et suo propinquiori vicino dabat ij. solidos.' Apparently the liability is absolute.

[2] Though Bracton can speak of *culpa* (*e.g.* f. 155, 'nec dolus nec culpa') this word is not received. As to *negligentia*, which Bracton, f. 146 uses in connexion with fire, this seems to have as its precursors *stultitia*, *insipientia* (Note Book, pl. 1249), Fr. *folie*.

[3] See the two learned articles on Agency by Mr Justice Holmes, Harv. L. R. iv. 346 : v. 1.

[4] See above, p. 509.

[5] Placit. Abbrev. 129 (Linc.); Rot. Parl. i. 24–5. In later days it was otherwise; the commander of a trespass could be treated as a principal, or, in other words, the rule as to principal and accessory was confined to cases of felony.

[6] The principal cases and dicta are conveniently collected by Mr Wigmore in Harv. L. R. vii. 330, 383.

of the Year Books and the days of Tudors and Stuarts, during which exceedingly few hints are given to us of any responsibility of a master for acts that he has not commanded[1], and, when our new rule is first taking shape, we see it working under cover of phrases which still thrust command to the forefront, phrases which teach that a master is liable for acts that he has 'impliedly,' as well as for those which he has 'expressly commanded.'

On the other hand, it is hardly to be doubted that, if we go back far enough, we shall see a measure of responsibility far severer than that which we now apply to 'masters' or 'employers,' applied to some superiors. A man was absolutely liable for the acts of his slaves—though some penal consequences he might be able to escape by a noxal surrender—and a householder was in all probability liable for what was done by the free members of his household. A lord, on the other hand, could not be charged with the acts of his free 'men,' his tenants or retainers, who formed no part of his family. The most that could be expected of him was that he should produce them in court so that they might 'stand to right' if any one accused them. Then already in the dim age that lies behind the Norman Conquest we seem to see the lords reducing their liability. In Cnut's day they would, if they could, ignore the difference between their slaves and those numerous free, but very dependent tenants who would soon be called *villani*[2]. At a yet earlier time the duty of producing their free men in court had been slipping from their shoulders. They had been allowed to substitute for it the duty of keeping their men in groups, such that each group would be solidly liable for the production of all its members[3]. At the end of the twelfth century almost every vestige of the lord's liability had disappeared. Anything that we could call slavery was extinct. The mere relationship between lord and villein did not make the one responsible for the acts of the other. The lord was not even bound to produce his villein in court. The villeins were in frankpledge. As to the liability of the groups of pledges,

<p 528> (margin note): Liability of slave-owner and house-father in old law.

---

[1] Y. B. 2 Hen. IV. f. 18 (Pasch. pl. 6), a case relating to the custody of fire, seems to be the most important case in the Year Books.

[2] Cnut, II. 20 § 1.

[3] Æthelstan, III. 7. We believe that this text points to the origin of frankpledge; but this much-debated point can not be discussed here.

we may perhaps see traces of a rule which would, not merely subject the tithing to an amercement if it failed to produce an accused member, but would exact from it a recompense for the wrong that he had done[1]. But in the thirteenth century the tithing has only to produce members charged with felony, and, if it makes default, it is merely amerced.

House-father's liability in Bracton's day.

Any theory therefore that would connect our 'employer's liability' with slavery has before it a difficult task. Between the modern employer and the slave-owner stand some centuries of villeinage, and the medieval lord was not liable for the acts of his villein. A more hopeful line of tradition may lie within the household. The householder of Bracton's day was bound to produce any member of his mainpast or household who was accused of felony, and, failing to do so, was amerced, but only amerced. We may detect, however, some scattered traces of a civil liability for wrongs, and very possibly other traces would be found were the rolls of our local courts systematically perused. In a book of precedents for pleas in manorial courts which comes [p. 529] from the last half of the thirteenth century we find that a defendant, who is charged with the act of two men who cut stubble in the plaintiff's close, pleads that these men were not of his mainpast but labourers hired from day to day[2].

Tort, crime and master's liability.

The king's courts, however, were approaching the field of tort through the field of crime. A criminal procedure which aimed solely at pure punishment, at loss of life or member, was being established, and the time had long gone by when a man could be made to answer for such an act as homicide if he had neither done nor taken part in, nor commanded, nor counselled the deed :—*quia quis pro alieno facto non est puniendus*, said Edward I.[3] To exact a *wer* from the slayer's master had been possible ; to send the master to the gallows—no one wished to

---

[1] Leg. Edw. Conf. c. 20. But this is not high authority.

[2] The Court Baron (Selden Soc.), pp. 36, 38, 53; Harvard Law Rev. vii. 332–3. Leg. Henr. 66 § 7: 'Si manupastus alicuius accusetur de furto, solus paterfamilias emendare potest, si velit, fracta lege sine praeiurante.' We read this to mean that the housefather may if he pleases defend an accusation for theft brought against his mainpast. The nature of his oath indicated by the last words of the clause we can not here discuss. The householder of Cnut's day was bound to produce a member of his family accused of crime and, failing to do so, had to pay the accused man's *wer* to the king, a far heavier penalty than an amercement of the thirteenth century; Cnut, II. 31; Leg. Henr. 41 § 6.

[3] Stat. West. II. c. 35.

do that. In Henry III.'s day disseisin was still for the king's court the one interesting misdeed that did not involve felony, and it is only about disseisin and wrongful distraint that Bracton has given us anything that can be called a doctrine of employer's liability. If we understand him rightly, he holds that if X's servants are guilty of disseising A, then X can not at once be charged with a disseisin; but it is his duty to make amends to A, and if X after the facts have been brought to his knowledge refuses to make amends, then he is a disseisor and can be sued. It is our misfortune that in this context we read only of disseisin and wrongful distraint, for these are wrongs of subtraction, and it is easy to say that if a man, when he knows what has happened, refuses to give up the land or beasts that his underlings have grabbed for him, he ratifies or 'avows' their act and becomes a participator in the wrong. We are not sure that Bracton means more than this[1]. What he would [p. 530] have said had the wrong consisted, not in the subtraction of a thing for the master's use, but in some damage to person, lands, or goods, we can not say for certain, but we imagine that he would have absolved the master if he neither commanded nor ratified the wrongful act. The only action to which such damage could have given rise was the penal *quare vi et armis.* Soon after his day this action came to the fore and for some centuries it reigned over our law of torts. Throughout the Year Books men are 'punished' for trespasses, and, when we are to be told that an action of trespass will not lie against the master, we are told that the master is not to be 'punished' for his servants' trespasses—*quia quis pro alieno facto non est puniendus*[2].

That our common law in thus sparing the master from civil liability was not in full harmony with current morality is possible[3]; and the local courts may have continued to enforce Identification of master and servant.

---

[1] Bracton, f. 158 b, 171, 172 b, 204 b. On the whole what Bracton says hardly goes beyond an application of the maxim *Ratihabitio retrotrahitur*, which he quotes, and which was current among the lawyers of Edward I.'s time; Y. B. 30–1 Edw. I. p. 129. See also Note Book, pl. 779, 781. Somersetshire Pleas, pl. 1427, 1437, 1497, cases heard by Bracton. These cases do not clearly indicate any other principle.

[2] Harv. L. R. vii. 387–391. The usual dictum in the sixteenth century is that if I send my servant to make a distress and he misuses the thing that he takes, I shall not be 'punished.'

[3] Mr Wigmore, Harv. L. R. vii. 384, sees for a century after 1300 'an undercurrent of feeling' in favour of the master's liability.

an old doctrine about the mainpast; but we gravely doubt
whether there was any wide discrepancy between the law of the
king's court and common opinion, and in particular we can not
believe that either law or morality was guilty of any theory of
'identification[1].' We see this best in the case in which there was
most temptation towards such a theory, the case of husband and
wife. Lawyers were always ready to proclaim that husband
and wife are one, but, as already said, they never threw much
real weight upon this impossible dogma[2]. Of course we do not
expect to hear that they hanged the husband for the wife's
felonies[3]: but they held that wrongs done by the wife died with
her. So of wrongs done by the monk; you can not sue the
abbot after the offender's death. But further, if we look for
the best legal ideas of the thirteenth century to Edward I.'s [p. 531]
statutes, we shall see no 'identification' of the servant with the
master and, what is more, no very strong feeling in favour of
'employer's liability.' It is true that a sheriff is in some cases
absolutely responsible for the acts of his underlings, in particular he must account to the king for all that they receive[4];
but we are never safe in drawing inferences about general
principles from the rigorous law that is meted out to royal
officers or royal debtors[5]. We see, however, that the lords of
franchises are not made responsible for all the unauthorized
acts of their bailiffs. If such a lord is guilty of taking out-
rageous toll, his franchise is to be seized into the king's hands;
but if his bailiff does the like without commandment, the
bailiff must pay double damages and go to prison for forty
days[6].

---

[1] Mr Justice Holmes, Harv. L. R. iv. 354 and v. 1, ascribes to this fiction a
greater efficacy than we can allow it, at all events within the sphere of tort.

[2] See above, p. 403. Y. B. 32–3 Edw. I. p. 474: 'the act of the wife is the
act of the husband.'

[3] Gloucestershire Pleas, pl. 244. In 1221 a husband escapes with a fine of
a half-mark for not having produced a wife accused of arson.

[4] Stat. West. I. c. 19: 'And let every sheriff beware that he have a receiver
for whom he will answer, for the king will betake himself for all [money
received] against the sheriff and his heirs.'

[5] Down to Henry II.'s day the exchequer would seize the chattels of knights
to satisfy a debt due from their lord to the king. Dial. de Scac. ii. 14.
Respondeat inferior.

[6] Stat. West. I. c. 31. See also cc. 9, 15. In 1256 Northumbrian jurors
present that the bailiff of Robert de Ros arrested a man and kept him in prison
for two days. 'Postea quia praedicti iuratores dicunt super sacramentum

To us however at this moment the chief interest of these statutes lies in their introduction of the phrase *Respondeat superior.* In no case does this phrase point to an absolute liability of the superior for wrongs done by the inferior, or even for those done 'in the course of his employment.' In all cases it points to a merely subsidiary liability of the superior, which can only be enforced against him when it is proved or patent that the inferior can not pay for his own misdeed[1]. This [p. 532] indicates, as we believe, what has first and last been one of the main causes of 'employer's liability.' Should we now-a-days hold masters answerable for the uncommanded torts of their servants if normally servants were able to pay for the damage that they do? We do not answer the question; for no law, except a fanciful law of nature, has ever been able to ignore the economic stratification of society, while the existence of large classes of men 'from whom no right can be had' has raised difficult problems for politics and for jurisprudence ever since the days of Æthelstan. However, our common law when it took shape in Edward I.'s day did not, unless we are much misled, make masters pay for acts that they had neither

suum quod ostensum fuit praedicto Roberto de Ros de praedicta captione, et ipse illam emendare noluit, ideo praedictus Robertus in misericordia et constabularius capiatur.' See Northumberland Assize Rolls, 115. The constable's act is not attributed to the castellan; he only became guilty when he refused to release the prisoner.

[1] Stat. West. II. c. 2: When beasts are replevied, the sheriff is to exact security for their return to the distrainor in case a return is awarded. If any exact pledges in any other form, he shall answer for the price of the beasts, and if a bailiff does this 'et non habeat unde reddat, respondeat superior suus.' Stat. West. II. c. 11: When an accountant is committed to gaol, if the keeper allows him to escape, the keeper must pay double damages. If the keeper can not pay, 'respondeat superior suus.' Articuli super Cartas (28 Ed. I.), c. 18: An escheator must answer for waste committed by a subescheator, if the latter can not pay for it. Stat. West. II. c. 43: The conservators of the liberties of the Templars and Hospitallers appoint subordinates to hold ecclesiastical courts, in which men are sued for matters cognizable in the king's courts. If the obedientiaries of the order offend in this matter, 'pro facto ipsorum respondeant sui superiores ac si de proprio facto suo convicti essent.' This last case is analogous to the others, for the obedientiary, being civilly dead, can not be sued. See also the ordinance as to the liability of the sheriff's clerk; Statutes, i. 213. The liability of the county to the king for sums due from the coroner is of the same kind, a subsidiary liability; see Fourth Institute, 114, where Coke speaks of *Respondeat superior.* But in the case of communities we come upon a different idea; the community is liable for wrongs done by any member of it in the prosecution of communal interests.

commanded nor ratified. Had it done so, it would have
'punished' a man for an offence in which he had no part[1].

Damage and injury. Besides trespasses in the narrow sense of the word, namely,
wrongs which give birth to the action *quare vi et armis*, our
law knows many other wrongs which are redressed in civil
actions. But these are, at least for the more part, infringements of proprietary rights or of seisin, and the actions for
them are, in the phrase that Bracton adopts, *rei persecutoriae*.
To what we have said of them in various parts of this book we
must here add nothing. The action, however, for the abatement of a nuisance deserves a word, because it gave Bracton
occasion to use a phrase that afterwards became famous. The
nuisance (*nocumentum*) that is to be actionable must do both [p. 533]
'damage' and 'injury.' If I erect a mill upon my land and so
subtract customers from your mill, I do you damage, but no
injury. We see here an incipient attempt to analyze the
actionable wrong; few similar attempts will be made for many
years to come[2].

We must now remark some notable defects in our nascent
'law of torts.'

Deceit. Protection against unlawful force has reached, at least in
theory, a high stage of perfection while protection against

---

[1] Bogo de Clare's case (1290), Rot. Parl. i. 24, is important. Action against
Bogo by a summoner of an ecclesiastical court who has been ill treated by
members of Bogo's mainpast and compelled to eat certain letters of citation.
Action dismissed, because plaintiff does not allege that Bogo did or commanded
the wrong. Thereupon, because this wrong was done within the verge of the
palace, the king takes the matter up and Bogo has to produce all his *familia*;
but after all he is dismissed as the offenders can not be found.

[2] As to the phrase *damnum absque iniuria*, see Pollock, Law of Torts,
5th ed. p. 142. Bracton, f. 221, 24 b, 45 b, 92 b, contrasts *iniuria* with *damnum*.
For him in this context (see f. 45 b) *iniuria* is *omne id quod non iure fit*. Our
transgressio or *trespass* has a fate similar to that of the Roman *iniuria*. It
will stand for *omne id quod non iure fit* (see above, p. 512), but under the
influence of the *quare vi et armis* begins to signify in particular one group of
actionable wrongs. Then *tort* was a very wide word. The formula of defence
shows us Fr. *tort et force* = Lat. *vis et iniuria* and, by means of a Scottish Book
(Leges Quatuor Burgorum, Statutes of Scotland, i. p. 338), we may equate this
with an Eng. *wrong and unlaw*. So far as we have observed, *iniuria* is hardly
ever used (except by Bracton in a few romance passages) to stand for anything
narrower than *omne id quod non iure fit*. Thus all our terms are at starting
very large and loose; still no medieval lawyer would have been guilty of that
detestable abuse of *injury* that is common among us now. One of the few
words descriptive of wrong that obtains a specific sense in the age with which
we are dealing is Lat. *nocumentum*, Fr. *nuisance.*

fraud is yet in its infancy. In the thirteenth century our
king's court had in general no remedy for the man who to his
damage had trusted the word of a liar. Already in John's
day it knew a writ of deceit (*breve de deceptione*)[1]; but for
a long time the only cause which will justify the issue of
such a writ is a deceit of the court (*deceptio curiae*). The
defendant is to answer, not only the private person whom he
has defrauded, but also and in the first instance the king;
he is charged with having in some fashion or another 'seduced'
or deceived the court. In modern terms we may say that the
cause of action is no mere fraud, but a fraudulent perversion
of the course of justice. Common as examples of 'deceit'
are the cases in which there is personation, the bringing or
defending of an action in the name of one who has given no
authority for the use of his name. Common also is the case
of the attorney who colludes with his client's adversary. In
these and similar cases the person who is defrauded can obtain
[p. 534] sometimes a money compensation, sometimes a more specific
remedy, the collusive proceedings being annulled; but the
punitive element in the action is strong; the defendant has
deceived the court and should be sent to gaol; he must answer
the king as well as 'the party grieved.' We must wait for
a later age before we shall see the court extending the action
of deceit beyond these narrow limits, and giving in a general
way relief to those who have suffered by placing faith in a
lie[2].

We can hardly suppose that in this case lowlier tribunals $\quad$ Fraud as
were doing the work that the king's court left undone. Even $\quad$ a defence.
as a defence we seldom read of fraud. Bracton indeed can
speak of the *exceptio doli*, just as he can speak of the *exceptio*
which is founded on *metus*[3]; but, while we should have no

---

[1] Select Civil Pleas, pl. 111 [A.D. 1201].

[2] Placit. Abbrev. p. 62 Buck.; p. 106 Kent; Note Book, pl. 10, 208, 500,
645, 1173, 1184, 1946; Reg. Brev. Orig. f. 112; Fitz. Nat. Brev. p. 96; Fitz.
Abr. *Disceit*. The following is an interesting instance: Coram Rege Roll,
Mich. 9–10 Edw. I. (No. 64) m. 46 d (unprinted): Adam is attached to answer
the king and Christiana, Adam's wife, why by producing a woman who
personated Christiana he levied a fine of Christiana's land, 'et unde praedicta
Christiana queritur quod praedictus Adam praedictam falsitatem et deceptionem
fecit ad exheredationem suam et deceptionem curiae domini Regis manifestam
...unde dicit quod deteriorata est et dampnum habet ad valentiam centum
librarum.' Adam, unable to deny the charge, goes to gaol.

[3] Bracton, f. 396 b, 398 b.

difficulty in finding cases which illustrate a growing doctrine of 'duress[1],' it would not be easy to come by instances in which a defendant relies upon fraud, except where the fraud consists in an abuse of the machinery of the law. Taking the execution of a charter as the typical 'act in the law,' we are warranted in believing that the person whose seal it bore might defend himself by alleging that he was tricked into sealing an instrument of one kind while he thought that it was an instrument of another kind[2]. In later days he might have said in such a case that the charter was 'not his deed[3]'; but the English *exceptio doli* seems to have stopped here. In truth the law would hardly allow that a man could protect himself against a document which bore the impress of his seal, even though he was ready to assert that the seal had been affixed without [p. 535] his authority and by the fraudulent act of another[4]. Our law, —though quite willing to admit in vague phrase that no one should be suffered to gain anything by fraud[5],—was inclined to hold that a man has himself to thank if he is misled by deceit: —'It is his folly.'

Defamation. The king's court gave no action for defamation. This in our eyes will seem both a serious and a curious defect in the justice that it administered. What is usually accounted the first known instance of such an action comes from the year 1356, and even in that instance the slander was complicated with contempt of court[6]. In 1295 a picturesque dispute between two Irish magnates had been removed to Westminster, and Edward I.'s court declared in solemn fashion that it would not entertain pleas of defamation; in the Irish court battle had been waged[7]. At the end of the middle ages we may see the

---

[1] Note Book, pl. 182, 200, 229, 243, 750, 1126, 1643, 1913; Bracton, f. 16 b.

[2] Bracton, f. 396 b: 'Item si per dolum, ut si donatorius fecit sibi cartam de feoffamento, ubi fecisse debuit cyrographum de termino.' Fleta, p. 424.

[3] Y. B. 30 Edw. III. f. 31. For later law, see *Thoroughgood's Case*, 2 Coke's Reports, 9 a.

[4] Glanvill, x. 12: 'et suae malae custodiae imputet si damnum incurrat per sigillum suum male custoditum.' The rule takes a milder form in Bracton, f. 396 b, Fleta, p. 424, and Britton, i. 163, 165.

[5] Reg. Brev. Orig. f. 227: 'et fraus et dolus nemini debent patrocinari.' Placit. Abbrev. p. 237 (26 Edw. I.): 'cum contemptus, fraus et dolus in curia Regis nemini debent subvenire.'

[6] Lib. Ass. f. 177, pl. 19 (30 Edw. III.).

[7] Rot. Parl. i. 133: 'et non sit usitatum in regno isto placitare in curia Regis placita de defamationibus.'

royal justices beginning to reconsider their doctrine and to foster an 'action on the case for words'; but they were by this time hampered by the rival pretensions of the courts Christian[1]. The tribunals of the church had been allowed to punish defamation as a sin, and the province which had thus been appropriated by the canonists was not very easily recovered from them until the Protestant reformation had weakened their hands[2].

We should be much mistaken, however, if we believed that the temporal law of the middle ages gave no action to the defamed. Nothing could be less true than that our ancestors in the days of their barbarism could only feel blows and treated hard words as of no account. Even the rude *Lex Salica* decrees that if one calls a man 'wolf' or 'hare' one must pay him three [p. 536] shillings, while if one calls a woman 'harlot,' and can not prove the truth of the charge, one must pay her forty-five shillings[3]. The oldest English laws exact *bót* and *wíte* if one gives another bad names[4]. In the Norman Custumal it is written that the man who has falsely called another 'thief' or 'manslayer' must pay damages, and, holding his nose with his fingers, must publicly confess himself a liar[5]. Shame was keenly felt. In almost every action before an English local court of the thirteenth century the plaintiff will claim compensation, not only for the damage (*damnum*) but also for the shame (*huntage, hontage, dedecus, pudor, vituperium*) that has been done him[6], and we may suspect that in the king's court this element was not

(margin: Defamation in the local courts.)

---

[1] Y. B. 22 Edw. IV. f. 20 (Trin. pl. 47); f. 29 (Mich. pl. 9); 12 Hen. VII. f. 22 (Trin. pl. 2).

[2] *Circumspecte Agatis*, Statutes, vol. i. p. 101; *Articuli Cleri*, Statutes, vol. i. 171. See *Palmer* v. *Thorpe*, 4 Coke's Reports, 20 a.

[3] Lex Salica, tit. 30 (Hessels and Kern, col. 181); Brunner, D. R. G. ii. 672.

[4] Hloth. and Ead. c. 11.

[5] Ancienne coutume, cap. 86 (ed. de Gruchy, p. 197); Somma, p. 207: 'nasum suum digitis suis per summitatem tenebit.' For Anjou, see Viollet, Établissements, i. 243.

[6] Select Pleas in Manorial Courts (Selden Soc.), pp. 13, 56, 138 ff.; The Court Baron (Selden Soc.), *passim*, especially p. 47, where even in an action of debt the plaintiff requires amends for shame as well as for damage. We may believe that the same formula had been used in the king's court, but that the practice of expressly asking a compensation for disgrace died out in the first half of the thirteenth century. Select Civil Pleas, pl. 183: in John's reign the Bishop of Ely has wronged the Abbot of St Edmunds, doing him shame to the amount of £100 and damage to the amount of 100 marks.

neglected when compensation was awarded[1]. But further, we find that in the local courts, not only were bad words punished upon presentment in a summary way, but regular actions for defamation were common[2]. We may gather that in such an action the defendant might allege that his words were true; *veritas non est defamatio*[3]. We may gather that the English for *meretrix* was actionable, though an interchange of this against the English for *latro* left one shilling due to the man[4]. We already hear that a slander was uttered 'of malice aforethought,' and sometimes a plaintiff alleges 'special damage[5].' But until further researches have been made among the records [p. 537] of our manorial courts, we shall know little of the medieval law of defamation. Probably in this matter those courts did good enough justice, and for this reason it was that no royal writ was devised for the relief of the slandered[6]. In later days, when the old moots were decaying, the ecclesiastical procedure against the sin of defamation seems to have been regarded as the usual, if not the only, engine which could be brought to bear upon cases of libel and slander, and in yet later days the king's court had some difficulty in asserting its claims over a tract of law that it had once despised[7].

[1] Thus when in 1256 Robert de Ros has to pay £20 in damages for having driven off to his castle two oxen and two horses belonging to the Prior of Kirkham, it is clear that he is not making compensation merely for 'pecuniary damage.' See Northumberland Assize Rolls, pp. 43–4.

[2] Select Pleas in Manorial Courts, pp. 19, 36, 82, 95, 109, 116, 143, 170; The Court Baron, pp. 48, 57, 61, 125, 133, 136.

[3] Select Pleas in Manorial Courts, p. 82.

[4] The Court Baron, p. 133.

[5] Rolls of the court of the Hundred of Wisbech, now in the Bishop's Palace at Ely, 34 Edw. I. (A.D. 1306): 'J. G. queritur de T. R. de placito quare...adivit Magistrum Gerardum de Stuthburi, Magistrum negotiorum Terrae Sanctae, apud Ely, et clericos suos ibidem, et ipsum J. accusavit *malitia praecogitata*, dicendo quod ipse J. debuit perturbasse negotium Terrae Sanctae, contradicendo ne quis legaret anulos et firmacula in subsidium Terrae Sanctae, per quam accusationem dictus J. fuit summonitus coram clericis praedicti Magistri...et adiudicatus fuit ad purgationem suam cum quinta manu ...pro qua purgatione redimenda dictus J. solvit xiij. denarios et ulterius expendidit catalla sua ad valentiam iij. solidorum, ad dampnum suum dimidiae marcae etc.'

[6] Bracton, f. 155, but in Roman phrase, speaks of an action for injurious words as a possibility: 'Fit autem iniuria, non solum cum quis pugno percussus fuerit...vero cum ei convitium dictum fuerit, vel de eo factum carmen famosum et huiusmodi.'

[7] If we were dealing with the law of the later middle ages, we should have to speak of the statutes against *scandalum magnatum*; Stat. West. I. c. 34;

Wrongful prosecution may be regarded as an aggravated Wrongful prosecution.
form of defamation. It is a wrong of which ancient law speaks
fiercely. In England before the Conquest a man might lose his
tongue or have to redeem it with his full *wer* if he brought a
false and scandalous accusation[1]. Probably the law only wanted
to punish the accuser who made a charge which he knew to be
false; but it had little power of distinguishing the pardonable
mistake from the wicked lie, and there was a strong feeling
that men should not make charges that they could not prove.
Roman influence would not tend to weaken this feeling. The
law of the later empire required that any one bringing a
criminal charge should bind himself to suffer in case of failure
the penalty that he had endeavoured to call down upon his
adversary[2]. So soon as our judicial records begin, we see that
[p. 538] an amercement is inflicted upon every unsuccessful plaintiff
pro falso clamore suo, whatever may have been the cause of his
failure. In the appeal of felony the appellor, vanquished in
battle, still pays the old *wíte* of sixty shillings to the king[3].
For a time, however, appeals were being encouraged, and we
may see an appellor excused from punishment *quia pugnavit pro
Rege*[4]. Under Edward I. the tide turned, and a statute decreed
that if the appellee was acquitted, his accuser should lie in
prison for a year and pay damages by way of recompense for
the imprisonment and infamy that he had brought upon the
innocent. This statute is a typical piece of medieval legislation.
It desires to punish malicious appeals; it actually punishes
every appeal that ends in an acquittal[5]. Even before this
statute an acquitted appellee may have had an action against
his accuser[6]. A few years later it was necessary to invent the
writ of conspiracy for use against those who were abusing the
new process of indictment[7]. In time past the offence of false

---

2 Ric. II. stat. 1, c. 5; 12 Ric. II. c. 11. See Rot. Parl. iii. 168–170; *Cromwell's
case*, 4 Coke's Reports, 12 b.

[1] Edgar, iii. 4; Cnut, ii. 16; Leg. Henr. 34 § 7. See Schmid, Gesetze,
p. 563; Brunner, D. R. G. ii. 675.

[2] Günther, Wiedervergeltung, i. 141.　　　[3] See above, vol. ii. p. 459.

[4] Note Book, pl. 1460.　　　[5] Stat. West. II. c. 12.

[6] Select Civil Pleas (temp. Joh.) pl. 181: action by an acquitted appellee
against one who procured the appeal.

[7] Articuli super Cartas, c. 10; Statutes, vol. i. pp. 145, 216; Rot. Parl.
i. 96. Coke, Sec. Inst. 383–4, 562, says that before the Edwardian statutes the
appellee had an action for damages and the writ of conspiracy was already
in existence. He relies however upon the fables in the Mirror.

judgment had been often placed beside that of false accusation; but even in Edgar's day the doomsman could free himself from punishment by swearing that he knew no better doom than that which he had pronounced[1]. By slow degrees the charge of false judgment became a means of bringing the decisions of the inferior courts before the supreme tribunal; it ceased to import moral blame, though it would lead to an amercement or in some cases to the suppression of a 'liberty.'

Forgery.　　　To account for the lenient treatment that forgers and perjurers received at the hands of our fully-grown common law is by no means easy. Forgery and perjury were common enough in the twelfth and thirteenth centuries. The escape of forgery from the catalogue of the felonies must have been narrow; Henry II. seems to put it on a par with arson, robbery and murder[2]. We have clear evidence that in 1221 a Jew who [p. 539] forged what purported to be a deed of the Prior of Dunstable was only saved from the gallows by a large payment made to the king[3]. Glanvill speaks as though the *crimen falsi* stood among the grave crimes[4]. But when once the royal lawyers have brought the counterfeiting of the king's seal or the king's money within the compass of high treason, they apparently think that they have done almost enough, though for a short while we hear that for a man to counterfeit his lord's seal is treason[5]. Fleta speaks of infamy, pillory and tumbrel in connexion with this offence[6]. So far as we can see, however, forgery was dealt with but incidentally and in the course of civil actions, and was merely a cause for an imprisonment redeemable by fine. What is more, the offence that is thus hit is not exactly that which we call forgery; it is not 'the making of a false document with intent to defraud'; rather it is the reliance on a false document in a court of law[7]. Civil procedure was not adapted for the purpose of tracing the false

---

[1] Edgar, iii. 3; Cnut, ii. 15 § 1; Leg. Will. i. 13, 39; Leg. Henr. 13 § 4.

[2] Ass. Northampt. c. 1.

[3] Ann. Dunstapl. 66; the record of this curious case is printed by Cole, Documents illustrative of Eng. Hist. p. 312.

[4] Glanvill, xiv. 7.

[5] Bracton, f. 119 b; Britton, i. 40, 41, 25; Fleta, 32.

[6] Fleta, p. 63 (falsely numbered).

[7] See *e.g.* Note Book, pl. 934: A litigant produces a charter which he says is twenty-four years old. The justices see from the state of the wax that it is not three years old. He is committed to gaol. Y. B. 20–1 Edw. I. p. 331: imprisonment for production of a false tally.

document to its source; and we have not observed any action based upon a fraud committed by forgery. Apparently a statute of 1413 was needed to give such a remedy[1]. Severe legislation does not begin until 1563[2]. Meanwhile a vast deal of harm must have been done by the negligent lenience of the law. The plea *Nient mon fet* was freely used by honourable gentlemen, while monks and burgesses did not scruple to impose upon the king's court would-be charters of the Anglo-Saxon time which had not even the dubious merit of cleverness.

Very ancient law seems to be not quite certain whether it Perjury. ought to punish perjury at all. Will it not be interfering with [p. 540] the business of the gods?[3] If a punishment is inflicted, this is likely to be the loss of the right hand by which the oath was sworn. Then the church asserted her interest in this sin. In Cnut's day the man who swore falsely upon a relic lost his hand or redeemed it with half his *wer,* and this ransom was divided in equal shares between his lord and the bishop[4]. The growing claims of the church tended to abstract this offence from the lay power, and at the same time tended to reduce even the moral guilt of a *periurium,* for this name was being given, not only to false assertory oaths but to those breaches of promissory oaths which the church was striving to draw within the pale of her jurisdiction[5]. Then at the same time a different stream of events was tending to make the temporal law careless of oaths, except oaths of one special kind, namely, the oaths of assize-recognitors. The main weight of the probative procedure of the king's courts was being thrown upon the oaths, not of the parties, nor of witnesses adduced by them, but of jurors. In most cases, however, even these jurors stood in no terror of a law against perjury, for the rule was established that if both the parties to the litigation had voluntarily 'put themselves' upon a jury, neither of them could complain of the verdict. On the other

---

[1] Stat. 1 Hen. V. c. 3.

[2] Stat. 5 Eliz. c. 14. For more of forgery at common law, see Coke, Third Instit. 169; Blackstone, Comment. iv. 247; Stephen, Hist. Crim. Law, iii. 180. The Star Chamber did much to supplement the meagre common law.

[3] Brunner, D. R. G. ii. 681. Kovalevsky, Droit coutumier Ossétien, p. 324.

[4] Cnut, II. 36; Leg. Henr. 11 § 6. Schmid, Gesetze, Glossar. s. v. *Meineid.*

[5] See above, vol. ii. p. 190. The author of the Mirror would make every kind of official misdeed a perjury, as being a breach of the offender's oath of fealty. This is ridiculous but instructive.

hand, 'assizes,' as distinct from 'juries,' are the outcome not of consent but of ordinance. An assize therefore may be attainted, that is to say, the verdict of the twelve men can be brought before another set of twenty-four men and the twelve will be punished and their verdict reversed if the twenty-four disagree with them[1]. The punishment for the false twelve looks upon paper a heavy punishment[2]. They are to be imprisoned and to lose their chattels; also they 'lose the law of the land,' that is to say they cease to be 'oath-worthy.' As a matter of fact we may sometimes see attainted jurors escaping with moderate [p. 541] fines[3]. The law seems to have no procedure which directly strives to distinguish among untrue verdicts those which are sworn with a knowledge of their falsehood. Bracton feels the gravity of this distinction, but leaves its application to the discretion of the justices, who should not deal very harshly with those who from ignorance or stupidity have sworn the thing that is not[4]. Here we may see one of the difficulties that beset a law against perjury. We do not want to punish with equal severity all persons who swear oaths that are untrue; but how to try their thoughts?

Perjury
and the
church.

During the rest of the middle ages the perjury of jurors seems to have been the only form of perjury that was punished by the lay courts, and this was punished only in a casual, incidental fashion in the course of attaints which were regarded mainly as a means for reversing untrue verdicts[5]. But in the twelfth and thirteenth centuries jurors were not the only men who swore in court. True that as yet no sworn evidence was laid before a jury; but still a principal swearer with his train of oath-helpers was often to be seen. For his and their immunity, for the consequent contempt into which compurgation fell and for the wide-spread immorality that its degradation occasioned, we can only account by saying that perjury was

---

[1] It seems perfectly clear from Bracton's text (especially f. 290 b) and the practice of his time that only an *assisa* could be attainted, never a *iurata*, unless perhaps one that had given a verdict against the king. Note Book, pl. 1294; Y. B. 21–2 Edw. I. 331. Bracton will not allow an attaint of a grand assize. See also 21–2 Edw. I. p. 429. But we learn from Glanvill, ii. 19, that the ordinance which established that assize had specially provided a punishment for jurors. We shall return to the attaint in our next chapter.

[2] Glanvill, ii. 19; Bracton, f. 292 b.

[3] Note Book, pl. 917.

[4] Bracton, f. 289. See also f. 292, and Britton, ii. 228.

[5] Stephen, Hist. Crim. Law, iii. 240.

a sin cognizable by the ecclesiastical courts[1]. We may see a few evanescent traces of an old practice whereby a swearer was 'levied from his oath[2].' His outstretched hand was seized, the charge of perjury made and battle offered. All this soon disappeared, for perjury, including breach of promissory oaths, was claimed by the ecclesiastical forum. A miserable jealousy blunted the edges of those two swords of which men were always speaking; neither power would allow the other to do anything effectual. The church could not keep up the character of the compurgators in her own courts. To say of a man that he was a common swearer before the ordinary was to blast his character[3]. And so our ancestors perjured themselves with impunity.

[p. 542]

§ 4.   *Ecclesiastical Offences.*

Some other crimes which old law had treated with great The sexual severity were appropriated by the church and so escaped from sins. lay justice. Almost the whole province of sexual morality had been annexed. Rape it is true was punished—though not always very severely—by the temporal courts[4], and in the manorial hall-moots the old fine for fornication, the *leger-wite*, was often exacted from the girl or from her father, but the payment of it, like the payment of *merchet*, was commonly regarded as a mark of villeinage. But fornication, adultery, incest and bigamy were ecclesiastical offences, and the lay courts had nothing to say about them, if we disregard the trifling *leger-wite* and some police discipline for common prostitutes who plied their trade in the neighbourhood of the king's house or among the clerks of Oxford[5]. If the church had left the

[1] Bracton, f. 290 b: 'satis est enim quod Deum expectent ultorem.' Britton, ii. 227.

[2] See above, vol. ii. p. 162.

[3] Munim. Gildh. i. 475: Witnesses in the civic court must be 'gentz de bone fame, et ne pas comune seutiers ne proeves devaunt lez ordinaires au Seint Poule ne aillours.'

[4] See above, vol. ii. p. 490.

[5] Fleta, p. 69. Edward I. ordained that no 'femme coursable' should dwell within the city of London: Munim. Gildh. i. 283. The London citizens used to arrest fornicating chaplains and put them in the Tun as night-walkers; in 1297 the bishop objected and the practice was forbidden: ibid. ii. 213. At a later time severe by-laws were made for the punishment of prostitutes, bawds, adulterers, and priests found with women: ibid. i. 457–9. In 1234 the king ordered the expulsion of prostitutes from Oxford: Prynne, Records, ii. 445.

matter to laymen, it is probable that some of these crimes would have been sternly, if not savagely, punished[1]. But the canonists had made such a capricious mess of the marriage law that the names of incest, bigamy and adultery had lost half their sting. Sometimes these offences were punished in the courts Christian by whipping and other bodily penances[2]; too often they were paid for with money. The church may take [p. 543] credit for an attempt to establish equality between the adulterous husband and the adulterous wife; but the outcome of this effort was rather a mitigation of her than an aggravation of his guilt.

Heresy.

It remains for us to speak of an offence of which few Englishmen were guilty, and about which therefore our courts seldom spoke. The first English statute that denounced the penalty of death against heretics was passed in the year 1401[3]. Whether before that statute the law that was in force in our land demanded or suffered that such persons should be burnt is a question that has been eagerly debated; on it in the days of Elizabeth and James I. depended the lives of Anabaptists and Arians; it has not yet lost its interest; but it is a question that buzzes in a vacuum, for until Lollardy became troublesome there was too little heresy in England to beget a settled course of procedure. In order to understand the controversy we must first look abroad.

Heresy on the continent.

On the mainland of Europe obstinate heresy had long before the date of our statute been treated as a crime worthy of death by burning. There is still some doubt among scholars as to the legal history of this punishment, in particular as to the abiding influence of ordinances issued by the first Christian emperors. They dealt separately with divers heretical sects;

---

[1] For adultery and incest in Anglo-Saxon and other old Germanic laws, see Brunner, D. R. G. ii. 662–6; Schmid, Gesetze, Glossar. s. v. *Ehebruch, Sibleger*. As to the mutilation of the man who commits adultery with another man's wife, see above, p. 490. German law of a later time still enforced this punishment: Günther, Wiedervergeltung, i. 261. We even hear from northern Switzerland of a bigamist being cut in half: ibid. 262. The worst forms of incest had been punished by death : Brunner, D. R. G. ii. 665. A queer story about the treatment of a fornicator by the woman's friends stands in Placit. Abbrev. 267.

[2] Regist. Palat. Dunelm. ii. 695: in 1315 a woman guilty of incestuous adultery is to be whipt six times round the market-place at Durham and six times round the church at Auckland.

[3] Stat. 2 Hen. IV. c. 15.

they condemned the Manicheans to death merely for being
Manicheans; they did not pronounce this pain against heretics
in general, but to teach heretical doctrines or frequent heretical
assemblies was a capital crime[1]. After the barbarian invasions
and the final disappearance of the Arian heresy the western
church enjoyed a long repose; but the law against the Manicheans was still being copied as part of the Lex Romana[2]. A
change came in the eleventh century; the Cathari appeared
upon the scene and with strange rapidity their doctrines spread
over Italy and southern Gaul. What we may call the medieval
period of persecution begins early in that century. In the
year 1022 heretics were put to death at Toulouse and at
Orleans[3]; we see a Norman knight active in bringing the
[p. 544] canons of Orleans to the stake[4]. Upon what theory of the
law their judges acted we do not precisely know; but it is to
be remembered that the medieval heretic was very generally
suspected, nor always wrongly, of being a Manichean. The
renewed study of Justinian's code confirmed men in their
persuasion that Manicheanism is a capital crime, and an
ingenious combination of the texts that were preserved in
that book would serve to prove that other heretics were in no
better case[5]. The prevailing doctrine seems to have been that
law human and divine demands the death of the obdurate
heretic, and this doctrine was enforced by church and state,
except where heresy was so pestilent that there was need for a
holy war, rather than for judicial decisions. At length there
was definite legislation. In the Lateran Councils of 1179 and
1215 the church uttered her mind. The impenitent heretic
when convicted by the ecclesiastical court is to be handed over
to the lay power for due punishment. The church does not
mention, does not like to mention, the punishment that is due;
but every one knows what it is[6]. The spiritual judge will even
go through the form of requesting that the victim's life may be
spared, in order that the 'irregularity' of blood-guiltiness may
be decently avoided; but the lay prince who pays heed to this
request will be guilty of much worse than an irregularity[7].

[1] Tanon, Histoire des tribunaux de l'inquisition en France, 127–133; Cod.
Theod. 16. 5; Cod. Iust. 1. 5; Lex Rom. Visig. ed. Hänel, pp. 256–8.

[2] Tanon, *op. cit.* 135.　　　　　[3] Tanon, *op. cit.* 13.

[4] C. Schmidt, Histoire de la secte des Cathares, p. 30.

[5] Tanon, *op. cit.* 130, 460.

[6] Tanon, *op. cit.* 462.　　　　　[7] Tanon, *op. cit.* 473.

Then, early in the thirteenth century, constitutions of that un-orthodox emperor Frederick II. spoke out plainly and fiercely against heretics[1], and, being promulgated and confirmed by papal bulls, they were received as law even in countries which lay beyond the limits of the empire. They became, as it were, a common law for the western church[2].

England and continental heresy.

These things concern us, for when in the fifteenth century [p. 545] the English canonist Lyndwood had to answer the question, Why are heretics burnt? his reply was in effect, 'Because certain constitutions of Frederick II. have been sanctioned by a decretal of Boniface VIII. which is part of the body of the Canon Law[3].' We must also remember that Englishmen of the thirteenth century, however orthodox they themselves might be, had heard much of heresy as of a terrible reality. They had praised the 'just cruelty' of Philip of Flanders[4]; they had watched the excesses of that 'hammer of heretics' Robert le Bugre[5]; already in 1214 King John had sent out

---

[1] Tanon, *op. cit.* 147. These constitutions extend over the years 1220–39.

[2] We have been relying on the work of M. Tanon; see especially pp. 441–463. An opposite opinion treats Frederick's constitutions as the first laws which punish heresy with death, and regards as the outcome of arbitrary power or of political necessities, the numerous cases of an earlier date in which heretics were burnt. According to this theory the decisive step was taken in the year 1231 when Gregory IX. published with his approval a constitution issued by Frederick in 1224. See Ficker, Die gesetzliche Einführung der Todesstrafe für Ketzerei, in Mittheilungen des Instituts für oesterreichische Geschichtsforschung, i. 179; Havet, L'hérésie et le bras séculier, Bibl. de l'École des chartes, vol. xli. pp. 488, 570, 603; Havet, Œuvres, ii. 117; also Lord Acton, Eng. Hist. Rev. iii. 776. The question is difficult because to the last the canon law never says in so many words that death is to be inflicted: it merely does this indirectly by approving the pious edicts of the emperor.

[3] Lyndwood, Provinciale, de Haereticis (5. 5) c. *Reverendissimae*, ad v. *Poenas in iure* (ed. 1679, p. 293): 'Sed hodie indistincte illi qui per iudicem ecclesiasticum sunt damnati de haeresi, quales sunt pertinaces et relapsi, qui non petunt misericordiam ante sententiam, sunt damnandi ad mortem per saeculares potestates, et per eos debent comburi seu igne cremari, ut patet in quadam constitutione Frederici quae incipit *Ut commissi* § *Item mortis* [= Const. of March 1232, Mon. Germ., Leges, ii. 288], et in alia constitutione ipsius quae incipit *Inconsutilem* § *Contra tales* [= Const. of 22 Feb. 1239, Mon. Germ., Leges, ii. 327]; quae sunt servandae, ut patet, e. ti. *Ut inquisitionis* in prin. li. 6 et c. fi. e. ti. [= cc. 18, 20 in Sexto 5. 2].' See Stephen, Hist. Cr. Law, ii. 448. Lyndwood does not think that the imperial constitutions as such are of force in England; but a constitution approved by the text of the Canon Law is a different matter. Sir James Stephen, p. 441, is wrong in thinking that Lyndwood's Frederick was Barbarossa.

[4] Ralph of Coggeshall, p. 122; Lea, History of the Inquisition, i. 112.

[5] Mat. Par. Chron. Maj. iii. 361, 520.

from England strict orders for the suppression of heresy in his French dominions[1]; repentant Cathari from Languedoc were frequent pilgrims to the shrine of St Thomas[2]; the ill-fated Raymond of Toulouse had married a daughter of our Henry II.; our great Earl of Leicester was the son of the ruthless crusader. A king of England, who held Gascony and had claims on the Quercy, was interested in the doings of papal inquisitors[3]; the machinery of English law was employed to enforce in England sentences of confiscation which had been pronounced in the south of France[4].

[p. 546]　　But we must speak of sentences passed in England[5]. The first heretics that we read of were some thirty foreigners; they seem to have been Flemings and to have belonged to some offshoot of the Catharan sect. They were condemned in a provincial council held at Oxford in or shortly before 1166 and were relinquished to the secular arm. By the king's orders they were whipt, branded in the face and exiled; some of them perished of cold and hunger; they made, it is said, but one convert here, and she recanted[6]. Then the Assize of Clarendon decreed that none should receive any of their sect and that any house in which they were entertained should be pulled down[7]. This is said to be the first law issued by any medieval prince

Heresy in England.

---

[1] Rot. Pat. Joh. p. 124.　　　　　[2] Lea, Hist. Inquisit. ii. 31.

[3] For the inquisition in the Quercy, see Lea, *op. cit.* ii. 30.

[4] Rot. Pat. 20 Hen. III. m. 11 d. *de vinis et catallis Ernaldi de Peregorde.* Rot. Pat. 26 Hen. III. pt. 1. m. 15, *de Stephano Pelicer de Agenensi.* These writs are referred to by Hale, P. C. i. 394, as if they related to sentences pronounced in England; but they do not. The first of them orders the arrest at Boston fair of wines belonging to Arnaud de Périgord who, as the king hears, has been convicted of heresy. The second of them orders the bailiffs of Bristol to restore to Stephen Pelicer certain goods of his that have been arrested, he having produced letters of the bishop of Agen and Arnaud guardian of the Friars Minor in Agen—the name of the famous Bernard de Cauz is here written but cancelled—testifying that he (Stephen) is not suspected of heresy. For a case in which Edward I.'s seneschal in Gascony had trouble with the inquisitors about some relapsed Jews, see Langlois, Le règne de Philippe le Hardi, 221.

[5] See Makower, Const. Hist. of Church, pp. 183 ff.

[6] Will. Newburgh, i. 131; Ralph of Coggeshall, 122; Diceto, i. 318; Mapes, De Nugis, 62; Schmidt, Histoire de la secte des Cathares, i. 97; Lea, Hist. Inquis. i. 113; Havet, Bibl. de l'École des chartes, xli. 510; Stubbs, Const. Hist. iii. 365.

[7] Ass. Clarend. c. 21. The destruction of houses plays a large part in the procedure against heretics on the continent; Tanon, *op. cit.* 519; Lea, *op. cit.* i. 481.

against heretics[1]; it was mild; the voice of the universal church had not yet spoken in the Lateran Councils. Then we are told that in 1210 an Albigensian was burnt in London; we are told this and no more[2]. A better attested case follows. In 1222 Stephen Langton held a provincial council at Oxford, and there he degraded and handed over to the lay power a deacon who had turned Jew for the love of a Jewess. The apostate was delivered to the sheriff of Oxfordshire, who forthwith burnt him. That sheriff was the unruly Fawkes of Breauté, then at the height of his power. His prompt action seems to have surprised his contemporaries; but it was approved by Bracton[3], who however did not write until after the constitutions of the Emperor Frederick had received the approval of the Pope, and the church was deeply committed to the infliction of capital punishment. In the same council the cardinal archbishop condemned to 'immuration,' that is, to close and solitary imprisonment for life, two of the laity, a man who had given himself out to be the Saviour of men, a woman [p. 547] who had called herself His Virgin Mother. All this seems to have been done in strict accordance with the continental procedure; the penitent fanatics were immured, the impenitent lover was burnt[4]. In 1240 the Dominicans at Cambridge arrested a Carthusian who would not go to church, said that the devil was loose and reviled the pope. The sheriff was ordered to take him from the hands of the Preaching Friars and bring him to Westminster. He was brought before the legate Otto, among whose assessors we may see the Hostiensis of canonical fame. What became of this man we do not know; but he said some things about the holy father which made the legate blush and amused Matthew Paris[5]. A little earlier the Dominicans were arresting

---

[1] Lea, *op. cit.* i. 114. Already in 1157 a synod at Reims had threatened the heretics with branding and banishment: Hefele, Conciliengeschichte, ed. 2, v. 568.

[2] Liber de Antiquis Legibus, p. 3: 'Hoc anno concrematus est quidam Ambigensis apud Londonias.'

[3] Bracton, f. 123 b.

[4] Maitland, The Canon Law in England, Essay VI. In 1240 a relapsed Jew was in prison at Oxford awaiting trial by the bishop: Prynne, Records, ii. 630. As to 'immuration,' see Tanon, *op. cit.* p. 485: 'Toutes ces prisons [the prisons in which heretics were confined] étaient désignées sous le nom particulier du mur, *murus, la mure, la meure*, et les prisonniers sous celui d'emmurés, *immurati*, en langue vulgaire *emmurats.*' See also Lea, *op. cit.* i. 486.

[5] Prynne, Records, ii. 560; Mat. Par. Chron. Maj. iv. 32.

heretics in Yorkshire and had to be told that this was the sheriff's business[1]. But even the trained scent of the Preachers could find little heresy in England, and they themselves were soon developing opinions which earned condemnation[2].

As to the text writers, Glanvill has no word of heresy; Bracton approves the fate of the apostate deacon[3]; Fleta holds that apostates, sorcerers 'and the like' should be drawn and burnt, while Christians who marry with Jews should be buried alive[4]; Britton would burn renegades and miscreants, and so would his glossator[5]; the author of the Mirror, who is at times frantically orthodox, treats apostasy, heresy and sorcery as the crime of *laesa maiestas divina*, treason against the heavenly King; according to him the punishment of heresy is fourfold, excommunication, degradation, disherison, incineration[6]. He holds too that heresy can be prosecuted by way of appeal in a temporal court and talks much nonsense about this matter. Britton admits an inquiry 'of sorcerers and sorceresses, of apostates and heretics' among the articles of the sheriff's turn; Fleta in this context speaks only of sorcerers and apostates[7]. In other copies of the articles we find no such inquiry[8]. All this suggests that lawyers, with an increasing horror, but no real experience, of heresy, think themselves at liberty to speculate about what ought to be done if heretics appear. According to the canon law the lay prince who determined a cause of heresy would be almost as guilty as would be he who refused to aid and complete the justice of the church[9].

Heresy in English text-books.

[p. 548]

We must carry our history a little further. In 1324 Richard Ledrede, a Franciscan friar who had become Bishop of Ossory, instituted a vigorous prosecution against certain sheep of his flock who were suspected of the heresy that consists of witchcraft.

Later cases of heresy.

---

[1] Prynne, Records, ii. 475.　　[2] Rashdall, Universities, ii. 527.

[3] Bracton, f. 123 b, 124.

[4] Fleta, p. 54. His words are 'contrahentes vero cum Judaeis vel Judaeabus.' In 1236 a Jew who had sexual intercourse with a Christian woman had to abjure the realm, while she was put to penance and abjured the town of Bristol; Note Book, pl. 1179.

[5] Britton, i. 42.

[6] Mirror, pp. 59, 135. The comparison of heresy to treason is found in a decretal of Innocent III. of 1199; c. 10, X. 5, 7.

[7] Britton, i. 179; Fleta, p. 113.

[8] See Stat. Walliae (Statutes, i. 57); and the apocryphal statute *De visu franciplegii* (ibid. p. 246); The Court Baron, pp. 71, 93.

[9] c. 18 in Sexto, 5. 2.

The chief offenders eluded him; they were of kin to men very powerful in Ireland who obstructed his efforts. At one time he was himself cast into prison. Incarceration stimulated his zeal. At length he triumphed. In the presence of the justiciar, chancellor and treasurer he tried his heretics. One miserable woman he caused to be flogged until she made an absurd confession about demonolatry and so forth. She and others remaining impenitent were committed to the flames, while in proper inquisitorial style the bishop condemned the penitent to wear crosses on their garments. The case is exceedingly interesting. We see on the one hand that the Anglo-Irish law was utterly unprepared to deal with heretics; it had no proper process for arresting the suspects and keeping them arrested; we see also that the king's judges and officers disliked the bishop's proceedings—not the less because he was an intruding Englishman;—but we see on the other hand that they had to give way, that they quailed before a prelate who resolutely flourished in their faces the imperious decretal of Boniface VIII. We have some satisfaction in reading that at a later time he himself was accused of heresy—perhaps the heresy of the 'Spiritual' Franciscans—and was driven from his diocese[1]. We are told that among the Minorites who in 1330 were martyred for resisting the decrees of John XXII. some were burnt in England 'in a wood'; but this story needs confirmation[2].

No English procedure apt for cases of heresy. The chief lesson that we learn from Bishop Ledrede's proceedings, namely that in England there was no machinery aptly suited for the suppression of heresy, is enforced by the case of the Templars. Edward II. urged on by Clement V., who had become the tool of Philip the Fair, suffered the admission into England of papal inquisitors and the use of torture. The Order was dissolved, the knights were dispersed, [p. 549] their wealth was confiscated; but, though the usual tales of

[1] See Proceedings against Dame Alice Kyteler (Camden Society, ed. Wright); Lea, Hist. Inquis. i. 354; iii. 456; Dict. Nat. Biog. *Lederede, Richard.* On pp. 23, 27 of the Proceedings we see the bishop producing 'Extra de haereticis, Ut Inquisitionis,' that is to say, the decretal of Boniface VIII. which appears as c. 18 in Sexto, 5. 2.

[2] Chron. de Melsa, ii. 323. The text may be corrupt; an execution 'in quadam sylva' would be very strange. See on this passage, Stubbs, Const. Hist. ii. 492, and compare Lea, *op. cit.* iii. 77.

devil-worship were told, they were not convicted and there was no burning[1].

Such are the principal cases of heresy that we find before the days of the Lollards. If now we ask what law about heresy was in force in England, we must in the first place answer that according to the law of the catholic church the man convicted by the bishop of his diocese as an impenitent or a relapsed heretic was to be delivered over to the secular power. We must add that the officer or the prince, who neglected to do what was implied in the bishop's sentence, was liable to excommunication, while if he persisted in his contumacy for a year, he himself was a heretic[2]. To ask what was the law of our temporal courts about this matter is to ask what would have been done in a case unprecedented or touched by very few precedents. The answer will vary from reign to reign, from pontificate to pontificate. If we ask it in the middle of the fourteenth century, when our parliaments were entering on a course of anti-Roman legislation, when statutes of Provisors and Praemunire were being passed, when the papacy in its Babylonish captivity had fallen from its high estate, when the theories of Ockham and Marsiglio were in the air, when England had repudiated her feudal dependence on Rome, when heresy no longer meant some strange, dualistic faith which rejected the Christian creeds, when Franciscans were heretics in the eyes of Dominicans, and Spirituals were heretics in the eyes of Conventuals, we may give a tolerant answer:—we see Wycliffe favoured at court and dying in peace at Lutterworth. But if we ask the same question at an earlier time, in Henry III.'s day, when the fate of the Counts of Toulouse was not forgotten, when the papacy was yet grand and terrible, when it could strike down an emperor the wonder of the world, when the flagrant heresy was Catharism, which to the popular mind implied devil-worship and nameless vices, when there were plausible and modern reasons for the doctrine that England was a papal fief, then we must say that the sheriff, the judge, the king, who neglected to enforce the church's law about this spiritual crime, would have been a bold man.

English law and heresy.

[p. 550] To the smaller, the technical, question 'whether there was a writ *de haeretico comburendo* at common law?' we must reply that no one has yet produced any such writ older than that

The writ for burning heretics.

---

[1] Lea, *op. cit.* iii. 298–301. [2] cc. 9. 13, X. 5. 7; c. 18 in Sexto, 5. 2.

which was made in the parliament of 1401 for the burning of William Sawtre, and that the events of that year, which we must not here discuss, suggest first that no such writ had theretofore been issued, secondly that the orthodox party was anxious that Sawtre should be burnt 'at common law' (that is to say, without any aid from the statute which they were on the point of obtaining), and thirdly that they had their way[1]. We must also remember that according to the doctrine of the canon law no such writ was requisite; the sheriff or other officer who received the 'relinquished' miscreant would be bound to burn him and would run a risk of excommunication if he waited for orders[2]. Under Elizabeth and James I., when there were no statutes which punished heresy with death, Sawtre's case and the case of the apostate deacon were the two precedents on which our lawyers based their theory that the writ lies at common law, though not as a writ 'of course.' Of the legality of the flames which then burnt the bodies of Arians and Anabaptists we must here say nothing, but assuredly it was hard to find any logical theory which would send heretics to death and yet not admit that papal decretals were still valid law in England[3].

Sorcery.

Closely connected with heresy is sorcery; indeed it is probable that but for the persecution of heretics there would have been no persecution of sorcerers. Here again therefore we find some difficulty in stating the law of England as it was in the twelfth and thirteenth centuries, for heresy was not trouble- [p 551] some and therefore we read little of diabolic arts[4].

[1] Stubbs, Const. Hist. iii. 357-8; Stephen, Hist. Cr. Law, ii. 445-450.

[2] Coke, 12 Reports, 56, admits this: 'and if the sheriff was present, he might deliver the party convict to be burnt without any writ *de haeretico comburendo.*'

[3] The discussion may be traced thus:—Fitzherbert, Natura Brevium, 269; Coke, 5 Reports, 23 a; 12 Reports, 56, 93 (not a book of high authority); 3rd Inst. 39; State Trials, v. 825; Hale, P. C. i. 383-410; Blackstone, Comm. iv. 44; Stephen, Hist. Cr. Law, ii. 437-469; Stubbs, Const. Hist. iii. 365-70; Stubbs, Lectures, 328-9; Lea, Hist. Inquis. i. 221-2; Makower, Verfassung der Kirche, Berlin, 1894, pp. 193 ff. The theory which would draw a distinction between a conviction before the ordinary and a conviction before a provincial council is founded only on what happened in two isolated cases, that of Sawtre and that of the apostate deacon; it has no warrant in medieval canon law. Again, the theory which holds that a cause of heresy is beyond the competence of the bishop's official rests, we believe, on a mistranslation of some words used by Lyndwood. As to this point, see L. Q. R. xiii. 214.

[4] As to the whole of this subject, see Lea, Hist. Inquis. vol. iii. ch. vi. vii.

The first Christian emperors had made savage laws against History of
sorcery. magicians and the like, and these, preserved in the Code, did much harm in after ages[1]. The Bible too enshrined that hideous text, 'Thou shalt not suffer a witch to live[2].' The Anglo-Saxon dooms, like the parallel folk-laws of the continent, have a good deal to say about sorcery[3]; the remnants of heathen rites were regarded as devil-worship, and in England the successive swarms of Norsemen were but slowly weaned from their old faith. Even Cnut had to legislate against the witchcraft which is heathenry[4]. But when once the western world had been safely won by the catholic religion and there was no longer any fear of a relapse into paganism, there came a time of toleration for those who dabbled in the black arts[5]. Doubtless if they compassed criminal ends by their practices, if, for example, they slew a man by maltreating a waxen image of him—and few doubted that such things were possible—they would be hanged or burnt[6]. Again, the mere practice of their arts was sinful; but no very severe measures would be taken if they did not obtrude themselves upon the notice of the church. The exact boundary between the legitimate and the illegitimate sciences was vague; astrology hovered on the border line. A little harmless necromancy would be met by blame that was tinctured by awe and admiration; bishops and even popes, it was whispered, had trifled with the powers of evil. In Henry I.'s day Archbishop Gerard of York was reputed a necromancer, and, when he died a sudden death with a book of astrology under his pillow, his body could not find burial in his cathedral; but then he had taken the wrong, the unclerical, side in the strife about investitures. It was not until the thirteenth century was at an end that the church [p. 552] began in various parts of the world a stringent prosecution of sorcerers. This grew out of the warfare against heresy.

The association of magic with heresy and rebellion was part of the imperial Roman heritage of the Church. Such charges were constantly made against the early Christians.

[1] Cod. Theod. 9. 16; Lex Rom. Visigoth. (ed. Hänel), p. 186; Cod. Iust. 9. 18.

[2] Exod. xxii. 18.

[3] Lea, *op. cit.* iii. 420; Brunner, D. R. G. ii. 678.

[4] Cnut, ii. 4.

[5] Lea, *op. cit.* iii. 422.

[6] Leg. Hen. 71. See Schmid's note on *invultuatio*, Gesetze, Glossar. p. 617; Brunner, D. R. G. ii. 679.

The sorcerer is a heretic and should be punished as such: John XXII. made this plain[1].

Sorcery in English law-books. In Edward I.'s day our English lawyers seem to have adopted the opinion that sorcerers ought to be burnt[2]. Britton and Fleta declare that an inquiry about sorcerers is one of the articles of the sheriff's turn[3]; but this is not borne out by other evidence[4]. A little later we read that it is for the ecclesiastical court to try such offenders and to deliver them over to be put to death in the king's court, but that the king himself ' as a good marshal of Christianity' may proceed against them if he pleases[5].

Cases of sorcery in England. Of actual cases we see but very few. In 1209 one woman appealed another of sorcery in the king's court; the accused purged herself by the ordeal of iron[6]. In 1279 a Northumbrian jury made the following curious presentment:—'An unknown woman, who was a witch (*sortilega*), entered the house of John of Kerneslaw at the hour of vespers and assaulted the said John because he signed himself with the cross above the candles when the *Benedicite* was said. And the said John defended himself as against the devil (*tanquam de diabolo*) and struck the witch with a staff so that she died. And afterwards by the judgment of the whole clergy she was burnt. Then John went mad, and, when he had recovered his wits and remembered what he had done, he fled.' Upon this presentment the judgment is that, since John is not suspected of any felony, he may return if he pleases, but that his chattels are forfeited for the flight[7]. Edward I.'s treasurer, Walter Langton, bishop of Lichfield, was accused before the pope of murder and adultery. A charge of sorcery, homage to Satan and the foul kiss was thrown in; but he cleared himself with compurgators. Another royal clerk, Adam of Stratton, was believed to have preserved nail-parings and other nasty things in a cabinet, which he made away with when he was arrested for offences less dubious than

---

[1] Lea, *op. cit.* iii. 453.

[2] Fleta, p. 54; Britton, i. 42, and the note from the Cambridge MS.

[3] Britton, i. 179; Fleta, p. 113.

[4] See above, vol. ii. p. 549.

[5] Note on Britton, i. 42.

[6] Placit. Abbrev. 62. It is possible that the charge was not of mere sorcery but of murder or mayhem effected by sorcery.

[7] Northumberland Assize Rolls (Surt. Soc.), 343.

[p. 553] sorcery[1]. The miserable beings whom the Bishop of Ossory sent to the stake were sorcerers as well as heretics; one of them was the first witch burnt in Ireland[2]. The bishop showed an all too close familiarity with the latest decretals. Many of the phenomena which characterize the witch trials of a later day appear already in this case—the hell-broth brewed from miscellaneous filth and the rest of it. Sorcery and devil-worship were charged against the Templars; but in England, as already said, they could not be convicted even after torture. In 1325 upwards of twenty men were indicted and tried in the King's Bench for having perpetrated a murder by tormenting a waxen image; the jury acquitted them[3]. In 1371 a man was brought before the King's Bench having been arrested in Southwark with a dead man's head and a book of sorcery in his possession. No indictment was found against him and he was let go; but the clerks made him swear that he never would be a sorcerer, and the head and book were burnt on Tothill at his cost[4]. But all this means very little.

A change came in the fifteenth century. In 1406, soon after our first statute against heretics, Henry IV. empowered the bishop of Norwich to arrest sorcerers and witches, and to keep them in prison after conviction until further order[5]. By this time a witch could be tried and burnt under the statute against heretics. Also the king's council began to take notice of sorcery, and accusations thereof were used for political purposes[6]. The epidemic which was raging on the continent reached our shores; but it came here late and mild. Where there is no torture there can be little witchcraft. Statutes were made by Henry VIII. and Elizabeth which condemned various forms of sorcery as crimes to be punished by the temporal courts[7]; but these statutes were neither so severe nor so comprehensive as the canon law; they seem to have been

Sorcery in later times.

---

[1] Barth. Cotton, 172.   [2] See above, vol. ii. p. 550.

[3] Proceedings against Alice Kyteler, Introduction, p. xxiii, where the record is printed.

[4] Y. B. 45 Edw. III. f. 17 (Trin. pl. 7).

[5] Proceedings against Alice Kyteler, Introduction, p. x, from the Patent Roll.

[6] Ibid. pp. xi–xx. Lea, *op. cit.* iii. 466–8. As to the witch of Eye, see also Coke, 3rd Inst. 44.

[7] Stat. 33 Hen. VIII. c. 8 (A.D. 1541), repealed by 1 Edw. VI. c. 12; Stat. 5 Eliz. c. 16 (A.D. 1562). See as to these statutes Stephen, Hist. Cr. Law, ii. 431.

occasioned by attempts to use divination for purposes that [p. 554] were regarded as treasonable[1], and very few people were done to death by them. A bloodier statute was passed by that erudite demonologist James I.[2]; but it was left for the Puritans in the moment of their triumph to enforce with cruel diligence this statute and the written law of God. The days of the Commonwealth were the worst days for witches in England[3].

But we have transgressed our limits. The thirteenth century seems to have been content to hold as an academic opinion that sorcerers, being heretics, ought to be burnt, if convicted by the courts of Holy Church[4]; but no serious effort was made to put this theory into practice. Sorcery is a crime created by the measures which are taken for its suppression.

Unnatural crime.

The crime against nature seems to have had a somewhat similar history[5]. It was so closely connected with heresy that the vulgar had but one name for both[6]. Possibly an old Germanic element appears when Fleta speaks of the criminal being buried alive[7]; but we are elsewhere told that burning is the due punishment[8], and this may betray a trace of Roman law[9]. It was a subject for ecclesiastical cognizance, and apparently there was a prevailing opinion that, if the church relinquished the offenders to the secular arm, they ought to be burnt[10]. As a matter of fact we do not believe that in England they were thus relinquished; in the twelfth century Anselm had been compelled to deal less severely with a prevailing vice[11]. The statute of 1533 which makes it felony affords an almost sufficient proof that the temporal courts had not

---

[1] Francis Hutchinson, Essay on Witchcraft (1718), pp. 173–6.

[2] Stat. 1 Jac. I. c. 12; Stephen, Hist. Cr. Law, ii. 433.

[3] Hutchinson, *op. cit.* p. 49: 'In this collection, that I have made, it is observable, that in 103 years from the statute against witchcraft in 33 Hen. VIII. till 1644, when we were in the midst of our civil wars, I find but about 15 executed. But in the 16 years following while the government was in other hands, there were 109, if not more, condemned and hanged.'

[4] Coke, 3rd Inst. 44 and Hale, P. C. i. 383 take this to have been the law.

[5] Coke, 3rd Inst. 58; Blackstone, Comm. iv. 215; Stephen, Hist. Cr. Law, ii. 429.

[6] Lea, Hist. Inquis. i. 115, also Oxford English Dictionary.

[7] Fleta, p. 54.   [8] Britton, i. 42 and the note from the Cambridge MS.

[9] Cod. Theod. 9. 7. 3. This passes into common knowledge through Lex Romana Visigothorum; see Hänel's ed. p. 178.

[10] Lea, Hist. Inquis. iii. 256.

[11] Letters of Anselm, Migne, Patrol. vol. clix. col. 95; Eadmer, p. 143.

[p. 555] punished it and that no one had been put to death for it for a very long time past[1].

We must not end this chapter without recording our belief that crimes of violence were common and that the criminal law was exceedingly inefficient. The justices in eyre who visited Gloucester in 1221 listened to an appalling tale of crime which comprised some 330 acts of homicide. The result of their visitation was that one man was mutilated, and about 14 men were hanged, while about 100 orders for outlawry were given. As the profits however of the minor offences, chiefly the offences of 'communities,' they raised some £430 by about 220 fines and amercements[2]. The period of which they took note was long and comprised a time of civil war. But even in quiet times few out of many criminals came to their appointed end. In 1256 the justices in Northumberland heard of 77 murders; 4 murderers were hanged, 72 were outlawed. They heard of 78 other felonies, for which 14 people were hanged and 54 were outlawed. In 1279 their successors in the same county received reports of 68 cases of murder, which resulted in the hanging of 2 murderers and the outlawry of 65, while for 110 burglaries and so forth 20 malefactors went to the gallows and 75 were left 'lawless,' but at large[3]. Thus, after all, we come back to the point whence we started, for, whatever the law might wish, the malefactor's fate was like to be outlawry rather than any more modern punishment.

Inefficiency of criminal law.

[1] Stat. 25 Hen. VIII. c. 6: 'forasmuch as there is not yet sufficient and condign punishment appointed and limited by the due course of the laws of this realm.'

[2] Gloucestershire Pleas, ed. Maitland.

[3] Page, Northumberland Assize Rolls, pp. xviii–xix.

CHAPTER IX.

PROCEDURE.

§ 1. *The Forms of Action.*

Our formulary system.

AFTER all that has hitherto been said, and now that we are nearing the end of our long course, we have yet to speak of the most distinctively English trait of our medieval law, its 'formulary system' of actions. We call it distinctively English; but it is also in a certain sense very Roman. While the other nations of Western Europe were beginning to adopt as their own the ultimate results of Roman legal history, England was unconsciously reproducing that history; it was developing a formulary system which in the ages that were coming would be the strongest bulwark against Romanism and sever our English law from all her sisters.

An English peculiarity.

The phenomenon that is before us can not be traced to any exceptional formalism in the procedure which prevailed in the England of the eleventh century. All ancient procedure is formal enough, and in all probability neither the victors nor the vanquished on the field at Hastings knew any one legal formula or legal formality that was not well known throughout many lands. No, the English peculiarity is this, that in the middle of the twelfth century the old, oral and traditional formalism is in part supplanted and in part reinforced by a new, written and authoritative formalism, for the like of which we shall look in vain elsewhere, unless we go back to a remote stage of Roman history. Our *legis actiones* give way to a formulary system. Our law passes under the dominion of a system of writs which flow from the royal chancery. What has made this possible is the exceptional vigour of the English kingship, or, if we look at [p. 557] the other side of the facts, the exceptional malleableness of a thoroughly conquered and compactly united kingdom.

The time has long gone by when English lawyers were tempted to speak as though their scheme of 'forms of action' had been invented in one piece by some all-wise legislator. It grew up little by little. The age of rapid growth is that which lies between 1154 and 1272[1]. During that age the chancery was doling out actions one by one. There is no solemn *Actionem dabo* proclaimed to the world, but it becomes understood that a new writ is to be had or that an old writ, which hitherto might be had as a favour, is now 'a writ of course[2].' It was an empirical process, for the supply came in response to a demand; it was not dictated by an abstract jurisprudence; it was conditioned and perturbed by fiscal and political motives; it advanced along the old Roman road which leads from experiment to experiment. Our royalism has debarred us from affixing to the various writs the names of the chancellors who first issued them or of the justices who advised their making; they have no names so picturesque as *Publiciana* or *Serviana*; but if a hundredth part of the industry that has been spent on Roman legal history were devoted to our plea rolls, we might with but few errors assign almost every writ to its proper decade[3].

Growth of the forms.

The similarity between these two formulary systems, the Roman and the English, is so patent that it has naturally aroused the suggestion that the one must have been the model for the other. Now it is very true that between the years 1150 and 1250 or thereabouts, the old Roman law, in the new medieval form that it took in the hands of the glossators, exercised a powerful influence not only on the growth of legal theory in England, but also on some of our English rules[4].

Our formulary system not of Roman origin.

---

[1] See above, vol. i. pp. 150, 195.

[2] For an instance, see above, vol. ii. p. 64.

[3] In some of the early MS. Registers we find by way of supplement a group of new writs which are ascribed to Bracton's master, William Raleigh; Maitland, History of the Register, Harv. L. R., iii. 175–6. See also Bracton, f. 222: 'breve de constitutione de Merton secundum quod tunc provisum fuit per W. de Ralegh iusticiarium.' Ibid. f. 437 b: 'consulitur heredi per tale breve per W. de Ralegh formatum pro Radulfo de Dadescomb.'

[4] We have admitted this as regards the novel disseisin, vol. i. p. 146, vol. ii. p. 46; the livery of seisin, vol. ii. p. 89; the treatment of the termor, vol. ii. p. 114; the conception of *laesa maiestas*, vol. ii. p. 503. One of our actions, namely, the *Cessavit per biennium* was borrowed; see vol. i. p. 353. Other

But before a case of imitation can be proved, or even supposed [p. 558] as probable, we must do much more than discover a resemblance between an English idea or institution and some idea or institution which at one time or another had a place in the Roman scheme. We must show a resemblance between English law and that Roman law which was admired and taught in the middle ages. The medieval civilians had little knowledge of and little care for the antiquities of the system that they studied. They were not historians; they had no wish to disinter the law of the republican or of the Antonine period. They were lawyers, and the Roman law that they sought to restore was the law of Justinian's last years. That was for them the law which, unless it had been altered by some emperor of German race, was still by rights the law of the Roman world. All that Justinian or any of his predecessors had abolished was obsolete stuff which no one would think of reviving. What they knew of the formulary system was that it had been swept away by imperial wisdom[1]. Therefore their influence was all in favour of a simple system of procedure, under which a magistrate would decide all questions of fact and law without any division of labour and without any formula. If they could have had their way in this country, the procedure of our temporal would have been, like that of our spiritual courts, a libellary procedure, which had no place either for the 'original writ' with its authoritative definition of the cause of action or for the 'issue' submitted to a jury.

Compari- son of Roman and English formulas.

But further, so soon as we begin to penetrate below the surface, the differences between the two formulary systems are at least as remarkable as the resemblances. For a moment our *cancellarius* with his *registrum brevium* looks very like the *praetor* with his *album,* but, while the *praetor* listens to both parties before he composes the formula, the chancellor when he issues the original writ has never heard the defendant's story, and in most cases the plaintiff obtains a writ 'as of course' by merely saying that he wants it and paying for it. So obvious

particulars might easily be mentioned. We have also admitted that the very idea of a science of law comes from civilians and canonists; see vol. i. pp. 131-5.

[1] Cod. 2. 57. 1: 'Iuris formulae aucupatione syllabarum insidiantes cunctorum actibus radicitus amputentur.' Contrast Bracton, f. 413 b: 'Tot erunt formulae brevium quot sunt genera actionum.' Ib. f. 188 b: 'Item procedere non debet assisa propter errorem nominis...item si erratum sit in syllaba.'

p. 559] is this, that we are soon compelled to change our ground, to compare, not the chancellor, but the justices with the *praetor*, and to see the Roman *formula*, not in the original writ, but in the 'issue' that is sent to a jury. However, a very slight acquaintance with our own history is enough to convince us that in this direction there can be no link of imitation between the two systems. Whatever likeness we may see between the jurors, when at the end of the middle ages they are becoming 'judges of fact,' and the *iudex* to whom the *praetor* committed a cause, there is no likeness whatever (beyond common humanity) between this *iudex* and those jurors of the thirteenth century who came to bear witness of facts or rights. Between the *Iudex esto* and the *Veniat iurata ad recognoscendum* there lies an unfathomable gulf[1].

Our forms of action are not mere rubrics nor dead categories; they are not the outcome of a classificatory process that has been applied to pre-existing materials. They are institutes of the law; they are—we say it without scruple—living things. Each of them lives its own life, has its own adventures, enjoys a longer or shorter day of vigour, usefulness and popularity, and then sinks perhaps into a decrepit and friendless old age. A few are still-born, some are sterile, others live to see their children and children's children in high places. The struggle for life is keen among them and only the fittest survive[2]. *(margin: Life of the forms.)*

The metaphor which likens the chancery to a shop is trite; we will liken it to an armoury. It contains every weapon of medieval warfare from the two-handed sword to the poniard. The man who has a quarrel with his neighbour comes thither to choose his weapon. The choice is large; but he must remember that he will not be able to change weapons in the middle of the combat and also that every weapon has its proper use and may be put to none other. If he selects a sword, he must observe the rules of sword-play; he must not try to use his cross-bow as a mace. To drop metaphor, our *(margin: Choice between the forms.)*

---

[1] If any point of contact is to be found between the jury and a Roman institution this must be sought at a remote period in the history of Gaul when Frankish kings borrow a prerogative procedure from the Roman *fiscus*. See vol. i. p. 141; also Brunner, D. R. G. ii. 525.

[2] Henceforward we shall give capital letters to the names of the forms, so that Debt will mean the form known as an action of debt.

plaintiff is not merely choosing a writ, he is choosing an action, [p. 560] and every action has its own rules[1].

Little law for actions in general. The great difference between our medieval procedure and that modern procedure which has been substituted for it by statutes of the present century lies here:—To-day we can say much of actions in general and we can say little of any procedure that is peculiar to actions of particular kinds. On the other hand, in the middle ages one could say next to nothing about actions in general, while one could discourse at great length about the mode in which an action of this or that sort was to be pursued and defended[2].

Modern and medieval procedure. It must not escape us that a law about 'actions in general' involves the exercise by our judges of wide discretionary powers. If the rules of procedure take now-a-days a far more general shape than that which they took in the past centuries, this is because we have been persuaded that no rules of procedure can be special enough to do good justice in all particular cases. Instead of having one code for actions of trespass and another for actions of debt, we have a code for actions; but then at every turn some discretionary power over each particular case is committed to 'the court or a judge.' One illustration will be enough. We lay down rules for actions in general about the times within which litigants must do the various acts which are required of them, for example, the time within which a defendant must 'enter an appearance,' or the plaintiff must deliver his statement of claim. Such rules would not be tolerable unless they were tempered by judicial discretion, and so a short clause about 'applications for an enlargement of time[3]' takes the place of the bulkiest chapter of our old law, the chapter on essoins, or excuses for non-appearance. That law strove to define the various reasonable causes which might prevent a man from keeping his day in court—the broken bridge, the bed-sickness (*malum lecti*), the crusade, the pilgrimage to Compostella. For every cause of delay it assigned a definite period:—even

---

[1] Britton, i. p. 152: 'Voloms...qe chescun bref eyt sa propre nature et qe nul ne soyt pledé par autre.'

[2] During cents. xvii., xviii. much was done by fiction towards introducing an uniform procedure in the only actions that were commonly used; but the first great statutory change was made by the Uniformity of Process Act, 2 & 3 Will. IV. c. 39.

[3] Rules of the Supreme Court, O. 64, R. 7.

[p. 561] a bed-sickness will not absolve a man for more than year and day[1]. But further, it here distinguished between the various forms of action. No essoin at all will be allowed to a man who is charged with a disseisin; the long essoin for year and day can only be allowed where there is a solemn question of 'right' in dispute and the litigants are in peril of being 'abjudged' from the debatable land for ever. Now it is just because we know that such rules as these, particular though they may be, are not particular enough, that we have recourse to an exceedingly general rule tempered by judicial discretion.

Let us not be impatient with our forefathers. 'Discretion' is not of necessity 'the law of tyrants,' and yet we may say with the great Romanist of our own day that formalism is the twin-born sister of liberty[2]. As time goes on there is always a larger room for discretion in the law of procedure; but discretionary powers can only be safely entrusted to judges whose impartiality is above suspicion and whose every act is exposed to public and professional criticism. One of the best qualities of our medieval law was that in theory it left little or nothing, at all events within the sphere of procedure, to the discretion of the justices. They themselves desired that this should be so and took care that it was or seemed to be so. They would be responsible for nothing beyond an application of iron rules. Had they aimed at a different end, they would have 'received' the plausibly reasonable system of procedure which the civilians and canonists were constructing, and then the whole stream of our legal history would have been turned into a new channel. For good and ill they made their choice. The ill is but too easily seen by any one who glances at the disorderly mass of crabbed pedantry that Coke poured forth as 'institutes' of English law; the good may escape us. But when we boast of 'the rule of law' in England, or give willing ear to the German historian who tells us that our English state is a *Rechtsstaat*, we shall do well to remember that the rule of law was the rule of writs. When Ihering assures the unamiable English traveller who fights a 'battle for right' over his hotel

No room for discretion in old procedure.

---

[1] The germs of these rules are to be found already in the earliest Germanic laws; Brunner, D. R. G. ii. 336.

[2] Ihering, Geist des römischen Rechts, ii. (2) § 45: 'Die Form ist die geschworene Feindin der Willkür, die Zwillingsschwester der Freiheit.'

bill, that his is the spirit that built up the Roman law[1], he [p. 562] speaks of nothing new. In the thirteenth century our justices kept to the old Roman road of strict adherence to 'word and form.' From the alien Corpus Iuris they turned aside, just because the spirit that animated them was (though they knew it not) *der Geist des römischen Rechts*[2].

The golden age of the forms. The last years of Henry III.'s day we may regard as the golden age of the forms. We mean that this was the time in which the number of forms which were living and thriving was at its maximum. Very few of the writs that had as yet been invented had become obsolete, and, on the other hand, the common law's power of producing new forms was almost exhausted. Bracton can still say *Tot erunt formulae brevium quot sunt genera actionum*[3]. A little later we shall have to take the tale of writs as the fixed quantity and our maxim will be *Tot erunt genera actionum quot sunt formulae brevium*[4]. Only some slight power of varying the ancient formulas will be conceded to the chancellor; all that goes beyond this must be done by statutes, and, when Edward I. is dead, statutes will do little for our ordinary private law. The subsequent development of forms will consist almost entirely of modifications of a single action, namely, Trespass, until at length it and its progeny—Ejectment, Case, Assumpsit, Trover,—will have ousted nearly all the older actions. This process, if regarded from one point of view, represents a vigorous, though contorted, growth of our substantive law; but it is the decline and fall of the formulary system, for writs are being made to do work for which they were not originally intended, and that work they can only do by means of fiction.

Number of the forms. How many forms of action were there? A precise answer to this simple question would require a long prefatory discourse, for we should have to draw some line between mere variations upon the one hand and the more vital differences upon the other; and after all when the line was drawn it would be an arbitrary line of our own drawing. We might easily raise the tale of forms to some hundreds, but perhaps we shall produce the right effect if we say that there were in common use

---

[1] Ihering, Der Kampf um's Recht (10th ed.), 45, 69.

[2] As to what happened in France when the reverence for 'word and form' disappeared, see Brunner, Wort und Form, Forschungen, pp. 272-3.

[3] Bracton, f. 413 b.   [4] See vol. i. p. 196.

p. 563] some thirty or forty actions, between which there were large differences[1].

A few statistics may set this matter before our readers in a clearer light. We will therefore make an analysis of the actions that were brought before the justices who in three different years near the end of our period made an eyre in Northumberland[2], while in the fourth column we give the results of an examination to which we subjected the roll of the Common Bench for the Easter term of 1271[3].

	Eyre 1256	Eyre 1269	Eyre 1279	Easter 1271
Miscellaneous Actions for Land[4]	25	14	12	185
Writ of Right[5]	8	1	2	12
Writ of Entry[6]	18	17	22	21
Novel Disseisin[7]	39	27	19	5
Mort d'Ancestor[8]	31	26	18	7
Aiel, Besaiel, Cosinage[9]	0	7	6	8
De Rationabili Parte[10]	0	0	1	2

---

[1] The nature of the difficulty can be briefly explained by reference to the most important instance. We may take as a single 'form' the Writ of Entry. Or we may make Writ of Entry a genus of which, (1) *sur disseisin*, (2) *sur intrusion*, (3) *cui in vita* etc. are species, and so we may make some twelve 'forms.' Or, taking each of these species separately, we may divide it into many forms, since the writ may be (*a*) in the *per*, (*b*) in the *per* and *cui*, and (*c*) in the *post*; and again it may be (i) *sine titulo*, *i.e.* for the first person who was deprived of the land, or (ii) *cum titulo* for his heir; so that we get six 'forms' within each species and thus force up the number of 'forms' of this one genus to seventy or eighty. See above, vol. ii. pp. 63, 67. Then if we distinguish between land and incorporeals we may rapidly increase this total by permutation and combination. A more familiar example would be raised by the question, Is Debt one form, while Detinue is another, and, if so, shall we count Debt in the *debet* and Debt in the *detinet* as two forms? See above, vol. ii. pp. 173, 206.

[2] Northumberland Assize Rolls (Surtees Society).

[3] Curia Regis Roll, No. 202. It would be long to explain exactly our method of computation. We believe that in the main the picture that we draw is truthful, but stress must not be laid on details.

[4] An entry relating to one of the initial stages of an action for land (*placitum terrae*) often leaves its form undetermined. These actions will for the more part be Writs of Right or of Entry; they will not be Possessory Assizes.

[5] See above, vol. ii. p. 62.   [6] See above, vol. ii. p. 63.

[7] See above, vol. ii. p. 47. This includes the assize of nuisance. Possessory Assizes rarely came before the Bench. They were taken by justices of Assize.

[8] See above, vol. ii. p. 56.   [9] See above, vol. ii. p. 57.

[10] For partition among parceners; proprietary.

	Eyre 1256	Eyre 1269	Eyre 1279	Easter 1271	
Nuper Obiit[1]	1	0	1	1	[p. 564]
Little Writ of Right[2]	0	0	0	1	
Monstraverunt[3]	0	0	0	2	
Right of Advowson[4]	0	0	0	1	
Darrein Presentment[5]	0	0	0	15	
Quare impedit, Quod permittat presentare, Quare non admisit[6]	0	0	1	14	
Assize Utrum[7]	0	0	0	6	
Quare eiecit infra terminum[8]	0	1	0	3	
De Rationabilibus Divisis[9]	0	1	0	0	
Dower[10]	9	12	12	189	
Formedon[11]	0	0	1	0	
Escheat[12]	0	0	0	1	
Quod permittat habere[13]	5	6	8	7	
Quod permittat fugare[14]	0	0	0	1	
Quod permittat prosternere[15]	0	1	3	0	
Quare levavit mercatum	0	0	0	1	
Quod reparari faciat stagnum	0	0	0	1	
De secta ad molendinum[16]	1	0	2	0	
Quo iure[17]	1	2	1	1	
Quod capiat homagium[18]	2	0	0	0	
Customs and Services[19]	4	4	4	15	
Mesne[20]	3	0	0	17	
Writs relating to wardships[21]	0	3	5	12	
De nativo habendo[22]	6	12	2	10	
De libertate probanda[23]	1	2	2	0	
Quare non permittit se talliari[24]	0	0	0	1	
Per quae servicia[25]	0	0	0	1	
Warantia Cartae[26]	18	6	10	26	

[1] For partition among parceners; possessory.

[2] See above, vol. i. p. 385. [3] See above, vol. i. p. 387.

[4] See above, vol. ii. p. 137. [5] See above, vol. ii. p. 137.

[6] See above, vol. ii. p. 139. [7] See above, vol. i. p. 247.

[8] See above, vol. ii. p. 107.

[9] For settling a disputed boundary; proprietary.

[10] This includes several different writs. [11] See above, vol. ii. p. 28.

[12] See above, vol. ii. p. 23. [13] For ways, rights of common, etc.

[14] Claiming a right to hunt. [15] For abatement of nuisances.

[16] To compel suit to a mill.

[17] Negatory of common rights; see above, vol. ii. p. 142.

[18] To compel receipt of homage. [19] See above, vol. ii. p. 125.

[20] See above, vol. i. p. 238.

[21] There are several different writs, some possessory, some proprietary.

[22] Affirming villeinage. [23] Negatory of villeinage.

[24] Claiming a right to tallage.

[25] Calling upon a tenant to say why he should not be attorned.

[26] Largely used for the purpose of levying fines; see above, vol. ii. p. 98.

	Eyre 1256	Eyre 1269	Eyre 1279	Easter 1271
De Fine Facto[1]	0	2	0	9
Waste[2]	0	0	0	1
Account[3]	0	0	1	8
Annuity[4]	2	5	2	18
Quare subtrahit[5]	0	0	0	1
Covenant[6]	7	10	6	35
Debt[7]	6	6	28[8]	53
Detinue[9]	2	1	3	11
Deceit[10]	0	1	0	1
Rescue[11]	0	0	2	2
Replevin[12]	1	0	0	35
Statutory Actions for unlawful distress[13]	0	0	0	11
Trespass[14]	6	3	9	85
Actions analogous to Trespass[15]	0	0	0	3
Appeal of homicide[16]	0	0	4	3
Appeal of robbery	1	0	5	4
Appeal of larceny (by approvers)	3	0	0	0
Appeal of wounds and mayhem	1	0	5	1
Appeal of rape	11	0	2	0
Appeal of imprisonment	1	0	0	1
Appeal of felony (unspecified)	4	0	0	1
Attaint[17]	1	0	3	0
Certification	0	0	1	0
False Judgment	1	0	0	6
Error	0	0	0	1
Prohibition[18]	0	0	0	11

[p. 565]

[1] See above, vol. ii. p. 100.

[2] See above, vol. ii. p. 9.   [3] See above, vol. ii. p. 221.

[4] See above, vol. ii. p. 133.   [5] An action for a corody.

[6] See above, vol. ii. p. 216.   [7] See above, vol. ii. p. 203.

[8] Mostly due to the activity of one money lender.

[9] See above, vol. ii. p. 172.   [10] See above, vol. ii. p. 534.

[11] For unlawfully rescuing distrained beasts.   [12] See below, p. 577.

[13] Given by various sections of the Statute of Marlborough.

[14] See above, vol. ii. pp. 167, 526.

[15] For interfering with rights of chase, for interrupting a court, etc.

[16] There is no criminal business on the roll of 1269 as printed. Appeals were still being heard by the [Common] Bench section of the High Court as well as Coram Rege. An appeal against several appellees is counted here as a single appeal.

[17] We shall speak below of this and the four following items.

[18] We believe that the only very important action not mentioned here is the royal Quo Waranto for the revocation of franchises. The Novel Disseisin and Mort d'Ancestor are not fairly represented. Hundreds of them are taken every year by justices of Assize.

[p. 566]

Differences between the forms. Now the differences between these various forms of action were such as would be brought out by answers to the following questions. (i) What is the 'original process' appropriate to this form, or, in other words, what is the first step that must be taken when the writ has been obtained? Is the defendant to be simply summoned, or is he at once to be 'attached by gage and pledges,' that is, required to give security for his appearance? Again, will the sheriff at once empanel an assize? (ii) What is the 'mesne process,' or, in other words, what is to be done if the defendant is contumacious? Will the land that is in dispute be 'seized into the king's hand' or will the compulsion be directed against the defendant's person? In the latter case what form will the compulsion take? Can he, for example, be exacted and outlawed, or can he only be distrained? (iii) Is a judgment by default possible? Can you, that is, obtain judgment against a defendant who has not appeared? (iv) What are the delays or adjournments[1]? (v) What essoins are allowed? Is this, for instance, one of those actions in which a party can delay proceedings by betaking himself to his bed and remaining there for year and day? (vi) Can a 'view' be demanded, that is to say, can the defendant insist that the plaintiff shall, not merely describe by words, but actually point out the piece of land that is in dispute? (vii) Can a warrantor be vouched? If so, may you only vouch persons named in the writ, or may you 'vouch at large[2]'? (viii) Must there be pleading and, if so, what form will it take? (ix) What is the appropriate form of trial or proof? Can there be wager of battle? Can there be wager of law—a grand assize—a petty assize—a jury? (x) What is the relief which the judgment will give to a successful plaintiff? Will it give him a thing or sum that he has claimed, or will it give him 'damages,' or will it give him both? (xi) What is the 'final process'? By what writs can the judgment be executed; for example, can outlawry be employed? (xii) What is the punishment for the vanquished defendant? Will he be simply amerced or can he be imprisoned until he makes fine with the king?

---

[1] Thus if an ordinary case comes before the court on the octave of Michaelmas, the next court-day to which it will be adjourned is the octave of Hilary; but an action of dower would be adjourned to a much nearer day. See Statutes, i. 208.   [2] See above, vol. ii. p. 71.

[p. 567]   If we addressed this catechism to the various actions, we might arrive at some tabular scheme of *genera* and *species,* for we should find that an answer to one of our questions would often imply an answer to others. Thus, to mention one instance, there is a connexion between trial by battle and the long essoin *de malo lecti,* so that we may argue from the former to the latter[1]. But many of these lines intersect each other, so that we must classify actions for one purpose in one manner, for another purpose in another manner. Often enough the sharpest procedural lines are drawn athwart those lines which seem to us the most natural.

An instructive example is worth recalling. There is one small family of actions which is marked off from all others by numerous procedural distinctions. It is the family of Petty Assizes. It has but four members, namely, the Novel Disseisin, the Mort d'Ancestor, the Darrein Presentment and the Utrum[2]. The procedure in these four cases is not precisely the same; the Novel Disseisin is swifter than the others; but still they have a great deal in common. In particular they have this in common :—the original writ directs the sheriff to summon a body of recognitors who are to answer a question formulated in that writ—formulated before there has been any pleading. Now if, instead of regarding procedure, we look at the substantive purposes that these actions serve, we see in Bracton's day little enough resemblance between the Mort d'Ancestor[3] and the Utrum, which has become 'the parson's writ of right[4].' On the other hand, there is the closest possible affinity between the Mort d'Ancestor and the action of Cosinage[5]. If I claim the seisin of my uncle, I use the one ; if I claim the seisin of a first cousin, I use the other. But procedurally the two stand far apart. The explanation is that the one belongs to Henry II.'s, the other to Henry III.'s day. The commonest cases are provided for by an ancient, the less common cases by a modern action. In the one place we find a round-headed, in the other a pointed arch. No theory of cathedrals in general will teach us where to look for the round-headed arches, though common sense assures us that as a general rule substructure must be older than superstructure ; and so no attempt to

---

[1] Bracton, f. 318 b, 346 b, 347.
[2] See above, vol. i. p. 149.
[3] See above, vol. ii. p. 56.
[4] See above, vol. i. p. 247.
[5] See above, vol. ii. p. 57.

[p. 568]

classify our actions will prevail if it neglects the element of
time and the historic order of development.

Attempts
to apply
Roman
classifica-
tion.
It was natural and perhaps desirable that English lawyers
should try to arrange these forms in the pigeon-holes provided
by a cosmopolitan jurisprudence, should try to distribute them
under such headings as 'criminal' and 'civil,' 'real' and
'personal,' 'possessory' and 'proprietary,' *ex contractu* and *ex
delicto*. The effort was made from time to time in desultory
wise, but it was never very fruitful. A few of the difficulties
that it had to meet deserve notice. We see that Bracton can
not make up his mind as to whether the Novel Disseisin is real
or personal. On the one hand, the compulsory process in this
assize is directed *in personam* and not *in rem*. In a Writ of
Right or a Writ of Entry the process is directed against the
thing, the land, that is in dispute. If the tenant, that is, the
passive party in the litigation, will not appear when summoned,
the land is 'seized into the king's hand,' and if there is continued contumacy then the land is adjudged to the demandant.
In a possessory assize it is otherwise; the land is not seized
before judgment. On the other hand, the plaintiff in the assize
is attempting to obtain the possession of a particular thing, a
piece of land, and, if he succeeds, this will be awarded to him.
Bracton therefore holds that the Novel Disseisin, though *rei
persecutoria*, is not *in rem* but *in personam*; it is founded on
delict, while as to the Mort d'Ancestor, that is *in personam* and
quasi ex contractu[1]. For all this, however, he speaks of the
Novel Disseisin as *realis*[2]. After his day less and less is
known of the Institutes; the reality of a real action is found
either in the claim for possession of a particular thing, or in a
judgment which awards to the plaintiff or demandant possession
of a particular thing. The Possessory Assizes are accounted
real actions, and at length even an action of Covenant, which
surely should be *in personam* and *ex contractu*, is called real
when the result of it will be that the seisin of a piece of land
is awarded to the plaintiff[3].

[1] Bracton, f. 103 b, 104.   [2] Bracton, f. 159 b.

[3] Even in Bracton, f. 439, Covenant is *in rem*: 'Actio...civilis...super
aliqua promissione vel conventione non observata vel finis facti...ubi prin-
cipaliter agitur in rem, ad aliquam rem certam mobilem vel immobilem
consequendam.' The action of Covenant Real was abolished in 1833 (Stat. 3 & 4
Will. IV. c. 27, sec. 36) among the 'real and mixed actions.' The same statute
spoke of Ejectment as though it were either real or mixed; but as a matter of

[p. 569]   After a brief attempt to be Roman our law falls back into old Germanic habits.   Old Germanic law, we are told, classifies its actions, not according to the right relied on, but according to the relief demanded.   It does not ask whether the plaintiff relies upon *dominium,* upon *ius in re aliena,* upon an obligation, contract or tort; it asks the ruder question—What does the plaintiff want; is it a piece of land, a particular chattel, a sum of money[1]?   Probably there is another very old line which answers to a difference between the various tones in which a man will speak when he has haled his adversary before a court of law.   He comes there either to demand (Lat. *petere,* Fr. *demander*) or to complain (Lat. *queri,* Fr. *se plaindre*); he is either a demandant or a plaintiff.   And so his adversary is either a tenant (Lat. *tenens*) or a defendant (Lat. *defendens*), being there either to deny (*defendere*) a charge brought against him or merely because he holds (*tenet*) what another demands.   Ancient law must, we should suppose, soon notice this distinction.   The *querela,* as distinct from the *petitio,* often comes from one who is with difficulty persuaded to accept money instead of vengeance, while the *petens* may have no worse to say of his opponent than that he has unfortunately purchased from one who could not give a good title.   This distinction we find in our classical common law; but it cuts across the line between those actions which seek for land and those which seek for money.   The active party in the Novel Disseisin is not a demandant; he is a plaintiff[2].   To have called him *petens* would have been impossible, for the Novel Disseisin is indubitably a possessory action, and it was common

early history Ejectment was an offshoot of Trespass and as personal as it could be.   If we make the distinction turn on the form of writ and declaration, then Ejectment is personal as late as 1852 (15 & 16 Vic. c. 76, sec. 168 ff.).   If, on the other hand, we look to the form of the judgment, then at the end of the middle ages Ejectment is becoming mixed, for a judgment will be given for possession of land and also for damages.   So in France when the clergy protested that they could not be sued by personal action in the temporal court, the royal lawyers maintained that the Novel Disseisin was, not personal, but real.   See the account of the dispute at Vincennes : Biblioth. S. Patrum, Paris, 1589, vol. iv. col. 1211.   Compare Grosseteste, Epistolae, p. 222.

[1] Laband, Die vermögensrechtlichen Klagen, p. 5 ff.   Above, vol. ii. p. 205, note 2, we have noticed Dr Heusler's assault on this doctrine.

[2] According to Bracton's usage, in the Novel Disseisin we have *querens* and *tenens,* in the Mort d'Ancestor *petens* and *tenens,* in the Darrein Presentment *querens* and *impediens* or *deforcians.*   Only in abstract disquisitions are *actor* and *reus* found.

knowledge that a possessory action can not be 'petitory.' On
the other hand, in early instances of the action of Debt the
active party is often put before us, not as complaining, but
as demanding[1], and, as we have seen, there were close affinities [p. 570]
between the action of Debt and the Writ of Right, the most
real and petitory of all real and petitory actions[2]. The man
who sues for a debt is regarded as merely asking for his own;
he ought not to speak in that angry tone which is excusable or
laudable in one who has been assaulted or disseised. But then
we have seen how Bracton, fixing for six centuries our use of
words, denied that the action for a specific chattel is an action
in rem, for the judgment will give the defendant a choice
between surrendering the chattel and paying its value[3].
Lastly, we have seen how possessoriness is regarded as a matter
of degree, how between the Possessory Assizes and the Writ
of Right there arise those Writs of Entry which for some are
possessory, for others proprietary, while for yet others they are
'mixed of possession and right[4].' 'Mixed' is a blessed word.
The impatient student who looks down upon medieval law
from the sublime heights of 'general jurisprudence' will say
that most of our English actions are mixed and many of them
very mixed.

Civil and
criminal.

Even between civil and criminal causes it was by no means
easy to draw the line, though Glanvill, under foreign influence,
points to it in the first words of his treatise[5]. We must repeat
once more that every cause for a civil action is an offence, and
that every cause for a civil action in the king's court is an
offence against the king, punishable by amercement, if not by
fine and imprisonment[6]. An action based on felony and aiming
at pure punishment, death or mutilation, has indeed become
very distinct from all the other actions; it has a highly
distinctive procedure and a name of its own; it is an Appeal
(*appellum*). The active party neither 'demands' nor 'complains'; he appeals (*appellat*) his adversary. But we have seen
how the action of Trespass is closely related to the Appeal, and
how the outlawry process which was once characteristic of the
Appeal is extended to Trespass and thence to more purely civil

---

[1] Note Book, pl. 52, 177, 325, 381, etc.　　[2] See above, vol. ii. pp. 206–7.
[3] See above, vol. ii. p. 174.　　[4] See above, vol. ii. p. 72.
[5] Glanvill, i. 1: 'Placitorum, aliud est criminale, aliud civile.'
[6] See above, vol. ii. p. 519.

actions[1]. We have also seen how in Edward I.'s day Trespass aimed at a punitive and exemplary result and how throughout the age of the Year Books men were 'punished' for their [p. 571] trespasses[2]. More native to our law was the distinction between Pleas of the Crown and Common Pleas, which was often supposed to coincide with, though really it cut, the more cosmopolitan distinction; but even this could not always be drawn with perfect neatness. Cnut's modest list of his 'rights over all men' has been wondrously expanded[3]; kings and royal justices are unwilling to close the catalogue of causes in which the crown has or may have an interest. Trespass *vi et armis*, even when in truth it had become as civil an action as civil could be, was still not for every purpose a Common Plea, for, despite Magna Carta, it might 'follow the king' and be entertained by the justices of his own, as well as by the justices of the Common Bench[4]. In these last days a statute was needed to teach us that an action of Quo Waranto is not a criminal cause[5], and even at the present moment we can hardly say that *crime* is one of the technical terms of our law[6].

Now to describe our medieval procedure in detail would be a task easy when compared with that of stating the broad outlines of the substantive law. Much we might say, for example, of essoins, for Bracton has written much, and his every sentence might be illustrated by copious extracts from the plea rolls. In all such matters the working lawyer of the thirteenth century took a profound and professional interest of the same kind as that which his successor takes in the last new rules of court. But our reader's patience, if not our own, would soon fail if we led him into this maze. Some also of the more important and the more picturesque sides of the old procedure have been sufficiently described by others; this will determine our choice of the few topics that we shall discuss[7].

Our course.

---

[1] See above, vol. ii. pp. 449, 466.

[2] See above, vol. ii. pp. 526, 531.		[3] See above, vol. ii. p. 453.

[4] Hale, Concerning the Courts of King's Bench and Common Bench, Hargrave's Law Tracts, p. 360. Novel Disseisin, Ejectment of Ward, and some other actions were in the same category.

[5] Stat. 47 & 48 Vic. c. 61, sec. 15.

[6] Stephen, Hist. Crim. Law, i. pp. 1–5. See also the large crop of decisions touching the meaning of 'any criminal cause or matter' in the Judicature Act, 1873, sec. 47.

[7] We shall, for example, pass backwards and forwards between civil and criminal procedure, just because most modern writers have sedulously kept them apart.

§ 2. *Self-help.*

Had we to write legal history out of our own heads, we [p. 572] might plausibly suppose that in the beginning law expects men to help themselves when they have been wronged, and that by slow degrees it substitutes a litigatory procedure for the rude justice of revenge. There would be substantial truth in this theory. For a long time law was very weak, and as a matter of fact it could not prevent self-help of the most violent kind. Nevertheless, at a fairly early stage in its history, it begins to prohibit in uncompromising terms any and every attempt to substitute force for judgment. Perhaps we may say that in its strife against violence it keeps up its courage by bold words. It will prohibit utterly what it can not regulate.

This at all events was true of our English law in the thirteenth century. So fierce is it against self-help that it can hardly be induced to find a place even for self-defence. The man who has slain another in self-defence deserves, it is true, but he also needs a royal pardon[1]. This thought, that self-help is an enemy of law, a contempt of the king and his court, is one of those thoughts which lie at the root of that stringent protection of seisin on which we have often commented. The man who is not enjoying what he ought to enjoy should bring an action; he must not disturb an existing seisin, be it of land, of chattels, or of incorporeal things, be it of liberty, of serfage, or of the marital relationship. It would be a great mistake were we to suppose that during the later middle ages the law became stricter about this matter; it became laxer, it became prematurely lax. Some of the 'fist-right,' as the Germans call it, that was flagrant in the fifteenth century would have been impossible, if the possessory assizes of Henry II.'s day had retained their pristine vigour. In our own day our law allows an amount of quiet self-help that would have shocked Bracton. It can safely allow this, for it has mastered the sort of self-help that is lawless[2].

[1] See above, vol. ii. p. 479.

[2] We are here differing from Mr Nichols who (Britton, i. 288) sees after Bracton's day a 'rapidly growing inclination on the part of the king's court to

[p. 573]   What may at first seem a notable exception to this broad prohibition of self-help lies in the process of extra-judicial distress (*districtio*); but we may doubt whether this should be regarded as a real exception. The practice of distraining one's adversary, that is, of taking things from him and keeping them, so that by a desire to recover them he may be compelled to pay money or do some other act, is doubtless very ancient. But among the peoples of our own race law seems to have very soon required that in general a *nâm* should not be taken until the leave of a court had been obtained and a great deal of forbearance had been shown[1]. Down one channel the extra-judicial develops into the judicial distress. The court not only licenses the process but sends an officer or party of doomsmen to see that it is lawfully performed, and at a later time the officer himself does the taking, and the beasts that are taken will be kept in the court's pound[2]. A distress without licence may perhaps be allowed when a man is found in the act of committing some minor offence which would not be a sufficient cause for a seizure of his body. In such a case you may, if you can, take his hat, his coat or the like; this may be your one chance of compelling him to appear in a court of law. In particular, however, if you find beasts doing damage on your land, you may seize them and keep them until their owner makes amends[3]. Down this channel the right becomes that carefully limited right to distrain what is 'damage feasant' (*damnum facientem*) which our law still knows in the present day[4].

repress the practice of recovering possession without judgment.' We see just the opposite inclination and think that the learned editor of Britton has been misled by Bracton's habit of calling four or five days *longum tempus*. The relaxation of possessory protection can not be doubted by any one who compares Bracton with Littleton. Ultimately the true owner has almost always at common law a right of entry; see The Beatitude of Seisin, L. Q. R. iv. 24, 286. Now-a-days the true owner always has a right of entry; all that he has to fear is statutes which make 'forcible entry' a crime. Yet our actual practice is not far from the ideal of the thirteenth century.

    [1] Sohm, Process der Lex Salica; Brunner, D. R. G. ii. 445; Viollet, Établissements, i. 185. For England, Ine, 9; Cnut, ii. 19; Leg. Will. i. 44; Leg. Henr. 51, § 3: 'et nulli sine iudicio vel licentia namiare liceat alium in suo vel alterius.' As to the word *nâm*, see Brunner, D. R. G. ii. 446.

    [2] As to judicial distress, see Brunner, D. R. G. ii. 452.

    [3] Brunner, D. R. G. ii. 531–5. In old days, however, the notion that the beast has offended and should be punished makes itself felt at this point.

    [4] Bracton, f. 158; Britton, i. 141; Note Book, pl. 1680.

But the landlord's power to distrain a tenant for rents or other services that are in arrear is the one great instance of a power of distress[1]. In the thirteenth century that power is [p. 574] being freely used and it is used extra-judicially: by which we mean that no order has been made by any court before the goods are seized. However, to all appearance there are many traces of a time when the landlord could not distrain until his court or some other court had given him leave to do so[2]. As a matter of fact we sometimes see lords obtaining a judgment before they seize the goods of their tenants. In England the transition from judicial to extra-judicial distress was in this case easy, because our law admitted that every lord had a right to hold a court of and for his tenants. Probably in the twelfth century most landlords had courts of their own. Their tenants were also their justiciables. A right to distrain a man into coming before your court to answer why he has not paid his rent may in favourable circumstances become a right to distrain him for not paying his rent, and the king's justices, who professed a deep interest in this process of distress, had no love for feudal justice. Here as in so many other cases a levelling process was at work; all landlords were put on a par and the right of distress began to look like a proprietary right. But we may at least be sure that the historical root of the landlord's right to take his tenant's chattels was no 'tacit hypothec.' At every point that right still bore a justiciary or 'processual' character. It was not a right of 'self-satisfaction[3].' The lord might not sell the beasts; he might not use them. When he has taken them they are not in his possession; they are, as the phrase goes, *in custodia legis*[4]. He must be always ready to show them; he must be ready to give them up if ever the tenant tenders the arrears or offers gage and pledge that he will contest the claim in a court of law. Nor can the lord

---

[1] The owner of a rent-charge has a similar power, but this is given him by express bargain. See above, vol. ii. p. 129.

[2] Leg. Henr. 51, § 3: 'et nulli sine iudicio vel licentia namiare liceat alium in suo vel alterius.' See Bigelow, Hist. Procedure, 202–8, and above, vol. i. p. 353.

[3] Brunner, D. R. G. ii. 451. Observe that when words are correctly used one does not distrain a thing; one distrains a man by (*per*) a thing.

[4] In early continental law the thing taken in distress sometimes became the property of the distrainor if the debtor did not redeem it within a fixed time.

take just what he likes best among the chattels that are upon
[p. 575] the tenement. On the contrary he is bound by rules, a breach
of which will make him a disseisor of his tenant[1]. Some of
these rules, which place chattels of a certain kind utterly
beyond the reach of distress, or suffer them to be taken only
when there are no others, are probably of high antiquity; but
we must not pause to discuss them[2].

Just because the power of extra-judicial distress is originally **Replevin.**
a justiciary power, the king's courts and officers are much concerned when it is abused. If the distrainor will not deliver
the beasts after gage and pledge have been offered, then it is
the sheriff's duty to deliver them. For this purpose he may
raise the hue, call out the whole power of the county (*posse
comitatus*) and use all necessary force[3]. 'When gage and
pledge fail, peace fails,' says Bracton[4]: in other words, the
distraining lord is beginning a war against the state and must
be crushed. The offence that he commits in retaining the
beasts after gage and pledge have been tendered, is known as
vetitum namii, or *vee de nam*[5]. It stands next door to robbery[6];
it is so royal a plea that very few of the lords of franchises have
power to entertain it[7]. It is an attack on that justiciary system
of which the king is the head. Disputes about the lawfulness of
a distress were within the sheriff's competence. He could hear
them without being ordered to do so by royal writ. But when
he heard them he was acting, not as the president of the county
court, but as a royal justiciar[8]. Before the end of the thirteenth
century the action based upon the *vee de nam* was losing some

---

[1] Bracton, f. 217.

[2] Co. Lit. 47; Blackstone, Comment. iii. 7. For parallel rules on the
continent, see Brunner, D. R. G. ii. 449.

[3] Bracton, f. 157; Britton, i. 137; Stat. West. I. c. 17.

[4] Bracton, f. 217 b: 'ubi deficiunt vadia et plegia deficit pax.'

[5] Blackstone, Comm. iii. 49, suggests that *de vetito namii* is a corrupt
reading of *de repetito namii*. This is a needless emendation. If you refuse to
give up a thing, you are said *vetare* that thing. See next note.

[6] Bracton, f. 157 b: 'cum iniusta captio et detentio contra vadium et
plegium dici poterit quaedam roberia contra pacem domini Regis, etiam plus
quam nova disseisina.' Ibid. f. 158 b: 'et notandum quod iniusta captio
emendari poterit per vicinos, iniusta autem detentio non, quia hoc est manifeste
contra pacem domini Regis et contra coronam suam.' Ibid. f. 217 b: 'si averia
capta per vadium et plegium vententur, vetitum illud non solum erit querenti
iniuriosum, immo domino Regi, cum sit contra pacem suam.' Britton, i. 139.

[7] Bracton, f. 155 b. See the Earl of Warenne's case, P. Q. W. 751.

[8] Bracton, f. 155 b; Britton, i. 136.

of its terrors; either party could easily procure its removal [p. 576] from the county court to the king's court[1]. Under the name of *Replegiare* or Replevin, an action was being developed which was proving itself to be a convenient action for the settlement of disputes between landlord and tenant; but it seems to have owed its vigour, its rapidity, and therefore its convenience to the supposition that a serious offence had been committed against the king[2].

Distress and seisin.

One other trait in our law of distress deserves notice. The power to distrain flows from seisin, not from 'right.' On the one hand, a lord or would-be lord must not distrain unless he can allege a recent seisin of those services the arrears of which he is endeavouring to recover. On the other hand, a recent, if wrongful, seisin of those services gives him the right to distrain[3]. We may say that even the negative self-help, which consists in a refusal to continue a compliance with unjust demands, is forbidden. The man who has done services must still do them until he has gone to law and disproved his liability. He may easily be guilty of disseising his lord[4].

§ 3. *Process.*

We have now to speak of the various processes which the law employs in order to compel men to come before its courts. They vary in stringency from the polite summons to the decree of outlawry. But first we must say one word of an offshoot of outlawry, of a species of summary justice that was still useful in the thirteenth century[5].

Summary justice.

When a felony is committed, the hue and cry (*hutesium et clamor*) should be raised. If, for example, a man comes upon a dead body and omits to raise the hue, he commits an amerciable offence, besides laying himself open to ugly suspicions. Possibly the proper cry is 'Out! Out!' and therefore it is

---

[1] Stat. West. II. c. 2.

[2] There was a tradition among the lawyers of Edward I.'s day that the plea *de vetito namii* was not so old as Henry II.'s time (P. Q. W. 232) but was invented under John (Y. B. 30–1 Edw. I. p. 222). The replevin writ in Glanvill, xii. 15, differs in important respects from that in Bracton, f. 157, and Reg. Brev. Orig. f. 81.

[3] Bracton, f. 158.   [4] See above, vol. ii. pp. 125–6.

[5] Brunner, D. R. G. ii. 481.

[p. 577] *uthesium* or *hutesium*[1]. The neighbours should turn out with the bows, arrows, knives, that they are bound to keep[2] and, besides much shouting, there will be horn-blowing; the 'hue' will be 'horned' from vill to vill[3].

Now if a man is overtaken by hue and cry while he has still about him the signs of his crime, he will have short shrift. Should he make any resistance, he will be cut down. But even if he submits to capture, his fate is already decided. He will be bound, and, if we suppose him a thief, the stolen goods will be bound on his back[4]. He will be brought before some court (like enough it is a court hurriedly summoned for the purpose), and without being allowed to say one word in self-defence, he will be promptly hanged, beheaded or precipitated from a cliff, and the owner of the stolen goods will perhaps act as an amateur executioner[5].

The hand-having thief.

In the thirteenth century this barbaric justice is being brought under control[6]. We can see that the royal judges do not much like it, though, truth to tell, it is ridding England of more malefactors than the king's courts can hang. The old rule held good that if by hue and cry a man was captured when he was still in seisin of his crime—if he was still holding the gory knife or driving away the stolen beasts—and he was brought before a court which was competent to deal with such cases, there was no need for any accusation against him, for any appeal or any indictment, and, what is more, he could not be heard to say that he was innocent, he could not claim any sort or form of [p. 578] trial[7]. Even royal judges, if such a case is brought before them,

Summary justice in the king's court.

---

[1] See Brunner, D. R. G. ii. 482, as to the various cries used for this purpose. The famous Norman *Haro* seems to mean *Hither*. See also Viollet, Établissements, i. 189.

[2] See the Writ of 1252 in Select Charters.

[3] Select Pleas of the Crown, p. 69: 'et tunc cornaverunt hutes.'

[4] Bigelow, Placita, p. 260.   [5] See above, vol. ii. p. 496.

[6] Palgrave, Commonwealth, p. 212; Y. B. 30–1 Edw. I. pp. 503, 545.

[7] Bracton, f. 137: 'haec est constitutio antiqua'; Britton, i. 37, 56. Good instances of the enrolments that will be made when the king's justices come round are these:—Northumberland Assize Rolls, p. 73: 'W. Y. burgavit domum T. F. in W. et furatus fuit...septem vellera... Et homines de eadem villa secuti fuerunt ipsum et ipsum decollari fecerunt praesente ballivo domini Regis. Catalla eiusdem...ix sol. vi. d.... Et super hoc veniunt ballivi Comitis Stratherne...et dicunt quod huiusmodi catalla pertinent ad eos, eo quod ipse recepit iudicium in curia sua.' Ibid. 78; 'S. de S....captus fuit cum quodam equo furato per sectam W. T. et decollatus fuit praesente ballivo domini Regis,

act upon this rule[1]. It is not confined to cases of murder and theft. A litigant who in a civil suit produces a forged writ is hanged out of hand in a summary way without appeal or indictment, and the only chance of exculpation given him is that of naming a warrantor[2]. Even in much later days if a man was taken 'with the mainour' (*cum manuopere*), though he was suffered and compelled to submit the question of his guilt or innocence to the verdict of a jury, he could be put on his trial without any appeal or any indictment[3].

Summary justice and outlawry. There is hardly room for doubt that this process had its origin in days when the criminal taken in the act was *ipso facto* an outlaw[4]. He is not entitled to any 'law'[5], not even to that sort of 'law' which we allow to noble beasts of the chase. Even when the process is being brought within some legal limits, this old idea survives. If there must be talk of proof, what has to be proved is, not that this man is guilty of a murder, but that he was taken red-handed by hue and cry. Our records seem to show that the kind of justice which the criminal of old times had most to dread was the kind which we now associate with the name of Mr Lynch[6].

Outlawry as process. We may now say a few last words of outlawry[7]. It was still the law's ultimate weapon. When Bracton was writing, a tentative use of it was already being made in actions founded on trespasses committed with force and arms. This was a novelty. In the past the only persons who were outlawed were [p. 579]

---

et praedictus equus deliberatus fuit praedicto W. qui sequebatur pro equo illo in pleno comitatu.' See also Thayer, Evidence, 71.

[1] Gloucestershire Pleas, pl. 174 ('non potest dedicere'), 189, 394 ('non potest defendere'); Select Pleas of the Crown, pl. 106, 124, 125, 169, 195; Note Book, pl. 136 ('non potest dedicere tunicam'), 138 ('non potest defendere') 1461, 1474, 1539.

[2] Note Book, pl. 1847, cited by Bracton, f. 414.

[3] Hale, P. C. ii. 156. In Stat. Walliae, c. 14, Edward I. concedes to the Welsh that a thief taken with the mainour shall be deemed convicted.

[4] Brunner, D. R. G. ii. 483. A gloss on the Sachsenspiegel says, 'Some are declared outlaw (*friedlos*) by a judge; others make themselves outlaw, as those who break into houses by night.' With reference to the closely analogous process of excommunication, we might speak of an outlawry *lata sententia*.

[5] Ass. Clarend. c. 12: 'non habeat legem.' But under this assize the man taken with the mainour may go to the ordeal if he be not of ill fame.

[6] The Halifax Gibbet Law, described by Stephen, Hist. Crim. Law, i. 265, is a relic of this old summary justice. Observe that Lynch law is not 'self-help.'

[7] See above, vol. ii. p. 449.

those who were accused of felony either by appeal or by indictment. An Appeal was a proceeding which was normally commenced in the county court without any writ. If the appellee did not appear, the ceremony of 'exacting' or 'inter-rogating[1]' him was performed in four successive county courts: that is to say, a proclamation was made bidding him 'come in to the king's peace,' and if he came not, then the dread sentence was pronounced. Then again, if any one was indicted before the king's justices and was not forthcoming, they would make inquisition as to his guilt and, being assured of this, would direct that he should be exacted and outlawed in the county court. In either case he might, it will be seen, remain contumacious for some five months without being put outside the peace[2]. Outlawry was still a grave matter. It involved, not merely escheat and forfeiture, but a sentence of death. If the outlaw was captured and brought before the justices, they would send him to the gallows so soon as the mere fact of outlawry was proved[3]. Therefore an important step in consti-tutional history was made in the year 1234 when the outlawry of Hubert de Burgh was declared null on the ground that he had been neither indicted nor yet appealed, though he had broken prison and the king was treating him as a rebel[4]. This weapon was as clumsy as it was terrible. There were all manner of cases in which a man might be outlawed without being guilty of any crime or any intentional contumacy. The exaction might, for example, take place in a county distant from his home. There was therefore great need for royal writs [p. 580] inlawing an outlaw and many were issued; but no strict line

---

[1] In our records *interrogetur* = *exigatur* = let him be demanded.

[2] Old English and old Frankish law would lead us to expect but three exactions. The London custom required but three, which were made at fortnightly intervals; but in cent. xiii. this was thought too hasty. See Munim. Gildh. i. 86; ii. 333–8. What is in substance the same procedure may be said to involve three, four or five exactions; for we may or may not count what happens at the first, or what happens at the last court as an exaction. See Bracton, f. 125 b; Gross, Coroners' Rolls, p. xli.

[3] The 'minor outlawry' for 'trespasses' that was being invented did not involve sentence of death. Bracton, f. 441.

[4] Note Book, pl. 857; Mat. Par. Chron. Maj. ann. 1234. Bracton, f. 127, is thinking of this case when he says: 'Item nulla [erit utlagaria] si ad praeceptum Regis vel sectam Regis fuerit quis utlagatus, nisi prius facta inquisitione per iustitiarios, utrum ille, qui in fuga est, culpabilis sit de crimine ei imposito vel non.'

could here be drawn between acts of justice and acts of grace[1].

Arrest.

From outlawry we may pass to arrest, which in our eyes may seem to be the simplest method of securing a malefactor's presence in court. Now of the law of arrest as it was in these early days we should like to speak dogmatically, for thus we might obtain some clue to those controversies touching 'the liberty of the subject' which raged in later ages. Our guides, however, the lawyers of the time, will not give us the help that we might hope for; they seem to be much more deeply interested in the essoin *de malo lecti* and other remunerative tithes of mint and cumin than in the law of arrest which does not directly concern those decent people who pay good fees.

Law of arrest.

The law of arrest is rough and rude; it is as yet unpolished by the friction of nice cases. Before we say more of it we must call to mind two points in our criminal procedure. In the first place, any preliminary magisterial investigation, such as that which is now-a-days conducted by our justices of the peace, is still in the remote future, though the coroners are already making inquest when there is violent death. This simplifies the matter. We have but to consider two or three cases. The man whose arrest we are to discuss either will have been, or he will not have been, already accused of an offence. In the former case he will have been either appealed or indicted. Secondly, there is no professional police force. The only persons who are specially bound to arrest malefactors are the sheriff, his bailiffs and servants and the bailiffs of those lords who have the higher regalities. The constables who are becoming apparent at the end of our period are primarily military officers, though it is their duty to head the hue and cry[2].

Arrest of felons.

The main rule we think to be this, that felons ought to be summarily arrested and put in gaol. All true men ought to take part in this work and are punishable if they neglect it. We may strongly suspect, however, that in general the only persons whom it is safe to arrest are felons, and that a man leaves himself open to an action, or even an appeal, of false [p. 581]

---

[1] Bracton, f. 127 b: 'de iure concomitante gratia ad omnia restituendi sunt.' Ibid. 132 b: 'recepi debet...ad pacem et sine difficultate, et aliquantulum de iure.' Ibid. 133: 'facit tamen rex aliquando gratiam talibus, sed contra iustitiam.'

[2] Writ of 1252 in Select Charters.

imprisonment if he takes as a felon one who has done no felony. In other words, it seems very doubtful whether a charge of false imprisonment could have been met by an allegation that there was reasonable cause for suspicion. This was not always the case, for before the end of Henry III.'s reign there were ordinances which commanded the arrest of suspicious persons who went about armed without lawful cause, and very probably the sheriff and his officers could always plead a justification for the caption of persons who were suspected, though not guilty, of felony[1]. The ordinary man seems to have been expected to be very active in the pursuit of malefactors and yet to 'act at his peril.' This may be one of the reasons why, as any eyre roll will show, arrests were rarely made, except where there was hot pursuit after a 'hand-having' thief[2].

When there had been an indictment of felony, the sheriff's duty was to arrest the indicted, and as the indictment might take place in the sheriff's turn, or some co-ordinate court which could not try felons, the arrest of some accused persons was thus secured. Then again, at the beginning of the eyre the names of those who were suspected of felony by the jurors were handed in to the justices, who ordered the sheriff to make arrests. But, as a matter of fact, those who thought that they were going to be indicted usually had an ample opportunity [p. 582] for flight and then they could only be outlawed. The law

Arrest of the accused.

---

[1] See Northumberland Assize Rolls, p. 108. In 1256 two women bring an action against Thomas of Bickerton, alleging that he arrested them and another woman, who has died in prison, as thieves and sent them to Newcastle gaol. Thomas defends himself by alleging that the three women stole a bushel of malt in his house. The jurors find that the dead woman committed the theft and that the two plaintiffs are innocent. Thomas has to make fine with the heavy sum of £40. No word is said by either party of 'probable cause.'

[2] The Assize of Clarendon, c. 2, speaks of the arrest of the indicted; it also, c. 16, orders the arrest of a waif or unknown man; even in a borough he must be arrested, if he has stayed there for more than one night. The ordinance of 1195 commands all men to arrest outlaws, robbers, thieves and the receivers of such. That of 1233, which institutes the night-watch, commands the arrest of the man who enters a vill by night and the man who goes armed. The ordinance of 1252 mentions also 'quoscunque perturbatores pacis nostrae, praedones et malefactores in parcis vel vivariis.' These documents are in the Select Charters. The oath taken by every youth (Bracton, f. 116) contained a promise, not only to join the hue and cry, but also to arrest any one who bought victuals in a vill in such wise as to found a suspicion that they were meant for the use of criminals ('et suspectus habeatur quod hoc sit ad opus malefactorum').

seems to believe much more in outlawry than in arrest. When there is an appeal of felony in the county court—and it is there that an appeal should be begun—we can see no serious effort made to catch the absent appellee. The process of 'exacting' him begins. If the fear of outlawry will not bring him in, we despair. Much had been done towards the centralization of justice; still the county boundary was a serious obstacle. The man outlawed in one shire was outlaw everywhere; but a sheriff could not pursue malefactors who had fled beyond his territory.

Mainprise. If a man was arrested he was usually replevied (*replegiatus*) or mainprised (*manucaptus*): that is to say, he was set free so soon as some sureties (*plegii*) undertook (*manuceperunt*) or became bound for his appearance in court. It was not common to keep men in prison. This apparent leniency of our law was not due to any love of an abstract liberty. Imprisonment was costly and troublesome. Besides, any reader of the eyre rolls will be inclined to define a gaol as a place that is made to be broken, so numerous are the entries that tell of escapes[1]. The medieval dungeon was not all that romance would make it; there were many ways out of it. The mainprise of substantial men was about as good a security as a gaol. The sheriff did not want to keep prisoners; his inclination was to discharge himself of all responsibility by handing them over to their friends.

Replevisable prisoners. The sheriffs seem to have enjoyed a discretionary power of detaining or releasing upon mainprise those who were suspected of felony; but the general rule had apparently been that, even after an appeal had been begun or an indictment had been preferred, the prisoner should be replevied unless he was charged with homicide. Glanvill seems to have regarded even this exception of homicide as one that had been introduced by ordinance, and he speaks as though a man appealed of high-treason would in the ordinary course of events be replevied[2]. The rigorous

---

[1] See *e.g.* Northumberland Assize Rolls, pp. 74, 76, 80, 89, 91, 96, 98.

[2] Glanvill, xiv. 1, says that one appealed of high treason is usually attached by pledges, if he can find them. 'In omnibus autem placitis de felonia solet accusatus per plegios dimitti praeterquam in placito de homicidio, ubi ad terrorem aliter statutum est.' Munim. Gildh. i. 113: 'Secundum antiquam legem civitatis [Londoniae] semper consueverunt replegiare homines rectatos de morte hominis.' See also Ibid. i. 296. So late as 1321 (Ibid. ii. 374) the Londoners asserted this custom of replevying men indicted of homicide, but

[p. 583] forest law introduced a second exception, for those who were 'taken for the forest' were to be detained. Again, the sheriff should not set at liberty any one who was imprisoned by the special command of the king or of his chief justiciar. A writ *De homine replegiando* soon came into currency. It told the sheriff to deliver the prisoner unless he had been taken at the special command of the king or of his chief justiciar, or for the death of a man, or for some forest offence, or for some other cause which according to the law of England made him irreplevisable[1]. Such a writ could apparently be obtained 'as of course' from the chancery. As we understand the matter, it did but remind the sheriff of what had all along been his duty: in other words, he was not bound to wait for a writ. It will be observed that this precept was so penned as to throw upon him the responsibility of deciding whether 'according to the law of England' the prisoner should be kept in custody. Four cases are specially mentioned as cases in which there should be no replevin; but he is warned that the list is not exhaustive. Clearly it is not, for we may say with certainty that this 'writ of course' would not warrant the delivery of a condemned felon, or of an outlaw. But we can see that in yet other cases a sheriff might be justified in refusing mainprise. The law was gradually growing less favourable to release. In one passage Bracton repeats Glanvill's words:—If a man has been appealed or indicted of any felony, other than homicide, he is usually replevied[2]. In another passage we find a far severer doctrine:—The man who has been taken for high treason is absolutely irreplevisable; the man who has been taken for any crime which is punished by death or mutilation will hardly be able to extort from the king the privilege of being released on bail[3]. The records of practice seem to show that some sheriffs were only too glad to dismiss prisoners from

the justices treated it as an intolerable infringement of common law. The Assize of Clarendon, c. 3, provides that an indicted man is to be replevied, if within three days he is demanded by his lord, his lord's steward or his lord's men. This reminds us that in the twelfth century a feudal force was making for replevin. The lords will not approve the detention of their men.

[1] This writ is in Bracton, f. 154: 'nisi captus sit per speciale praeceptum nostrum, vel capitalis iustitiarii nostri, vel pro morte hominis, vel foresta nostra, vel pro aliquo retto quare secundum legem Angliae non sit replegiandus.'

[2] Bracton, f. 123.   Compare f. 139.

[3] Bracton, f. 437.   Observe that there is room for a variety of opinions.

custody[1]. Then in 1275 one of Edward I.'s momentous statutes, [p. 584] after accusing the sheriffs both of retaining those who were, and releasing those who were not, replevisable, and after admitting that the law about this matter had never been precisely determined, proceeded to lay down rules which correspond rather with Bracton's severer than with his more lenient doctrine, and these statutory rules became the law for the coming centuries[2].

Action of
the king's
court.

In later days our interest in 'the liberty of the subject' finds its focus in the king's courts at Westminster. Our question is: What will these courts do with those men who have not been sentenced to imprisonment but who are in prison? If we ask this question of the thirteenth century, we suppose too perfect a centralization. In theory, no doubt, the central court had a control over the whole province of criminal justice. We can see, for example, that it will sometimes direct a sheriff to send up prisoners to Westminster for trial, though this is a rare event and such mandates generally come from the chancery, not from the justices, and are to be considered rather as governmental than as judicial acts[3]. We may also believe that if a man who thought himself unlawfully imprisoned by the sheriff or by some lord of a franchise made his voice heard in the king's court, the justices had power to order that his body should be brought before them and to liberate him if they were persuaded that his detention was wrongful. But we have seen no definite machinery provided for this purpose, nor do our text-writers speak as if any such machinery was necessary. The central power for the time being seems to fear much rather that there will not be enough, than that there will be too much imprisonment of suspected malefactors, while upon merely lawless incarceration the appeal or action for false imprisonment[4] seems a sufficient check. Those famous words *Habeas corpus* are making their way into divers writs, but for any habitual use of them for the purpose of investigating

---

[1] See *e.g.* Gloucestershire Pleas (A.D. 1221), pl. 245 : prisoners for homicide delivered by the sheriff for five marks.

[2] Stat. West. I. c. 15. For commentaries on this famous statute, see Coke, Second Instit. 185 ; Hale, P. C. ii. 127 and Stephen, Hist. Crim. Law, i. 233.

[3] See *e.g.* Rot. Cl. 429. Approvers are often moved about from prison to prison.

[4] See above, vol. ii. p. 488.

[p. 585] the cause of an imprisonment we must wait until a later time[1].

In particular, we must not as yet set the king's court in opposition to the king's will. His justices were his very obedient servants. As we have lately said[2], a memorable triumph for law over arbitrary power was won in 1234 when the royal court by the mouth of William Raleigh declared null and void that outlawry of Hubert de Burgh which the king had specially commanded. But this victory was only gained after a revolt and a change of ministry. The man committed to gaol *per mandatum domini Regis* would have found none to liberate him. The luckless Eleanor of Britanny was kept in prison to the end of her days. Her one offence was her birth; she had never been tried or sentenced; but we may safely say that none of the king's justices would have set her free[3].

There is, however, another writ that deserves mention. We have seen how in Glanvill's time homicide was the only crime for which men were usually detained as irreplevisable. But even in this case the law of the twelfth century showed no love for imprisonment, and a writ was framed for the relief of the incarcerated appellee, the writ *de odio et atia*. Unfortunately the mention of this writ compels us to unravel a curious little node in which the history of provisional imprisonment is knotted with the history of pleading and the history of trial. We must be brief.

In the twelfth century the only mode of bringing a felon to justice has been the appeal; the only mode of meeting an appeal has been a direct negation, and the normal mode of proof has been battle. But the king has his royal inquest-procedure for sale, and the canonists are teaching our English lawyers how to plead *exceptiones*, that is to say, pleas that are not direct negations of the charge made by the plaintiff. Now sometimes a defendant will plead such an *exceptio* and buy from the king the right to prove it by a verdict of the country.

Royal control.

The writ de odio et atia.

Origin of the writ.

[1] We shall see hereafter (p. 593) that a *Habeas corpus* was at one time a part of the ordinary mesne process in a personal action.

[2] See above, vol. ii. p. 581.

[3] Mat. Par. Chron. Maj. iv. 163: 'obiit Alienora filia Galfridi...in clausura diutini carceris sub arcta custodia reservata.' Coke's laborious attempt (Second Instit. 187) to make *le maundement le roy* of Stat. West. I. c. 15, mean the order of the king's court will deceive no student of history. See Stephen, Hist. Crim. Law, i. 234, note 3.

One of these 'exceptions' is the plea of spite and hate (*de odio* [p. 586] *et atia*)[1]. The appellee asserts and undertakes to prove that the appeal is, if we use modern terms, no *bona fide* appeal, but a malicious prosecution[2]. Sometimes, if not always, he alleges a particular cause for the spite and hatred[3]. He is not directly meeting the appeal by denying his guilt, he is raising a different question. This having been raised, he obtains a writ directing that an inquest shall be taken. Is he appealed of spite and hatred or is there a true, that is, a *bona fide* appeal?

Effect of the writ. Such is the writ *de odio et atia*. Suppose now that the jurors testify in favour of the appellor. The appellee is not convicted; he can still meet the appeal with a direct negation and go to battle[4]; meanwhile he will remain in prison. Suppose on the other hand that the verdict is favourable to him, then the appeal will be quashed and he can obtain a writ directing the sheriff to let him out of prison. But the king is now asserting his right to have every one who is appealed of felony arraigned at his suit, even though the appeal has broken down. So our appellee will not be wholly acquitted; he will be replevied and must come before the king's justices when next they make their eyre.

Later history of the writ. In a few years a great part of this procedure has become obsolete. Trial by jury has made further encroachments on trial by battle. The appellee has gained the right to submit, not merely special pleas, but the whole question of his guilt or innocence to a verdict of the country. Also the Great Charter has ordained that the writ *de odio et atia* shall issue as of course and that no fee shall be taken for it—so rapidly popular

[1] It seems possible that this famous formula occurred first in some fore-oath *de calumnia* which could in some instances be required of a plaintiff. See Leg. Will. i. cc. 10, 14: 'li appelur jurra...que pur haur nel fait.' The A.-S. form may have been 'ne for hete ne for hóle'; Schmid, App. x. c. 4.

[2] The question is 'Utrum appellatus sit de morte illa odio et atia, vel eo quod inde culpabilis sit.' Sometimes the contrast is between an appeal *ex odio et atia* and *verum appellum*, where *verum* implies, not the truth of the accusation, but the good faith of the accuser.

[3] Select Pleas of the Crown, pl. 84: 'Et dicit quod ipse R. facit hoc appellum...per attiam et vetus odium, unde tres causas ostendit. Quarum prima est... Alia causa... Tertia causa...' Ibid. pl. 87: 'Et dicit quod ipse W. appellat eum per odium et athiam quia ipse quaesivit versus eum dedecus et damnum ut de uxore sua.' Bracton, f. 123: 'et si de odio et atia, quo odio et qua atia.'

[4] Select Pleas of the Crown, pl. 91, 92, 93.

[p.587] have the recent improvements in royal justice become[1]. Henceforth the writ sinks into a subordinate place. It merely enables a man, who is imprisoned on a charge of homicide, to obtain a provisional release upon bail when an inquest has found that the charge has been preferred against him 'of spite and hatred[2].'

We have spoken, perhaps too indifferently, of 'mainprise' and of 'bail.' There was some difference between these two institutions, but at an early time it became obscure[3]. Bail implied a more stringent, mainprise a laxer, degree of responsibility[4]. English, Norman and French tradition seem all to point to an ancient and extremely rigorous form of suretyship or hostageship which would have rendered the surety liable to suffer the punishment that was hanging over the head of the released prisoner[5]. In Normandy these sureties are compared to gaolers, and a striking phrase speaks of them as 'the Duke's living prison[6].' In England when there is a release on bail

Mainprise and bail.

---

[1] Articles of the Barons, c. 26 ; Charter, 1215, c. 36. We know from Bracton, f. 121 b, 123, that the writ of inquest which is to be denied to no one is the writ *de odio et atia*.

[2] The story here told is substantially that which was first told by Brunner, Entstehung der Schwurgerichte, p. 471. The publication of excerpts from the earliest plea rolls have gone far to prove the truth of his brilliant guess, which has been confirmed by Thayer, Evidence, 68. See Gloucestershire Pleas, pl. 76, 434 ; Select Pleas of the Crown, pl. 25, 78, 81–4–6–7–8, 91–2–3–4–5, 104, 202–3 ; Note Book, pl. 134, 1548. Our classical writers missed the track because they were inclined to treat trial by jury as aboriginal. As regards the later history of the writ, Foster (Crown Cases, 285) and Sir James Stephen (Hist. Crim. Law, i. 242 ; iii. 37) have contended that it was abolished in 1278 by Stat. Glouc. c. 9, which deals with homicide by misadventure. This doctrine can hardly be true, for the writ is mentioned as an existing institution in 1285 (Stat. West. II. c. 29) and in 1314 (Rot. Parl. i. 323). Coke, Second Instit. 43, and Hale, P. C. ii. 148, certainly supposed that the writ could be issued in their own days. Coke thought that it had been abolished by Stat. 28 Edw. III. c. 9, and restored by Stat. 42 Edw. III. c. 1. The writ with which the Statute of Gloucester deals had nothing whatever in it about *odium et atia*; it directly raised the issue 'felony or self-defence [or misadventure].' See above, p. 481. The writ *de odio* went out of use as gaol-deliveries became frequent.

[3] Hale, P. C. ii. 124.

[4] Bracton, f. 139 : 'non est per plegios dimittendus, nisi hoc fuerit de gratia, et tunc per ballium, scilicet, corpus pro corpore.'

[5] Fitz. Abr. tit. *Mainprise*, pl. 12 ; Hale, P. C. ii. 125 ; Ancienne coutume, cc. 68, 75 (ed. de Gruchy, pp. 163, 180); Somma, p. 168 ; Esmein, Histoire de la procédure criminelle, 55.

[6] Ancienne coutume, p. 180 ; Somma, p. 188 : 'viva prisonia Ducis Normanniae': 'la vive prison au Duc de Normendie.' On the other hand, a

the sureties are often said to be bound *corpus pro corpore*[1]. [p. 588]
However, so far as we can see, whether there has been bail
or whether there has been mainprise, the sureties of the
thirteenth century, if they do not produce their man, escape
with amercement. The undertaking to forfeit a particular sum
and the formal recognizance, which afterwards become familiar,
seem to be very rare in this age[2]. The strict theory seems
to be that all the chattels of the sureties are at the king's
mercy, while in case of bail they may have to render their own
bodies to gaol. Very often the prisoner was handed over to
a tithing; sometime a whole township was made responsible
for his appearance[3].

Sanctuary and abjuration. One of the commonest results of the attempt to catch a
criminal was his flight to sanctuary and his abjuration of the
realm. This picturesque episode of medieval justice has been
so admirably described by other hands that we shall say little
about it[4]. Every consecrated church was a sanctuary. If a
malefactor took refuge therein, he could not be extracted; but
it was the duty of the four neighbouring vills to beset the holy
place, prevent his escape and send for a coroner. The coroner
came and parleyed with the refugee, who had his choice between submitting to trial and abjuring the realm. If he chose
the latter course, he hurried dressed in pilgrim's guise to the
port that was assigned to him, and left England, being bound
by his oath never to return. His lands escheated; his chattels
were forfeited, and if he came back his fate was that of an
outlaw. If he would neither submit to trial nor abjure the
realm, then the contention of the civil power was that, at all
events after he had enjoyed the right of asylum for forty days,

prison is sometimes spoken of as a pledge, *e.g.* Select Pleas of the Crown,
pl. 197: 'plegius Eustachii gaola de Flete.'

[1] Bracton, f. 139. See the bail-bond for Nicholas Seagrave, Rot. Parl. i. 173.

[2] Hale, P. C. ii. 124: 'Always mainprise is a recognizance in a sum certain.'
This was not so in cent. xiii. Any eyre roll will show that the regular
punishment for defaulting mainpernors was amercement. Munim. Gildh. i.
92, 115: in London the mainpernor forfeited his *wer* of 100 shillings. This
will be an old trait.

[3] Gloucestershire Pleas, pl. 45: 'et villata de P. cepit in manum habendi
eum, et non habuit, ideo in misericordia.' Ibid. pl. 71: 'et thethinga sua
cepit in manum habendi eos.' Ibid. pl. 219: 'Gaufridus...captus fuit et postea
commissus Rogero de Cromwelle de Horsheie et thethingae suae... Et Rogerus
et thethinga sua in misericordia pro fuga.'

[4] Réville, L'Abjuratio regni, Revue historique, vol. 50, p. 1 (1892).

[p. 589] he was to be starved into submission; but the clergy resented this interference with the peace of Holy Church. However, large numbers of our felons were induced to relieve England of their presence and were shipped off at Dover to France or Flanders[1].

In contrast to the procedure against felons by way of Appeal which is begun with 'fresh suit,' we have the civil procedure which is begun by Original Writ[2]. Here the original writ itself will indicate the first step that is to be taken, in other words, the 'original process'; and the subsequent steps (the 'mesne process'), which will become necessary if the defendant is contumacious, will be ordered by 'judicial' writs which the justices issue from time to time as defaults are committed. Throughout, the sheriff acts as the court's minister; he does the summoning, attaching, distraining, arresting; but his action is hampered by the existence of 'liberties' within which some lord or some borough community enjoys 'the return of writs.' Civil process.

Our readers would soon be wearied if we discoursed of mesne process. Its one general characteristic is its tedious forbearance[3]. Very slowly it turns the screw which brings pressure to bear upon the defendant. Every default that is not essoined is cause for an amercement, but the law is reluctant to strike a decisive blow. If we would understand its patience, we must transport ourselves into an age when steam and electricity had not become ministers of the law, when roads were bad and when no litigant could appoint an attorney until he had appeared in court[4]. Law must be slow in order that it may be fair. Every change that takes place in Forbearance of medieval law.

---

[1] For the right of asylum under the continental folk-laws see Brunner, D. R. G. ii. 610; for A.-S. law see Schmid, Gesetze, p. 584. M. Réville holds that the law of abjuration is developed from ancient English elements and passes from England to Normandy. It must have taken its permanent shape late in the twelfth century. Some leading passages are Leg. Edw. Conf. c. 5; Bracton, f. 135 b; Britton, i. 63; Fleta, p. 45; Mat. Par. Chron. Maj. vi. 357. For early cases see Select Pleas of the Crown, pl. 48, 49, 89, etc.; Gross, Coroners' Rolls *passim*.

[2] In Bracton's day men are already beginning to make appeals in the king's central courts. In this case a writ issues which directs arrest or, in some cases, attachment. Bracton, ff. 149, 439, regards criminal and civil procedure as two variations on one theme.

[3] Reeves, Hist. Engl. Law, ch. vii, has written at length of this matter.

[4] See above, vol. i. p. 213.

procedure is an acceleration[1]. Were we to say more we should
have to tell of the formal summons which is made in the [p. 590]
presence of witnesses, and then of the various kinds of 'attachment'—for a man may be attached 'by his body' or 'by gage
and pledge[2]'—of the various kinds of distress which will take
away his chattels and deprive him of the enjoyment of his
land. We see much that is very old and has been common
to the whole Germanic race, as for example the principle that
a man is entitled to three successive summonses; but a few
words as to the real and a few as to the personal actions of
Bracton's day must suffice[3].

Process in real actions. If we reduce the process in the real action to its lowest
terms, it consists of Summons and *Cape* and Judgment by
Default. If the tenant does not appear when summoned, then
a writ (*Magnum Cape*) goes out bidding the sheriff seize the
debatable land into the king's hand and summon the tenant
to explain his default[4]. If at the new day that has been thus
given to him he fails to appear, or fails to heal (*sanare*) his
former default, then the land is adjudged to the demandant,
and the tenant's only chance of recovering it will lie in a new
action begun by writ of right. We have put the simplest case
of pure contumacy. An almost infinite number of other cases
are conceivable as we permute and combine all the possibilities
of essoin and default. But the broad general idea that runs
through the maze is that the land will be taken from the
contumacious tenant, and, after an interval, which gives him
another opportunity of submitting to justice, it will be adjudged to his adversary. But even when this has been done
we see the extreme patience of medieval law. A judgment by

---

[1] See Stat. Marlb. c. 7 (Writs of Wardship); c. 9 (Suit of Court); c. 12
(Dower, *Quare impedit* etc.); c. 13 (general as to Essoins); c. 23 (Account).

[2] The Court Baron (Seld. Soc.), p. 79: 'duplex est attachiamentum per
corpus videlicet et per manucaptores sive per plegios.' The Scottish tract
Quoniam attachiamenta (Acts of Parl. i. 647) is full of instruction for Englishmen.

[3] For the antiquities of 'original and mesne process,' see Brunner, D. R. G.
ii. 332, 452, 457, 461. In the oldest stage the summoning is done by the
plaintiff himself; it is a *mannitio* as opposed to the *bannitio* of later days which
proceeds from the court. In England the triple summons can be traced thus:—
Æthelst. ii. 20; Edg. iii. 7; Cnut, ii. 25; Leg. Will. i. 47; Leg. Will. iii. 14;
Leg. Henr. 51, § 1; Glanvill, i. 7; Select Pleas in Manorial Courts, pp. 114–5;
but it was common elsewhere; Tardif, Procédure civile et criminelle, p. 53.

[4] In Glanvill's day (i. 7) three successive summonses preceded the *Cape*.

default—unless indeed the default was committed at the very
 p. 591] last stage of the action[1]—will not preclude the defaulter from
reopening the dispute by a proprietary writ[2].

When there was no specific thing that could be seized and Process in
personal
adjudged to the plaintiff as being the very thing that he actions.
demanded, the law had at its command various engines for
compelling the appearance of the defendant. Bracton has
drawn up a scheme which in his eyes is or should be the
normal process of compulsion; but we can see both from his
own text and from the plea rolls that he is aiming at generality
and simplicity, and also that some questions are still open[3].
The scheme is this:—(1) Summons, (2) Attachment by pledges,
(3) Attachment by better pledges, (4) *Habeas corpus*, (5) a
Distraint by all goods and chattels, which however consists
in the mere ceremony of taking them into the king's hand;
(6) a Distraint by all goods and chattels such as to prevent
the defendant from meddling with them; (7) a Distraint by
all goods and chattels which will mean a real seizure of them
by the sheriff, who will become answerable for the proceeds
(issues, *exitus*) to the king; (8) Exaction and outlawry[4].

Bracton however has to argue for the use of outlawry. He Outlawry
in civil
has to suggest that there can be a minor outlawry just as there process.
can be a minor excommunication: in other words, that a form of
outlawry can be employed which will not involve a sentence

---

[1] Bracton, f. 367.

[2] Our *Cape in manum* corresponds to the *Missio in bannum Regis* of
Frankish law; Brunner, D. R. G. ii. 457; but whereas in the old Frankish
procedure the land stays in the king's hand for a year and a day, in the England
of Glanvill's day the period for replevying the land has already been cut down
to a fortnight; Glanvill, i. 16.

[3] Bracton, f. 439-41; Reeves, Hist. Eng. Law (ed. 1814), i. 480.

[4] The Bractonian process which inserts a *Habeas corpus* between Attachment
and Distress is fully illustrated by Note Book, pl. 526, 527, 1370, 1376, 1407,
1408, 1420, 1421, 1446. A little later this *Habeas corpus* seems to disappear,
but the writ of Distress commands the sheriff *quod distringat etc. et habeat
corpus*, see *e.g.* Northumberland Assize Rolls, pp. 51, 59, 60, 178, 199 etc.
Then Stat. Marlb. c. 12 and Stat. West. I. c. 45 accelerated the procedure by
cutting away all that intervened between First Attachment and Grand Distress.
Thus we pass to the process described by Britton, i. 125–134. Bracton's
scheme does not provide for any 'imprisonment upon mesne process'; the
sheriff is not directed, as he is by the later *Capias*, to take the defendant's
body and keep it safely; but the *Habeas corpus* would, we suppose, justify
the sheriff in arresting the defendant when the court-day was approaching in
order to bring him into court.

of death[1]. At a little later time a distinction is here drawn. In some of the forms of action, for example Trespass *vi et* [p. 592] *armis,* there can be arrest (*Capias ad respondendum*) and, failing this, there may be outlawry; in other forms 'distress infinite' is the last process[2]. At a yet later stage, partly by statute, partly under the cover of fictions, *Capias* and Outlawry became common to many forms, and 'imprisonment upon mesne process' was the weapon on which our law chiefly relied in its struggle with the contumacious[3].

No judgment against the absent in a personal action.

One thing our law would not do: the obvious thing. It would exhaust its terrors in the endeavour to make the defendant appear, but it would not give judgment against him until he had appeared, and, if he was obstinate enough to endure imprisonment or outlawry, he could deprive the plaintiff of his remedy. Now this is strange, for Bracton had pointed to the true course. 'It would, so it seems, be well to distinguish between pecuniary actions arising from contract and actions arising from delict. In the former case it would be well to adjudge to the plaintiff seisin of enough chattels to satisfy the debt and damages, and also to summon the defendant; and then, if he appeared, his chattels would be restored to him and he would answer to the action, and if he did not appear the plaintiff would become their owner. And in the case of delict it would be well that the damages should be taxed by the justices and paid out of the defendant's rents and chattels[4].' Now, at all events in the case of Debt, this course had sometimes been taken in the early part of the century[5]. But Bracton was speaking to deaf ears. Our law would not give

---

[1] Bracton, f. 441, proposes to use outlawry in such actions as Debt and Covenant as well as in Trespass. For early cases of outlawry in Trespass, see Note Book, pl. 85, 1232.

[2] Britton, i. 132. Northumberland Assize Rolls (A.D. 1269), p. 179: in Debt the sheriff reports that the defendant has no land open to distress: 'ideo inde nichil'; there is no more to be done. Ibid. pp. 273-7-9: in 1279 we see the *Capias* in trespass.

[3] The extension of the *Capias* is best studied in Hale's tract Concerning the Courts of King's Bench and Common Pleas, printed in Hargrave's Law Tracts, p. 359. See also Blackstone, Comm. iii. 279 ff.

[4] Bracton, f. 440 b. We have abbreviated the passage.

[5] Note Book, pl. 900. For an earlier age see Laws of William (Select Charters), c. 8: 'Quarta autem vice si non venerint, reddatur de rebus hominis illius, qui venire noluerit, quod calumniatum est, quod dicitur *ceapgeld*, et insuper forisfactura Regis.'

judgment against one who had not appeared. Seemingly we have before us a respectable sentiment that has degenerated [p. 593] into stupid obstinacy. The law wants to be exceedingly fair, but is irritated by contumacy. Instead of saying to the defaulter 'I don't care whether you appear or no,' it sets its will against his will:—'But you shall appear.' To this we may add that the emergence and dominance of the semi-criminal action of Trespass prevents men from thinking of our personal actions as mere contests beween two private persons. The contumacious defendant has broken the peace, is defying justice and must be crushed. Whether the plaintiff's claim will be satisfied is a secondary question[1]. Near six centuries passed away before Bracton's advice was adopted[2].

Passing by the trial of the action, in order that we may say a few words about the 'final process,' we must repeat once more that the oldest actions of the common law aim for the more part, not at 'damages,' but at what we call 'specific relief[3].' By far the greater number of the judgments that are given in favour of plaintiffs are judgments which award them seisin of land, and these judgments are executed by writs that order the sheriff to deliver seisin. But even when the source of the action is in our eyes a contractual obligation, the law tries its best to give specific relief. Thus if a lord is bound to acquit a tenant from a claim for suit of court, the judgment may enjoin him to perform this duty and may bid the sheriff distrain him into performing it from time to time[4]. In Glanvill's day the defendant in an action on a fine could be compelled to give security that for the future he would observe his pact[5]. The history of Covenant seems to show that the judgment for specific performance (*quod conventio teneatur*) is at least as old as an award of damages for breach of contract[6]. We may find a local court decreeing that a rudder is to be made in accordance with an agreement[7], and even that one man is to serve another[8]. Nor can we say that what is in substance an

Specific relief.

---

[1] To this may be added that the judgment by default in Debt (Note Book, pl. 900) may be a sign that the action has been regarded as 'real.'

[2] Stat. 2 Will. IV. c. 39, sec. 16.   See Co. Lit. 288 b for a curious apology.

[3] See above, vol. ii. p. 523.   [4] Note Book, pl. 837.

[5] Glanvill, viii. 5.   [6] See above, vol. ii. pp. 216–220.

[7] The Court Baron (Selden Soc.), p. 115.

[8] Select Pleas in Manorial Courts, p. 157.

'injunction' was as yet unknown. The 'prohibition' which forbids a man to continue his suit in an ecclesiastical court on pain of going to prison[1], is not unlike that weapon which the courts of common law will some day see turned against them [p. 594] by the hand of the chancellor[2]. But further, a defendant in an action of Waste could be bidden to commit no more waste upon pain of losing the land[3], and a forester or curator might be appointed to check his doings[4]. The more we read of the thirteenth century, the fewer will seem to us the new ideas that were introduced by the chancellors of the later middle ages[5]. What they did introduce was a stringent, flexible and summary method of dealing with law-breakers. The common law has excellent intentions; what impedes it is an old-fashioned dislike for extreme measures.

Final process.

When judgment has been given for a debt, the sheriff will be directed to cause the sum that is needful to be made (*fieri facias*) out of the goods and chattels of the defendant, or levied (*levari facias*) out of his goods and the fruits of his land. But our common law will not seize his land and sell it or deliver it to the creditor; seignorial claims and family claims have prevented men from treating land as an available asset for the payment of debts. A statute of 1285 bestowed upon the creditor a choice between the old writ of *fieri facias* and a new writ which would give him possession of one half of his debtor's land as a means whereby he might satisfy himself[6]. It is not a little remarkable that our common law knew no process whereby a man could pledge his body or liberty for payment of a debt, for our near cousins came very naturally by such a process, and in old times the *wíte-þeów* may often have been working out by his labours a debt that was due to his master[7].

[1] Bracton, f. 410.

[2] Of course there is this difference: a prohibition could, and still can, be sent to the judge ecclesiastical (*ne teneat placitum*) as well as to the party (*ne sequatur*), while the chancery could lay no 'injunction' on the courts of common law.

[3] Note Book, pl. 540. Such judgments as this were rendered unnecessary by Stat. Glouc. c. 5, Stat. West. II. c. 14, which enabled the plaintiff to recover the wasted land.

[4] Note Book, pl. 56; Bracton, f. 316, 316 b; Second Instit. 300.

[5] Holmes, Early English Equity, L. Q. R. i. 162.

[6] Stat. West. II. c. 18.

[7] Kohler, Shakespeare vor dem Forum der Jurisprudenz, *passim.*

Under Edward I. the tide turned.   In the interest of commerce
a new form of security, the so-called 'statute merchant,' was
[p. 595] invented, which gave the creditor power to demand the seizure
and imprisonment of his debtor's body[1].

What some modern practitioners may think the most in-   Costs.
teresting topic of the law was as yet much neglected.   We
read little or nothing of 'costs.'   No doubt litigation was
expensive, as we know from the immortal tale which Richard
of Anesty has bequeathed to us of the horses that he lost and
the loans that he raised in his endeavour to get justice from
Henry II.[2]   It is highly probable that in some actions in which
damages were claimed a successful plaintiff might often under
the name of 'damages' obtain a compensation which would
cover the costs of litigation as well as all other harm that
he had sustained[3]; but we know that this was not so where
damages were awarded in an action for land[4], and in many
actions for land no damages, and therefore no costs, could be
had[5].   It is only under statute that a victorious defendant can
claim costs, and at the time of which we write statutes which
allowed him this boon were novelties[6].   *In expensarum causa
victus victori condemnandus est*[7]—this is a principle to which
English, like Roman, law came but slowly.

---

[1] Stat. 11 Edw. I. (Acton-Burnel); 13 Edw. I.; Statutes, vol. i. pp. 53, 98.
If we are to have from comparative jurisprudence any grand inductive law as
to the legal treatment of debtors, it can not possibly be of that simple kind
which would see everywhere a gradually diminishing severity.   May not the
mildness of our English law in cent. xiii. be due to its refusal to cultivate
the old formal contract, the *fides facta*?

[2] Palgrave, Eng. Commonwealth, p. ix; Hall, Court Life, p. 129.

[3] Coke, Second Instit. 288; Blackstone, Comment. iii. 399.   Sometimes on
a compromise costs were paid *eo nomine*; Note Book, pl. 439, 1430.

[4] Stat. Glouc. c. 1.   The profits of the land had been the measure of
damages.   In various actions this statute gave to a successful plaintiff damages
which were to cover 'the costs of his writ purchased.'

[5] See above, vol. ii. p. 524.

[6] Stat. Marlb. c. 6 gives the defendant damages and costs in an action
charging him with a feoffment destined to defraud his lord of a wardship.

[7] Cod. 3. 1. 6.   For costs awarded in an ecclesiastical suit, see Note Book,
pl. 544.

§ 4. *Pleading and Proof.*

Ancient
modes of
proof.

We are now to speak of what happens when two litigants of the twelfth or thirteenth century have at length met each other in court. But first we must glance at the modes of proof which those centuries have inherited from their predecessors[1]. [p. 596] In so doing we must transfer ourselves into a wholly different intellectual atmosphere from that in which we live. We must once for all discard from our thoughts that familiar picture of a trial in which judges and jurymen listen to the evidence that is produced on both sides, weigh testimony against testimony and by degrees make up their minds about the truth. The language of the law, even in Bracton's day, has no word equivalent to our *trial*. We have not to speak of trial; we have to speak of proof[2].

The ordeal.

The old modes of proof might be reduced to two, ordeals and oaths; both were appeals to the supernatural. The history of ordeals is a long chapter in the history of mankind; we must not attempt to tell it. Men of many, if not all, races have carried the red-hot iron or performed some similar feat in proof of their innocence[3]. In Western Europe, after the barbarian invasions, the church adopted and consecrated certain of the ordeals and composed rituals for them[4]. Among our

[1] See Brunner, Zeugen- und Inquisitionsbeweis (Forschungen, p. 88); Wort und Form (ibid. p. 260); Entstehung der Schwurgerichte; Bigelow, History of Procedure; Thayer, Evidence, ch. 1; Lea, Superstition and Force.

[2] See Thayer, Evidence, p. 16. Our Eng. *try* comes from Fr. *trier*. This (see Diez, s.v. *trier*) comes from a Lat. *tritare*, a frequentative from *terere*. The Fr. *trier* begins to appear in the law books of cent. xiii., chiefly in connexion with the practice of challenging jurors; the challenges are tested or *tried*. See *e.g.* Britton, i. 30. Then the Lat. forms *triare, triatio* are made from the Fr. word. In the vulgate text Bracton, f. 105, is made to say 'ubi triandae sunt actiones'; but the MSS. have the far more probable *terminandae*. A similar mistake may be suspected in Fleta, p. 236, § 4.

[3] Patetta, Le Ordalie, Turin, 1890; Lea, Superstition and Force (3rd ed.), p. 249 ff.; Brunner, D. R. G. ii. 399. In Paul's Grundriss d. german. Philol. ii. pt. 2, p. 197, von Amira has argued that the German races had no ordeals until after they had accepted Christianity. Dr Liebermann has recently discovered the ordeal of the cauldron in the laws of Ine: Sitzungsberichte der Berliner Akademie, 1896, p. 829.

[4] The rituals are collected in Zeumer, Formulae Merovingici et Karolini Aevi (Monum. Germ.), 4to. p. 638. An English ritual is given in Schmid, Gesetze, p. 416.

own forefathers the two most fashionable methods of obtaining
a *iudicium Dei* were that which adjured a pool of water to
receive the innocent and that which regarded a burnt hand as
a proof of guilt.   Such evidence as we have seems to show that
the ordeal of hot iron was so arranged as to give the accused
a considerable chance of escape[1].   In the England of the
[p. 597] twelfth century both of the tests that we have mentioned
were being freely used; but men were beginning to mistrust
them.   Rufus had gibed at them[2].   Henry II. had declared that
when an indicted man came clean from the water, he was none
the less to abjure the realm, if his repute among his neighbours
was of the worst[3].   Then came a sudden change.   The Lateran
Council of 1215 forbad the clergy to take part in the ceremony[4].
Some wise churchmen had long protested against it; but
perhaps the conflict with flagrant heresy and the consequent
exacerbation of ecclesiastical law had something to do with the
suppression of this old test[5].   In England this decree found a
prompt obedience such as it hardly found elsewhere; the ordeal
was abolished at once and for ever[6].   Flourishing in the last
records of John's reign, we can not find it in any later rolls[7].
Our criminal procedure was deprived of its handiest weapon;
but to this catastrophe we must return hereafter.

---

[1] The only statistical information that we have comes from a Hungarian
monastery which kept a register of judgments in cent. xiii.   This is said to
show that it was about an even chance whether the ordeal of hot iron succeeded
or failed.   See Dareste, Études d'histoire du droit, pp. 259–264.   In certain
cases our English procedure gave the appellee a choice between bearing the iron
and allowing the appellor to bear it.   See Select Pleas of the Crown, pl. 24, and
Glanvill, xiv. 6.   This seems to show that the result could not be predicted
with much certainty.

[2] Eadmer, Hist. Nov. 102; Bigelow, Placita, 72.   Of fifty men sent to the
ordeal of iron all had escaped.   This certainly looks as if some bishop or clerk
had preferred his own judgment to the judgment of God, and the king did well
to be angry.

[3] Ass. Clarend. c. 14.

[4] Concil. Lateran. IV. c. 18.

[5] Concil. Lateran. IV. c. 3 deals with heretics; c. 8 defines the new
procedure by inquisition; c. 18 abolishes the ordeal.

[6] See the letters patent of 26th Jan. 1219; Foedera, i. 154: 'cum prohibitum
sit per ecclesiam Romanam iudicium ignis et aquae.'   England was for the
moment at the pope's foot.

[7] Rolls of the King's Court (Pipe Roll Soc.), 80, 86, 89 etc.   Select Pleas of
the Crown, *passim*.   Note Book, pl. 592: 'quia ante guerram [1215] habuerunt
iudicium ignis et aquae.'   Thayer, Evidence, 37; Lea, *op. cit.* 421.

Proof by battle.

The judicial combat[1] is an ordeal, a bilateral ordeal. The church had shown less favour to it than to the unilateral ordeals, perhaps because it had involved pagan ceremonies[2]. Therefore we hear nothing of it until the Normans bring it hither. In later days English ecclesiastics had no deep dislike for it[3]. It was a sacral process. What triumphed was not brute force but truth. The combatant who was worsted was a [p. 598] convicted perjurer.

Proof by oath.

The ordeal involves or is preceded by an oath; but even when the proof is to consist merely of oaths, a supernatural element is present. The swearer satisfies human justice by taking the oath. If he has sworn falsely, he is exposed to the wrath of God and in some subsequent proceeding may perhaps be convicted of perjury; but in the meantime he has performed the task that the law set him; he has given the requisite proof. In some rare cases a defendant was allowed to swear away a charge by his own oath; usually what was required of him was an oath supported by the oaths of oath-helpers[4]. There are good reasons for believing that in the earliest period he had to find kinsmen as oath-helpers[5]. When he was denying an accusation which, if not disproved, would have been cause for a blood-feud, his kinsmen had a lively interest in the suit, and naturally they were called upon to assist him in freeing himself and them from the consequences of the imputed crime. The plaintiff, if he thought that there had been perjury, would have the satisfaction of knowing that some twelve of his enemies were devoted to divine vengeance. In course of time the law no longer required kinsmen, and we see a rationalistic tendency which would convert the oath-helpers into impartial 'witnesses to character.' Sometimes the chief swearer must choose them from among a number of men designated by the court or by his opponent; sometimes they must be his neighbours. Then again, instead of swearing positively that his oath is true, they may swear that it is true to the best of their

[1] Brunner, D. R. G. ii. 414; Lea, *op. cit.* 101 ff.; Neilson, Trial by Combat; Thayer, Evidence, 39.

[2] Brunner, D. R. G. ii. 416.

[3] See above, vol. i. pp. 50, 74. Note Book, pl. 551: in 1231 the bishop of London produces his champion. Neilson, *op. cit.* pp. 50–1.

[4] Brunner, D. R. G. ii. p. 378; for England, Schmid, Gesetze, pp. 563–7.

[5] Brunner, D. R. G. ii. p. 379; Lea, *op. cit.* ch. iv.; Leg. Henr. 64, § 4.

knowledge[1]. In some cases few, in others many helpers are demanded. A normal number is 12; but this may be reduced to 6 or 3, or raised to 24, 36, 72[2]. A punctilious regard for
[p. 599] formalities is required of the swearers. If a wrong word is used, the oath 'bursts' and the adversary wins. In the twelfth century such elaborate forms of asseveration had been devised that, rather than attempt them, men would take their chance at the hot iron[3].

Besides the oaths of the litigants and their oath-helpers, the law also knew the oaths of witnesses; but apparently in the oldest period it did not often have recourse to this mode of proof, and the oaths which these witnesses proffered were radically different from the sworn testimony that is now-a-days given in our courts[4]. For one thing, it seems to have been a general rule that no one could be compelled, or even suffered, to testify to a fact, unless when that fact happened he was solemnly 'taken to witness[5].' Secondly, when the witness was adduced, he came merely in order that he might swear to a set formula. His was no promissory oath to tell the truth in answer to questions, but an assertory oath. We shall see hereafter that the English procedure of the thirteenth century expects a plaintiff to be accompanied by a 'suit' of witnesses of this kind, witnesses who are prepared to support his oath in case the proof is awarded to him.

Oaths of witnesses.

[1] Compare on the one hand the A.-S. oath, Schmid, Gesetze, p. 406 ('On þone Drihten, se áð is clǽne and unmǽne þe N. swór'), with the formula used in the London of cent. xiii. ('quod *secundum scientiam suam* iuramentum quod fecit fidele est'), Munim. Gildh. i. 105. The same change took place in the canon law and was consecrated by Innocent III.; c. 13, X. 5. 34; Lea, *op. cit.* 71–2.

[2] Brunner, D. R. G. ii. 384. The question whether when a man is said *iurare duodecima manu* he has twelve or only eleven compurgators, must, according to Dr Brunner, be answered sometimes in the one, sometimes in the other way. The inclusive reckoning seems to be the older, and is sanctioned by the Statutum Walliae, c. 9, where eleven helpers are required; but in London during cent. xiii. the other reckoning prevailed; Munim. Gildh. i. 104–5. In the last reported English case of compurgation, *King* v. *Williams* (1824), 2 Barnewall & Cresswell, 538, the court declined to aid the defendant by telling him how many helpers were needed; he produced eleven helpers, whereupon the plaintiff withdrew from his suit.

[3] Leg. Henr. 64, § 1; Brunner, Forschungen, 328.

[4] Brunner, D. R. G. ii. 391; Schmid, Gesetze, Glossar. s.v. *gewitnes*; Thayer, Evidence, 17.

[5] Brunner, D. R. G. ii. 395.

Such being the modes of proof, we must now understand
that the proof is preceded by and is an attempt to fulfil a
judgment. The litigants in court debate the cause, formal
assertion being met by formal negation. Of course it is
possible that no proof is necessary and the action will be, as
we should say, 'decided upon the pleadings.' So soon as the
plaintiff has stated his claim, the defendant will perhaps
declare that he is not bound to give an answer, because the
plaintiff is an outlaw, or because the plaintiff has omitted some
essential ceremony or sacramental phrase[1]. But if an un- [p. 600]
exceptionable assertion is met by an unexceptionable answer,
then the question of proof arises. The court pronounces a
judgment. It awards that one of the two litigants must prove
his case, by his body in battle, or by a one-sided ordeal, or by
an oath with oath-helpers, or by the oaths of witnesses. It has
no desire to hear and weigh conflicting testimony. It decrees
that one of the two parties shall go to the proof. It sets him
a task that he must attempt[2]. If he performs it, he has won
his cause. Upon this preliminary or 'medial' judgment[3]
follows the wager[4]. The party to whom the proof is awarded
gives gage and pledge by way of security for the fulfilment of
the judgment. The doomsmen have declared for law that he
must, for example, purge himself with oath-helpers; thereupon
he 'wages,' that is, undertakes to fulfil or to 'make' this 'law[5].'

[1] Brunner, D. R. G. ii. 346.

[2] A beautiful example of this award of the proof is given by Modbert's suit
in the court of the Bishop of Bath in 1121; Bigelow, Placita, p. 114; Bath
Chartularies (Somerset Rec. Soc.), pt. 1, pp. 49–51.

[3] Bigelow, History of Procedure, p. 288, has introduced the term 'medial or
proof judgment' as an equivalent for the *Beweisurteil* of German writers.

[4] Brunner, D. R. G. ii. 365. Even in the present century the form of the
record of an action showed the old medial judgment. Any one who for the
first time saw such a record might well believe that, after the oral altercation
in court was at an end, the court adjudged that proof should be made by a
jury; for the record, after stating the pleadings, went on to say, 'Therefore it is
commanded to the sheriff that he do cause twelve men to come etc.' In the
thirteenth century this order for a jury is still regarded as a judgment.
'*Consideratum est* quod inquiratur per sacramentum xii. hominum' says the
record; Note Book, pl. 116.

[5] As to this use of *lex*, see Brunner, D. R. G. ii. 376. We may suppose that
the judgment began with some such words as the *Nous vous dioms pur lei* of
our Year Books. Then it would be easy to transfer the *lex*, *lei* or *law* to the
probative task imposed by the judgment. Salmond, Essays in Jurisprudence,
p. 17.

A great part of the jurisprudence of the wise has consisted in rules about the allotment of the proof[1]. Their wisdom has consisted in ability to answer the question—'These being the allegations of the parties, which of them must go to the proof and to what proof must he go?' It is in the answer to this question that a nascent rationalism can make itself felt. The general rule seems to have been that the defendant must [p. 601] prove[2]. If the accusation against him was a charge of serious crime, he would perhaps be sent to a one-sided ordeal; but usually he would be allowed to swear off the charge with oath-helpers, unless he had been frequently accused. The difficulty of the oath or of the ordeal would vary directly with the gravity of the charge. Then again, there were some defences, in particular that of a purchase in open market, which could be proved by witnesses. Lastly, it was possible for a plaintiff to cut off the defendant from an easy mode of proof by an offer to undergo the ordeal or by a challenge to battle[3]. There were some stringent rules about these matters; still it is here, and only here, that we can see an opening for the play of reason, for an estimate of presumptions and probabilities. When once the proof has been awarded, when once a *lex* has been decreed, formalism reigns supreme.

Now this old procedure was still the normal procedure in the days of Glanvill; and even in the days of Bracton, though it was being thrust into the background, it was still present to the minds of all lawyers. A new mode of proof was penetrating and dislocating it, namely, the proof given by the verdict of a sworn inquest of neighbours or proof by 'the country.' The early history of the inquest we have already endeavoured to tell when we were regarding its constitutional or political side[4]. The revolution which it worked in our legal procedure and in our notions of proof now claims our attention. First however, we should notice that the days of Glanvill and Bracton were critical days for the law of proof in other countries besides England. In many lands men were dissatisfied with the old

---

[1] Brunner, D. R. G. ii. 369.

[2] Brunner, D. R. G. ii. 370. Æthelr. ii. 9, § 3. Fleta, p. 137: 'Et in hoc casu semper incumbit probatio neganti.'

[3] See the offers of proof in Domesday Book collected in Bigelow, Placita, pp. 37–46.

[4] See above, vol. i. pp. 138–150.

formal tests. The catholic church was dissatisfied with the ordeal and was discovering that the oath with helpers, though it had become the *purgatio canonica,* would allow many a hardy heretic to go at large. And everywhere the reformers have the same watchword—*Inquisitio.* What is peculiar to England is not the dissatisfaction with waged 'laws' and supernatural probations, nor the adoption of an 'inquisition' or 'inquest' as the core of the new procedure, but the form that the inquest takes, or rather retains. By instituting the Grand Assize and the four Petty Assizes Henry II. had placed at the disposal of [p. 602] litigants in certain actions that inquest of 'the country' which ever since the Norman Conquest had formed part of the governmental machinery of England. His reforms were effected just in time. But for them, we should indeed have known the inquest, but it would in all likelihood have been the inquest of the canon law, the *enquête* of the new French jurisprudence[1].

The plaintiff's count. The litigants are in court. All pleading is as yet oral pleading, though when a plea has been uttered it will be recorded on the roll of the court. When the parties stand

---

[1] Trial by jury became in this century the theme of a large controversial literature, for the more part German. At the present time the student will hardly find occasion to pursue this debate further back than Brunner's Entstehung der Schwurgerichte (1871), and Zeugen- und Inquisitionsbeweis (Forschungen, p. 88): but much useful material was collected by Biener, Das englische Geschworengericht (1852). In this country light began to dawn when Reeves, Hist. Engl. Law (ed. 1814, i. 249), said that the *iudicium parium* of Magna Carta does not point to trial by jury. But the decisive step was taken by Palgrave, English Commonwealth (1832), chap. VIII. Among more recent books dealing with this matter are Forsyth, History of Trial by Jury (1852), and Bigelow, History of Procedure (1880). Lately Mr J. B. Thayer has published in Harv. L. Rev. v. 249, 295, 357, three articles so full and excellent that we shall make our own sketch very brief, and insist only upon what seem to us to be the more vital or the more neglected parts of the story. We are glad to hear that Mr Thayer is about to publish his papers in a collected form. (We can now add that they are published as Part 1 of a Treatise on Evidence, Boston, 1896.) As to France, the important Ordinance of St Louis substituting for trial by battle an *enquête* of witnesses will be found in Viollet, Établissements, i. 487. It is dated in 1257-8 by J. Tardif, Nouv. rev. hist. de droit, 1887, p. 163. See also Biener, Beiträge zu der Geschichte des Inquisitions-Processes ; Esmein, Histoire de la procédure criminelle en France, ch. ii. When all has been said, the almost total disappearance in France of the old *enquête du pays* in favour of the *enquête* of the canon law, at the very time when the *inquisitio patriae* is carrying all before it in England, is one of the grand problems in the comparative history of the two nations.

opposite to each other, it then behoves the plaintiff[1] to state his case by his own mouth or that of his pleader. His statement is called in Latin *narratio,* in French *conte*; probably in English it is called his *tale*[2]. It is a formal statement bristling with sacramental words, an omission of which would be fatal.

[p. 603] For example, if there is to be a charge of felony, an irretrievable slip will have been made should the pleader begin with 'This showeth to you Alan, who is here,' instead of 'Alan, who is here, appeals William, who is there[3],' and again in this case the 'words of felony' will be essential. In a civil action begun by writ, the plaintiff's count must not depart by a hair's-breadth from the writ or there will be a 'variance' of which the defendant will take advantage[4]. On the other hand, the brief statement that the writ contains must be expanded by the count. Thus a writ of Debt will merely tell William that he must say why he has not paid fifty marks which he owes to Alan and unjustly detains; but the count will set forth how on a certain day came this William to this Alan and asked for a loan of fifty marks, how the loan was made and was to have been repaid on a certain day, and how, despite frequent requests, William has refused and still refuses to pay it. The count on a Writ of Right will often be an elaborate history[5]. A seisin 'as of fee and of right' with a taking of 'esplees' will be attributed to some ancestor of the demandant, and then the descent of this right will be traced down a pedigree from which no step may be omitted.

It is not enough that the plaintiff should tell his tale: he must offer to prove its truth. In an Appeal of Felony he offers proof 'by his body[6]'; in a Writ of Right he offers proof 'by the body of a certain free man of his *A. B.* by name' who, or whose father, witnessed the seisin that has been alleged; in other

The offer of proof.

---

[1] As we must speak very briefly, we shall use *plaintiff* to cover *appellor* and *demandant*, while *defendant* will include *appellee* and *tenant*.

[2] The book whose Latin title is *Novae Narrationes* was also known as *Les Novels Tales* (Y. B. 39 Hen. VI. f. 30). As to the use of the Roman terms *demonstratio* and *intentio*, see Pike, Introduction to Y. B. 12–3 Edw. III. pp. lxxiv–lxxxiii.

[3] Britton, i. 103.

[4] See *e.g.* Note Book, pl. 921.

[5] Bracton, f. 372 b.

[6] It is not unknown about the year 1200 that the appellor will offer proof by the body of another person; Select Pleas of the Crown, pl. 84.

cases he produces a suit (*secta*) of witnesses[1]. No one is entitled to an answer if he offers nothing but his bare assertion, his *nude parole*. The procedure in the Appeal of Felony is no real exception to this rule. The appellor alleges, and can be called upon to prove, fresh 'suit' with hue and cry, so that the neighbourhood (represented in later days by the coroner's rolls) is witness to his prompt action, to the wounds of a wounded man, to the torn garments of a ravished woman. It should not escape us that in this case, as in other cases, what the plaintiff relies on as a support for his word is 'suit.' This [p. 604] suggests that the suitors (*sectatores*) whom the plaintiff produces in a civil action have been, at least in theory, men who along with him have pursued the defendant. Be that as it may, the rule which required a suit of witnesses had been regarded as a valuable rule; in 1215 the barons demanded that no exception to it should be allowed in favour of royal officers[2].

The suit.

And now we must observe the manner in which the suitors are introduced. If Alan is bringing an action against William, his count, unless there is a provocation to battle, will end with some such words as these:—'And if William will confess this, that will seem fair to Alan: but if he will deny it, wrongfully will he deny it, for Alan has here suit good and sufficient, to wit, Ralph and Roger[3].'

Function of the suitors.

When we first obtain records from the king's court, the production of suit is beginning to lose its importance, and we know little as to what the suitors did or said when they had thus been introduced to the court. But we may gather from the Norman books that each of them in turn ought to have stepped forward and said: 'This I saw and heard and [by way of

---

[1] Thayer, Evidence, 10 ff. In a Writ of Right the demandant can not offer proof by his own body 'desicut non potest esse secta sui ipsius'; Note Book, pl. 1935.

[2] Articles of the Barons, c. 28; Charter, 1215, c. 38: 'Nullus ballivus ponat de cetero aliquem ad legem simplici loquela sua, sine testibus fidelibus ad hoc inductis.' In 1217 after *legem* the words *manifestam vel iuramentum* were added. See Bémont, Chartes, p. 55. Also see Fleta, p. 137. The *lex manifesta* does not necessarily point to an unilateral ordeal; it may well stand for trial by battle. See Thayer, Evidence, pp. 11, 37; Brunner, Schwurg. p. 178.

[3] Bracton, f. 297; Britton, ii. 257; The Court Baron (Seld. Soc.), pp. 20, 23; Y. B. 20–1 Edw. I. pp. 451–3. In a French book (Jostice et Plet) a similar formula occurs: 's'il le conoist, biau men est; s'il le nie, jou sui prez dou mostrer et de l'avérer': Brunner, Forschungen, p. 309.

proof] I am ready to do what the court shall award[1].'   At this
stage the suitors make no oath and are not questioned.   They
are not yet making proof; the proof will not be made until the
court has spoken after hearing what the defendant has to say.
And so in the Writ of Right the proffered champion will speak
thus: 'This I saw and heard—or, this my father saw and heard
and of this when dying he bade me bear witness[2]—and this I
am ready to prove by my body when and where the court shall
award.'

[p. 605]   As regards the number of suitors requisite when no battle Number
was offered, the only rule of which we find a trace is the *Testis* of the suitors.
unus, testis nullus, which—so men thought—could be deduced
from holy writ[3].   This would make two suitors sufficient; but
as a matter of fact we find three, four, six, seven, ten, eleven,
thirteen produced[4].   The reason for these numerically weighty
suits will appear when we describe the modes of defence.

The time has now come when the defendant must speak, The defence.
and as a general rule the only plea that is open to him is a
flat denial of all that the plaintiff has said.   He must 'defend'
all of it, and in this context to defend means to deny[5].   In
the past he has been bound to 'defend' the charge word by
word with painful accuracy[6].   By the end of the thirteenth
century he is allowed to employ a more general form of negation.   He may, for example, in an appeal of homicide say
such words as these: 'William, who is here, defends against
Alan, who is there, the slaying and the felony and all that is
against the king's peace word by word[7].'   In a writ of right

---

[1] Somma, p. 157; Ancienne coutume, c. 62, ed. de Gruchy, p. 150.   Compare
Lyon, Dover, ii. 292.

[2] Glanvill, ii. 3.   Note Book, pl. 185.

[3] Note Book, pl. 396, 790, 1603.   For the history of *Testis unus, testis
nullus*, see Viollet, Établissements, i. 203.

[4] Note Book, pl. 890, 1065, 265, 279, 194, 1390, 1919; Northumberland
Assize Rolls, 56.

[5] See Oxford Engl. Dict.   In cent. xiii. *defendere* is currently used in both its
two senses (1)=protect, and (2)=deny with accusative of thing denied or with
a *quod* which introduces the statement that is denied.   See *e.g.* Note Book,
pl. 1467: 'Et Robertus defendit *quod* nullum placitum secutus fuit...et *hoc*
offert defendere...Consideratum est quod defendat *se* xii. manu.'

[6] Brunner, Forschungen, 311; Esmein, Histoire de la procédure criminelle,
p. 45.

[7] Britton, i. 101–2.   Note Book, pl. 1460 gives a full form including the
words 'nec per ipsum fuit morti appropiatus nec a vita elongatus, nec idem

he will say : ' William, who is here, defends against Alan, who is there, his [Alan's[1]] right and the seisin of Bertram [Alan's ancestor] and all of it word by word.' In an action for trespass he will say ; ' William, who is here, defends against Alan, who [p. 606] is there, and against his suit [of witnesses] the tort and the force and all that is against the peace, and the damages and all that he [Alan] surmiseth against him word by word.' Such is the ' defence[2].'

Thwert-ut-nay. For reasons that will appear hereafter, the ' defence' is losing its old meaning. Men are beginning to regard it as a mere formal preamble which serves to introduce the more material part of the defendant's answer. They call this clause a defence of ' the words of court,' that is of the formal, technical words, and when they enrol it they make a free use of the *&c.*[3]. But it seems to tell us plainly that as a general rule all ' exceptions ' or ' special pleas,' all answers which are not flat negations of the plaintiff's story are novelties[4]. In 1277 the burgesses of Leicester obtained from their lord, Earl Edmund, a charter remodelling the procedure of the borough court. One of the grievances of which they complained was this, that a defendant was treated as undefended unless, before he said anything else, he met the plaintiff's tale with a *thwert-ut-nay*,

---

Rogerus [*appellator*] hoc vidit.' In a case of felony the appellee must make a ' defence' before he seeks counsel and may afterwards repeat his defence more formally by the mouth of a serjeant. Munim. Gildh. i. 114 : '' Roberia et pax fracta et raptus et felonia...omnia ista et talia defendenda sunt ante consilium captum et post consilium.' See Brunner, Forschungen, 319. It is clear from Britton, i. 102, that the appellee may have a serjeant to speak his defence.

[1] We are abbreviating this form. The record will say that the tenant *venit et defendit ius suum,* but as Blackstone, Comm. iii. 297, has rightly remarked, this means that he defends (=denies) the demandant's right. Note Book, pl. 86: there are two demandants; the tenant ' venit et defendit ius *eorum.*'

[2] See the forms in the Court Baron (Seld. Soc.) which are very full. On early plea rolls the words of ' defence' are but hinted at, unless in the particular case some objection was taken to them. Therefore negative inferences from these rolls should be sparingly drawn. In the Court Baron, pp. 41, 48, 84, we see a defendant vanquished because he omits the words ' and his suit.'

[3] As to the phrase *verba curiae, les moz [paroles] de la court,* see Y. B. 32–3 Edw. I. pp. xxxv, 105 ; Select Pleas in Manorial Courts, pp. 82, 113. We are not satisfied with the suggestion that the phrase should really be the *words of course* ; but already in 1292 *paroles de la court* seems to mean formal words which must be used but may not be taken very seriously ; Y. B. 20–1 Edw. I. p. 281.

[4] An assertion that for some reason or another one is not bound to answer *et ideo non vult inde respondere* we do not here count as an answer.

that is, a downright No. A downright No has been in the past the one possible answer; it is still the indispensable preliminary to every possible answer[1].

[p. 607]   Now we will suppose for a while that our defendant really wishes to rely upon a downright No. In that case, as we understand the matter, one of the things that he may do is to demand an examination of the plaintiff's suit of witnesses[2]. Perhaps he can object that no suit at all has been produced. This in the early years of the thirteenth century is done successfully with a frequency that is somewhat curious. In such cases the defendant protests that he need not answer the 'nude parole' (*simplex dictum, simplex vox*) of the plaintiff[3]. If, on the other hand, a suit has been produced, the defendant may demand that it be heard[4]. We take it that in the old procedure, which was vanishing, this would have led to a formal and indisputable oath on the part of the suitors. If they had duly pronounced the requisite words, the defendant would have been vanquished, though he might perhaps have charged them with perjury and provoked them to battle[5]. But in the thirteenth century the procedure is not so formal; the suit can be 'examined.' This implies, not merely, that suitors

Examination of the plaintiff's suit.

---

[1] Records of the Borough of Leicester, ed. Bateson, pp. 156–8: 'E pur ceo ke usé fu avaunt ces oures quant les parties deveient pleder e le pleintif aveit dit sa querele, si le defendant taunt tost cum la parole ly fust issue de la buche ne deist *thwerthutnay* il fu tenu cum non defendu, e ceo apelerent *swareles*....... E pur ceo ke avaunt fu usé ke le defendaunt ne poeit a la pleinte le pleintif autre chose respundre for tut granter ou tut dire *thwerthutnay*.......' Mr W. H. Stevenson tells us that the forms *thwertutnay* and *swareles* [=*indefensus, non defendu*] seem to point to a Scandinavian [Old Norse] influence. The idea of a *thwertutnay* is preserved in our *traverse*; it is the 'defence *tut atrenche*' of our Y. BB., *e.g.* 32–3 Edw. I. pp. 3, 375. In the Scots Leges Quatuor Burgorum (Act of Parl. i. p. 338) we read that in defending 'wrong and unlaw' a *twertnay* is used. The Earl of Chester had conceded to his tenants that if any of them was impleaded by the earl's officers without a suit, 'per tweitnic [*corr.* twertnie?] se defendere poterit.' This charter is known from an *Inspeximus*, Rot. Pat. 28 Ed. I. m. 22.

[2] In Note Book, pl. 396, a defendant loses his right to object to the nullity of the plaintiff's *secta* by making a 'full defence.' See also The Court Baron (Seld. Soc.), p. 84. But other cases seem to show that a defendant had to do a good deal in the way of 'defending' even though he was going to rely on an objection of this kind. See Note Book, pl. 424, 479, 574, 1693; Northumberland Assize Rolls, p. 275.

[3] See *e.g.* Note Book, pl. 57, 494, 1868; Y. B. 20–1 Edw. I. p. 69.

[4] See *e.g.* Note Book, pl. 1693.

[5] See above, vol. ii. pp. 162-3.

can be rejected for good cause, as being villeins, interested persons or the plaintiff's attorneys[1]—this could have been done even in earlier days—but also that the court will give audience to the suitors one by one and try to discover whether they really know anything about the facts. If they break down under examination, if they know nothing, if they disagree, 'the suit is null' and the plaintiff fails[2].

The defendant's offer of proof.

But the defendant who called for an examination of the plaintiff's *secta* was, we take it, throwing away every other defensive weapon[3]. He has chosen a test and must abide by the choice. He will probably desire that 'the proof' should be [p. 608] awarded to him rather than to his adversary. He must therefore offer to make good his downright No. When battle has been offered, he must—for we are at present neglecting as novelties all forms of the jury—accept the offer. Having 'defended' the charge, he professes his willingness to defend it once more, in some cases by his own body, in others by the body of a certain freeman of his, *C. D.* by name, 'when and where the court shall consider that defend he ought.' When there has been no offer of battle, he will follow up his defence by the words: 'And this he is ready and willing to defend when and where he ought as the court shall consider.' In the former case the court will award a wager of battle. In the latter case the court will award to the defendant some other 'law,' to wit, an oath with helpers; he must at once wage this law, that is, find gage and pledges that he will on a later day 'make' this law by performing the task that has been set him. The court will fix the number of the compurgators that he must produce, and this may in some cases depend upon the number of suitors tendered by the plaintiff[4].

---

[1] Note Book, pl. 740, 941, 953.

[2] Note Book, pl. 424, 479, 574, 613, 649, 761, 762, 1693, 1848.

[3] Bracton, f. 315 b, and Fleta, p. 137, allow a defendant to go to the proof with oath-helpers after there has been an 'examination' of the plaintiff's *secta*. We are inclined to regard this procedure, which goes near to 'admitting evidence on both sides,' as an innovation. The judges seem to be trying for a short while to make something reasonable out of the *secta*. Little comes of the effort, because the habit of referring questions to 'the country' is growing rapidly. At Sandwich the plaintiff in Debt seems to have been allowed to go to the proof with three suitors, even though the defendant desired to wage law. It was otherwise in Trespass. See Lyon, Dover, ii. 292–4.

[4] Bracton, f. 315 b: 'duplicatis ad minus personis iuratorum.' Fleta, p. 137,

Such have been the modes whereby a man made good his Special pleading.
thwert-ut-nay. In Bracton's day they are being concealed from
view by an overgrowth of special pleading and the verdicts of
jurors. But the background of the law of pleading and trial
still is this, that the defendant must take his stand upon a
downright No, whereupon there will be a wager of battle or
of some other law[1].

[p. 609]　For some time past, however, a new idea has been at The exception.
work. We have here no concern with the ancient history of
the Roman *exceptio*; but must notice that in what became
a classical passage Justinian used words which might well
bewilder the medieval lawyer[2]. Knowing little or nothing
of any system of 'equity' which could be contrasted with a
system of 'law,' he could not mark off a proper sphere for

---

repeats this rule, but holds that twelve is the maximum number of helpers that
can be required.

[1] In later days a defendant, even though he is going to deny the competence
of the court, or the validity of the writ, or the ability of the plaintiff, is bound
to begin by 'defending the wrong [or, in some cases, the force] and injury.'
This is called a 'half defence.' If he defends more than this, if he makes a
'full defence,' he is apt to lose his right of raising these 'dilatory exceptions.'
If, *e.g.* he 'defends the damages,' he waives all objections to the ability of the
plaintiff. In course of time some of these subtleties were evaded by a formula
which made use of the convenient *&c.* See Co. Lit. 127 b; 2 Wms. Saund.
209 b, note c; Stephen, Pleading (ed. 1824), 430–4. It is difficult to pursue this
doctrine into Bracton's age, because the *&c.* is already being used on the roll.
On very old rolls there is sometimes no 'defence' at all when a dilatory
exception is pleaded. See Y. B. 21–2 Edw. I. pp. 9, 167. Sometimes, on the
other hand, we see what looks like a full defence. The art of enrolling with
mechanical regularity was not perfected in an hour. We have seen above
(p. 609, note 2) that there was a defence even when the plaintiff produced no
sufficient *secta* and the defendant was going to rely upon this defect. It seems
to us that the ancient reasons for giving no answer are (under the influence of
the exotic *exceptio*) being mixed up with the new kinds of answer that are being
introduced. In the end the form of a defendant's plea is quaintly illogical, if
we take all its words seriously. For instance, if he is going to plead in abatement, he will come and defend (= deny) the wrong and injury and then, after
suggesting certain facts, will go on to ask the court whether he need answer,
just as if a denial were no answer. On the whole our evidence seems to point to
a time when the defendant's only choice lay between (1) refusing to answer and
(2) relying on a downright No. Compare Brunner, Forschungen, pp. 316–8;
D. R. G. ii. 346. The supposed rule that in Dower there is no 'defence'
(Stephen, Pleading, 431–4) seems to be a mere matter of words. See *e.g.* Note
Book, pl. 1383: 'Et W. venit et defendit quod non debet inde dotem habere';
but in later days *defendit* in this context gave way to *dicit.*

[2] Inst. 4. 13 pr.: 'saepe enim accidit ut, licet ipsa persecutio qua actor
experitur iusta sit, tamen iniqua sit adversus eum cum quo agitur.'

exceptiones, and was apt to believe both that every kind of answer to an action was an *exceptio,* and that Roman law allowed an almost unlimited licence to the pleaders of *exceptiones*[1]. This new idea set up a ferment in England and elsewhere. When the old rigid rules had once been infringed, our records became turbid with 'exceptions,' and a century passed away before our lawyers had grasped the first principles of that system of pleading which in the future was to become the most exact, if the most occult, of the sciences[2].

Exceptions in assizes.

Now the region in which the 'exception' first obtained a [p. 610] firm footing was to all seeming one which we have been neglecting, namely, the new and statutory procedure of the Petty Assizes. These, it will be remembered, are actions in which there need not be any pleading at all; they are regarded as summary actions which touch no question of 'right.' The plaintiff obtains a writ which directs that recognitors shall be summoned to answer on oath a particular question. The recognitors appear; if they answer that question in the plaintiff's favour, he obtains seisin[3]. From the first, however, it must have been plain that in some instances a gross injustice would thus be done to the defendant. We will put a simple case. Alan brings an assize of Mort d'Ancestor on the seisin of his father Bernard against William. The question stated in the writ will be this: 'Did Bernard die seised in his demesne as of fee, and is Alan his next heir?' Now it is possible that both clauses of this question ought to receive an affirmative answer, and yet that William ought not to be turned out of possession; for the case may be that on Bernard's death Alan, his son and heir, entered and afterwards enfeoffed William. It would be scandalous if Alan, despite his own act, could now

---

[1] Bethmann-Hollweg, Civilprozess des gemeinen Rechts, vol. vi. p. 55; Fournier, Les officialités au moyen âge, 160–1. Azo distinguishes between a laxer and a stricter use of the term *exceptio.* 'Large ponitur pro omni defensione quae reo competit, etiamsi nulla actori competat actio.... Stricte vero ponitur et proprie pro ea defensione quae competit reo contra actionem competentem in eum.' This doctrine is repeated by later civilians and canonists; but they seem to use *exceptio* habitually in the large sense which makes it cover any and every kind of answer.

[2] The elements of this science were in its last days admirably explained by H. J. Stephen, Principles of Pleading, a book which contains some excellent historical remarks. We purposely use a copy of the first edition, which was issued in 1824, while as yet the system was unreformed.

[3] See above, vol. i. pp. 144–9 ; vol. ii. pp. 47, 56, 137.

recover the land; and yet he will do this if the assize proceeds. Therefore we must allow William an opportunity of asserting that for some reason or another the assize ought not to proceed (*quod non debet assisa inde fieri*)[1], and if we are justified in appropriating the Roman word *exceptio* for any English purpose, we may surely use it in this context. William will show cause against the further continuance of that procedure which the writ has ordained; this plea of his we call an *exceptio*. It is soon evident that the Mort d'Ancestor and the Darrein Presentment can often be 'elided' by 'exceptions' of this character[2].

[p. 611]   But we do not stop here, for we begin to see that the assize-formulas contain words which are rapidly acquiring a technical import, such as 'disseised,' 'free tenement,' 'as of fee' and so forth. A defendant may well fear that, with such phrases before them, the jurors, though they ought to answer the question in his favour, will give his adversary a verdict. The defendant, for example, has ejected a tenant in villeinage, who forthwith brings the Novel Disseisin against him. The jurors ought to say that the plaintiff has not been disseised from a 'free tenement.' But will they do so, unless their attention is specially directed to the villein character of the tenure? So we allow the defendant to raise this point; we allow him to do so by way of an assertion that the assize should not proceed; this assertion we call an *exceptio*. Obviously our *exceptio* is becoming a very elastic term[3].

Elasticity of the exception.

[1] For an early (1194) instance of this formula, see Rolls of the King's Court (Pipe Roll Soc.), p. 68.

[2] For an early instance, see Select Civil Pleas, pl. 122. It is in this context that Glanvill, xiii. 11. 20, introduces the term *exceptio*. As to the large sphere left for exceptions by the formula of Darrein Presentment, see above, vol. ii. pp. 137–8. In course of time the justices began to require that the plaintiff in an assize should give some explanation of his case, see above, vol. ii. p. 49; but on the rolls of the early part of cent. xiii., if there is any pleading at all, the defendant begins it with *Non debet assisa inde fieri*. This is the reason why there is no 'defence' to an Assize: Stephen, Pleading, p. 434. There is nothing to deny, for the plaintiff has not spoken.

[3] See the whole of Bracton's treatment of the exceptions to assizes, ff. 187 b–210, 240–245 b, 266 b–274. The Note Book is full of examples; a single one (pl. 270) may serve to show the form of the *exceptio* and the wide scope that is given to it. The defendant *dicit quod assisa non debet inde fieri*, and states as his reason certain facts whence he concludes that the plaintiff was never seised of free tenement (*quod nullum liberum tenementum inde habere possit*). Thus in form we get from the defendant an assertion that a question

From the province of the Petty Assizes the *exceptio* spread
with great rapidity throughout the domain of the other actions[1].
For one thing, the old reasons for refusing to answer were
brought under the new rubric. From of old a defendant must
have had some power of urging such reasons: for example,
of saying, 'I will not answer, for this court is not competent
to decide this cause,' or 'I will not answer you, for you are an
outlaw.' Under the influence of the romano-canonical procedure
these preliminary objections were now called exceptions; they
were 'temporary' or 'dilatory' exceptions. A classification of [p. 612]
exceptions and a theory about the order in which they should
be propounded was borrowed. First you must except to the
jurisdiction of the court, then to the person of the judge, then
to the writ, then to the person of the plaintiff, then to the
person of the defendant, and so on[2]. About all this much
might be said, and it would be interesting to trace the fortunes
in England of this once outlandish learning[3]. But we must
hasten to say that in a very short time we find the defendant
propounding by way of exception, pleas that we can not regard
as mere preliminary objections, for they are directed to the
heart of the plaintiff's case; these are 'peremptory' or 'perpetual' exceptions, the 'special pleas in bar' of later law. For
a while the utmost laxity prevails. Of this the best examples
are to be found among the Appeals. By way of exception to
an appeal of homicide the appellee is suffered to plead that the
appeal is not a 'true' (that is, not a *bona fide*) appeal but is
the outcome of spite and hatred (*odium et atia*)[4]. A climax
seems to be reached when an appellee pleads an *alibi* by way of
exceptio: a climax we say, for the plea of *alibi* can be nothing
but an argumentative traverse of the charge that has been

ought not to be asked because it ought to be (but perhaps will not be) answered
in his favour.

[1] In speaking of *exceptions* rather than of *special pleas* we are following the
records of this age. The technical usage of *plea* (*placitum*) which makes it
stand for the first utterance of the defendant (provided that utterance is not
a demurrer) seems to be comparatively recent. That utterance is often called
responsum, response. But throughout the Y. BB. of Edw. I. the word *excepcioun*
is constantly used, and apparently stands for any first utterance of the
defendant, at all events if that utterance is not a simple negation See *e.g.*
Y. B. 20–1 Edw. I. p. 275, where *excepcioun* and *respounce* are contrasted.

[2] See Bracton, ff. 399 b, 400 b, 411 b, 413, 415 b, 429 b.

[3] For the ultimate form of the doctrine, see Stephen, Pleading, pp. 63, 429
and Note 78.　　　　　　　　　　　　　　　　[4] See above, vol. ii. p. 587.

made against him, a charge that he will already have traversed
in large and explicit words by his 'defence[1].' And here we may
see how exotic the *exceptio* once was, though it is now flourishing but too luxuriantly in our soil:—it is always, or almost
always, preceded by a *thwert-ut-nay*, that is by a flat denial of
the plaintiff's assertions[2].

[p. 613] The exception may be met by a replication, the replication Laxity of
by a triplication and so on *ad infinitum*. We may occasionally _{placeholder}
find long debates between the parties[3]. Not only are they
long, but, if judged by the standard of a later time, they are
loose and irregular. The pleaders must be charged with many
faults which would have shocked their successors; they habitually 'plead evidence,' they are guilty of argumentativeness and
duplicity[4]. The curious rule which in later days will confine a

---

[1] Bracton, f. 148: 'Item excipere poterit quod anno et die quo hoc fieri
debuit fuit alibi extra regnum vel in provincia in tam remotis partibus quod
verisimile esse non poterit quod hoc quod ei imponitur fieri posset per ipsum.'
Select Pleas of the Crown, pl. 84: 'Et Thomas totum defendit...et dicit quod
die illo...fuit ipse...apud L....et inde ponit se super patriam.' Rec. Off. Assize
Roll, No. 82 (Cambridgeshire, 45 Hen. III.) m. 32: an appellee accused of
committing a crime at Cambridge, 'petit sibi allocari quod quando factum fieri
debuit, si factum esset factum, fuit apud Ely et non apud Cauntebrig...et, istis
sibi allocatis, ponit se super patriam, praeterquam super villam de Cauntebrig.'
However, in this last case the appellee had to join battle, was vanquished and
hanged. Y. B. 21–2 Edw. I. p. 391: in a civil action a litigant tries to plead an
alibi by way of exception; but is driven to a direct traverse. Long afterwards
the criminal practice of Scotland treated an *alibi* as a preliminary exception
that must be disposed of before the evidence for the prosecution could be heard.

[2] See above, p. 611, note 1. Observe how a special plea is pleaded to an
action of debt. Note Book, pl. 177: 'Et W. venit et defendit contra eum et
contra sectam suam quod nihil ei debet. Sed verum vult dicere. Dicit quod
bene potest esse quod etc.' The phrase *Sed veritatem vult dicere* is commonly
used to usher in a 'confession and avoidance.' The defendant first denies
everything, but then 'wishes to tell the truth,' and admits that there is some
truth in the plaintiff's case.

[3] Note Book, pl. 716, cited by Bracton, f. 436, is a good specimen. Under
Edward I. the answer to an *excepcion* is currently called a *replicacion*; Y. B.
21–2 Edw. I. pp. 142, 426. We have not met with *triplication* except in the
text books, nor with *rejoinder* and *rebutter*, which seem to belong to a later
day.

[4] Stephen, Pleading, Note 38, has remarked these faults. His examples
might now be indefinitely multiplied. Under Edward I. objections to duplicity
are becoming common. There is a regular formula by which what we should
call evidence is pleaded: *et hoc bene patet quia*. See *e.g.* Note Book, pl. 612,
669, 979, 1565, 1616, 1663. In Northumberland Assize Rolls, pp. 12, 191, will
be found two early instances of the phrase *absque hoc*, but it is not as yet a
technical phrase. See also Y. B. 30–1 Edw. I. p. 199. Under Edward I. the

man to a single 'plea in bar[1]' appears already in Bracton, justified by the remark that a litigant must not use two staves to defend himself withal[2]. But this rule had not always been observed; defendants were allowed a second staff, at all events if, when using the first, they expressly reserved the right of picking up another[3].

The exception and the jury.

These men are drunk with the new wine of Romanism :— [p. 614] such may be the comment which a modern reader will make when for the first time he watches the exploits of our ancient pleaders. But we ought to see that there is an under-current of good sense running beneath their vagaries. The extension of the *exceptio* is the extension of a new mode of proof; it is the extension of a mode of proof which will become famous under the name of trial by jury.

Proof of exceptions.

He who excepts must, like a plaintiff, offer to prove his case[4]. It may be that he can rely upon the record of a court or upon a charter; but in general the modes of proof that would seem open to him would be a 'suit' of witnesses or, in appropriate cases, a single witness who is ready to do battle[5].

term *traverse* is common and we may find *demur* (Y. B. 20–1 Edw. I. p. 323; 21–2 Edw. I. p. 163), *tender an averment* (21–2 Edw. I. p. 263), *the issue of a plea* (33–5 Edw. I. 297).

[1] Stephen, Pleading, pp. 151, 290 and Note 57.

[2] Bracton, f. 400 b: 'sicut posset se pluribus baculis defendere, quod esse non debet, cum ei sufficere debeat tantum probatio unius [peremptoriae exceptionis].' Y. B. 33–5 Edw. I. p. 359: 'vous ne averez point deus bastons.' This seems an allusion to trial by battle. Bracton, f. 301 b, 302, permits a defendant in Dower to plead another plea after failing in the allegation that the husband is still living. But this point seems to have been questionable.

[3] See *e.g.* Note Book, pl. 272. Writ of Right against a prior; he first excepts on the ground of royal charters; 'et si curia consideraverit quod super hoc debeat respondere, dicet aliud.' Judgment, 'quod prior dicat aliud.' He pleads another plea, 'et si curia consideraverit quod debeat respondere super cartas sine Rege, dicet aliud.' The attempt to retain a right 'dicere aliud' is not very uncommon. The limits of the rule against two peremptory exceptions were doubtful in 1292; Y. B. 20–1 Edw. I. pp. 457, 463; 21–2 Edw. I. p. 593. At present we are inclined to think that the rule which holds a defendant to have been totally defeated if any one issue of fact is found against him is a rule which punishes a liar for having lied. See Bracton, f. 432: 'amittet rem quae petitur propter mendacium.' If so, the rule was but slowly defined, for an appellee who had been beaten on the issue of *odium et atia* was allowed to join battle. See above, vol. ii. p. 588.

[4] Bracton, f. 399 b: 'Nam qui excipit videtur agere.' Dig. 44. 1. 1: 'Agere etiam is videtur, qui exceptione utitur: nam reus in exceptione actor est.' Stephen, Pleading, Note 84.

[5] Observe how alternative proofs are offered. Note Book, pl. 95: 'et inde

At this point, however, the procedure of the Petty Assizes once more became of decisive importance. In other actions when the litigants are pleading they stand in the presence of the justices, but there are no recognitors, no representatives of 'the country' at hand. If, however, the action is a Petty Assize, then when the litigants first meet each other in court they stand in the presence of the twelve men who have been summoned to answer the formulated question. If now the defendant 'excepts,' a method of testing the truth of his 'exception' is within easy reach. The recognitors have been summoned to answer one question, but why should they not answer another? The facts alleged in the exception are as likely to be within their knowledge as the facts suggested by the plaintiff's writ. The transition is the easier because, as [p. 615] we have explained above[1], the defendant's so-called 'exception' is often a statement which, if it were true, would preclude the jurors from giving an affirmative answer to the original question. One example will suffice. The recognitors in an assize have been summoned to say whether Richard disseised John[2]; Richard asserts that the assize should not proceed, because John gave the land by feoffment to Richard's villein and the villein surrendered it to Richard, who entered by reason of this surrender. Now if this assertion is true, Richard did not disseise John. Richard, however, is desirous that the question which the jurors are to answer should be the question that he has defined. Of course if John consents to this change there is no difficulty; but further, we can say that he ought to consent, and that, if he will not, his action should be dismissed, for his case is that he was disseised by Richard, and this he can not have been if Richard's story is true. Of the verdict of twelve men as a mode of deciding this dispute the plaintiff can not complain, for he himself has invoked it. Thus it becomes common that a question raised by pleading should be answered by a jury and that a litigant should find himself

---

producit sectam, et si hoc non sufficit ponit se super iuratam patriae.' Ibid. pl. 116: 'et inde producit sectam...et si hoc non sufficit offert dirationare per corpus...' The Norman Custumal, c. 105 (100), ed. de Gruchy, p. 317, gives us much information as to the defendant's *secta* (*lex probabilis*); we shall return to it hereafter. Somma, p. 325.

[1] See above, vol. ii. p. 613.

[2] Note Book, pl. 1256.

driven, on pain of losing his cause, to accept the offer that his opponent makes of submission to a verdict[1].

The jury and the appeal.

The offer of a verdict of the country as proof of an exception soon invades the other actions. The excipients desire that this should be so, for if they offered proof by a *secta* of witnesses, this would very properly be met by a wager of law[2]. The king also gains by the new procedure for it is a royal commodity and he sells it. Far into the thirteenth century men will sometimes offer him money if they want an inquest[3]. Very often, again, the plaintiff is quite willing that the exception should be submitted to a verdict, either because he is [p. 616] confident in the righteousness of his cause, or because he is by no means certain of being able to make a law. But, even if unwilling, he may be compelled to give a reluctant consent to the intervention of a jury. The exception is a novelty, and plaintiffs have in this case no traditional right to any of the antique modes of proof.

The exception and the denial.

One last line had yet to be crossed: that, namely, which divides the exception from the mere denial. However broad this line should have been, practice had reduced it to the utmost tenuity. If to a charge of homicide the plea of an *alibi* is a proper *exceptio*, we can hardly deny the name *exceptio* to the plea 'I am not guilty.' In the department of criminal law the forces which worked in favour of the jury were at their strongest. For one thing, the king was interested in all breaches of his peace, and he trusted to inquests rather than

---

[1] When an *assisa* is turned into a *iurata ex consensu partium* it is often plain that the original recognitors answer the new question, for the record shows no trace of any 'jury process' subsequent to the pleading. See *e.g.* Note Book, 87, 93, 1256, 1833, 1899, 1924. Sometimes, however, a new jury will be summoned after the pleading. See pl. 205 and the marginal note, also pl. 51. This subject is discussed by Mr Pike in his Introduction to Y. B. 12–13 Edw. III. pp. xli–lxxi.

[2] Bracton, f. 400 b, § 9.

[3] See *e.g.* Note Book, 86, 90, 134, 145, 233, 241, 316, 895, etc. On the other hand in 1220 (pl. 102) William Marshall offers the enormous sum of a thousand marks for the privilege of fighting Fawkes of Breauté. Before the end of Henry III.'s reign a litigant can generally get a jury for nothing. If he makes a payment, this is for something unusual, *e.g.* a jury drawn from two counties. But even in the nineteenth century the tenant in a writ of right could purchase an advantage by tendering 6s. 8d. to the king at the proper moment. See Y. B. 20–1 Edw. I. p. 293; Littleton, sec. 514. This was actually done so late as 1833 in *Spiers* v. *Morris*, 9 Bingham, 687.

to the arms of appellors.   Secondly, an appeal generally came before justices in eyre who were presiding over an assembly in which every hundred of the county was represented by a jury which had come there to answer inquiries.   Indeed the justices as a general rule first heard of the appeal because it was 'presented' to them by a jury.   Thirdly, the abolition of the ordeal in 1215 had left a gap.   When men are appealed by women or by other non-combatants, the truth of the appeal can no longer be tested, as it once was[1], by fire or water, and the duel is out of the question, so the verdict of a jury appears as the only possible mode of proof.   If then in such a case the appellee may have recourse to this test, why not in others?   An objection on the part of the appellor could be met by the argument that, not he, but the king was the person primarily interested in a breach of the king's peace, and that the king wished for proof by verdict.   By Bracton's day the right of the appellee to 'put himself upon his country for good and ill,' that is, to submit to a verdict the general question of his guilt, [p. 617] seems to have been conceded; but even Bracton is doubtful whether an accusation of poisoning, an act done in secret, could be met in this manner[2].

In civil causes also we begin to find defendants desirous of referring to a jury what in substance, if not in form, is a general negation of the plaintiff's statements.   In some instances they are expected to do this.   For example, when there is a charge of 'waste' by cutting down trees or the like, the court holds that a general negation should be made good by a verdict rather than by a 'law,' for it might well fall out that the formal negatory oath would be a flagrant denial of visible facts[3].   And then, in contrast to the old actions into which the

The jury and the general issue.

---

[1] Select Pleas of the Crown, pl. 4, 9, 11, 19, 24, 68.

[2] Bracton, ff. 142 b, 137 b.   The practice of allowing the appellee to put himself upon the country for good and ill, if he will purchase this privilege from the king, seems to be establishing itself about the year 1200.   See Select Pleas of the Crown, pl. 59, 64, 78, 81.   Towards the end of Henry III.'s reign the appellor rarely has a chance of urging any theoretical right to a duel that he may have, for the justices as a matter of course quash the appeal for informality and arraign the appellee at the king's suit.   We write this after perusing various unprinted eyre rolls.   See also Chadwyck-Healey, Somersetshire Pleas, p. 136.   In Normandy the appellor's right to a duel was more respectfully treated: Somma, p. 177; Ancienne coutume, c. 69 (ed. de Gruchy, p. 171); Brunner, Schwurgericht, 475.

[3] Bracton, f. 315 b.   So far as we have observed, Waste is the first action

jury must slowly work its way, we see newer actions which, if we may so speak, are born into an atmosphere of trial by jury. Two of these are of special importance. The Writs of Entry, which look like an infringement of feudal principles, are defended by the statement that they deal with recent events well known to the neighbours[1]. The action of Trespass is a semi-criminal action in which the king has an interest, and when it comes into being men are no longer suffered to wage their law in the king's court by way of answer to a charge of breaking his peace[2]. Before the end of Henry III.'s reign it is a common incident in most kinds of litigation that the parties agree to submit to 'the country' some question that has been raised by their pleadings. The proposal is made by the one [p.618] party and accepted by the other. The one 'puts himself upon the country, and,' says the record, 'the other does the like.' In the hands of the second or third generation of professional pleaders, of serjeants at law[3], the system of pleading begins to recrystallize in a new shape. Trial by jury is now its centre, and very soon it has become so peculiarly English that legists and decretists would be able to make nothing of it. We must not explore its later history, but of its nucleus, the trial by twelve men, a few more words must be said[4].

in which a defendant habitually pleads what we should call 'the general issue' and puts himself upon a jury. See Note Book, pl. 388, 443, 485, 580, 640, 717, 718, 880, 1371. In this action the inquest procedure is specially appropriate, for usually the verdict is taken, not by the justices in court, but by the sheriff on the spot where the alleged waste was committed.

[1] See above, vol. ii. p. 65, and Bracton, f. 317 b.

[2] Stat. Walliae (1284) c. 11 (Statutes, i. 66): 'Et cum vix in placito transgressionis evadere poterit reus quin defendat se per patriam, de consensu partium inquirat veritatem iustitiarius per bonam patriam.' In the first days of Trespass a wager of law was not unknown: Somersetshire Pleas, pl. 572.

[3] See above, vol. i. p. 214.

[4] We agree with H. J. Stephen (Pleading, Note 38) that anything that could be called a formulated science of pleading is hardly to be traced beyond the time of Edward I. Our theory of the part played in earlier times by the Romanesque *exceptio* may be open to dispute. To anyone who knows only the *exceptio* of classical Roman law the statement that the English 'general issue' is in its origin an 'exception' would seem an absurd paradox. Nevertheless we believe that it would be near the truth. A plea of *alibi* was regarded by Bracton as an *exceptio*, and from *alibi* to *Not guilty* the step is of the shortest. Here we find the reason why a plea of the general issue contains a two-fold denial. Take the form that was still used in our own century: 'And the said *C.D.* comes and defends the force and injury when etc. *and says* that he is not guilty of the said trespasses above laid to his charge, or any part thereof, in

A grand assize is composed of twelve lawful knights of the Composition of the jury. district in which the disputed tenement lies, who have been chosen in the presence of the justices by four knights, who have been chosen by the sheriff [1]. This double election is peculiar to a grand assize, a solemn process safeguarded by precautions
[p. 619] against the sheriff's partiality. To form a petty assize or an ordinary jury, twelve free and lawful men of the neighbourhood are summoned directly by the sheriff [2]. In the case of a jury summoned after there has been pleading, he is bidden to choose those 'through whom the truth of the matter may be best known [3].' The litigants have an opportunity of 'excepting' to or challenging the jurors, and our law has borrowed for this purpose the canonist's scheme of 'exceptions to witnesses [4].' The jurors must be free and lawful, impartial and disinterested, neither the enemies nor the too close friends of either litigant [5]. We must not think of them as coming into court ignorant, like their modern successors, of the cases about which they will have to speak. In every case the writ that summons them—whether it be an 'original' writ calling for an assize, or a 'judicial' writ

manner and form as the said *A.B.* hath above complained. And of this the said *C.D.* puts himself upon the country.' To state this more briefly, *C.D.* denies that he trespassed *and says* that he did not trespass. A modern denial, suggested by the practice of excepting, is tacked on to the ancient denial, the Defence or *Thwert-ut-nay*. The rules as to the use of the three phrases 'Et hoc paratus est verificare,' 'Et de hoc ponit se super patriam' and 'Et petit quod hoc inquiratur per patriam,' are not so old as the time of which we speak. Thus *e.g.* Northumberland Assize Rolls, pp. 236, 244, a defendant 'petit quod inquiratur,' and a plaintiff 'ponit se super patriam.' An affirmative plea often ends with a 'ponit se super patriam.' The rule (Stephen, Pleading, pp. 247–8) which in later days allows the defendant to 'put himself' on the country, while the plaintiff must 'pray' for an inquiry, suggests that defendants acquired an absolute right to a jury while plaintiffs still had to pay if they wanted one; but we have failed to verify this suggestion.

[1] Glanvill, ii. 10–12; Bracton, f. 331 b. For an early case of election, see Select Civil Pleas, pl. 212. It is abundantly clear that, whatever may have been the practice at a later time, the grand assize was a body of twelve, not of sixteen knights: in other words, the four electors took no part in the verdict.

[2] For the petty assizes, see Glanvill, xiii. 3, 19, 33; Bracton, f. 179, 238, 253 b.

[3] The classical words are 'per quos rei veritas melius sciatur.' See Bracton, f. 316 : 'qui melius sciant et velint veritatem dicere.'

[4] Glanvill, ii. 12.

[5] Bracton, f. 185. Jurors are often removed as being too poor; *e.g.* Select Civil Pleas, pl. 126, 253. Of the 'peremptory challenges' of our later criminal procedure we have seen nothing in this age.

issued after the litigants have ended their pleadings—will define some question about which their verdict is wanted[1].

That in old times 'the jurors were the witnesses'—this doctrine has in our own days become a commonplace. For the purposes of a popular exposition it is true enough. Nevertheless it does not quite hit the truth. If once the jurors had been called *testes*, if once their *veredictum* had been brought under the rubric *testimonium*, the whole subsequent history of the jury would have been changed, and never by imperceptible degrees would the jurors have ceased to be 'witnesses' and become 'judges of fact[2].' In all probability a time would have come when the justices would have begun to treat these *testes* [p. 620] in the manner in which witnesses ought to be treated according to our ideas: each witness would have been separated from his fellows and questioned about his belief and its grounds. The court, instead of receiving the single verdict of a jury, would have set itself to discuss the divergent testimony of twelve jurors. Where there was flat contradiction it might have been puzzled; still the simple device of counting heads was open to it, and at all events it might have insisted that each juror whose testimony was received should profess a first-hand knowledge of the facts about which he spoke, for already the elementary truth that 'hearsay' is untrustworthy had been apprehended[3]. Therefore we have to explain why the history of the jury took a turn which made our jurors, not witnesses, but judges of fact, and the requisite explanation we may find in three ancient elements which are present in trial by jury so soon as that trial becomes a well-established institution. For

---

[1] In other words, the 'issue' will be embodied in the *Venire facias*. See for some elaborate instances, Bracton, f. 325.

[2] The verb *testari* is often used of jurors; *e.g.* Northumberland Assize Rolls, p. 72: 'et iuratores testantur quod...non sunt culpabiles.' But *recognoscere* and *dicere* are from the first the usual words. The term *recognoscere* seems to imply a calling to mind, a recalling. The Constitutions of Clarendon were a *recordatio vel recognitio* of the king's rights. We must remember, however, that in good Latin *recognoscere*, if it will stand for *recollect*, will also stand for *examine, investigate*. When at length English became the language of formal records, *recognoscere* was rendered by *recognize*. Any other translation of it would be dangerous; but *to find* is our best modern equivalent.

[3] See *e.g.* Select Pleas of the Crown, pl. 29 (A.D. 1202): 'Et hoc offert probare...sicut ille qui non vidit hoc sed per alios habet eum suspectum. Nullum est appellum.'

want of better names, we may call them (1) the arbitral, (2) the communal, and (3) the quasi-judicial elements.

(1) Jurors are not arbitrators. We have seen, however, that the verdict of jurors becomes a common mode of proof only because litigants 'put themselves' upon it, and that the summons of a jury (in the narrow sense of that term which opposes *iurata* to *assisa*) is always in theory the outcome of consent and submission. Both litigants have agreed to be bound by a verdict of the country. They might perhaps have chosen some other test. We may, for example, see a plaintiff and a defendant 'putting themselves' upon the two witnesses named in a charter, or upon the word of some one man[1]. Now in such a case neither of the litigants can quarrel with the declaration that he has invoked. He has called for it, and must accept it. So with the verdict of the country; he has asked for it, and by it he must stand or fall. It is, says Bracton, 'his own proof' and therefore he can not reprobate it[2]. If he produced as compurgators men who at the last moment refused to help him in his oath, he could not force them to give an explanation of their conduct. So with the jurors; it is not for him to ask them questions or expose their ignorance, for he has put himself upon their oath. What he can not do for himself, the court will not do for him. The justices are not tempted to analyze the process of which an unanimous verdict is the outcome; that verdict has been accepted in advance by the only persons whom it will affect[3].

Arbitral element in the jury.

[p. 621]

---

[1] Note Book, pl. 255 (A.D. 1227). The question is whether Philip de Colombiers was of sound mind when he executed a charter. Two witnesses named in the charter are still living. 'Et omnes ponunt se super illos duos testes. Et ideo vicecomes...illos venire faciat...ad recognoscendum si... Philippus tempore quo fuit compos sui...cartam illam fecit vel non.' These witnesses are, like jurors, to come *ad recognoscendum.* Curia Regis Rolls [Rec. Off.] No. 140, Pasch. 34 Henr. III. m. 17: The defendant asserts that the plaintiff 'assigned' him to pay money to the Earl of Oxford. The plaintiff denies this, 'et de hoc ponit se super ipsum Comitem.' The defendant does the like. A writ is sent to the Earl. 'Et venit Comes in propria persona sua et recordatur' that the assignment was made.

[2] Bracton, f. 290 b. Therefore a *iurata* can not be attainted. When this rule was altered in 1275 (Stat. West. I. c. 38) it was already becoming evident that the consensual origin of the *iurata* was a fiction.

[3] The arbitral element is clearly seen in a case of John's day in which the Bishop of Ely and the Abbot of St Edmund's 'put themselves' upon a jury of eighteen knights, of whom six are to be chosen by each litigant, while the remaining six are named by Hubert Walter and Geoffrey Fitz Peter: Select

Communal
element in
the jury.

(2) The verdict of the jurors is not just the verdict of twelve men; it is the verdict of a *pays*, a 'country,' a neighbourhood, a community[1]. There is here a volatile element which we can not easily precipitate, for the thoughts of this age about the nature of communities are vague thoughts, and we can not say that 'the country' is definitely *persona ficta*. Still we may perceive what we can not handle, and, especially in criminal procedure, the voice of the twelve men is deemed to be the voice of the country-side, often the voice of some hundred or other district which is more than a district, which [p. 622] is a community. The justices seem to feel that if they analyzed the verdict they would miss the very thing for which they are looking, the opinion of the country.

Quasi-
judicial
element in
the jury.

(3) Lastly, we may already detect in the verdict of the jurors an element which we can not but call quasi-judicial. Whatever theory may have prevailed[2], the parties to an action are often submitting to 'the country' questions which the twelve representatives of the country will certainly not be able to answer if they may speak only of what they have seen with their own eyes[3]. Some of the verdicts that are given must be founded upon hearsay and floating tradition[4]. Indeed it is the

Civil Pleas, pl. 183. Again, when Edward I. in his Carta Mercatoria (Munim. Gildh. ii. 207) grants that a foreign merchant may have six foreign merchants on the jury, we see the arbitral element. Already the idea is that a jury, taken as a whole, should be impartial, while its component parts should in some sort represent the interests of both litigants. Even in our own century when a jury was summoned, the sheriff was told to call in the twelve men 'because as well (*quia tam*) the said *C.D.* as the said *A.B.*, between whom the matter in variance is, have put themselves upon that jury.' This *quia tam* clause in the *Venire facias* seems almost as old as the *iurata*; Bracton, f. 325.

[1] The early submissions to a verdict vary slightly in their form. See *e.g.* Select Civil Pleas, pl. 27: as to one question a litigant 'ponit se super legale visnetum'; as to another question 'simili modo ponit se inde super iuratam patriae.' Though our Latin uses *patria*, our French uses *pays*, which descends from Latin *pagus*. The 'country' of this formula is not our father-land but 'the country-side.'

[2] According to Glanvill, ii. 17, the recognitors of a Grand Assize may base their verdict upon what their fathers have told them. But jurors (in the narrower sense) should speak 'de proprio visu et auditu'; Bracton, f. 317 b.

[3] See *e.g.* Note Book, pl. 628 (A.D. 1231): 'Et Ricardus...dicit quod omni tempore a conquestu Angliae ibi communam habuit...et inde ponit se super patriam.'

[4] See *e.g.* Note Book, pl. 798: 'Iuratores dicunt quod quaedam Margeria... praesentavit quemdam Robertum Luvel xl. annis elapsis et eo amplius.' Ibid. pl. 769: a strange tale of what happened before 1188 told in 1233. Placit.

duty of the jurors, so soon as they have been summoned, to
make inquiries about the facts of which they will have to speak
when they come before the court[1]. They must collect testimony; they must weigh it and state the net result in a verdict.
Bracton sees that this is so; he even, though in a loose,
untechnical sense, speaks of the jurors as deliberating and
'judging,' and he speaks of the result of their deliberations,
when it takes the form of a general verdict, as a 'judgment[2].'

[p. 623]   It is to the presence of these three elements that we may
ascribe the ultimate victory of that principle of our law which
requires an unanimous verdict. We can not treat this as an
aboriginal principle. In the old Frankish inquests the sworn
neighbours sometimes gave a single verdict, while in other
cases each man's evidence was taken separately and recorded
separately[3]. We have here a plastic institution, which can
assume divers shapes in Normandy and England and Scotland.
A little inquisitory zeal on the part of the king's commissioners
might turn it into a mere examination of witnesses, whose
divergent testimonies would be weighed by the court. Or
again, their voices might be counted without being weighed and
the verdict of the majority accepted. For a long time we see
in England various ideas at work[4]. If some of the recognitors

Unanimity of the jury.

Abbrev. p. 155: in 1264 jurors speak of Richard I.'s day. Select Civil Pleas,
pl. 41: in 1200 a litigant wants a verdict as to what happened before 1135; his
adversary refuses to submit to a verdict 'de tam antiquo tempore.'

[1] This is made plain by the writ which tells the sheriff to summon jurors to
appear before the court to 'recognize' some matter, 'et se ita inde certificent
quod iustitiarios nostros inde reddant certiores'; Bracton, f. 325. Britton, ii.
87: 'issint qe chescun jurour distingtement soit garni en touz pointz, sur quel
point il se deit aviser avaunt soen vener en nostre court.'

[2] Bracton, f. 185 b: 'de veritate discutiant [iuratores] et iudicent.' Ibid.
f. 289: 'Eodem modo potest iurator falsum facere iudicium et fatuum cum
iudicare teneatur per verba in sacramento contenta... Et si iustitiarius
secundum eorum [*scil.* iuratorum] iudicium pronunciaverit, falsum faciet
pronunciationem.' Ibid. f. 290 b: 'Si autem iuratores factum narraverint
sicut rei veritas se habuerit, et postea factum secundum narrationem suam
iudicaverint, et in iudicio erraverint, iudicium potius erit fatuum quam falsum,
cum credant tale iudicium sequi tale factum.' This makes it possible for men
of a later age to see in the verdict of a jury the promised *iudicium parium*; see
above, vol. i. p. 173. This mistake is being made already in Edward I.'s day;
Y. B. 30-1 Edw. I. p. 531. A knight's demand for a *iudicium parium* is
supposed to be satisfied by knights being put upon the jury.

[3] Brunner, Forschungen, 231–242; D. R. G. ii. 524.

[4] Brunner, Schwurgericht, 363–371; Gierke, D. G. R. ii. 481; Thayer,
Evidence, p. 86.

profess themselves ignorant, they can be set aside and other men can be called to fill their places[1]. If there is but one dissentient juror, his words can be disregarded and he can be fined :—*Testis unus, testis nullus*[2]. In the assize of novel disseisin, which in no wise touches 'the right,' we are content with the verdict of seven men, though the other five have not appeared or have appeared and dissented[3]. But gradually all these plans are abandoned and unanimity is required. The victory is not complete until the fourteenth century is no longer young[4]; but, from the moment when our records begin, we seem to see a strong desire for unanimity. In a thousand cases the jury is put before us as speaking with a single voice, while any traces of dissent[5] or of a nescience confessed by some only of the jurors are very rare. 'You shall tell us,' says a judge in 1293, 'in other fashion how he is next heir, or you shall remain shut up without meat or drink until the morrow[6].'

Why is unanimity desired? The arbitral and communal principles are triumphing. [p. 624] The parties to the litigation have 'put themselves' upon a certain test. That test is the voice of the country. Just as a corporation can have but one will, so a country can have but one voice : *le pays vint e dyt*[7]. In a later age this communal principle might have led to the acceptance of the majority's verdict. But as yet men had not accepted the dogma that the voice of a majority binds the community. In communal affairs they demanded unanimity; but minorities were expected to give way. Then at this point the 'quasi-judicial' position of the jurors becomes important. No doubt it would be wrong for a man to acquiesce in a verdict that he knew to be false; but in the common case—and it becomes commoner daily—many of the jurors really have no first-hand knowledge of the facts about which they speak, and there is no harm in a juror's joining in a verdict which expresses the

[1] Glanvill, ii. 17 ; Bracton, f. 185 b. [2] Select Civil Pleas, pl. 241.

[3] Bracton, f. 179 b, 255 b. Britton, i. 31, speaking of criminal cases, says that if the majority of the jurors know the facts and the minority know nothing, judgment shall be given in accordance with the voice of the majority.

[4] Y. B. 41 Edw. III. f. 31 (Mich. pl. 36).

[5] Note Book, pl. 376, 524 ; Placit. Abbrev. 279, Kanc.; 286, Norf. See the important records in the note to Hale, P. C. ii. 297.

[6] Y. B. 21–2 Edw. I. p. 273.

[7] Y. B. 21–2 Edw. I. p. 225. This is a rare phrase; but *assisa venit* and *iurata venit* are from the first the proper phrases, and they put before us the body of twelve men as a single entity.

belief of those of his fellows who do know something. Thus a professed unanimity is, as our rolls show, very easily produced. Nor must it escape us that the justices are pursuing a course which puts the verdict of the country on a level with the older modes of proof. If a man came clean from the ordeal or successfully made his law, the due proof would have been given; no one could have questioned the dictum of Omniscience. The *veredictum patriae* is assimilated to the *iudicium Dei*[1]. English judges find that a requirement of unanimity is the line of least resistance; it spares them so much trouble. We shall hardly explain the shape that trial by jury very soon assumed unless we take to heart the words of an illustrious judge of our own day :—' It saves judges from the responsibility—which to many men would appear intolerably heavy and painful—of deciding simply on their own opinion upon the guilt or innocence of the prisoner[2].' It saved the judges of the middle [p. 625] ages not only from this moral responsibility, but also from enmities and feuds. Likewise it saved them from that as yet unattempted task, a critical dissection of testimony. An age which accepts every miracle and takes for sober history any tale of Brutus or Arthur that anyone invents must shrink from that task. If our judges had attempted it, they would soon have been hearing the evidence in secret[3].

As to the manner in which the jurors came to their verdict, Verdict we know that as a general rule they had ample notice of the and question which was to be addressed to them. At the least a evidence. fortnight had been given them in which to 'certify themselves' of the facts[4]. We know of no rule of law which prevented them from listening during this interval to the tale of the litigants; indeed it was their duty to discover the truth. Then, when the day of trial had come, we take it that the parties to the cause had an opportunity of addressing the jurors

---

[1] This comes out in the phrase ' to put oneself on God and the grand assize,' which is as old as 1293 (Y. B. 21–2 Edw. I. p. 217) but not, so far as we know, much older. Compare too the prisoner's statement that he will be tried ' by God and his country,' of which, however, we can not give any early example. The idea persists that somehow or another an appeal to God must be allowed.

[2] Stephen, Hist. Crim. Law, i. 573.

[3] This happened in France. Viollet, Établissements, i. 274 : ' les baillis avaient fait triompher le système commode pour eux de la procédure occulte.'

[4] Britton, ii. 87.

collectively[1]. In our very first Year Books we see that documents can be put in 'to inform the jury,' and it is to documents thus used that, so far as we are aware, the term 'evidence' was first applied[2]. Again, we know of no rule of law which would have prohibited the jurors from listening in court to persons whom the litigants produced and who were capable of giving information, though we do not think that as yet such persons were sworn[3]. It is difficult to discover the truth about this matter, because, even in the nineteenth century, the formal 'record' will say no word of any witnesses and will speak as though the jurors had agreed on a verdict before they came into court. But certain it is that already under Henry III. a jury would often describe in detail events that took place long ago and acts that were not done in public. Separately or collectively, in court or out of court, they have listened to [p. 626] somebody's story and believed it. This renders possible that slow process which gives us the trial by jury of modern times. We may say, if we will, that the old jurors were witnesses; but even in the early years of the thirteenth century they were not, and were hardly supposed to be, eye-witnesses.

Jurors and witnesses.
Great importance has been attributed by modern historians to the peculiar procedure that prevailed when the genuineness of a charter was denied[4]. The witnesses whose names stood at its foot were summoned along with a body of neighbours. These *testes* and these *iuratores* were to join in a verdict. The appropriateness of this procedure we shall understand if we observe that the question submitted to this composite body was in the oldest days very rarely the simple question whether a certain man had set his seal to a certain parchment; it was generally the more complex question whether he had made a 'gift' of land, and the verdict spoke of seisin[5]. A similar

---

[1] Y. B. 20–1 Edw. I. p. 243: 'dites ceo en evidence de lassise.' Placit. Abbrev. 145 (A.D. 1258): jurors in an assize say that they know nothing about the alleged pedigree of Maud the plaintiff 'nisi tantum ex relatu attornati ipsius Matillidis.'

[2] Y. B. 20–1 Edw. I. pp. 17, 21; 21–2 Edw. I. p. 451: 'la chartre put estre boté avant en evidence de ceo a la grant assyse.' This practice may perhaps go back as far as 1200; see Jocelin of Brakelond (Camd. Soc.), p. 91.

[3] In old collections of oaths (*e.g.* Court Baron, p. 77) we find a witness's oath to tell truth in answer to questions.

[4] This is admirably described by Thayer, Evidence, p. 97.

[5] See the early case, Select Civil Pleas, pl. 59: 'And John puts himself upon the witnesses of the charters and upon the neighbourhood, as to whether

composite body was sometimes called in when the dispute was as to the manner in which a woman had been endowed at the church door[1]. We are very far from denying that this practice of calling the *testes* of a deed to assist in the trial played a considerable part in the transformation of the jury. It brings out in an emphatic manner the contrast between *testes* and *iuratores*. But this procedure was adapted only to a small class of disputes, and would have exercised no general influence if the jurors in other cases had been steadily regarded as first-hand witnesses[2].

[p. 627]   The principle that the jurors are to speak only about matter of fact and are not concerned with matter of law is present from the first. They are not judges, not doomsmen; their function is not to 'find the doom' as the suitors do in the old courts, but to 'recognize,' to speak the truth (*veritatem dicere*). Still this principle long remains latent and tacit. A plain utterance of it would imply an analysis of concrete disputes that was foreign to the old procedure[3]. That procedure would, for example, have allowed a defendant to swear to the statement 'I do not owe you penny or penny's-worth,' a statement which, to our thinking, can not be of pure fact. The recognitors in a grand assize were called upon to say

[margin: Fact and law.]

Jollan had any entry into that land, except through Alice, whom he had in ward.' Note Book, pl. 188, 205, 222, 250, 269, 332, etc. So clean an issue as *Non est factum* was rare in the first days of special pleading.

[1] Note Book, pl. 91, 154, 631, 1603, 1707. Thayer, Evidence, p. 98.

[2] The theory which saw an historical link between the modern witness who testifies before a jury and the plaintiff's *secta* has been sufficiently disproved. See Brunner, Schwurgericht, p. 428. The *secta* and the jury never come into contact. The *secta*, if produced at all, is produced in court before any question for a jury is raised or any summons for a jury issued. Curia Regis Roll, No. 140 (Pasch. 34 Hen. III.), m. 10, gives an interesting case from Huntingdonshire. Ten jurors and seven charter-witnesses appear; the jurors say that a feoffor, Simon by name, was *non compos sui*; the witnesses say *compos*. One litigant offers the king twenty marks that eight jurors of Northamptonshire and eight of Huntingdonshire 'qui habuerunt notitiam de praedicto Simone' may be added. The other litigant offers ten marks for eight jurors from Bedfordshire and eight from Buckinghamshire. The four sheriffs are ordered to send eight jurors apiece.

[3] The famous maxim 'ad quaestionem iuris respondent iudices, ad quaestionem facti iuratores,' seems to have been attributed by Coke to Bracton. It has not been traced beyond Coke, who, as Mr Thayer says, 'seems to have spawned Latin maxims freely.' See Thayer, Law and Fact, Harv. L. Rev. iv. 148–9.

whether the demandant had greater right than the tenant, and in so doing they had an opportunity of giving effect to their own opinions as to many a nice point of law[1]. To all appearance they usually gave their answer in two or three words; they declared that the *mere dreit* was with the one party or with the other, and they proffered no reason for their belief[2]. We must not suppose that in such a case they followed the ruling of the justices. The justices were powerless to help them. The demandant, it is true, had set forth the title on which he relied; but the tenant had contented himself with a sweeping denial. The recognitors, being his neighbours, might know something about his case and were morally bound to investigate it; the justices knew no more than he had told them, and he had told them nothing[3].

Special verdicts.

Perhaps when the Possessory Assizes were first instituted the questions that were formulated in their writs were regarded as questions of pure fact, for example the question whether one [p. 628] man was the next heir of another. Heirship may at one time have seemed to be a simple physical fact, just as sonship may appear as a simple physical fact, until we have perceived that the only sonship with which the law is, as a general rule, concerned involves a definition of marriage. Very soon, however, the separation of matter of fact from matter of law had begun. Sometimes the jurors felt that, though they knew all that had happened in the world of sense, they yet could not answer the question that the writ put to them. They knew that Ralph had ejected Roger, they knew what services Roger had been performing, and yet they would not take upon themselves to say whether Ralph had 'disseised' Roger from his 'free tenement.' So, with the terrors of an attaint before their eyes, they asked the aid of the justices and, as we should say, returned a 'special verdict[4].'

[1] They might, however, state pure facts and these might be a sufficient foundation for a judgment. Glanvill, ii. 18.

[2] For verdicts of a Grand Assize with reasons, see Note Book, pl. 769, 960, 1701.

[3] Bracton, f. 185 b, says that when a Petty Assize is taken without pleading the justices are to give no instruction to the jurors.

[4] Special verdicts in Petty Assizes are found at an early time. For an example from John's reign, see Select Civil Pleas, pl. 179: 'Iuratores dicunt quod rei veritatem inde dicent, et audita rei veritate, iudicent iustitiarii.' See also Note Book, pl. 144, 339, 1032, 1033, 1193, 1258. In pl. 1792 [A.D. 1222] the jurors after stating facts 'dicunt quod nesciunt quis eorum fuit in seisina.'

The once popular doctrine which represents the justices as encroaching on the province that belonged to the jurors will not commend itself to students of the thirteenth century. Neither jurors nor justices had any wish to decide dubious questions. The complaint is, not that the justices are unwilling to receive a monosyllabic verdict, but that special verdicts are rejected:—they force the jurors into statements which explicitly answer the words of the writ, and thereby in effect require an oath about matter of law. The statute of 1285 forbids them to do this, while at the same time it allows the jurors to return general verdicts if they choose to risk their goods and their liberty[1]. When the jurors gave a special verdict they often had to answer a long string of questions [p. 629] addressed to them by the justices. The questions and the answers are recorded[2]. The justices desire to obtain all the relevant facts. On the other hand, they seem never to question the jurors as to their means of knowledge, though it is obvious enough that the twelve men can not have seen with their own eyes all the events that they relate.

We very much doubt whether in the thirteenth century Englishmen were proud of trial by jury, whether they would have boasted of it in the faces of foreigners, whether they regarded it as a check upon the king. We must wait for Sir John Fortescue to sing the lauds of the trial by twelve men. Jury service was oppressive. The richer freeholders obtained charters which exempted them from it, until in 1258 men said that in some counties there were not knights enough to make up a Grand Assize[3]. The poorer freeholders groaned under a duty which consumed their time and exposed them to the enmity of powerful neighbours. Edward I. relieved those

---

A common practice was that the jurors should state facts and add that therefore there was (or was not) a disseisin. See *e.g.* pl. 318: 'iuratores dicunt quod...et ideo dicunt quod idem *A.* eum iniuste disseisivit sicut breve dicit.' By a verdict in this form the jurors might escape the punishment ordained for perjury, though they would perhaps be amerced for a 'fatuous' oath if they drew a wrong inference of law. See Bracton, f. 290 b. But general verdicts in Petty Assizes were still common in Edward I.'s day. Occasionally a special verdict was given even in a Grand Assize; Note Book, pl. 251, 1865–6.

[1] Stat. West. II. c. 30.

[2] A good example of the way in which the jurors were catechized will be found in Northumberland Assize Rolls, p. 254.

[3] Oxford Petition, c. 28; Prov. West. c. 8; Stat. Marlb. c. 14.

whose lands were not worth twenty shillings a year[1]. None the less, it was seen that Henry II.'s Possessory Assizes had admirably done their appointed work, and the procedure which they had introduced was extended from case to case as men lost faith in the older kinds of proof. Much was at stake during those wakeful nights in which the Novel Disseisin was being fashioned[2]. Thenceforth the inquest, which might only have been known as an engine of fiscal tyranny, was associated with the protection of the weak against the strong, the maintenance of peace and seisin[3]. We may say that it suited Englishmen well; it became a cherished institution and was connected in their minds with all those liberties that they held dear; but what made it possible was the subjection of the England of the Angevin time to a strong central government, [p. 630] the like of which was to be found in no other land[4].

Fate of the older proofs.

We have been turning our faces towards the rising sun, and must now glance back at the fate of those institutions which trial by jury displaced[5].

Trial by battle.

Before the accession of Edward I. the judicial combat was already confined to that sphere over which its ghost reigned until the year 1819[6]. The prosecutor in the Appeal of Felony, the demandant in the Writ of Right[7], offered battle, the one by his own, the other by his champion's body, and the defendant might accept the offer, though by this time he could, if he pleased, have recourse to a verdict of his neighbours instead of staking his cause on a combat. Even in the Norman days 'battle did not lie' if there was no charge of crime and less

---

[1] Stat. West. II. c. 38. There was further legislation in 1293; Statutes, vol. i. p. 113.

[2] Bracton, f. 164 b: 'de beneficio principis succurritur ei per recognitionem assisae novae disseisinae multis vigiliis excogitatam et inventam.'

[3] In the Très ancien coutumier, pp. 17–18, the person against whom the jury is demanded is represented as some 'comes vel baro vel aliquis potens homo' who desires to grab land from his tenants or neighbours, while the plaintiff is an 'impotens homo.' 'Potens vero...in misericordia remanebit et impotens suam habebit terram.'

[4] The inquest procedure of the Karolingian times seems to have been exceedingly unpopular. Brunner, D. R. G. ii. 526.

[5] Thayer, The Older Modes of Trial, Harv. L. Rev. v. 45.

[6] 59 Geo. III. c. 46.

[7] Writ of Right must here be taken to include Customs and Services (Note Book, pl. 895), and *De rationabilibus divisis*, but not Writ of Right of Dower. See Bracton, f. 347.

than ten shillingsworth of property was in dispute[1]. As a means of proving debts[2] and 'levying' would-be swearers from the oath[3] it disappeared soon after Glanvill's day. That the oath of the demandant's witness and champion was almost always false was notorious, though we have met with a man who at the last moment refused to take it[4]. Does this induce our legislators to abolish the battle? No, it induces them to abolish the material words in the oath that made the champion a witness[5]. We see one hireling losing his foot for entering into warranty in an *actio furti*[6]; but for civil causes professional pugilists were shamelessly employed. Apparently there were men who let out champions for hire. Richard of Newnham, whose services were highly valued about the year 1220, might be retained through his 'master' William of [p. 631] Cookham[7]. We doubt whether in Bracton's day the annual average of battles exceeded twenty. There was much talk of fighting, but it generally came to nothing. The commonest cause for a combat was the appeal of an 'approver' (*probator*): that is, of a convicted criminal who had obtained a pardon conditional on his ridding the world of some half-dozen of his associates by his appeals. Decent people, however, who were in frankpledge and would put themselves upon a jury were not compelled to answer his accusations[8].

The rules of the duel have been so well described by others *Rules of the duel.* that we shall say little of them[9]. The combatants' arms of offence are described as *baculi cornuti, bastons cornuz*. It has

---

[1] Leg. Henr. 59, § 16; compare Brunner, D. R. G. 418; Viollet, Établissements, i. 184.

[2] Glanvill, x. 12; above, vol. ii. pp. 204–206.

[3] See above, vol. ii. p. 162.

[4] Note Book, pl. 980.

[5] Stat. West. I. c. 41: 'pur ceo que rarement avient que le champion al demandaunt ne seit perjurs.'

[6] Select Pleas of the Crown, pl. 192.

[7] Note Book, pl. 185, 400, 551. The names of Stephen the Englishman, Duncan the Scot and William Champneys occur from time to time as those of 'witnesses' who have seen a great deal. For contracts with champions, see Neilson, Trial by Combat, pp. 50–4; also Chron. de Melsa, ii. 100; Winchcombe, Landboc, i. 49–50. As to the champion's homage—for in theory he must be his employer's 'man'—see Bracton, f. 79 b.

[8] Bracton, f. 152–3; Select Pleas of the Crown, pl. 109, 140, 190, 198, 199; Note Book, pl. 1159, 1431, 1447, 1472, 1517.

[9] In particular, see Neilson, Trial by Combat, where most of the English stories are collected.

been commonly assumed that this means staffs 'tipped with horn'; but Dr Brunner has lately argued that the weapon thus described was really the old national weapon of the Franks, the war-axe (*francisca, bipennis*) which in its day had conquered Gaul[1]. The burden of the proof was on the combatant who fought for an affirmative proposition[2]; his adversary won if the stars appeared before the fight was over.

Wager
of law. The oath with oath-helpers[3], though it had been driven out of many fields, was by no means uncommon. The perdurance into modern times of this antique procedure as a special peculiarity of the two actions of Debt and Detinue has suggested rationalistic attempts to discover characteristics of those actions which make them unfit for submission to a jury. The simple truth is that they are old actions, older than trial by jury. In [p. 632] Bracton's day wager of law still appears as a normal mode of defence, and the charge that is thus denied is often one which in our eyes could easily be decided by 'the country.' In particular it is the common method of proving that one has never been summoned to appear in court[4], that one has not sued in court Christian after receipt of a royal prohibition[5], that one is not detaining a ward from his guardian[6], that one has not broken a final concord, or a covenant[7], that one has not detained beasts against gage and pledge[8]; we may even see it used in an action of trespass[9]. Nor is it always the defendant who wages his law; if the defendant pleads an affirmative plea, the plaintiff will deny it and prove the denial with oath-helpers[10]. However, the argument that you can not wage your law about facts that are manifest is beginning to prevail.

---

[1] Brunner, D. R. G. ii. 417. The evidence consists in part of the well-known sketch drawn on an English plea roll and reproduced, not for the first time, as a frontispiece for Select Pleas of the Crown, and a very similar picture found in the Berlin MS. of Beaumanoir. In a very late case the weapon had 'a horn of yryn i-made lyke unto a rammys horne'; Neilson, *op. cit.* 155.

[2] Generally the plaintiff must prove, but *Reus in exceptione actor est.* See Select Pleas of the Crown, pl. 87, where an appellee is ready either to deny the charge or to prove an exception, and offers different champions for the two purposes.   [3] Thayer, Harv. L. Rev. v. 57.

[4] Note Book, pl. 7, 1436; Bracton, f. 366.

[5] Note Book, pl. 143, 536, 629, 788, 799, 1467, etc.; Bracton, f. 410.

[6] Note Book, pl. 731, 742, 763, 1125, 1151.

[7] Note Book, pl. 396, 1097, 1101, 1457, 1579.

[8] Note Book, pl. 477, 741; Bracton, f. 156.

[9] Somersetshire Pleas, pl. 572.

[10] Note Book, pl. 184, 1549, 1574.

There has, for example, been doubt as to whether the commission of waste can be thus disproved. Bracton holds that it can not; otherwise the oath of the swearers would prevail against the evidence of our senses[1]. In the seignorial courts trespasses as well as debts are denied with wager of law[2]; indeed the lords have very little lawful power of compelling free men to serve as jurors.

In the city of London and in some other towns which enjoyed a chartered immunity from change, we find that even against accusations of felony the citizens still purge themselves with oath-helpers. They do this in the thirteenth, they talk about doing it in the fourteenth century. The London custom knew three 'laws': the great law for homicide, the middle law for mayhem, the third law for the smaller deeds of violence[3]. The great law required the accused to swear six times, each oath being supported by six helpers, so that in all thirty-seven persons swore. Three oaths, each backed by six compurgators, satisfied the middle law, while a single oath with six helpers was all that the third law required. This third law was sufficient even in a case of homicide if there was no appeal and the accused was being subjected to trial merely at the king's suit[4]. The accused did not choose his own helpers; they were chosen for him in his absence by the mayor and aldermen, or the mayor and citizens in the folkmoot, but he had an opportunity of rejecting for reasonable cause any of the persons who were thus selected. If the chief swearer was to escape, then each of the helpers swore that to the best of his knowledge and belief his principal's exculpatory oath was true. It is evident that 'the great law' must have been a severe, though a capricious test. In course of time a mitigation seems to have been introduced, and the accused was allowed to give a single oath at the head of his six-and-thirty backers, instead of swearing six times at the head of six groups[5]; but still he would be hanged if any one of the six-and-thirty refused his testimony. The Londoners probably discovered that they

Marginal note: Oath-helpers in criminal cases.

Marginal note: [p. 633]

---

[1] Bracton, f. 315 b; Note Book, pl. 580.

[2] Select Pleas in Manorial Courts, pp. 7, 8, 9, etc.; The Court Baron, pp. 21, 26, 28, etc.

[3] Mun. Gild. i. 56–9, 90–2, 102–4–6–7, 110–1: ii. 321. For Lincoln, see Select Pleas of the Crown, p. 39.

[4] Mun. Gild. i. 91.

[5] Contrast Mun. Gild. i. 57 with Ibid. i. 111.

had made a mistake in adhering to this ancient custom and that the despised foreigner, who was tried by a jury of forty-two citizens chosen from the three wards nearest to the scene of the supposed crime, had a better chance of escape than had the privileged burgher[1]. In the fourteenth century it was said that the citizen had his choice between 'the great law' and a jury of twelve[2].

Decay of the trial by oath. We see in this instance that the old set task of making a law might be very difficult. In the king's court and the seignorial courts the swearer was allowed to choose his own assistants—usually eleven or five—and the process fell into bad repute[3]. The concentration of justice at Westminster did much to debase the wager of law by giving employment for a [p. 634] race of professional swearers. In the village courts, on the other hand, it would not be easy for a man of bad repute to produce helpers; his neighbours would be afraid or ashamed to back his negations. And so we seem to see that many defendants in these courts prefer to put themselves upon a jury rather than to wage a law. The compurgatory process was still the means by which guilt was disproved in our English ecclesiastical courts; we have seen above that they allowed it to become a farce[4].

The decisory oath. The practice of 'deferring' and 'referring' a 'decisory oath' was widely received on the Continent as a part of the Roman procedure. Bracton had heard of it; but it never struck root in our common law[5]. However, at a later day we find that in

---

[1] Mun. Gild. i. 102, 106–7. It is to be regretted that the learned editor of this book has confused wager of law and trial by jury. The text distinguishes them sharply. The foreigner 'ponit se super veredictum' and the jurors swear 'de veritate dicenda.'

[2] Mun. Gild. ii. 321. Apparently wager of law in Trespass was abolished in the civic courts by Edward I. during the time when the city was in his hands. Ibid. i. 294. In 1270 the Earl of Warenne or his men slew Alan de la Zouche in Westminster Hall before the justices; he was allowed to escape with *wer* and *wite* (to use the old terms) after swearing with twenty-five knights as compurgators that the deed was not done of malice aforethought or in contempt of the king; Ann. Wint. 109; Wykes, 234. Purgation with thirty-six oath-helpers in criminal causes was allowed at Winchelsea in the fifteenth century; Palgrave, Engl. Commonwealth, p. cxvii. See also the custumals in Lyon's Dover, ii. 300, 315, etc.

[3] Records of Leicester, ed. Bateson, p. 158. In Leicester so late as 1277 the defendant has to choose his helpers from among the plaintiff's nominees. This is abolished as too onerous a task.

[4] See above, vol. i. pp. 443–4; vol. ii. pp. 395–6.

[5] Bracton, f. 290 b. We have seen no instance on any plea roll.

the London civic courts the defendant can call upon the plaintiff to swear to his cause of action, or the plaintiff can call upon the defendant to swear to an affirmative plea that he has pleaded, and in either case the oath, if sworn, is 'peremptory,' that is, it gives victory to the swearer[1]. The oath *de calumnia* is another institution that we refuse to borrow, though to all seeming the fore-oath of the Anglo-Saxon dooms, which we allowed to perish, was a kindred institution[2].

One other mode of trial remains to be mentioned. For a moment it threatened to be a serious rival of trial by jury. The common law of a later day admits in a few cases what it calls a trial by witnesses; we should now-a-days call it a trial by judge without jury[3]. How did it arise and why did it become very unimportant? *Trial by witnesses.*

We have seen that a plaintiff had to produce a suit of witnesses, and that a defendant might call for an examination of these suitors. Now when the 'exception' was yet new, it seems to have been thought—and this was very natural—that, if the defendant pleaded an affirmative plea, he might offer to prove by a suit the facts on which he relied[4]. And so, again, [p. 635] the plaintiff will sometimes offer suitors for the support of a replication[5]. In the parallel law of Normandy we see as a flourishing institution this production by the defendant of backers for the proof of an affirmative exception. If, for example, a plaintiff demands a debt, and the defendant pleads that he has paid it, the latter can prove his affirmative plea by a formal oath supported by four fellow-swearers[6]. In England the defendant's offer of suit soon begins to give way to a vaguer offer of 'verification,' which leads to a proof by jury. If his offer of suit had been accepted, there would, we take it, have been here, as in Normandy, a purely unilateral test :—the defendant would *The excipient's suit.*

---

[1] Munim. Gildh. i. 217–8.

[2] See the oath in Schmid, Gesetze, App. x. c. 4; Brunner, D. R. G. ii. 344.

[3] Thayer, Evidence, p. 17; Blackstone, Comment. iii. 336.

[4] Bracton, f. 301 b; Note Book, pl. 68, 79, 233, 613, 882, 1002, 1311, 1863. In pl. 233 [A.D. 1224] a defendant who produces no suit for his affirmative plea is allowed to purchase a jury, as the plaintiff does not object.

[5] Note Book, pl. 123.

[6] Somma, p. 325 : Ancienne coutume, c. 125 (122), ed. de Gruchy, pp. 317–22. In Normandy an affirmative plea is proved by a *lex probabilis*, a negative plea by a *deraisnia* equivalent to our wager of law. See Bigelow, Hist. Procedure, p. 304. It is curious that, while in Normandy *disrationare* or *derationare* is applied to disproof, in England it generally points to affirmative proof.

have sworn, his suitors would have sworn and he would have gone quit.

Rival suits.

But we see the English court occasionally adopting a more rational procedure. There is a bilateral production of witnesses. In 1234 a curious cause was evoked from the hundred of Sonning. A stray mare had been arrested; one William claimed it, and produced sufficient suit; it was delivered to him on his finding security to produce it if any other claim was made within year and day. Then one Wakelin appeared, claimed the mare and produced suit. The hundred court did not know to whom the proof should be awarded; so the matter was removed into the king's court. That court heard both suits and examined the witnesses one by one. Wakelin's men told a consistent, William's an inconsistent story, and the case was remitted to the hundred with an intimation that William's suit proved nothing[1]. Again, in one very common kind of action, namely, the action for dower, we repeatedly find suit produced against suit, both when the defence is that the would-be widow's husband is still alive and when it is asserted that she was endowed in some mode other than that which she has described. In these cases the court seems to think that each party is urging an affirmative allegation, that the two sets of witnesses should be examined, and that the more convincing testimony should prevail[2].

Fate of trial by witnesses.

But, for some reason or another, this mode of trial did not [p. 636] flourish in England. Very soon it seems to be confined to one small class of cases, namely, that in which a would-be widow is met by the plea that her husband is still alive[3]. Witnesses are produced on the one side to prove his death, on the other to prove his life, and the weightier or more numerous suit carries the day. A reason for the survival of this 'trial by witnesses' within these narrow bounds we may find perhaps in the idea that widows are entitled to a specially speedy justice, or perhaps in the difficulty of submitting to any English 'country' the question whether a man, who might have gone beyond the seas, was still alive. But any such explanation will

[1] Note Book, pl. 1115; Thayer, Evidence, p. 21.

[2] Bracton, f. 301 b, 304; Note Book, pl. 265, 279, 345, 356, 457, 518, 545, 898, 1065, 1102, 1307, 1586, 1595, 1604, 1919. See also the procedure in Replevin described by Bracton, f. 159. Records of Leicester, ed. Bateson, p. 159: in 1277 it is established that the plaintiff's suit is to be examined.

[3] Thayer, Evidence, p. 23.

leave us facing a serious problem, namely, why this rational procedure, this procedure which might easily have been converted into such an *enquête* of witnesses as Saint Louis ordained, soon fell out of the race. In Bracton's book it looks like a serious rival of trial by jury, while in later books and records we read of it only as of an anomaly. At this point some would say much of national character; we prefer to fall back once more on the antiquity and popularity of the Possessory Assizes. Henry II. lived before Saint Louis and before Innocent III. The reformation of procedure begins in England at a very early time, while the canon law is still trusting the old formal probations. The main institute of our new procedure is the 'inquest of the country.' This has taken possession of England before people have thought of balancing the evidence given by two sets of witnesses. For a moment ' trial by witnesses ' gains a foot-hold in this country under the influence of men like Bracton, who have heard of the new canonical inquest and who would make something rational out of the ancient *secta*; but the ground is already occupied. English judges have by this time fashioned a procedure which is far less troublesome to them, and which has already won a splendid success in the protection of every freeholder's seisin. In a few years they will be regarding the plaintiff's production of a *secta* as a mere formality and one which may be safely neglected; they will not allow the defendant to object that no *secta* has been tendered, and so the phrase 'and thereof he produces suit,' though [p. 637] men will be writing it in the nineteenth century, becomes a mere falsehood[1].

A few miscellaneous 'proofs' there were. Certain questions were decided by the certificate of the bishop, such as the question whether a church was 'full,' that is, whether it had a properly constituted parson[2], and the question whether two people were lawfully married, or whether a child was legitimate[3]. If it was asserted that a litigant was not of full age, the justices would sometimes trust their own eyes; if they doubted, he made his proof by a suit of twelve witnesses, some of whom

Other proofs

---

[1] Y. B. Edw. II. f. 242, 582; 17 Edw. III. f. 48 (Mich. pl. 14); Thayer, Evidence, p. 14.

[2] Note Book, pl. 111, 173, 296, 1428, etc.; Bracton, f. 241 b.

[3] See above, vol. ii. p. 367.

were his kinsmen and some his neighbours[1]. In the chancery when a youth, who has been in ward to the king, goes to sue for possession of his lands, the witnesses whom he adduces to prove his full age are examined : that is to say, they are asked how they come to remember the time of his birth, and they answer with talk of coincidences[2]. This rational examination of witnesses is of some interest to those who explore the early history of the chancery. Sometimes about a small and incidental question the justices also will hear witnesses one by one and contrast their testimony; but this is rare[3]. Lastly, one can only prove that a man is a villein by producing kinsmen of his who are self-confessed villeins[4]. This is a procedure favourable to freedom; the man whose liberty is at stake should not be driven to put himself upon a verdict of the 'free and lawful.'

Questions of law.

Of course in many cases there is no need for any proof. In the language of a somewhat later age the parties have 'demurred[5]'; the relevant facts are admitted and there is between them only a question of law. Very often the defendant raises some 'dilatory exception' to the writ, or to the person of the plaintiff and craves a judgment (*petit iudicium*) as to whether he need give any answer[6]. More rarely the defendant [p. 638] pleads facts which attack the core of the plaintiff's case, and the plaintiff, though unable to deny those facts, still asserts that he is entitled to a judgment. Here a judgment must be given 'on the count counted and the plea pleaded' (*par counte counté et ple pledé*)[7]. The first class of cases which brings this procedure to the front seems to be that in which two kinsmen are disputing about an inheritance but have

---

[1] Bracton, f. 424 b; Note Book, pl. 46, 687, 1131, 1362; Northumberland Assize Rolls, p. 230. The oath of these witnesses is a formal assertory oath, very like that of a Norman *lex probabilis*.

[2] See *e.g.* Calend. Geneal. pp. 184, 197, 203.

[3] Note Book, pl. 10: Men who profess that they summoned a litigant are examined separately and contradict each other.

[4] See above, vol. i. p. 426.

[5] For early occurrences of this word, see Y. B. 20–1 Edw. I. p. 323; 21-2 Edw. I. p. 163.

[6] Select Civil Pleas, pl. 24 [A.D. 1201]: 'petunt considerationem curiae utrum debeant respondere.' For a long time, however, anything that could be called a regular 'joinder in demurrer,' which involves an express statement by both pleaders of their desire for a judgment, is, to say the least, very rare upon the rolls.

[7] Bracton, f. 279. Note Book, pl. 1383 : 'ita quod per narrationem narrare et responsum dare recuperavit...seisinam.'

admitted each other's pedigrees. Here there is a pure question of law for the court[1]. But, as already said[2], the contrast between matter of law and matter of fact is as yet by no means sharp. Between men who have not admitted each other's pedigrees or who do not trace descent from a common stock, the whole question of 'greater right' will be left to a grand assize.

When Henry III. died, the verdicts of jurors were rapidly expelling all the older proofs. We have analyzed the trials of civil causes which took place before the justices in eyre at Newcastle in the years 1256, 1269 and 1279 with this result :— Victory of the jury.

Verdicts of Grand Assizes	1	Wagers of Battle	0
Verdicts of Petty Assizes	57	Wagers of Law	1
Verdicts of *Iuratae*	22	Trials *per parentes*[3]	1
Verdicts of Attaint Juries	1		

Very little remained to be done, and between 1272 and 1819 (when the battle was abolished)[4], very little was done to remove the remaining archaisms. The justices ceased, as we have lately said, to pay any heed to the production of 'suit.' Wager of law was driven out of a few actions in which it would [p. 639] still have been permitted in Bracton's time, while the two actions to which it clung until 1833[5], namely, Debt and Detinue, were slowly supplanted for practical purposes by the progeny of Trespass. Meanwhile, as is well known, the whole nature of trial by jury was changed. There was real change, but there was formal permanence. If we read the enrolled words which describe a trial by jury of Blackstone's or of a much later day, we are reading a bald translation of a record of Edward I.'s time. When a legal formula serves fifteen or twenty generations it has not been unsuccessful.

It remains that we should speak of a form of criminal procedure which had the future before it, that, namely, which The presenting jury.

---

[1] Glanvill, ii. 6: 'per verba [=*counte counté*] placitabitur et terminabitur in curia ipsa.'

[2] See above, vol. ii. p. 629.

[3] Northumberland Assize Rolls, p. 196. This trial took place in the county court.

[4] Stat. 59 Geo. III. c. 46.

[5] Stat. 3 & 4 Will. IV. c. 42, sec. 13 ; Thayer, Evidence, p. 25.

is initiated by a presentment or indictment. We have seen above how the old Frankish inquest was put to this among other uses; it could be employed for the collection of a *fama publica* which would send those whom it tainted to the ordeal. We have seen that the Frankish church had adopted this process in its synodal courts[1]. We have said—but this must still be a matter of doubt—that it may have been occasionally used in England before the year 1166 when Henry II. issued his Assize of Clarendon[2]. That ordinance must now be our starting point.

Fama publica.

Let us first ask what it is that the king desires to collect from the oaths of jurors. Does he want accusations of crime? Not exactly accusations. A man who has an accusation to bring can bring it; it will be called an Appeal. Does he then want testimony against criminals? Not exactly testimony. The jurors will not have to swear that *A. B.* has committed a theft, nor even that they believe him to be guilty. No, they are to give up the names of those who are defamed by common repute of theft or of certain other crimes, of those who are *publicati, diffamati, rettati, malecrediti* of crimes. This is of some importance. The ancestors of our 'grand jurors' are from the first neither exactly accusers, nor exactly witnesses; they are to give voice to common repute[3].

Composition of the presenting jury.

The machinery that Henry II. set in motion for this purpose [p. 640] was not invented by him. It involved the oath of twelve knights, or, failing knights, twelve good and lawful men, of every hundred, and the oath of four lawful men of every vill. This is in the main the same machinery that the Conqueror employed when Domesday Book was to be made. About every matter there are to be two sets of swearers, certain men of higher rank who represent a hundred, certain men of lower

---

[1] See above, vol. i. p. 142.

[2] See above, vol. i. pp. 151–3.

[3] The word *rettatus* is common on the early rolls as describing the position of one against whom the jurors make a presentment, while the charge against him seems to be a *rettum*. A little later *rettatus* degenerates into *rectatus*, the notion being that the person against whom the charge is made is 'brought to right,' made to 'stand to right.' Diez thinks that *rettatus* (Fr. *retté*) comes from *reputatus*. Le très ancien coutumier (p. 43) gives *reptatus*, and also (pp. 53–4) uses the active *reptare* to describe the action of an accuser. In our English documents *rettatus, publicatus, diffamatus, malecreditus* seem to be approximately equivalent.

rank who represent a vill or several vills[1]. Upon the working of this scheme some light is thrown by what we see the sheriff doing at a later time. Henry's ordinances, if they instituted the procedure which takes place before the justices in eyre, also instituted the accusatory procedure of the sheriff's turn[2]. Now in the thirteenth century we find in the sheriff's turn a procedure by way of double presentment, and we may see it often, though not always, when a coroner is holding an inquest over the body of a dead man[3]. The *fama publica* is twice distilled. The representatives of the vills make presentments to a jury of twelve freeholders which represents the hundred, and then such of these presentments as the twelve jurors are willing to 'avow,' or make their own, are presented by them to the sheriff[4]. This duplex process will, if we think it over, seem appropriate to the matter in hand. The highly respectable knights or freeholders of the hundred are not likely to know at first hand much about the crimes that have been committed among the peasantry or of the good or ill repute of this or that villein. On the other hand, it is not to be tolerated that free men should be sent to the ordeal merely by the oaths of the unfree, and undoubtedly in the thirteenth century many or most of the representatives of the vills were men whom the lawyers called serfs. This is of some importance when we trace the pedigree of the indictment. From the very first the legal forefathers of our grand jurors are not in the majority of cases supposed to be reporting crimes that they have witnessed, or even to be the originators of the *fama publica*. We should be

[p. 641] guilty of an anachronism if we spoke of them as 'endorsing a bill' that is 'preferred' to them; but still they are handing on and 'avowing' as their own a rumour that has been reported to them by others[5].

Then early in the thirteenth century, if not before the end of the twelfth, we have the coroners also making inquests by

The coroner's inquest.

---

[1] D. B. iv. 497 (Liber Eliensis); Ass. Clarend. c. 1; Ass. Northampt. c. 1.

[2] Ass. Clarend. c. 1: 'Et hoc inquirant iustitiae coram se et vicecomites coram se.'

[3] Gross, Coroners' Rolls, pp. xxx ff., and cases there cited.

[4] Britton, i. 178–182.

[5] See in Reg. Brev. Orig. f. 99 a writ whence we learn that in cent. xiv. or xv. the reeve and four men of the vill were still charged with the duty of 'informing the jurors.'

means of some four or six vills or townships. This they do whenever there is a sudden death, and, if the sworn representatives of the vills declare that some one is guilty of homicide, he is arrested and put in gaol. The results of these inquests are recorded on the coroner's roll, and that roll will be before the justices when next they make their eyre. Also we must notice that it is the coroner's duty to secure by 'attachment' the presence before the justices in eyre of the persons who found the dead body and of those who were in any house where a violent death occurred[1].

Present-ments and ordeal.

But we must turn to the doings of the justices in eyre. When we first see them at their work they have before them a jury of twelve hundredors, and if this jury presents a crime, or rather a reputation of crime, then the justices turn to the representatives of the four vills that are nearest to the scene of the misdeed and take their oath. Why reference should be made to just four vills we can not say. Perhaps the underlying notion is that they are the four quarters, east, west, north and south of the neighbourhood[2]. Almost always the townships agree with the hundredors, probably because the hundredors have derived their information from the townships. The result of such agreement is that the defamed man goes to the ordeal[3].

Practice of the eyres.

If we are to understand the working of this procedure when [p. 642] the ordeal is no more, we must draw some exacter picture of a session of the justices in eyre. In the first half of the thirteenth century almost all the high criminal justice that was being done was being done at such sessions. True that an appeal of felony was sometimes begun before or evoked to the Bench[4];

---

[1] The apocryphal statute *De officio coronatoris* ascribed to 4 Edw. I. (Statutes, i. p. 40) seems to be an extract from Bracton's treatise, f. 121, slightly altered; it is very possible, however, that Bracton made use of some ordinance or set of official instructions. See Gross, Coroners' Rolls (Selden Soc.), where the duties of the coroner are fully and learnedly discussed and illustrated.

[2] Leg. Edw. 24 (22) § 1; Leg. Will. I. 6, 21 § 2; Gross, Coroners' Rolls, p. xl.

[3] One entry from the roll of the Cornish eyre of 1201 (Select Pleas of the Crown, pl. 5) will suffice as an example. 'Hundredus de Estwivelisira. Iuratores dicunt quod malecredunt W. F. de morte A. de C. ita quod die praecedente minatus fuit ei de corpore et catallis suis. Et iiij. villatae iuratae proximae malecredunt eum inde. Consideratum est quod purget se per aquam per assisam.'

[4] Bracton, f. 149; Select Pleas of the Crown, pp. 38–81, 120–140.

but the central court had little to do with indictments.   True
also that, as time went on, justices were sent with ever increasing regularity to deliver the gaols; but the work of gaol-
delivery seems to have been light—for few men were kept
in prison—and it was regarded as easy work which might be
entrusted to knights of the shire[1].   Bracton's treatise *De Corona*
is a treatise on the proceedings of justices in eyre.

When the justices begin their session[2] they have before The jury
them the sheriff, the coroners, and the bailiffs of the hundreds and the articles.
and liberties.   They have before them what is in theory 'the
whole county,' that is to say, all the suitors of the county court
who have neither sent excuse nor failed in their duty[3].   They
have before them a jury of twelve men representing each
hundred; the boroughs, and some privileged manors, also send
juries.   The process whereby these juries were selected was
this : the bailiff of the hundred chose two or four knights who
chose the twelve[4].   There are also present the reeve and four
men from every township.   Thereupon the juries of the various
hundreds are sworn.   The oath that they take obliges them
to say the truth in answer to such questions as shall be
[p. 643] addressed to them on the king's behalf and to obey orders.
Then the articles of the eyre[5] are delivered to them in writing
and days are given them for bringing in their verdicts[6].   The
justices are opening what will be a prolonged session; it may

---

[1] See above, vol. i. p. 200.   For modern doctrine as to the powers given by
a commission of gaol delivery, see Hale, P. C. ii. 34–5.   We suspect that those
powers were gradually enlarged by interpretation.   At any rate it is plain that
in Henry III.'s reign, despite gaol deliveries, the main part of the criminal
work fell on the justices in eyre.   See Munim. Gildh. i. 296–7.   The inferior
position of the justices of gaol delivery is vividly illustrated by a writ of 1292 ;
Rot. Parl. i. 86.

[2] Writs of summons will be found in Rot. Cl. i. 380, 476 (A.D. 1218–21);
Select Charters (A.D. 1231); Bracton, f. 109; Y. B. 30–1 Edw. I. p. lv.

[3] For the defaulters at the Northumbrian eyre of 1279 (*Edmundus frater
Regis* is among them) see Northumberland Assize Rolls, 326, 356.

[4] In the eyre of 1194 four knights elected by the county elect two knights of
the hundred who choose ten others to serve with them ; see the writ in Select
Charters.   In later days the electors are named by the bailiffs; Bracton, f. 116 ;
Fleta, p. 23; Britton, i. 22; Statutes of the Realm, i. 232; Northumberland
Assize Rolls, 128, 395 ; Y. B. 30–1 Edw. I. p. lviii.

[5] See above, vol. ii. p. 520.

[6] Bracton, f. 116 ; Britton, i. 22.   We are right in saying 'verdicts.'   The
answers to the articles are often called *veredicta*.

well last for a month and more[1]. Some of these juries will
not be wanted again for many days[2]. They have also been
told in private that they are to hand in to the justices a
schedule of the suspects, the *malecrediti*, in order that the
justices may order their arrest. We have some evidence that
such a schedule, a *rotulus de privatis*[3], was delivered to the
justices at once, so that the *malecrediti* might be captured
before the jurors returned to answer the articles.

Present-
ments in
the eyre.

We will now suppose that a jury is ready to answer. Unless
we are mistaken, it will have put its answer into writing and
will deliver this writing to the justices; but none the less it will
have to make an oral reply to every article, and any variance
between what it has written and what it says will bring down
an amercement upon it[4]. The justices already know a great
deal touching the matters about which the jurors should speak,
for they have in their possession the sheriff's rolls and the
coroners' rolls, which tell of appeals begun in the local courts
and of inquests held on the bodies of dead men. The catechi-
zation of the jurors is a curious process. We are reminded of
a schoolmaster before whom stands a class of boys saying their
lesson. He knows when they go wrong, for he has the book.
Every slip is cause for an imposition unless his pupils have
purchased a favourable audience. In the fourteenth century,
when eyres were becoming rare, this practice had degenerated
into an extortionate absurdity. In 1321 a ward-jury of the
city of London was expected to recite all the crimes that had
been committed during the last forty-four years and to know [p. 644]
the value of every homicide's chattels. If it disagreed with
the coroners' rolls, it was amerced, and yet it had given the
justices and clerks five marks, more or less, for a breakfast[5].

---

[1] Bracton, f. 116. In 1321 the eyre in the city of London dragged on its
slow length for twenty-four weeks and then was brought to a premature end;
Munim. Gildh. ii. p. c.

[2] Gloucestershire Pleas, p. xxvi.

[3] Gloucestershire Pleas, p. 60. In the Kentish eyre of 1278 the jurors had
one day in which to deliver their *privetez* and a longer time for providing an
answer to the articles; Y. B. 30–1 Edw. I. p. lx. In the sheriff's turn the
presentments of felony are made privily, other presentments openly; Britton,
i. 182.

[4] Select Pleas of the Crown, pl. 62, 71; Somersetshire Pleas, pl. 950; Britton,
i. 23, gloss from the Cambridge MS.; Munim. Gildh. ii. 370.

[5] Munim. Gildh. ii. 370.

But, even in earlier times, when the eyres were more frequent, the jurors often had to speak of misdeeds and misadventures that were seven years old.

Among the miscellaneous mass of presentments that they make about the doings of unknown or fugitive malefactors, about accidental deaths which give rise to a deodand, about purprestures, about the usurpation of franchises and so forth, there will usually be a few, but only a few, which we can call indictments for felony of persons who can be brought before the court. What happens in these cases? Before the abolition of the ordeal in 1215 the justices, having received the statement of the hundred-jurors, turn to the representatives of the four neighbouring vills, who at this point are sworn to make true answer. If these *villani* agree with the hundredors in declaring that the person in question is suspected of a felony, then he goes to the water[1]. We can not be quite so certain as to what happens in Henry III.'s time, for about this point there has been in our own day some difference of opinion. The man against whom the presentment is directed will be asked how he will acquit himself of the charge. By this time there is but one mode of trial or proof open to him, namely, a verdict of the country. His choice lies between consenting and refusing to put himself for good and ill upon the oath of his neighbours. This is a test to which in 1215 appellees and defendants are frequently submitting their *exceptiones*. We will suppose then that our suspect thinks that a trial is the least of two evils and puts himself upon his country. Now as we read the rolls[2] and Bracton's text[3] what normally happens is this :—The hundred jury without being again sworn,—it has already taken a general oath to answer questions truly—is asked to say in so many words whether this man is guilty or no. If it finds him guilty, then 'the four townships' are sworn and answer the same question. If they agree with the hundredors, sentence is passed. This we believe to have been

Indictments for felony.

[p. 645]

---

[1] Select Pleas of the Crown, pl. 5, 6, 10 etc.

[2] Besides the Gloucestershire Pleas (1221), the Northumberland Assize Rolls (1256, 1279) and the Somersetshire Pleas which are in print, we have looked through various unprinted rolls, in particular Assize Rolls, Nos. 82 (Cambridge-shire eyre of 45 Hen. III.), 912 (Sussex eyre of 47 Hen. III.), 569 (Norfolk eyre of 53 Hen. III.).

[3] The critical passages are on f. 116, 143, 143 b.

the normal trial. But there were many juries about, for every hundred had sent one, and upon occasion the justices would turn from one to another and take its opinion about the guilt of the accused. By the end of Henry III.'s reign it is common that the question of guilt or innocence should be submitted to the presenting jury, to the jury of another hundred and to the four vills. They are put before us as forming a single body which delivers an unanimous verdict[1].

The second jury.

It may seem unfair that a man should be expected to put himself upon the oath of those who have already sworn to his guilt. But this is not exactly what the jurors have done. They have not sworn that he is guilty, they have not even sworn that they suspect him, they have only sworn that he is suspected (*rettatus, malecreditus*). They would have exposed themselves to an amercement had they said nothing of his ill fame, for this would very possibly have come to the ears of the justices through other channels; and yet, when asked to say [p. 646]

---

[1] Thus *e.g.* Northumberland Assize Rolls, 106, 115. The county is divided into two wards, viz. North of Coquet and South of Coquet. 'Balliva de Northekoket venit per duodecim......Ricardus de C. captus pro morte G. F.... ponit se super patriam. Et iuratores ex parte australi de Koket et similiter iuratores ex parte boriali de Koket simul cum villatis propinquioribus dicunt... quod culpabilis est ; ideo etc.' Select Pleas of the Crown, pl. 179. Gloucestershire Pleas, pl. 52 : the juries of three hundreds find a man not guilty. We could give numerous examples of this from unprinted rolls ; a few must suffice. Assize Roll, No. 82 (45 Hen. III.), m. 23. 'Hundredum de Chileford venit per duodecim...J. O. rettatus de morte W....ponit se super patriam...Et xii. iuratores istius hundredi et de hundredis de R. et W. una cum villatis de eisdem hundredis dicunt super sacramentum suum quod...in nullo est culpabilis.' Ibid. m. 28 d : 'Et duodecim iuratores de hundredo de R. in quo praedicta transgressio fieri debuit, et similiter xii. iuratores de hundredo de C. ex habundanti de officio iustitiariorum super hoc requisiti, dicunt....' Ibid. m. 33 d : 'Et xii. iuratores istius hundredi [de F.] simul cum iuratoribus de C. et S. et quatuor villatis propinquioribus dicunt...' Assize Roll, No. 912 (47 Hen. III.) m. 36 : 'P. de K. captus fuit per indictamentum xii. iuratorum hundredi de S. et modo venit et...ponit se super xii. istius hundredi de S. Et xii. iuratores simul cum xii. de H. et quatuor villatae propinquiores dicunt super sacramentum suum...' Ibid. m. 43 d : 'Et offerunt dom. Regi i. marcam pro habenda inquisicione hundredi propinquioris simul cum isto hundredo.' Assize Roll, No. 569 : 'Et per sic quod hundreda de C. et S. adiciantur isti hundredo offert dom. Regi x. libras, et recipiuntur.' See also Somersetshire Pleas, p. 27. It seems to us that at the end of the reign when the jury of a second hundred is called up, this is still regarded as a favour granted to the accused. But it is often granted and is not always purchased with money. See Gross, Coroners' Rolls, p. xxxi.

directly (*praecise dicere*) whether he is guilty or no, they may acquit him. However, the notion is growing that a man's 'indictors' will not be impartial when they try him. Britton allows the accused, in case of felony, to challenge jurors who are his indictors[1]. As a complement to this, we find jurors, in case of misdemeanour, amerced for denying in what we should call their verdict a statement of the guilt of the accused contained in what we should call their indictment of him[2]. In 1352 a statute was necessary to establish the general principle that a man's indictors are not to be put upon the inquest which tries him, be it for felony or for trespass[3]. Another change was going on. Just at the time when the accused was acquiring a right to challenge his indictors, 'the four townships' were ceasing to perform their old function. We see them in full activity on some of the latest eyre rolls of Henry III.'s reign, while on some of the rolls of his son's time they are no longer mentioned as part of that *patria* which says that men are guilty or not guilty[4]. A great deal yet remained to be done before that process of indictment by a 'grand jury' and trial by a 'petty jury' with which we are all familiar would have been established. The details of this process will never be known until large piles of records have been systematically perused. This task we must leave for [p. 647] the historian of the fourteenth century. Apparently the

---

[1] Britton, i. 30. The challenge is only allowed where there is 'peril de mort.'

[2] Assize Roll, No. 915 (Sussex eyre of 7 Edw. I.) m. 13 d : 'Hundredum de E. venit per xii...Iuratores praesentant quod W.' committed an assault and battery. 'Postea venit W. et...ponit se super patriam. Et xii. iuratores dicunt super sacramentum suum quod...non est culpabilis... Ideo inde quietus. Et quia xii. iuratores modo dedicunt id quod prius dixerunt, in misericordia.' A similar case stands on m. 29. Another will be found in Palgrave, Commonwealth, p. clxxxviii. None of these are cases of felony, and we believe that, while the hundredors were expected to present all public suspicions of felonies, they were deemed to pledge their oaths to the truth of any charges of 'trespass' to which they gave utterance.

[3] Stat. 25 Edw. III. stat. 5, c. 3 ; Rolls of Parliament, ii. 239.

[4] We have looked at Assize Rolls, Nos. 621 (Northampton, 13 Edw. I.) and 915 (Sussex, 7 Edw. I.) without discovering cases in which the *villatae proximae* were spoken of as an element in the body that tries the accused. At present we do not think that 'the four townships' can be said to become the petty jury of later days. See Gross, Coroners' Rolls, p. xxxii. The practice of swearing in these villagers seems to be abandoned as the accused acquires his right to a second jury of free and lawful men.

change was intimately connected with the discontinuance of those cumbrous old eyres which brought 'the whole county' and every hundred and vill in it before the eyes of the justices[1].

Refusal
of trial.

But what if the suspect would not put himself upon the country? It is clear that for a long time after 1215 the law did not know what to do with him. The abolition of the ordeal had disturbed all its arrangements. We take it that under the old procedure a man who refused to go to the ordeal to which he had been sent might have been put to death, though rather perhaps as an outlaw than as a convict:—he had renounced the 'law' declared by the court. It was a different thing to sentence a man who had been allowed no chance of proving his innocence by any of the world-old sacral processes. 'No one is to be convicted of a capital crime by testimony,' said the author of the *Leges Henrici*[2]. These words represent a strong feeling: mere human testimony is not enough to send a man to the gallows. In 1219, when the first eyre of Henry III.'s reign was in progress, the king's council was compelled to meet the needs of the moment by instructions sent to the justices[3]. A man charged with one of the gravest crimes is to be kept in prison for safe custody, but the imprisonment is not to endanger life or member. If the crime is of a middle sort and the accused would under the old law have gone to the ordeal, then he may abjure the realm. If the crime is light, then he may find pledge to keep the peace. Not one word is said about compelling people to abide a trial, or of trying by jury men who have not put themselves upon the country. All details are expressly left to the discretion of the justices[4].

---

[1] The practice of putting men upon their trial to answer indictments preferred in the sheriff's turn and inquisitions taken by the coroners seems to play a part in the transforming process. In the old eyres the hundred-juries were expected to 're-present' all these presentments of felony.

[2] Leg. Henr. 31 § 5: 'Et nemo de capitalibus placitis testimonio convincatur.'

[3] Foedera, i. 154, from the Patent Roll.

[4] As to this important document, see Palgrave, Commonwealth, p. 207 and Thayer, Harv. L. Rev., v. 265. Palgrave thinks that 'the royal advisers may even have meditated the introduction of proceedings analogous to those of the Civil and Canon Law.' Happily in 1219 the canonical *inquisitio* was yet in its infancy.

[p. 648]   One expedient which occurred to some of the justices was *Peine forte et dure.* that of taking the verdict of an exceptionally strong jury and condemning the prisoner, if found guilty, even though he had refused to stand the test.   Martin Pateshull twice took this course in the Warwickshire eyre of 1221.   The prisoner refused trial, but the twelve hundredors and twenty-four other knights having sworn to his guilt, he was hanged[1].   This procedure seems to have been in advance of the age.   In the next year the court at Westminster merely committed to prison a man accused of receiving felons, though the townships and the knights of the shire had declared him guilty[2].   Bracton does not like to speak out plainly about this matter.   He talks of compelling a man to put himself upon the country and of deeming him undefended and quasi-convict if he refuses[3].   The parallel Norman custumal betrays the same difficulty.   In Normandy, if a man is defamed of murder, he is kept in fast prison for year and day with little enough to eat or drink, unless in the meanwhile he will submit to an inquest of the country[4].   A similar expedient was adopted in England, but probably there was for many years much doubt as to the exact nature of the means that were to be employed in order to extort the requisite submission.   On such of the rolls of Henry III.'s last years as we have searched we see all the suspects putting themselves upon the country with an exemplary regularity which can only be the result of some powerful motive.   In 1275 Edward I. found it necessary to declare that notorious felons who were openly of ill fame and would not put themselves upon inquests should be kept in strong and hard prison as refusing to stand to the common law of the land[5].   Soon

[1] Select Pleas of the Crown, pl. 153, 157.   See the note to Hale, P. C. ii. 322.

[2] Note Book, pl. 136.   At the same time it sent another man to the gallows; but he had been taken with the mainour, *seisitus de latrocinio.*   See also pl. 67, 918, 1724, and Gloucestershire Pleas, p. xxxix.

[3] Bracton, f. 142 b, 143 b.

[4] Ancienne coutume, c. 68 (ed. de Gruchy, p. 167) : 'per iustitiarium debet arrestari et firmo carcere debet observari usque ad diem et annum cum penuria victus et potus (*à peu de menger et de boire*) nisi interim super hoc patriae inquisitionem se offerat sustinere.'   Somma, p. 172.   At a later time torture was used ; Brunner, Schwurgericht, p. 474.

[5] Stat. West. I. c. 12 : 'seient remis en la prison forte et dure.'   Compare the *firmo carcere* of the Norman custom.   But in England we do not see the limit of year and day.   Ann. Dunstapl. 377 (A.D. 1293) : 'Et aliqui milites et

afterwards we learn that their imprisonment is to be of the [p. 649] most rigorous kind; they are ironed, they lie on the ground in the prison's worst place, they have a little bread one day, a little water the next[1]. A few years later we hear that the prisoner is to be laden with as much iron as he can bear[2], and thus in course of time the hideous *peine forte et dure* was developed[3].

Present-
ments of
minor
offences. We have been speaking of indictments or presentments of felony[4]. So far as we can see, if the justices in eyre receive a presentment of any of the minor offences, they give the incriminated person no chance of denying his guilt, but at once declare him to be 'in mercy.' If, for example, the jurors present that *J. S.* has broken the assize of wine, then *J. S.* is put in mercy; and so if he is said to have 'fled for' a crime of which he was not guilty, a forfeiture of his chattels is decreed. It is thus that the justices raise hundreds of pounds by thousands of amercements[5]. This also is the procedure of the local courts, the turns and leets. In them, for example, the jurors will often begin with the stereotyped presentment that 'all the ale-wives have broken the assize'; the women are not suffered to deny this charge. So it is if the village jury presents that a man has drawn blood or used 'villein words.' In all these cases when the punishment will be only an amercement, the presentment is treated, not as an accusation, but as testimony and conclusive testimony. We believe that in Henry III.'s day anything that we could call the trial of a

nobiles sunt suspensi; quidam autem, eligentes poenitentiam secundum statutum, miserabiliter defecerunt.'

[1] Britton, i. 26; Fleta, p. 51, does not mention the irons.

[2] Y. B. 30–1 Edw. I. p. 511 (Cornish eyre of 1302). See also Ibid. pp. 499, 503, 531.

[3] Palgrave, Commonwealth, pp. 268, clxxxix; Thayer, Evidence, 70–81; Stephen, Hist. Crim. Law, i. 299–300; Pike, Hist. of Crime, i. 468. We do not think it proved that under Henry III. the man who refused trial suffered worse than a rigorous imprisonment. In 1293 a prisoner is spoken of as undergoing *poena statuti* because of his refusal to put himself upon the country; Staffordshire Collections, vol. vi. pt. i. p. 260.

[4] Hale, P. C. ii. 152: '*Presentment* is a more comprehensive term than *indictment*.' All the answers given by jurors to the articles of the eyre or of the turn are presentments. The usage of Bracton's day seems to restrict the term *indictati* to those who are presented as *malecrediti* of some *felonia*. It will be remembered that at the present day every *indictment* is a presentment. The grand jurors 'upon their oaths present that etc.'

[5] See above, vol. ii. p. 557.

p. 650] man upon an indictment for misdemeanour was exceedingly rare[1]. Slowly, when the procedure in cases of felony was well established, the doctrine gained ground that the person charged with an offence punishable by imprisonment might traverse the presentment of the jurors and 'put himself' upon the country[2]; but, so long as many of the minor misdeeds were punished by amercement in the old local courts, there were many presentments that were not traversable[3].

We must return for a moment to indictments of felony. We would fain describe what happened when the accused had put himself upon the country. The curt brevity of our records allows us to say but little. An appellee might make his answer by the mouth of a professional pleader; but no counsel was allowed to one who was arraigned at the king's suit[4]. A man who confessed a felony in court or before a coroner was condemned upon his confession, and the coroner's record of his confession was indisputable. We have found upon the rolls a good many recorded confessions of crime, and it may have been considered the justices' duty to urge the accused to tell the truth[5]; but when a prisoner had acknowledged his guilt before a coroner, and afterwards protested that his self-accusation was won from him by duress, we may see

The nature of the trial.

---

[1] See above, vol. ii. p. 522.

[2] An example from 1279 will be found in Northumberland Assize Rolls, p. 340. A presentment has been made that a coroner took money for not doing his duty. He puts himself on a jury and is acquitted. Some other cases are referred to above, vol. ii. p. 649, note 2.

[3] The later doctrine of presentments will be found in Hale, P. C. pt. 2, ch. 19: 'Regularly all presentments or indictments before justices of the peace, *oyer* and *terminer*, gaol-delivery, etc. are traversable... If a presentment be made *super visum corporis* that *A* killed *B* and fled, this presentment of the flight is held not traversable... If before justices in eyre...an escape be presented upon a vill...this is held to be not traversable... A presentment in a leet of bloodshed or the like' [is not traversable, unless it] 'concerns the freehold, as presentments of nuisances, or such matters as charge the freehold.' Hale's 'or the like' would in cent. xiii. cover a wide field of petty misdemeanours. Palgrave, Commonwealth, 268: 'The presentment or declaration of those offences which fell within the cognizance of the Hundred Jury or the Leet Jury...was final and conclusive; no traverse or trial by a second Jury, in the nature of a Petty Jury, being allowed.'

[4] Britton, i. 102; Y. B. 30–1 Edw. I. p. 530; cf. Leg. Henr. 46–9; 61 § 18, 19.

[5] The Court Baron (Seld. Soc.) p. 64. This appears also in a manual describing the practice of the king's justices: Camb. Univ. Lib. Mm. 1. 27, f. 128.

the justices sending for his gaoler and some of his fellow [p. 651]
prisoners and taking their evidence as to the alleged extortion[1].
Probably no fixed principle prevented the justices from questioning the accused; but there are no signs of their having
done this habitually[2]. We may take it that he could address
the jurors collectively. Sometimes, before putting himself upon
their oath, he will have urged an *alibi* and have prayed that his
submission to a verdict may be subject to this plea[3]. It is by
no means impossible that if there were at hand men who could
speak of facts telling in his favour, they would have been
permitted to say their say before the jury, though they would
not have been sworn[4]. A special verdict in a criminal case,
unless it deals with homicide by misadventure or in self-defence,
is a great rarity; but we have before now given an instance in
which the jurors found the bare facts and left the justices to
decide whether there had been larceny[5]. Another great rarity
is a case in which any difference of opinion among the jurors is
recorded. In entry after entry they are reported to say unani-
mously that the man is guilty or is not guilty, and this although
the trying body often consists of no less than forty-four men,
that is to say, of two hundred-juries and of the five representatives of each of four vills. This unanimity is no doubt somewhat
fictitious. If some of the jurors have a clear opinion and others
know nothing about the matter, probably the latter give way
and an unanimous verdict is recorded. The justices would sometimes lecture the jurors about the gravity of their duties[6], but
were not in a position to give them much advice or assistance;

---

[1] Y. B. 30–1 Edw. I. p. 543. This is a notable instance of the justices
hearing evidence. See Thayer, Harv. L. Rev. iv. 148.

[2] Sometimes (*e.g.* Select Pleas of the Crown, pl. 197) an appellee is
questioned, in order to see whether the case is one which should be tried by
battle. Cole, Documents, p. 312 : a Jew charged with forgery is questioned.
For this case see above, vol. ii. p. 540.

[3] The form is this : ' Petit sibi allocari quod fuit apud B......et, hoc allocato,
ponit se super patriam.' We have given one example above, vol. ii. p. 498,
note 7, and have seen others.

[4] See above, vol. ii. p. 627. We agree with Mr Thayer (Evidence, p. 13)
in thinking that the case (Gloucestershire Pleas, pl. 394) on which Sir James
Stephen relied (Hist. Crim. Law, i. 259) to show that witnesses were called in
criminal trials is not a case of trial at all. It is an example of the procedure
against a hand-having malefactor who refuses trial.

[5] See above, vol. ii. p. 498, note 7.

[6] Y. B. 30–1 Edw. I. p. 528.

[p. 652] nor, despite what Bracton says[1], do the justices seem to have been at pains to interrogate the jurors as to their knowledge and means of knowledge. The prisoner had put himself upon the oath of the jurors; a professedly unanimous verdict would satisfy the justices; it was the test that the prisoner had chosen. On the whole, trial by jury must have been in the main a trial by general repute. That in quiet times it pressed hardly on the accused, we do not believe; acquittals seem to have been much commoner than convictions in the last days of Henry III.

Now and again there would be scandal, panic, hasty hanging. Matthew Paris tells how in 1249 the parts of Winchester had become a den of thieves, who robbed the merchants of Brabant, attacked the king's own baggage train and made themselves drunk with the king's own wine. A royal justice could get no indictments; the jurors were in league with the criminals. The king came to Winchester, assembled the free-holders of the county in the castle, raged and stormed against them: he would try the whole county for treason by all the other counties of England. William Raleigh, once a justice but now a bishop, thundered the anathema. The gates of the castle were suddenly closed. A jury of twelve was sworn in and deliberated long. The jurors made a most inadequate presentment. They were forthwith committed to prison under sentence of death as manifest perjurers. Another jury was sworn in. After a lengthy and secret confabulation, the string of their tongues was loosened and in mortal terror they denounced many rich and theretofore respected folk and even some members of the king's household. From thirty to a hundred men were hanged. One William Pope turned approver and by six successful battles ridded the world of six of his associates. An indelible mark of infamy was set upon the county, says Paris[2].

Difficulties of trial by jury.

Such events as these must at times have tempted the king and his advisers to think that the inquest of twelve was a clumsy machine and to look abroad and see what was being done in France. Was not an inquest of a quite other kind possible? Our king was a frequent, if unwilling, litigant in

The collection of evidence.

---

[1] Bracton, f. 143.
[2] Mat. Par. Chron. Maj. v. 56–60; Historia Anglorum, iii. 46–7.

the court of his sovereign lord[1]. Certainly upon a grand [p. 653]
occasion some endeavour would be made to collect the evidence
of individual witnesses touching a crime. This we learn from
a valuable document that has come down to us among the rolls
of the king's court. In 1235 one Henry Clement, who had
come over to England as an envoy to the king sent by some
of the Irish nobles, was slain in the neighbourhood of the palace
at Westminster. He had bragged, so it was said, of having
brought about the death of Richard Marshall, and suspicion fell
on the Marshalls and their adherents. On the roll in question
we find the evidence given—in at least some cases it was
given upon oath—by a large number of witnesses. They tell
what they saw; they tell how Clement had said that his life
was threatened; they know very little, but there is some vague
testimony against William de Marisco. Then twenty-four
jurors from the parts of Westminster, Charing and Tothill say
that they know nothing and have heard nothing. The immediate effect of this proceeding seems to have been a decree of
outlawry against William de Marisco and others. He took to
open piracy, held Lundy Island against all comers and in the
end was hanged, drawn and quartered as a traitor, for among
other charges against him was that of having sent an assassin to
kill the king[2]. Now had inquests of this kind become common,
inquests in which witnesses were separately examined, indictment and trial by jury would have had to struggle for existence
and would very possibly have been worsted in the conflict.
Happily the jury was by this time firmly rooted in our civil
procedure.

The
canonical
inquisition.
It is not a little remarkable that a criminal procedure which
makes use of two 'inquests' or 'inquisitions,' one for the purpose of indictment, another for the purpose of trial, appears in
the end as the most emphatic contrast that Europe can show to
all that publicists mean when they speak of an 'inquisitory'
procedure. Let us glance for a moment at its one great rival.
The normal criminal procedure of the classical Roman law was
accusatory, and for a long time the normal criminal procedure
of the canon law was accusatory. It was not unduly favourable

---

[1] Olim, i. p. 521: in 1269 our king has got the worst of an *inquesta* about a
disseisin, and is condemned to pay 830 pounds. See also ibid. p. 559.

[2] Curia Regis Roll, No. 115 (18–9 Henry III.) m. 33 d; E. H. R. x. 294.

[p. 654] to accusers; on the contrary, the accuser bound himself to undergo the *poena talionis* in the event of his failing to furnish a complete proof of the guilt of the accused, and the law's conception of a complete proof was narrow and rigorous[1]. In course of time other modes of procedure were placed beside the *accusatio.* The ecclesiastical judge might proceed *ex officio* against those who were defamed by general report and compel them to submit to the *purgatio canonica*, that is to say, to swear away the charge with oath-helpers. Again, he might send to the ordeal (*purgatio vulgaris*) persons who were charged with offences by the synodal jurors[2]. Here for a moment, as we have already seen[3], the history of the canon law comes into close contact with the history of our English temporal procedure. But in the twelfth century all these methods were breaking down. Innocent III. introduced a new procedure, the inquisition. The judge proceeds *ex officio* either of his own mere motion, or on the suggestion of a promoter (*inquisitio cum promovente*); he collects testimony against the suspect, testimony which the suspect does not hear; it is put in writing[4]. But even this weapon was too feeble for that warfare against heresy in which the church was by this time engaged. The work of suppressing this crime was committed to the friars, more especially to the Dominicans, and the procedure by way of inquisition soon assumed in their hands all its worst characteristics. Every safeguard of innocence was abolished or disregarded; torture was freely used. Everything seems to be done that can possibly be done to secure a conviction. This procedure, inquisitory and secret, gradually forced its way into the temporal courts; we may almost say that the common law of Western Europe adopted it[5]. When in the eighteenth century French philosophers and jurists rebelled against it and looked about them for an accusatory, contradictory, public procedure, a procedure which knew no torture,

---

[1] Tanon, Histoire des tribunaux de l'inquisition, 255–263; Fournier, Les officialités au moyen âge, 233–251.

[2] Tanon, *op. cit.* 264–281; Fournier, *op. cit.* 262.

[3] See above, vol. i. pp. 141, 151.

[4] Tanon, *op. cit.* 281–290; Fournier, *op. cit.* 266 ff.; Biener, Beiträge zu der Geschichte des Inquisitions-Processes, 38 ff. The two decretals which organize the new procedure come from the years 1199 and 1206. The latter was reissued as Concil. Lat. IV. c. 8.

[5] Esmein, Histoire de la procédure criminelle en France, 284, 315.

they looked to ancient Rome and modern England[1]. Fortunate [p. 655] in her unblemished orthodoxy, England at the critical moment had escaped the taint of the *inquisitio haereticae pravitatis*[2].

English and foreign inquisitions.

The escape was narrow. In England, as elsewhere, a system which left the prosecution of offences to 'the party grieved' was showing its insufficiency. A new procedure was placed by the side of the old, and the new was in name an inquisitory procedure. It is to 'inquire of,' as well as to 'hear and determine' criminal causes that the king's justices are sent through the shires. They 'make' or they 'take' inquests or inquisitions (*inquisitiones*). We may even represent them as collecting testimony behind the backs of those whe are defamed. Happily, however, the reforms of Henry II. were effected before the days of Innocent III. Our new procedure seems to hesitate for a while at the meeting of two roads. A small external impulse might have sent it down that too easy path which the church chose and which led to the everlasting bonfire[3]. All that was necessary was that the sworn declarations of the hundredors should be treated as testimony. As regards some matters of small importance this was done. There were, as we have lately seen, some 'presentments' that were not 'traversable': in other words, a man was convicted upon the testimony of jurors taken behind his back and was allowed no opportunity of denying the charge. But where the imputation is grave, the words of the jurors are treated not as testimony but as a mere accusation[4]. The new procedure becomes as accusatory as the old; the Appeal and the Indictment are regarded as institutions of the same order. The English judge who is instructed to 'inquire of' felonies discharges himself of this duty by collecting accusations, not testimony. Then when, having 'inquired,' he proceeds to 'hear and determine,' he treats the jury as a whole

---

[1] Esmein, *op. cit.* 359.

[2] Tanon, *op. cit.* p. ii.: 'Les traits généraux que nous relevons dans la justice inquisitoriale sont ceux que revêt la procédure criminelle commune, non seulement en France, mais dans les principaux groupes des nations européennes au moyen âge, l'Italie, l'Espagne, l'Allemagne, les Pays-Bas. Un seul pays fait exception: c'est l'Angleterre... Or l'Angleterre est précisément le seul de ces pays dans lequel l'inquisition ne se soit pas établie, et qui ait ainsi échappé à la contagion de ses tribunaux.'

[3] Fortescue de Laudibus, c. 22: 'Semita ipsa est ad gehennam.'

[4] Rot. Parl. i. 75: 'inquisitio talis est inquisitio ex officio et quasi quoddam accusamentum.'

[p. 656] that can not be broken up.   Even now he is not going to weigh testimony; he is going to take a verdict.

How narrow the escape was we may see from that Norman custumal which is the next of kin to our English law books[1]. There, when the man defamed of murder has been induced to submit himself to an inquest, the judge causes twenty-four men who may be supposed to know the facts to come before him. He does this suddenly, without telling them why they are wanted, lest the kinsmen of the suspect should tamper with them.   Then he takes each of them apart before four impartial knights, examines him as to what he knows and his answer is put in writing.   Then the suspect is given his chance of challenging these men and striking them off the 'jury.'   Then in public session the evidence that was taken in secret is read aloud; each witness is asked whether he abides by his testimony, and, if there are twenty who say that the suspect is guilty, he is condemned.   This, it will be seen, is by no means a stringent procedure; it would have been far from satisfying a Dominican inquisitor; still the suddenness of the inquest, the separate and secret examination of the jurors, we do not find in England, and we may learn how the *iurea patriae* was at one time a plastic institution which might take different forms in two sister lands.

The inquest in Normandy.

We escaped secrecy and torture; but we were not very far from torture in the days when the *peine forte et dure* was invented.   Prominent enough in the late Roman law books, it had made its way into those of the Germanic folk-laws that were most deeply tinged by Romanism, though in general they only applied it to slaves.   After this, little is heard of it for a very long time until the renewed study of the classical jurisprudence unearthed and sanctioned it[2].   Then it stole into the courts both temporal and ecclesiastical.   The appearance of heresy, a crime committed, not by deed nor by word, but by thought, provided for it an all too ample field.   It came to the relief of a law of evidence which made conviction well-nigh impossible.   The canonists were evolving a law, and a rigorous law, of evidence.   'Full proof' consists of the accordant testimony of two unexceptionable witnesses who have themselves

Torture and the law of evidence.

---

[1] Somma, p. 174; Ancienne coutume, c. 68 (ed. de Gruchy, p. 167).

[2] Lea, Superstition and Force, pt. iv.   Esmein, Histoire de la procédure criminelle en France, 93–100.

seen the crime committed. At all events in the case of serious [p. 657 crimes, full proof, proof clearer than the noon-day sun, is requisite. Such proof was rarely to be had, more especially as large classes of mankind were incapable of testifying. One must eke out a 'half proof' by the confession of the accused, and to obtain this torture is used[1]. Luckily for England neither the stringent rules of legal proof nor the cruel and stupid subterfuge became endemic here. Whether we may ascribe to our ancestors any unusual degree of humanity or enlightenment is very doubtful. During the anarchy of Stephen's reign the 'devils' who lived in the castles had shown an ingenuity in the invention of torments which would have won praise from the inquisitors of a later age; but those 'devils' were extorting money, not evidence[2]. The *peine forte et dure* was barbarous enough and clumsy enough. But our ancestors had not been corrupted by the persecution of heretics. Foreign criminalists in the middle ages and in later times are for ever dwelling on the weakness of the law, on the difficulty of obtaining convictions unless the state takes to itself every advantage in its struggle with the prisoner. Of this we hear little in England, though we can see that an enormous quantity of crime went unpunished[3]. Our law seems to think itself quite strong enough. This difference was in a great measure due to the absence of any 'theory of legal proofs' such as that which hampered our neighbours. Our criminal procedure took permanent shape at an early time and had hardly any place for a law of evidence. It had emancipated itself from the old formulated oaths, and it trusted for a while to the rough verdict of the countryside, without caring to investigate the

[1] Tanon, Histoire des tribunaux de l'inquisition, 362–384.

[2] A.-S. Chron. ann. 1137. Pike, Hist. of Crime, i. 427, cites from the Pipe Roll of 34 Hen. II.: 'Petrus filius Ade reddit compotum de xxxv. marcis, quia cepit quandam mulierem et eam tormentavit sine licentia Regis.' This certainly seems to hint that torture could be used if the king pleased. Edward II. tried to throw upon the law of the church all responsibility for the torture of the Templars; Lea, Hist. of the Inquisition, iii. 300. It is of course well known that at a later time torture was used in England as an engine of state; but it never became a part of the ordinary machinery of the law, and its legality could be denied; Lea, Superstition and Force, 567–70; Spedding, Evenings with a Reviewer, ii. 100 ff.; Gardiner, Hist. Engl. 1603–42, ii. p. 275.

[3] See above, vol. ii. p. 557.

logical processes, if logical they were, of which that verdict was the outcome[1].

[p. 658] A few miscellaneous matters we have yet to notice.

Of the king as a litigant we must add but little to what has been said above[2]. His exchequer[3] collected his debts for him, attacking his debtors and (if need were) their debtors; but for lands and advowsons he often brought in his own court actions of the ordinary kind[4]. He had, however, an objectionable habit of using a *Quo Waranto* for land[5]—objectionable, we say, because this compelled a defendant to disclose his title as against a plaintiff who had disclosed none[6]. On the other hand, the *Quo Waranto* for franchises was defensible, for there is a sound presumption that all royal powers should be in the king's hands. Under Edward I. this prerogative writ was being taught to know its proper place[7].

Omitted points.

The king as a litigant.

---

[1] Bracton sometimes alludes to the canonical theory of proof, *e.g.* on f. 302, where he speaks of 'praesumptio ex semiplena probatione'; but that theory would not fit into our system, which handed over everything to the verdict of a jury, and was even beginning to treat with contempt the *secta* of eye-witnesses which the plaintiff was supposed to produce. In much later days our law can work out for itself a doctrine of evidence, which is all its own and is fashioned to suit trial by jury; it can do this just because in its days of adolescence it knew little of witnesses and therefore did not take over that theory of legal proof which lay ready to its hand in the works of the canonists. As to this 'théorie des preuves légales,' as French writers call it, see Esmein, *op. cit.* p. 260 fol. It attempted far more than is attempted by our modern English rules which merely 'admit' or 'exclude' evidence; it tried to assign a relative, and almost numerical, value to the various kinds of testimony. See the passage which M. Esmein, p. 369, quotes from Voltaire: 'Le parlement de Toulouse a un usage bien singulier dans les preuves par témoins. On admit ailleurs des demipreuves...mais à Toulouse on admet des quarts et des huitièmes de preuves.'

[2] See above, Book ii. ch. 2 § 13.

[3] See above, vol. i. pp. 190, 193.

[4] Note Book, pl. 199 (Right of Advowson), 187 (Darrein Presentment), 785 (Quare Impedit), 628 (Quo Iure), 1124 (Entry), 1220 (Escheat), 903 (Wardship).

[5] There are numerous cases in the Note Book. Sometimes when a subject brings a writ which contains the words *quo waranto*, this is really a writ of intrusion (see Bracton, f. 160 b) and the plaintiff's title is stated.

[6] Bracton, f. 372 b, quoting Cod. 3. 31. 11, would allow a *quo waranto* merely for the purpose of discovering whether the defendant holds *pro herede* or *pro possessore*, so that the plaintiff may know what other action he must bring. We have seen above (vol. i. p. 217, note 5) how the maxim *Cogi possessorem etc.* was current in the court of Edward I.

[7] Placit. Abbrev. p. 199 Norf.; Plac. de Quo War. 681, 686.

Criminal informations.

Could the king put a man on his trial for a crime though no indictment had been found against him? There seems to us to be clear evidence that this was done by Edward I., but not very frequently. Though there has been no indictment and no appeal, a man is called before the court and accused by the king's serjeant of treason or of felony. This evidence, however, comes to us from a somewhat later time than that [p. 659] which we are endeavouring to describe, and as the origin of 'criminal informations' has been the theme of hot debate, we will say no more of it in this place[1].

Voucher to warranty.

One of the commonest episodes in litigation about land is the voucher (*vocatio*) of a warrantor[2]. When the demandant (*D*) has counted against the tenant (*T*), the latter, instead of defending the action, will call in some third person (*V*) to defend it. If *V* admits that he is bound to warrant *T*, or if the court decides that he is thus bound, then *T* retires from the contest and *D* proceeds to count against *V*. If *D* succeeds in his contest with *V*, the judgment will be that *D* is to have the land in dispute and that *T* is to recover from *V* an exchange in value (*excambium ad valentiam*), that is to say, other land of equal value to that which he (*T*) has lost[3].

Counter-pleading.

When *V* first comes before the court, instead of admitting, he will perhaps deny the duty of warranting *T*. In that case he is said to 'counterplead the warranty' and there will then be a debate, trial and decision of this preliminary question before *D* can go on with his action. As a general rule our common law gave *D* no right to protest against the voucher of

[1] Oxford City Documents (Oxf. Hist. Soc.), p. 204; roll of Oxford eyre of 1285: 'Robertus le Eyr serviens dom. Regis pro dom. Rege iusticiariis dom. Regis hic monstravit quod Mag. Nicholaus de Wautham contra fidelitatem suam...[a charge of treason follows]...et petit iustitiam de eo ut de seductore ac proditore dom. Regis.' The famous case of Nicholas Segrave, Rot. Parl. i. 172, Memoranda de Parl. 1305 (ed. Maitland), p. 255, can only be read as an information for treason. An instance of an information for felony which sends a man to the gallows occurs in Mem. de Parl. p. 280. For later history see Stephen, Hist. Crim. Law, i. 295.

[2] Glanvill, iii. 1–5; Bracton, f. 257 b–261 b, 380–399 b. In the Novel Disseisin there can be no voucher of a person not named in the writ; Glanvill, xiii. 38. In Glanvill's day there seems to have been doubt as to whether there could be a voucher in any of the new possessory actions: Ibid. xiii. 30. But a voucher in the Mort d'Ancestor soon became very common.

[3] For instances illustrating the exchange, see Note Book, pl. 196, 284, 600, 633, 945, 1717, 1803.

a warrantor, and as the first warrantor could vouch a second, and the second a third, the hearing of the original claim might be long delayed. A statute of Edward I.[1] gave D in numerous cases the right to 'counterplead the voucher,' that is, to insist that V's appearance should not be awaited, and that T must himself defend the action.

[p. 660]

This process of voucher may seem very curious to us; for we may well think that the question whether D has greater right than T should take precedence of the question whether in that case T should receive compensation from a third person. A clue to the original meaning of the voucher we shall perhaps obtain if we observe that even in Bracton's day it was a feature which the actions for land had in common with the antique *actio furti*[2]. When the defendant in such an action alleged that he had purchased the goods which the plaintiff was demanding, he was bound to name the seller in order that the provenience of the goods might be traced backwards to a thief. Now it is said that in remote times the only action for land was, like the old *actio furti*, a punitive action; it aimed at a *wíte* as well as at restoration. The plaintiff desired, not merely to recover his land, but to attack the original wrong-doer who took his land away from him. Thus the process of voucher was at first a process which in the interest of plaintiffs strove to bring before the court the real offender in order that he might pay for his offence[3]. Howbeit, very long ago warranty had become one of the most powerful of those forces which had given society its feudal form. The gift of land implied protection, defence, warranty for the donee. If he was impleaded, his battle would be fought for him by a high and mighty lord. To gain the right to vouch such a lord as their warrantor many men would be content to give up their land and take it back again as rent-paying tenants[4]. In Bracton's day a tenant had as a general rule a right to call upon his feoffor, who would also

Explanation of the voucher.

---

[1] Stat. West. I. c. 40; Second Instit. 239.

[2] See above, vol. ii. p. 164.

[3] Brunner, D. R. G. ii. 516. This seems to be the origin of the rule (Britton, ii. 108) that if an action is successfully brought by D against T, in which T has vouched V, who has vouched W, the only person to be amerced is W: 'le dreyn garraunt remeigne en nostre merci.' Here 'le dreyn garraunt' is the original wrong-doer, and he owes the *wíte*.

[4] See above, vol. i. p. 306.

be his lord, for warranty. He had this right if he had done
homage to his feoffor, or if he had a charter of feoffment containing the usual formula *Sciatis me dedisse*; but the recipient
of homage would sometimes expressly stipulate that there was
to be no warranty[1], and, on the other hand, promises of warranty [p. 661]
were often inserted in charters in order either to make assurance
doubly sure or to bind the feoffor's 'assigns' and benefit the
'assigns' of the feoffee[2].   The duties of a lord who was bound
'to warrant, acquit and defend' his tenant were brought home
to him, sometimes by voucher, sometimes by the action of
Warantia Cartae[3].

Proceed-
ings of an
appellate
kind.

Nothing that was, or could properly be, called an appeal
from court to court was known to our common law.   This was
so until the 'fusion' of common law with equity in the year
1875.   Long ago both in France and in England the verb
appellare had been used to describe the action of one who
brings a criminal charge against another; such an action is an
appellum, 'an appeal of felony[4].'   In the twelfth century, under
the influence of the canon law, Englishmen became familiar
with appeals (*appellationes*) of a quite other kind; they appealed
from the archdeacon to the bishop, from the bishop to the
archbishop, from the archbishop to the pope[5].   The graduated
hierarchy of ecclesiastical courts became an attractive model.
The king's court profited by this new idea; the king's court
ought to stand to the local courts in somewhat the same
relation as that in which the Roman curia stands to the courts
of the bishops[6].   It is long indeed before this new idea bears
all its fruit, long before there is in England any appeal from

---

[1] Bracton, f. 390 b; Note Book, pl. 196.

[2] Bracton, f. 37; Note Book, pl. 804; Y. B. 20–1 Edw. I. p. 233. The Statute
De Bigamis (4 Edw. I.), c. 6, laid down rules about this matter which became
the basis of the later law.   See Second Instit. 274.

[3] For this action see Bracton, f. 399.   It is common in the Note Book.   In
after days it is often used by one who has been turned out of possession by
an Assize of Novel Disseisin.   In that Assize he had no chance of vouching
his feoffor.

[4] See for France, Esmein, Histoire de la procédure, 24.

[5] Const. Clarend. c. 8: 'De appellationibus si emerserint, ab archidiacono
debent procedere ad episcopum...'

[6] Bracton, f. 412: 'Sicut dominus Papa in spiritualibus super omnibus
habeat ordinariam iurisdictionem, ita habet Rex in regno suo ordinariam in
temporalibus.'

court to court; but we must here notice the various processes which have about them more or less of an appellate character.

First we may once more mention the reversal of a verdict Attaint. by the process of Attaint (*convictio*). The twelve jurors are accused before twenty-four jurors. If convicted of a false oath, [p. 662] they are severely punished; if their oath was but 'fatuous,' some mercy is shown them; but in either case the verdict of the twenty-four is substituted for the verdict of the twelve. In Bracton's day, however, this procedure was, at least as a general rule, confined to cases in which the recognitors of a Petty Assize had answered the question specified in the original writ, for if both litigants had put themselves upon a verdict, neither could dispute it[1].

A process known as a Certification is employed when jurors Certification. have given an obscure or an incomplete verdict. They are summoned to Westminster 'to certify the justices' as to the oath that they have made. In this way a verdict given before justices of assize is sometimes brought before the central court. If the jurors admit that they have blundered, they may be punished, but recourse to an Attaint is necessary if they are to be charged with perjury[2].

The king's court was not superior to the ecclesiastical courts; Prohibition. it could not reverse their judgments. It could, however, and would prohibit them from meddling with a temporal dispute[3], and the ecclesiastical judge who infringed a royal prohibition could be haled before the justices and punished. Archdeacon Bracton speaks of this offence as *laesa maiestas*[4]. We have seen that the king's court would send certain questions to be tried by the bishop. This gave it an interest in the proceedings which took place before him, and it seems to have claimed some power of directing his conduct of the cause[5]; it could at all events maintain the principle that, if the bishop was acting on

---

[1] See above, vol. ii. pp. 541, 623. We are at one with Brunner (Schwurgericht, 372) and Thayer (Evidence, 143) in thinking that the attaint-procedure is from the first a royal favour which has to be purchased.

[2] For instances, see Note Book, pl. 63, 382, 431, 771, 856, 1209, 1265, 1281, 1928; Somersetshire Pleas, pl. 1491, 1514.

[3] See above, vol. ii. p. 199.

[4] Bracton, f. 410.

[5] See the writs in Bracton, f. 302 b, 307.

the authority of a royal writ, there could be no appeal from his to any higher tribunal[1].

Removal of actions. From the inferior courts, communal and seignorial, no appeal lay to the king's court. But there were various processes by which actions begun in those courts could be removed before judgment; also, when a decision had been given, a complaint of 'false judgment' could be made. The action for freehold, which in theory should be begun in a feudal court, was from Henry II.'s time onwards subordinate to royal control[2]. The 'original' writ threatened the lord with the sheriff's interference. The demandant by a formal oath, which the royal justices were reducing to an absurdity, could prove that his lord had made 'default in justice,' and then the action was removed to the county court; the lord could seldom procure a restoration of the action when once it had been removed[3]. The tenant could stay all proceedings in the inferior courts by putting himself upon the king's grand assize and obtaining a 'writ of peace[4].' From the county court an action could be removed into the royal court by a writ known from its cardinal word as a *Pone*[5]. The plaintiff could obtain such a writ as a matter of course, the defendant only for some good cause such as the sheriff's partiality, the theory being that plaintiffs have nothing, while defendants have much, to gain by mere delay. [p. 663]

False judgment. If a judgment had been given by an inferior court, the method by which it could be questioned was the complaint of 'false judgment.' This takes us back to very old days when a litigant who is dissatisfied with a proposed doom will at once charge the doomsman who utters it with falsehood[6]. But in course of time the rule had been established that the complaint of false judgment was a royal plea and could only be urged in the king's court[7]. In England this principle was upheld, and

---

[1] Note Book, vol. i. p. 112; Rot. Parl. i. 16. Sometimes the king's court would order the absolution of an excommunicate. Note Book, pl. 1143.

[2] See above, vol. i. pp. 146, 147.

[3] Glanvill. xii. 7; Bracton, f. 329, 330; Britton, ii. 326–332; and see also the story about Becket and John the Marshal, Materials for the Life of Becket, i. 30; iii. 50.

[4] Glanvill, ii. 7–9; Bracton, f. 331; Britton, ii. 335.

[5] Bracton, f. 330 b; Britton, ii. 336; Hengham Magna, c. 4.

[6] Brunner, D. R. G. ii. 356–365. The A.-S. phrase for this process seems to have been *to forsake the doom*; Edgar, I. 3; Cnut, II. 15, § 2.

[7] Leg. Henr. 10, § 1.

it delivered us from some of the worst results of feudalism; the great lords had no control over the courts held by their tenants. But in the thirteenth century the complaint of false judgment still retained many an archaic trait. The unsuccessful litigant obtained a writ (*breve de falso iudicio*) which commanded the sheriff or the other president of the incriminated court to cause a 'record' to be made (*recordari facias loquelam*) of the proceedings and to send four suitors of the court to bear this record before the king's justices[1]. Then a debate takes place, not between the two litigants, but between the complainant and the four suitors who represent the court. Very commonly he denies the truth of their record; he offers battle and they offer battle, the champions being, at least in theory, two suitors of the court who were 'within its four benches' when the judgment was given; but we suspect that a county keeps some doughty pugilist in its pay for these emergencies[2]. Generally the justices manage to find some reason for declaring that there shall be no battle. They are beginning to treat the complaint of false judgment as a means of correcting the errors of the lower courts, and they give ear to the successful party as well as to the complainant[3]. But still the procedure is directed against the lower court; the county, the hundred or the manor is amerced if its judgment is annulled, and in appropriate cases it has to pay damages[4]. By a false judgment a lord may lose for ever the right to hold a court[5]. If the truth of the record is admitted, the question as to the falsehood of the judgment appears as a matter of law which the justices decide. In most cases the question turns

[p. 664]

---

[1] Sometimes they will put their record into writing and bring the parchment with them; Note Book, pl. 243.

[2] Glanvill, viii. 9, thinks that the man who pronounced the impugned doom should do the fighting. The procedure is well illustrated by Note Book, pl. 40, 592, 824, 834, 955, 1019, 1412, 1436, 1672. For 'the four benches' see Northumberland Assize Rolls, 196. In 1219 the Surrey champion was Stephen English, who in the next year was waging another battle; Note Book, pl. 40, 1360.

[3] Note Book, pl. 1436, a long and instructive record.

[4] Note Book, pl. 1412: 'Willelmus...dixit quod per recordum illud et per falsum iudicium deterioratus fuit et damnum habuit ad valenciam x. marcarum....Consideratum est...quod W. recuperavit damnum suum x. marcarum versus comitatum [Sussexiae].'

[5] Glanvill, viii. 9; comp. Edgar, iii. 3; Cnut, ii. 15, § 1; Leg. Will. i. 39, § 1.

on a point of procedure; the judgment that is impugned is a 'medial' or 'interlocutory' judgment, and the king's court will sometimes take the case in hand and direct its future course[1].

The king's court can not be charged with a false judgment; but gradually as it breaks into segments and throws off wandering satellites, something like an appeal from one segment to another or from the satellite to the central nucleus [p. 665] becomes possible[2]. In the early years of the thirteenth century the possessory assizes are often 'taken' by four knights of the shire[3]. These justices of assize, while acting under their commission, are royal justices; but they are not professional lawyers. The central court seems to hesitate in its dealings with them. On the one hand, they can not be accused of false judgment; on the other, they can be directed to bear record of their doings before the central court; they can be amerced for their errors and their errors can be corrected[4]. Even justices in eyre, among whom there will generally be some members of the permanent tribunal[5], can be thus dealt with[6]. But the central court itself is throwing out branches[7]. Above 'the Bench' rises the court held *coram ipso Rege.* In 1235 the Abbot of St Augustine's at Bristol brought 'before the king himself' a case in which the justices of the Bench had in his opinion been guilty of a mistake. They were summoned before the king and pleaded ignorance. Their proceedings were set aside[8]. The idea of a complaint against a judgment which is not an accusation against a judge is not easily formed. But gradually in Edward I.'s day as the king's court assumed a triple form—Common Bench, King's Bench, King in Council[9],—

---

[1] See *e.g.* Note Book, pl. 824, 1436.

[2] Compare Esmein, Histoire de la procédure, 27.

[3] See above, vol. i. p. 200.

[4] For this procedure, see Note Book, pl. 281, 512, 871, 917, 976, 1285, 530 ('ad iudicium de iustitiariis'), 564 ('et ideo iustitiarii in misericordia').

[5] See above, vol. i. p. 201.

[6] Note Book, pl. 67 (A.D. 1219): the justices in eyre are brought before the Bench and the Council to answer for having unlawfully condemned a man to death; they are amerced and the disherison is annulled. See also pl. 1069.

[7] See above, vol. i. pp. 190—192.

[8] Note Book, pl. 1166: 'Et quia fuit ostensum domino Regi...quod ipsi iustitiarii ita male processerunt, vocati fuerunt coram Rege et ibi cognoverunt quod ita processerunt, sed nesciverunt in dicto negotio melius procedere.'

[9] Maitland, Memoranda de Parliamento (1305), pp. lxxix–lxxxvii. Pike, History of the House of Lords, ch. iv.

and as the work of taking assizes and delivering gaols fell more and more into the hands of the permanent justices, men became familiar with the notion of a 'procedure in error' which does not call for a defence from the judges who are said to have made the mistake[1].

[p. 666]The distinction that we still draw between 'courts of record' and courts that are 'not of record' takes us back to early times when the king asserts that his own word as to all that has taken place in his presence is incontestable[2]. This privilege he communicates to his own special court; its testimony as to all that is done before it is conclusive[3]. If any question arises as to what happened on a previous occasion the justices decide this by recording or bearing record (*recordantur, portant recordum*). Other courts, as we have lately seen, may, and, upon occasion, must bear record; but their records are not irrefragable; the assertions made by the representative doomsmen of the shire-moot may be contested by a witness who is ready to fight[4]. We easily slip into saying that a court whose record is incontrovertible is a court which has record (*habet recordum*) or is a court of record, while a court whose record may be disputed has no record (*non habet recordum*) and is no court of record[5]. In England only the king's court—in course of time it becomes several courts—is a court of record for all purposes, though some of the lower courts 'have record' of some particulars[6], and sheriffs and coroners 'have record' of certain transactions, such as confessions of felony[7]. In the old

Records and courts of record.

---

[1] Even in Edward I.'s time, however, the justices sometimes come before the king in council almost in the character of defendants; *e.g.* Rot. Parl. i. 41. The old idea that an appeal is a complaint against the judge seems to have endured in northern France until very late days; Viollet, Établissements, i. 279.

[2] Note Book, pl. 239 [A.D. 1224]: 'quia testificatio domini Regis per cartam vel viva voce omnem aliam probationem excedit.' A strong statement of this doctrine that the king's word exceeds every other record was made by Edward I.'s council in 1292; Rot. Parl. i. 74.

[3] Brunner, D. R. G. ii. 523. Leg. Henr. 31, § 4; 49, § 4; Glanvill, viii. 9. In Leg. Will. I. 24 the privilege is confined to the court in which the king sits in person, 'la u le cors le rei seit.'

[4] See above, vol. ii. p. 667.

[5] Glanvill, viii. 9: 'nulla curia recordum habet generaliter praeter curiam domini Regis.' Compare for French law Viollet, Établissements, i. 221.

[6] Glanvill, viii. 11: 'recordum habet comitatus de plegiis, vel plagis datis et receptis in ipso comitatu.'

[7] See *e.g.* Bracton, f. 140 b; Select Pleas of the Crown, pl. 194, 195, 201.

days, when as yet there were no plea rolls, the justices when they bore record relied upon their memories[1]. From Normandy we obtain some elaborate rules as to the manner in which record is to be borne or made; for example, a record of the exchequer is made by seven men, and, if six of them agree, the voice of the seventh may be neglected[2]. In England at [p. 667] an early time the proceedings of the royal court were committed to writing[3]. Thenceforward the appeal to its record tended to become a reference to a roll[4], but it was long before the theory was forgotten that the rolls of the court were mere aids for the memories of the justices[5]; and, as duplicate and triplicate rolls were kept, there was always a chance of disagreement among them[6]. A line is drawn between 'matter of record' and 'matter in *pays*' or matter which lies in the cognizance of the country and can therefore be established by a verdict of jurors[7].

Function of the judges.

The behaviour which is expected of a judge in different ages and by different systems of law seems to fluctuate between two poles. At one of these the model is the conduct of the man of science who is making researches in his laboratory and will use all appropriate methods for the solution of problems and the discovery of truth. At the other stands the umpire of our English games, who is there, not in order that he may invent

[1] Glanvill, viii. 8. If the justices could not remember the levying of a fine, the court would act as though none had been levied. As to the recording of fines, see above, vol. ii. p. 100.

[2] Somma, pp. 310 ff. Ancienne coutume, cc. 103–7 (ed. de Gruchy), pp. 251–6.

[3] See above, vol. i. p. 169.

[4] Note Book, pl. 307: 'et inde ponit se super iustitiarios.' Ibid. pl. 583: 'et inde ponit se super rotulos.' Ibid. pl. 1411: 'et ponit se super recordum curiae et super rotulos.' Ibid. pl. 1285: one out of four justices of assize has no record (*recordum habere non potest*) without his fellows. We are not at all sure that the justices of assize of the first half of cent. xiii. usually kept rolls. See in Y. B. 32–3 Edw. I. pp. 361–7 a curious story about the unwritten record of a court baron.

[5] Bracton, f. 352 b. Y. B. 7 Hen. VI. f. 29 (Pasch. pl. 22). In 1292 the bare word of Beckingham, J. is preferred to the roll of Weyland, J. who has been guilty of forging records; Rot. Parl. i. 84–5.

[6] Note Book, vol. i. p. 65; Select Pleas of the Crown, p. ix.

[7] In some old cases the appeal to the court's memory is spoken of as a voucher to warranty. Note Book, pl. 88: 'vocavit curiam domini Regis ad warantum.' Ibid. pl. 829: 'et inde vocat ad warantum rotulos ipsorum iustitiariorum.'

tests for the powers of the two sides, but merely to see that
the rules of the game are observed. It is towards the second
of these ideals that our English medieval procedure is strongly
inclined. We are often reminded of the cricket-match. The
judges sit in court, not in order that they may discover the
truth, but in order that they may answer the question, 'How's
that?' This passive habit seems to grow upon them as time
goes on and the rules of pleading are developed. In Bracton's
day they not unfrequently addressed questions to the parties
in the hope of obtaining admissions and abbreviating the
[p. 668] suit. The answers given to these questions were enrolled,
and judgments were expressly based upon them[1]. In some
other respects, unless we are misled, they wielded discretionary
powers which were not exercised by their successors. Third
parties are allowed to intervene[2], or are summoned in the
course of the action[3], in a manner which would have seemed
strange to the practitioners of a later age. The judges conceived themselves to be endowed with certain 'equitable'
powers[4], and as yet the rules for the intricate game of special
pleading had not been formulated. But even in a criminal
cause, even when the king is prosecuting, the English judge
will, if he can, play the umpire rather than the inquisitor. No
rule of law prevented him from questioning the prisoner, and
probably he did this from time to time; but in general he was
inclined to throw as much responsibility as he could upon the
jurors or upon the God of battles.

Often the judgment that is enrolled is *motivé*, or, to use   *Considér-*
another French term, it is preceded by *considérants*; it has a   *ants.*
preamble which states the *ratio decidendi*. Usually this does
but sum up the concrete facts on which the court relies.
Thus, for example:—'And whereas the plaintiff has not produced sufficient suit, therefore it is considered that he take
nothing by his writ.' But occasionally a major premiss, a rule

[1] Note Book, pl. 296, 303, 350, 477, 550, 797, etc.
[2] Note Book, pl. 483, 525, 642, 750, 815, 821, etc.
[3] Note Book, pl. 253, 256, 273, 581, 586, 687, 713, 748, etc.
[4] See above, vol. i. p. 189. In Note Book, pl. 273, third parties are summoned 'per consilium curiae,' a phrase which, as we have noted above, points
to judicial discretion. See Bracton, f. 12 b: 'de equitate tamen per officium
iustitiariorum.' Ibid. f. 247 b: 'et hoc provenit non per iudicium sed per
consilium curiae.'

of law, is stated in abstract terms.   We have above set forth
the notable judgment in which Edward I.'s court inferred that
adultery had been committed and gave its reasons for refusing
to send the question to a jury[1].   One other example must
suffice: ' And for that Ralph [the would-be lord who is claiming
Thomas as his villein] has avowed his writ and his count and
has produced as suit but one male and two women, and for that
the said women are not to be admitted to proof because of their
frailty, and also because a male, who is a worthier person than
females, is being claimed, therefore it is considered that the
said Thomas and his heirs do go hence quit and free of the said [p. 669]
Ralph and his heirs for ever, and that Ralph be in mercy[2].'
We may regret that such recitals are not found upon the rolls
of a later day; the Year Books hardly supply their place[3].

Caution of
the judges.
The justices of Edward I.'s time seem to have been cautious
men; they were exceedingly unwilling to decide nice points of
law.   When in turning over their records we come upon a case
which raises a pretty question, our hopes are too often dashed
by a *Concordati sunt,* which tells us that the parties after all
their pleadings have made a compromise.   Bracton advises the
justices of assize to induce the litigants to make peace if the
jurors can not give a clear and decisive verdict[4].   The king's
court knew that to lay down a new rule was no light matter,
though it could not know that it was fashioning law for many
centuries and for many lands.

Last
words.
That we have written at wearisome length of one short
period of legal history, this is an accusation that we could not
'defend' with a *thwert-ut-nay,* while an attempt to confess and
avoid it might aggravate our guilt.   But whatever this book
may deserve, the law of the age that lies between 1154 and 1272
deserves patient study.   For one thing, it is a luminous age

---

[1] See above, vol. ii. p. 395.

[2] Northumberland Assize Rolls, p. 275 (A.D. 1279).   See also Note Book,
pl. 564, 1273.

[3] Coke, Fourth Instit. 4, says that this practice was abandoned under
Edward III., when 'the great casuists and reporters of cases (certain grave
and sad men) published the cases.'   But we now know that cases were being
reported under Edward I. at a time when *considérants* were frequent on the
rolls.

[4] Bracton, f. 186: 'tutius erit quod partes inducantur ad concordiam.'

throwing light on both past and future.   It is an age of good
books, the time of Glanvill and Richard FitzNeal, of Bracton
and Matthew Paris, an age whose wealth of cartularies, manorial
surveys and plea rolls has of recent years been in part, though
only in part, laid open before us in print.   Its law is more
easily studied than the law of a later time when no lawyer
wrote a treatise and when the judicial records had grown to so
unwieldy a bulk that we can hardly hope that much will ever
be known about them.   The Year Books—more especially in
their present disgraceful plight—must be very dark to us if we
can not go behind them and learn something about the growth
of those 'forms of action' which the fourteenth century inherited
as the framework of its law.   And if the age of Glanvill and
Bracton throws light forward, it throws light backward also.
[p. 670] Our one hope of interpreting the *Leges Henrici*, that almost
unique memorial of the really feudal stage of legal history, our
one hope of coercing Domesday Book to deliver up its hoarded
secrets, our one hope of making an Anglo-Saxon land-book
mean something definite, seem to lie in an effort to understand
the law of the Angevin time, to understand it thoroughly as
though we ourselves lived under it.

But we wrong this age if we speak of it only as of one that
throws light on other ages.   It deserves study for its own sake.
It was the critical moment in English legal history and therefore in the innermost history of our land and our race.   It was
the moment when old custom was brought into contact with
new science.   Much in our national life and character depended
on the result of that contact.   It was a perilous moment.   There
was the danger of an unintelligent 'reception' of misunderstood
and alien institutions.   There was the danger of a premature
and formless equity.   On the other hand, there was the danger
of a stubborn *Nolumus*, a refusal to learn from foreigners and
from the classical past.   If that had not been avoided, the crash
would have come in the sixteenth century and Englishmen
would have been forced to receive without criticism what they
once despised.   Again, we have stood at the parting of the
ways of the two most vigorous systems of law that the modern
world has seen, the French and the English.   Not about what
may seem the weightier matters of jurisprudence do these sisters
quarrel, but about 'mere matters of procedure,' as some would
call them, the one adopting the canonical inquest of witnesses,

the other retaining, developing, transmuting the old *enquête du pays.* But the fate of two national laws lies here. Which country made the wiser choice no Frenchman and no Englishman can impartially say: no one should be judge in his own cause. But of this there can be no doubt, that it was for the good of the whole world that one race stood apart from its neighbours, turned away its eyes at an early time from the fascinating pages of the *Corpus Iuris,* and, more Roman than the Romanists, made the grand experiment of a new formulary system. Nor can we part with this age without thinking once more of the permanence of its work. Those few men who were gathered at Westminster round Pateshull and Raleigh and Bracton were penning writs that would run in the name of kingless commonwealths on the other shore of the Atlantic Ocean; they were making right and wrong for us and for our children.

INDEX.